MENTAL MODELS

TOWARDS A COGNITIVE SCIENCE OF LANGUAGE, INFERENCE, AND CONSCIOUSNESS

P. N. JOHNSON-LAIRD

MEDICAL RESEARCH COUNCIL
APPLIED PSYCHOLOGY UNIT,
CAMBRIDGE

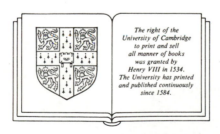

The right of the
University of Cambridge
to print and sell
all manner of books
was granted by
Henry VIII in 1534.
The University has printed
and published continuously
since 1584.

CAMBRIDGE UNIVERSITY PRESS

CAMBRIDGE

NEW YORK   PORT CHESTER

MELBOURNE   SYDNEY

Published by the Press Syndicate of the University of Cambridge
The Pitt Building, Trumpington Street, Cambridge CB2 1RP
40 West 20th Street, New York, NY 10011, USA
10 Stamford Road, Oakleigh, Melbourne 3166, Australia

First published 1983
Reprinted 1985, 1987, 1990

Printed in Great Britain at the University Press, Cambridge

British Library cataloguing in Publication Data
Johnson-Laird, P. N.
Mental models.
1. Cognition
I. Title
153.4   BF311

ISBN 0 521 24123 5   hardback
ISBN 0 521 27391 9   paperback

J.W.A.

Contents

Acknowledgements

Any book that reports psychological research depends on a highly collaborative effort. This book is no exception, and I am grateful for help from several different quarters.

The research itself was carried out in collaboration with many individuals – students, assistants and colleagues. My principal collaborators were Bruno Bara, Charles Bethell-Fox, Kate Erhlich, Alan Garnham, Dave Haw, Kannan Mani, Jane Oakhill, Mick Power, Gerry Quinn, Mark Steedman, Patrizia Tabossi, Scott Warman, and Til Wykes. Without their work, and of others mentioned in the text, this book would not exist.

Many people have contributed indirectly to the research by making available their expertise. My brother, Andy Johnson-Laird, president of Control-C Software Inc., was a one-man surgical team for my hardware and software problems. My colleagues in the Laboratory of Experimental Psychology at Sussex University have provided both moral and intellectual support. Steve Isard, Christopher Longuet-Higgins, and Arnold Smith, in particular, have given me much advice on computational theory, programming, and semantics. Bob Boakes, Mic Burton, Anne Cutler, Denis Norris, Keith Oatley, Donia Scott, Stuart Sutherland, and many others, listened with sympathy and made helpful suggestions. Others, too, have contributed indirectly to the content of the book. Its intellectual background was decisively shaped by my work with Peter Wason on thinking and reasoning, and later by a five-year research project with George A. Miller on the psychology of lexical semantics. The two topics of reasoning and meaning – between which I alternated for many years – have at last come together in the present book; I hope that it does justice to what I learned from these earlier collaborations. Another impetus came from the Sloan Foundation's decision to invest in Cognitive Science. Phil Gough and Stan Peters invited me to four Sloan Foundation workshops on semantics at the University of Texas at Austin, and there I discovered that linguists and logicians were actively concerned with developing psychologically realistic theories of meaning. It was at these meetings that I was able to talk to Emmon Bach, Jon Barwise, Hans Kamp, David Lewis,

vi

ACKNOWLEDGEMENTS

Barbara Partee, Stan Peters, Bas van Fraassen, and Bob Stalnaker about
the problems of reconciling model-theoretic semantics with what goes on
in people's heads when they understand discourse. I also had the opportunity *en route* to present my ideas to George Miller's lively research
seminar at Rockefeller University. Herb Clark, Ivan Sag, and Julius
Moravcsik, invited me to Stanford as a Sloan fellow for the spring term
of 1980. They were marvellous hosts; and the audience for my talks on
inference and meaning were highly stimulating. It was their evident
enthusiasm for the rather half-baked ideas I was advancing – and they did
not fail to point out where the shortcomings were – that first gave me the
idea of writing this book.

Several colleagues (as well as the publishers' readers) have read the
entire manuscript. Chuck Clifton, who visited Sussex from the University
of Massachusetts at Amherst, first gave me the benefit of his expertise on
the chapter on parsing – I duly rewrote it entirely – and then volunteered
to read the complete book. His comments boosted my morale and he
tactfully saved me from many errors. Alan Garnham went through the
manuscript with the finest of combs. His own independent work on mental
models was a continual stimulus; he also brought to my attention the
relevance of Wittgenstein's concept of a 'criterion' to semantic theory. Eric
Wanner, who is both a distinguished psycholinguist and an editor for
Harvard University Press, read two complete drafts, made some 'architec-
tural' suggestions of singular merit, and gently nudged me in the direction
of an explanatorily adequate theory. Other colleagues have read one or
more chapters, and I am especially grateful to Stuart Sutherland for advice
on the earlier chapters, to Gerald Gazdar for his guidance on the chapter
on grammar, to Elizabet Engdahl for her critique of the chapter on parsing,
to Stan Peters for his detailed comments on the chapter on model-theoretic
semantics, and to Keith Oatley for his generous advice on the chapter on
consciousness.

The production of the book has depended on the skill of many people,
to whom I am most grateful. Both Jeremy Mynott of Cambridge University
Press and Eric Wanner of Harvard University Press have been more than
any author has the right to expect from a publisher, smoothing the way
towards the eventual completion of the book in innumerable practical and
helpful ways. Pauline Marsh of Cambridge University Press, who subedited
the book, was responsible for many improvements in style. I am similarly
indebted to Stella Frost and Susanne Westgate for their rapid and precise
typing and retyping of the manuscript.

My research has been supported for ten years by the Social Science Research Council of Great Britain. In 1978, they awarded me a grant that paid my salary for three years and thus freed me from the usual academic duties; they allowed me to devote the last six months of this period to writing the first draft of the book. I thank the members of the psychology committee and the linguistics panel for this support. I also want to thank Anne Kauder and her colleagues at the SSRC for helping me to cope with many day-to-day problems that arose during the grant. The Science and Engineering Research Council very kindly supported my computing costs in a grant awarded to N. S. Sutherland.

Finally, the writing of the book depended on the help, forbearance, and support of my family. They made life possible for me and suffered my long-term absences from normal domestic life with amused sympathy. I dedicate the book to them: Mo, Ben, and Dorothy.

Prologue

— Why is it that we cannot think everything at once but are forced to have one thought after another? Our memories exist together, yet we cannot call them to mind all at once, but only one at a time.

— Why are there silences when we think aloud? Aren't we thinking at those moments, or are we unable to put our thoughts into words? It seems unlikely that thoughts should be grossly intermittent, so what barrier prevents them from being articulated?

— Why can't we become aware of the rules of language and thought by introspection? We can gain access to unconscious conflicts by free-associating on the psychoanalyst's couch: why won't the same method work for cognitive processes?

— Why is it that when we consciously characterize a concept, we try to do so in a cold-blooded, cut-and-dried fashion like lawyers defining a tort, whereas, as Wittgenstein pointed out, if we are prepared to look and see how ideas are used in daily life, we often find nothing so clear-cut, only indefinite and open-ended concepts?

— What happens when we understand a sentence? We are aware of understanding it, and still more aware of having failed to do so. Why can't we follow the mental process of comprehension as we can follow the action of tying a shoelace?

— Why is it that the words that are most frequently used in conversation are precisely the ones that have many different meanings? In a rationally designed language, ambiguous words would be avoided and, if they had to be admitted, they would be used the least frequently.

— When you believe that a sentence make perfect sense, why don't you notice the grammatical error that occurs in it (as in this one)? Surely you must analyse the grammatical relations in any sentence (including this one) in order to recover its meaning?

— What is the meaning of the word *possible*? You are familiar with it, and have no difficulty in using or understanding it in a typical sentence. But, now that you are asked what it means, you are tongue-tied for a moment and then can only offer a synonym rather than an analytical definition.

— How is it possible for you to make a valid deduction even if you have not learned logic? Is there an innate mental logic? Or have you somehow picked up rules of inference from other people? If so, how did *they* acquire them?

All of these phenomena, and many more besides, present problems to anyone who wants to understand human psychology. Yet they are not always recognized as problems, and indeed their solutions may strike you as trivial. 'It's obvious why we cannot think of more than one thing at a time', you may be tempted to say 'it's because . . . well, we are just made that way.' I share your feelings about the matter – it ought to be obvious, but sadly, it is not. Nor are answers to any of the other questions readily forthcoming, though again one feels that they ought to be. That is the nature of many problems about the mind: we are so familiar with the outcome of its operations, which are for the most part highly successful, that we fail to see the mystery. The phenomena above, however, are not merely mysteries. I shall argue that they provide us with singular clues to the nature of human mentality. What these clues signify will gradually be unravelled in the course of this book, so that by the end of it all of the questions will have answers. Lying behind those answers is the central idea on which the book is based: the idea that human beings construct mental models of the world, and that they do so by employing tacit mental processes.

This idea is not new. Many years ago Kenneth Craik (1943) proposed that thinking is the manipulation of internal representations of the world. This deceptively simple notion has rarely been taken sufficiently seriously by psychologists, particularly by those studying language and thought. They certainly argue that there are mental representations – images, or strings of symbols – and that information in them is processed by the mind; but they ignore a crucial issue: what it is that makes a mental entity a representation *of* something. In consequence, psychological theories of meaning almost invariably fail to deal satisfactorily with referential phenomena. A similar neglect of the subtleties of mental representation has led to psychological theories of reasoning that almost invariably assume, either explicitly or implicitly, the existence of a mental logic.

The assumption that there is some system of logic in the mind may seem innocuous; in fact, it runs the risk of paradox, for how could such a logic be acquired by someone who was not already able to reason soundly? A variety of answers have been given to this question, but, as we shall see, none of them will do.

Perhaps there is no logic in the mind, and perhaps humanity is intrinsically irrational. The follies of the human condition certainly lend credence to this view. Yet it must be false. A species incapable of valid inference could never have invented logic.

The main purposes of the present book are accordingly: (1) to solve the puzzle of mental logic; (2) to explain the nature of mental representations and how they relate language to the world; (3) to trace the process by which the meanings of sentences are constructed from the meanings of their parts according to the grammatical relations between them; (4) to discover how the interpretation of discourse is built up from the meanings of sentences; and (5) to elucidate the nature of intentionality and self-awareness. The plan of the book follows exactly the same organization of topics: thought, meaning, grammar, discourse, and consciousness. What knits these problems together, and articulates the solutions to them, is a concept and a methodological commitment.

The concept is that of *recursive* mental processes that enable human beings to understand discourse, to form mental models of the real and the imaginary, and to reason by manipulating such models. Recursion is a concept from computational theory, which will be explained in the opening chapter. Indeed, computational ideas play a crucial part throughout, culminating in the final chapter in a new theory of consciousness.

The methodological commitment is to Cognitive Science. I believe, perhaps with undue pessimism, that the mind is too complicated to be seen clearly, or to be studied with advantage, from the perspective of a single discipline. The scientific understanding of cognition depends on a synthesis; and the research to be reported here is an attempt to bring together some of the ideas and methods of experimental psychology, linguistics, and artificial intelligence. I did not make a deliberate decision to adopt a particular methodology: I had the good fortune to work alongside gifted colleagues with backgrounds in different disciplines, and their various techniques seemed to be producing results. With hindsight, I should describe how one learns from both experiments and intelligent software in terms of the distinction that philosophers draw between the correspondence and the coherence theories of truth. An assertion is true according to the first theory if it corresponds to some state of affairs in the world; true according to the second if it coheres with a set of assertions constituting a general body of knowledge. Experiments provide information about correspondence with the facts, but they exert a dangerous pull in the direction of empirical pedantry, where the only things that count are facts, no matter how limited their purview. Computer programs provide information about the coherence of a set of assumptions, but they exert a dangerous pull in the direction of systematic delusion, where all that counts is internal consistency, no matter how remote from reality. Give up one approach and you turn into a Gradgrind, the teacher in Dickens's novel *Hard Times*, whose only concern is with the facts; give up the other and you become an architect for the Flat Earth Society. Those, at least, are the dangers.

Sadly, many experimental psychologists make no use of computer modelling. They eschew it, I suspect, largely because there is no obvious way of interrelating programs and empirical findings. There are no general techniques for measuring the degree of discrepancy between the performance of a program and a human protocol, or for using such discrepancies to modify the program in a way that systematically improves its performance. Moreover, it may be too easy to pass Turing's (1950) test and to devise a program that responds in a way that is indistinguishable from human performance. As Weizenbaum (1976) found to his dismay, his program ELIZA, which engages in 'therapeutic discourse', fooled a number of people into believing that there was a real therapist sitting at a computer terminal in another room. Yet ELIZA works in a way that is very distant from actual processes of thought: it is a brilliant and salutary conjuring trick – it is a dissimulation, not a simulation. The appeal of Artificial Intelligence is, in part, that it can rid itself of the difficulties – if not the invidiousness – of comparing human beings with computer programs. Although the methods implemented in a pure AI program, say, for proving theorems, are likely to interest a psychologist, any resemblance to human mentality may be entirely coincidental.

How, then, is one to avoid becoming either a Gradgrind or a Flat-Earther? In my view, it is essential to maintain a clear distinction between theories and programs. General theories about the mind should be couched in the vernacular of cognitive science. Such theories tend to be vague roughly in proportion to their comprehensiveness. No matter. Explicit models of parts of the theory can and should be developed in the form of computer programs. Such programs should not be thought of as studies in either computer simulation or artificial intelligence. On the contrary, the point of a program should be to develop the general theory. It is thus fruitful to tackle only a small part of the theory at any one time: the program is small and easy to modify; it embodies principles rather than *ad hoc* 'patches'; and it allows the theory to be readily discerned within it. The development of such a program is truly a dialectical process, which leads to revisions in the general theory, and which can even give rise to experimentally testable predictions. What the program does is not as important as the effects of developing it on the programmer's thinking. As Jackson Pollock once remarked about his painting, it is the process that matters, not the end product. Reasoned argument alone is seldom responsible for a permanent change in behaviour, even in the methodological habits of scientists. Example is more powerful than precept, and I can only hope that the present book provides a modest example of the value of this approach.

The book is addressed to anyone who is seriously interested in a scientific understanding of how the mind works. Its origin was a series of seven talks that I gave to an audience of cognitive scientists at Stanford University early in 1980, but it has undergone several metamorphoses since then. It was always written with such a readership in mind, but it contains its own intellectual 'life-support system' in the form of explanations of the technical notions that it draws on from logic, linguistics, and computer science. I have tried to keep the formal notation to a minimum, often isolating it within tables or figures, but some mathematically innocent readers may nevertheless find these tutorial sections hard going. They can be skipped with no essential loss in continuity provided that readers are prepared to take on trust some of the claims made elsewhere in the book. For those who, on the contrary, want to follow up these matters in greater detail, there are suggestions for further reading after the main text. My aim is, above all, to communicate *ideas* rather than the minutiae of experiments and computer programs.

1

The nature of explanation

Introduction

Is psychology possible? Psychologists may be the last to know the answer to this question. They seldom raise it. Yet one plausible conjecture is that the mind must be more complicated than any theory proposed to explain it: the more complex the theory, the still more complex the mind that thought of it in the first place. It follows that psychology is biting off something that is too big for it – it is trying to bite off its own head – and can never succeed. This idea is a variation on the old joke that in a democracy the people are always more stupid than their leaders. The more stupid the leaders, the still more stupid are the people for having elected them. The joke is patently false; the psychological claim is more subtle and perplexing. However, the fact that psychologists have been convinced for a hundred years or more that they are not wasting their time shows that nature has at least contrived matters so that the discipline seems to be feasible: cognition appears to be comprehensible. A prima facie reason for the same conclusion is that human beings seem to have a privileged access to the mind, because they are able to introspect. The technique was much used by the pioneers of experimental psychology; unfortunately, it yields only data to be explained, not an explanation itself. In order to see why, one needs to consider both introspection and, more importantly, the nature of explanation.

It is logically possible that the whole of psychology might have been obvious to us; we might have been able to open up our minds introspectively and to examine our complete mental stocks and abilities. In fact, we cannot inspect fundamental cognitive operations. Suppose, for instance, that you are told two things about a group of people in a room:

Some of the children have balloons
Everyone with a balloon has a party hat

and you have to formulate a conclusion that necessarily follows from them. Like most people, you should have little difficulty in drawing a valid conclusion, but do you have introspective access to how you did so? Some

1

people are wholly unable to say how they drew the inference; others make such observations as, 'You told me that some of the children had balloons, and that everyone with a balloon had a party hat, and so it was obvious that some of the children – those with balloons – had party hats.' The conclusion is undoubtedly obvious, very much more obvious than which of the many possible methods of deduction people actually use in drawing it. Protocols from more complicated problems are likewise invariably silent on a number of matters, and it is these silences that betray the fact that introspections are at best glimpses of a process rather than detailed traces of its operations.

Introspection is not a direct route to understanding the mind and, as far as we know, there is no such route. Psychologists have available only a number of indirect methods, such as observing the characteristics and time course of behaviour. The phenomena that can be demonstrated in the psychological laboratory are only clues, but it is the progressive revelation of these clues that has convinced researchers that they are making progress in explaining human mentality.

Explanation depends, of course, on understanding: if you do not understand something, you cannot explain it. It is easier to give criteria for what counts as understanding than to capture its essence – perhaps because it has no essence. Understanding certainly depends on knowledge and belief. If you know what causes a phenomenon, what results from it, how to influence, control, initiate, or prevent it, how it relates to other states of affairs or how it resembles them, how to predict its onset and course, what its internal or underlying 'structure' is, then to some extent you understand it. The psychological core of understanding, I shall assume, consists in your having a 'working model' of the phenomenon in your mind. If you understand inflation, a mathematical proof, the way a computer works, DNA or a divorce, then you have a mental representation that serves as a model of an entity in much the same way as, say, a clock functions as a model of the earth's rotation.

The first modern formulation of this thesis is to be found in Kenneth Craik's remarkably prescient book, *The Nature of Explanation*, published in 1943. In that work, Craik proposed that human beings are processors of information. He wrote that they make use of three distinct processes in reasoning:

1. A 'translation' of some external process into an internal representation in terms of words, numbers, or other symbols.

2. The derivation of other symbols from them by some sort of inferential process.

3. A 'retranslation' of these symbols into actions, or at least a recognition of the correspondence between these symbols and external events, as in realizing that a prediction is fulfilled.

Although the digital computer had yet to be invented, Craik anticipated the analogy between it and the brain. After describing the three components of reasoning, he wrote:

One other point is clear; this process of reasoning has produced a final result similar to that which might have been reached by causing the actual physical processes to occur (e.g. building the bridge haphazard and measuring its strength or compounding certain chemicals and seeing what happened); but it is also clear that this is not what has happened; the man's mind does not contain a material bridge or the required chemicals. Surely, however, this process of prediction is not unique to minds, though no doubt it is hard to imitate the flexibility and versatility of mental prediction. A calculating machine, an anti-aircraft 'predictor', and Kelvin's tidal predictor all show the same ability. In all these latter cases, the physical process which it is desired to predict is imitated by some mechanical device or model which is cheaper, or quicker, or more convenient in operation. Here we have a very close parallel to our three stages of reasoning – the 'translation' of the external processes into their representatives (positions of gears, etc.) in the model; the arrival at other positions of gears, etc., by mechanical processes in the instrument; and finally, the retranslation of these into physical processes of the original type.

By a model we thus mean any physical or chemical system which has a similar relation-structure to that of the processes it imitates. By 'relation-structure' I do not mean some obscure non-physical entity which attends the model, but the fact that it is a physical working model which works in the same way as the processes it parallels, in the aspects under consideration at any moment. . .

My hypothesis then is that thought models, or parallels, reality – that its essential feature is not 'the mind', 'the self', 'sense-data', nor propositions but symbolism, and that this symbolism is largely of the same kind as that which is familiar to us in mechanical devices which aid thought and calculation. . .

If the organism carries a 'small-scale model' of external reality and of its own possible actions within its head, it is able to try out various alternatives, conclude which is the best of them, react to future situations before they arise, utilize the knowledge of past events in dealing with the present and future, and in every way to react in a much fuller, safer, and more competent manner to the emergencies which face it.

Like clocks, small-scale models of reality need neither be wholly accurate nor correspond completely with what they model in order to be useful. Your model of a television set may contain only the idea of a box that displays moving pictures with accompanying sound. Alternatively, it may embody the notion of a cathode-ray tube firing electrons at a screen, with the beam scanning across the screen in a raster controlled by a varying electro-magnetic field, and so on. You may conceive of an electron as nothing more than a negatively charged particle whose trajectory is influenced by a magnetic field. There may be no need for you to have any deeper understanding, because you can grasp the way the set works without having to reduce everything to its fundamental principles. A person who repairs television sets is likely to have a more comprehensive model of them than someone who can only operate one. A circuit designer is likely to have a still richer model. Yet even the designer may not need to understand the full ramifications of quantum electro-dynamics – which is just as well, because nobody completely understands them.

There are no complete mental models for any empirical phenomena. What must be emphasized, however, is that one does not necessarily increase the usefulness of a model by adding information to it beyond a certain level. If a television set is represented as containing a beam of electrons that are magnetically deflected across the screen, then this component of the representation serves an explanatory function. It accounts, for example, for the distortion of the picture that occurs when a magnet is held near the screen. Other components of the model may serve no such function. One imagines, say, each electron as deflected by a magnetic field much as a ball-bearing is diverted from its course by a magnet, but there is no representation of the nature of magnetism: the 'picture' is just a picture, which simulates reality rather than models its underlying principles. A model has, in Craik's phrase, a similar 'relation-structure' to the process it models, and hence it can be useful explanatorily; a simulation merely mimics the phenomenon without relying on a similar underlying relation-structure. Many of the models in people's minds are little more than high-grade simulations, but they are none the less useful provided that the picture is accurate; all representations of physical phenomena necessarily contain an element of simulation.

Why theories should be expressed as effective procedures

On the view developed here, to understand a phenomenon is to have a working model of it, albeit a model that may contain simulated components. This thesis applies at two quite distinct levels: it is an assumption about what underpins our ordinary understanding of phenomena, but it is equally an assumption about the goal of psychology. Psychologists aim to understand the mind, and thus they seek to develop a 'working model' of how it operates.

All explanations must take something for granted. When one person successfully explains something to another, what is conveyed is a 'blueprint' for the construction of a working model. Obviously, a satisfactory blueprint for one individual may be grossly inadequate for another, since any set of instructions demands the knowledge and ability to understand them. The explanation may take too much for granted. In most domains of expertise, there is a consensus about what counts as a satisfactory explanation – a consensus based on common knowledge and formulable in public criteria. In the physical sciences, for example, explanations are couched in the language of mathematics.

What should be the criteria for explanations of cognition? In the past, psychologists have allowed that just about any form of description is satisfactory – not necessarily true, but at least worth taking seriously as a putative explanation, especially if it is associated with empirical predictions. But should cognitive scientists be satisfied that the following examples constitute potential explanations?

1. Thinking consists in envisaging, realizing structural features and structural requirements; proceeding in accordance with, and determined by, these requirements; thereby changing the situation in the direction of structural improvements, which involves that gaps, trouble-regions, disturbances, superficialities, etc., be viewed and dealt with structurally; that inner structural relations – fitting or not fitting – be sought among such disturbances and the given situation as a whole and among its various parts; that there be operations of structural grouping and segregation, of centering, etc...

2. The relation of thought to word is not a thing but a process, a continual movement back and forth from thought to word and from word to thought. In that process the relation of thought to word undergoes changes which themselves may be regarded as development in the functional sense. Thought is not merely expressed in words; it comes into existence through them. Every thought tends to connect something with something else, to establish a relationship between things. Every thought moves, grows, and develops, fulfills a function, solves a problem. This flow of thought occurs as an inner movement through a series of planes. An analysis of thought and word must begin with an investigation of the different phases and planes a thought traverses before it is embodied in words.

3. When there is an external disturbance, the subject succeeds in compensating for this by activity. The maximum equilibration is thus the maximum of activity, and not a state of rest. It is a mobile equilibration, and not an immobile one. So equilibration is defined as compensation; compensation is the annulling of a transformation by an inverse transformation. The compensation which intervenes in equilibration implies the fundamental idea of reversibility, and this reversibility is precisely what characterizes the operations of intelligence.

Even granted an intimate familiarity with the terminology and concepts of the three great psychologists from whose works these extracts were culled (respectively, Wertheimer, 1961, p. 235; Vygotsky, 1962, p. 125; and Piaget, 1962, p. 120), it is impossible to be sure that the empirical claims they made necessarily follow from their theories. The derivation of the predictions inevitably calls for the exercise of intuition. Theoretical intuitions are very valuable (to those who have them), but if they are needed to work out what a theory predicts, there is a strong possibility that they are responsible for the predictions, and that the theory itself has no explanatory value. It is not a signpost, but a crutch on which the theorist leans in order to point the way.

There is one criterion that would avoid this danger. The theory should be describable in the form of an *effective procedure*. The concept comes from the theory of computability. If a procedure can be carried out by a simple machine, plainly it does not require any decisions to be made on the basis of intuition or any other such 'magical' ingredient: it is an effective procedure. If a theory is expressed in this form and it is still not obvious what its predictions are, then they in turn should be derivable by an effective procedure from the formulation of the theory. The general criterion, of course, is intended to apply to all scientific theories; it has yet to be satisfied by many psychological hypotheses. Indeed, in contemporary psychology the experimental expertise of a Galileo is often to be found alongside qualitative explanations like those of Aristotle. If the long promised Newtonian revolution in the study of cognition is to occur, then qualitative explanations will have to be abandoned in place of effective procedures.

The concept of an effective procedure is important in what follows, both as a criterion of explanation and as motivating some crucial features of psychological explanations themselves. There are several ways in which the idea can be made more precise by rendering explicit the nature of a 'simple machine', that is, a device that takes for granted as little as possible. Two ways are of intrinsic interest and worth describing in detail because they will crop up again and again in this book. A *Turing machine* is a hypothetical device that takes for granted the notions of writing a symbol on a memory tape, reading a symbol from it, shifting the tape one square to the left or to the right, and changing the machine from one internal state to another as a function of the symbol read on the tape and the current state of the machine. The machine is indeed the abstract ancestor of the modern programmable digital computer. The apparatus of *recursive functions* takes for granted three simple sorts of function and three procedures for constructing new functions out of old ones. Since these matters are somewhat technical, I have relegated them to the final part of the chapter, which may be skipped without much loss of continuity. What the reader should bear in mind, however, is that Turing machines and recursive functions turn out to be equivalent in that anything that can be computed by a Turing machine can be computed by recursive functions. Other formulations of the notion of an effective procedure turn out to be equivalent, too, and thereby corroborate *Turing's thesis* that the result of any effective procedure can be computed by a Turing machine. The thesis cannot be proved because the notion of an effective procedure is an informal and pre-theoretical one. All the different analyses of it so far have turned out to be equivalent, though someone may yet discover a new definition that encompasses more than can be computed by a Turing machine.

Effective procedures are made precise within a mathematical framework, and the reader may thus suspect that I am arguing that psychological theories must necessarily be mathematical in form. The suspicion is groundless, because effective procedures can be defined for entities other than numbers. In particular, psychological theories may make use of linguistic representations or other systems of symbols and invoke procedures for manipulating them. Effective procedures of this sort can always be modelled by a Turing machine or a set of recursive functions: if there is a finite number of different symbols, or a method of representing any symbol by finite means, then a symbol can be translated into binary code, and so for each operation on words or symbols there is a corresponding computable function.

There is one final complication that I have not so far mentioned. A function is an abstract notion – a mapping from one set to another – whereas an effective procedure specifies how to carry out the mapping. There are many different effective procedures for any given computable function. In fact, it is easy to show that there are, technically speaking, an infinite number of possible procedures for calculating any computable function (Rogers, 1967, p. 9). Most of them are trivial variations produced by inserting otiose evaluations of identities, but there are genuinely different procedures: e.g., in the lowly function of subtraction, 'borrowing' can be handled either by subtracting 1 from the upper digit or by adding 1 to the lower digit. Hence, even if we knew exactly what function a particular mental process computed, it would still be a problem to identify the procedure used to compute it (cf. Marr, 1977). My proposed criterion for psychological theories is that they count as putative explanations only if it is possible to formulate them as effective procedures – or at least those parts of them giving rise to empirical predictions. The criterion has to be applied at the level of procedures because, as we shall see in the final section of the chapter, there are functions that cannot be effectively computed, and there is no general test for whether any arbitrary function is computable.

The criterion implies that a theory can be implemented in the form of a computer program. It does not imply that it should be – other formulations may be equivalent in force, e.g., axiomatic statements of the theory. Still less does the criterion imply that the whole theory must be stated as an effective procedure. It is a bonus if it can be, but formulating a large-scale theory in this way may require too many *ad hoc* decisions to be worth the effort. It might be supposed that by stressing computability, the criterion implies that human beings are nothing but computers. It has no such implication. The fact that a psychological theory is computable does not imply that human beings are – so to speak – computable. First, there may be certain aspects of human mentality that cannot be captured in any theory. The phenomenal experience of consciousness, for example, may prove to be a matter about which no theory yielding determinate predictions can be made (though I shall attempt to rebut this view in the last chapter). Second, it may turn out that the concept of an effective procedure is ultimately extended to embrace more than the set of currently computable functions, and that only this richer notion of effectiveness suffices to account for mental phenomena. Either of these two possibilities would breach the simple equation of the mind with a computer program. The first possibility places a permanent barrier on the expansion of psychological knowledge – it puts limits on what can be known. The second possibility seems very remote. In so far as there can be a science of the mind it will almost certainly be restricted to accounts that can be formulated as computer programs. To abandon this criterion is to allow that scientific theories can be vague, confused, and, like mystical doctrines, only properly understood by their proponents.

The doctrine of functionalism

Cognitive science aims to understand the mind, and hence it aims to construct a 'working model' of a device for constructing working models. But a model's usefulness, as I argued earlier, is not enhanced by extending it beyond a certain level, and that moral applies equally to models of the mind. They will not be improved by embodying knowledge beyond a certain level. In the extract quoted from *The Nature of Explanation*, Craik wrote: 'By a model we thus mean any physical or chemical system which has a similar relation-structure to that of the processes it imitates. By 'relation-structure' I do not mean some obscure non-physical entity that attends the model, but the fact that it is a physical working model which works in the same way as the processes it parallels...' Craik's notion of 'relation-structure' evidently concerns the way in which the model functions, and the importance of this idea has become clear since the development of programmable computers. Once you know the way in which a computer program works, your understanding of it is in no way improved by learning about the particular machine on which it runs on this occasion or that. The same program may be translated into completely different codes for controlling different makes of computer that operate in different ways, and yet it is the same program that computes the same function however it is physically realized – whether the machine uses cogs, hydraulic valves, vacuum tubes, or silicon chips.

There is a major lesson for cognitive science here, which has been drawn by a number of authors, notably Miller, Galanter, and Pribram (1960, Chapter 14), Putnam (1960), Fodor (1968), and Oatley (1978): the mind can be studied independently from the brain. Psychology (the study of the programs) can be pursued independently from neurophysiology (the study of the machine and the machine code). The neurophysiological substrate must provide a physical basis for the processes of the mind, but granted that the substrate offers the computational power of recursive functions, its physical nature places no constraints on the patterns of thought. This doctrine of *functionalism*, which can be traced back to Craik, and even perhaps ultimately to Aristotle, has become commonplace in cognitive science.

No one is likely to confuse a program embodying a piece of physics with the actual physical process that is being simulated. A program that represents a wave breaking on the shore is manifestly different from a real wave, and it would be absurd to criticize the program on the grounds that it was not wet. Moreover, no sane person is likely to assume that the real wave is controlled by a computer program: it is governed by physical forces that are simulated by the program. All theories are abstractions, of course, but there is a more intimate relation between a program modelling the mind and the process that is modelled. Functionalism implies that our understanding of the mind will not be further improved by going beyond the level of mental processes. The functional organization of mental

9

processes can be characterized in terms of effective procedures, since the mind's ability to construct working models is a computational process. If functionalism is correct, it follows not only that scientific theories of mentality can be simulated by computer programs, but also that in principle mentality can be embodied within an appropriately programmed computer: computers can think because thinking is a computational process. It is sometimes said that the computer is just the latest piece of machinery – following clockwork, steam engines, and telephone exchanges – to be used as a metaphor for the mind. However, if both Turing's thesis and functionalism are correct, any future theory of the mind will be completely expressible within computational terms. The computer is the last metaphor; it need never be supplanted.

Mental models and criteria for explanations

In this introductory chapter, I have made a claim about mental representations that applies at two distinct levels. At the first level, human beings understand the world by constructing working models of it in their minds. Since these models are incomplete, they are simpler than the entities they represent. In consequence, models contain elements that are merely imitations of reality – there is no working model of how their counterparts in the world operate, but only procedures that mimic their behaviour. When men invented numbers, they neither grasped, nor needed to grasp, all of their mathematical properties. A limited model of arithmetic is useful, which is fortunate because there can be no consistent formal system that captures all of it. Likewise, to take a more mundane example, many mental representations are kinematic or dynamic; they take place in time, yet no one has much of an explanatory model of time itself. Models either make a direct use of time, or else they simulate it. We use or mimic time; we do not have an explanation of it; we merely work with it so well that we think we understand it.

At the second level, since cognitive scientists aim to understand the human mind, they, too, must construct a working model. It happens to be of a device for constructing working models. Like other models, however, its utility is not improved by embodying more than a certain amount of knowledge. The crucial aspect of mental processes is their functional organization, and hence a theoretical model of the mind need concern only such matters. But the mere possession of a model guarantees very little. It may mean no more than that the model mimics mental phenomena, and hence that a psychological theory based on it merely describes those phenomena accurately. I have argued that a scientific explanation must be formulable as an effective procedure, but that criterion, too, is a very weak condition on the adequacy of a theory. It ensures only that the theory is not a woolly phantasy. A psychological theory of mental models should also be – in Chomsky's (1965) terms – explanatorily adequate. It must lay down explicit constraints on the class of possible mental models: it must list the elements and operations from which mental models can be composed. Hence such a theory would provide a potential, though abstract, account of how children acquire mental models. Some mental models may be highly artificial and acquired only by dint of deliberate cultural training, e.g., models governing domains of pure mathematics. Other models, however, are presumably natural, acquired without explicit instruction, and used by everyone in the course of such universal processes as inference and language comprehension. To say what makes certain models natural and others artificial, one indeed needs an explanatorily adequate theory. My goal is to develop such a theory, and I shall describe one in Chapter 15.

The theory is not cut from whole cloth, and it would be misleading to present it all of a piece as an a priori conjecture. My starting-point will be Craik's intuitive idea of an inner mental replica that has the same 'relation-structure' as the phenomenon that it represents. I shall apply this idea to the rich and revealing test case of mental inference, both formal and informal, in order to discover what kinds of working hypotheses about mental models yield a descriptively adequate account of reasoning. These hypotheses will evolve informally at first, but their feasibility will be tested by computer modelling, and their credibility will be tested by experimental studies. Eventually, an explanatory theory of mental models will emerge, partly as a result of extending the theory to cope with comprehension, and partly as a result of factoring out the essential components of the models that I introduce.

It is important to draw a clear distinction between the criterion of effectiveness, the need for explanatory adequacy, and the doctrine of functionalism. The criterion of effectiveness is a methodological recommendation – the requirement that theories be stated explicitly and in a way that takes little for granted. The need for explanatory adequacy is a special condition on psychological theories: there are biological constraints on the nature of mental processes and representations, and a theory should account for what is possible within those constraints. The doctrine of

11

functionalism, however, is an empirical conjecture that the workings of the mind are intrinsically computational. It does, indeed, imply that the mind is nothing but a computer, though not necessarily one akin to any known artefact. If human beings are at least as complicated as Turing machines and their individual processes of thought differ as a result of their genes and their experience, then their behaviour is most unlikely ever to become wholly predictable, because there is no effective procedure that can predict the behaviour of an arbitrary Turing machine. There is thus little danger of creating a psychology capable of modelling an individual's thoughts – an eventuality likely to destroy the spontaneity and significance of life. But there are no a priori reasons for supposing that it is impossible to develop scientific theories of general psychological abilities. The remainder of this book is an argument to the effect that the construction of mental models, the communication of their contents, and reasoning on the basis of such representations, are nothing more than computational processes.

An outline of the theory of computability

This final section of the chapter gives an informal outline of the theory of Turing machines and recursive functions. It is designed for readers who are not mathematicians, but it can be skipped with little loss in continuity, though in that case a number of the subsequent arguments in the book will have to be taken on trust. Readers who wish to pursue the details further than I can take them here will find a starting point in the suggestions for further reading.

The logician Alan Turing (1936) devised a simple hypothetical machine, which operates in a way that takes as little as possible for granted. It reads and writes symbols on a tape divided into a series of separate squares, rather like a strip cut from a child's arithmetic book. The tape is used to feed data into the machine, to store symbols as a memory, and to output the results of computations. The machine can do just three things:

1. Read the symbol on the square of the tape that it is currently scanning.
2. Replace the symbol on the square by another symbol.
3. Shift the tape one square to the left or one square to the right. The tape never runs out; it is potentially infinite since new squares can always be added as needed.

A Turing machine recognizes only a finite number of symbols, which can always be translated unambiguously into a simple binary notation: any square on the tape can contain either a '1' or else a blank (symbolized by a '0' henceforth). The machine itself can be in any one of a finite number of different states; the theory is not concerned with the physical realization of these states – they might be different positions of cogs, or different voltages in various electronic components – since it is a piece of abstract mathematics applying to the performance of any such machine. Hence, the different states can be represented by numbers. The immediate action of any Turing machine is determined solely by the state it is in and the symbol it is scanning. The behaviour of a machine is accordingly characterized by a finite set of instructions, which each specify what action the machine carries out (and what state it shifts to) as a function of its present state and the symbol it is scanning. Each instruction therefore specifies the following four items: the present state of the machine, the symbol on the scanned square, the action to be carried out, and the next state of the machine (as a consequence of carrying out the instruction). Table 1.1 describes a simple Turing machine for adding positive integers, where each integer is represented by a string of 1's, e.g., 3 is represented by a string of three 1's, 1110, with the 0 acting as a punctuation marker for the end of a number. The machine takes an input tape that represents the two numbers to be added (for example, $2+1$ as represented by the tape 11010). It erases the initial symbol (yielding 01010), replaces the punctuation marker with a 1 (01110), and finally shifts the tape back to the beginning of the string that represents the result (1110). There are many other effective procedures for addition, and many other equivalent ways of defining Turing machines.

Mathematically speaking, addition is a function that here takes two arguments from the set of positive integers (1, 2, 3, . . .) and produces for each such pair a unique value which is also a positive integer. The notion of a function can be generalized to any mapping from one set of entities to another in which there is always a unique result corresponding to each of the values of the input arguments for which the function is defined – a trivial function, for example, might return the value zero for any input argument (or set of arguments if the function takes several of them). Just as a function may take several arguments, so it may deliver an ordered set of outputs, e.g., a function might deliver descriptions of persons, consisting of gender, height, weight, and date of birth. What a function does not produce is different output values (e.g., two dates of birth) for a given argument (e.g., a person): there is a unique value associated with each of the input arguments. If a function is not defined for a particular input, it

Table 1.1. *A Turing machine for adding two positive integers. The machine is started in its initial state scanning the leftmost 1 of a string of 1's representing the first integer, followed by a 0, and then a string of 1's representing the second integer*

Present state	Symbol scanned	The machine has the following set of instructions: Action carried out	Next state
1	1	Replace symbol by 0	1
1	0	Move tape one place to left	2
2	1	Move tape one place to left	2
2	0	Replace symbol by 1	3
3	1	Move tape one place to right	3
3	0	Move tape one place to left	4

A more perspicuous way of representing the same machine is by a state diagram in which each state is represented within a circle, and an arrow stands for an instruction with the symbol scanned on the left of the colon and the action on the right of the colon:

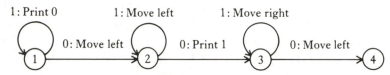

Given an input tape of 11010, which represents $2+1$, the machine carries out the following actions, where the arrow head represents the symbol currently scanned and the number in the circle the state of the mcahine:

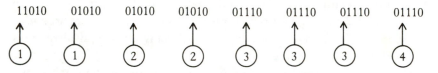

At this point, the computation halts because there is no instruction for state 4; the machine ends scanning the leftmost of a string of 1's equal to the result of the addition.

fails to return anything for that input – the Turing machine goes on computing for ever without yielding a value.

What is surprising about these simple machines is how much they can do. You might suppose that if a machine had access to more than one tape, or to two or three- or still higher-dimensional tapes, then it would be able to compute a whole new set of functions. Likewise, you might suppose that its power would be increased by allowing several machines to compute in parallel or by having instructions that *did* yield different outcomes for the same input configuration (the state of the machine and the symbol scanned). The latter condition gives rise to a non-deterministic machine, containing such pairs of instructions as:

Present state	Symbol scanned	Action carried out	Next state
2	1	Replace symbol by 0	3
2	1	Replace symbol by 1	2

which are not deterministic because they need the machine to 'choose' between two different actions. In an actual machine, non-determinism would be a nuisance – brought about, say, by a loose connection – but in computational theory it can be useful. We can stipulate that a machine always makes the correct choice between alternatives, and we need not worry about the basis of this magical ability. (As we will see in Chapter 13, this form of non-determinism can be simulated by several methods in a computer program.) Yet, these complications in the basic design of a Turing machine affect only the nature of the procedure that can be used to compute a function, not what is computable. Anything that can be computed by using several tapes, a set of machines operating in parallel, or non-deterministic machines, can also be computed by a single one-tape deterministic machine. The notion of an effective procedure is therefore made precise in the theory of Turing machines.

Despite the power of Turing machines, there are functions that neither they nor any other device can compute. The existence of such functions is established by an argument that I shall only sketch here. Any Turing machine is completely described by its set of instructions, and it is easy to establish a simple method of representing a machine as a string of symbols on a tape. For example, let the first instruction of the machine in Table 1.1 be represented as:

$$10 \quad 1 \quad 00 \quad 1 \quad 00000$$

according to the following principles. There is an initial string of 1's corresponding to the number of the present state, followed by 0 to act as a punctuation mark; next there is a 1 or 0 to represent the symbol scanned; next there is a pair of digits to represent one of the four possible actions (11 = replace a symbol by 1, 00 = replace a symbol by 0, 10 = move tape to the right, 01 = move tape to the left); finally, there is a string of 1's corresponding to the number of the next state, followed by a string of five 0's to indicate the end of an instruction. I have used spaces to separate the different parts of the instruction, but the spacing is purely for legibility. A machine as a whole can be represented by the string corresponding to

15

all of its instructions. The machine in Table 1.1 is represented by:

10100100000	100011100000	1101011100000
11001111100000	111011011100000	1110001111100000

If you have followed this account of Turing machines, you could reconstruct the sequence of computations carried out by a simple machine. You could take the specification of the machine and work out what happens when it is fed a specific input tape (as in the example in Table 1.1). You look at the first instruction and see whether the symbol to be scanned corresponds to the first symbol on the data tape. If it does, you carry out the first instruction – rewriting the symbol, or shifting the tape – and then you jump to the first instruction corresponding to the next state of the machine, and so on. If the symbol to be scanned does not correspond to the first symbol on the tape, you look at the next instruction, and so on until you find a match. This process of imitating a machine from its specification can itself be expressed as an effective procedure. It is therefore possible to specify a Universal Turing machine which, if presented with a tape representing any arbitrary machine, will imitate that machine by carrying out exactly the same computations as it would do. Table 1.2 presents a simple flow diagram showing the sequence of operations that a Universal machine goes through in imitating a specific machine. A digital computer and its program stand in much the same theoretical relation to one another as do a Universal Turing machine and a tape representing a specific Turing machine.

Since each string of symbols representing a machine can be readily interpreted as a number, the set of tapes representing all possible Turing machines can be put into numerical order. There are an infinite number of tapes, but they are enumerable, i.e., the numerical ordering can be matched one-to-one with the integers 1, 2, 3, ... *ad infinitum*, because each tape is really just a binary representation of an integer. A Turing machine such as the one for addition can be thought of as an effective procedure for computing a function from integers to integers, since it starts and finishes with some set of numbers on its tape. It is an interesting question whether every such function from integers to integers can be computed by a Turing machine, and, in fact, the answer has been shown to be negative. Unlike the set of all possible Turing machines, which can be counted, the set of all possible functions from integers to integers is not enumerable; there are more functions than can be put into a numerical order. It sometimes comes as a shock to non-mathematicians to learn that

16

Table 1.2 *A flow diagram for a Universal Turing machine*

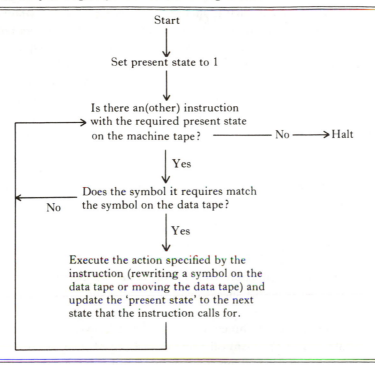

Note. There are many possible designs for the machine. The present design assumes a device that takes two separate tapes as its input: one is a description of the machine to be simulated (the machine tape), and the other is the input data that the simulated machine is to work on (the data tape). The universal machine is started scanning the leftmost squares of the two tapes.

infinity has different sizes. There is an infinity of integers, but it is smaller than the infinity of functions from integers to integers. The proof depends on showing that any putative list of such functions leaves some functions out: a list could of course be mapped one-to-one onto the integers. (The proof is a variation on Cantor's celebrated 'diagonalization' method of showing that the real numbers are not enumerable: see, e.g., Boolos and Jeffrey, 1974, Chapter 2.) Since there are more functions than can be listed, it follows that there are more functions than Turing machines, and hence that there are functions that are not computable. An important function that cannot be computed is one that would decide for any arbitrarily selected Turing machine and input tape whether or not the machine ultimately halts if it begins computing on the leftmost symbol of the input tape. The paradox of a machine that computed this function is evident if you consider what it should do in trying to decide whether or not it itself stops computing given some arbitrarily selected data tape. If it does not halt when it is given the tape, its specification requires it to halt in order to deliver this message. Obviously, there is a self-contradiction here: it has to halt to indicate that it doesn't halt. In summary, you can construct a Universal machine that can compute anything that any machine can compute; but you cannot construct a machine that can predict the behaviour of any machine, and, in particular, whether or not it halts given an input tape.

A second way of analysing the notion of an effective procedure is in terms of the theory of recursive functions developed by the logician Kurt Gödel and others. Let us suppose there is some method – its details can be taken for granted – for computing three simple things:

1. The zero function, which returns the value 0 given an input of any natural number (0, 1, 2, 3, . . .).

2. The successor function, which returns the number that follows any natural number (e.g., the successor of 0 is 1, the successor of 1 is 2, and so on).

3. The set of identity functions, each of which given a string of input arguments returns the identical value of just one of them as specified by its position in the string. Thus, there is an identity function that takes one argument and returns its value; there is an identity function that takes two arguments and returns the value of the first of them; there is an identity function that takes two arguments and returns the value of the second of them; and so on for functions that take any finite number of arguments and return the value of one of them. Identity functions are therefore very useful for manipulating strings of items.

More complex functions can be built up by combining these basic functions in three different ways.

The first method is the simple *composition* of functions: the outputs of one or more functions become the inputs for another function. For example, the function +2, which adds 2 to any number, can be defined by composing the successor function:

The flow diagram here indicates that the successor of x is assigned as the new value of x, and this output then becomes the input to the second function, which performs the same operation again. The function $+2$ is thus given by successor(successor(x)). In general, composition can make use of any number of functions; it corresponds to the standard device in computer programming of calls to subroutines, which compute the required values.

The second method for combining functions is the operation of *primitive recursion*. A recursive definition is a method of defining something in terms of itself, as the following highly simplified definition of a sentence illustrates:

Sentence = Sentence *and* Sentence

Sentence = Noun phrase   Verb phrase

The first line, which defines conjunction, looks like a circular definition. And it *is* a circular definition, but not viciously so. It can be applied to Sentence to yield:

Sentence *and* Sentence

and then to one of the Sentences in this structure to yield, say, the structure:

Sentence *and* (Sentence *and* Sentence)

This process could go on indefinitely. Finally, the second line of the definition specifies the internal structure of each Sentence:

Noun phrase Verb phrase *and* Noun phrase Verb phrase *and*
Noun phrase Verb phrase

With further rules to provide the proper analyses of noun phrases and verb phrases, we have the machinery we need to decide that:

John arrived and Mary left and the party ended

fits the definition of a sentence.

The basic idea of a primitive recursive definition of a function is to specify its value for the successor of n in terms of its value for n. The factorial function n! (where, for example, $3! = 3 \times 2 \times 1$) can be defined thus:

Factorial $(0) = 1$

Factorial $(n + 1) = (n + 1)$ (Factorial (n))

It follows from this definition that:

$$3! = 3(2!)$$
$$2! = 2(1!)$$
$$1! = 1(0!)$$
$$0! = 1$$

Hence $3! = 3 \times 2 \times 1 \times 1$

19

The idea can be generalized to functions that take more than one input argument.

The actual computation of primitive recursive functions can be carried out in two main ways. First, a high-level programming language such as ALGOL, LISP, or POP-2, allows a programmer to define a function recursively. For example, the factorial function can be specified in POP-2 by a direct use of a recursive definition:

> Function FACTORIAL n;
> If n = 0 then 1;
> Else n × FACTORIAL (n − 1); Close;
> End

The language enables a function to call itself in this way in a manner that closely follows the computation of 3! in the example above. Programmers often use the term 'recursion' to refer just to this self-referential aspect of computation that is allowed in certain languages: a recursive function is one that can call itself during the process of its execution. Second, a primitive recursive function can be computed by a simple repetitive or 'iterative' loop based on a conditional instruction. Here is a flow diagram of such an iterative loop for computing the factorial of n, which exemplifies all the main features of this method of computation:

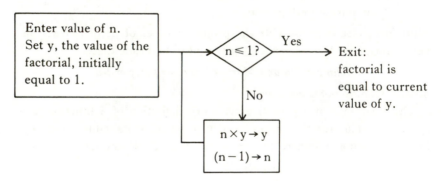

Thus, a primitive recursive loop begins with some initial conditions, which here consist in setting the initial value of the factorial equal to 1. Thereafter, the procedure continues to loop round calculating the value of the function until the conditional test is satisfied. In the present case, the factorial is computed by multiplying its current value by the current value of n and then subtracting 1 from n, and this process continues until n is reduced to 1.

20

The principle feature of a primitive recursive loop is that the maximum number of iterations is determined from the outset; in the case of the factorial loop, the number of iterations is equal to $n-1$, where n is the value of the input argument. Such loops, of course, are specific instances of the Test–Operate–Test–Exit (TOTE) unit of Miller, Galanter, and Pribram (1960).

The third operation for forming new functions out of old is still more powerful. It is known as *minimization* (or *minimalization*) and it consists in defining the value of a new function to be equal to the smallest value of an argument for which another given function returns the value 0 (see Davis, 1958, p. 38ff.). Suppose, for example, we wish to determine the largest integer not exceeding half the size of x (where x is a positive integer): e.g., the smallest integer not exceeding half of 5 is 2. This function is readily defined as:

$$\text{The minimization of y in the expression } x \dotminus 2y \dotminus 1$$

where the dotted subtraction sign, as in $x \dotminus y$, denotes a function that works like ordinary subtraction except when x is smaller than y, in which case, the answer is 0. For example, if $x=5$, then the smallest value of y for which $5 \dotminus 2y \dotminus 1$ yields 0 is $y=2$. The way to compute the value of a minimized function is to compute the successive values of the given function: $f(x, 0)$, $f(x, 1)$, $f(x, 2), \ldots$, and so on until an input value is reached for which the function yields the outcome 0. This form of computation is familiar to programmers as a 'while'-loop. The largest integer not exceeding half the size of x is computed by the following while-loop:

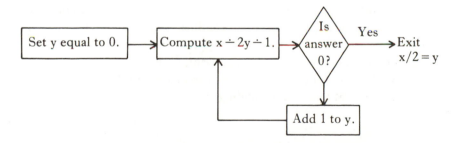

There is an initial assignment of 0 to y, and then the given function is evaluated. Therefore, if the answer is 0, the current value of y is the required result of the largest integer not exceeding half the size of x. However, *while* the answer is not 0, the procedure in the loop increments the value of y, and works out the value of the given function again. Hence,

21

the values of f(x, 0), f(x, 1), f(x, 2), ... go on being computed until the result is 0.

Once again, minimization is a special case of a TOTE unit, but it is more complicated than primitive recursion, because when the while-loop is entered there is no way of knowing how many iterations will have to be executed, or indeed whether the procedure will ever terminate with a value for the new function. So, whereas primitive recursion always yields a function that is defined for all input arguments (provided that the functions that it employs are so defined), minimization may yield a function that is undefined for certain input values. The vast majority of computer programs are primitive recursive – it can be dangerous to run the risk of having a program that goes into an infinite loop for certain inputs – but there are some functions that are defined for all inputs and that can only be computed by using minimization. A further index of the power of minimization is that if the set of basic functions (zero, successor, and identity) is extended to include addition, multiplication, and the subtraction function $(x \div y)$, then primitive recursion can be dropped as a building-block without making any difference to the set of functions that can be computed.

It is a remarkable fact that the functions that can be computed by combining the three basic sorts of function by the operations of composition, primitive recursion, and minimization (the so-called 'partial recursive functions' or 'recursive functions' for short) turn out to be identical to those that can be computed by Turing machines. The potency of the three sorts of operation has implications for the actual programming of computers. Composition, primitive recursion, and minimization, can be translated into computer programs as subroutines, simple iterative loops, and while-loops, respectively. It follows, as the proponents of 'structured' programming have emphasized (e.g., Dahl, Dijkstra, and Hoare, 1972), that any computer program whatsoever can be built up from a set of basic functions and just these three building-blocks.

22

2

The doctrine of mental logic

In any science it is useful to have a number of test cases – phenomena that must be explained by a proposed theory if it is to count as having any explanatory value. There are many phenomena that might be treated as test cases for cognitive science, but one of them embodies most of the major theoretical goals of the discipline and the specific topic of mental models.

Imagine the following scenario:

Person A asks: Where's the university?

Person B replies: Some of those people are from there.

Person A goes up to the group of people indicated by B and asks them the same question.

A's behaviour depends on a chain of inferences that includes at its centre the following deduction:

Some of those people are from the university. Any person from the university is likely to know where the university is.

∴ Some of those people are likely to know where the university is.

The first premise derives from B's reply; the second premise derives from general knowledge; the conclusion derives from a process of reasoning.

The ability to reason, as befits a test case, lies at the heart of human mentality: *Homo sapiens* is a rational creature, and there are many occasions in life that call for inferential skill. They include: decisions about courses of action; the evaluation of assumptions and hypotheses; the pursuit of arguments and negotiations; the weighing of evidence; the solution of problems; and, above all, the development of science, culture, and technology. It is, of course, no more possible to define inferential thinking than to define life. Such matters can be elucidated only by a theory. It is useful, however, to give a working definition that delimits the domain of study. An *inference* is a process of thought that leads from one set of propositions to another. Typically, it proceeds from several premises to a single conclusion, though sometimes it may be an immediate step from a single premise to a conclusion. The propositions are usually expressed verbally, though in the case of some practical inferences the premises may consist of a perceived or imagined state of affairs and the conclusion may consist of a course of action. The process of thought in a *deduction*, such as the one in the test case, is based on principles designed to establish a logical relation between the premises and the conclusion.

My test case for cognitive science is to account for the mental processes that occur in deductive inference. This explanatory goal draws together many of the puzzles that currently confront us – the recognition of words, the parsing of syntactic structure, the semantic interpretation of sentences, the process of reasoning, and the conscious grasp of conclusions. My starting point will be the central role of mental models in the psychology of reasoning, but before I begin to describe this novel approach I must outline the orthodox view that it is designed to replace – the doctrine of mental logic.

Logic and mental logic

Logically speaking, the deductions of daily life are invariably trivial. You might therefore imagine that it is neither important nor difficult to give a satisfactory explanation of them. You would be wrong. There is a fundamental riddle to be resolved: how is it possible for people to reason validly, that is, to draw a conclusion that must be true given that the premises are true? Psychologists have solved the riddle by postulating that there is a logic in the mind. An extreme form of this idea of a mental logic is that 'reasoning is nothing more than the propositional calculus itself' (Inhelder and Piaget, 1958, p. 305). But some version of the doctrine appears to have been held by every psychologist who has considered that human beings are capable of rational thought. It is also embodied in the nineteenth-century claim that the laws of thought are nothing else but the laws of logic.

Where does mental logic come from – how is it acquired? It might seem that in order to learn logic you would need to be able to reason validly; but, of course, if you can reason validly then you might not need logic. The doctrine of mental logic accordingly solves one riddle only to create another.

Several conjectures have in fact been made about how the mind acquires a logic. Some theorists have drawn a parallel between learning language and learning logic. Children encounter valid inferences in verbal guise and, it is said, they abstract rules of inference from them in the same way that they acquire grammatical rules. Adults, alas, are not noted for sustained

24

public demonstrations of logical thinking, and so this conjecture presumes that children can tell the difference between valid and invalid inferences, or else begs the question by assuming that Adam and Eve somehow obtained the distinction and passed it on to their offspring by applying the well-known principles of 'Old Testament' Behaviourism. Although such pedagogical procedures may be useful in extending deductive ability to new patterns of inference, they cannot account for the acquisition of logical competence itself. There is consequently a natural temptation to propose that it is inborn, just as the principles of universal grammar are supposed to be innate. This appeal to the powers of evolution proceeds by default: there is no direct evidence for it whatsoever, merely the lack of any alternative that its proponents find convincing.

Piaget has attempted to account for the development of logical thinking without relying either on the conventional principles of learning theory or on innate structures (see, e.g., Beth and Piaget, 1966). He argues that children construct logic by internalizing their own actions and by reflecting upon them. The mastery of propositional thinking ultimately grows from the mental operations engendered by this reflective process. There is much in Piaget's work that is illuminating, but he has never described the developmental process in a form that constitutes an *effective procedure*. The relation between his theory and his observations is consequently problematical. This flaw runs through all of his work like a geological fault: it seems that one can step easily from hypotheses to data, but at any moment these two massive bodies of dogma and description are threatened by total dislocation.

Granted the mystery of its origins, a logic in the mind none the less remains an appealing notion. It has had no serious competitors. Yet it provokes a number of so far unanswered questions, and my immediate purpose is to deal with them in detail, and to come to a considered opinion about the doctrine of mental logic.

The most glaring problem is that people make mistakes. They draw invalid conclusions, which should not occur if deduction is guided by a mental logic. The main response to this discrepancy is a direct assault on the phenomena. Mary Henle (1978) forthrightly declares: 'I have never found errors which could unambiguously be attributed to faulty reasoning.' She suggests that mistakes arise because people misunderstand or forget premises, and because they import additional and unwarranted factual assumptions into their reasoning. They fail to stick to pure logic, though they are capable of it. Even with the most charitable interpretation of my own (and others') inferential performance, I believe that this defence is mistaken. However, there are no criteria independent of controversy by which to make a fair assessment of whether an error violates logic. It is not clear what would count as crucial evidence, since it is always possible to provide an alternative explanation for an error. Perhaps for this reason, Henle's defence has exerted a considerable influence on psychologists studying reasoning. It is tendentious for the best of reasons: it rests on an immovable conviction that conscious thought is rational. Yet even if Henle's claim could be given more substance by the development of a theory of performance that explains how logical knowledge may be vitiated in practice, there are still grounds for abandoning the doctrine.

If there is a mental logic, it is natural to ask which particular brand of logic it is. This question was not raised in the last century, because it then appeared that there was only one kind of logic. Modern logicians have developed more powerful methods, and have discovered how to formulate many different logics. It turns out, for instance, that there are an infinite number of distinct modal logics governing the concepts of possibility and necessity. Perhaps there is more than one mental logic; some logicians certainly consider that natural language cannot be accommodated within a single logic. All of these riches are difficulties in disguise, because the task for psychology is to discover which of the infinite variety of logics is in the mind.

Even if the particular brand of mental logic had been isolated, there would still be the problem of discovering the nature of its mental specification. Any given logic can be formulated in a number of different ways. An *axiomatic* treatment proceeds by specifying:

1. A vocabulary of symbols.

2. A set of syntactic rules that recursively define well-formed expressions.

3. A set of well-formed expressions that are to be taken as axioms.

4. A set of rules of inference that enable new well-formed expressions to be derived from others.

A derivable conclusion is one that can be obtained from premises using only the axioms and the rules of inference. This specification, which is illustrated for the propositional calculus in Table 2.1, is *formal*, or *syntactic*, in that the rules of inference concern only well-formed strings of symbols, not what they mean or whether they denote truths or falsehoods. A *semantics* for the logic can be separately formulated: the basic expressions of the

26

Table 2.1 *An axiomatization of the propositional calculus*

Vocabulary

not	:	corresponding to negation
&	:	corresponding to conjunction
or	:	corresponding to inclusive disjunction, i.e., p or q (or both)
→	:	corresponding to implication, i.e., not-p or q, and in some uses: if p then q
(	:	left bracket
)	:	right bracket
p, q, r...	:	variables denoting propositions

Grammar
1 Any variable is a well-formed formula.
2 If A is a well-formed formula, then not-A is too.
3 If A and B are well-formed formulas, then so are (A & B), (A or B), and (A → B).

Axioms
1 (p → (q → p))
2 ((p → (q → r)) → ((p → q) → (p → r)))
3 (not-not-p → p)

Rules of inference
1   If A → B and A have been derived, then B can be derived (*modus ponens*)
2 Given a well-formed formula A containing a variable, p, then any well-formed formula B can be uniformly substituted for each occurrence of p in A (substitution).

---

language, the variables, are assigned a truth value, so that the value of any individual propositional variable is either *true* or *false*. Next, it is stipulated that for any formula A, the value of not-A is *true* if and only if the value of A is *false*, that the value of A & B is *true* if and only if A is *true* and B is *true*; and so on. The logical terms are thus defined in such a way that the interpretation of a complex expression can be built up compositionally from the interpretations of its constituents. Like conjunction, the other connectives of the calculus are functions from the truth values of constituents to the truth value of the proposition formed from them by the particular connective. The semantics is accordingly *truth-functional*; nothing more is at stake than truth values, and functions from truth values. (In actual usage, of course, words such as *and* and *or* often imply temporal relations.) A simple way to display these functions is to use a 'truth table', which shows the truth value of a proposition formed with a particular connective as a function of each possible combination of truth values of its constituent propositions. Thus, the truth table for conjunction takes

27

the following form:

p	q	p & q
True	True	True
True	False	False
False	True	False
False	False	False

It shows that $p \& q$ is true if and only if its constituents (p, q) are both true.

Validity is a semantic notion: an inference is valid if and only if it yields a true conclusion from true premises; whereas derivability is a syntactic notion. A logic is said to be *complete* if those inferences that are valid are derivable; it is said to be *sound* if those inferences that are derivable are valid. The propositional calculus can be formulated in ways that have both of these desirable characteristics.

A given logic can be axiomatized in a variety of different ways, depending on the choice of axioms and rules of inference. The choice will have no bearing on which inferences are valid, but it will affect the relative ease with which their derivations can be made. The mental specification of logic will accordingly have psychological consequences, since the difficulty of making a particular inference may vary markedly depending on whether or not a certain rule of inference is included in the system.

Axiomatic treatments of logic can be contrasted with what is known as the method of *natural deduction*. The fundamental semantic principle governing all logic is that an argument is warranted provided that there can be no counter-example to it – that is, an inference is valid if there is no interpretation of the premises that is consistent with a denial of the conclusion. Natural deduction provides a method for making a systematic search for such interpretations of the premises. The ideal in any logic is a *decision procedure* that for any inference reveals after a finite number of steps that the inference is valid or invalid. There are several such decision procedures for the propositional calculus. But in the case of the more powerful quantificational calculus, which we shall encounter later, only one half of the decision procedure is possible: the search for a counter-example can always be known to be fruitless after a finite number of steps, i.e., it is always possible to show that the inference is valid, but a search for an interpretation of the premises that is consistent with a denial of the conclusion can continue *ad infinitum*. There is a practical consequence of this asymmetry. In computer programs for evaluating inferences, there is a premium on discovering that an inference is valid as soon as possible:

while a program is still searching for a counter-example, there is no way of knowing whether it will ultimately deliver a verdict or has gone into an infinite loop.

The method of natural deduction is based on inference schemata, which are really semantically motivated counterparts to rules of inference, except that there is no premium on economy, and schemata are freely introduced for each logical connective. Table 2.2 presents some examples of inference schemata for the propositional calculus. The method is indeed intended to be natural, and several psychologists have used it as the basis for psychological theories of reasoning (Johnson-Laird, 1975a; Osherson, 1975; Braine, 1978; Rips, 1982). There is, however, no convincing evidence in favour of this approach (or any other) to the logic of the mind. It is very difficult to discover which logic, in which particular format, is to be found there.

Table 2.2 *Some examples of inference schemata for the propositional calculus*

1	A, B	
	∴ A & B	
2	A or B, not-A	
	∴ B	
3	A → B, A	
	∴ B	
4	A → B, not-B	
	∴ not-A	
5	A & B	
	∴ A	
6	A	
	∴ A or B	
7	not-A	
	∴ A → B	
8	not-not-A	
	∴ A	

The effect of content on reasoning

The underlying assumption of any formal logic, of course, is that deductions are valid in virtue of their form, not their content. Any inference, for example, that has the following form:

$$p \text{ or } q$$
$$\text{not-}p$$
$$\therefore q$$

29

is valid regardless of the specific propositions denoted by p and q. If such a rule of inference is laid down in the mind, it should apply whatever the content of the propositions. There are a number of cases, however, where the content of a problem does affect inferential performance. The most dramatic examples occur in a task invented by Peter Wason, which we jointly investigated (see Wason and Johnson-Laird, 1972).

The task seems simple. The experimenter lays out four cards in front of a subject, displaying the following symbols:

$$E \quad K \quad 4 \quad 7$$

The subject already knows that each card has a number on one side and a letter on the other side. The experimenter then presents the following generalization:

If a card has a vowel on one side then it has an even number on the other side.

The subject's task is to select those cards that need to be turned over in order to find out whether the generalization is true or false. The order of turning over the cards is not at issue: each card must be considered on its merits, i.e., on whether it is relevant to determining the truth value of the generalization.

Although the problem is easy to understand, it is hard to solve. The reader is advised to try it before proceeding any further.

Nearly every subject appreciates the need to turn over the card bearing the vowel: if it has an even number on its other side then the generalization is unscathed, but if it has an odd number on its other side then the generalization is plainly false. Likewise, most subjects realize that there is no need to select the card bearing the consonant, since the generalization has no implications for such cards. Some subjects choose the card bearing the even number; other subjects do not. If this card is turned over to reveal a vowel, the generalization is unscathed; if it is turned over to reveal a consonant, it would seem to be equally unscathed. Hence, it is not really necessary to turn over this card, but its selection is a venial sin of commission. The serious mistake arises with the card bearing the odd number. Very few subjects elect to turn it over, and this sin of omission is puzzling because if the card has a vowel on its other side then the generalization is blatantly false. In other words, the reason for selecting the card with the odd number on it is precisely the same as the reason for selecting the card bearing the vowel: both might reveal cases of a vowel combined with an odd number, and thus refute the generalization.

Quite why subjects fail to make the correct selection is mysterious. A number of factors appear to be at work, including an uncertainty about whether the generalization implies its converse, a tendency to consider properly only those cards bearing values explicitly referred to in the generalization, and a propensity towards seeking confirmation rather than disconfirmation. The task is sufficiently complicated to have engendered a sizeable body of studies with results that are not always totally consistent (see Evans, 1982, for an excellent review).

Critics have argued that the selection task is a trick (Cohen, 1981), that subjects are right to ignore the falsifying instance (Wetherick, 1970), and that the task is so complicated that even the correct selections are made only by chance (Finocchiaro, 1980). Such arguments are again tendentious. Their motive is to defend rationality. Moreover, they lose their point in the light of the effects of content on performance.

Wason and I explored a number of changes in procedure and materials in a vain attempt to improve performance in the task until we discovered that a seemingly simple change in content produced a striking effect. When the subjects were presented with four cards representing journeys, i.e., a destination on one side and a mode of transport on the other, there was a significant gain in insight (Wason and Shapiro, 1971). Hence, with the cards:

Manchester   Sheffield   Train   Car

and the general rule:

Every time I go to Manchester I travel by train

over 60% of the subjects appreciated the need to turn over the card with 'car' on it. If this card has 'Manchester' on its other side, then the rule is plainly false. In the control group, only just over 12% of the subjects made the equivalent choice with the abstract materials. A further study showed that experience with realistic materials failed to transfer positively to abstract materials (Johnson-Laird, Legrenzi, and Legrenzi, 1972). In one realistic condition in this experiment, there was a set of envelopes, including one that was face down and sealed, one that was face down and unsealed, one that was face up with a 50 lire stamp on it, and one that was face up with a 40 lire stamp on it. The subjects were told that there was a general postal regulation:

If a letter is sealed, then it has a 50 lire stamp on it

and they were asked to imagine that they were sorting letters to make sure they conformed to the regulation. Their task was to determine which envelopes it was necessary to turn over to find out whether or not they violated the rule. In this condition, the subjects, who were English, had no difficulty in appreciating that it was necessary to turn over the envelope with the 40 lire stamp on it. (If it was sealed, then plainly it contravened the regulation.) They performed almost as well in another realistic condition with the rule:

A letter is sealed only if it has a 5d. stamp on it

where again they realized that they needed to turn over an envelope with a 4d. stamp on it to check whether it was in accordance with the regulation. But, although the trials with the realistic materials alternated with trials with abstract materials, there was no apparent transfer: the subjects continued to fail to select the potentially falsifying item.

There have been many replications of the effect of realistic materials on increased insight into the selection task (e.g., Lunzer, Harrison, and Davey, 1972; Gilhooly and Falconer, 1974; Van Duyne, 1974), and variations in the type of content have been shown to yield different degrees of insight (Van Duyne, 1976; Pollard and Evans, 1981). But there have also been failures to demonstrate improved performance with realistic materials (Manktelow and Evans, 1979; Reich and Ruth, 1982; Brown, Keats, Keats, and Seggie, 1980; Griggs and Cox, 1982). There are a number of factors that may account for the discrepancy. One obvious possibility is that it arises as a result of 'experimenter' effects. The standard administration of the selection task is certainly open to such effects. Some of the more notable failures to obtain an effect of realistic materials occurred with group testing, and any procedure that reduces the onus on the subjects to think is likely to yield a poorer performance. However, there is at least one study that employed the optimal technique of individual face-to-face testing by a naive experimenter, and this experiment replicated the facilitating effect of a realistic rule (Pollard, 1981).

Another conjecture is that realistic materials improve performance only if the subjects can recall past experiences with the content of the rule. There are several variations on this hypothesis. At one extreme, the subjects merely have to remember the answer, and do not have to reason at all (Manktelow and Evans, 1979). Responses of that sort may have occurred in certain conditions in some experiments. But the inadequacy of this version of the 'memory cue' explanation is obvious from the very first results on realistic materials; subjects had surely never encountered such rules as 'Every time I go to Manchester I travel by train', or 'If a letter is sealed, then it has a 50 lire stamp on it.' A weaker version of the hypothesis is therefore more plausible: subjects can be cued to make the correct selections by their memory for analogous rules and their counter-examples (Griggs and Cox, In press). The fact that the relation between the terms in the rule must be a familiar one supports this proposal. Thus, such rules as 'Every time I think of Ottawa I remember car' (Bracewell and Hidi, 1974) and 'If I eat haddock, then I drink gin' (Manktelow and Evans, 1979) do not lead to insight into the task. Similarly, when the familiarity of the rules is manipulated, insight into the task is correlated with it. For example, with subjects in Florida, the local law 'If a person is drinking beer, then the person must be over 19' yields better performance than its unfamiliar contrapositive or converse (Cox and Griggs, 1982). A striking result with one and the same rule is that English subjects over the age of 45, who may remember the postal regulation concerning sealed envelopes, performed well in a recent replication of the envelope experiment, but subjects under the age of 45, who may never have encountered the regulation, performed no better than with abstract materials (Golding, 1981). However, direct personal experience of the rule is not necessary. In a study carried out by D'Andrade (cited by Rumelhart and Norman, 1981; and replicated by Mandler, 1981) the subjects had to imagine that they managed a store; they showed insight with the 'sensible' principle:

If a purchase exceeds $30, then the receipt must have the signature of the manager on the back

but they lacked insight with an arbitrary principle. In a further replication, Griggs and Cox demonstrated a significant degree of insight with such negated rules as:

If a purchase does not exceed $30, then the receipt must have the signature of the manager on the back.

Such a rule is the opposite of 'sensible', but perhaps its clear violation of common sense suffices, as Wason (In press) has suggested, to trigger the correct inference.

Memory is plainly important for correct performance in the selection task: no effect of content can be explained without appeal to previous experience. What is crucial, however, is that insight into the task reflects an effect of content on the process of deduction. If subjects already possess a mental model of the relation expressed in the general rule, or a model that can be readily related to the rule, they are much more likely to have an insight into the task. This phenomenon is an embarrassment to any psychological theory that assumes that generalizations are falsified by recourse to formal rules of inference.

The doctrine of mental logic commits one to the view that faced with a complex situation:

the subject will ask himself two kinds of questions: (a) whether fact x implies fact y. . . To verify it, he will look in this case to see whether or not there is a counterexample x and non-y. (b) He will also ask whether it is really x which implies y or whether, on the contrary, it is y which implies x . . . (Piaget, in Beth and Piaget, 1966, p. 181)

The subjects in the card-turning task do, indeed, search for counter-examples, but their search is only comprehensive with realistic materials that relate to an existing mental model. Their conspicuous failure with abstract materials is difficult to reconcile with syntactic principles of inference that are independent of content. A mental logic would provide the same formal guide to performance in both cases, and at the very least would have to be supplemented by principles sensitive to content and leading to conclusions of a different form.

Semantic information and inferential heuristics

One final problem for mental logic must be confronted. Suppose that psychologists had successfully determined its nature, its mental specification, and the causes of errors and effects of content. Could they then retire from the field to contemplate other mysteries of nature? Unfortunately not. Any set of premises implies an infinite number of different valid conclusions. Many will be wholly trivial, such as a simple conjunction of the premises; only a few, if any, are likely to be drawn spontaneously in ordinary circumstances. Given the premises:

If there is no error message, then the program is compiled.
There is no error message

most people draw the conclusion:

The program is compiled.

They do not draw such equally valid conclusions as:

There is no error message or the program is compiled.
There is no error message and, if there is no error message, then the program is compiled.
There is no error message or if there is no error message, then the program is compiled

34

and so on. No sane person would draw such conclusions. Psychologists must therefore specify the heuristic principles that govern the particular valid deductions that are drawn. These principles must lie outside logic altogether, because they determine which of a potentially infinite set of valid deductions the inferential mechanism produces.

Some years ago, when I suggested a psychological theory of reasoning based on natural deduction (Johnson-Laird, 1975a), I drew a distinction between major inference schemata, such as:

$$A \text{ or } B, \text{ not-}A$$

$$\therefore B$$

and auxiliary inference schemata, such as:

$$A$$

$$\therefore A \text{ or } B$$

A sensible person does not spontaneously advance valid arguments of the form:

A: My aunt's name is Grace.

∴ A or B: Hence, my aunt's name is Grace or your weight is 160 lb.

However, the schema underlying this inference can be abandoned only at the cost of requiring more complex schemata for deductions of the following sort:

If A or B then C:

If the plane is late or the flight is diverted, the airline makes a public announcement.

A: The plane is late.

∴ C: Hence, the airline makes a public announcement

where it is necessary to show that the simple premise, A, establishes the truth of the antecedent of the conditional premise, A or B. My idea was accordingly that auxiliary inference schemata are never used on their own, but only as an immediate precursor to the use of a major schema. This manoeuvre was transparently *ad hoc*. It describes the sorts of inferences that people draw rather than explains why they draw them. A more promising approach to the required inferential heuristic can be based on the concept of *semantic* information.

Psychologists are familiar with the statistical concept of information which derives from the work of Hartley, Shannon, and others, but which has to do with the relative probabilities of messages, not their meanings. It is possible, however, to develop a measure of semantic information, on the basis of the assumption that the more states of affairs a proposition rules out, the more information it conveys. The assumption can be traced back to medieval philosophy; the most sustained attempt to use it to develop a calculus is to be found in the work of Bar-Hillel and Carnap (1952). The present account, which was independently formulated, is much less ambitious since it is restricted to the propositional calculus, but it thereby avoids some intractable problems (see Hintikka, 1973).

Within the propositional calculus, a simple categorical proposition, p, rules out merely the state of affairs corresponding to its negation, *not-p*; a conjunction, p & q, rules out rather more states of affairs, namely *not-p & q, p & not-q*, and *not-p & not-q*; a disjunction, *p or q or both*, rules out rather fewer states of affairs, namely, *not-p & not-q*. Since a proposition is either true or else false within the propositional calculus, there are only four possible contingencies concerning the truth values of two arbitrary propositions, p and q:

p	q
True	True
True	False
False	True
False	False

The greater the number of contingencies that a proposition eliminates, the greater the amount of semantic information that it conveys. If we express this measure as the proportion of contingencies that are ruled out, then it remains constant regardless of the number of propositions entering into the truth table. A simple categorical always eliminates 0·5 of the contingencies in the table, as does its negation. A conjunction eliminates 0·75 of them. A disjunction eliminates 0·25 of them. These figures are in a rank order that corresponds to most people's intuitions about the relative informativeness of such propositions: disjunctions are less informative than straightforward categorical assertions, which in turn are less informative than conjunctions. There is an effective procedure for computing the semantic informativeness of any complex proposition, which is described in Table 2.3.

Although ordinary individuals are unlikely to compute semantic information accurately, relying instead on a rough-and-ready assessment, the concept is important in understanding the psychology of deduction. No valid inference can yield a conclusion with a greater amount of semantic information than contained in the premises. A heuristic that appears to

Table 2.3 *An effective procedure for computing the semantic informativeness of any proposition within the framework of the propositional calculus*

1 The semantic informativeness of any proposition A, no matter how many connectives it contains, is given by the following simple formula:

$$\text{Informativeness (A)} = 1 - P(A)$$

where P(A) denotes the 'truth-table' probability of A. This probability is equivalent to the proportion of contingencies in the truth table that are consistent with the proposition; its complement, semantic informativeness, is the proportion that are inconsistent with it, i.e., that the proposition eliminates.

2 The truth-table probability of a proposition is calculated according to the ordinary laws of probability theory on the assumption that the a priori probabilities of all the simple propositions involved in the premises equal 0·5. In general, the truth-table probability of a negative proposition is given by:

$$P(\text{not-A}) = 1 - P(A)$$

the truth-table probability of a conjunction (of independent events) is given by:

$$P(A \& B) = P(A) \cdot P(B)$$

the truth-table probability of a disjunction is given by:

$$P(A \text{ or } B) = P(A) + P(B) - P(A \& B)$$

and the truth-table probability of an implication is given by:

$$P(A \rightarrow B) = P(\text{not-A or } B)$$

However, the following special cases should be noted:

$$P(A \& \text{not-A}) = 0 \qquad \text{(contradictions)}$$
$$P(A \text{ or not-A}) = 1 \qquad \text{(tautologies)}$$
$$P(A \& A) = P(A \text{ or } A) = P(A) \quad \text{(redundancies)}$$

It is a straightfoward matter to specify a recursive function that uses these principles to compute the truth-table probability of any arbitrary proposition.

govern the inferences that people actually draw can now be stated: *No conclusion contains less semantic information than the premises on which it is based or fails to express that information more parsimoniously.* Propositional inference is thus essentially a matter of expressing the same semantic content as the premises with greater linguistic economy, that is, using fewer connectives and fewer occurrences of categorical propositions. For example, premises of the form:

> p or q or r
> if p and not-r then q
> either r and q, or else not-r and not-q
> if r then p

validly imply:

> p and q and r

This conclusion contains the same semantic content as the premises, and the same amount of semantic information (0·875), but it expresses it with maximum economy. The heuristic explains why people do not make inferences of the form:

$$p$$
$$\therefore \ p \ or \ q$$

The conclusion contains less information, and is less parsimonious, than the premises. Likewise, the heuristic explains why, given premises of the form:

$$p$$

$$q$$

people claim that nothing of interest follows. They refrain from drawing the conclusion:

$$p \ and \ q$$

because it is less economical linguistically than the premises on which it is based.

There is one other general principle to be added. Given premises of the form:

$$p$$

$$not\text{-}p \ or \ q$$

one can validly infer:

$$p \ and \ q$$

which contains exactly the same content as the premises. However, the conclusion that individuals usually draw is stated in categorical form:

$$q$$

which contains less semantic information than the premises. The abbreviation reflects the principle that it is not normally necessary to repeat a simple categorical premise – p, in this case – in drawing a conclusion. The reasoner can take it for granted: to repeat it would be to violate the convention that in ordinary discourse speakers need not state the obvious – a convention that, as the philosopher Paul Grice (1975) has observed, forms part of the general co-operative principle by which discourse proceeds. Only if the conclusion is taken together with the unrepeated categorical premise is the heuristic of not losing information observed.

It is important to bear in mind the interplay between the inferential heuristic and the Gricean principle. The heuristic is a constraint that governs inferences: it filters out trivia. The Gricean convention governs the formulation of conclusions: it filters out unnecessary repetitions. People do not draw the conclusion:

$$p \text{ and } q$$
$$\therefore \; p$$

because they would thereby lose information. They make inferences such as:

$$\text{if } p \text{ then } q$$
$$p$$
$$\therefore \; p \text{ and } q$$

but they express the conclusion parsimoniously as:

$$\therefore \; q$$

Conclusions

The doctrine of mental logic can certainly be formulated in a way that meets the methodological criterion of effectiveness: a number of authors, notably Rips (1982), have expressed versions of the doctrine as effective procedures. The trouble with mental logic is thus empirical. There are six main problems:

1. People make fallacious inferences. Attempts have been made to explain these mistakes away, but it is difficult to assess the merit of such proposals.

2. Which logic, or logics, are to be found in the mind? There is no definitive answer to this question. For the most part, psychologists have been happy to postulate mental counterparts to certain calculi of modern logic, but they have produced no decisive evidence to corroborate such assumptions.

3. How is logic formulated in the mind? The main attempt to answer this question concerns propositional reasoning. Several investigators have suggested schemes based on natural deduction, but again it is difficult to obtain direct empirical evidence relevant to this issue.

4. How does a system of logic arise in the mind? Neither the principles of learning theory nor the assumptions of Piagetian lore appear to provide an adequate answer. By default, it seems that our logical apparatus must

be inborn, though there is no account of how it could have become innately determined.

5. What evidence there is about the psychology of reasoning suggests that deductions are not immune to the content of the premises. When individuals have a relevant mental model of a relation, they are more likely to reason about it validly. This phenomenon requires the introduction of considerable theoretical machinery if the doctrine of mental logic is to be sustained.

6. People follow extra-logical heuristics when they make spontaneous inferences. They appear to be guided by the principle of maintaining the semantic content of the premises but expressing it with greater linguistic economy. This principle is likely to be an intrinsic part of the mental machinery for inference rather than a constraint tagged on *ad hoc*. Theories of mental logic have largely ignored the problem. They have concentrated on the evaluation of given conclusions rather than on their spontaneous production. In fact, an effective procedure that produces valid conclusions will be able, if it is to be of any use, to evaluate them, too. (The converse does not hold.) To evaluate a given conclusion, one adds its negation to the set of premises. If the conclusion is valid, the procedure will signal that the premises are now inconsistent. In the next chapter, I shall describe a procedure for generating non-trivial conclusions that can be used in this way.

Although the doctrine of mental logic is by no means refuted, I believe that the time has come for a radically different conception of inference. It is worth giving up, not the thesis that human beings are capable of rational thought, but the idea that what underlies this ability is a mental logic. There can be reasoning without logic. More surprisingly, perhaps, there can be valid reasoning without logic. Indeed, once the search for mental rules of inference is abandoned it is possible to make better sense of the psychology of reasoning, and, as we shall see, to develop a theory of the inferential mechanism from which the heuristic principles described in this chapter are an automatic consequence.

3

Reasoning with propositions

The thesis that I shall defend is that reasoning ordinarily proceeds without recourse to a mental logic with formal rules of inference. In order to sustain this claim, I need to show how an alternative procedure is possible for each of the important varieties of deductive inference. The simplest inferences depend on the interrelations between propositions, not on their internal structures. Many English words can connect clauses expressing propositions, and there are at least two of them, *and* and *or*, that can be used with truth-functional meanings like the connectives of the propositional calculus. I shall deal first with such propositional inferences before going on to consider more complex deductions.

Logicians have argued about whether the meaning of a connective is specified wholly by the inferences that it warrants. If this principle were to hold, one could introduce Prior's (1960) delightful connective *tonk*, which has the property of allowing any conclusion whatsoever to be inferred from any premise. It is defined by the inference schemata:

$$1 \quad \frac{A}{\therefore \ A \text{ tonk } B} \qquad 2 \quad \frac{A \text{ tonk } B}{\therefore \ B}$$

Hence, the following deductions are valid:

Man is mortal
∴ Man is mortal tonk arithmetic is complete (From schema 1)
∴ Arithmetic is complete. (From schema 2)

What is the meaning of *tonk*? It seems that the question is not answered merely by giving schemata that specify its inferential properties. This conclusion is borne out by a well-known result concerning the interpretation of the propositional calculus. For reasons that I shall explain later (in Chapter 9), in one interpretation of the propositional calculus (an Intuitionistic one applied to mathematics), the assertion of a proposition, p, means that a proof of p can be constructed, and the negation of a proposition, *not-p*, means that a proof of the absurdity of p can be constructed. The propositional connectives can then be redefined in these terms, e.g., p &

41

not q means that *p* is provable and that *q* is provably absurd. It turns out, however, that even with this new interpretation, all the derivable theorems of the standard propositional calculus still hold (see Kneale and Kneale, 1962, p. 678). Since these theorems are derivable using the standard rules of inference (or inference schemata), the moral is plain: the meaning of a connective is not defined merely by specifying rules of inference for it.

Psychologically speaking, children are likely to learn the meaning of a connective before they learn about its inferential behaviour. At the heart of its meaning is its contribution to the truth conditions of sentences in which it occurs. For example, an assertion of the form 'A or B', is true if and only if 'A' is true or 'B' is true. This formulation is circular because the word *or* also occurs in the defining expression. In the formal statement of the semantics of the propositional calculus, the second occurrence of the term would be in the vocabulary of the meta-language (not the language being defined). Children master the meaning of the inclusive sense of *or* by learning that the connective corresponds to the concept of disjunction. They acquire in effect a term that corresponds in meaning to the following truth table:

A	B	Truth value of 'A or B' in English
True	True	True
True	False	True
False	True	True
False	False	False

They learn in short that a disjunction is true if at least one of its constituent propositions is true. The truth table spells out the set of possible models of the disjunction.

Once children have grasped the truth conditions of a connective, they can in principle make deductions without needing to learn any formal rules of inference. For example, given premises of the form:

$$p \text{ or } q$$
$$\text{not-}p$$

the first premise rules out any models in which both *p* and *q* are false, as can be ascertained from the truth table for *or*, and the second premise eliminates any models in which *p* is true. Hence, the premises have eliminated three of the possible models:

p	q	
True	True	Eliminated by the premise *not-p*
True	False	Eliminated by the premise *not-p*
False	True	
False	False	Eliminated by the premise *p or q*

As Sherlock Holmes remarked, when you have eliminated the impossible, whatever remains must be the truth. In the present case, what remains is the only possible model of the premises, in which p is false and q is true. The following conclusion is accordingly valid:

not-p and q

This inference was made without using either rules of inference or inference schemata. All that it required was a semantics for the connective – its truth conditions, and the ability to use these truth conditions to eliminate contingencies from a set of possible models.

Once you have understood the meaning of a connective – in the case of propositional connectives, the function from the truth values of the constituents to the truth value of the proposition as a whole – you have sufficient knowledge to grasp the logical properties of that connective. They emerge directly from its meaning. Rules of inference, of course, are designed to reflect the semantics of connectives; they provide a piece of formal machinery that automatically weeds out contingencies (as does the procedure described above). But from a psychological point of view, the two methods are distinct. It is one thing to learn the truth conditions of a term and to put this knowledge to work in eliminating models; it is quite another to learn formal rules of inference and to use them as a syntactic template by which to derive a new conclusion. This distinction becomes sharper when we consider the problem of how inferential heuristics guide a reasoner to a specific conclusion; it becomes sharper still when we meet connectives that have unambiguous truth conditions but vagaries in their logical properties; it becomes absolute when we encounter higher-order logical calculi that are provably 'incomplete', that is to say, for which it is impossible to devise formal rules that capture the complete set of valid deductions.

The psychological inadequacies of truth tables

Although a table of contingencies corresponds to a set of models, the method of eliminating entries that are inconsistent with premises is psychologically implausible, because the systematic evaluation of the table is likely to exceed the capacity of working memory. Moreover, considerable ingenuity is required to dream up the method in the first place, and most of us are not sufficiently ingenious, as is shown by the popularity of reasoning puzzles that become trivial by recourse to this method. These puzzles are typically devised by constructing a contingency table and then thinking up a series of propositions that eliminates all but one (or a few) of its entries. Table 3.1 illustrates the method.

Table 3.1 *How to devise a logical puzzle*

---

1 Construct a table of contingencies for a number of propositions which specifies all the possible combinations of truth values that they could have, e.g.:

	p	q	r
1	True	True	True
2	True	True	False
3	True	False	True
4	True	False	False
5	False	True	True
6	False	True	False
7	False	False	True
8	False	False	False

2 Devise a set of propositions that eliminate all but one (or a few) of the contingencies. For example:
i   *If r then p* eliminates contingencies 5 and 7.
ii *Either r and q or else not-r and not-q* eliminates contingencies 2, 3, 6 and 7.
iii *If p and not-r then q* eliminates contingency 4.
iv *p or q or r*, where *or* is used inclusively, eliminates contingency 8.
There is only one contingency, 1, that has not been eliminated, and it is therefore the correct conclusion:

p and q and r

3 Think up an appropriate content for *p*, *q*, and *r*, and state the puzzle in terms of it:
    the following four assertions are all true of a particular situation:
    1 If the airport has been closed then the plane is late.
    2 Either the airport has been closed and the flight diverted or else the airport hasn't been closed and the flight not diverted.
    3 If the plane is late and the airport hasn't been closed, then the flight has been diverted.
    4 At least one of the following has happened: the plane is late, the flight has been diverted, the airport has been closed.
    What conclusion can you draw?
    (Answer: The plane is late and the flight has been diverted and the airport has been closed.)

For a naive subject, who knows no formal logic, a problem such as the one in Table 3.1 is wellnigh impossible to solve without recourse to pencil and paper, and even then it is difficult. No subject that I have ever tested has re-invented the complete notion of truth tables – it takes a Peirce or a Wittgenstein to invent them in the first place. Indeed, few people seem to realize spontaneously that only eight contingencies are at stake in the problem. This point was brought home to me most forcefully by an experiment that I have often carried out in laboratory classes. The subjects have to discover the rule by which three switches control a light. In fact, the rule is always a simple 'truth-function' of two of the switches, e.g., the light comes on provided switch 1 is down or else 2 is down. The aim of the experiment is to investigate differences in the difficulty of conjunction, disjunction, and implication, and, in general, its results establish that the fewer the combinations that make the light come on, the easier is the task. The relevant finding here, however, is the surprising difficulty of the task and the unsystematic way in which intelligent subjects tackle it. The performance of a typical subject is illustrated in Table 3.2. After the last trial shown in this protocol, the subject announced that the rule was that switch 2 had to be down and switch 1 up. This conjecture is, in fact,

Table 3.2 *A protocol of a typical subject's performance in trying to determine the rule relating the positions of three switches to the state of a light*

A '1' indicates that the subject moved the switch down, and a '0' indicates that the subject moved the switch up. Only after the position of the switches has been set is the subject able to see the effect on the light.

Switch 1	Switch 2	Switch 3	Effect on the light
1	0	0	On
0	1	0	On
0	0	1	Off
1	1	0	Off
0	1	1	On
0	0	0	Off
0	0	1	Off
0	1	1	On
0	0	1	Off

At this point, after 32 seconds on the task, the subject announces a rule: 'Switch 2 has to be down and switch 1 up to make the light come on.'

inconsistent with the very first pattern of switch positions that the subject had tried. Moreover, the subject never even tested what happened with either of the following two switch positions:

1	0	1	(Light comes on)
1	1	1	(Light does not come on)

There are a number of phenomena at work, including the load on memory, but the critical point is that subjects do not spontaneously examine the combinatorial possibilities in a systematic and exhaustive fashion – notwithstanding Piaget's claim that this ability develops at the stage of formal operations around the age of twelve.

With such limited ability on an overt 'truth table', it is unlikely that ordinary individuals consult mental truth tables in carrying out propositional inferences. There is, however, another possibility.

An effective procedure for propositional reasoning

Another effective procedure that I have devised makes valid propositional inferences without relying on either rules of inference or contingency tables. It is exemplified by the form of reasoning that occurs in the following case. Given the premises:

If the communications protocol is incorrect or the Baud rate is wrong, then the printer won't work.

The communications protocol is incorrect

a reasoner may go through the sequence of steps:

The fact that the protocol is incorrect renders the antecedent of the conditional true.

If the antecedent of a conditional is true, and the conditional is true (which it is, because it is a premise), then the consequent of the conditional follows. Hence, the printer won't work.

At first sight, this process may seem as though it depends on formal rules of inference, but the repeated reference to truth values is a good clue that the deduction is not merely a result of a syntactic process of derivation. In fact, the procedure depends on a knowledge of the truth conditions of connectives, an ability to substitute a truth value for a proposition, and a capacity to work out the resulting effects of making such a substitution in a complex proposition. People probably cannot inspect a complete mental truth table for a given connective. Nevertheless, they do know, for example, that if there is an inclusive disjunction between two propositions:

The communications protocol is incorrect or the Baud rate is wrong (or both)

and one of the propositions is true, then the disjunction as a whole is true. Similarly, they know that if one of the propositions is false, then the only way in which the disjunction as a whole could be true is if the other proposition is true. They possess the ability to evaluate the meaning of a complex proposition from a knowledge of the truth values of its constituents: they are capable of constructing such meanings compositionally. Although I have developed a computer program that implements this effective procedure in the list-processing language, POP-10 there are grounds – as we shall see – for supposing that it has only a limited range of application to the psychology of everyday inference.

The input to the program consists in a set of premises, such as:

> not(p or q)
>
> p or r
>
> q or s

where the variables can be taken to stand for propositions. Its output is either a valid conclusion – s and r, in this case – or else a response to the effect that nothing of any interest follows from the premises. There are always an infinite number of conclusions that could be drawn – a disjunction of all the premises, their conjunction, and so on – but the program refrains from making trivial deductions.

Suppose that the program is given premises of the form that occurred in the problem about the printer:

> if p or q then r
>
> p

Its first step is to find the premise that conveys the greater amount of information, according to the procedure described in the previous chapter. In this case, the procedure yields the premise p. The next step is to search for another premise that contains p as a constituent. Whenever one premise occurs as a constituent of another more complex premise, the program substitutes the value *true* in place of the constituent in the complex premise. Hence, in the present case, the complex premise becomes:

> if true or q then r

(In the case of a negative premise, *not-p*, if p occurs as a constituent of another premise the value *false* is substituted for it.) Once the substitution of a truth value for a constituent has been made, a compositional semantics is called into play in order to work out the effects on the status of the complex premise. The truth conditions for *or* (in its inclusive sense) establish that whenever one disjunct is true the disjunction as a whole is

47

true. This knowledge enables the compositional semantics to simplify the antecedent of the conditional above to:

if true then r

The conditional can be simplified still further by the compositional semantics, because whenever a conditional is true and its antecedent is true, then the consequent must hold. This step reduces the conditional to the simple conclusion:

r

The premises are actually equivalent in their semantic content to:

p and r

But, by carrying out the compositional semantics directly on the premise into which the substitution of the truth value has occurred, the program automatically delivers a conclusion in accordance with the Gricean maxim of not stating the obvious: there is no need to introduce additional machinery to suppress the restatement of the simple premise p.

A further example shows the program failing – as it should – to draw a trivial conclusion. Given the premises:

p or q

p

a truth value is substituted for the occurrence of p in the first premise:

true or q

The truth conditions for *or* (in its inclusive sense) establish that whenever one disjunct is true the disjunction as a whole is true, and the compositional semantics accordingly simplifies the disjunction to:

true

This end product is trivial since it merely establishes that the premises are consistent with one another, and the program therefore responds that nothing of interest follows. It draws the same moral if it is presented with such premises as:

p

q

since it is unable to make a substitution. If the program is given the inconsistent premises:

p and q

not-p

the result of the substitution is:

false and q

and the truth conditions for *and* allow a simplification to:

false

This end product indicates that the premises are inconsistent. The fact that inconsistencies simplify to *false* can be used to advantage if a given conclusion is to be evaluated. The negation of this conclusion is added to the premises, and if the final outcome is *false*, the conclusion must be valid because its denial leads to a contradiction. And so a program that generates spontaneous conclusions can always be used in this way to evaluate given conclusions.

In summary, the program can be divided into three major steps:

Step 1: Find the maximally informative premise that has yet to be tried. This search makes use of the measure of semantic information based on the number of contingencies that a proposition rules out (see Chapter 2). If all the premises have been tried with no result, then no inference is made.

Step 2: If the premise chosen in step 1 is a constituent of a second premise, substitute the value *true* for its occurrence in the second premise. Otherwise, if the premise from step 1 is negative and the component that is negated occurs as a constituent of a second premise, substitute the value *false* for it in the second premise. Otherwise, return to step 1.

Step 3: Use the semantics of the connective immediately governing the substituted truth value to simplify the premise compositionally; continue the process of simplification until it can go no further. If the final result is the value *true*, then the premises are consistent and nothing of interest follows from them; if the final result is the value *false*, then the premises are self-contradictory; if the final result is a proposition, then it is the conclusion to be drawn.

In the previous chapter, I outlined the case for an inferential heuristic governing propositional reasoning: no conclusion should contain less semantic information than the premises on which it is based or fail to express that information more parsimoniously. This heuristic is merely a constraint that appears to characterize the inferences that people draw. The program automatically abides by this constraint, though it operates without the use of rules of inference and *a fortiori* without the distinction between major and auxiliary inferences. The direct use of semantic composition ensures that no information is lost from the premises and that any

forthcoming conclusion states the information they contain more parsimoniously. Likewise, the program operates on the more complex premise,
and thus automatically abides by the Gricean principle of not restating
simple premises unnecessarily. Its performance is in accordance with logic
and with the inferential heuristics, but they are nowhere incorporated
within it as explicit principles.

Not all propositional inferences derive from treating one premise
categorically, i.e., as a constituent of another. An inference of the following
form:

$$p \text{ and } q$$
$$\text{not-}p \text{ or } r$$
$$\text{not-}q \text{ or } s$$
$$\therefore r \text{ and } s$$

contains no premise that can be treated categorically. But, as soon as the
first premise is broken down into its two separate constituents, each of
them can be exploited by the categorical procedure. The conclusions that
it produces can be combined using whatever connective occurred in the
first premise – in this case, a conjunction – provided that the connectives
are truth-functional and symmetric. Since *if p then q* is not symmetric,
i.e., not equivalent to *if q then p*, conditionals have to be translated into
their equivalent symmetric form, *not-p or q*. The procedure can be used
recursively in order to make a deduction from a complex premise, such as:

$$p \text{ or } q, \text{ and } r$$

The premise is split into two conjuncts, *p or q* and *r*, and their inferential
consequences followed up. This process, in turn, requires splitting up *p
or q* into two and following up their consequences.

It might be thought that the procedure for splitting up complex premises
introduces formal rules of inference. In fact, no logical rules are involved
at all. If the mysterious connective *bonk* is added to the list of acceptable
connectives, then the premises:

$$p \text{ bonk } q$$
$$\text{not-}p \text{ or } r$$
$$\text{not-}q \text{ or } s$$

will lead to the conclusion:

$$r \text{ bonk } s$$

Since there are no rules of inference for *bonk*, then *a fortiori* there are no rules of inference for the program to rely on in drawing this conclusion. The truth conditions of *bonk*, however, will have to be specified if it is to be used in simple categorical inferences. In short, every type of deduction in the standard propositional calculus can be carried out without the use of formal rules of inference.

The real nature of propositional reasoning

Is the effective procedure embodied in the program psychologically real – does it correspond to the way in which people actually make inferences? The answer must be a qualified one. Results from some subjects strongly suggest that they reason by substituting truth values and simplifying premises compositionally. Given the problem about the printer, for example, they typically make such observations as: 'The fact that the communications protocol is incorrect [the categorical premise] tells you that this [the antecedent of the conditional] is true and so the printer won't work [the consequent of the conditional].' It is possible, of course, that such introspections are actually based on the syntactic manipulation of formal rules such as *modus ponens*, but there is no good reason for making this assumption. Indeed, the compositional procedure is certainly superior to any theory based on rules of inference or inference schemata. It solves at a stroke the problems of which particular rules of inference are in the mind, how they are mentally represented, and how children acquire them. These questions simply do not arise, because logic is banished from the mind. Of course, it is necessary to explain how the truth conditions of connectives are mentally represented, and how they are acquired; but these questions would still have to be answered even if there were mental rules of inference. Hence, one is trading a system of formal rules, and the machinery for manipulating them, for the simple principle of substituting truth values for premises, and the ability to pursue the consequences of such substitutions. Likewise, the procedure predicts with a single mechanism both which inferences are made and how they are made, whereas if theories of mental logic were ever to confront the problem, they would be forced to make extra assumptions about the heuristics that rule out trivial conclusions. Like such theories, however, the procedure is only as real as the phenomenon of truth-functional reasoning.

In fact, people do not ordinarily think in a truth-functional way: it is a possible mode of thought rather than a habitual one. They are generally more interested in interrelating events within a model of causal or intentional relations. Suppose, for example, that someone asserts:

The government will change its policies only if the rate of inflation doesn't increase.

Either unemployment increases or else the rate of inflation increases.

One is likely to conclude:

If unemployment increases then the rate of inflation won't increase and the government will change its policies.

But such an inference does not follow validly from a purely truth-functional interpretation of the premises. What does follow is:

If the government changes its policies then the rate of inflation won't increase and unemployment will increase.

The first premise is of the form *p only if q* and is truth-functionally equivalent to *if p then q*, but the interpretation *if q then p*, though unwarranted, is most plausible. When I gave subjects such problems, they found it extremely difficult to draw truth-functionally correct conclusions (see Wason and Johnson-Laird, 1972, Chapter 7). They tried instead to establish some sensible model of the causal relations between the events. When their mental model pulled in one direction and truth-functional relations pulled in another, the mental model prevailed. Once again, the content of a problem affected the conclusions that were drawn.

The proponents of mental logic might argue that its underlying reality is obscured by matters of fact and by reinterpretations of the premises according to general knowledge. A better defence might be that the propositional calculus is just a small part of mental logic: there is also a causal logic, an intentional logic, and a logic of tense and time. Yet even this revised doctrine, though it correctly emphasizes the importance of an interpretative framework, fails to explain the phenomena. Consider, for example, the following evidence that might be established at a trial:

The victim was stabbed to death in a cinema while he was watching the afternoon showing of *Bambi*.

The suspect was travelling to Edinburgh on a train when the murder took place.

Plainly, the evidence, if true, provides a good alibi, and even children can recognize the force of the argument. How does one make the deduction? I have often given the premises to students in seminars. Their initial reaction is indeed that the suspect is innocent. When I ask why, they point out all sorts of unstated assumptions that they have used, such as:

One person cannot be in two places at the same time.
There are no cinemas on any trains travelling to Edinburgh.
The murder referred to in the second premise is the same as the one referred to in the first premise.

Someone may suggest that perhaps the suspect might have been taken off the train by helicopter, flown to the cinema to perpetrate the crime, and then flown back to the train and lowered down to reboard it. This scenario, however, is ruled out by the second premise, which asserts that the suspect was on the train *when* the murder took place. If I ask the students 'Are you absolutely sure of the suspect's innocence?', someone is likely to point out that a confederate might have carried out the murder. When this possibility is eliminated, the consensus is usually again that the suspect is innocent. But when I persist, 'Are you really sure?', a student may ask to be reminded about how the murder was committed. (Somebody once suggested that perhaps the murderer used a very long knife!) Eventually, someone may volunteer that the suspect could have used a radio-controlled robot. Once this scenario has been ruled out, everyone is convinced that the suspect could not have carried out the murder.

What these observations imply, of course, is that the inference is *not* made by recourse to a mental logic – not even a logic of *when* and *while*. On the contrary, people reason by constructing a representation of the events described by the premises. This mental model is based on the meanings of the premises (hence the continual attempts to establish precisely what they mean) and also on implicit inferences from general knowledge. If you are sceptical about the latter claim, then ask yourself whether you thought of the suspect as an adult or a child, and as male or female. (Most people tacitly infer that the suspect is an adult male.) The resulting model of the murder depicts the events in the cinema going on contemporaneously with the suspect's train journey to Edinburgh: one event overlaps the other in time, but they occur in different places. The model suggests that the suspect could not have committed the crime. This putative conclusion – with some prodding by the experimenter – is then tested by searching for an alternative scenario in which the suspect *is* guilty. When all other possibilities have been rejected, the judgment of innocence is sustained.

The models that people use to reason are more likely to resemble a perception or conception of the events (from a God's-eye view) than a string of symbols directly corresponding to the linguistic form of the premises. Reasoning is not a matter of recovering the logical forms of the premises and then applying rules of inference to them in order to derive a conclusion. It is here not even a matter of substituting truth values for constituents of propositions and working out their compositional consequences. The heart of the process is interpreting premises as mental models that take general knowledge into account, and searching for counter-examples to conclusions by trying to construct alternative models of the premises. The only truth-functions that people think about in daily life are those that arise when the world behaves in a truth-functional way, e.g., in the 'logic' of electrical circuitry and simple switches. Real assertions in real contexts only occasionally give rise to truth-functional conclusions.

Connectives that are not truth-functions

The effective procedure for propositional reasoning embodies one fundamental principle that I shall argue governs the psychology of reasoning: the logical properties of connectives derive from their meanings. This principle is vindicated by the behaviour of terms whose 'logic' lies outside the truth-functions of the propositional calculus. The meaning of *because*, for example, is obviously not truth-functional. It may be true that:

Edward insulted Maggie

and that:

Maggie ignored Edward

but these truths fail to establish the truth (or falsity) of:

Edward insulted Maggie because she ignored him

or:

Maggie ignored Edward because he insulted her.

The truth of these assertions depends on one event (the second) being the cause or reason for the other (the first), and their mere occurrence does not in itself establish the required relation between them.

A similar principle applies to the connective that has excited more psychological studies of reasoning than any other: *if*. The meaning of *if* is indeed problematical – does it have one meaning or many? Does it have a truth-functional meaning or not? I shall consider it as a representative sample of the problems that arise beyond the pale of pure logic.

One ingenious conjecture – Martin Braine's (1978) – tries to reconcile a uniform meaning for *if* with the doctrine of mental logic. Braine, who was anticipated in part by Ryle (1949, Chapter 5), argues that assertions of the form *if p then q* are merely stating a rule of inference to the effect that *q* can be inferred from *p*. Conditionals are thus supposed to have the force of an inference schema:

$$\frac{p}{\therefore\ q}$$

though they provide in themselves no information about the basis for the inference. For example, the conditional:

If Norman is in town, then he is staying at the Grand Hotel

sanctions the inference:

> Norman is in town.
> ∴ He is staying at the Grand Hotel.

Unfortunately, although it may be true that whenever *q* follows from *p* the assertion *if p then q* is true, the converse is false. There are many conditionals that do not have the force of warranting inferences. The assertion:

If you want to meet Norman, then he's at the Grand Hotel

can hardly be said to warrant the inference:

> You want to meet Norman.
> ∴ He's at the Grand Hotel.

The consequent is true *simpliciter* given that the conditional is true, and the antecedent is not a premise but a stipulation of the conditions in which the consequent is likely to be of relevance to the addressee (cf. Austin, 1961).

A striking feature of conditionals is that their antecedents always *state* conditions, whereas their consequents can serve a variety of illocutionary functions:

If your spouse comes to the party {
then you will come, too.
then will you come, too?
then do come, too!
}

It is obvious that a conditional with a question as its consequent hardly serves as a rule of inference. Indeed, any formulation of the semantics of conditionals in terms of truth conditions is too restrictive. What is required is a more general account of the meaning of *if* that will accommodate statements, questions, and requests in the consequent clause.

Although some philosophers have attempted to provide a precise formulation of the truth conditions of conditionals, and particularly to cope with the problem of just which hypothetical states of affairs are picked out by their antecedents, there are no grounds for supposing that such precision mirrors the ordinary meaning of the connective. It is no accident that the logical properties of conditionals are still under debate. An apparent failure in transitivity, as in Lewis's (1973) example:

If J. Edgar Hoover had been born in Russia, then he would have been a Communist.

If J. Edgar Hoover had been a Communist, then he would have been a traitor.

∴ If J. Edgar Hoover had been born in Russia, then he would have been a traitor

can be explained on the grounds that the 'possible worlds' in which Hoover was born in Russia are more far-fetched than some of those in which he was a Communist (as Lewis claims), or on the grounds that the two premises have different contexts: Hoover would only have been a traitor if he had been a Communist while remaining an American (see Kratzer, 1978; Braine, 1979). The following two assertions, however, could be true in the same context:

If you need any money, there's a pound note in your wallet.

If there's a pound note in your wallet, then you don't need any money

but the transitive inference is unacceptable:

∴ If you need any money, then you don't need any money.

The solution to the problem of *if* is to search, not for a single uniform logic of the term, but for a single uniform semantics from which its logical vagaries emerge. Such an analysis will strengthen both the case against mental logic and the case for the fundamental semantic principle that the meaning of a term gives rise to its logical properties. I am going to consider: first, how conditionals are interpreted; second, their analysis in a 'possible worlds' semantics, which I shall reject as unrealistically abstract; and, third, an alternative analysis in terms of mental models.

An old idea in philosophy is that the way to interpret a conditional is to add its antecedent to your stock of beliefs, and then assess whether or not its consequent is true. If you believe that there is a causal or necessary connection from the antecedent to the consequent, then you will hold that the consequent is true, and hence that the conditional as a whole is true.

If you already believe that the consequent is true, then it should remain a part of your beliefs, and you will consider the conditional true, too. Hence, a causal or necessary connection may be relevant to your assessment of a conditional, but it is not an indispensable part of the process. This idea of a 'thought experiment' triggered by a conditional was formulated by Ramsey (1931). But it works only where you have no prior opinion about the truth of the antecedent of the conditional. Stalnaker (1968) accordingly suggested the following extension to the procedure. Where you believe the antecedent to be true, your evaluation of the conditional is equivalent to your belief about its consequent. Where you believe the antecedent to be false, its addition to your stock of beliefs will require some of them to be modified in order to avoid inconsistency, and which particular modifications you make will be determined on pragmatic grounds. A general procedure for conditionals can thus be summarized as follows: add the antecedent to your stock of beliefs; adjust your other beliefs, where necessary, to maintain consistency; and evaluate the conditional as true or false depending on whether its consequent is true or false. Stalnaker also proposed a set of truth conditions for conditionals congruent with this method of evaluation. A conditional *if p then q* is true if and only if *q* is true in that 'possible world' in which *p* is true but which otherwise differs minimally from the actual world. (If *p* is true in the actual world, then the evaluation of *q* is with respect to the actual world; if *p* is self-contradictory, then *q* is evaluated with respect to a special 'absurd' world in which all contradictions are true.) For example, a conditional such as:

If Russia invades West Berlin, then NATO will use nuclear weapons

is true provided that:

NATO will use nuclear weapons

is true in that particular 'possible world' that most resembles the actual world given that within it:

Russia invades West Berlin.

Although the notion of a 'thought experiment' is on the right lines, there are a number of difficulties in its detailed formulation. 'Possible worlds', which will be considered in greater depth in Chapter 8, are highly abstract, and since any proposition is either true or false in a given possible world, each possible world goes far beyond what any individual can apprehend. Moreover, the idea that the truth of a conditional depends on one particular possible world – the one that most resembles the actual world given the truth of the antecedent within it – takes abstraction beyond the realm of feasibility. In one possible world, for example, Russia invades West Berlin and that morning I have a headache; in another possible world, Russia invades West Berlin and that morning I have no headache (and everything else is the same). It seems an unmerited philosophical scruple to suppose that the truth of the conditional depends in principle on which of these two possibilities is closer to reality. Happily or unhappily, the state of my head has no bearing on whether NATO uses nuclear weapons. Indeed, as Lewis (1973) points out, there is no guarantee that possible worlds can be ranked in terms of their resemblance to reality. Unfortunately, Lewis's own solution is to move in the direction of still greater abstraction. He proposes that round any given world there is a sort of Ptolemaic universe of concentric spheres of possible worlds. The nearer a sphere is to the world at its centre, the greater the similarity of its members to that central world, but there may not be a closest sphere: the series may get closer and closer without limit. Again, one can ask what guarantee there is that possible worlds can even be ranked in terms of their similarity to a central world. A variation of a paradox discovered by the economist Kenneth Arrow establishes that world A can be closer than world B to the centre on two out of three characteristics, and world B can be closer than world C to the centre on two out of three characteristics, and yet it need not follow that world A is closer than world C to the centre. The real problem, however, is that universes of possible worlds are metaphysical luxuries that have nothing to do with the way in which people ordinarily understand conditionals.

The inappropriateness of an analysis in terms of 'possible worlds' is vividly demonstrated by conditionals that require necessarily false antecedents to be entertained for the sake of argument. The conditional:

If the subsets of an infinite set could be enumerated, then the real numbers could be enumerated

is a reasonable claim that is true for the sake of many arguments. But the conditional:

If a door can be both open and not open, then the real numbers could be enumerated

is a blatant *non sequitur*. To imagine that both conditionals are evaluated by reference to an 'absurd world' is to avoid the problem of distinguishing between them. The point is that if one considers what it would be like to be able to enumerate the subsets of an infinite set, there is a close parallel with what it would be like to be able to enumerate the real numbers. The impossibility of both enterprises is established by the same sort of mathematical argument (Cantor's 'diagonalization'). There is, of course, no such parallel between the two clauses of the second conditional.

What really happens when people interpret a conditional? Certainly, they do not add its antecedent to their stock of beliefs, and then evaluate its consequent. They do not have ready access to their stock of beliefs: it might take hours for them to review even a sample of their relevant views. A more plausible alternative is that they use those beliefs *provoked* by their interpretation of the conditional to construct a mental model of a scenario in which the antecedent is realized, and then interpret the consequent with respect to that model or to a scenario based on it. What complicates matters, however, is that the interpretation of the consequent may well affect the interpretation of the antecedent.

From the standpoint of an abstract theory of semantics, such as a 'possible worlds' theory, it is entirely legitimate to postulate that the context of a sentence can include any relevant item of knowledge. But this assumption sets a dangerous precedent for psychological theories of meaning, because it suggests that just the right information is sitting there waiting to be used in interpreting the sentence. In fact, listeners generally do not know before they hear an utterance what knowledge will be relevant to its interpretation, and their search for relevant information is guided by their current interpretation, such as it is, of the utterance. Hence, a sentence in effect defines its own context for the listener (see Johnson-Laird, 1967, for a formulation of this idea). A conditional is a particularly good example of a sentence that defines its own context, because it normally does so in a three-fold way: once for its antecedent, once for its consequent, and once for the relation between them.

A mental model based on the antecedent of a conditional is a fragment of many possible worlds, that is, it is consistent with many alternative complete specifications of how the world might be, because many propositions will be neither true nor false in the fragment. The mental model elicited by the antecedent:

If Russia invades West Berlin . . .

represents certain protagonists – the leaders of Russia and the USA, their military commanders and militia, and so on, but it will not contain any representation of many other individuals, and in particular the question of whether or not I have a headache will not arise with respect to it. The mental model elicited by the consequent:

. . . NATO will use nuclear weapons

can, of course, be evaluated in isolation, as when one considers in what circumstances NATO might use nuclear bombs. But the force of the conditional is plainly that the antecedent and consequent are related, and that the event described in the consequent will occur as a result of the event described in the antecedent.

Once a mental model primarily based on the antecedent has been constructed, the consequent of the conditional is evaluated with respect to the model. Hence, if the consequent is an assertion, its truth value in the model or in its projection in time to subsequent events, determines the truth value of the conditional as a whole. If the consequent is a question, it is answered with respect to the model. And if the consequent is a request, it is carried out (by a helpful listener) if and when the model corresponds to reality. What complicates this account is that the model of the antecedent may be influenced by the interpretation of the consequent. Both of Quine's (1960) revealing examples:

If Caesar had been in command in Korea, he would have used the atom bomb

and:

If Caesar had been in command in Korea, he would have used catapults

can be true. In the first case, the consequent suggests a model representing Caesar's 'hawkish' personality; in the second case, the consequent suggests a model representing the military technology of his day. Granted these respective models, then of course the conditionals may well be taken to be true.

According to this theory of conditionals, what underlies their meaning is the ability to envisage states of affairs that may or may not correspond to reality, that is, the ability to construct mental models of possible, hypothetical, and imaginary situations. A possible situation is one that may or may not be the case; a hypothetical situation is one – either possible or imaginary – that is assumed for the sake of argument; and an imaginary situation is one that is either physically or logically impossible. *If* is a verbal cue to consider such situations, and the content, the grammatical mood of the clause, and the context, usually make clear the intended status of the antecedent. An antecedent such as:

If the government resigns . . .

is intended to designate a possible event (in relation to the current context). The antecedent:

If the government were to resign . . .

is intended to designate a hypothetical event (in relation to the current context). And the antecedent:

If the government had resigned . . .

is intended to designate a once possible, but now imaginary event, to be taken hypothetically (in relation to the current context).

The contrast between antecedents denoting possible states of affairs and those denoting imaginary states of affairs is reflected in the difference between such conditionals as:

If *The Ancient Mariner* wasn't written by Coleridge, then it was written by Wordsworth

and:

If *The Ancient Mariner* hadn't been written by Coleridge, then it would have been written by Wordsworth.

The mental model of the possible event denoted by the indicative antecedent leaves open the possibility that Coleridge did not write the poem. The counterfactual antecedent takes for granted that Coleridge did write the poem, and invites us to consider an imaginary state of affairs in which he did not. Given an antecedent that is to be taken hypothetically, it is obviously anomalous to couple a request with it:

If your spouse were to come to the party, then do come, too.

Although the procedure for interpreting conditionals is a uniform one, it inevitably gives rise to vagaries in their logical properties. This phenomenon arises from the use of background knowledge in interpreting the antecedent and the consequent and in evaluating the relation between them. If the model of the antecedent is irrelevant to the truth of the consequent, but suggests a certain attitude on the part of the addressee, then the antecedent may be stipulating a condition on the relevance of the consequent that is intended to be true *simpliciter*:

If you need any money, there's a pound note in your wallet.

Stalnaker (1968) argued that the falsity of the antecedent is never sufficient reason to affirm a conditional, even an indicative conditional. But a conditional that presents two compatible alternatives, and that has a negative antecedent:

If Pat isn't here, then Ron is

is a case to the contrary. It is rendered true by the mere falsity of its antecedent (Pat is here) or by the truth of its consequent (Ron is here). It is thus in effect a truth-functional implication, equivalent in force to the disjunction:

Pat is here or Ron is here (or both).

Other conditionals present pairs of conditions that stand or fall together in the light of general knowledge:

If you are over the age of eighteen then you are eligible to vote.

This conditional is in effect a truth-functional equivalence: the antecedent implies the consequent, and the negation of the antecedent implies the negation of the consequent. The majority of conditionals, however, make no claims about what is the case if their antecedents are false. The assertion:

If Norman is in town, then he is staying at the Grand Hotel

is true if Norman is indeed in town and staying at the Grand, false if he is in town and not staying there, and neither true nor false if he is not in town.

In short, conditionals are not creatures of a constant hue. Like chameleons, as I once put it, they take on the colour suggested by their surroundings. Their logical properties are determined in part by the nature of the propositions that they interrelate. The crux is, not that *if* is ambiguous, though some critics have taken that to be my point, but rather that *if* has a single unequivocal semantics that leaves a role to be played by the interpretation of the clauses that it connects. It is the varying nature of the known links between them that gives rise to the chameleon-like properties of the conditional.

Conclusions

Human beings evidently need to acquire the meanings of connectives if they are to use them appropriately in discourse. But these meanings also suffice to give rise to logical properties. With truth-functional connectives, there are at least two effective procedures for making valid inferences without recourse to rules of inference or inferential schemata. One procedure relies on eliminating the contingencies that the premises rule out. Another procedure, which I described in the form of a program, is based on substituting truth values for premises, and working out the compositional effects of the substitutions from the meanings of the connectives. This procedure automatically abides by the inferential heuristics governing the conclusions that people draw spontaneously. Like the theories based on inference schemata, however, it presents too narrow a view of ordinary reasoning. Rather than thinking in a truth-functional way, individuals are more likely to construct a mental model of the states of affairs described in premises, relying on both their general knowledge and their knowledge of the context. A uniform semantics for a word such as *if* may therefore give rise to considerable variation in its logical behaviour, and this phenomenon is difficult to reconcile with the presence of a logic in the mind.

The indirect case against mental logic is a strong one, since the procedural account of reasoning is more parsimonious and clears up some long-standing riddles. However, the case for mental models has so far largely consisted in arguments for the feasibility of this mode of inference. For empirical support for the theory, it is necessary to turn to a more complex form of deduction.

4

Theories of the syllogism

Syllogisms are deductions based on two premises. Each premise and conclusion is in one of four forms:

All X are Y   (A universal and affirmative assertion)
Some X are Y   (A particular and affirmative assertion)
No X are Y   (A universal and negative assertion)
Some X are not Y   (A particular and negative assertion)

Thus, a typical syllogism has the following abstract logical form:

All B are A
All B are C
∴ Some A are C.

The occurrence of the so-called 'middle' term, B, in both premises enables an inference to be drawn, because it interrelates the information in the two premises. There are only four possible arrangements of the middle term in the premises:

A – B   B – A   A – B   B – A
B – C   C – B   C – B   B – C

I shall refer to these four arrangements as the 'figures' of the premises. (The term is a traditional one, but it is usually applied to the premises *and* the conclusion.)

Aristotle, who on his own account was the first person to write on logic, successfully formulated a theory of syllogisms. Logic has, of course, advanced enormously since his day, and syllogisms have been relegated to an unimportant suburb of the subject, particularly since 1879 – the year in which Gottlob Frege, the great German logician, published his *Begriffsschrift*, in which he introduced the general theory of quantifiers. The year 1879 was also, of course, the year in which Wilhelm Wundt opened the first psychological laboratory, and syllogisms have been studied experimentally for eighty years or more. Psychology, alas, is not logic, and Aristotle remains in advance of much of the recent psychology of reasoning.

The logic of syllogisms is simple. There are only 64 formally distinct pairs of syllogistic premises (4 forms of first premise × 4 forms of second premise × 4 figures). But my use of a syllogism in Chapter 2 in presenting inference as a test case for cognitive science was no accident. The psychology of syllogisms is not simple: some of them are very easy and some, very hard. If, after so many years of experimental study, we are still unable to explain the psychology of syllogisms, then perhaps the task of understanding the mind is too difficult for us. My goal in this chapter is to show that current accounts of this form of inference are indeed inadequate; in the next, I shall present an alternative theory that makes good their deficiencies. My first task, however, is to lay out more explicitly the criteria against which to assess the adequacy of any psychological theory of reasoning.

The goals of a psychological theory of reasoning

There are seven goals that are sufficiently exhaustive to provide useful criteria for evaluating any theory of reasoning:

1. *A descriptively adequate theory must account for the evaluation of conclusions, the relative difficulty of different inferences, and the systematic errors and biases that occur in drawing spontaneous conclusions.* A theory that only accounts for the evaluation of given conclusions may have nothing to contribute to the problem of what determines which particular inferences people tend to make spontaneously.

2. *The theory should explain the differences in inferential ability from one individual to another.* In the past, psychologists have generally been content to account for such differences by appealing to 'general intelligence' or to some other factors derived from mental tests (e.g., Guilford, 1959; Frandsen and Holder, 1969). They have been happy to treat some dimension derived from a factor analysis of test performance as a primitive and unanalysed commodity that gives rise to the observed differences in reasoning ability. This approach seems to be fundamentally mistaken in that we know more about the mental processes underlying reasoning than about the factors that determine test performance. Psychometric data are too gross to elucidate the intricacies of complicated cognitive processes. The validity of such factors as 'verbal ability' and 'spatial–abstract' ability that emerge from the factor analysis of test scores is debatable (Levy, 1973). Indeed, the use of factor analysis in investigating differences in thought

65

processes is like the use of a paint spray as a pen. The only sensible way to proceed is in the opposite direction – to employ experiments to take to pieces the different cognitive skills that underlie performance in mental tests (e.g., Hunt, Lunneborg, and Lewis, 1975).

3. *The theory should be extensible in a natural way to related varieties of inference rather than apply solely to a narrow class of deductions.* A good theory of propositional inferences ought to be readily extensible to inferences based on other connectives. A good theory of syllogistic inference ought to be extensible to deductions based on other sorts of assertion, e.g., 'Most authoritarians are dogmatic', or assertions containing more than one quantifier, e.g., 'There is someone in the team whom no one else likes.' What is at stake here is the fact that inferences in daily life do not come in separate packets labelled according to particular logical calculi.

4. *The theory should explain how children acquire the ability to make valid inferences.* If a theory proposes that a sophisticated logical notation is used as a mental representation, then it should offer some account of how such an apparatus is acquired.

5. *The theory must allow that people are capable of making valid inferences, that is, they are potentially rational.* A theory is inadequate if it permits valid inferences to occur only by chance or as a result of processes that do not suffice to establish validity. The basis of this criterion is that if people were intrinsically irrational then the invention of logic, mathematics, and much else besides, would be inexplicable. Hence:

6. *The theory should shed some light on why formal logic was invented and how it was developed.*

7. *The theory should ideally have practical applications to the teaching of reasoning skills.*

To revert to the Chomskyan terminology that I introduced in Chapter 1, if a theory is *descriptively* adequate, it accounts for the difficulties and errors that occur in reasoning (criterion 1) and for individual differences in ability (criterion 2). If a theory is *explanatorily* adequate, it is extensible (criterion 3), it accounts for how children acquire the ability to reason (criterion 4), and it allows for the potential rationality of human beings (criterion 5). Optimally, a theory should also illuminate both the development of formal logic (criterion 6) and the pedagogy of reasoning (criterion 7). After I have presented some of the phenomena that occur in syllogistic reasoning, I shall use these criteria to evaluate a number of different theories of the process of inference.

The figural effect in syllogistic reasoning

Some syllogisms are easy and some are hard, as I have already mentioned, and this is easy to illustrate. Nearly everyone is able to formulate a valid conclusion that follows from the premises:

Some of the artists are beekeepers.
All of the beekeepers are chemists.

You should pause for a moment and come to your own conclusion about what the premises necessarily imply – imagine that they refer, say, to a large group of people attending a meeting. You shouldn't use pencil and paper, but work out your answer mentally. Likewise, you shouldn't employ any of your technical knowledge of logic. Be warned: the only person whom I have ever known to get the answer wrong is a distinguished philosopher who tried to exploit his logical expertise!

The following syllogism is very different. Few people are able to cope correctly with the premises:

All of the bankers are athletes.
None of the councillors are bankers.

You might again attempt to work out what conclusion, if any, follows validly from them.

To return to the first problem, a valid conclusion from its premises is:

Some of the artists are chemists

or conversely, and equally validly:

Some of the chemists are artists.

The reader almost certainly drew the first of these conclusions rather than the second. My collaborators and I have found a very strong preference of this sort in our experiments; and audiences in Europe and America presented with the problem have invariably yielded the same massive bias. The effect does not depend on the order of the two premises: switch them around and it is equally powerful. It depends on the figure of the premises, that is, on the arrangement of the terms within the syllogism. The figure of the terms in this problem about artists ($=$A), beekeepers ($=$B), and chemists ($=$C) is:

$$A - B$$
$$B - C$$

and the conclusion that people favour takes the form:

$$A - C$$

67

rather than its converse:

$$C - A$$

The figural effect that we have just sampled will be an important diagnostic in assessing the descriptive adequacy of psychological theories of the syllogism.

The second and harder of the two problems above, which concerned the athletes, bankers, and councillors, has the valid conclusion:

Some of the athletes are not councillors.

The converse conclusion:

Some of the councillors are not athletes

is *not* valid. Each of the following responses is wrong, too:

None of the athletes is a councillor.
None of the councillors is an athlete.
'There is no valid conclusion of interest.'

Few readers are likely to have produced the valid conclusion above. (I will explain later in the chapter why it is valid.) Janellen Huttenlocher and I spent more than one afternoon at Teachers College, Columbia University, establishing our own fallibility with such problems. Not a single subject in the experiment we designed drew the correct conclusion from premises of this sort, and our subjects were highly intelligent university students (see Johnson-Laird, 1975a; Johnson-Laird and Steedman, 1978). The figure of the premises is worth noting. There are three terms: athletes (= A), bankers (= B), and councillors (= C), and the figure has the form:

$$B - A$$
$$C - B$$

The figural effect in this case is conducive to conclusions of the form:

$$C - A$$

The valid conclusion, however, has the form:

$$A - C$$

The figural effect is evidently a common factor at work in determining both the bias towards one of the two possible conclusions for the first problem and the difficulty of drawing the correct conclusion for the second problem. The effect is most noticeable in the form of the conclusions, valid or invalid, that subjects draw spontaneously. Table 4.1 presents the results of our experiment in which every subject was given all 64 possible

Table 4.1 *The effect of the figure of the premises on the form of the conclusions, both valid and invalid, drawn in an experiment on syllogistic reasoning: the balance of responses were of the form 'There is no valid conclusion' (from Johnson-Laird and Steedman, 1978)*

Form of conclusion	Figure of premises			
	A – B B – C	B – A C – B	A – B C – B	B – A B – C
A – C	51%	5%	21%	32%
C – A	6%	48%	21%	18%

pairs of premises, each with a different lexical content. The table states the percentages of the two forms of conclusion for the four different figures of the premises: the balance of the percentages corresponds to responses of the form 'There is no valid conclusion.' There is a very significant bias for the first two figures, but no very pronounced bias for the other two.

The figural effect is probably the most reliable phenomenon to occur in syllogistic reasoning – we have yet to encounter a subject who fails to show it. Nevertheless, it had not been reported nor, I suspect, observed before the present studies. It is surprising that so robust an effect was not detected for eighty years, but there are two instructive reasons for the oversight. First, the experimental studies from Störring (1908) onwards always used 'objective' techniques in which the subjects had either to evaluate a given conclusion or else to choose a response from a multiple choice. Second, all of the studies relied on the Scholastic logic of the medieval Schoolmen. In logic, the 'figure' of a syllogism refers to the arrangement of terms in the premises *and* the conclusion, and the Scholastics recognized four figures, which in the notation of this chapter are as follows:

$$
\begin{array}{cccc}
A-B & B-A & A-B & B-A \\
\underline{B-C} & \underline{C-B} & \underline{C-B} & \underline{B-C} \\
\therefore \; C-A & \therefore \; C-A & \therefore \; C-A & \therefore \; C-A
\end{array}
$$

Since the order of the premises has no effect on logic, the Scholastics adopted the convention that the subject of the conclusion is always stated in the second premise. The combination of 'objective' experimental technique and Scholastic logic made it impossible to observe the figural effect. The individuals tested in experiments were not allowed to draw conclusions in their own words; and there were no syllogisms in which the subject of the conclusion occurred in the first premise. It was sometimes noted (see

69

Frase, 1968; Dickstein, 1978) that problems in the figure:

$$
\begin{array}{c}
B - A \\
C - B \\
\hline
\therefore\ C - A
\end{array}
$$

seemed easier than those in the figure:

$$
\begin{array}{c}
A - B \\
B - C \\
\hline
\therefore\ C - A
\end{array}
$$

But, of course, no one could appreciate that the difference had as much to do with the form of the conclusions as with the form of the premises. It was impossible to observe that syllogisms in the figure:

$$
\begin{array}{c}
A - B \\
B - C \\
\hline
\therefore\ A - C
\end{array}
$$

were easier than those in the figure:

$$
\begin{array}{c}
B - A \\
C - B \\
\hline
\therefore\ A - C
\end{array}
$$

These figures were never tested because they were not part of Scholastic logic.

Unlike the Schoolmen and the psychologists, Aristotle knew that syllogisms in the figure:

$$
\begin{array}{c}
A - B \\
B - C \\
\hline
\therefore\ A - C
\end{array}
$$

were easy. He admitted this figure into his canon. Indeed, he regarded syllogisms of the following sort:

$$
\begin{array}{c}
\text{All A are B} \\
\text{All B are C} \\
\hline
\therefore\ \text{All A are C}
\end{array}
$$

as perfect. Their validity, unlike that of other syllogisms, was immediately self-evident. In this judgment, Aristotle shows himself to have been an outstanding student of the psychology of reasoning; modern experimentalists have only recently caught up with his intuitions.

Syllogisms in daily life

If you are doubtful about the value of psychological experiments, you may well be saying to yourself at this point, as a number of critics have said to me: 'The trouble with syllogisms is that they are very artificial.' And, of course, you may be right. But, you insist, 'Psychologists shouldn't study artificial arguments, because they never occur in daily life.' Here, again, you could well be right. And so, you conclude, dismissively, 'Psychologists shouldn't study syllogisms. The author is wasting his time and mine in writing about them; he should study the sorts of inferences that people actually make.' This argument, of course, is itself a syllogism. And the fact that sceptics use syllogisms to argue against syllogisms suggests on the contrary that they surely merit investigation. They certainly can be artificial – a rigid and ceremonial way of dressing up an argument – and it is sometimes dangerous to study artificial problems in the psychological laboratory. On other occasions, however, such studies may lead to genuine insights into the way the mind works. Moreover, as Kate Ehrlich has shown in an unpublished study, figural effects are equally evident when syllogisms are presented in the informal style of everyday discourse.

A more subtle objection to syllogisms was put forward by Bertrand Russell (1927):

This form of inference does actually occur, though very rarely. The only instance that I have ever heard of was supplied by Dr. F. C. S. Schiller. He once produced a comic number of the philosophical periodical *Mind*, and sent copies to various philosophers, among them to a certain German, who was much puzzled by the advertisements. But at last he argued: 'Everything in this book is a joke, therefore the advertisements are jokes.' I have never come across any other case of new knowledge obtained by means of a syllogism. It must be admitted that, for a method which dominated logic for two thousand years, this contribution to the world's stock of information cannot be considered very weighty.

This argument contains an element of sophistry. In the first place, no branch of logic – not even the powerful machinery of the mathematical logicians – is much use in discovering new knowledge. The reason is that logic merely specifies what inferences are valid, and does not dictate which particular conclusions should be drawn from a given set of premises. There are always, as we have seen, infinitely many valid conclusions than can be drawn from any set of premises. It is for this reason that I argued that an inferential heuristic, constraining the particular conclusions that are drawn, is so crucial a part of a psychological theory of reasoning. The heuristic guides the reasoner to conclusions that are not trivial and perhaps novel.

Russell's joke also creates the misleading impression that syllogisms are rarely employed in everyday life. This claim is false. In introducing my 'test case' for cognitive science, I have already illustrated how syllogisms crop up quite naturally in ordinary thought. Indeed, whenever an argument about a specific entity hinges on a general assertion, the chances are that its deductive form is that of a syllogism:

(1) Do you have a TV set?
   Yes.
   Do you have a licence for it?
   No.
   Well, it requires a licence.
   Why?
   All TV sets are required by law to have a licence.

(2) Any point on which a player serves out of turn is a 'let'.
   A player served out of turn on this point.
   Hence, this point is a 'let'.

(3) Some arguments that are likely to be hard to understand are syllogisms.
   No argument that is used spontaneously in daily life is likely to be hard to understand.
   Therefore, some syllogisms are not used spontaneously in daily life.

It is just as well that the last of these arguments is sound: certain syllogisms are too difficult for most of us to grasp.

The 'atmosphere' effect and the 'conversion' hypothesis

The early experimental studies of syllogisms concerned potential sources of error. The most important alleged source, judging from its durability in the literature, is the 'atmosphere' created by the premises. The idea that there might be such an effect was first put forward by Woodworth and Sells (1935) and Sells (1936). They observed that their subjects were prone to evaluate as valid the following sort of deduction:

> If all x's are y's;
> And if all z's are y's;
> Then all z's are x's.

The cause of the mistake might be, they supposed, that both premises contain the quantifier *all*, and could accordingly create an 'atmosphere' conducive to the acceptance of a conclusion containing the same quantifier.

Other sorts of premises also seemed to create an atmosphere favourable to conclusions that were superficially congruent with them. The initial statement of the hypothesis was cumbersome, but Woodworth and Schlosberg (1954, p. 846) provided a succinct formulation:

(1) Whenever there is a negative premise, there is a negative atmosphere. Otherwise, the atmosphere favours affirmative conclusions.
(2) Whenever there is a 'particular' premise, i.e. containing the quantifier *some*, there is a particular atmosphere. Otherwise, the atmosphere favours universal conclusions.

These two principles are exemplified in the prediction for premises of the form:

No A are B
Some B are C.

Since one premise is negative and the other is particular, their atmosphere should predispose subjects to either of the following conclusions:

Some A are not C
Some C are not A

though only the second of them is valid. The same predictions follow for premises in the figure:

No B are A
Some B are C.

Hence, the atmosphere hypothesis takes no account of figure.

Woodworth and Sells appreciated that there must be more to syllogistic reasoning than the atmosphere effect, because it is inimical to rational thought. They likened it to the 'set' created by a nearby word that gives rise to elementary grammatical blunders, e.g., 'Analysis of such substructures of relations have (sic) provided relationships. . . .' Indeed, the atmosphere effect, if it genuinely exists, must overlay the basic mechanism of inference. Subjects are more likely to accept valid conclusions that conform to atmosphere than to accept invalid conclusions that conform to it, and this difference reflects the existence of an inferential mechanism independent of the atmosphere effect itself. Likewise, there is considerable variation in its apparent strength from one figure to another.

The evidence that counts most strongly against the atmosphere hypothesis is that subjects often respond that there is no valid conclusion. Such a response contravenes the hypothesis, because there are always at least two possible conclusions congruent with the atmosphere of the premises. Yet subjects even claim that there is no conclusion to certain premises for which there *is* a valid conclusion, and, moreover, one that is in accordance with the atmosphere. Here, for example, are the results that we obtained with one such syllogism (see Johnson-Laird and Steedman, 1978). Its premises were of the form:

Some B are A
No C are B

and our 20 subjects were divided between the following responses:

No valid conclusion	(Incorrect: 12 subjects)
No C are A	(Incorrect: 4 subjects)
Some C are not A	(Incorrect: 2 subjects)
Some A are not C	(Correct: 2 subjects)

Atmosphere favours the last two of these responses; but the majority of the subjects declared that there was no valid conclusion. Such evidence casts considerable doubt on the reality of the effect.

Another potential source of error is the alleged tendency, originally noted by Chapman and Chapman (1959), to make illicit conversions of premises. A premise of the form:

Some A are B

validly implies its converse:

Some B are A.

Similarly, a premise of the form:

No A are B

validly implies its converse:

No B are A

But the remaining two forms of premise:

All A are B

and:

Some A are not B

do not validly imply their respective converses. There is experimental evidence that subjects presented with symbolic assertions such as 'All x's are y's' do fall into the trap of assuming that the converse is valid (Wilkins, 1928). However, it is one thing to catch subjects out in this way, and quite another to assume that they spontaneously make such conversions. If subjects were automatically to convert every premise – an assumption once adopted by Revlis (1975), though he now holds to it less strongly (personal communication) – then premises in the figure:

$$A - B$$
$$B - C$$

should be just as likely to elicit a conclusion in the form $C - A$ as in the form $A - C$. The conversion hypothesis is ruled out as a general mechanism by the figural effect.

Entities that are the same have properties in common; and entities with properties in common may be the same. This sort of plausible thinking was also advanced by Chapman and Chapman (1959) as a source of error. They argued that subjects assume on such grounds that the following form of inference is valid:

Some A are B

Some C are B

∴ Some C are A.

While plausibility certainly enters into the deliberations of daily life, the part it plays in conscious deduction is again overshadowed by the figural effect. The point is directly established by the data given in Table 4.2.

Table 4.2 *The numbers of subjects (out of 20) drawing two alternative invalid conclusions from four sorts of syllogistic premises (from Johnson-Laird and Steedman, 1978)*

	Form of premises			
	Some A are B Some B are C	Some B are A Some C are B	Some A are B Some C are B	Some B are A Some B are C
∴ Some A are C	7	1	4	3
∴ Some C are A	0	9	1	0

They show – wholly typically, as subsequent experiments have confirmed – that figures to which the Chapman's hypothesis does not apply, such as:

Some A are B

Some B are C

yield just as many, if not more, errors. The errors presumably arise for some other reason.

The drawback with all of these conjectures about the causes of error is that their alleged effects must be superimposed on an underlying deductive mechanism that is left unspecified. Hence, a full account of this mechanism might suggest a quite different explanation of deductive mistakes. What I want to do in the rest of this chapter is to outline and to evaluate the current theoretical accounts of the underlying mechanism. Much of the recent theorizing is extremely intricate, but my aim is to delineate the main ideas accurately rather than to describe the details.

The logical origins of psychological theories of the syllogism

There are only a few obvious sources for a theory of the mental machinery for syllogistic inference. One possibility is that there is a mental logic equivalent to the quantificational calculus – that branch of logic deriving from Frege's work and which embraces the syllogism and much else besides. There have been no proposals of this sort, perhaps because the rules of inference for the calculus are not intuitively obvious, and because it seems too powerful for a psychological model – to invoke it would be like employing a computer to work out small change. (Ironically, there are some simple inferences, as I shall show in Chapter 6, that are well within our capability but that cannot be derived within the standard 'first order' quantificational calculus.) During the course of two thousand years, however, a number of procedures have been devised for determining the validity of any arbitrary syllogism. Aristotle offered some general principles: that, e.g., at least one premise must be universal and at least one premise must be affirmative. He did not attempt to state a comprehensive set of rules, but rather made use of a method of 'reducing' any syllogism to one of a perfect form of self-evident validity. The Scholastic and later logicians developed a comprehensive set of rules that acted as a sieve to catch just those syllogisms that are valid. Five such rules suffice:

1. If both premises are affirmative, then the conclusion is affirmative.
2. If one premise is negative, then the conclusion is negative.
3. If both premises are negative, then there is no valid conclusion.
4. The middle term must be *distributed* in at least one premise.
5. No term may be *distributed* in the conclusion if it is not *distributed* in the premise in which it occurs.

The notion of distribution referred to in the last two rules is reasonably straightforward. A term is distributed in an assertion if it is necessary to take into account the entire class of entities that it subsumes in order to determine whether the assertion is true. In an assertion of the form *All A are B*, the A term is distributed because all of its members must be considered in order to determine whether the assertion is true; but the B term is not distributed, because it is not necessary to consider all of its

76

members, as there may be B's that are not A's. Following the same general principle, the distributed terms for the four forms of assertion have been italicized in the following list:

All *A* are B
Some A are B
No *A* are *B*
Some A are not *B*.

The only case that is perhaps not immediately obvious is the last. However, if someone asserts that:

Some of the students are not team members

then the entire set of team members must be considered to make sure that there are some of the students who are not included in it.

The notion of distribution is central to the traditional lore of the syllogism, and one reason for mentioning it here, and indeed for going into these rules of the syllogism, is to draw attention to their similarity to the atmosphere hypothesis. Rules 1 and 2 are identical to the principle governing whether the atmosphere is affirmative or negative. Rules 4 and 5 ensure that whenever one of the premises is particular (i.e., contains the quantifier *some*), the conclusion, if any is warranted, is also particular. This similarity indeed suggests that a proper account of the inferential machinery might yield an alternative explanation of deductive errors that does not rely on the atmosphere hypothesis. That claim, however, should not be taken to imply that the traditional rules of the syllogism constitute a complete psychological theory: they do not specify how to draw conclusions, but only whether given conclusions are valid.

There are two other traditional decision procedures for syllogisms. The first is the method of Euler circles, and the second is the more elegant method of Venn diagrams. With the exception of my theory of mental models, all current psychological theories of the syllogism turn out to be variations on these two methods.

Syllogistic theories based on Euler circles

Euler circles are a geometrical analogy that the eighteenth-century mathematician Leonhard Euler used in teaching logic to a German princess. (The technique was in fact invented by Leibniz; it is often confused with the method of Venn diagrams.) The basic idea is to use a circle as a model of a set of entities. Hence, each of the four forms of syllogistic premises can be represented diagrammatically. A premise of the form *All artists are beekeepers* requires two separate diagrams:

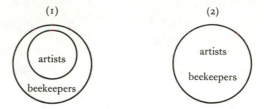

The first diagram represents the case where the set of artists is properly included within the set of beekeepers, i.e., there are beekeepers who are not artists, and the second diagram represents the case where the two sets have identical members. An assertion of the form *Some artists are beekeepers*, where *some* is taken to mean *at least some* and thus does not rule out *all*, requires four separate diagrams:

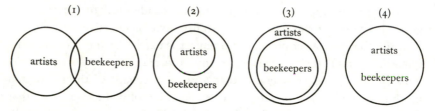

An assertion of the form *No artists are beekeepers* requires one diagram:

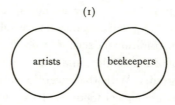

where there is no overlap between the two circles. Finally, an assertion of the form *(At least) some artists are not beekeepers* requires three diagrams:

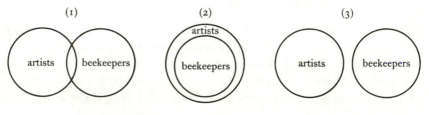

In order to make an inference, it is necessary to consider all the different ways in which the respective diagrams for the two premises can be combined. A conclusion is valid only if it holds for each of the possible combinations. I shall illustrate the process by deriving the correct conclusion for the difficult syllogism that was presented at the beginning of the chapter.

The two premises are:

All of the bankers are athletes.
None of the councillors are bankers.

The first premise requires two separate diagrams:

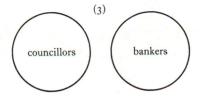

and the second requires one diagram:

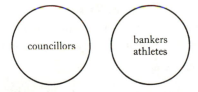

Diagram 2 can be combined with diagram 3 in only one way:

There is a similar combination of diagrams 1 and 3:

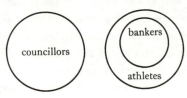

However, the number of different combinations is greater than the simple product of the number of diagrams for the first premise and the number of diagrams for the second. There are other ways of combining diagrams 1 and 3. The circle representing athletes can overlap the circle representing councillors:

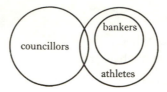

or the circle representing the athletes can completely enclose the circle representing councillors:

This combination, which is consistent with the premises, shows that it is wrong to conclude:

Some of the councillors are not athletes

for here all the councillors are athletes. In all four of these different combinations, however, at least some of the athletes are not councillors, namely, those athletes who are bankers. The conclusion:

Some of the athletes are not councillors

is accordingly valid.

The first comprehensive theory about the mental processes underlying syllogistic inference, which was proposed by James R. Erickson (1974), assumed that ordinary people who are untrained in logic form mental models that are isomorphic to Euler circles, and that they base their conclusions on combined models of the premises. Certain aspects of the theory are plausible, but it suffers from one severe problem: Euler diagrams can be combined in a large number of different ways. In order to deal with this combinatorial embarrassment, Erickson was forced to adopt a number of expedients. He assumed that subjects do not always consider the full set of distinct ways in which a single premise can be represented. Similarly, in one version of his theory, he suggested that subjects construct only one of the many possible combinations of the representations of the two premises. This combination is selected at random from the total set of possibilities, which are assumed to be equi-probable. When subjects formulate a conclusion, then according to Erickson they are prey to the atmosphere effect. That assumption is necessary because, if not all combinations are constructed, there will be occasions when an overlap between two sets, A and C, as illustrated here:

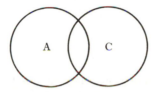

needs to be interpreted as *Some A are C*, and other occasions when it needs to be interpreted as *Some A are not C*. To invoke the atmosphere effect to save subjects' rationality is a paradoxical remedy.

The theory accounts for some of the errors that subjects make in syllogistic reasoning, but there is at least one important class of mistakes that it leaves unexplained. Subjects often respond that there is no valid conclusion, and that response counts against the simple version of the theory in which only one combination is constructed, because a conclusion always follows from a single combination. However, subjects also respond *incorrectly* that there is no valid conclusion, and this phenomenon counts against the full-scale model in which all combinations are considered. The assumption that subjects consider only some of the possible representations for individual premises, and the consequent invocation of the atmosphere effect, make it still harder to explain erroneous responses that there is no valid conclusion.

One way in which to try to circumscribe the combinatorial problem of Euler circles is to express their content in a symbolic language, because strings of symbols are often computationally more tractable than topological representations. This motive perhaps lies behind a theory put forward by Robert Sternberg and his colleagues (e.g., Guyote and Sternberg, 1978). The theory assumes that subjects represent the content of premises accurately and completely. An assertion of the form *All A are B* requires two separate Euler diagrams:

(1)

(2)

A

B

A

B

Corresponding to diagram 1, Sternberg postulates the following symbolic representation:

$$a1 \subseteq B$$
$$a2 \subseteq B$$
$$b1 \subseteq A$$
$$b2 \subseteq \bar{A}$$

The first two assertions represent set A included in set B: a1 and a2 are disjoint and exhaustive subsets of A, and $\subseteq$ stands for the inclusion relation. (Sternberg uses his own notation, which I have ignored here, since it is equivalent to the standard notation of set theory.) The second two assertions represent a subset of B included in A, and a subset of B not included in A, i.e., included in its complement, not-A. The components taken together yield the correct logic for diagram 1:

$$A \subset B \qquad \text{(A is \textit{properly} included in B)}$$

The representation of diagram 2 takes a comparable form except, of course, that there $A = B$.

Although it is easier in principle to combine strings of symbols than sets of diagrams, the process that Sternberg postulates for combining the representations of premises is very complicated. It calls for four separate steps, which I have spelled out in Table 4.3 primarily to illustrate their complexity. The steps depend on two heuristic rules. First, where x is a subset of Y, and Y has a subset included in Z, then x may be a subset of Z. Second, where x is not a subset of Y, and Y has a subset included in Z, then x may or may not be included in Z. In summary, the four steps carry out the following operations: the first step forms a set of possible combined representations, the second and third eliminate those that are incompatible with the premises, and the fourth compiles the set of possible pairings of whatever remains. The process of combination in the simplified example of Table 4.3 requires eight separate applications of the rules in

Table 4.3 *A summary of the four steps in Sternberg's syllogistic theory illustrated with a simplified example*

There are two rules for forming and testing combinations:

1. If $x \subseteq Y$ and Y has a subset $y \subseteq Z$, then possibly $x \subseteq Z$.
2. If $x \subseteq \bar{Y}$ and Y has a subset $y \subseteq Z$, then $x \subseteq Z$ or $x \subseteq \bar{Z}$.

Step 1: Apply the rules to the premise representations to yield the set of possible combinations.

Premise 1	Premise 2	The set of possible combinations

$$a1 \subseteq B \qquad b1 \subseteq C$$
$$a2 \subseteq \bar{B} \qquad b2 \subseteq \bar{C}$$

$$\Rightarrow \quad \begin{matrix}1.\\ \begin{pmatrix} a1 \subseteq C \\ a2 \subseteq C \end{pmatrix}\end{matrix} \quad \begin{matrix}2.\\ \begin{pmatrix} a1 \subseteq C \\ a2 \subseteq \bar{C} \end{pmatrix} \text{ or: } \begin{pmatrix} a1 \subseteq \bar{C} \\ a2 \subseteq C \end{pmatrix}\end{matrix} \quad \begin{matrix}3.\\ \begin{pmatrix} a1 \subseteq \bar{C} \\ a2 \subseteq C \end{pmatrix}\end{matrix}$$

$$b1 \subseteq A \qquad c1 \subseteq B$$
$$b2 \subseteq A \qquad c2 \subseteq B$$

$$\Rightarrow \quad \begin{matrix}4.\\ \begin{pmatrix} c1 \subseteq A \\ c2 \subseteq A \end{pmatrix}\end{matrix}$$

Step 2: Apply the rules to the possible combinations and premise 2 to eliminate combinations inconsistent with premise 2 (All but combination 1 survive.) Example:

Combination 1   Premise 2

$$a1 \subseteq C \qquad c1 \subseteq B$$
$$a2 \subseteq C \qquad c2 \subseteq B$$

$$\Rightarrow \quad \begin{pmatrix} a1 \subseteq B \\ a2 \subseteq B \end{pmatrix} \quad \begin{matrix}\text{inconsistent with premise 1}\\ \therefore \text{ eliminate combination 1.}\end{matrix}$$

Step 3: Apply the rules to premise 1 and possible combinations to eliminate combinations inconsistent with premise 2

Premise 1   Combination 2

$$b1 \subseteq A \qquad a1 \subseteq C$$
$$b2 \subseteq A \qquad a2 \subseteq \bar{C}$$

$$\Rightarrow \quad \begin{pmatrix} b1 \subseteq C \\ b2 \subseteq \bar{C} \end{pmatrix} \quad \begin{matrix}\text{consistent with premise 2}\\ \therefore \text{ combination 2 survives.}\end{matrix}$$

The only other combination to survive is 4.

Step 4: Find a verbal description, if any, that fits all of the surviving combinations.

2.   4.

$$a1 \subseteq C \qquad c1 \subseteq A$$
$$a2 \subseteq \bar{C} \qquad c2 \subseteq A$$

only one pairing of combinations corresponding to *All C are A*:

the first step; they yield four possible relations between the subsets of A and C. After a further eight applications of the rules and four tests for consistency, one of these possibilities is eliminated in the second step. After a further six applications of the rules and three tests for consistency, another possibility is eliminated in the third step. One operation of combination yields the final representation in the fourth step. An actual inference of the form:

$$\text{All B are A}$$
$$\underline{\text{All C are B}}$$
$$\therefore \ \text{All C are A}$$

would be still more complicated than the example in Table 4.3, because each premise requires two distinct representations. Since subjects can make this inference in about three seconds, the reader may be forgiven for wondering why the theory does not simply translate the premises directly into the notation:

$$B \subseteq A$$
$$C \subseteq B$$

and utilize the transitivity of set-inclusion to deduce:

$$C \subseteq A$$

The answer is that Sternberg wishes to give an account of the errors that subjects make.

Sternberg postulates three main causes of error, two of which resemble Erickson's assumptions. What is strange about Sternberg's theory, however, is that having made some complicated proposals about the combination of representations, it does not locate the causes of error in those processes. The theory assumes that the rules of combination are applied entirely without error. Where then do subjects go wrong?

First, according to Sternberg, subjects fail to consider *all* the different representations of the premises. The four forms of premise can be ordered in terms of the number of Euler diagrams that they require in order to be accurately represented:

No X are Y	1 diagram
All X are Y	2 diagrams
Some X are not Y	3 diagrams
Some X are Y	4 diagrams

Sternberg argues that human reasoners always consider at least one, but never more than four combinations of representations, because of some inherent limitation on the processing capacity of working memory. It follows from this assumption that people are irremediably irrational in making the inference:

$$\text{Some A are B}$$
$$\underline{\text{All B are C}}$$
$$\therefore \ \text{Some A are C.}$$

They may reach the right conclusion, but they cannot do so for the right reasons since their unaided minds cannot consider all eight possible combinations of the representations of the premises. The theory thus fails to be explanatorily adequate because it cannot account for rationality with an inference that is easily seen to be valid. The only sensible moral is that it must be a mistake to assume so many different models for premises that all their combinations cannot in principle be constructed and evaluated.

The second source of error according to Sternberg arises in choosing a description to characterize the final set of combined representations. The description must be consistent with all the representations, and if there is no possible description, then the syllogism is labelled 'indeterminate', i.e., it yields no valid conclusion of interest. There are occasions, however, when two different descriptions are consistent with the representations. The choice between them is supposed to be affected by a bias towards descriptions that refer to the fewest possible states of affairs (i.e., the smallest number of diagrams as shown in the list above), and by a bias towards descriptions that correspond to the 'atmosphere' of the premises.

Guyote and Sternberg (1978, p. 35) claim that there are never more than two labels consistent with the final combined representations. This claim is at best misleading and at worst false: it is true only if the subjects' responses are restricted to the four Scholastic figures of the syllogism – a restriction that indeed applies to the syllogisms used in Sternberg's experiments. A simple counter-example to the general claim is provided by the following premises:

All A are B

No B are C

which yield validly any one of the *four* conclusions:

No A are C

No C are A

Some A are not C

Some C are not A.

Hence, the final representations are here consistent with four different descriptions. By failing to consider two of them, Sternberg's theory is unable to give any account of the figural effect and is therefore descriptively inadequate.

The third putative source of error also arises in the course of choosing a description for the final combined representations. If the initial components (i.e., those that relate subsets of A to the set C) of the final representations are not identical to one another, then reasoners become confused about whether or not there is a single description that is consistent with all of them. This confusion can lead to a response that there is no valid conclusion – even if one is justified.

One important feature of Sternberg's work is that he has used his theory to develop an account of individual differences in reasoning ability. He formulated a mathematical model that ascribes seven probabilities to each of the key decisions that affect the likelihood of error. The first four such parameters correspond respectively to the probabilities of constructing one, two, three, or four, combinations of the premise representations, and the remaining parameters concern the process of selecting a description to match the final combined representations. He and his collaborators gave subjects tests of verbal reasoning, abstract reasoning, and spatial reasoning, from which they obtained (by a principal components factor analysis) two main factors that they labelled 'verbal ability' and 'spatial–abstract' ability. They then divided their subjects into four groups on the basis of whether they scored high or low on these two factors. They went back to their mathematical model and estimated the parameter values that gave the best fit with the results for each of these four groups. Differences in the verbal ability factor had no effect on the values of the parameters, but differences in the spatial–abstract factor had a significant effect on the probability of constructing one or more combined representations.

How much does this finding tell us about individual differences? I fear the answer is: very little. Even Guyote and Sternberg make only a limited claim: 'This relationship between spatial–abstract ability and ability to form and integrate transitive chains provides evidence that the representations used in solving syllogisms may be spatial or abstract in nature, rather than verbal.' The role of the mathematical model is tangential to this claim, since only the spatial–abstract factor correlated significantly with a direct score of accuracy in syllogistic reasoning. Moreover, since the parameter values were estimated from groups of subjects working on a set of problems, they hardly have any psychological reality within the minds of the individual subjects. To suppose otherwise would be like using actuarial data on suicides to provide parameters for a mathematical model of the mental processes underlying an individual's decision to commit suicide. People kill themselves for many different reasons, but it does not follow that any individual considers *all* such potential reasons before making a decision. The mathematical model provides us with an account of a 'group mind'. It perhaps tells us something about the group's working memory, and the group's form of mental representations – ironically, that people are probably using a spatial model, not a linguistic-like string of symbols as assumed by the theory. In short, it is a model of actuarial data, not of individual minds. Such models are commonplace in cognitive psychology; they are often the best that we can do. Nevertheless, they should not be confused with genuine explanations of differences in ability.

Sternberg's is the best of the theories based on Euler circles. It is ingenious, but implausible and limited in its application. Its ingenuity resides in its apparently successful translation of Euler circles into an equivalent notation using strings of symbols, and in its deployment of rules for manipulating the notation that appear to be sound. Although it correctly emphasizes the importance of alternative models of the premises, it fails to be descriptively adequate because it gives no account of the figural effect, and at best only an actuarial account of individual differences. It fails to be explanatorily adequate because it implies that human reasoners are intrinsically irrational, and because it is restricted to a narrow class of inferences. Finally, the theory's complexity is implausible, particularly given that certain major components are supposed to function without error and that no account of how children acquire such skills is provided.

Syllogistic theories based on Venn diagrams

The problem with Euler circles as a logical tool is that there is no simple algorithm for ensuring that one has considered all the different ways of combining the representations of the premises. A superior topological method was invented by a nineteenth-century cleric, John Venn. He, too, uses circles to represent sets of entities, but his method is more systematic than Euler's. He represents all the possible combinations of the premises as distinct areas in a single diagram. If a premise rules out a particular subset, then the corresponding region is shaded out in the diagram. The premise *All A are B* rules out the existence of A's that are not B's, and the Venn diagram thus takes the following form:

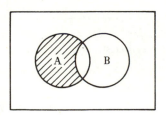

The square as a whole represents the complete universe of discourse. The left-hand circle represents the set A, the right-hand circle represents the set B, and the shaded area indicates that a subset is empty – there are no members of set A outside set B. (In accordance with standard logical practice, a universal assertion of the form *All A are B* is not taken to imply the existence of A's: it has the force of *Any A is a B*, which may be true even if there are no A's.) If a premise asserts that a subset is not empty, then a cross is marked in the corresponding region of the diagram. A Venn diagram of *Some A are B* thus takes the form:

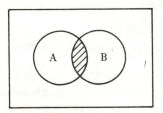

where the cross indicates that the intersection is not empty – there are A's that are B's. A Venn diagram of *No A are B* takes the form:

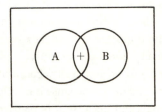

where the shading indicates that the intersection is empty. A Venn diagram of *Some A are not B* takes the form:

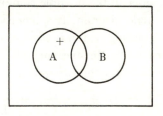

In order to evaluate a syllogism such as:

> All A are B
> No C are B
> ∴ No A are C

the Venn diagram has a circle for each set:

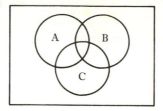

The diagram is then filled in according to the information in the premises. The result in this case is shown in Figure 4.1. Since the conclusion fits the resulting diagram, the inference is valid.

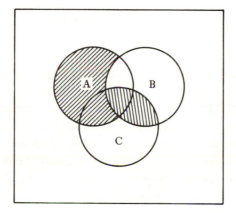

Figure 4.1 A Venn diagram appropriately shaded to represent the premises *All A are B, No C are B*. The shaded portions represent subsets whose existence is ruled out by the premises.

Allen Newell (1981) has presented a theory of syllogistic inference based on the approach to problem solving that Herb Simon and he have developed (Newell and Simon, 1972). The theory assumes that there is a problem 'space', and a set of 'operators' that can be used to move from one position in the space to another. An appropriate operator is selected by a 'means-ends' analysis. This is a well-known heuristic that uses a characterization of the current goal (the 'end' to be attained) in order to select an operator likely to be useful in achieving it (the 'means' to be employed). In presenting Newell's theory, I shall describe it as a symbolic equivalent of Venn diagrams, though Newell himself makes no use of them in his exposition.

The theory assumes that there are four stages in evaluating a given syllogism.

First, the premises are represented in a symbolic form that corresponds to a Venn diagram. Newell's representations are not Venn diagrams but strings of symbols that appear to correspond directly to them in much the same way that the strings in Sternberg's theory correspond to Euler circles. The premise *All A are B* is accordingly represented by the following triplet of strings:

$$\text{Nec A} + \text{B} +, \text{Pos A} - \text{B} +, \text{Pos A} - \text{B} -$$

Each string corresponds to part of the Venn diagram: Nec A + B + indicates that necessarily there exists something that is both A and B: Newell departs from orthodox logical practice in taking universal assertions to establish necessary existence. Pos A − B + indicates that possibly there is something that is not A but is B. Pos A − B − indicates that possibly there is something that is not A and not B. The fact that the premise renders it impossible for there to be things that are A but not B is represented by the absence of any string concerning A + B −. As Newell correctly points out, the latter convention makes the notational system vulnerable to errors of omission. It also makes it incapable of representing the distinction between 'No' and 'I don't know' as answers to the question 'Are there A's that are not B's?' If the absence of information is used to represent impossibility, there is no obvious way to represent ignorance.

The second step consists in combining representations according to a heuristic that indicates the existence of possible objects. The easiest way to understand the heuristic is to consider again the Venn diagram in Figure 4.1 constructed from the premises:

All A are B
No C are B.

The diagram suggests that four different sorts of entity may exist. In particular, there may be:

A's that are B's but not C's:	Pos A + B + C −
B's that are neither A's nor C's:	Pos A − B + C −
C's that are neither B's nor A's:	Pos A − B − C +
Entities that are not A's, B's, or C's:	Pos A − B − C −

The corresponding 'operator' formulated by Newell takes two strings as input and produces a new string as output. To produce the output above, it has to yield such derivations as:

$$\text{Nec A} + \text{B} +, \text{Pos B} + \text{C} - \Rightarrow \text{Pos A} + \text{B} + \text{C} -$$

and the appropriate symbolic rule is relatively easy to formulate. In fact, it is not really necessary to generate all the possible outputs in order to evaluate a given conclusion, and Newell argues that those states that are generated could be selected by a means–ends analysis.

The third step in the process determines whether a possible entity produced by the heuristic necessarily exists. In the example above, the first premise establishes that there are necessarily A's that are B's, and the heuristic suggests the possibility that these same objects are not C's, i.e., Pos A+ B+ C−. If the existence of objects in the complementary class, A+ B+ C+, can be ruled out for certain, then necessarily the objects that are A's and B's are not C's. An inspection of Figure 4.1 shows indeed that there are no objects of the sort A+ B+ C+: that portion of the diagram is shaded. Hence, it follows:

$$\text{Nec } A+ B+ C-$$

Newell specifies an operator that can carry out the equivalent search among the strings of symbols.

Finally, in the fourth step, an operator is used to recognize that an object is an instance of the given conclusion. The conclusion *Some A are not C* is represented as Nec A+ C−; the operator recognizes that Nec A+ B+ C− is an instance of it, and that the deduction is accordingly valid. In fact, a conclusion of the form *No A are C* also follows from the premises.

Newell suggests that errors may arise in encoding the premises, or in working memory, but he makes no specific predictions about them. His account is an illustration of an approach to syllogisms that derives from work on problem solving rather than a fully-fledged theory, and indeed it is plainly both descriptively and explanatorily inadequate. Moreover, there is an alternative and simpler theory on the same general lines. The theory rests on the close relation between Venn diagrams and the truth tables of the propositional calculus (see Chapter 2). A table such as:

A	B	All A are B
+	+	+
+	−	−
−	+	+
−	−	+

is isomorphic to a truth table for *not-A or B*, though obviously it receives a different semantic interpretation. Hence a simple algorithm can be based on the idea, described in Chapter 3, of making propositional inferences by eliminating contingencies from a truth table. The premises:

1. All A are B
2. No C are B

eliminate the following items in the table of contingencies for A, B, and C:

A	B	C	
+	+	+	– eliminated by premise 2
+	+	–	
+	–	+	– eliminated by premise 1
+	–	–	– eliminated by premise 1
–	+	+	– eliminated by premise 2
–	+	–	
–	–	+	
–	–	–	

The contingencies that survive correspond directly to the four unshaded areas of Figure 4.1, and the assertion *No A are C* holds over all of them. All that is needed to complete the theory is a procedure that establishes the positive existence of certain contingencies. Thus, for example, the assertion *Some A are B* calls for the following table:

A	B	
+	+	– established by premise
+	–	
–	+	
–	–	

Hence, the premises:

1. Some A are B
2. All B are C

call for the following table of contingencies:

	A	B	C	
Premise 1 establishes:	+	+	+	
	+	+	–	– eliminated by 2
	+	–	+	
	+	–	–	
	–	+	+	
	–	+	–	– eliminated by 2
	–	–	+	
	–	–	–	

92

Premise 1 establishes that the first or second contingency is fulfilled, and premise 2 eliminates the second contingency. From what remains, it is clear that *Some A are C*. As a psychological theory, this procedure for syllogistic inference suffers from the same drawback as its propositional analogue – the difficulty of mentally manipulating tables of contingencies.

Conclusions

None of the theories of syllogistic inference survives the battery of criteria for descriptive and explanatory adequacy. Both Erickson's and Sternberg's theories contain the plausible idea that the difficulty of a syllogism is proportional to the number of different representations that its premises require. The problem is that neither Euler circles nor Venn diagrams are natural mental models. They are sophisticated mathematical notations that depend on mapping sets of individuals into sets of points in a Euclidean plane. Ironically, they have a limited range of application and cannot handle premises with more than one quantifier, e.g., 'Everyone loves someone.' Some syllogistic premises require several different Euler diagrams and the combinatorial cost is too great for Erickson's theory to be compatible with human rationality. The problem persists even if, as in Sternberg's theory, the diagrams are translated into strings of symbols. And this manoeuvre calls for symbolic rules of such intricacy that the theory appears to step away from mental models back towards a system of formal rules of inference. Venn diagrams are a still more sophisticated notation built on the essential machinery of representing sets as circles in the plane. As my tabular version of the theory illustrates, however, the procedure is close to the manipulation of truth tables. Hence it suffers from the same drawback as its propositional analogue – the difficulty of holding in mind all the various contingencies.

The present theories are too fragile to bear the weight of human reason. Erickson and Sternberg tamper with the logical machinery in order to account for deductive errors, and thereby give up the chance to achieve rationality. Newell holds fast to logical power, but fails to explain systematic error. The dilemma to be resolved is to allow for both rationality and human error. If my diagnosis is correct, what is needed is both a simpler and a more natural conception of a mental model.

5

How to reason syllogistically

In this chapter, I am going to describe a theory of syllogistic inference that my colleagues and I have gradually developed over the last seven years (see Johnson-Laird, 1975a; Johnson-Laird and Steedman, 1978; Johnson-Laird and Bara, 1982). It may seem surprising that it has taken so long to explain how people derive conclusions from what are, formally speaking, only sixty-four different pairs of premises. But the theory is, I believe, essentially correct; it is both descriptively and explanatorily adequate according to the criteria introduced in the previous chapter. Its various versions have been modelled in computer programs, and it has been corroborated by independent experimental results. It is in fact a special case of a more general theory of reasoning, but it is worth concentrating first on syllogisms because they straddle the boundary of human logical competence – some are literally child's play while others are beyond the ability of all but the most expert reasoners.

The externalization of syllogistic inference

Let us begin by considering an imaginary method of externalizing the process of deduction. Suppose you want to draw a conclusion from the premises:

All the artists are beekeepers
All the beekeepers are chemists

without relying on Euler circles or Venn diagrams. One way in which to proceed is to employ a group of actors to construct a 'tableau' in which some of them act as artists, some as beekeepers, and some as chemists. To represent the first premise, every person acting as an artist is also instructed to play the part of a beekeeper, and, since the first premise is consistent with there being beekeepers who are not artists, that role is assigned to other actors, who are told that it is uncertain whether or not they exist. In short, a tableau of the following sort is set up:

$$artist = beekeeper$$
$$artist = beekeeper$$
$$artist = beekeeper$$
$$(beekeeper)$$
$$(beekeeper)$$

There are three actors playing the joint roles, and two actors taking the part of the beekeepers who are not artists – the parentheses designate a directorial device establishing that the latter may or may not exist. Obviously, the numbers of actors playing the different roles is entirely arbitrary. The tableau is easily extended to accommodate the second premise:

All the beekeepers are chemists.

Those actors playing beekeepers are instructed to take on the role of chemists, and an arbitrary number of new actors are introduced to play the role of chemists who are not beekeepers – a type which, once again, may or may not exist:

$$artist = beekeeper = chemist$$
$$artist = beekeeper = chemist$$
$$artist = beekeeper = chemist$$
$$(beekeeper) = (chemist)$$
$$(beekeeper) = (chemist)$$
$$(chemist)$$

At this point, if you were asked whether it followed that *All the artists are chemists*, you could readily inspect the tableau and determine that this conclusion is indeed true. All that you have done is to externalize and to combine the information in two premises. Deductive inference, however, requires more than just the construction of an integrated representation of the premises: it calls for a search for counter-examples. A more complicated example will illustrate this point.

Consider how a troupe of actors could represent the premises:

None of the authors are burglars.
Some of the chefs are burglars.

The first premise is represented by two distinct groups acting as the authors and the burglars, and they are instructed that they are never allowed to take on each other's role. The two groups are, as it were, fenced off from each other:

```
author
author
author
- - - - - - - - - - - - - - - -
burglar
burglar
burglar
```

The tableau indicates that no author is identical to any burglar. The information in the second premise, *Some of the chefs are burglars*, is added by extending the tableau in a straightforward way, where *some* is taken to mean *at least some*:

```
author
author
author
- - - - - - - - - - - - - - - -
          burglar = chef
          burglar = chef
         (burglar)  (chef)
```

It is tempting, at this point, to conclude that *None of the authors are chefs*, or conversely, that *None of the chefs are authors*. (Six subjects out of twenty drew conclusions of this form in an experiment reported by Johnson-Laird and Steedman, 1978.) Both conclusions are certainly consistent with the tableau. But neither is warranted, because there is another way of representing the premises:

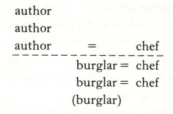

```
author
author
author        =        chef
- - - - - - - - - - - - - -
     burglar = chef
     burglar = chef
    (burglar)
```

You can check for yourself that this interpretation is wholly consistent with the premises (*None of the authors are burglars*, and *Some of the chefs are burglars*), yet it invalidates the previous conclusions and suggests instead that *Some of the authors are not chefs*. However, there is still another possibility. There could be several chefs who are not burglars, and each author could be identical to such a chef:

$$
\begin{array}{rcl}
\text{author} & = & \text{chef} \\
\text{author} & = & \text{chef} \\
\text{author} & = & \text{chef} \\
\hline
& \text{burglar} = & \text{chef} \\
& \text{burglar} = & \text{chef} \\
& (\text{burglar}) &
\end{array}
$$

The tableau is still consistent with the premises, but what it shows is that the conclusion that *Some of the authors are not chefs* is invalid. There is no other assignment of roles that is compatible with the premises, and you might therefore suppose that there is no valid conclusion (as did six subjects in the experiment). But in all three of the tableaux it is the case that at least *Some of the chefs are not authors*. This conclusion is accordingly valid. (It was drawn by seven subjects.)

An effective procedure for syllogistic inference

The idea of employing actors to take on different parts suggests, of course, a hypothesis about how people might actually make inferences. Instead of arranging an external tableau, they could construct a mental model – an internal tableau containing elements that stand for the members of sets in just the same way that the actors did. A general procedure for making inferences in this way requires three main steps.

1. *Construct a mental model of the first premise.* The representation of a universal affirmative assertion has the following structure:

$$
\begin{array}{ll}
\text{All of the X are Y:} & x = y \\
& x = y \\
& (y) \\
& (y)
\end{array}
$$

where the number of tokens corresponding to x's and y's is arbitrary, and the items in parentheses represent the possible existence of y's that are not x's. The representations of the other forms of syllogistic premise are straightforward:

$$
\begin{array}{llll}
\text{Some of the X are Y:} & \quad & x = y \\
& & x = y \\
& & (x) \quad (y) \\
\text{None of the X are Y:} & & x \\
& & \underline{x} \;\underline{}\;\underline{}\;\underline{}\;\underline{} \\
& & \qquad y \\
& & \qquad y \\
\text{Some of the X are not Y:} & & x \\
& & \underline{x} \;\underline{}\;\underline{}\;\underline{}\;\underline{} \\
& & (x) = y \\
& & \qquad y \\
\end{array}
$$

It should be noted that each premise requires only a single mental model.

A crucial point about mental models is that the system for constructing and interpreting them must embody the knowledge that the number of entities depicted is irrelevant to any syllogistic inference that is drawn. In the case of numerical or proportional inferences, however, the numbers or proportions will matter. The procedure must accordingly have an independent way of keeping track of which particular proposition is being modelled. Human reasoners appear to retain a superficial representation of the propositions expressed by the premises – one that is close to their linguistic form – but from the errors they make, they appear to make inferences by manipulating mental models rather than by deploying rules of inference on these superficial representations.

2. *Add the information in the second premise to the mental model of the first premise, taking into account the different ways in which this can be done.* In addition to the purely interpretative skills required to construct mental models, reasoners must appreciate the fundamental semantic principle underlying valid deduction: an inference is valid if and only if there is no way of interpreting the premises that is consistent with a denial of the conclusion. This principle motivates the search for alternative ways of adding the information from the second premise.

For some syllogisms, there is only one possible integrated model. For example, a premise of the form *Some of the A are B* yields the model:

$$
\begin{array}{l}
a = b \\
a = b \\
(a) \quad (b)
\end{array}
$$

and a second premise of the form *All of the B are C* can be integrated only by forming the model:

$$a = b = c$$
$$a = b = c$$
$$(a) \quad (b) = c$$
$$(c)$$

from which it follows that *Some of the A are C*. There is no alternative model of the premises that violates this conclusion.

For other syllogisms, it is necessary to construct and evaluate two models. For example, premises of the form:

Some of the A are not B

All the C are B

can be represented by the model:

$$a$$
$$\underline{a} \; _____$$
$$(a) = b = c$$
$$b = c$$
$$(b)$$

In this model, the conclusion *Some of the A are not C* is true because the A's above the broken line are not C's, and the converse conclusion *Some of the C are not A* is also true because there is at least one C that is not linked to an A. The search for an alternative model to falsify these putative conclusions yields a second model:

$$a$$
$$\underline{a} \; \_\_\_\_\_$$
$$(a) = b = c$$
$$(a) = b = c$$
$$(b)$$

This model rules out the second conclusion because all the C's are A's, but there is no way to destroy the first conclusion, *Some of the A are not C*, which is accordingly valid.

Still other premises yield three different models. For example, the premises:

All of the B are A

None of the B are C

yield the model:

```
        c
        c
      _ _ _ _ _
          b = a
          b = a
```
(a)

which suggests the conclusion *None of the C are A*, or its converse *None of A are C*. The search for a counter-example yields the model:

```
        c
        c   =   a
      _ _ _ _ _
          b = a
          b = a
```
(a)

which falsifies both of these conclusions and suggests instead that *Some of the C are not A* or conversely that *Some of the A are not C*. The search for a counter-example to these conclusions yields:

```
        c   =   a
        c   =   a
      _ _ _ _ _
          b = a
          b = a
```
(a)

which shows that only the conclusion *Some of the A are not C* is valid. The last model by itself, of course, suggests the invalid conclusion that *All of the C are A*, but that conclusion is ruled out by the previous models. Although these premises have three models, they do not all have to be constructed *ab initio*: an entirely feasible strategy, as illustrated here, is to construct one model and then to try out various modifications of it that are consistent with the premises.

Since the procedure is based on the assumption that each of the four forms of syllogistic premise is represented by just one mental model, it avoids the explosion of combinatorial possibilities that so embarrasses the theories based on Euler circles. The assumption is feasible provided that optional entities are directly represented within a model, as in the representation of *All A are B* as:

$$a = b$$
$$a = b$$
(b)

Is it logically possible to extend this notion so that instead of the three models required by the last example just one model suffices? Such a model might have the following form:

$$
\begin{array}{c}
c \quad (= a) \\
\underline{c \quad (= a)} \\
b = a \\
b = a \\
(a)
\end{array}
$$

However, its correct interpretation requires a new notational principle to be introduced in order to make plain that both, one, or neither of the identities above the broken line may apply. Such a device is merely a notational variation on the present theory: it is still necessary to consider three logically distinct possibilities corresponding to all, some, or none of the c's being identical to a's.

Syllogisms never require more than three different mental models to be constructed, and Table 5.1 presents the number of models that are required for each of the twenty seven pairs of premises that yield a non-trivial valid conclusion. The table indicates when such a conclusion is contrary to the figural effect, and should therefore be harder to draw. It also presents the percentages of correct responses made by subjects in an experiment designed to test the theory (see Johnson-Laird and Bara, 1982). Every subject was presented with each of the sixty-four possible premises with a different sensible content and asked to state what conclusion, if any, followed from the premises. The results will be analysed later in the chapter together with those from other experiments.

3. *Frame a conclusion to express the relation, if any, between the 'end' terms that holds in all the models of the premises.* An 'end' term is one which occurs in only a single premise, unlike the 'middle' term which occurs in both premises. If there is no such relation between the end terms, the only valid conclusions that can be drawn are trivial ones, such as a conjunction or disjunction of the premises, and subjects generally respond that there is no valid conclusion.

The difficulty of syllogistic inference depends on the number of mental models of the premises

If every step of the procedure is carried out correctly, then as a computer implementation of it (in POP-10) shows, the result is a completely rational

Table 5.1 *The number of mental models required for the twenty-seven pairs of premises yielding valid conclusions, and the number of subjects out of twenty drawing the correct conclusions in an experiment reported by Johnson-Laird and Bara (1982). The entries show where premises have a valid conclusion that runs contrary to the figural effect*

FIRST PREMISE

SECOND PREMISE	All the A are B	Some of the A are B	None of the A are B	Some of the A are not B
All the B are C	1 model All the A are C: 19	1 model Some of the A are C: 18 Some of the C are A: 0	3 models (contrary to figure) Some of the C are not A: 0	
Some of the B are C		3 models Some of the A are not C: 4	3 models (contrary to figure) Some of the C are not A: 1	
None of the B are C	1 model None of the A are C: 14 None of the C are A: 3			
Some of the B are not C				
All the C are B			1 model None of the A are C: 8 None of the C are A: 5	2 models Some of the A are not C: 7
Some of the C are B			3 models Some of the C are not A: 1	
None of the C are B	1 model None of the C are A: 8 None of the A are C: 4	3 models Some of the A are not C: 0		
Some of the C are not B	2 models Some of the C are not A: 4			

FIRST PREMISE

SECOND PREMISE	All the B are A	Some of the B are A	None of the B are A	Some of the B are not A
All the B are C	2 models Some of the A are C: 0 Some of the C are A: 0	1 model Some of the C are A: 10 Some of the A are C: 3	3 models Some of the C are not A: 0	2 models Some of the C are not A: 0
Some of the B are C	1 model Some of the A are C: 9 Some of the C are A: 4		3 models Some of the C are not A: 2	
None of the B are C	3 models Some of the A are not C: 0	3 models Some of the A are not C: 3		
Some of the B are not C	2 models Some of the A are not C: 9			
All the C are B	1 model All the C are A: 15		1 model None of the C are A: 12 None of the A are C: 2	
Some of the C are B	1 model Some of the C are A: 19 Some of the A are C: 1		3 models Some of the C are not A: 6	
None of the C are B	3 models (contrary to figure) Some of the A are not C: 0	3 models (contrary to figure) Some of the A are not C: 0		
Some of the C are not B				

and error-free performance. A mistake in any step may, or may not, vitiate the conclusion. Since the first and third steps are common to the comprehension and production of much discourse, they are likely to be relatively free of error. The task of drawing a valid conclusion should be relatively easy when there is only one possible integrated model: even an individual who does not appreciate the need to search for counter-examples should make the correct response. The major source of difficulty should be the construction and evaluation of alternative models. This process places an additional load on working memory – the memory system that is used for holding the mental models while they are manipulated. The greater the number of models to be considered, the harder it should be to construct and to evaluate them. Hence, the task should be harder when it is necessary to construct two models, and harder still when it is necessary to construct three models.

Working with various colleagues – principally Janellen Huttenlocher, Kate Ehrlich, and Bruno Bara – I have carried out a number of experiments on inference in which subjects have been asked to state what, if anything, follows from a series of syllogistic premises. We have used premises with sensible contents, but which do not predispose the subjects to any particular conclusions on a factual basis. Table 5.2 summarizes the results of three of our experiments. In experiment 1, twenty students at Teachers College, Columbia University were given all sixty-four possible pairs of premises. In experiment 2, twenty students at Milan University were also given the sixty-four pairs of premises. And in experiment 3, a further twenty Milanese

Table 5.2 *The percentages of correct valid conclusions that were drawn in three different experiments on syllogistic reasoning. The percentages are shown as a function of the number of different models that have to be constructed to yield the correct conclusion*

	Premises requiring one model	Premises requiring two models	Premises requiring three models
Experiment 1	92	46	27
Experiment 2	80	20	9
Experiment 3	62	20	3

Note. Experiment 1 is reported in Johnson-Laird and Steedman (1978); Experiments 2 and 3 are reported in Johnson-Laird and Bara (1982). The data from Experiment 2 on individual valid problems were presented in Table 5.1. In Experiment 1, twenty American subjects were given all sixty-four possible pairs of premises; and, in Experiment 2, twenty Italian subjects were also given the sixty-four pairs of premises. In Experiment 3, a further twenty Italian subjects were given only ten seconds to respond to each problem.

104

students were given the same problems but had only ten seconds to respond to each of them. The table shows the percentages of correctly drawn valid conclusions as a function of the number of mental models that have to be constructed to make the right response for the right reason. Despite the variety of conditions and subjects in the experiments, there was a highly reliable trend in each of them: the greater the number of models to be considered, the harder the task of drawing a valid conclusion.

Subjects do indeed attempt to assess alternative models of the premises, but often the task exceeds the capacity of their working memories. It is difficult to hold in mind one model whilst attempting to construct and to evaluate an alternative model. This conclusion is corroborated by the nature of the errors that the subjects make. They almost invariably (i.e., 90% or more) respond with a conclusion that is congruent with only *some* of the possible models of the premises.

The figural effects

There is one other major factor that affects syllogistic inference: the figure of the premises. The figural effects consist in a bias towards certain forms of conclusion, and an increase in the difficulty and latency of drawing correct conclusions over the four figures. These phenomena are important because they cannot be readily explained in terms of atmosphere, illicit conversion, or the theories based on Euler circles and Venn diagrams. But they can be accounted for in terms of the processes that occur in forming an integrated mental model of premises. If the two occurrences of the middle term are in a figure that readily permits the two premises to be integrated, the task is relatively easy; if they are in a figure that does not permit an immediate integration, then additional operations have to be carried out to make it possible, and the premises that require these additional operations are harder to integrate. These additional operations have been modelled in the computer program too. The fundamental assumption on which they are based is that working memory operates on a 'first in, first out' basis. For example, it is easier to recall a list of digits in the order in which they were presented – the first digit recalled first, the second digit recalled second, and so on – than in the opposite order (see Broadbent, 1958, p. 236). The same principle applies to syllogisms, and the natural order in which to state a conclusion is the order in which the terms were used to construct a mental model of the premises.

With premises in the A – B, B – C figure, the two instances of the middle term, B, occur one after the other, and it is easy to construct a mental model of the first premise and then immediately to integrate the information from the second premise. For example, with premises of the form:

Some of the A are B
All of the B are C

a reasoner can form a model of the first premise:

$$a = b$$
$$a = b$$
$$(a)\ (b)$$

and then immediately integrate the content of the second premise by substituting c's for b's:

$$a = c$$
$$a = c$$
$$(a)\ (c)$$

This procedure of substituting one type of token for another was deliberately omitted in the account of the theory earlier in the chapter, but it is an essential part of the explanation of the figural effects, because the substitution requires an appropriate ordering of the terms within the premises: there has to be temporal contiguity between the original items (b's) and the ones that replace them (c's). Since the a's preceded the c's into working memory in the example, the 'first in, first out' principle leads to a conclusion of the form *Some of the A are C* rather than its equally valid converse. The same principle applies to any premises in the A – B, B – C figure, and thus favours conclusions of the form A – C rather than C – A (cf. Table 5.3).

With premises in the B – A, C – B figure, the two instances of the middle term do not occur one after the other. They are separated and therefore the process of substitution cannot occur. A natural way to proceed, however, is to construct a model of the second premise, C – B, renew the interpretation of the first premise, B – A, and then substitute the information it contains in the model of the second premise. The reordering of the premises brings together the two occurrences of the middle term. For example, with premises of the form:

All of the B are A
Some of the C are B

reasoners are unable to make an immediate substitution, because of the separation of the two occurrences of the middle term. They accordingly construct a model of the second premise:

$$c = b$$
$$c = b$$
$$(c) \ (b)$$

make a renewed interpretation of the first premise, and substitute its information in the model:

$$c = a$$
$$c = a$$
$$(c) \ (a)$$
$$(a)$$

On the 'first in, first out' principle of working memory, the resulting mental model will yield a conclusion of the form *Some of the C are A*. In general, premises in this figure should produce a bias towards C – A conclusions (cf. Table 5.3).

The two remaining figures are still more complicated. There are two possible routes by which to integrate premises in the A – B, C – B figure. Reasoners can construct a model of the first premise, A – B, and then switch round the order of the terms in their interpretation of the second premise to B – C so that the two instances of the middle term occur one after the other. Alternatively, they can construct a model of the second premise, C – B, renew their interpretation of the first premise, then switch it round to B – A so as to make the substitution possible. Switching round an interpretation must not be confused with the operation of converting a premise, though the two notions are similar. The converse of *Some A are B* is *Some B are A* and they are equivalent in that when one is true the other is true; the converse of *All A are B* is *All B are A*, and they are not equivalent. If reasoners simply formed the converse of an expression, they would often fall into error. Although various theorists have argued that illicit conversions are a source of error (see Chapter 4), the idea of switching round an interpretation concerns only the order of information in working memory. The interpretation of *All the A are B* takes the form:

$$a = b$$
$$a = b$$
$$(b)$$
$$(b)$$

107

If this interpretation is switched round, it takes the form:

$$b = a$$
$$b = a$$
$$(b)$$
$$(b)$$

This revision is logically accurate: an illicit conversion would only occur if the tokens representing the possibility of b's that were not a's were dropped in the process. The purpose of the operation is to ensure that the two instances of the middle term occur one after the other.

In the remaining figure, B – A, B – C, there are again two alternative procedures. Reasoners may switch round a model of the first premise to A – B, form a model of it, and then substitute the information from the second premise, B – C, in the model. Alternatively, they may switch round a model of the second premise to C – B, renew their interpretation of the first premise, B – A, and substitute its information in the model.

The operations that are required to form a mental model from premises in the four figures are summarized in Table 5.3. The bias they create towards one particular form of conclusion for the asymmetric figures, $\begin{matrix} A - B \\ B - C \end{matrix}$ and $\begin{matrix} B - A \\ C - B \end{matrix}$, is highly reliable. The slight bias towards A – C conclusions for the symmetric figures, $\begin{matrix} A - B \\ C - B \end{matrix}$ and $\begin{matrix} B - A \\ B - C \end{matrix}$, probably reflects a preference both for constructing an initial model from the first premise and for a process that requires fewer operations.

Two basic operations are required to construct a model of the premises in the $\begin{matrix} A - B \\ B - C \end{matrix}$ figure: building an initial model and integrating the information from the second premise. A third operation of renewing the interpretation of a premise is required for premises in the $\begin{matrix} B - A \\ B - C \end{matrix}$ figure. A more complex operation is required by both procedures for premises in the $\begin{matrix} A - B \\ C - B \end{matrix}$ figure: switching round the interpretation of a premise so that information about its end term can be substituted in the model. Finally, a still more complex operation is required by both procedures for premises in the $\begin{matrix} B - A \\ B - C \end{matrix}$ figure:

Table 5.3 *The operations required to form an integrated model of premises in the four figures, together with the predicted and obtained response bias*

	Figure of premises					
	A – B B – C	B – A C – B	A – B C – B		B – A B – C	
Operations						
Switch round	—	—	—	Premise 2	Premise 1	Premise 2
Build model	Premise 1	Premise 2	Premise 1	Premise 1	Premise 1	Premise 2
Renew	—	Premise 1	—	Premise 1	—	Premise 1
Switch round	—	—	Premise 2	Premise 1	—	—
Integrate	Premise 2	Premise 1	Premise 2	Premise 1	Premise 2	Premise 1
Predicted reponse bias:	A – C	C – A	A – C	C – A	A – C	C – A
Obtained response bias:						
Experiment 1	89%	91%	50%	50%	64%	36%
Experiment 2	93%	86%	55%	45%	62%	38%
Experiment 3	94%	66%	56%	44%	73%	27%

switching round the interpretation of a premise as a whole as a prerequisite for constructing an initial model.

Since the complexity of the operations required to form a mental model increases over the four figures, there should be a corresponding increase in the difficulty of drawing a valid conclusion, and in the latency of responses. An experiment carried out by Johnson-Laird and Bara (1982) was specifically designed to test these predictions (see Experiment 2 of Table 5.2). There was a reliable decline in the percentages of correct conclusions over the four figures: 51%, 48%, 35%, and 22% respectively. As Table 5.2 shows, the percentages of correct responses where three models had to be constructed were too small to allow us to obtain reliable estimates of latency, while premises requiring two models only occur in the two symmetric figures and hence their data did not enable us to test the latency prediction. However, the trend in latencies for the premises requiring one model reliably confirmed the prediction; over the four figures, the means were 11·6, 12·9, 18·7, and 22·1 seconds respectively.

An alternative explanation of the figural effects

In principle, there are many other possible explanations for the effects of figure on the form of conclusions, their accuracy, and their latency. I believe, however, that the present theory is correct in its essentials, and to substantiate this claim I shall consider an alternative account and some further experimental results.

Many psychologists confronted with the figural effects assume that they somehow reflect the order of the premises and their 'given – new' structure, that is, the position of the given information and the new information in the premises. In fact, this superficially appealing hypothesis fails to account for the phenomena. It is certainly true that the optimal ordering of given and new information corresponds to the figure:

$$A - B$$
$$B - C$$

with the given information in the second premise, B, referring back to the most recent new information in the first premise. The hypothesis predicts that the other figures, which violate this optimal ordering, should be harder to understand, but it does not explain the trend in difficulty over the remaining figures. Likewise, it does not account for the bias in the form of the conclusions.

A further difficulty for the 'given – new' explanation of the figural effects derives from a series of experiments reported by Ehrlich and Johnson-Laird (1982). In one condition of these experiments, the subjects had to remember premises of the form:

A is on the right of B
B is in front of C
C is on the left of D

in order to draw a corresponding diagram. These experiments, which will be reported in Chapter 14, were primarily concerned with quite a different matter, but one of the independent variables was the figural arrangement of the terms, A, B, C, D, which in fact designated common objects. Figure had no consistent effects on reading times or on memory for the premises, as reflected in the accuracy of the diagrams. It therefore seems that figural effects occur primarily when an inference has to be made, and in particular when a direct link has to be established between the end terms – with the middle term dropping out of the final representation of the conclusion.

If figural effects are a consequence of the operations required to make inferences, then they should occur in all forms of deduction. There should be figural effects, for example, in simple three-term series problems of the form:

Alice is taller than Bertha.
Bertha is taller than Carol.

Indeed, in his classic paper, Ian Hunter (1957) proposed that the difficulty of such problems exactly reflected their figural arrangement. Yet, despite the many studies of three-term problems, there had been no investigation of the conclusions that subjects spontaneously state in their own words until Bruno Bara, Patrizia Tabossi and I carried out two experiments using this procedure in order to test whether there was a figural bias on such conclusions.

One factor that affects the difficulty of three-term series problems is that there is, as Herb Clark has established, a difference in the ease of understanding such pairs of expressions as *taller than* and *shorter than* (see Clark and Clark, 1977). *Taller than* is a neutral expression that implies nothing about the absolute heights of the entities it relates, whereas *shorter than* suggests that these entities are short rather than tall. This contrast between the neutral or 'unmarked' term and its 'marked' antonym is clearest in the difference between such questions as 'Which of the two is the taller?' and 'Which of the two is the shorter?', and in the fact that *tallness* rather than *shortness* is the name of the dimension as a whole. In general, unmarked terms are easier to grasp than marked terms. Hence, in order to obviate this factor in our experiments, we used problems in which the relational term is its own converse:

> Alice is related to Bertha
> Bertha is related to Carol

where it was clear to the subjects that the premises were about blood-relationships. The experiments showed that there was a general bias towards A – C conclusions, and that, as predicted, premises in the A – B, B – C figure enhanced this bias (77% A – C conclusions), whereas those in the B – A, C – B figure eliminated it (only 47% A – C conclusions).

Evidently, the figural effect is not peculiar to syllogisms, but truly mirrors the task of combining premises in working memory. The present theory seems to give a comprehensive account of it.

Syllogisms that yield no valid conclusions interrelating end terms

There are thirty-seven out of the sixty-four pairs of syllogistic premises for which there are no valid conclusions interrelating end terms. In principle, their correct evaluation requires a reasoner to discover that the alternative models of the premises have nothing in common, but the right response may sometimes be made for the wrong reason.

If both premises are particular, i.e., contain the quantifier *some*, then they can be interpreted by alternative models that support contradictory conclusions. For example, the premises:

Some of the A are B
Some of the B are C

are readily interpretable both where identities are maximized:

$$a = b = c$$
$$a = b = c$$
$$(a) \quad (b) \quad (c)$$

and where they are not:

$$a = b$$
$$a \quad = b \quad (c)$$
$$(a) \quad b = c$$
$$\quad \quad b = c$$

112

Hence, it is readily apparent that such premises do not support a valid conclusion interrelating the end terms. When both premises are negative, they likewise support blatantly inconsistent models. For example, the premises:

None of the A are B
None of the B are C

yield both the model:

$$a$$
$$a \: \_\_\_\_\_$$
$$b$$
$$b \: \_\_\_\_\_$$
$$c$$
$$c$$

and the model:

$$a = c$$
$$a = c \: \_\_\_\_$$
$$b$$
$$b$$

in which there is no relation between the end items common to both interpretations.

The remaining premise pairs require three models to be constructed if the correct response of 'No valid conclusion' is to be guaranteed. For example, the premises:

All of the A are B
Some of the B are not C

yield a model:

$$a$$
$$a$$
$$\_\_\_\_$$
$$(c)$$
$$c$$

which suggests that *None of the A are C*, or its converse. They also yield another model:

$$a \: \_\_\_\_$$
$$a = c$$
$$c$$

which rules out the previous conclusions and suggests instead that *Some of the A are not C* or its converse. These conclusions are only falsified by constructing a third model of the premises:

$$b$$
$$- - - - -$$
$$a = c$$
$$a = c$$

The second and third models taken together suggest that at least *Some of the A are C*, or its converse; these conclusions are eliminated only by bearing in mind the first model.

In summary, the theory establishes three main categories of problem for which there is no valid conclusion interrelating the end terms. There are no grounds for supposing that it should be easier to construct two inconsistent models from two particular premises than from two negative premises, or vice versa. The two sorts of problem require independent skills. What can be predicted, however, is that both should be easier than problems that definitely require three models to be constructed to refute putative conclusions. As Table 5.4 indicates, the results of the experiments reliably confirmed this prediction.

Table 5.4 *The percentages of correct responses to premises with no valid con-clusions in three experiments. The percentages are shown as a function of the number of models that have to be constructed in order to guarantee the correctness of the response*

	Premises requiring two models	Premises requiring three models
Experiment 1	68	40
Experiment 2	46	18
Experiment 3	71	40

Inference and working memory

The theory of mental models implies that two principal factors affect the difficulty of making an inference: the number of models to be constructed, and the figural arrangement of terms within the premises. As the results of our experiments show, both factors affect performance highly significantly, but they do not interact. Their effects do add up, however, to produce a peculiarly difficult variety of syllogism. Four pairs of premises out of the sixty-four require three models to be constructed that have in common only a conclusion that runs counter to the 'first in, first out' principle underlying the figural effect. Here is an example of such a problem, which the reader may recall from the previous chapter:

All of the bankers are athletes.
None of the councillors are bankers.

There are three ways of integrating the premises in a mental model:

```
        a           a           a
        a           a           a
       (a)
     _ _ _ _     _ _ _ _     _ _ _
        c         c = a       c = a
        c           c         c = a
```

The first model suggests the conclusion:

None of the councillors are athletes

which was drawn by twelve subjects in Experiment 1 – the experiment that yielded the best overall performance. Two subjects drew the converse conclusion. The second model shows that both these conclusions are invalid and suggests instead:

Some of the councillors are not athletes

which was drawn by a further two subjects. The third model shows that this conclusion is invalid, too. Four subjects may have succeeded in constructing this model, since they responded that there was no valid conclusion. Not a single subject, however, appreciated that there is a conclusion that covers all three models, though it runs counter to the figure of the premises:

Some of the athletes are not councillors.

These results are characteristic for the four most difficult syllogisms of all – those that run counter to figure and require three models to be evaluated.

The effects of both number of models and figure arise from an inevitable bottleneck in the inferential machinery: the processing capacity of working memory, which must hold one representation in a store, while at the same time the relevant information from the current premise is substituted in it. This problem is not obviated by allowing subjects to have the written premises in front of them throughout the task: the integration of premises has to occur in working memory, unless the subjects are allowed to use paper and pencil so as to externalize the process.

The effect of number of models on inferential performance, so amply confirmed by the studies of syllogisms, is also detectable in other sorts of inference. In an experiment carried out by Johnson-Laird and Wason (1970) the task was to check whether a *description* of the contents of an envelope was correct. The subjects selected diagrams one at a time from a set laid out in front of them, and they were told by the experimenter whether or not each such diagram was in the envelope. The subjects could use this information to determine whether the description was true or false. The logically prudent strategy in this task is to concentrate on diagrams that do *not* fit the description on the envelope: if such a diagram is in the envelope, plainly the description is false. Some subjects, however, choose diagrams that fit the description. That choice is uninformative once it is known that the envelope contains something, because there is no reason why a diagram that fits the description should not also be outside the envelope. What the experiment showed was that a complex disjunctive description:

There is a dot which is not connected to any dot or every dot is connected to every dot

had a striking effect on the subjects' insight into the task. A subject would perform perfectly with other descriptions, only to lose that insight on the very next trial when the disjunctive description occurred. The effect did not seem to be merely a function of the presence of a negation or of several quantifiers, because the subjects were able to cope with such descriptions as:

There is a dot connected to a dot to which no other dot is connected.

The crucial factor seemed to be that this description could be represented in a single mental model of a prototypical relation:

where the required dot, A, is connected to another dot, B, that has no other connections. The disjunctive description, however, contains two mutually exclusive states of affairs:

There is a dot which is not connected to any dot

or:

Every dot is connected to every dot.

Hence, it can be represented only by keeping in mind a disjunction of two alternative prototypical relations:

which satisfies the first disjunct, and:

which satisfies the second. As Wason and I wrote:

it is possible that this [disjunctive description] occupies a greater amount of short-term memory than a single complex rule, and thus leaves a smaller amount of 'computing space' available for handling the selection of the diagrams. (Johnson-Laird and Wason, 1970, p. 58)

More recently, Baddeley and his colleagues have made a comprehensive examination of the role of working memory in simple verbal inferences. They have found that when subjects are asked to hold in mind a string of digits, their performance in reasoning tasks is adversely affected in comparison with a control group that had no such load on memory (see Baddeley and Hitch, 1974; Hitch and Baddeley, 1976). It is therefore plausible to suppose that the effect of having to construct a greater number of models has its *locus* in working memory.

Individual differences in reasoning ability

What causes people to differ in their ability to make inferences? That they do differ is, of course, evident from the longstanding use of syllogisms in tests of intelligence. Yet no one knows for certain what aspects of mental processing make one person a good reasoner and another a poor reasoner. Whatever the general merit of investigating 'individual differences' by way of mental tests, their use is unfortunately of little value in the study of reasoning. The data they yield are, as I argued in Chapter 4, too gross to elucidate differences in mental processes from one individual to another.

The theory of mental models offers an explanatory framework that helps both to make sense of differences in reasoning ability and to go beyond a merely 'actuarial' account of mental processes. It specifies the separate components underlying inferences and places constraints on the possible differences between individuals. The theory assumes that inferences depend on three component skills: (1) the ability to form an integrated model of the premises; (2) the appreciation that an inference is sound only if there are no counter-examples to it, together with the capacity to put this principle into practice, and (3) the ability to put into words the common characteristics of a set of mental models. Bruno Bara and I have explored the differences in the protocols of subjects carrying out syllogistic inferences, and I shall summarize the outcome of our research.

The only way to convey the 'feel' of the results is to present data from individual subjects. Table 5.5 gives the percentages of valid conclusions drawn by twenty American students, and Table 5.6 gives the percentages for twenty Italian students (the results are from Experiments 1 and 2 reported earlier). Both tables show the percentages as a function of the number of mental models that have to be constructed to draw a valid conclusion. Fortuitously, the two samples of subjects differed in their inferential ability. The most striking overall pattern in the two samples of data is the decline in performance as the number of models to be constructed increases: thirty-three out of the forty subjects conform precisely to this predicted trend, and of the remainder only two showed competence

Table 5.5 *The percentages of correct conclusions drawn by twenty American subjects in an experiment on syllogistic reasoning. The percentages are shown as a function of the number of models to be constructed in order to draw a valid conclusion (Johnson-Laird and Steedman, 1978)*

| Subjects | The number of models to be constructed | | | |
	One model (n = 10)	Two models (n = 5)	Three models (n = 12)	Overall percentages (n = 27)
1	100	80	75	85
2	100	60	58	74
3	90	60	42	63
4	90	80	33	63
5	90	80	33	63
6	100	80	25	63
7	100	60	33	63
8	100	40	33	59
9	90	80	17	56
10	100	60	17	56
11	100	40	25	56
12	80	60	25	52
13	100	60	8	52
14	100	0	25	48
15	100	20	17	48
16	90	20	17	44
17	80	20	17	41
18	80	0	17	37
19	70	0	25	37
20	80	20	0	33
Overall %	92	46	27	55

Table 5.6 *The percentages of correct conclusions drawn by twenty Italian subjects in an experiment on syllogistic reasoning. The percentages are shown as a function of the number of models to be constructed in order to draw a valid conclusion (Johnson-Laird and Bara, 1982)*

	The number of models to be constructed			
	One model	Two models	Three models	Overall percentages
Subjects	(n = 10)	(n = 5)	(n = 12)	(n = 27)
1	100	20	33	56
2	80	20	42	52
3	100	20	17	48
4	90	40	8	44
5	90	40	8	44
6	70	40	17	41
7	70	20	25	41
8	90	20	8	41
9	100	20	0	41
10	90	40	0	41
11	80	20	8	37
12	80	40	0	37
13	90	20	0	37
14	90	0	8	37
15	70	20	0	30
16	80	0	0	30
17	60	20	0	26
18	70	0	0	26
19	50	0	0	19
20	40	0	0	15
Overall %	80	20	9	37

contrary to the predictions – subjects 1 and 2 in the Italian sample were able to cope with three-model problems, but not two-model problems. I will now examine the individual data in the light of the three main components of the theory.

The process of forming an integrated mental model of premises is nothing more than the proper comprehension of discourse: it is required in order to grasp the full impact of what a speaker has to say. The ability to carry it out should be common to all native speakers of a language, and, since it and its complementary skill of putting models into words suffice for competency with syllogisms requiring only one model, it is hardly surprising that the subjects were almost universally able to cope with these syllogisms. Every single subject performed more accurately with them than with any other sort (for those who relish significance levels, the chance probability of such a result is less than one in a billion). The main difficulty in constructing an integrated model is that a representation of one premise must be held in working memory while information from a representation of the other premise is combined with it. The two subjects (19 and 20) in the Italian experiment who failed to do better than chance with one model were quite unable to cope, as one would expect, when the premises required more than one model to be constructed. Likewise, the figural arrangement of terms had a striking effect on their performance: they could only form a model for premises of the A – B, B – C and B – A, C – B figures. With premises in the other figures, which require interpretations to be switched round, they either declared erroneously that there was no valid conclusion or else forgot one of the end terms and mistakenly replaced it with a middle term so as to form a conclusion that was blatantly inconsistent with one of the premises. Their tendency to assert that there was no valid conclusion if (and only if) the figures required interpretations to be switched round gave rise to a spuriously good performance with syllogisms that have no interesting conclusions in these figures.

Only where a valid inference depends on constructing alternative models of the premises are genuine differences in *inferential* ability to be observed. A reasoner must appreciate the need to construct and to evaluate alternative models, and must be able to carry out this procedure within the processing limitations of working memory. An important general point is that the subjects' performance with valid syllogisms and their performance with invalid syllogisms is not reliably correlated ($\tau = 0.11$, $p > 0.2$, for the American subjects; $\tau = -0.13$, $p > 0.2$, for the Italian subjects). The lack of a correlation arises from the responses to those premises for which more than one model can be constructed, which include, of course, all the problems for which there is no valid conclusion. A few subjects seem not to appreciate the need to consider alternatives. The hallmark of their performance is a string of erroneous conclusions and a reluctance to respond that there is no valid conclusion. None of the Americans fell into this category: even subject 20 got 32% of the problems with no valid conclusion correct. There were, however, three Italian subjects (13, 14 and 15) who performed poorly with premises requiring more than one model and who responded correctly to the problems lacking a valid conclusion on less than 20% of occasions. Subject 15, in particular, got only two of these thirty-seven problems correct, otherwise drawing a conclusion based on a single model of them. Other subjects perceive the need to construct alternatives, and are able to do so, but are wholly incapable of assessing them. The hallmark of their performance is a tendency to respond 'No valid conclusion', whether or not it is justified. They accordingly perform spuriously well with premises that do not yield a conclusion, but fall down badly with premises that require assessing more than one model to yield a valid conclusion. Any subject who performs better with invalid syllogisms than with valid syllogisms is showing symptoms of this syndrome. Among the Americans, four subjects (11, 14, 17 and 18) showed marked signs of it: e.g. subject 17 got 89% of the invalid problems correct, but also tended to respond 'No valid conclusion' to valid problems which required more than one model to be constructed. The two most striking instances of the syndrome among the Italians were subject 16 (81% of the invalid syllogisms correct) and subject 17 (62% of the invalid syllogisms correct).

Most subjects are able to construct some alternative models, but from time to time they fall down in assessing what, if anything, they have in common. They are particularly prone to error in those figures that require interpretations to be switched round, failing to detect either that a putative conclusion is violated by one alternative model or else that there is a conclusion common to all the alternatives. It is noteworthy that only one out of the forty subjects in the two experiments showed any competence in dealing with the most difficult syllogisms of all, namely, those with three models where the conclusion runs counter to figure.

There are several other differences in performance between the subjects, including their susceptibility to figural effects, which I shall not analyse here. My point has been to establish that the theory of mental models at least provides a framework suitable for describing individual differences, and even suggests some explanations for them. Indeed, Jane Oakhill and I have recently confirmed in an unpublished study that there is a reliable correlation ($\rho = 0.7$) between a simple measure of the processing capacity of working memory – the number of pairs of letters (e.g. IB) that can be converted in a fixed interval of time into those that are two places later in the alphabet (KD) – and accuracy in syllogistic reasoning. Of course, there are other general personal characteristics, such as impulsivity, that are likely to affect reasoning ability just as they affect the performance of any other intellectual task.

Children's ability to reason syllogistically

Such is Piaget's influence on the study of intellectual development that the majority of psychologists, whether or not they subscribe to his theories, probably believe that children learn to reason formally by the age of 11 to 12 years – the age of Piaget's putative stage of 'formal operations'. There have been many studies which establish that children are able to make deductions at a much earlier age than is dreamt of in Piagetian lore (see, for example, Mehler and Bever, 1967; Bryant and Trabasso, 1971; Donaldson, 1978). But what is equally important is that there are varieties of deduction that are mastered only after the age of twelve. The best evidence comes from the study of syllogisms.

Debbie Bull and I designed an experiment to investigate the ability of two groups of intelligent children (nineteen 9- to 10-year-olds and nineteen 11- to 12-year-olds) to draw their own conclusions from syllogistic premises. It was not possible to use all sixty-four pairs of premises – the task would have been too gruelling – but we carefully selected twenty pairs (of which sixteen yielded valid conclusions) in order to examine the children's general competence. The experiment showed that there was only a slight difference between the abilities of the two groups, that the children were just as susceptible to the effects of figure as adults, but that, unlike most adults, they could only draw valid conclusions that depended on constructing one mental model. The older group responded correctly on 58% of the one-model problems – there were eight such problems and a child had to get four of them right to perform reliably better than chance. Not one of these older subjects drew a correct conclusion to the two-model problem or to the six three-model problems. The younger group responded correctly to 41% of the one-model problems, three subjects (16%) responded correctly to the two-model problem, and not a single subject responded correctly to the three-model problems. In short, some of the children were competent with one-model problems, three of them might have been competent with the two-model problem, but none of them was competent with three-model problems. The syllogism that elicited the best performance from both groups was of the form:

$$\begin{array}{l} \text{All the A are B} \\ \text{All the B are C} \\ \therefore \ \text{All the A are C.} \end{array}$$

Doubtless, Aristotle would have predicted this result, because the syllogism is in the form that he considered to be perfect.

Granted that the children taking part in the experiment are intelligent – and the teachers selected the brightest of their children – then they should at a later stage develop a logical ability on a par with the adults that we have tested: they should improve significantly in their ability to reason syllogistically.

122

Educational applications: how to improve reasoning ability

Educationalists have developed a variety of methods designed to improve the ability to reason. They include the pedagogical use of stories illustrating logical principles (Lipman and Sharp, 1978), the deployment of special reasoning problems (Feuerstein, Hoffman, and Miller, 1980), and various courses on thinking and problem solving (e.g., Whimbey and Lochhead, 1980). Psychologists have become increasingly involved in such matters, especially since the start of the project to raise the intelligence of the entire population of Venezuela (the international newsletter *Human Intelligence* has published several reports on this project, which includes work carried out by researchers at Harvard University, Bolt Beranek and Newman, Inc., and many other research organizations). Applied psychologists need to devise an economical technique for assessing the strengths and weaknesses of an individual's inferential skills, and they need to implement effective remedial procedures that will overcome the various deficiencies underlying poor performance. The work that my colleagues and I have carried out has two main implications. First, it is important to diagnose and to distinguish between weaknesses in reasoning ability that result from the following factors:

1. Cultural or personal characteristics that underlie apparently poor performance, but that have nothing whatsoever to do with basic intellectual ability (cf. Luria, 1977; Scribner, 1977).
2. Linguistic impairments that make it difficult to understand and to remember verbal permises, or to put into words conclusions that have been drawn.
3. Failures to appreciate the fundamental principle of valid inference, or to understand that a reasoning test calls for conclusions that follow of necessity.
4. An inability to construct integrated representations of the premises, or to evaluate alternative representations, as a result of a limited working memory.

Such deficiencies are readily detectable if subjects are asked to state what conclusions follow of necessity from the sixty-four different pairs of syllogistic premises. The premises should each be presented with a sensible everyday content that does not predispose subjects to any particular conclusion on the basis of general knowledge. If the test is followed up by a 'debriefing' session in which the subjects are asked to explain the

123

reasons for their fallacious conclusions, it is relatively easy to identify the causes of their particular problems.

Second, our work suggests that the most common cause of difficulty in reasoning for individuals living in a literate society is the limited processing capabilities of working memory. Its effects have been apparent in every subject that we have tested (see, e.g., Tables 5.5 and 5.6). It must be emphasized, however, that there is a spontaneous improvement in reasoning ability simply as a consequence of practice (with no feedback). The subjects whose data are reported in Table 5.5 were tested again one week later. They were given no forewarning that they would be retested, but their overall performance increased by 10%, and nineteen out of the twenty subjects returned an improved score. One striking differential effect of practice occurred with the valid conclusions drawn from premises in the most difficult figure, B – A, B – C. Here, there was an overall improvement of 20%, and half of it was due to a decline in erroneous responses to the effect that there was no valid conclusion. The result of practice must in part be to increase the efficiency of the encoding operations of working memory, enabling subjects to switch round the interpretation of a premise. The B – A, B – C figure is difficult according to the mental model theory, precisely because it is always necessary to switch round the interpretation of at least one premise. Subjects who earlier were unable either to form alternative integrated models, or to assess their implications, improved with practice. Experience with the task may also produce a growing awareness of general principles governing the logical properties of the problems. Some subjects may notice, for example, that two negative conclusions never yield a valid conclusion and in this way they may begin to perform like logicians and no longer need to construct mental models.

Some commentators on our work have suggested that diagrams of mental models might serve a useful pedagogical function in teaching people the principles of deduction. Although the prospect is appealing, it may be dangerous. Whenever I have presented a reasoning problem informally, I have noticed the difficulties that people get themselves into if they use Euler circles. The problem is that there is no simple algorithm for using them that one can learn as one learns, say, the algorithm for long multiplication. Merely drawing circles does not guarantee that all their possible combinations will be considered exhaustively. The same problem applies to the notation of mental models – if there were a simple algorithm that guaranteed an exhaustive search, doubtless most of us would have mastered it when we first learnt to reason. Educators are probably better advised to ensure that their students understand the fundamental principle of inference and get plenty of opportunities to put it into practice – at least until someone should chance upon an effective way of increasing the processing capacity of working memory.

Conclusions

This chapter has outlined a theory of syllogistic inference based on the assumption that reasoners construct integrated mental models of the premises. These models have an important structural property deriving from a constraint on the set of possible mental models: a *natural* mental model of discourse has a structure that corresponds directly to the structure of the state of affairs that the discourse describes. The sophisticated notations of Euler circles and Venn diagrams lack this property, and consequently they are not natural mental models. For example, a premise such as:

All the artists are beekeepers

describes a state of affairs in which one finite set of individuals is mapped into another. A natural mental model likewise contains one finite set of individual tokens mapped into another. Neither Euler circles nor Venn diagrams, however, contain finite sets of individual tokens: they map finite sets of individuals into infinities of points. Because any syllogistic premise can be represented in a single mental model of the present sort, the theory avoids the combinatorial problems that bedevil Euler circles, and similarly the maximal load on working memory (three different models) is considerably less than would be required for Venn diagrams (eight different contingencies). The theory has been corroborated experimentally and the results that have been presented establish its descriptive adequacy according to the criteria introduced in Chapter 4: it accounts for the relative difficulty of different syllogisms and for the systematic errors and biases in performance (criterion 1); it describes the characteristic patterns of individual differences (criterion 2); and it also has some implications for pedagogy (criterion 7). The theory extends to other sorts of deductive inference, and I propose to evaluate the explanatory adequacy of the general theory rather than the specific instance of it presented here.

6

Inference and mental models

At the end of a lecture on ethics, Epictetus, the Stoic philosopher, recommended the study of logic to his audience because it was useful. One of his listeners was unconvinced, and asked: 'Sir, would you *demonstrate* the usefulness of the study of logic?' Epictetus smiled and replied: 'That is my point. How could you, without the study of logic, test whether my demonstration would be valid or not?'

The late Yehoshua Bar-Hillel, who recounts this story, comments that if the audience had signed up to take the course in logic that Epictetus announced, then they must surely have been very disappointed. Epictetus had shown merely that there was a need for a theory that would make it possible to test the validity of arguments in ordinary language, not that he possessed such a theory. Indeed, as Bar-Hillel (1970) emphasizes, logic until very recently was insufficiently powerful to cope with natural language.

There is another, very different, moral to the anecdote about Epictetus. His audience may or may not have been disappointed by his course, but doubtless they were capable of thinking rationally in any case. Valid inferences were made long before the invention of logic; and they can be made without relying, consciously or unconsciously, on rules of inference. This point will be clarified in assessing the general theory that inferences are based on mental models. In the previous chapter, a special case of the theory concerning syllogisms was shown to be descriptively adequate. In this chapter, I shall describe the general theory of inference, which incorporates the machinery for the 'test case' of syllogisms, and evaluate its logical and psychological properties in the light of the explanatory criteria that any adequate theory of reasoning should satisfy. In particular, I shall consider the variety of inferences with which it deals – implicit and explicit – how children master them, and how validity is captured within the theory without recourse to rules of inference.

Implicit inferences

There is an important distinction between two sorts of inference that oc
in daily life. On the one hand, the inferences that I have so far consideı
mostly require a conscious and cold-blooded effort. You must make a
voluntary decision to try to make them. They may take time and they are
at the forefront of your awareness: they are *explicit*. On the other hand,
the inferences that underlie the more mundane processes of intuitive
judgment and the comprehension of discourse tend to be rapid, effortless,
and outside conscious awareness: they are *implicit*. Suppose, for example,
you were to read in the paper:

There was a fault in the signalling circuit. The crash led to the deaths
of ten passengers . . .

then you might well infer that the passengers were killed in the crash.
The text does not make this assertion, and it might even continue:

because they were arrested after the accident, and subsequently shot as
spies.

Plainly, you jumped to a conclusion based partly on the content of the
passage and partly on your general knowledge. You make such inferences
automatically, almost involuntarily, and often without being aware of what
you are doing. Since a valid inference is one for which, if the premises
are true, the conclusion must be true, an important feature of these
inferences is that they are usually invalid.

There are many sorts of inference, but any adequate psychological theory
of reasoning must recognize the distinction between *implicit* and *explicit*
inferences. When theorists have tried to formulate theories of thinking,
however, there has been a strong tendency for them to concentrate on
explicit rather than implicit reasoning. In the seventeenth century, Pascal
(trans. Krailsheimer, 1966, p. 211) observed:

It is rare for mathematicians to be intuitive or the intuitive to be mathematicians,
because mathematicians try to treat intuitive matters mathematically, and make
themselves ridiculous, by trying to begin with definitions followed by principles,
which is not the way to proceed in this kind of reasoning. It is not that the mind
does not do this, but it does so tacitly, naturally and artlessly, for it is beyond any
man to express it and given to very few even to apprehend it.

The point is well taken: psychologists had largely overlooked implicit
inferences until attempts to program computers to understand discourse
revealed their ubiquity. The credit for this discovery must go to Charniak,

Minsky, Schank, and Winograd, and to their colleagues on this side of the Atlantic, Isard, Longuet-Higgins, and Wilks.

Without an ability to make implicit inferences, written and spoken discourse would be beyond anyone's competence. In order to understand the following passage, it is necessary to make a variety of inferences:

The pilot put the plane into a stall just before landing on the strip. He just got it out of it in time. Wasn't he lucky?

Every word in the first sentence, apart perhaps from the articles and prepositions, is ambiguous, and the appropriate meanings can be recovered only by making implicit inferences from linguistic context and general knowledge. To make sense of the second sentence, a number of inferences have to be made to determine the referents of the pronouns: the first *it* refers to the plane, and the second, to the stall. The third sentence is not to be taken as a question, though it is interrogatory in form: an inference from the context establishes that it has the force of an assertion. At the point at which most of these inferences are made they can seldom be securely established: they are plausible conjectures rather than valid deductions. Many psychologists are accordingly inclined to suppose that they must depend on the computation of probabilities. However, there is no need to suppose that individuals compute probabilities in determining, say, that a pronoun refers to one entity rather than another. The mechanism is more likely to consist of a device that constructs a *single* mental model on the basis of the discourse, its context, and background knowledge. Such knowledge is embodied in the model by default, that is, it is maintained in the model provided that there is no subsequent evidence to overrule it. No attempt is made to search for an alternative model unless such evidence arises. It is for this reason that the process can be very rapid; it becomes as automatic as any other cognitive skill that calls for no more than a single mental representation at any one time. And it is also for this reason that implicit inferences lack the guarantee, the mental imprimatur, associated with explicit deductions. Hence, the fundamental distinction between the two types of inference is whether or not there is a deliberate search for alternative models of the discourse.

The acquisition of implicit inferential ability

If the present account of implicit inferences is correct, then children must acquire the ability to make such inferences in order to understand discourse.

This hypothesis has been borne out by a number of experimental studies. Til Wykes, a former student of mine, showed that young children (about 4 years old) have considerable difficulty in correctly acting out with glove puppets such pairs of sentences as:

Susan needed Mary's pencil.
She gave it to her.

The task is much easier for them if gender can be used as a cue:

Susan needed John's pencil.
He gave it to her.

In general, the greater the number of pronouns in a sentence, the harder it is for young children to understand it properly. They appear to adopt a syntactically-based procedure for assigning referents to pronouns rather than an inferential one. They assume that a pronoun is co-referential with the subject of the previous clause (see Wykes, 1981). In a further study, we discovered that children are poor at making implicit inferences to work out the meaning of such sentences as 'The Smiths saw the Rocky Mountains flying to California' (Wykes and Johnson-Laird, 1977). Similarly, children presented with a sentence such as:

The man stirred his cup of tea

tend not to infer spontaneously that the man used a *spoon* to stir his tea. In all these cases, it was clear from control studies that the children are able to make the relevant inferences. The point is that they do not do so as a matter of course in understanding discourse.

The ability to make implicit inferences is equally important, of course, for reading. Jane Oakhill, another former student, has shown that an important distinction between excellent and average readers is precisely this inferential ability. In one study, Oakhill (1982) gave a sample of 168 children (aged 7 to 8 years) a variety of vocabulary and reading tests. She was then able to select two groups matched on vocabulary and phonic skills, but differing considerably in their ability to understand what they read. The two groups of children were then tested in an experiment on their ability to make inferences when *listening* to simple stories. Each story consisted of three sentences, such as:

The car crashed into the bus.
The bus was near the crossroads.
The car skidded on the ice.

After the children had heard eight such stories, their memory for them

129

was examined in a recognition test. A child who has built up an integrated mental model on the basis of implicit inferences is likely to assume that the sentence:

The car was near the crossroads

had originally occurred in the story. Given the nature of the original events, this inference is extremely plausible. But a sentence such as:

The bus skidded on the ice

is much less plausibly inferred, since there is no reason to make this inference in building a model of the events in the story. The results of the recognition test using such sentences showed, as expected, that the good readers tended to make more errors based on plausible inferences than did the average readers. Good readers, however, performed better than average readers in recognizing the original sentences from the stories and in rejecting the implausible inferences. It seems that good readers are more likely than average readers to make implicit inferences in order to build up a mental model of a story. This study obviously tells us nothing about causal direction: good readers may be good because they spontaneously make inferences, or they may make such inferences because they are good readers as a result of other factors. In a series of additional experiments, however, Oakhill failed to find any other major difference in the abilities of her two groups of readers.

One addendum to this work is worth noting. The procedure is based on one devised by Paris and his colleagues (e.g., Paris and Carter, 1973) though these investigators were not concerned with differences in reading ability. Their studies have been criticized on the grounds that the sentences used in the memory tests allowed children to detect the new sentences, which had not occurred in the original stories, solely on the grounds that they contained new words that also had not occurred in the original stories. The materials used by Oakhill, as the example above shows, were carefully selected so as to obviate this criticism.

Reasoning without rules of inference

Logical thinking in daily life is most likely to occur in explicit inferences. From a semantic standpoint, the natural way to think of logic is as a set of procedures for establishing the validity of a given inference, that is, as a method for showing systematically that there is no interpretation of the premises that is consistent with the denial of the conclusion. From a formal or syntactic standpoint, a logic contains a set of rules of inference, or inferential schemata, that allow conclusions to be formally derived from premises. Explicit inferences based on mental models, however, do not need to make use of rules of inference, or any such formal machinery, and in this sense it is not necessary to postulate a logic in the mind. This claim, as I know from the reaction of audiences to whom it has been addressed, is both hard to understand and hard to believe – it is viewed as almost on a par with the Pelagian heresy in some quarters. That the doctrine of original sin may be mistaken is hardly a new idea, but perhaps there is something novel in the notion that the doctrine of mental logic may be wrong – the major tradition in psychology, culminating in the work of Jean Piaget, has always firmly implanted formal logic in the mind.

The crux of the matter is that a system of inference may perform in an entirely logical way even though it does not employ rules of inference, inferential schemata, or any other sort of machinery corresponding to a logical calculus. The rest of the argument is simple once this point is grasped, so let me labour it awhile.

I am going to describe a hypothetical procedure for making syllogistic inferences from affirmative premises which is related to the theory presented in the previous chapter, but which is designed to illustrate in the clearest and most elementary way the feasibility of reasoning without formal rules of inference. The first step in the procedure is to construct a finite model that satisfies the first premise and a finite model that satisfies the second, taking care to use the same number of items to represent the middle term in both models. Next, the procedure forms an integrated model by joining the two in virtue of the items representing the middle term. It then formulates a conclusion that is true of the resulting model and that interrelates the two end terms. So far, of course, it has not employed any logic: the conclusion may well be blatantly invalid. For example, given the premises:

$$\text{All the A are B}$$
$$\text{All the C are B}$$

the procedure forms the model:

$$a = b = c$$
$$a = b = c$$
$$\text{(b)}$$
$$\text{(b)}$$

131

and draws the erroneous conclusion:

All the A are C.

However, it now begins an exhaustive series of tests whose outcome, if any, will be a valid conclusion. It selects an end item in the model at random. If there is an identity between that end item and a middle item, it destroys it and seeks to form a new identity between the end item and a middle item hitherto unrelated to the class of end items. In the example, the procedure might select the second token corresponding to C, destroy its present identity and establish a new one:

$$a = b = c$$
$$a = b$$
$$(b) = c$$
$$(b)$$

If the end item selected at random is not initially linked by an identity to a middle item – an eventuality that could arise with other premises – then the procedure seeks to establish such a relation. In either case, it then checks whether the resulting model is still consistent with the premises, and, if it is, whether the model is consistent with the current conclusion. Where the model is consistent with the premises but not consistent with the conclusion, as in the example, that conclusion is rejected as invalid. The procedure formulates (if possible) a new conclusion covering the current model and all the previous models consistent with the premises. It then samples a new end item at random and carries out the whole process again. Since the model is finite, then, provided that the procedure records the selections that it has made, there will eventually be no more items to select. If there is any conclusion still remaining at that point, then it is valid.

This procedure is extremely wasteful even for the restricted set of inferences with which it can cope. It constructs many models that violate the truth conditions of the premises, and which are therefore useless. Yet, although it works randomly, it does make a complete search. It embodies the general semantic principle that lies behind all logics, though not explicitly formulated within any of them: an inference is valid if and only if there is no interpretation of the premises that falsifies the conclusion. However, the procedure does not employ any formal logical apparatus. That is why it has to search for falsifications at random and wastes most of its time looking at models that are not even relevant to the question of validity.

What about the machinery for searching for end items, destroying identities, and testing truth conditions – does it perhaps incorporate a formal logic? Once again, the answer is negative. All that is required is the ability to construct models, to search for entities in them, and to generate descriptions of them – in short, the basic computational power described in Chapter 1 in terms of Turing machines and recursive functions. Such functions do not in themselves constitute a logic: they can be used to model either logical or illogical processes. They can even be used to develop a theory of human inference that allows for both rationality and errors.

The general theory of explicit inference based on mental models assumes that human reasoners can construct finite models of premises, formulate putative conclusions on the basis of them, and search for models of the premises that are counter-examples to such conclusions. If the search is systematic and exhaustive, then the conclusion is valid. But human reasoners often fail to be rational. Their limited working memories constrain their performance. They lack the guidelines for systematic searches for counter-examples; they lack secure principles for deriving conclusions; they lack a logic. Since even the most intelligent individuals have difficulty with certain syllogisms, and are aware of it, they have an obvious motivation to try to externalize and to systematize the search for counter-examples. Hence, the theory is compatible with the development of logic as an intellectual tool.

When Aristotle invented logic, his method was to determine which pairs of syllogistic premises yielded valid conclusions (see Kneale and Kneale, 1962). An inference of the form:

> Every man is an animal
> No stone is a man
> ∴ No stone is an animal

certainly yields a true conclusion. In order to determine whether inferences of this form were *valid*, Aristotle changed the content of the premises whilst holding their form constant, e.g.:

> Every man is an animal
> No horse is a man
> ∴ No horse is an animal.

The conclusion is manifestly false, but the inference is identical in form to the previous example. Since the form can lead to false conclusions from true premises, it must be invalid. Instead of searching for interpretations

133

of premises that are counter-examples to conclusions, Aristotle held form constant and searched for premises with a content that was incompatible with the corresponding conclusion. He used his semantic intuitions to determine the set of valid syllogisms, and then he developed a logic – a set of principles for deriving validity.

The power of mental models

A major advantage of natural mental models over other, more sophisticated, forms of representation such as Euler circles, Venn diagrams, and even the first-order predicate calculus, is that they can represent the content of any sentences for which the truth conditions are known. I shall illustrate this point by considering inferences based on relations and on different sorts of quantifiers.

Relational expressions such as *greater than*, *father of*, *next to*, *equals*, *loves*, have a number of different logical properties. A relation such as *greater than* is transitive because it permits an inference of the form: if x is greater than y, and y is greater than z, then x is greater than z. In more general terms, the transitivity of a relation R guarantees the validity of an inference of the form:

$$xRy \text{ and } yRz \quad \therefore \quad xRz$$

A relation such as *father of* is intransitive because it leads to the negation of such a conclusion:

$$xRy \text{ and } yRz \quad \therefore \quad \text{not } (xRz)$$

A relation such as *next to* is neither transitive nor intransitive. A second set of properties concerns the symmetry of relations. A relation such as *next to* is symmetric because if x is next to y, then it follows that y is next to x. A relation such as *greater than* is asymmetric because if x is greater than y then it follows that y is not greater than x. A relation such as *not greater than* is neither symmetric nor asymmetric. A third set of properties concerns the reflexiveness of relations. A relation such as *equals* is reflexive because for any entity x, it is always the case that x equals x. A relation such as *taller than* is irreflexive because for any entity x, it is never the case that x is taller than x. A relation such as *loves* is neither reflexive nor irreflexive since it fails to guarantee either conclusion – some individuals love themselves, and some do not.

134

Psychologists have devoted most of their study of relations to the topic of transitivity. An argument of the sort:

Alice is taller than Betty
Betty is taller than Carol
∴ Alice is taller than Carol

is treated by logicians as technically invalid, since it lacks a premise to the effect that *taller than* is transitive. Advocates of mental logic are accordingly forced to argue either that there is a general schema of transitivity:

For any x, y, and z, if xRy and yRz then xRz

to which particular relations such as *taller than* become linked, or else that specific schemata are acquired for each transitive relation in the form of specific rules or 'meaning postulates':

For any x, y, and z, if x is taller than y, and y is taller than z, then x is taller than z.

Granted a knowledge of the principle of transitivity, children might readily learn to which relations it applies. The problem, however, is to explain the acquisition of the principle itself. Once the idea of mental logic is given up, that problem is reduced to one of accounting for how the meanings of relational terms are learned. This problem, as I shall show, is more tractable.

The relational expressions *more than*, *taller than*, *bigger than*, *kinder than* and their cognates are all transitive, asymmetric, and irreflexive. It follows that the differences in meaning between them cannot be distinguished merely on the basis of their logical properties. An account of their semantics is needed in any case, since a complete specification of the meaning of a relational assertion such as:

There are more a's than b's

must specify its truth conditions. If the domain of discourse consists of sets of entities, then a semantics for this assertion can be specified in terms of a one-to-one mapping. The assertion is true if and only if each *b* can be put into a one-to-one correspondence with an *a*, but there remain outstanding a's not within the mapping. If you have acquired this semantics for *more than*, then you can interpret the assertion 'There are more a's than b's by forming a mental model containing some representative number

135

of members of the two classes with the following mapping between them:

a——b
a——b
a——b
a

Likewise, you can interpret the assertion 'There are more b's than c's in the same manner:

b——c
b——c
b

So, if you combine your two interpretations, taking pains to ensure that there were the same number of b's in both, you will form the following unified representation:

You could also readily ascertain that the truth conditions of the assertion 'There are more a's than c's' are satisfied by your mental representation. Hence, the semantics of the relation ensure that whenever there are more *a*'s than *b*'s and more *b*'s than *c*'s then there are more *a*'s than *c*'s. You can make the transitive inference by building a mental model of this sort even though you have neither a meaning postulate for transitivity nor an internal logic of relations. In the same way, a mental model establishes the asymmetry and irreflexiveness of *more than*: if there are more *a*'s than *b*'s then the converse cannot hold; and there can never be more *a*'s than *a*'s. The logical properties of a relation emerge naturally from its meaning.

The same principle of emergent logical properties applies to other relational terms. In the case of length, for example, the truth conditions of 'a is longer than b' can be specified either in terms of the cardinality of the units of measurement, i.e., the number of units for *a* are more than the number for *b*, or in terms of a direct comparison between the major axes of *a* and *b*. The assertion 'a is longer than b' is true if and only if the major axis of *a* is coextensive with a proper part of the major axis of *b*. If you have acquired this semantics, then you can construct a mental model in which *a* and *b* are lined up so that *b*'s axis is coextensive with only part of *a*'s axis. There are obvious problems about the direct encoding of real numbers, since the continuum is infinitely and uncountably dense and could not be directly represented in a finitary device such as the human brain. However, it is plausible to suppose that lengths are mentally represented by a digital approximation. This principle would permit an alternative representation of 'a is longer than b' in which *a* and *b* are located in appropriate positions on a single 'dimension' corresponding to length – a format that has been postulated by several authors (De Soto, London, and Handel, 1965; Huttenlocher, 1968), and that could apply to such relations as 'better than', 'prettier than', 'kinder than'. A combined representation of separate premises, whether in terms of axes or a unitary dimension of length, would readily yield a transitive conclusion.

Piagetian theorists have assumed that there is a transitivity schema and that it derives from the notion of serial order: 'transitivity is an ordinal qualitative property' (Youniss, 1975, p. 234). Although it is true that serial orders give rise to transitivity, there are a number of transitive relations that do not depend on orderings, e.g., 'is included in', 'is an ancestor of', 'is identical to'. Their transitivity follows from their semantics, and can be readily grasped from an appropriate mental model: for instance, a model in which *a* is included in *b* and *b* is included in *c* readily yields the conclusion that *a* is included in *c*. It is accordingly a mistake to try to reduce the representation of all transitive relations to a system based on an underlying ordinal dimension.

Turning to quantifiers, mental models cope naturally with the interpretations of specific numbers and such terms as *most, many, several,* and *a few.* Janet Fodor (1982) has argued for a very similar form of mental representation in order to distinguish between the meaning of such quantifiers as *every* and *all.* Mental models can certainly provide the necessary interpretations for inferences that hinge on relative sizes, e.g.,

All fascists are authoritarians.
Most authoritarians are dogmatic.

These premises are representable by the following type of tableau:

$$f = a$$
$$f = a = d$$
$$f = a = d$$
$$f = a = d$$
$$a = d$$
$$a \quad d$$

which suggests the conclusion:

Most fascists are dogmatic.

137

People readily make these sorts of inference even though their validity is problematical. It seems to depend on the relative sizes of sets. The following premises are superficially of the same form as those in the example above, but they are unlikely to elicit a comparable conclusion:

All archbishops are tories.
Most tories are middle class.

Even if these premises were true, one knows that the number of archbishops is very small in comparison to the number of tories. Hence, the premises are entirely compatible with the model:

$$a = t$$
$$a = t$$
$$t = m$$
$$\vdots \quad \vdots \quad \vdots$$
$$t = m$$

In cases of this sort, there is a positive advantage in using mental models rather than a mental logic to make inferences. A logic will either sanction an inference or not (though the particular status of the inference may not be obvious). A system of mental models more accurately reflects the uncertainty of inferences that depend on proportions: a conclusion of debatable status is forthcoming, since the search for refutations can be guided by general knowledge.

The distinction between class-membership and class-inclusion is represented straightforwardly in a mental model. The premise:

Jock is a Scotsman

calls for the following sort of model:

$$s$$
$$j = s$$
$$s$$
$$s$$
$$s$$

where j represents Jock, and the s's represent the complete class of Scotsmen, since there is no optional element signifying that the term is not distributed. The premise:

Scotsmen are widely scattered around the world

asserts that the class of Scotsmen is included in the class of classes whose members are widely scattered around the world. This assertion can be represented by a model in which the class of Scotsmen as a whole is identified with a class of individuals widely scattered around the world:

$$
\left.\begin{array}{l}
s \\
s \\
s \\
s \\
s
\end{array}\right\} = \begin{array}{l}
w \\
w \\
w \\
w
\end{array}
$$

where the brace indicates that the set of individuals that it embraces is identified with a member of the class of w's, classes of entities whose members are widely scattered. The two models can be combined:

$$
\begin{array}{l}
\quad\; s \\
j = s \\
\quad\; s \\
\quad\; s \\
\quad\; s
\end{array}\left.\right\} = \begin{array}{l}
w \\
w \\
w \\
w
\end{array}
$$

But since it is the class of Scotsmen as a whole that is identified with a class of entities scattered around the world, there is no way of forming an identity that yields the conclusion that Jock is widely scattered around the world. Class-inclusion, however, is represented in a way that automatically yields a transitive inference. The premises:

Jock is a Scotsman
Scotsmen are human beings

are representable as:

$$
\begin{array}{l}
s = h \\
s = h \\
j = s = h \\
s = h \\
\quad\;\; h \\
\quad\;\; h
\end{array}
$$

and a direct link is established between j (Jock) and h (a human being). It follows that Jock is a human being.

Mental models also accommodate assertions containing multiple quantifiers. A statement such as 'Some professors attended all the meetings' can be represented in the following way:

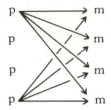

where an arrow between a token representing a professor and a token representing a meeting stands for the relation x attends y. The model supports the conclusion that *All of the meetings were attended by at least one professor*. The point to be emphasized about such deductions is that they cannot even be represented using Euler circles or Venn diagrams, which are not sufficiently powerful to cope with relations whose arguments are quantified. Human reasoners have difficulty with syllogisms and, not surprisingly, they are soon overwhelmed by inferences that depend on multiple quantification. Nevertheless, they can interpret multiply quantified assertions reasonably accurately, and make simple inferences from them (see Johnson-Laird, 1969a, b), and this limited ability can be captured by the present approach to reasoning.

Certain everyday deductions in natural language cannot be proved within the standard quantificational calculus. The simple inference:

More than half the musicians were classically trained

More than half the musicians were in rock groups

∴ Some of the musicians were both classically trained and in rock groups

is particularly instructive. It is easy enough for children to make, but it cannot even be formulated within the standard first order quantificational calculus in which the variables that can be quantified range over individuals – a fact that follows directly from a theorem proved by Barwise and Cooper (1981) to the effect that there is no way to define *more than half the x's* in terms of *more than half of all things* and the operations of the calculus (even if the domain is finite). Such a deduction can be formulated within the higher-order quantificational calculus in which variables can range over sets, but this calculus is not *complete*. That is to say, there is no way to formalize the calculus so that all valid inferences are derivable within it. If there can be no formal logic that captures all the valid deductions, then *a fortiori* there can be no mental logic that does either. It is a remarkable fact that natural language contains terms with an implicit 'logic'

140

that is so powerful that it cannot be completely encompassed by formal rules of inference. It follows, of course, that any theory that assumes that the logical properties of expressions derive directly from a mental logic cannot give an adequate account of those that call for a higher-order predicate calculus. This failure is a final and decisive blow to the doctrine of mental logic. The inference in the example above is readily made on the basis of a mental model in which the two predicates apply respectively to more than half the entities designated as musicians:

$$
\begin{array}{lllll}
m & = & c & & \\
m & = & c & & \\
m & = & c & = & r \\
m & & & = & r \\
m & & & = & r
\end{array}
$$

There is no way to satisfy the two premises that does not create an overlap.

One final example shows the importance of mental models in logical controversy. The philosopher Jaakko Hintikka (1974) has observed that the sentence:

Some relative of each villager and some relative of each townsman hate each other

appears to be entirely synonymous with the corresponding sentence in which the noun phrases have been swapped round:

Some relative of each townsman and some relative of each villager hate each other.

The order of the quantifiers in the corresponding expressions in the quantificational calculus does matter: there, the two expressions are not equivalent. Hintikka accordingly claimed that the sentences call for a logic with 'branching' quantifiers, i.e., quantifiers whose order is immaterial. Both sentences are satisfied by the following model:

$$
\begin{array}{l}
v \ldots r \text{——} r \ldots t \\
v \ldots r \text{——} r \ldots t
\end{array}
$$

where the v's denote villagers, the t's denote townsmen, the r's denote other people, the dotted line stands for the relation of being *a relative of* someone, and the solid line stands for the relation of *mutual hatred*. Hintikka's claim is debatable, but the moral I want to draw does not depend on whether he is right or wrong. It is that the only way to tease out the logic of such sentences is to construct models of them. The cases that are genuinely problematical to modern logicians naturally elicit the same strategy that was employed by Aristotle. The logician first relies on semantic intuitions to make pre-theoretical judgments about inferences, and only subsequently sets up formal machinery to codify those judgments. If there are assertions that require branching quantifiers, there is no doubt that inferences that depend on them can be made by recourse to mental models. The question of the validity of such inferences depends initially on the exercise of intuitions, and this exercise, I contend, relies on the mobilization of mental models or their external counterparts.

The acquisition of explicit inferential ability

The mystery of how the ability to reason develops is so perplexing that some theorists, like Piaget, consider that children think in an essentially different way from adults, whereas others take the diametrically opposite point of view and postulate an innate logical ability. Perhaps the chief proponent of the latter doctrine is Jerry Fodor (1975, 1980). The essence of his argument is that there are and can be no theories of how concepts are acquired *ab initio*, but only theories that might explain how people can build up new beliefs inductively on the basis of the concepts they already possess. In particular, a child at a stage of development corresponding, say, to propositional logic, could not pass by way of learning to a stage corresponding to a more powerful logic such as the quantificational calculus. This transition is impossible, says Fodor.

Why? Because to learn quantificational logic we are going to have to learn the truth conditions of such expressions as '(x)Fx' [i.e. for any x, x is F]. And, to learn those truth conditions, we are going to have to formulate, *with the conceptual apparatus available at stage 1*, some such hypotheses as '(x)Fx' *is true if and only if* . . . But of course, such a hypothesis can't be formulated with the conceptual apparatus available at stage 1; that is precisely the respect in which propositional logic is weaker than quantificational logic . . .

  If you think about this, you will see that this is an entirely general form of argument, one that shows that it is *never* possible to learn a richer logic on the basis of a weaker logic, if what you mean by learning is hypothesis formation and confirmation. Yet I say again that learning must be nondemonstrative inference [i.e. inductive inference]; there is nothing else for it to be. And the only model of nondemonstrative inference that has ever been proposed anywhere by anyone is hypothesis formation and confirmation. (Fodor, 1980, pp. 148–9)

The moral that Fodor draws is an extreme version of nativism – no concept is invented; all concepts are innate. Alas, any argument that purports to explain the origins of all intellectual abilities by postulating that they are innate merely replaces one problem by another. No one knows how deductive competence could have evolved according to the principles of neo-Darwinism.

In fact, the claim that there is no way in which the logical power of the mind could be increased by learning is ambiguous. Any computable function can be characterized in terms of the three sorts of primitive recursive functions (the zero, identity, and successor functions) and the three operations that create new functions out of old (composition, recursion, and minimization – see Chapter 1). Hence, any computable procedure whatsoever can be constructed out of these functions. One way in which to think of learning is as a procedure that discovers a way in which to combine old functions so as to create new ones. The system starts with an inborn set of functions and an inborn set of procedures for combining them, and learning consists in constructing functions that the system did not hitherto possess out of the functions that it did possess. There is accordingly both a sense in which the system does not increase in power – it always had the power of a Universal Turing machine – and another sense in which it *does* increase in power – hitherto it was unable, say, to make a transitive inference, but now it can do so. We can see why it is not necessary to accept Fodor's conclusion. First, there is no need to assume that stage 1 is weaker in *computational* power than stage 2: in stage 1, an individual has a weaker logic than in stage 2, but does possess the capacity to construct a more powerful logic. Second, one must not confuse *what* is learned with *how* it is learned. When Pythagoras first proved his celebrated theorem, he learned something new – a certain proposition, which he may have believed to be true, was *necessarily* true. How Pythagoras discovered his proof may indeed have depended on all sorts of inductive procedures, but this supposition in no way infects what Pythagoras learnt. In general, it may be true, as Fodor claims, that learning must be a process of non-demonstrative inference, but it does not follow that all that can be learned is the inductive confirmation, or disconfirmation, of a belief. To argue otherwise is to argue that one can never learn necessary truths – they are all, as Plato supposed, inborn.

The real problem of learning is to explain the discovery of useful ways of combining old functions. Imagine an artificial learning system based on the standard recursive functions, which proceeds by using composition, recursion, and minimization, first on the set of primitive functions and then on the functions that it has created in this way. The system can in principle construct any of the denumerably infinite number of computable functions, but, like the volumes in Borges's library of Babel, most of these functions will be useless. The system has to be guided by a set of heuristics that determine what is useful. Given such heuristics, even a process of trial and error could learn how to do addition and multiplication by combining the basic recursive functions. (Such a process has indeed been implemented in a computer program by David Fallside, a former student of mine at Sussex.) The mind almost certainly has a rich set of native functions, together with specific procedures for guiding the process of constructing new functions out of old. Likewise, just as the environment may select among innately specified concepts (Fodor, 1980, p. 151), it may also help to place constraints on the combinations of functions that the mind pursues.

The conclusion to be drawn is not that nativism should be abandoned – there must be an innate armamentarium of data and procedures. And Fodor is right to argue that stages in inferential ability cannot possibly be associated solely with mental logics of increasing power. Where he is wrong, however, is in his stronger thesis that *in principle* all concepts are innate and that inferential skill cannot be learned.

Because the theory of mental models has no need of mental logic, it does not have to explain the initial development of reasoning ability by way of the acquisition of rules of inference. What children learn first are the truth conditions of expressions: they learn the contribution of connectives, quantifiers, and other such terms to these truth conditions. And, until they have acquired this knowledge about their language, they are in no position to make verbal inferences. Once they have learned such truth conditions, there may still be impediments that prevent them from realizing their full inferential competence. The reason that 12-year-olds are unable to cope with more complex syllogisms may depend, for example, on the limited processing capacity of their working memories. This system has yet to develop to its greatest power.

Conclusions

In this chapter, I have outlined a general theory of inference based on mental models, and I have established the following points:

1. The theory embraces both implicit and explicit inferences. Implicit inferences depend on constructing a single mental model; explicit inferences depend on searching for alternative models that may falsify putative conclusions. Since the interpretation of premises as mental models provides a powerful representational system, the theory is also extensible to most,

if not all, classes of arguments deployed by speakers of natural language.

2. The theory solves the central paradox of how children learn to reason, namely, how they could acquire rules of inference before they were able to reason validly. The paradox is resolved because it rests on a false assumption: children need neither acquire rules of inference (*pace* Piaget) nor possess them innately (*pace* Fodor) in order to make valid deductions. It is possible to reason validly without logic.

3. The theory is entirely compatible with the fact that human beings are capable of making valid deductions.

4. It is also compatible with the origins of logic. It assumes that people make inferences without recourse to a mental logic. Certain inferences cause them difficulty, however, and therefore provide the motivation for the search for systematic principles governing validity.

These four points correspond to the criteria that any explanatorily adequate theory of reasoning must satisfy. After I had introduced them in Chapter 4, I pointed out that the fundamental dilemma yet to be resolved by any theory of reasoning was to allow for rationality in ideal conditions and for human error in less than ideal conditions. The theory of mental models dispels this dilemma. The remaining lacunae in the theory concern how sentences containing complex quantifiers or several quantifiers are translated into mental models; how these models are manipulated in searching for counter-examples; and what constraints apply to the set of possible models – cf. the notation of mental models, which was quietly expanded in order to deal with the membership of one class within another.

The first of these gaps calls for an effective procedure. There are many feasible algorithms for translating complex and multiple quantifiers into models, and for manipulating those models; and a search for models that are counter-examples to putative conclusions will either succeed or fail in a finite number of steps granted that any mental model is finite in size. (Reasoning about infinite sets such as the natural numbers calls for a different approach that will be described later in the book.) Hence there is no doubt that appropriate algorithms exist. The problem of determining *which* algorithm is used in inference is difficult to solve because people who are untrained in logic find these particular inferences very hard.

Before the second of these gaps can be filled, and the set of possible mental models delineated (in Chapter 15), it will be necessary to examine both the way in which models differ from other representations and the process of understanding natural language.

## 7

Images, propositions, and models

In the first decade of this century, there was a long controversy over the existence of 'imageless thoughts' – mental processes that have no sensory or imaginal content. It lasted until psychologists became so disenchanted with mentalistic notions that they abandoned them for forty years in pursuit of Behavior. With the revival of interest in imagery, a new controversy has arisen over whether images have any explanatory value in psychological theorizing. Perhaps it should be dubbed the 'thoughtless imagery' controversy because, like its inglorious predecessor, it threatens to be prolonged and infertile. I shall propose a resolution of the controversy during the course of this chapter, though I suspect that both parties to the dispute may find my arguments unacceptable – an eventuality that will reinforce my conviction that they owe us some account of how the issue between them could be settled in principle. My thesis is that different types of representation are logically distinguishable at some level of analysis, and, moreover, that they exist as different options for encoding information. In particular, I shall argue that there are at least three major kinds of representation – mental models, propositional representations, and images. I shall outline a theory that relates mental models both to propositional representations and to images, which are treated as a special class of models. However, my primary purpose in entering the debate is to draw a clear contrast between mental models and propositional representations interpreted in a more traditional and narrower sense than has become customary among some cognitive scientists. There are empirical methods, as I shall show, for determining which form of representation subjects make use of on a given occasion.

Images and symbolic representations

No one doubts the conscious phenomena of imagery. Many people report that they can use their imaginations to form a visual image of an object or scene. Such images can be mentally rotated at a rate of about sixty degrees per second (Shepard, 1978); they can be suppressed by concurrent visual tasks (Brooks, 1967); they can be used to represent spatial information and to solve problems (Kosslyn, 1980); they are a useful aid to memory (Paivio, 1971; Bower, 1972). What is problematical is the ultimate nature of images as mental representations. They cannot be pictures-in-the-mind, because a picture requires a homunculus to perceive it, and this requirement leads to the slippery slope of an infinite regress – big homunculi need little homunculi to perceive their pictures-in-the-mind, and so on *ad infinitum*. What images really are is a matter that divides psychologists into two opposing schools of thought.

First, there are those such as Paivio, Shepard, and Kosslyn, who argue that images are a distinct sort of mental representation. There is a consensus among these 'imagist' psychologists on four points:

1. The mental processes underlying the experience of an image are similar to those underlying the perception of an object or picture.

2. An image is a coherent and integrated representation of a scene or object from a particular viewpoint in which each perceptible element occurs only once with all such elements being simultaneously available and open to a perception-like process of scanning.

3. An image is amenable to apparently continuous mental transformations, such as rotations or expansions, in which intermediate states correspond to intermediate states (or views) of an actual object undergoing the corresponding physical transformation. Hence, a small change in the image corresponds to a small change (of view) of the object.

4. Images *represent* objects. They are analogical in that structural relations between their parts correspond to the perceptible relations between the parts of the objects represented.

Second, there are those who argue that images are epiphenomenal and that there is only a single underlying form of mental representation, strings of symbols that correspond to propositions (e.g., Baylor, 1971; Pylyshyn, 1973; Palmer, 1975). These 'propositionalist' theorists are also agreed on four points:

1. The mental processes leading to the strings of symbols that correspond to an image are similar to those underlying the perception of an object or picture.

2. The same element or part of an object may be referred to by many of the different propositions that constitute the description of the object. Such a description may be represented as a set of expressions in a logical

calculus (with access to a general procedure for making inferences), or it may be represented in a semantic network.

3. A propositional representation is discrete and digital, but it can represent continuous processes by small successive increments of variables, such as the angle of an object's major axis to the frame of reference. Hence, a small change in the representation will correspond to a small change in the appearance of the object.

4. Propositions are true or false of objects. They are abstract in that they do not directly correspond to either words or pictures. Their structure is *not* analogous to the structure of the objects they represent.

In short, the critics of imagery allow that an image can be constructed from its underlying propositional representation, but assert that the image is epiphenomenal – it does not introduce any new information, but merely makes the stored information easier to manipulate.

It is evident that many of the claims about images and propositional representations are very similar. Their underlying processes can be akin to the perception of an object or picture. They can form coherent and integrated representations. A small change in them can correspond to a small change in the appearance of an object. The only major divergence is that images are said to represent objects, whereas propositions are said to be true or false of them. The overall similarity between the two formats has led some commentators to conclude that the controversy is neither fundamental nor resolvable (see Norman and Rumelhart, 1975).

It is, of course, a universal truth in any science that there can always be more than one theory that explains the data: no observations can ever establish definitely that a single unique theory is the correct one. Einstein and Infeld make this point most vividly:

Physical concepts are free creations of the human mind, and are not, however it may seem, uniquely determined by the external world. In our endeavour to understand reality we are somewhat like a man trying to understand the mechanism of a closed watch. He sees the face and the moving hands, even hears its ticking, but he has no way of opening the case. If he is ingenious he may form some picture of a mechanism which could be responsible for all the things he observes, but he may never be quite sure his picture is the only one which could explain his observations. He will never be able to compare his picture with the real mechanism and he cannot even imagine the possibility of the meaning of such a comparison. (Einstein and Infeld, 1938, p. 152, cited by Zukav, 1979).

The same limitations on knowledge apply *a fortiori* to psychology, and to theories about mental representations. And here there is a special case of the argument to be considered.

148

Anderson's mimicry theorem

John Anderson (1978) has argued that it is impossible to evaluate any claim for a particular sort of mental representation unless the *processes* that operate on this representation are specified in the theory. He bases this claim on a theorem that he proves: given any theory of mental representations and processes, it is always possible to construct an alternative theory making use of a different sort of representation that behaves in an entirely equivalent way. For instance, a theory based on the rotation of images can be mimicked by one based on propositional representations. In fact, 'mimicry' is not the right word to describe the manoeuvre in Anderson's proof: rather the second theory invades the first and takes it over like a virus taking over an organism's machinery for producing DNA. This embedding of one theory within another can be illustrated by a specific example.

Let us suppose that according to one theory stimuli are encoded as images that can be mentally rotated by certain specified processes, and that according to another, stimuli are encoded as sets of propositions. The imaginal theory is embedded within the propositional theory by postulating that a stimulus is subject to the following sequence of operations:

1. The stimulus is encoded as a set of propositions.
2. The inverse of the function that encodes stimuli as sets of propositions is applied to the propositional representations in order to recover the original stimulus, or, more accurately, a representation of its sensory image.
3. The perceptual encoding function of the imaginal theory is applied to this representation in order to obtain an image of the stimulus.
4. The image is rotated according to the process employed by the imaginal theory.
5. The inverse of the function encoding the stimulus as an image is applied to the rotated image in order to obtain a representation of the corresponding sensory stimulus.
6. The perceptual encoding function of the propositional theory is applied to the rotated sensory stimulus to recover the corresponding set of propositions.

This embedding of an imaginal theory within a propositional theory is summarized in Figure 7.1. A decision about whether the resulting propositions correspond to the comparison stimulus presented by the experimenter can be made by using exactly the same sort of stratagem.

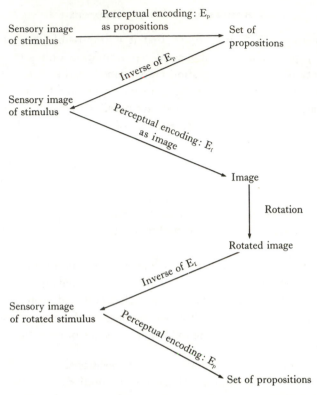

Figure 7.1 The embedding of an imaginal theory within a propositional theory according to Anderson's procedure.

The feasibility of embedding one theory within another in this way requires that the various functions are computable. Because the process of perception is almost certainly a many-to-one mapping, i.e., a function that delivers the same representation for many stimuli that are physically different, there is no guarantee that the inverse of the function will yield the original sensory image of the stimulus. Hence, the theorem also requires the existence of a one-to-one mapping between the respective representations of the two theories. This assumption ensures that the inverse of the propositional encoding can yield any of the differing stimuli that might have given rise to the original representation, and it will not matter which of them is selected, because they will all be treated as equivalent by the imaginal theory too. If one theory encodes stimuli into classes that do not correspond one-to-one with the encodings of the other theory, then of course the whole system of mappings breaks down and the theorem ceases to hold. Hence, considerable care needs to be taken in drawing conclusions on the basis of the theorem, and, as we shall see in Chapter 11, even its author is not immune to making false claims on its basis.

The fact that one theory can mimic another by taking it over wholesale is plainly trivial. What is of interest is the possibility of a more direct method of mimicry that does not depend on embedding one theory within another. However, there is no guarantee that such a method can always be found, and Anderson makes only the modest claim: 'it seems we can usually construct [the required operation] more simply than its formally guaranteed specification'. The theorem certainly does not establish that the controversy between imagists and propositionalists is futile. It can be resolved; but not perhaps in the way intended by the controversialists. Under one interpretation of 'propositional representations' the issue is almost completely emptied of empirical content; under another, which I advocate, the controversy is resolved in favour of the imagists.

How to reduce images to strings of symbols: the Turing machine argument

If a 'propositional representation' is interpreted to mean a mental representation consisting of a string of symbols composed from a finite vocabulary, there is a simple way to show that the mind uses only propositional representations. The argument depends on two assumptions, both introduced in Chapter 1. The first assumption is that any psychological theory should be formulable as an effective procedure: it should be computable. The second assumption is Turing's thesis that anything that can be effectively computed is computable by the machines that he described. This is an assumption that cannot be proved, because of the open-ended nature of the concept of effectiveness; but it has yet to be falsified, and, as I noted, it has been strongly corroborated by the equivalence of several independent definitions of computability. It follows from the two assumptions that any psychological theory that postulates complex mental representations, such as images or mental models, can be translated into the notation of a Turing machine. The only form of representation required by that device is a linear string of symbols ('0', '1'). Hence, any theory can be couched in a form that makes use only of strings of symbols.

The fact that a psychological theory can be expressed in a form that uses only one kind of symbolic representation does not entail that such a formulation is correct. What it does imply, however, is that claims about imagery are unlikely to be settled by psychological experiment. Suppose that ultimately the brain carries out all its computations on strings of symbols in a code: then, indeed, regardless of what happens at a higher level of representation, the brain uses only propositional representations. To establish that this claim is false, it would be necessary to show that the brain's 'machine' code is intrinsically richer – that, for example, it uses two-dimensional items or some sort of analogue medium of computation. There is no evidence for any such claim, nor is there likely to be any psychological experimentation that can address the issue. Hence, on this interpretation of a 'propositional representation', to characterize a theory as relying on propositional representations is to make a physiological claim rather than a psychological one.

Levels of description

Although some commentators see the question of the machine's code and architecture as fundamental, from the standpoint of functionalism it trivial-izes the controversy between the imagists and the propositionalists. Pyly-shyn (1981), for instance, argues that images are epiphenomenal and not part of the functional architecture of the machine because they are 'cogni-tively penetrable', i.e., the way in which they govern behaviour can be influenced in a rationally explainable way by beliefs, goals, and tacit knowledge. Hence, he claims, images depend on a cognitive rule-governed process that acts on semantically interpreted representations rather than on the intrinsic properties of an underlying analogue medium. All these assumptions can be granted to Pylyshyn, though whether anything from ulcers to short-term memory fails to be 'cognitively penetrable' might be difficult to determine. The real trouble is that Pylyshyn has pitched the battle in the wrong place. To see why, one only has to consider how a thoroughgoing materialist (cf. Churchland, 1981) might react to Pylyshyn's recourse to beliefs, goals, and tacit knowledge. Such notions, the materialist might say, are epiphenomenal and not part of the functional architecture of the machine because they are 'imagistically penetrable', i.e., the way in which they govern behaviour can be influenced in a rationally explainable way by images. The moral is plain: images and beliefs are both high-level constructs, and it is a mistake to argue that they are epiphenomenal just because they can 'penetrate' each other.

The level at which a particular mental entity is described is indeed a source of much confusion in theoretical discussions. A theorist might propose, for example, that a mental image consists of a two-dimensional array built up from some internal description. Such a hypothesis is informal, but at a high level – the level at which psychological discourse is normally conducted. A specification of the theory at a lower level would describe the underlying representation of the arrays and the otherwise invisible machinery that makes them possible. From the standpoint of functionalism, however, the neurophysiological embodiment of the array is irrelevant even if it is expressed within a uniform propositional code. There is an analogy with computer programming here: an array is a structure in which elements can be accessed and updated by giving appropriate ordered sequences of integers corresponding to co-ordinate values. Programmers need to know no more: they can devise algorithms for manipulating arrays simply by thinking of them as n-dimensional spaces where each location is specified by an n-tuple of integers. There is, of course, no corresponding physical array of locations in the computer. That would be wholly unnecessary. All that matters is that the physical embodiment should *function* as an array, that is, there is a set of locations that can be used as an array. Its elements can be accessed as an array, and its contents displayed or manipulated as an array. The machine code that controls a particular computer as it processes an array is a translation of the program into a low-level description in which these functional principles are no longer evident. Likewise, the redescription of a theory of imagery at the level of a Turing machine – the lowest theoretical level – almost entirely obscures its operational principles.

The moral is that although at one level a psychological process may use only strings of symbols, at a higher level it may use various sorts of representation. The reason why the mind might rely on different representations in this way is revealed by considering why high-level programming languages include such data-structures as arrays. Arrays do not increase the computational power of the language, since – to make the point again – the only representation that in principle is ever needed is a string of symbols. The point of introducing arrays is to make the programmer's task of developing and testing new software easier. The programmer can solve problems in terms of arrays and can entirely ignore the detailed machinery on which they rely. There is no reason to suppose that the human mind is organized on different lines. It, too, needs to develop new procedures and it can do so very much more easily if it can work directly with high-level structures, such as spatial representations, ignoring the details of their ultimate representation in the brain. Hierarchy, as Simon (1969) has argued, is a pre-requisite for intelligence.

Function is critical in another way. It can distinguish between two representations that have the same content and the same structure. One illustration can be drawn from computer programming. A programming language may contain a function, ISFUNC, which returns the value *true* (1) when it is applied to something that is a function, and the value *false* (0) when it is applied to something that is not a function:

$$ISFUNC(ADD) \Rightarrow 1$$
$$ISFUNC(5) \Rightarrow 0$$

This function can be applied to itself, and since it *is* a function, the value returned is true:

$$ISFUNC(ISFUNC) \Rightarrow 1$$

In this case, the same expression is put to two quite different uses: in one, it serves as a function to evaluate an expression, and in the other, it serves merely as an expression, i.e., as data to be used by the function. This contrast is familiar to philosophers of language as a distinction between the *use* of an expression and its *mention*. The expression 'is four words long' can be applied to various quotations to yield true or false assertions, e.g., '"To be or not to be" is four words long' is a false assertion. The predicate can also be applied to its own quotation: '"Is four words long" is four words long' is a true assertion, and the same expression is both mentioned and used.

There is an important psychological moral here, too. Mental representations may differ, not just in their intrinsic properties such as their structure or content, but also in the function that they serve. One and the same image of, say, an elephant smoking a cigar could function on one occasion as part of the interpretation of a fairy-story, and on another occasion as a mnemonic for the paired associate: *elephant – cigar*. The significance of an image depends on the processes that construct and interpret it.

How to distinguish between mental models and propositional representations

Suppose you are lost in the maze at Hampton Court Palace. You come to a turning and for a moment you are not sure which way to go. You recognize that you have been at this point before, and, in your imagination, you turn right, proceed down an alley, and are then confronted by a dead end. And so this time around, you decide to turn left. What you did, I assume, was to reconstruct a route through the maze on the basis of a mental model of it. You may hardly have experienced any imagery at all; or you may have had a succession of vivid images like a snippet from an imaginary film that culminates in the leafy cul-de-sac. In either case, there was nothing 'propositional', in the philosophical sense of the word, about your reasoning: there was no process based on the representation of verbal propositions. You navigated your way through your model of the maze much as a rat in a psychological laboratory might have done. However, you might have made your decision in a very different way. You might have recalled that the way to get out of the maze is to keep turning left at every available opportunity, and, since you were faced with such an opportunity, you might accordingly have elected to turn left. This method makes use of a mental representation of verbal propositions.

The two methods illustrate the contrast between exploiting a mental model (perhaps with accompanying imagery) and making use of a propositional representation. But this is a narrower sense of propositional representation than mere reduction to a string of symbols. Indeed, philosophers have generally taken propositions to be the conscious objects of thought – those entities that we entertain, believe, think, doubt, etc., and that are expressed by sentences (see Gale, 1967 for a history of the term). Since I am concerned, not with the nature of the 'machine code' of the brain, which may well consist of strings of symbols from a finite alphabet, but with the types of higher level of representation, I propose to revert henceforth to the traditional philosophical terminology: a propositional representation is a mental representation of a verbally expressible proposition.

To understand a proposition is to know what the world would be like for it to be true. Since a proposition is true or false of the state of affairs to which it refers, a propositional representation is the representation of a function from states of affairs to truth values. And the most general way to represent a function is to express it in a language. This mental language must have a vocabulary, a grammar, and a semantics (cf. Kintsch, 1974; Fodor, 1975). Its vocabulary must relate to that of natural language. Its grammar is likely to have evolved as a result of many unknown factors. For example, the syntax of sentential conjunction could be:

$$K(p, q)$$

where K is the conjunctive connective and p and q are propositional variables. It could be one of the other natural alternatives:

$$pKq$$

or:

$$(p, q)K$$

The particular form that was selected is unlikely ever to be discovered, but, granted that it is linked to the appropriate semantics, it can be treated as an essentially arbitrary choice.

The crucial problem for the mental language is the nature of its semantics. Propositions can refer to the world. Human beings, of course, do not apprehend the world directly; they possess only an internal representation of it, because perception is the construction of a model of the world. They are unable to compare this perceptual representation directly with the world – it *is* their world, as was the thrust of the quotation from Einstein and Infeld. Propositions can also refer to imaginary or hypothetical worlds. One proposition may be false of such a world given that others are true of it. Human beings can evidently construct mental models by acts of imagination and can relate propositions to such models. A principal assumption of the theory which I am developing is that the semantics of the mental language maps propositional representations into mental models of real or imaginary worlds: *propositional representations are interpreted with respect to mental models*. In due course, I shall describe how this process of interpretation is carried out, but here I want to pursue the contrast between the different forms of representation, and in particular some potential differences between their structure and content.

The structure and content of mental representations

Unlike a propositional representation, a mental model does not have an arbitrarily chosen syntactic structure, but one that plays a direct representational role since it is analogous to the structure of the corresponding state of affairs in the world – as we perceive or conceive it. However, the analogical structure of mental models can vary considerably. Models of quantified assertions may introduce only a minimal degree of analogical structure, such as the use of separate elements to stand for individuals. Alternatively, models of spatial layouts such as a maze may be two- or three-dimensional; they may be dynamic and represent a sequence of events; they may take on an even higher number of dimensions in the case of certain gifted individuals. One advantage of their dimensional structure is that they can be constructed, and manipulated, in ways that can be controlled by dimensional variables. But a propositional representation, as Simon (1972) pointed out, can be scanned only in those directions that have been encoded in the representation. Simon also drew attention to the fact that people who know perfectly well how to play noughts-and-crosses (tic-tac-toe) are unable to transfer their tactical skill to number scrabble, a game that is isomorphic to noughts-and-crosses. Just as they can scan an external noughts-and-crosses array, so they can scan its internal representation, but that process is irrelevant to the game of number scrabble.

There is plainly a relation between images and mental models, and I shall assume that images correspond to *views* of models: as a result either of perception or imagination, they represent the perceptible features of the corresponding real-world objects. In imagining, say, a rotating object, the underlying mental model of the object is used to recover a representation of its surfaces, reflectances, and so forth – what the late David Marr (1982), in referring to the process of perception, called the '$2\frac{1}{2}$-D sketch'. Mental rotations in depth appear to be just as easy as those in the picture plane. Hence, as Hinton (1979) argues, when you form an image, you must compute the projective relations from the model to the $2\frac{1}{2}$-D sketch: a model underlies an image.

A characteristic difference in the *contents* of mental models, images, and propositional representations, concerns their specificity. Models, like images, are highly specific – a characteristic which has often drawn comment from philosophers. You cannot form an image of *a triangle in general*, but only of a specific triangle. Hence, if you reason on the basis of a model or image, you must take pains to ensure that your conclusion goes beyond the specific instance you considered. Hume (1896, Vol. I) made the point, somewhat optimistically, in this way:

For this is one of the most extraordinary circumstances in the present affair, that after the mind has produced an individual idea, upon which we reason, the attendant custom, revived by the general or abstract term, readily suggests any other individual, if by chance we form any reasoning that agrees not with it. Thus, should we mention the word triangle, and form the idea of a particular equilateral one to correspond to it, and should we afterwards assert, *that the three angles of a triangle are equal to each other*, the other individuals of a scalenum and isosceles, which we overlooked at first, immediately crowd in upon us, and make us perceive the falsehood of this proposition . . .

Although a model must be specific, it does not follow that it cannot be used to represent a general class of entities. The interpretation of a specific model depends upon a variety of interpretive processes, and they may treat the model as no more than a representative sample from a larger set. Once again, the *function* of the model cannot be ignored: a specification of structure and content must always be supplemented by an account of the processes using the model if one is to formulate what the model represents. However, since language is inherently vague, the content of models invariably embodies some arbitrary assumptions, whereas there is no such need in the construction of propositional representations.

Pylyshyn (1973), echoing many philosophers from Hume onwards, has pointed out a major difference between images and propositional representations:

It would be quite permissible . . . to have a [propositional] mental representation of two objects with a relation between them such as 'besides'. Such a representation need not contain a more specific spatial relation such as 'to the left of' or 'to the right of'. It would seem an unreasonable use of the word 'image' to speak of an image of two objects side by side, without the relation between them being either 'to the left of' or 'to the right of'.

This distinction is useful because it has empirical consequences: a propositional representation should be able to handle both determinate and indeterminate spatial relations with equal ease, whereas a mental model should handle determinate relations more readily than indeterminate ones. The only way to form a model of one object beside another that is neutral with respect to left and right would be to construct a set of such analogue representations corresponding to the various possibilities. A picture may be worth a thousand words, but a proposition is worth an infinity of pictures.

Since models, images, and propositional representations are functionally and structurally distinguishable from one another, it follows that there is indeed a useful theoretical distinction between different kinds of representations.

Evidence for propositional representations and mental models

Suppose that you are reading Conan Doyle's (1905) well-known story, 'Charles Augustus Milverton', which recounts how Sherlock Holmes and Dr Watson set out to burgle the house of the eponymous blackmailer, 'the worst man in London', and you come upon the following passage:

With our black silk face-coverings, which turned us into two of the most truculent figures in London, we stole up to the silent, gloomy house. A sort of tiled veranda extended along one side of it, lined by several windows and two doors.

'That's his bedroom', Holmes whispered. 'This door opens straight into the study. It would suit us best, but it is bolted as well as locked, and we should make too much noise getting in. Come round here. There's a greenhouse which opens into the drawing room'.

The place was locked, but Holmes removed a circle of glass and turned the key from the inside. An instant afterwards he had closed the door behind us, and we had become felons in the eyes of the law. The thick, warm air of the conservatory and the rich, choking fragrance of exotic plants took us by the throat. He seized my hand in the darkness and led me swiftly past banks of shrubs which brushed against our faces. Holmes had remarkable powers, carefully cultivated, of seeing in the dark. [!] Still holding my hand in one of his, he opened a door, and I was vaguely conscious that we had entered a large room in which a cigar had been smoked not long before. He felt his way among the furniture, opened another door, and closed it behind us. Putting out my hand I felt several coats hanging from the wall, and I understood that I was in a passage. We passed along it, and Holmes very gently opened a door upon the right-hand side. Something rushed out at us and my heart sprang into my mouth, but I could have laughed when I realized that it was the cat. A fire was burning in this new room, and again the air was heavy with tobacco smoke. Holmes entered on tiptoe, waited for me to follow, and then very gently closed the door. We were in Milverton's study, and a portière at the farther side showed the entrance to his bedroom.

It was a good fire, and the room was illuminated by it. Near the door I saw the gleam of an electric switch, but it was unnecessary, even if it had been safe, to turn it on. At one side of the fireplace was a heavy curtain which covered the bay window we had seen from outside. On the other side was the door which communicated with the veranda. A desk stood in the centre, with a turning-chair of shining red leather. Opposite was a large bookcase, with a marble bust of Athene on the top. In the corner, between the bookcase and the wall, there stood a tall, green safe, the firelight flashing back from the polished brass knobs upon its face.

You may have noticed that some of the details stand out in considerable clarity – the cat that frightened Dr Watson, the cigar smoke, the shining red chair, and the firelight glinting off the knobs of the safe. You may also have observed that Holmes does *not* make one of his celebrated deductions. In fact, the omission is deliberate on my part because I want you to try to make a deduction. Here is a simple plan of the house with the veranda running down one side of it:

The question is: which way did Holmes and Watson make their way along the veranda – from right to left, or from left to right?

About one out of every hundred people to whom I have read this passage (in various lectures) can spontaneously give the right answer for the right reason. Most people's representations are too partial to provide the necessary information. Yet, if you read the passage again with the aim of solving this riddle, you will probably be able to construct a sufficiently complete mental model to answer it easily. (The solution, for those who are still perplexed, can be found at the end of the chapter.) There thus appear to be different levels of comprehension. It might be argued that the difference is merely one of detail – the extent to which you furnish your representation of the house with all the paraphernalia mentioned in the story – but the phenomena are also compatible with a difference in kind. What you have to do in order to make the required inference is to build up a mental model of the spatial layout. The fact that you are unlikely to be able to draw the correct conclusion unless you are forewarned lends support to the idea that discourse can be represented either in a propositional form close to the linguistic structure of the discourse, or in a mental model that is closer to a representation of a state of affairs – in this case the plan of a house – than to a set of sentences.

Kannan Mani and I have investigated the hypothesis about levels of representations in a series of experiments, and I shall describe just one of them (see Mani and Johnson-Laird, 1982). Our basic idea was that subjects would tend to form a mental model of a spatially determinate description, but would not do so for an indeterminate description consistent with more than one spatial layout – especially if their task was to check whether the description corresponded to a diagram. They might easily form the 'wrong' model, that is, one that did not match the diagram, though it was equally consistent with the indeterminate description.

The subjects heard a series of spatial descriptions, such as:

The spoon is to the left of the knife.
The plate is to the right of the knife.
The fork is in front of the spoon.
The cup is in front of the knife.

After each description, they were shown a diagram such as:

spoon   knife   plate
fork   cup

and they had to decide whether the diagram was consistent or inconsistent with the description. (If you think of the diagram as depicting the arrangement of the objects on a table top, then obviously this example is consistent

160

with the description). Half the descriptions that the subjects received were determinate, as in this case, and half were spatially indeterminate. The indeterminate descriptions were constructed merely by changing the last word in the second sentence:

The spoon is to the left of the knife.
The plate is to the right of the spoon.
The fork is in front of the spoon.
The cup is in front of the knife.

This description is consistent with two radically different diagrams:

spoon	knife	plate		spoon	plate	knife
fork	cup			fork		cup

After the subjects had judged the descriptions and diagrams, they were given an unexpected test of their memory for the descriptions. On each trial, they had to rank four alternatives in terms of their resemblance to the original description: the original description, an inferrable description, and two 'foils' with a different meaning. The inferrable description for the example contained the sentence:

The fork is to the left of the cup

in place of the sentence interrelating the spoon and the knife. The description is therefore not a paraphrase of the original, but it can be inferred from the layout corresponding to the original description in the case of both the determinate and the indeterminate descriptions. This inference is only likely to be made if the subjects construct mental models, and, moreover, ones that are symmetrical. If they were to construct an asymmetrical model of, say, the determinate description above:

spoon	knife	plate
fork		

            cup

then they might well fail to consider that the fork is to the left of the cup.

The subjects remembered the gist of the determinate descriptions very much better than that of the indeterminate descriptions. The percentage of trials on which they ranked the original and the inferrable descriptions prior to the confusion items was 88% for the determinate descriptions, but only 58% for the indeterminate descriptions. All twenty of the subjects conformed to this trend, and there was no effect of whether or not on a particular trial a diagram had been consistent with a description. However, the percentages of trials on which the original description was ranked higher than the inferrable description was 68% for the determinate descriptions, but 88% for the indeterminate descriptions. This predicted difference was also highly reliable.

Evidently, subjects tend to remember the gist of determinate descriptions better than that of indeterminate descriptions, but they tend to remember the verbatim detail of indeterminate descriptions better than that of determinate descriptions. This 'cross-over' effect is impossible to explain without postulating at least two sorts of mental representation. A plausible account of the pattern of results is indeed that subjects construct a mental model of the determinate descriptions, but abandon such a representation in favour of a superficial propositional one as soon as they encounter an indeterminacy in a description. Models are easier to remember than propositions, perhaps because they are more structured and elaborated (cf. Craik and Tulving, 1975) and require a greater amount of processing to construct (cf. Johnson-Laird and Bethell-Fox, 1978). But models encode little or nothing of the linguistic form of the sentences on which they are based, and subjects accordingly confuse inferrable descriptions with the originals. Propositional representations are relatively hard to remember, but they do encode the linguistic form of sentences. Hence, when they are remembered, the subjects are likely to make a better than chance recognition of verbatim content. The controversy is resolved: there is an empirical distinction between mental models and propositional representations.

The representation of indeterminate discourse

Indeterminate descriptions are not necessarily represented in a propositional form on every occasion. Our experiments deliberately employed a task that was likely to favour a propositional representation whenever an indeterminacy occurred. However, there are other potential ways of coping with indeterminate discourse. Consider, for example, the following typical description of a room:

I have a very small bedroom with a window overlooking the heath. There is a single bed against the wall and opposite it a gas fire with a gas ring for boiling a kettle. The room is so small that I sit on the bed to cook. The only other furniture in the room is a bookcase on one side of the gas fire next to the window – it's got all my books on it and my portable radio – and a wardrobe. It stands against the wall just near to the door, which opens almost directly onto the head of my bed.

The text creates a reasonably clear impression of the room, but is radically indeterminate in that it is consistent with a potentially infinite number of alternative rooms. The problem is not merely a question of the dimensions of the room and furniture: the actual layout itself is not described in a way that permits a unique reconstruction of the spatial relations between the objects. How, then, is such a passage mentally represented? A number of theorists have struggled with this problem, which was first brought home to me on reading Miller's (1979) discussion of it. As he points out, one can analyse the interpretation of discourse by assuming that each successive sentence reduces the number of alternative possibilities that are compatible with the passage. In the present framework of mental models, however, there are at least four different strategies for coping with indeterminacy.

First, you can simply stop constructing a model as soon as you detect an indeterminacy. In fact, you are only likely to detect the indeterminacy if you *are* trying to construct a model. This strategy was evidently adopted by most of the subjects in our experiments. Its likely cost is that memory for the passage will be poor.

Second, you can try to cope with indeterminacy by constructing alternative models representing the different possibilities. Unfortunately, a descriptive passage such as the example above is likely to require a combinatorially explosive number of alternatives, and, as our studies of reasoning showed, people find it difficult to keep in mind even a few alternatives. Hence, this strategy is unlikely to be employed except when the numbers are very small.

Third, you may be able to represent the indeterminacy within a mental model by introducing a propositional-like element of notation. A good example of this idea is provided by the representation for quantified assertions. The reader will recall that an assertion of the form *All the A are B* was represented in a model containing an arbitrary number of individuals, such as:

$$a = b$$
$$a = b$$
$$(b)$$
$$(b)$$

where the parenthesized elements represent the possibility of there being B's that are not A's. In fact, this is an instance of referential indeterminacy, and the use of parentheses is supposed to correspond to some mental

163

tagging of the elements to indicate that the corresponding individuals may, or may not, exist. Plainly, this mental tagging introduces a propositional-like notation into an analogical model. Kosslyn (1980) has also argued for a similar admixture of image-like and propositional-like elements. Unfortunately, it is difficult to represent spatial indeterminacy within a dimensional model. For example, the indeterminate description:

A is on the left of B, which is to the right of C

could receive a mental representation equivalent to:

where the arrows represent the relations expressed explicitly in the assertion. But such a format makes no essential use of the analogical properties of the model. That is to say, the representation consists of one particular model of the description supplemented by a propositional representation of the description: the latter renders the former redundant. The same problem arises with notations of the following variety:

$$A\begin{pmatrix} C \\ B \end{pmatrix}$$

where the propositional force of the parentheses (that the relation between B and C is indeterminate) destroys the analogical nature of the model. If, then, you were to make use of such a system to represent the description of the room in the example above, there would be so many propositional notations that it would be pointless to embed them within a dimensional framework.

Fourth, you may plump for one specific model of the discourse, perhaps on the basis of an implicit inference. If this interpretation does not conflict with the subsequent discourse, there is clearly no problem. If there is such a conflict, however, you can attempt to reconstruct an appropriate alternative model. This procedure is a demanding one, and obviously depends on access to the previous discourse. You may be forced to abandon the whole enterprise in some confusion. One observes anecdotally both of these outcomes when travellers receive detailed instructions about a route; and Stenning (1981) has found that subjects do tend to make specific assumptions about, say, the direction of a turn when it is not specified explicitly in the description of a route.

There can be little doubt that the radical reconstruction of a mental model is seldom called for in everyday discourse, as Grice (1975) has emphasized, there is a convention that speakers tend to abide by: they do not deliberately mislead their listeners. In other words, if you construct a mental model on the basis of my discourse, then I am likely to order the information in my description so as to prevent you from going astray. I owe you an account that you can represent in a single model without running into a conflict with information that I only subsequently divulge. Of course, no speaker is likely to be able to live up to this principle all the time but nevertheless it is followed on most occasions. A mental model is in essence a representative sample from the set of possible models satisfying the description.

Conclusions

This chapter has presented a case for the existence of at least three types of mental representation: propositional representations which are strings of symbols that correspond to natural language, mental models which are structural analogues of the world, and images which are the perceptual correlates of models from a particular point of view. The distinction is a high-level one; doubtless, everything can be reduced to a uniform code in the language of the brain just as the data structures of a high-level programming language can be reduced to patterns of bits in the machine code of a computer, and the most complex of algorithms can be reduced to manipulations on strings of symbols by a Turing machine.

Why should the mind make use of these various media? The previous chapters of the book have shown how propositions and models enter into the process of inference. Mental models provide a basis for representing premises, and their manipulation makes it possible to reason without logic. The search for alternative interpretations, however, demands an independent representation of the premises, a representation that is propositional in form. The rest of the book will develop the theory of mental models to provide an integrated account of the processes underlying meaning and the comprehension of discourse. This account prepares the way for an explanatorily adequate theory of the nature of mental models and of the role they play in consciousness and self-awareness.

In this chapter, I have assumed that descriptions are initially represented propositionally, i.e., by expressions in a mental language, and that the semantics of the mental language maps these propositional representations into mental models. I have given no indication of how either of these two processes works. My first task will be to specify the semantic theory, and my second will be to describe the process by which linguistic expressions are translated into propositional representations.

The solution to the riddle about Holmes and Watson is that they must have walked along the veranda from right to left. After they broke into the house round the corner from one end of the veranda, they passed through various rooms and along a corridor, and then they turned *right* into Milverton's study and saw the door that communicated with the veranda. By a nice coincidence, Sheila Jones, a leading investigator of imagery, lives in the house in Hampstead that is generally believed to be the 'model' for Conan Doyle's story.

8

Meaning in model-theoretic semantics

The reader will recall that my long-term goal is to give an account of all the mental processes that occur in making a deduction such as:

Some of those people are from the university.
Any person from the university is likely to know where the university is.
∴ Some of those people are likely to know where the university is.

So far, I have described how such inferences can be made by constructing and evaluating mental models, and I have argued that there are psychological grounds for supposing that mental models are constructed by a semantics that operates on superficial propositional representations of the premises. In general terms, this process consists in mapping strings of symbols into models. It therefore resembles a way of doing semantics that was developed by logicians to specify the meaning of the ideal languages of logic and mathematics, but that is increasingly used in the analysis of natural languages. The method is known as 'model-theoretic' semantics. Model-theoretic semantics lays out the structure of semantic interpretations with a pure but almost unreal clarity. It embodies one central principle that almost certainly applies to natural languages, the principle of compositionality that can be traced back to the work of the founder of modern logic, the great German logician, Gottlob Frege. This chapter is accordingly intended to describe the basic principles of the method – as a precursor to an account of how the corresponding psychological processes of semantic interpretation occur. It is written within the spirit of an 'ecumenical' principle proposed by Stanley Peters: model-theoretic semantics should specify what is computed in understanding a sentence, and psychological semantics should specify how it is computed.

The principle of compositionality

Frege (1892) drew a distinction between the *sense* of an expression and its *reference*. The *reference* of an expression is what it stands for in the world;

167

the *sense* of the expression is more problematical in Frege's work, since he talked only of its containing 'the mode of presentation' of the reference. However, he recognized that the sense of an expression is a part of its meaning – the part that concerns the way in which the expression connects up with its reference – and is different from the connotative 'colouring' of a term, which distinguishes, say, *a quick dip in the briny* from *a rapid swim in the sea* but does not affect reference. Frege's informal and somewhat obscure notions of sense and reference have been replaced by the concepts of *intension* and *extension* in formal semantics, and I shall anticipate my subsequent account of them by adopting this usage. To take Frege's example, the two expressions *the Morning Star* and *the Evening Star* have the same extension in our universe, normally the planet Venus, but different intensions, since one means the 'star' observed in the morning and the other means the 'star' observed in the evening. Frege took the extension of a declarative sentence to be its truth value, and its intension to be the conditions which must hold for the sentence to be true. In an idealized language such as the predicate calculus of formal logic, which Frege invented, one expression in a sentence can be replaced by another with the same extension without affecting the truth value of the sentence as a whole. For example, if the assertion 'The teacher punished William' is true, then the assertion 'Mr Brown punished William' is true provided that *the teacher* and *Mr Brown* have the same extension. However, as Frege pointed out, this principle does not hold invariably in natural language. The assertion 'Henry believes that the Morning Star is a planet' could be true, but the assertion 'Henry believes that the Evening Star is a planet' could be false. Henry might not know that *the Morning Star* and *the Evening Star* have the same extension, and hence one expression cannot be sub- stituted for another in a statement of his beliefs. Frege argued that in such contexts a constituent refers not to its usual reference but to its usual sense: the indirect extension of a constituent is its intension rather than its extension. Here, he sought to preserve a principle that has become central to model-theoretic semantics: *the intension of a sentence can be built up compositionally from the intensions of its constituents in a way that depends only on their grammatical mode of combination.* This basic principle of compositionality has been discovered more than once, in one guise or another, and what it amounts to is the idea that the meanings of words can be combined according to the grammatical relations between them so as to yield the meanings of the constituents containing the words. The meaning of the noun phrase *old men*, for example, is obtained by combining the meanings of *old* and *men* according to the grammatical analysis of the noun phrase, and the meaning of the sentence *old men forget* is obtained from the meanings of the noun phrase *old men* and the verb phrase *forget* as a function of the grammatical analysis of the sentence. The ingredients are the meanings of the words in the sentence; the recipe is its syntactic structure. (Idiomatic expressions such as 'kick the bucket' receive a unitary interpretation that does not depend on compositionality.)

The principle of compositionality ought to have empirical consequences, but they will depend on what intensions are associated with words and on what grammatical analyses are assigned to sentences. With such degrees of freedom, the consequences may at best be testable only very indirectly. The chief argument in favour of the principle is an appeal to elegance. A speaker can understand a potentially infinite number of different sentences, and such an ability must depend on finite means, because the brain is a finite device. The set of sentences can be recursively specified by grammatical rules. The meanings of the sentences must also be specified in some way as a function of the meanings of the finite number of words in the language. There is therefore a considerable aesthetic appeal in assigning meanings to sentences in a way that runs in parallel with the assignment of their syntactic structures. That appeal, however, has been resisted by a number of authors, including both Russell (1905) and Chomsky (1977).

Models of a language

The development of Frege's ideas was largely the work of logicians. They showed how to formulate a rigorously compositional semantics for a formal language by providing it with a semantic interpretation with respect not to the real world, but to a *model*. This recourse to models is useful because a given logical calculus can apply to quite different models, and because it shelves the question of how language relates to reality and the ultimate nature of truth. However, a *model* of a language in formal semantics is an abstract construct: it consists of a function from the syntactically well-formed expressions of the language to elements in some specified *model structure* such as the set of natural numbers or of some other sort of entity. Mental models are analogous to model structures, but, as we shall see, there are important differences between them. Table 8.1 illustrates the basic principles of model-theoretic semantics by providing a model for a very small fragment of English. In the model each proper name is assigned an interpretation consisting of a corresponding individual in the model

Table 8.1 *A simple model-theoretic semantics for a very small fragment of English*

The syntax of the fragment

Basic words:

Nouns:	'Anne', 'Charles', 'Diana'
Intransitive verb:	'smiles'
Transitive verb:	'loves'

Syntactic rules:

1 If N is a noun and V_I is an intransitive verb, then $N+V_I$ is a well-formed sentence, where '+' denotes a simple concatenation of words.
2 If N and M are nouns and V_T is a transitive verb, then $N+V_T+M$ is a well-formed sentence.
3 If S_1 and S_2 are sentences, then S_1+'and'$+S_2$ is a sentence.

The semantics of the fragment

There is a model structure consisting of the following set of individuals: Princess Anne, Prince Charles, and Lady Diana, which for convenience will be designated here as {a, c, d}.

Lexical rules:

1 'Anne' is assigned a as its interpretation in the model.
2 'Charles' is assigned c as its interpretation in the model.
3 'Diana' is assigned d as its interpretation in the model.
4 'Smiles' is assigned as its interpretation in the model a set of individuals corresponding to those who smile: {c, d}.
5 'Loves' is assigned as its interpretation in the model a set of ordered pairs corresponding to who loves whom: {⟨a, a⟩, ⟨c, d⟩, ⟨d, c⟩}.

Compositional rules:

1 A sentence of the form $N+V_I$ is true with respect to the model if and only if the individual constituting the interpretation of N is a member of the set comprising the interpretation of V_I.
2 A sentence of the form $N+V_T+M$ is true with respect to the model if and only if the ordered pair consisting of the interpretation of N followed by the interpretation of M is a member of the set comprising the interpretation of V_T.
3 A sentence of the form S_1+'and'$+S_2$ is true with respect to the model if and only if S_1 is true with respect to the model and S_2 is true with respect to the model.

---

structure. An intransitive verb is likewise assigned an interpretation consisting of a set of individuals: the interpretation of *smiles*, for instance, consists of a set containing the individuals c and d, thereby indicating that Charles and Diana smile. This interpretation of the verb can be equivalently expressed as a *characteristic* function, which returns the value true or false for each individual in the model, depending on whether or not that individual is a member of the set in question. Generally speaking, the characteristic function for *smiles* will change from one moment to the next as some individuals start smiling and others stop, but for simplicity I have introduced a model structure representing one moment of time. A transitive verb is interpreted as a set of ordered pairs of individuals, e.g., the ordered pair $\langle c, d \rangle$ in the interpretation of *loves* indicates that Charles loves Diana. The interpretation of this verb can also be treated as a characteristic function from the complete set of ordered pairs of individuals to a truth value; and the function for *loves* yields the value *true* for $\langle a, a \rangle$, $\langle c, d \rangle$ and $\langle d, c \rangle$, and the value *false* for all the remaining ordered pairs. The rules of syntax permit such sentences as 'Anne smiles', 'Charles loves Charles and Diana smiles', 'Anne loves Charles and Diana loves Charles and . . .'. There is no bound on the length of a sentence, because the rule introducing *and* is recursive. The truth value for a sentence is similarly built up recursively by rules that operate in parallel to the syntactic rules: first, the lexical entries provide an interpretation for the basic words in a sentence, and second, the compositional rules build up an interpretation of complex expressions such as sentences or clauses from the interpretations of their constituents. For example, consider the interpretation of the sentence:

Charles loves Diana and Diana smiles.

Its structure is built up by the syntactic rules in the way shown in Figure 8.1. The proper names pick out the corresponding individuals in the model, and the ordered pair of individuals named in the first clause is a member of the set that is the interpretation of the verb, and the individual named in the second clause is a member of the interpretation of the verb. Hence each clause is true, and this condition in turn fulfils the semantic rule 3 for conjunction, and thereby yields a true sentence.

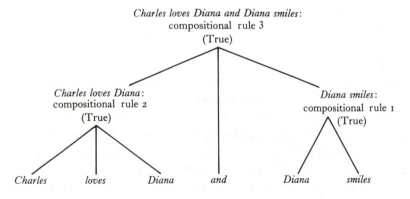

Figure 8.1 The structure of a sentence generated by the grammar of Table 8.1.

Possible worlds

The full development of model-theoretic methods and their extension to the analysis of natural language was made possible by two major developments. First, Tarski (1956, originally published in 1936) defined the notion of truth for a formal language and showed how to cope with sentences such as 'Every mother has a child who loves her', where the relative clause 'who loves her', unlike the clauses in the conjunction above, cannot have a truth value in isolation. Tarski's solution was to introduce a more general notion, *satisfaction*, which applies to such constituents, and to use it in turn to define truth. An ordered pair of individuals in a model structure, say, Anne and Diana, satisfies the expression 'who loves her', only if the pair is a member of the set of pairs assigned as the interpretation of the verb *loves*, and the second member of the pair is female. Second, Hintikka (1963), Kripke (1963a, b), and others showed how to formulate a model-theoretic semantics for the so-called 'modal' logics of necessity and possibility. A fundamental assumption that goes back to Leibniz is that a proposition which is *necessary* is one that is true in all possible worlds, and that a proposition which is *possible* is one that is true in at least some possible world(s). Logicians talk of 'possible worlds' rather than the more cumbersome 'possible states of affairs'; they take the real world to be a member of the set of possible worlds. What Kripke and the others introduced was the idea that not every possible world has to be entertained in considering necessity and possibility: an assertion is necessarily true in a particular world if and only if it is true in all possible worlds that are *accessible* from that world. Different assumptions can be made about the logical properties of the accessibility relation, and depending on them the resulting semantics corresponds to different modal logics that had been axiomatized, but not, hitherto, given a model-theoretic interpretation.

The introduction of possible worlds into model-theoretic semantics provides one way in which to clarify the Fregean distinction between intension and extension. The intension of a predicate – the property that it captures – can be treated as a function from the set of possible worlds to sets of individuals; the extension of the predicate is the particular set of individuals to which it applies in the particular possible world under consideration. Psychologically, one would want to know what information is in the 'body' of the function corresponding to the intension of predicate, i.e., what has to be computed in order to specify the individuals possessing the property. This problem is finessed in model-theoretic semantics, which merely posits the existence of such functions without indicating how they would work. The intension of a sentence – the proposition that it expresses – can be treated as a function from the set of possible worlds to truth values (*true* and *false*); the extension of the sentence is its truth value in the particular possible world under consideration. The sentence 'Hitler is dead' is true in the actual world, but false in some other possible worlds. The proposition that it expresses is accordingly captured by its division of the set of possible worlds into those in which it is true and those in which it is false.

In fact, this account is over-simplified, because the proposition expressed by a sentence in ordinary language generally depends on the context in which it occurs – the time and place, the speaker and listener, and so on. Thus, the sentence 'You look tired' expresses different propositions depending on its context, particularly the person to whom it is addressed. This notion of context can also be treated as a possible world (Kamp, 1971; Kaplan, 1977). The meaning of a sentence is accordingly a function from the set of possible worlds representing contexts to the specific propositions expressed by the sentence in the different contexts. These different propositions in turn have different truth values in different possible worlds. The proposition expressed by a particular use of the sentence above may be true in the actual world, i.e., the addressee does look tired, but obviously it could be false in other possible states of affairs.

The abstract account of context, as a possible world, as I remarked in discussing conditionals in Chapter 3, sets a dangerous example for psychology. It suggests that context is an external inert 'object' – a set of indices corresponding to time, place, speaker, addressee, and all the other relevant referents – that waits passively to be used in the interpretation of an utterance. This conception is doubly misleading. First, the notion of *the* context overlooks the fact that an utterance generally has at least two contexts: one for the speaker and one for the listener. The differences between them are not merely contingent, but, as I shall show in analysing discourse (in Chapter 14), a crucial datum for communication. Second, just about any item of information could be relevant to the interpretation of an utterance – a fact that was once used to argue that there could be no theory of contextual effects (Katz and Fodor, 1963). Certainly, listeners generally have no way of knowing what will be relevant until they hear the utterance. In this sense, a sentence defines its own context when it is uttered (Johnson-Laird, 1967). Of course, there is a current model of the discourse that provides essential contextual information, but an utterance may well cause listeners to search their memories for relevant background. If, for instance, I ask you:

Do you love Lady Diana?

then your knowledge that Lady Diana is married to Prince Charles, etc., plays a vital part in determining what question you are being asked. You are not being asked whether you love her in the same sense that you love family and friends (unless, that is, you are Prince Charles and I am Prince Philip), but whether you 'love' her as a public personality. The relation between you and Lady Diana is part of the context of the utterance, and you have to recover that knowledge to which the sentence directs you in order to grasp its significance. There is a mental mechanism that retrieves the relevant information with striking efficiency, though how it works is largely unknown.

Montague grammar

The application of model-theoretic semantics to natural language is principally the work of Montague (1974) and other like-minded theorists. It has relied on the use of 'possible worlds' in order to cope both with sentences expressing modal notions and with other sorts of expression whose extensions, as Frege foresaw, cannot be built up compositionally from the extensions of their constituents. Assertions about propositional attitudes such as beliefs or wants, and terms like *alleged* and *former*, for example, cannot be treated in a simple extensional manner. Montague integrated a variety of techniques in formal semantics in order to analyse various 'fragments' of English. One of his major aims was to establish that the principle of compositionality could be made to work in a rigorous way for natural language. He used a system of different semantic *types* that were constructed to run in parallel to the different grammatical categories of his theory. There are two basic types: e, entities, and t, truth values; but complex types can be built up recursively for any function from one type to another. As Table 8.1 illustrated, a set designated by an intransitive verb can be represented by its *characteristic* function, which returns the value *true* or *false* for each individual in the model depending on whether or not that individual belongs to the set in question. Hence, such terms are of the type $\langle e, t \rangle$ since they are interpreted as functions from entities (type e) to truth values (type t). The underlying simplicity of Montague's scheme is overlaid by several factors, including his somewhat rebarbative notation; and readers with little taste for technicalities may omit what follows without too much loss in continuity.

In the analysis of noun phrases, Montague uses an approach which, though familiar to logicians (see Mostowski, 1957), is different from the normal method illustrated in Table 8.1. The idea is to treat all the different sorts of noun phrase, such as *Betty, a woman, every woman, no one*, in the same uniform way. The syntactic rules for specifying noun phrases can then be matched one-to-one with semantic rules according to the compositional principle. Since the extension of a predicate such as *smiles* is interpreted as a set of individuals, the extension of each predicate that applies, say, to Betty consists of a set of individuals, included in which, of course, is Betty herself. Only Betty will be a member of all of these sets, because if two individuals are in exactly the same extensions of predicates they must be identical. Hence the denotation of the noun phrase *Betty* is a set of sets, viz., the set of all the sets of which *Betty* is a member. (As Barwise (1980) has pointed out, if you want to have your cake and eat it, you can treat the proper noun *Betty*, as opposed to the noun phrase *Betty*, as picking out the relevant individual in the model in the simple way illustrated in Table 8.1.) This way of treating noun phrases as of the type $\langle\langle e, t\rangle, t\rangle$, i.e., sets of sets, is illustrated in detail in Table 8.2. It can be readily extended to deal with any sort of noun phrase. Thus, the extension of *every woman* consists of all the sets in the model that contain every woman; the extension of *a woman* consists of all the sets that contain at least one woman; the extension of *no one* consists of all the sets that contain no persons (in a richer model they will contain other sorts of entity such as inanimate objects). The procedure may seem mystifying at first, but it is perfectly sensible, and has several advantages over the more traditional approach since it can cope with noun phrases like *most women* and *few people*, and with noun phrases that include relative clauses like *every woman who has had a child*.

An important syntactic function of noun phrases is to serve as the subject of a sentence. Hence, semantically, any given noun phrase divides verb phrases into two: those which yield a true sentence (with respect to a given possible world) when combined with the noun phrase, and those which yield a false sentence (with respect to a given possible world) when combined with the noun phrase. Noun phrases are accordingly of type $\langle\langle e, t\rangle, t\rangle$ because they denote functions that map sets $\langle e, t\rangle$ that correspond to the interpretations of verb phrases to truth values $\langle t\rangle$. This parallel should be noted: syntactically, a sentence S consists of an NP combined

Table 8.2 *The semantic treatment of noun phrases as sets of sets.*

Determiners

'Some' is interpreted as a function that is applied to the set N, corresponding to the interpretation of the noun, and that yields the set of all sets in the model that have at least one member in common with N.

'Every' is interpreted as a function that is applied to the set N, corresponding to the interpretation of the noun, and that yields the set of all sets in the model that include N.

Noun phrases

Suppose that the model consists of the set {a, b, c}, corresponding to Alice, Betty, and Cecil, and the following lexical assignments:

'woman': {a, b}
'man': {c}
'smiles': {a, c}
'loves': {⟨a, b⟩, ⟨c, b⟩, ⟨b, a⟩}

The following interpretations can then be made:

'Some woman': {{a}, {b}, {a, b}, {a, c}, {b, c}, {a, b, c}}
'Every woman': {{a, b}, {a, b, c}}
'Betty': {{b}, {a, b}, {b, c}, {a, b, c}}

Sentences

A sentence is true if and only if the set corresponding to its predicate is a member of the set comprising the interpretation of its subject noun phrase. The sentence 'Some woman smiles' is accordingly true in the model because the interpretation of 'smiles' is a member of the set comprising the interpretation of 'some woman', but the sentence 'Betty smiles' is false because the interpretation of 'smiles' is not a member of the interpretation of 'Betty'.

Where the predicate is a verb phrase containing an object noun phrase, as in 'loves Betty', it is interpreted as the set of x's such that the interpretation of the object noun phrase has as a member the set of all y such that ⟨x, y⟩ is in the verb's interpretation. The interpretation of 'loves' is: {⟨a, b⟩, ⟨c, b⟩, ⟨b, a⟩} and the only x's in the appropriate pairs are a and c. Hence, the interpretation of 'loves Betty' is {a, c}. The sentence 'Some woman loves Betty' is therefore true in the model, since the interpretation of its predicate is a member of the set comprising the interpretation of its subject noun phrase, but the sentence 'Betty loves Betty' is false because its predicate's interpretation is not a member of its subject's interpretation.

---

with a VP; semantically, its interpretation of type $\langle t \rangle$ is a result of combining an NP's interpretation, of type $\langle \langle e, t \rangle, t \rangle$, with a VP's interpretation, of type $\langle e, t \rangle$. In general, if something of semantic type $\langle a, b \rangle$ is combined with something of type $\langle a \rangle$, then the result is of type $\langle b \rangle$. As Table 8.2 shows, a sentence such as *Betty smiles* is true if the set of individuals denoted by the verb *smiles* is a member of the set denoted by the noun phrase *Betty*. Once again, this way of proceeding may seem counter-intuitive, but a moment's thought should clarify matters. If one of Betty's properties is that she smiles at the moment of time embodied in the model, then one of the sets denoted by the noun phrase *Betty* will consist of all the individuals smiling at that time. Hence, the set comprising the denotation of the verb *smiles* will indeed be a member of the set denoted by the noun phrase *Betty*, provided that the sentence is true. This principle holds equally for the interpretation of the other sorts of noun phrase, as the reader may readily check by experimenting with the model in Table 8.2.

There are several further layers of complexity in Montague's approach. Clearly, a model cannot usefully represent just a single moment of time in a single world: it is necessary to introduce a set of possible worlds indexed by moments of time. It is possible to interpret certain modal logics as governing, not possible worlds, but moments of time. Depending upon the properties of the accessibility relation between moments of time, so the resulting logic treats time as discrete or continuous. However, Montague regarded the structure of time as a contingent matter and assumed merely a simple ordering relation, $\leq$, over moments of time. The extension of a sentence is its truth value in a particular moment in a particular world.

To capture the synonymity of pairs of expressions such as *seek* and *try to find*, Montague introduces a 'meaning postulate' that stipulates the required relation. This takes the form of a postulate specifying that in any world and at any time someone *seeks* something if and only if they *try to find* it, and Montague's semantics for noun phrases allows that a search need not be for a particular entity. A meaning postulate is a stipulation in the semantics that constrains the set of interpretations: it rules out certain otherwise possible worlds, in this case worlds in which an individual seeks something without trying to find it. Montague also uses meaning postulates to ensure that a proper name picks out the same individual in all possible worlds. (The question of whether a proper name does denote the same individual in every possible world has attracted much philosophical attention: see, e.g., Kripke, 1972. The whiff of medieval disputation associated with the topic is a consequence of the abstract nature of model-theoretic semantics.) Finally, to ensure the greatest possible generality, Montague treats all expressions intensionally at first: the semantic rules build up intensions compositionally. Some expressions, of course, are extensional in that their truth values depend only on the extensions of their constituents – e.g., *Charles loves Diana* has a truth value that depends only on the extensions of *Charles*, *loves*, and *Diana*. If an expression is extensional in this way, then its extensionality is also stipulated by meaning postulates.

In his treatment of quantification, Montague (1974) showed how to translate a fragment of natural language into a formal language – a tensed intensional logic, for which he provided a model-theoretic interpretation. Table 8.3 briefly summarizes the main notation of this logic for those readers with an interest in such technicalities. However, there is no need for a translation into an intermediate language: a model-theoretic semantics can be provided for natural language directly, as Montague (1974) showed for the fragment characterized in his paper on English as a formal language.

There are a number of important methodological principles that distinguish Montague grammar from other theories of language. Logicians had previously taken the view that natural language did not wear its logic on its sleeve. There were, for example, allegedly important differences between the semantics of noun phrases such as *No woman* and *Betty*. Montague introduced a new conception of natural language, as a system that could be analysed as a formal language in which constituents with the same syntactic role can be treated as having the same basic semantics, and distinguished if need be by meaning postulates. Indeed, he assumed that the rules of semantic interpretation should run in parallel to the rules of syntax. Chomsky (1957) established the need for recursive rules in the grammar of a language, and there is a similar need for recursive rules to capture the meanings of sentences. Montague exploited a direct relation between the two sorts of rules, with each semantic *type* corresponding to a syntactic category, and each compositional rule corresponding to a grammatical rule. Designers of programming languages have an actual choice of whether or not to follow this strategy, and in the early days of high-level programming languages at least one language unwisely had its syntax specified independently from its semantics (Hamish Dewar, personal communication). Experience has shown that compositionality on a rule-by-rule basis works best for programming languages. Chomsky (1977), however, has rejected the compositional principle and defended the autonomy of syntax in natural language; he argues that syntax is not a means for ensuring the proper composition of meaning-bearing elements. Such is the power of an analysis in terms of functions – as is illustrated by the two radically different treatments of the semantics of noun phrases in Tables 8.1 and 8.2 – that it is unclear how much empirical content there is in this controversy.

Table 8.3 *The notation of Montague's intensional logic*

1 *Quantifiers and connectives*

Montague makes use of the familiar truth-functional connectives, which he designates in the following way: ∧ for conjunction, ∨ for inclusive disjunction, → for implication ('if'), ↔ for equivalence ('if and only if'). He also makes use of the standard universal quantifier, 'for any x', which he symbolizes $\bigwedge x$; and the standard existential quantifier, 'there exists an x', which he symbolizes $\bigvee x$.

2 *Lambda calculus*

Montague relies on Church's lambda calculus, which provides a way of designating functions, properties, and relations, rather than their values. $(\lambda x)(x^2)$ designates the function that squares a number, and thus $(\lambda x)(x^2)(3)$ designates the value obtained when the function is applied to 3, viz., 9. Likewise, $(\lambda x)(\text{Woman }(x))$ designates the characteristic function for woman, i.e., the set of x's that are women, and $(\lambda x)(\text{Loves}(x, \text{Anne}))$ designates the set of individuals that love Anne. Hence, $(\lambda x)(\text{Loves}(x, \text{Anne}))(\text{Betty})$ asserts that Betty is in the set of individuals who love Anne. The rules of the lambda calculus permit the conversion of formulas to their equivalents, e.g., $(\lambda x)(x^2)(3)$ can be converted to 3^2, and $(\lambda x)(\text{Woman}(x))$ (Betty) can be converted to Woman(Betty).

3 *Intensions*

Montague uses the symbol '∧' as a prefix to any symbol in order to form a new expression with an extension that is the *intension* of the prefixed symbol. If b is a constant whose extension in the model is an individual (corresponding, say, to Betty), then $\hat{b}$ denotes an individual concept, i.e., the function that picks out Betty in any world at any time. He uses the symbol ''' to denote the function from English to intensional logic – e.g., *smiles'* is the constant into which the word 'smiles' is translated. Because Montague operates at the level of intensions, *smiles'* designates not the characteristic function for the set of individuals that smile, but rather the characteristic function for the corresponding set of individual concepts. Montague uses $\hat{P}$ as a special notation for (λP) to designate the set of properties P. $\hat{P}[P\{x\}]$ designates the set of properties P such that x possesses P.

4 *Examples of the notation*

Betty : $\hat{P}[P\{\hat{b}\}]$, i.e., the set of properties such that the individual picked out by the function $\hat{b}$ has those properties.

Every woman : $\hat{P}\bigwedge x [woman'(x) \to P\{x\}]$, i.e., the set of properties P such that for any x if x is designated by the function *woman'*, x has those properties.

Some woman : $\hat{P}\bigvee x [Woman'(x) \land P\{x\}]$, i.e., the set of properties such that there exists an x in the set designated by the function *woman'*, and x possesses those properties.

Every woman smiles : $\hat{P}\bigwedge x [woman'(x) \to P\{x\}]$ ($\hat{smiles'}$), i.e., the property of individual concepts expressed by 'smiles' is in the set of properties corresponding to every woman. Since this is an extensional expression, it can be reduced by λ-conversion to the customary formula: for any x, if x is a woman then x smiles. In general, extensional formulas will have exactly the same extensions as they would in Table 8.1.

Model-theoretic semantics and the psychology of meaning

The power of model-theoretic semantics resides in its explicit and rigorous approach to the composition of meanings. It provides a theory of semantic properties and relations, e.g., a set of premises *entails* a conclusion if and only if the conclusion is true in every model in which the premises are true. Its techniques enable a theorist to formulate a precise account of how the meaning of a sentence is composed from the meanings of its constituents according to the syntactic relations between them. But those techniques inevitably demand that certain idealizations be made about language: this price must, of course, be paid by any scientific theory. Some of the idealizations are trivial; but not everything is for the best in the best of all 'possible worlds' semantics. Some idealizations definitely compli-cate the 'ecumenical' use of model-theoretic semantics as a guide to psycho-logical semantics. One such idealization is the mapping of language to model without any reference to the human mind, and this omission gives rise to certain intractable difficulties with the semantics of sentences about *beliefs* and other such propositional attitudes. The difficulties are readily resolved within the framework of mental models (see Chapter 15). Another important idealization is the notion that there is a function that directly provides each basic lexical item with an interpretation in the model structure. The use of a direct assignment of interpretations to the basic lexical items does indeed seem a plausible simplification granted that when theorists lay down the law about meanings, they generally attempt to specify the necessary and sufficient conditions for the application of a term. If the vocabulary of natural language is truly explicable in this way, then simple lexicography should reveal the required sets of necessary and sufficient conditions, and the assumption that basic intensions can be taken as primitive and unanalysed functions is a justified way of avoiding unnecessary lexical analysis. As Thomason wrote in his introduction to Montague's (1974) collected papers:

We should not expect a semantic theory to furnish an account of how any two expressions belonging to the same syntactic category differ in meaning. 'Walk' and 'run', for instance, and 'unicorn' and 'zebra' certainly do differ in meaning, and we require a dictionary of English to tell us how. But the making of a dictionary demands considerable knowledge of the world. The task of explaining the particular meanings of various basic expressions will obviously presuppose, if not factual information, at least a minutely detailed terminology for classifying things of all kinds. Perhaps even pictures or a museum of representative specimens would have to be counted as 'terminology' – after all, there are words in English such as 'meter' and 'yard'.

Unfortunately, Thomason is wrong in supposing that one can look to lexicographers, and to dictionaries of English, to find out the difference in meaning between such words as *walk* and *run*. Dictionaries can provide competent speakers of a language with useful clues to the meaning of a word, but their limitations for certain words have been known to dictionary-makers for a very long time (see Dr Johnson's satirical definition of *horse* as 'an equine quadruped', and *network* as 'anything reticulated or decussated, at equal distances, with interstices between the intersections'). Moreover, the meanings of words do not, unlike their counterparts in model-theoretic semantics, map simply into the world.

The interpretation of basic lexical items by entities in the model-structure is handled by a function that operates by fiat: there is no need to specify how a predicate such as *woman* is mapped into a model. This idealization masks an important difference between model structures and mental models. If a model-theoretician wishes to take cognizance of the fact that all women are necessarily adults, then it is a simple matter to add a meaning postulate to that effect: the postulate rules out any model-structure in which a woman is not adult. As we shall see, some psychologists have been tempted to assume that meaning postulates are the natural way to handle the mental lexicon too. In the case of a mental model, however, it is necessary to assume that there must be functions that (1), construct a model containing an entity satisfying the predicate *woman*, (2), evaluate a given model to determine whether it contains an individual satisfying the predicate *woman*, and so on. Moreover, a psychologist is naturally going to be concerned with how those functions work – indeed, Chapter 11 lays out a theory of precisely this sort. What has too often been overlooked is that once the functions carrying out semantic interpretations are given some 'body' in this way, it is no longer necessary to use meaning postulates to constrain the interpretations of lexical items. For example, the body of the function that determines whether or not an individual in a mental model is a *woman* will naturally be able to check *en passant* that the individual is adult: only adults can be women. This point is so important that I shall come back to it again. Meanwhile, it need hardly be added that the relation of expressions to the model-structures of formal semantics is very different from their relation to the world. That relation is a matter which we must now take up because, whatever it is, it is the basic ingredient in the recipe for sentence meaning.

9

What is meaning?

When one descends from the heights of formal semantics, where the light has an unreal clarity, to the low-lying realities of psychology, the atmosphere is, to say the least, somewhat murky. Meanings as model-theoretic interpretations are idealizations – abstract theoretical fictions, though none the less useful for all that. The principle of compositionality can certainly be borrowed by an account of the psychology of meaning. However, there is one puzzle about meaning finessed in model-theoretic semantics that has to be solved before we can pursue the analogy between model-structures and mental models any further: what exactly is the meaning of a word? This question calls for a semantic analysis of meanings, and it is distinct from the psychological question: how is the meaning of a word mentally represented? The first question has some claim to priority because at least one answer to it is, paradoxically, that meanings are entities that cannot be in the mind. Hence, I propose to answer this question in the present chapter, and to discuss the question of mental representation in the next chapter. Only when I have tried to resolve the mystery of lexical meaning will I turn to the formulation of a semantics that maps propositional representations into mental models.

The true nature of meaning has puzzled thinkers from the very beginnings of philosophy, and there are several intertwined themes running through the history of its analysis that need to be disentangled. The most crucial one for our purposes is the contrast between the claims of Psychologism, the view that meanings are mental constructions imposed on the world, and those of Realism, the doctrine that meanings are determined by the nature of the world and are wholly independent from the way in which the mind works. This controversy is as entrenched as any of the standard philosophical disputes, and it would take an audacious writer indeed to claim to have settled it. That is not my goal. Instead, I have only the more modest aim of resolving the controversy in so far as it affects the psychology of meaning.

Realism and Psychologism

The philosophy of Realism, which can be traced back to Plato, holds that meanings are independent of the mind. Its most important defender in modern times was Frege (1953, originally published 1884), who argued that one should always distinguish between the truth conditions of a proposition and an account of the mental processes by which one becomes conscious of them. He considered that words are correlated with actual entities in the universe. Hence, nouns refer to 'objects', which include physical objects, numbers and points in space; and predicates and relational terms refer to more complex 'concepts', which are abstract rather than mental entities. But in all these cases, the referents of expressions are real entities awaiting discovery rather than mental constructs awaiting invention. A concept is accordingly an entity that is true of some objects and false of others; it is defined by the essential characteristics of the objects of which it is true.

In pursuing the consequences of Realism, Frege took great care to separate, on the one hand, sense and reference, and, on the other hand, the *idea* associated with a sign. He wrote:

If the reference of a sign is an object perceivable by the senses, my idea of it is an internal image, arising from memories of sensory impressions which I have had and acts, both internal and external, which I have performed. Such an idea is often saturated with feeling; the clarity of its separate parts varies and oscillates. The same sense is not always connected, even in the same man, with the same idea. The idea is subjective: one man's idea is not that of another. There results, as a matter of course, a variety of differences in the ideas associated with the same sense. A painter, a horseman, and a zoologist will probably connect different ideas with the name, 'Bucephalus'. This constitutes an essential distinction between the idea and the sign's sense, which may be the common property of many and therefore is not part of the individual mind. For one can hardly deny that mankind has a common store of thoughts which is transmitted from one generation to another. (Frege, 1892)

The doctrine that there is a *real* sense of a sign, distinct from any individual's idea of it, which somehow society is able to possess as public property and to pass down to the next generation, is likely to perplex any psychologist. How can the sense of a sign be the property of many and passed from generation to generation without entering the mind? And yet, if it does enter the mind – and Frege and his successors certainly assumed that meanings did enter the mind – then in what way is it different from

183

an idea? The fact that people may have different ideas about the object denoted by a sign does not imply that necessarily they cannot possess a common idea about the sense of the sign.

A very different doctrine of meaning was promulgated by the Swiss linguist Ferdinand de Saussure, the father of both structuralism and modern linguistic theory. In his lectures from 1907 to 1911 at the University of Geneva, which were published posthumously (see de Saussure, 1960), he took the view that a sign consists of a form (the 'signifier') that is mentally associated with a concept (the 'signified'). In the case of natural language, the particular sound-form that is bound to a concept is arbitrary in that there is no natural connection between them except in cases of onomatopoeia. However, the particular semantic value that a concept has depends on what other concepts exist. Indeed, de Saussure insists that it is only possible to define a concept in terms of its relations to other concepts. (He made the same point about phonemes – the basic sounds of a language – and this assumption underlies the modern phonological theory of distinctive features.) Hence, the French word *mouton* and the English word *sheep* can have the same signification – an expression that de Saussure seems to have used to mean the extension of a sign – because they can both be used to refer to a sheep; but they differ in semantic value because English contains the word *mutton* for referring to meat, whereas there is no equivalent word in French. The concepts for which there are signs plainly differ from one language to another, and are by no means immutable, but capable of change from one generation to another. 'If words stood for pre-existing concepts', de Saussure (1960, p. 116) observed, 'they would all have exact equivalents in meaning from one language to the next, but this is not true'. He here advanced an implicit argument against both Realism and the extreme form of Nativism that holds that all concepts are innate (see, e.g., Jerry Fodor, 1980). While de Saussure evidently took the same view as Frege that language transcends what occurs in any individual's mind, he did not adopt the philosophy of Realism in which there is some objective realm that provides the necessary and sufficient conditions that define the sense of any term. On the contrary, de Saussure claimed that the links between words and mental concepts reflect the relational nature of the organization of the lexicon. They are associations that bear the stamp of societal approval; meanings are determined by the structures of the mind. A more extreme brand of Psychologism asserts that language deals not with the world but with a world-view. One species of this argument with which psychologists are familiar is the doctrine of linguistic relativity promulgated by Whorf (1956). Another species of it is that the laws of logic are nothing but the principles by which the mind works.

Meanings as necessary and sufficient conditions

Before we can follow the controversy between Realism and Psychologism any further, we must take up the questions of whether the concepts corresponding to words consist of necessary and sufficient conditions. Obviously, both language and thought necessitate treating different things as though they were the same for some purposes, and mental concepts provide the machinery for subsuming entities under a common heading. Until recently, philosophers and psychologists alike have assumed that the different entities subsumed by a concept necessarily have some element (or elements) in common, and that this set of elements suffices to define the concept. Although this notion is identical to Frege's thesis that there are essential characteristics for the application of each word, an earlier source is the work of John Locke. Locke (1961, originally published 1706) took the view that there is an objective reality, but human understanding of it is at best partial and invariably dependent on 'ideas' that mediate between reality and understanding. Words stand for ideas, and hence general words stand for general ideas. Locke accounted for the origin of general words by a process of abstraction in which idiosyncratic details are gradually dropped to leave behind only what holds in common:

For, let anyone reflect, and then tell me wherein does his idea of 'man' differ from that of 'Peter' and 'Paul', or his idea of 'horse' from that of 'Bucephalus', but in the leaving out something that is peculiar to each individual, and retaining so much of those particular experiences as they are found to agree in? Of the complex ideas signified by the names 'man' and 'horse', leaving out but those particulars wherein they differ, and retaining only those wherein they agree, and of those making a new distinct complex idea, and giving the name 'animal' to it, one has a more general term that comprehends, with man, several other creatures. (Locke, 1961, Vol. I, Book III, Chapter 3, Sec. 9)

Locke went on to stress that what is general and universal does not belong to the real existence of things, but is an invention of human understanding.

This notion of a concept might almost be a 'blueprint' for the psychological investigation of conceptual thinking. Most of the studies in the literature have indeed employed a technique in which the subjects have to discover the common element that characterizes some particular concept. Hull, who used this procedure, argued that the meaning of a word such as *dog* is 'a characteristic more or less common to all dogs and not common to cats, dolls, and teddy bears'. As a result of diverse pairings of word and exemplar, a child gradually acquires a knowledge of the common element. 'But to the child the process of arriving at this meaning or concept has been largely unconscious' (Hull, 1920). The Russian psychologist L. S. Vygotsky independently took a very similar view, arguing that children, schizophrenics, and certain brain-damaged patients, are not capable of the abstract thought required to isolate the common element from the mass of irrelevant attributes (see Vygotsky, 1962). Nearly all the standard procedures for investigating conceptual thinking in the laboratory have their origins in the studies of these pioneers (see Campbell, Donaldson, and Young, 1976). The procedures take for granted that the processes by which subjects deliberately seek to acquire explicit concepts are similar to those that occur in the implicit acquisition of concepts in everyday life. They are based on the assumption that simple concepts are definable as sets of necessary and sufficient conditions, and that complex concepts are definable as Boolean functions – negation, conjunction, disjunction, and their combinations – of simple concepts. Hence, psychologists have investigated the acquisition of such concepts as A and B, not-C, D or E, where A, B, C, etc., denote simple characteristics such as round, large, and green. The fact that disjunctive concepts are very difficult to learn appeared to vindicate the 'common element' thesis (Bruner, Goodnow, and Austin, 1956) – a concept such as *green or square* subsumes instances such as a green circle and a red square that have no element in common.

An alternative view is that these studies are not representative of what occurs in the ordinary acquisition of concepts (see Johnson-Laird and Wason, 1977, p. 177). The discrepancy hinges on several points. First, the concepts that are used in daily life are seldom Boolean functions of independent characteristics. On the contrary, they tend to have a relational structure that cannot even be captured within a Boolean algebra. Thus, the everyday concept of a table is not just a conjunction of a top and some legs: the legs *support* the top. When such relational concepts are used in the laboratory, they yield a significant improvement in performance – e.g., children leap a whole developmental stage in Piaget's classification (Markham and Seibert, 1976). Second, in the unlikely event that you want to teach somebody the concept of, say, *green or square*, you would not do so by using the standard experimental procedure in which they chose a sequence of different stimuli, such as a red circle, a green triangle, a blue square, and you tell them which items are instances of the concept. You

186

would instead give them a direct definition of the concept. The experimental procedure is appropriate only for those concepts that are indefinable, e.g., styles of music, or varieties of wine. Studies using such materials have only recently begun to be carried out (see Smith and Medin, 1981). Third, if an ordinary concept has a common element, then it is likely to concern function rather than form. Experimental studies, however, have often failed to distinguish between a concept and the perceptual characteristics of its exemplars.

Some of these criticisms were anticipated by workers in the Gestalt tradition. In opposition to Hull, Smoke (1932, p. 5) wrote, 'As one learns more and more about dogs, his concept of "dog" becomes increasingly rich, not a closer approximation to some bare "element" . . . No learner of "dog" ever found a "common element" running through the stimulus patterns through which he learned.' Smoke's own view was that what one learned was 'the total pattern' which constituted the concept. This notion, like much of Gestalt psychology, was by no means clear. It is only now, some fifty years later, that cognitive science has become equipped to offer an explicit analysis of what perhaps Smoke had in mind.

Criteria and schemata

The historical see-saw between Realism and Psychologism can be seen most vividly at play in the works of Wittgenstein. In his earlier philosophy, Wittgenstein (1922) advanced a Realist theory of semantics: the meaning of a proposition is its truth conditions. If a proposition is true, then it corresponds to a state of affairs in the world. How you come to know the truth conditions, and even whether you are able to come to know them, are wholly irrelevant to semantics; similarly, the state of affairs in the world that renders a proposition true is entirely independent of the operations of the mind.

After he had written the *Tractatus*, Wittgenstein ceased to be interested in philosophy for some years, because he was convinced that he had solved its essential problems. What woke him from his slumbers, according to Herbert Feigl, was his attendance in Vienna in 1928 at a lecture given by L. E. J. Brouwer, the founder of Intuitionism. In the lecture, as it is summarized by Hacker (1972), Brouwer argued that the human mind imposes order on reality and constructs mathematics, science, and language. Language serves the social and communicative function of expressing the individual's will. To know the meaning of a statement is not just to know its truth conditions, but to grasp what would count as its proof or verification, that is, the conditions under which the statement is warranted. Logical principles are also human constructions rather than eternal verities reflecting the a priori structure of reality. You may not be warranted in asserting either a proposition or its negation, if that proposition concerns the existence of a mathematical property possessed by a natural number. The assertion is warranted only if you can show how to construct a number with the required property; its negation is warranted only if you can show that such a construction is impossible, and, since you cannot establish the latter condition by examining each of the infinite set of numbers, it calls for a demonstration of the self-contradictory nature of the property in question. Brouwer's semantics thus leads him to reject the principle that either a proposition or its negation is true – the so-called law of the excluded middle.

How far Wittgenstein was directly influenced by Brouwer is a matter for conjecture. However, a plausible interpretation of his later philosophy – an interpretation advanced by Dummett (1959), Hacker (1972), and Baker (1974) – is that he shifted from one end of the see-saw to the other, from Fregean Realism to a generalized Intuitionistic theory. Certainly, one of the main elements of his later philosophy is his rejection of the idea that concepts can be defined in terms of essential characteristics or necessary and sufficient conditions. In a well-known passage of his *Philosophical Investigations*, he wrote:

Consider for example the proceedings that we call 'games'. I mean board-games, card-games, ball-games, Olympic games, and so on. What is common to them all? – Don't say: 'There *must* be something common, or they would not be called "games"' – but *look and see* whether there is anything common to all. – For if you look at them you will not see something that is common to *all*, but similarities, relationships, and a whole series of them at that. To repeat: don't think, but look! – Look for example at board-games, with their multifarious relationships. Now pass to card-games; here you find many correspondences with the first group, but many common features drop out, and others appear. When we pass next to ball-games, much that is common is retained, but much is lost. – Are they all 'amusing'? Compare chess with noughts and crosses. Or is there always winning and losing, or competition between players? Think of patience. In ball games there is winning and losing; but when a child throws his ball at the wall and catches it again, this feature has disappeared. Look at the parts played by skill and luck; and at the difference between skill in chess and skill in tennis. Think now of games like ring-a-ring-a-roses; here is the element of amusement, but how many other characteristic features have disappeared! And we can go through the many, many other groups of games in the same way; can see how similarities crop up and disappear.

And the result of this examination is: we see a complicated network of similarities overlapping and criss-crossing: sometimes overall similarities, sometimes similarities of detail.

I can think of no better expression to characterize these similarities than 'family resemblances'; for the various resemblances between members of a family: build, features, colour of eyes, gait, temperament, etc. etc. overlap and criss-cross in the same way, – And I shall say: 'games' form a family. (Wittgenstein, 1953, pp. 31–2)

If there are no essential characteristics corresponding to a term, then on what basis is it applied? Wittgenstein talked of *criteria*. The notion is controversial and rejected by some critics (e.g., Chihara and Fodor, 1965), but Hacker (1972) and Baker (1974) offer an illuminating interpretation. Criteria are fixed neither by experience, which supports inductive generalizations, nor by logical necessity, which supports entailments. They are fixed by convention. Hence, the criterial relation does not fall into any orthodox logical category: it is weaker than entailment but stronger than an inductive generalization. A natural way in which to construe criteria is as *default* values (Minsky, 1975), that is, as characteristics of an object that can be assumed unless there is evidence to the contrary. Thus, the criteria for the application of the term *dog* – those characteristics that can be taken for granted – include having four legs, fur, a tail, the ability to bark, and so on. Yet, plainly, these are not necessary conditions of doghood – a dog can have three legs or lack a tail. Likewise, they are not inductions based on observation. They could not be, for you would need to know what counts as a dog before you could carry out such a survey. They are part of the concept of a dog, part of what Wittgenstein called the 'grammar' of things. Moreover, since criteria are determined by what it is possible to think, it follows that truth and falsity are not independent of human cognitive capacity.

If concepts depend on criteria, then contrary to Frege's doctrine, they have no clear-cut boundaries. They have 'blurred edges', and are no more circumscribed by their criteria than a game is completely specified by its rules. Hence, when you teach someone the meaning of a word, you describe examples of its range of application. You begin with typical cases, and deal with border-line ones by reference to the norm. You try to convey a *schematic* model corresponding to the concept. In the *Critique of Pure Reason*, Kant wrote:

In truth, it is not images of objects, but schemata, which lie at the foundation of our pure sensuous conceptions. No image could ever be adequate to our conception of triangles in general. For the generalness of the conception it never could attain to, as this includes under itself all triangles, whether right-angled, acute-angled, etc., whilst the image would always be limited to a single part of this sphere. The schema of the triangle can exist nowhere else than in thought, and it indicates a rule of the synthesis of the imagination in regard to pure figures in space.

Hence, a schema is not an image, but a model that underlies the ability to form an image. In a Kantian vein, Wittgenstein asks himself whether there might not be samples of a colour or an object that function as schemata – say, a schematic leaf, or a sample of *pure* green. And he answers: 'Certainly there might. But for such a schema to be understood as a *schema*, and not as the shape of a particular leaf, and for a slip of pure green to be understood as a sample of all that is greenish and not as a sample of pure green – this in turn resides in the way the samples are used' (Wittgenstein, 1953, p. 35). And, of course, precisely this point was borne out in the notion of mental models as representative samples.

The notion that a concept might be represented by a schema, and moreover a schema that specifies, *not* a set of necessary and sufficient conditions, but the typical or default characteristics of the items it subsumes, has surfaced from time to time in psychology. In one of the first studies of concept attainment, Fisher (1916) reported the development of schematized and conventional images corresponding to an idealized picture of the conceptualized object. Bruner, Goodnow, and Austin (1956) talked of a 'typical instance' of a concept, and reported that subjects had less difficulty in setting a colour wheel to the typical colour of an eating-orange than to the acceptable boundaries of the colour. This phenomenon was replicated in an influential cross-cultural study carried out by Berlin and Kay (1969). They asked native speakers of twenty different languages to trace out the boundaries (in an array of coloured chips) of each of the language's basic colour terms, and also to pick out the best example of each colour. There was little agreement from one speaker to another about the boundaries of colours, and even an individual subject's choices would vary from one session to another. But there was a reliable consensus about the best exemplars of a colour, and this agreement extended to a considerable degree over the twenty different languages. These results suggest that there are indeed 'focal points' in the space of possible colours. This work was followed up in a variety of studies by Eleanor Rosch (e.g., Rosch, 1976, though cf. Lucy and Shweder, 1979), who argued that many natural categories are mentally represented by *prototypes*, i.e., schemata of their most characteristic members. Real objects, unlike the concepts studied in the psychological laboratory, have features that are correlated – feathers tend to be found on wings, and scales on fins – and the pattern of correlations is reflected in the schema. A crucial datum corroborating the theory is that not all instances of a concept are deemed equally representative – a robin is a prototypical bird, whereas a chicken is not – and such judgments seem to depend on 'distance' from the schema.

Are meanings in the mind?

The fact that many words lack necessary and sufficient conditions for their application might be thought to vindicate Psychologism in its long battle with Realism. Not so. Indeed, the very phenomenon has been used by Hilary Putnam to advance the strongest possible Realist thesis: *meanings are not in the mind*.

Putnam (1970) starts with the familiar observation that there are words whose meanings cannot be analysed into sets of necessary semantic components. The meaning of *lemon*, for instance, might be decomposed into such characteristics as: round, yellow, having peel, having a tart taste, and so on. Yet none of these components is necessary: a green lemon is still a lemon, a sweet peel-less lemon is still a lemon. Hence, the meaning of *lemon* cannot be captured by such meaning postulates as:

for any x, if x is a lemon, then x has peel

because the purpose of meaning postulates is to specify necessary truths (see Chapter 8). The set of characteristics is to be explained instead by a theory, scientific or pre-scientific, of the 'essential nature' of lemons. Putnam dubs those words whose meanings depend on such theories of underlying structure 'natural kind terms'. In telling someone what the meaning of *lemon* is you generally sketch a *simplified* theory of what it is to be a lemon: you describe a typical lemon, a normal member of the class of lemons. Such a description, according to Putnam, provides a stereotype for lemons that will help the listener to recognize them. Hence, Putnam's notion of a stereotype seems to correspond to a schematic model defined in terms of default values. The stereotype does not specify the extension of the word, though if the stereotype were to change, then the word *lemon* would certainly have changed its meaning. The extension, Putnam claims, is determined by some test – though no particular test may be necessary – or by providing a sample. There are tests, for example, for establishing whether or not something is *gold*. However, there is a division of linguistic labour: these tests are known only to experts, and are not part of the stereotype governing the ordinary use of the word. Certain core facts are thus necessary and sufficient to convey to someone else the use of a word, namely, the stereotype and the extension – though often nothing need be said about the extension, since listeners know that they can consult an expert in case of difficulty.

In subsequent papers, Putnam (1973, 1975) tackles the question of what initially determines the extension of a natural kind term. He adopts a position, independently reached by Kripke (1972), that the extension is fixed by the ostensive reference that accompanied the original giving of the name, that is, it is fixed by the actual properties of the object(s) used in defining a natural kind term for the first time. This fixing occurs regardless of whether the underlying properties of the object were known to the original users of the term. It is easy to see that the same stereotype could be associated with terms that have different extensions. Putnam considers a number of imaginary instances of the phenomenon. One example is based on a world that is a counterpart to ours except that the extension of *water* is not H_2O but a different substance. Speakers in both that world and ours may have had exactly the same stereotypical concept of *water* in the seventeenth century, yet the extension of the term was totally different in the two worlds. The remainder of Putnam's argument against the mental embodiment of meaning is straightforward. By definition, the extension of a term is specified by its intension. Since a stereotype does not determine an extension, it cannot be an intension; and since a stereotype is the only concept of many terms that speakers possess, it follows that speakers do not possess intensions. Intensions cannot be mental objects: *meanings*, in Putnam's words, *just ain't in the head*.

Mental meanings

I began this chapter by asking what the meaning of a word is, and in pursuing this question I have been led progressively further away from psychology to the point where its answer appears to have nothing to do with what is in anyone's mind. Something at least is to be found in the mind, and something that has to do with the meanings of words. I have no quarrel with the thesis that stereotypes, i.e., schemata defined by default values, rather than sets of necessary and sufficient conditions, are our only mental baggage for some words, but I do want to attempt to qualify Putnam's conclusion and to restore the study of meaning to psychology.

A natural kind term such as *water* may have been introduced originally in order to refer to a particular sort of stuff, in ignorance of its essential nature, and regardless of what that nature turned out to be. In this case, it is true that the original users of the term did not know its extension, and so its intension could not have been in their minds. Like those who introduced the term, most of us also have nothing more than a stereotype, yet we believe with Michael Faraday that 'water is one individual thing – it never changes'. Chemists armed with appropriate tests can identify pure water: they provide the rest of us with a more determinate extension for the term. But even that extension should not be confused with what water *really* is: according to Putnam and Kripke, water is the same in all possible worlds (the term is technically, though maladroitly in this instance, a 'rigid designator') and its extension is fixed by the underlying structure of the actual stuff that was picked out ostensively when the term was introduced.

Unfortunately, there is no reason to suppose that the current chemical tests for water are infallible. As Putnam (1975) allows: 'whether something is or is not the same liquid as *this* may take an indeterminate amount of scientific investigation to determine. Moreover, even if a "definite" answer has been obtained either through scientific investigation or through the application of some "common sense" test, the answer is *defeasible*: future investigation might reverse even the most "certain" example.' Hence, some ingenious scientists – elsewhere in the universe, perhaps – may already have discovered a whole aspect of chemistry unknown to us. What we call *water* is really a set of different substances for which they have no generic name. This imagined situation raises the interesting question: which of these different substances is the 'real' water, that is, the substance that was used in the original dubbing ceremony when the term was introduced? An answer is most unlikely to be forthcoming, and, I submit, could never be established definitively. It follows that no one will ever know whether the true extension of water has been discovered.

Putnam has considered a related problem. He discusses the case of jade, which is evidently two different substances, jadeite and nephrite, with the same textural properties. The solution here, he says, is to say that there are two sorts of jade. But, there are equally plausible alternatives – perhaps adopted elsewhere in the universe – one is to abandon the use of the term altogether in favour of separate terms for each substance, and another is to restrict the term to just one of the two substances, the one that is the 'real' jade in the Putnamian sense.

Any natural kind term may suffer the hypothetical fate outlined above for *water*. But there is a more drastic possibility against which language itself cannot legislate: it is possible, though admittedly highly unlikely, that the whole notion of natural kinds turns out to be mistaken. What I have in mind is not Putnam's account of the phenomenon, but the phenomenon itself. Perhaps God will ultimately reveal that there is no common underlying structure, or 'essential nature', for any natural kind term. What would happen then? Of one thing we can be sure: people would not cease to refer to a certain class of liquids as *water*. The illusion of an underlying structure would be maintained by the superficial characteristics of water. Perhaps the intentions of those who originally coined the term would have been thwarted, but its usefulness would continue as long as there were bits of stuff around that possessed the requisite superficial characteristics.

Putnam (1975) admonishes us to avoid the mistake of assuming that the instances of a natural kind necessarily have a common underlying structure. It could indeed turn out that *water* has only superficial characteristics common from one drop to another. As Putnam says, the necessary and sufficient condition for being water would then be the possession of enough of these superficial characteristics. There are two aspects of this thesis worthy of comment. First, following Kripke (1972), Putnam takes the view that it is *conceivable* that water is not H_2O, but that it is not logically possible; that is, once the empirical discovery has been made that water *is* H_2O then this truth is a logically necessary one, true in all possible worlds. Hence, if water is truly H_2O, then it is necessarily H_2O, but the grounds for holding that water *is* H_2O are defeasible along the lines sketched above. We do not know that we know its true extension – perhaps we do, perhaps we don't. Second, the thesis that there are necessary and sufficient conditions for classes defined only by their superficial characteristics seems unrealistically Realist in tone. A more plausible doctrine is that they too have an intension consisting of a schema.

The major element of 'science fiction' in Putnam's theory is the notion, which he has taken from Kripke's (1972) account of names, that extensions are transmitted by a causal chain stretching back to their original introduction. This doctrine may apply to proper names. Natural kind terms, however, can change their extensions over time. For example, the word *tree* originally designated oak trees, and the word *cattle* first meant property, then moveable property, then livestock, and only finally bovine animals. The cause of such changes is little understood, but their existence seems beyond doubt. Speakers come to use words in ways that no longer coincide with their original uses, and so the extensions of natural kind terms are not immutable. This fact obviously makes it harder to recover the intentions of those speakers who introduced a term that now functions to denote a natural kind. They may have intended it to do so, or they may have intended it to pick out a class of entities only on the basis of superficial appearance. *Most likely, they were simply not aware of what they were doing, and the nature of the distinction never crossed their minds.*

Scepticism about the causal chain account of the transmission of meaning should not be allowed to affect the status of natural kind terms. There *are* words that are used to refer to classes of entity whose underlying nature is elucidated only by a theory. Natural language would be a poor instrument for communication, or for externalizing thought, if it only contained terms specifying classes in virtue of sets of necessary and sufficient conditions. It is very useful to be able to point at some substance and say, 'Let's call that kind of stuff, whatever it is, *blodge* from now on.' However, the true intension of such a word – always supposing that it has one – is not very interesting: either it is in an expert's mind (though no one can know for sure that the right meaning is there), or it is in no one's mind and accordingly an idle wheel in the intellectual traffic of the world. All that it is necessary to acknowledge is that *some* words are used to refer to entities without anyone knowing for certain what the essential nature of these entities is, or indeed whether they have one. If the extension of a word is fixed ostensively or by reference to a sample, then a plausible empirical hypothesis is that each natural kind term refers to a class whose members bear a superficial perceptual resemblance to one another. The class must generally be sufficiently homogeneous to merit baptism, though the speaker introducing the term may intend to designate a class sharing some as yet unknown underlying structure. If this structure remains unknown, then the only factor likely to maintain the use of the term is superficial resemblance.

The nature of intensions

The moral of these deliberations is that the nature of meaning differs from one word to another: intensions are not uniform. The moral is obvious in the case of words coming from different parts of speech. What, perhaps, is less clear is that even in the case of common nouns there are important differences in meaning. Some nouns are 'analytic' in that their meaning comprises a set of essential conditions that support necessary truths. The noun *uncle*, for example, supports the truth of 'An uncle is a brother of a parent.' If you are sceptical about this claim, as some philosophers such as Quine (1953) tend to be, then perhaps you will allow that speakers can introduce a technical term that is defined by stipulation as a set of necessary and sufficient conditions. My favourite examples come from the London Building Amendment Act, 1939, wherein one discovers the following definitions (here freely paraphrased):

A warehouse class of building is a warehouse, manufactory, brewery, distillery, or any other building exceeding 150,000 foot cube which is neither a public nor a domestic building.
A public building is a hotel, hospital, school, or any building open to the general public exceeding 250,000 foot cube.
A domestic building is one which is not a public building or a warehouse class of building.

These definitions clearly support necessary truths.

Other nouns such as *apple*, *silver*, and *yeti*, are indeed natural kind terms. Their true intensions are unknown, and their mental representations consist of schemata specified by default values that correspond to simple theories of their designata.

Still other nouns like *home*, *chair*, and *melody*, have what I shall call a 'constructive' semantics. The intensions of these words are mental constructions, imposed on the world, and although they designate entities in the world those entities do not possess an underlying structure that determines their membership of the extension. Constructive terms have no objective correlates in reality; their meaning is a matter of convention and is open to social negotiation, particularly in the case of dubious exemplars. The names of artifacts are also constructive, because what is central to their specification is their intended function rather than their intrinsic structure. What counts as a chair or an automobile is not determined by the essential structure of the *real* classes of these entities; it depends solely on schemata that different exemplars resemble to a greater or lesser degree. There is no need for tests known only to experts and no fixing of extensions by the ostensive use of samples.

Other parts of speech contain items with a constructive semantics. Consider, for example, the spatial preposition *at*. As Miller and I discovered in writing *Language and Perception*, it is one of those annoying little words that seems sufficiently close to being a primitive to defy analysis. Indeed, Bennett (1975) takes it as primitive in his analysis of prepositions; and

196

other definitions in the literature include:

x is at y: x is near or in y, with the constraint that x is portable relative to y, and y is not a geopolitical area. (Cooper, 1968)

x is at y: x is contiguous or juxtaposed with the place of y, where the dimensionality of y is not significant. (Leech, 1969)

The problem is to determine the truth conditions of the following sorts of sentence:

John is at the window.
The chair is at the table.
The bicycle is at the repair shop.

Even with simple circular discs, as Lucy Velicogna and I found (in an unpublished experiment), the meaning of *at* is not simple: there is a region of uncertainty between those arrangements of the discs for which subjects will definitely accept an assertion of the form *a is at b* and those arrangements for which they definitely reject it in favour of *a is near b* – a phenomenon that casts doubt on Cooper's definition above; the actual distances depend on the relative sizes of the discs. Miller and I suggested:

to say 'x is at y' is to say that x is included in the region of y, that is, x is where it can interact with y socially, physically, or in whatever way x's conventionally interact with y's.

If this analysis is on the right lines – and it certainly has complexity on its side in comparison to its rivals in the literature – then underlying the meaning of *at* is an indefinitely large series of relations concerning the ways in which x's of one sort interact prototypically with y's of another sort. The term is clearly constructive: its semantics is conventional and ultimately a construction of the human mind rather than a direct mapping onto some objective relation in the world. Of course, the 'rules of the game' are often incomplete, and so there is an indefinite number of problematical cases. Some of them can be eliminated on the grounds that the relevant entities do not normally interact in any way:

The chair is at the ocean liner.
Bill is at Australia.

But others such as:

Ann is at Beryl

require us to consider the taxonomic organization of the mental lexicon, a matter to which I shall return at the end of the chapter.

The nature of extensions: vagueness and fuzzy sets

If certain words depend on schematic models defined by default values rather than by necessary and sufficient conditions, then what is the nature of their corresponding extensions? Putnam (1975) suggests that the elucidation of extensions calls for the apparatus of fuzzy sets, and several linguists and psychologists have independently adopted this approach (e.g., Lakoff, 1972; Halff, Ortony and Anderson, 1976). However, despite its appeal, I shall argue that it is mistaken.

In orthodox set theory, on which model-theoretic semantics relies, an entity is either a member of a set or not; in fuzzy set theory, membership can be partial ranging over the real number continuum, or some less dense set of numbers, from zero to unity. It follows that truth values must similarly range over the same continuum in order to cope with assertions about set membership (e.g., 'John is a tall man').

What does it mean to say that a sentence has a truth value of, say, 0·75? Some people find the question genuinely perplexing; some are only puzzled by the perplexity of others. None the less, it is important to distinguish between three theoretically different states of affairs:

1. An uncertainty about something that is intrinsically determinate.

2. A certainty of the exact indeterminacy of something that is intrinsically indeterminate.

3. An inability to decide an issue because it is outside the 'rules of the system'.

If you are uncertain about whether Homer existed, you are in the first state of mind. If you know that the probability of an unbiased coin coming down heads is 0·5, you are in the second state of mind. If you cannot decide whether the size of the goalkeeper's gloves is permissible, because the laws of the game say nothing explicitly about the matter, you are in the third state of mind. Likewise, you may be uncertain about the truth value of a particular sentence, such as 'Shakespeare wrote *Hamlet*', or you may be unable to decide the truth value of a sentence because the meaning of a word in it is constructive and does not legislate for the relevant case, as in 'A lightshade is a piece of furniture.' What seems incoherent is the idea that a truth value is something that is intrinsically indeterminate, and that you can be absolutely certain that a sentence has a truth value of, say, 0·75. Of course, a generic assertion may be true three times out of four for the specific instances that it covers, but that condition is a very different matter. One says, 'Three out of four marriages end in divorce', and agrees that this proposition is true (or false). One does not say, '"Marriages end in divorce" expresses a proposition that has a truth value of 0·75.' The fact that the *evaluation* of a proposition may vary over a continuum from absolute conviction to absolute rejection creates an atmosphere conducive to thinking that truth values may similarly vary, but degree of conviction should not be confused with truth value.

A further difficulty with fuzzy sets is that truth-functional connectives have to be redefined for them. For example, the connective *and* in its logical sense is a simple truth function: *p and q* is true if and only if *p* is true and *q* is true. But if *p* and *q* can have intermediate truth values, then it is necessary to specify the resulting truth value of *p and q*. Rescher (1969) has shown that there is no satisfactory way of framing such a semantics. Supposing that both *p* and *q* have truth values of 0·5, what truth value should be assigned to *p and q*? Presumably it cannot be greater than 0·5, since a conjunction of two propositions can hardly have a stronger truth value than either of them, and it must be greater than zero, since a conjunction of two intermediate values can hardly be completely false. If a proposition *r* has a truth value of 0·25, then presumably the truth value of *not-r* should be at least as large if not larger: it would have the truth value of 0·75 if the negation of a proposition is true to exactly the same extent that the proposition itself fails to be true. It follows from these two principles that any self-contradiction of the form *p and not-p* will have a truth value greater than 0 – e.g., if *p* has a value of 0·25, *not-p* has a value greater than 0·25, and the conjunction of the two is greater than zero. This consequence is absurd, because a self-contradiction surely merits a truth value of zero. However, if *p* has a value of 0·5 and the truth value of *p and not-p* is set as zero, how can one avoid *p and p* having a truth value of zero? All the obvious ways of specifying rules for *and* and *not* do violence to our intuitions about natural language. These arguments count decisively against the adoption of a fuzzy-set semantics for natural language (see Osherson and Smith, 1981, for other, though related, shortcomings of fuzzy logic).

A much more fruitful analogy for dealing with the 'blurred edges' of extensions comes from probability theory. If the probability of an *event p* equals 0·5, and the probability of an *event q* equals 0·5, then what is the probability of *p and q*? If you are not familiar with probability theory, you may be stumped for a moment. But, suppose that *p* is the event of an unbiased coin coming down heads, and *q* is the event of the same coin coming down tails: then the probability of *p and q* is zero. Suppose, now,

199

that p is the probability of the coin coming down heads and q is the probability of the same coin coming down with the date uppermost, where head and date are on the same side: then obviously the probability of p and q is $0\cdot5$. Finally, consider the case where p is the event of the coin coming down heads and q is the event of another unbiased coin also coming down heads. Then the probability of p and q equals $0\cdot25$ since there are four possible joint outcomes (head + head, head + tail, tail + head, tail + tail). These examples establish that a knowledge of the respective probabilities of p and q is not sufficient to estimate their joint probability, which is determined by the extent to which one event is dependent on the other. This analogy suggested to Hans Kamp (1975) an alternative way of treating vagueness.

Kamp starts from the assumption that some predicates are vague: speakers of a language may be uncertain about whether a predicate applies to a particular object. For example, it may be unclear whether or not Mary is tall, and consequently the assertion 'Mary is tall' will be neither true nor false. The trouble with such a 'truth gap' is that an assertion such as:

Either Mary is tall or Mary is not tall

should nevertheless be true. Van Fraassen (1969) suggested a way out of the problem: truth gaps are filled in using all the different ways which are possible without logical inconsistency. Hence, in some completions of truth gaps the sentence 'Mary is tall' will be true, and in the other remaining completions it will be false. In every completion, however, the semantics for *or* will ensure that the disjunctive assertion above will come out true. This method of filling in truth gaps can be adopted for discourse as well as for individual sentences. If, for example, there are truth gaps for both the following assertions:

Mary is tall
Julia is tall

then there will be a set of completions in which both Mary and Julia are classified as tall, another in which Mary is tall but Julia is not, and so on. Kamp adopts the sensible principle that if, say, Mary is actually taller than Julia, then Julia should never be classified as tall without Mary being classified as tall too.

Kamp formalizes a theory of vagueness based on these assumptions within the framework of model-theoretic semantics, and he shows how truth values ranging from 0 to 1 can be assigned to sentences. Each vague sentence has a set of completions associated with it, and the proportion of interpretations in which it is true can be interpreted as its truth value. The conjunction of two vague assertions has associated with it a set of completions in which both conjuncts are true: this set is simply the intersection of the corresponding sets for the two conjuncts, but its proportional size will depend on the independence of the two conjuncts in just the way that is required to yield sensible truth values for *p and not-p* and *p and q*. Although the proportions can be interpreted as truth values, Kamp has agreed (personal communication) that it might be better to treat them as degrees of certainty in the truth value of a proposition.

Is vagueness a problem?

The pervasiveness of vagueness in language is undeniable and it has often been treated as a problem by logicians, lawyers, and others with a vested interest in precision. In fact, vagueness is a solution rather than a problem. But, in order to understand the problem that vagueness solves, one must distinguish between different varieties of vagueness.

A speaker can be deliberately imprecise in answering a question and thereby fail to provide the requisite information. Similarly, a metaphor or figure of speech may be misleadingly vague. However, the alleged problems of vagueness arise not in these uses of language, but from its fundamental semantics. An extension may be vague as when one asks whether Mary is tall, or a relation between intensions may be vague as when one asks whether a lightshade is an item of furniture. These two phenomena, which I shall call 'extensional vagueness' and 'intensional vagueness', should be considered separately though they have roots in common.

Certain aspects of language are extensionally precise. A proper name, if it picks out anyone, picks out one and only one individual. If all predicates were extensionally precise, however, then the boundaries between classes of objects in the world would be mapped with absolute precision. Such a mapping would have to be easy to use and to remember, and, like an Act of Parliament, it would have to legislate for future states of affairs. Those who laid down the law about animals, vegetables, and minerals, would have to do so for entities that they had never encountered and that would exist only in the future as a result of the development of new varieties. This demand is unrealistic, particularly in the light of the way in which children acquire the meanings of words. It would be a massive undertaking to specify such boundaries, and learning them would be likely to defeat any ordinary human being.

An alternative way of specifying extensions is plainly called for – one that is easy to acquire, open to the future, and simple to use. It is based on two cardinal principles: the representation of classes of entities by schemata, and the taxonomic interrelation of schemata. Our concepts of objects and properties consist of specifications of the criteria of typical instances. The boundaries of a word's extension are set, not by its schema, but by the nature of the particular taxonomy in which the schema occurs. Whether something is to count as a *dog* depends on its similarity to typical dogs, typical cats, typical foxes, and so on; whether something is to count as a *table* depends on its similarity to typical tables, benches, desks, and so on. This idea goes back in part to de Saussure, and the variety of taxonomic relations was explored in depth by Miller and Johnson-Laird (1976). The most clear-cut relations are hierarchies created by class-inclusion, e.g., poodle – dog – mammal – animal – physical object, and contrastive sets, e.g., the basic colour terms. But many semantic fields have a complex structure. Table 9.1 shows a simplified version of the decision table that we proposed for capturing the interrelations between the spatial concepts corresponding to *in*, *on*, *at*, and *with*. An assertion such as:

Ann is at Beryl

Table 9.1 *A decision table representing the semantic relations underlying the concepts corresponding to* in, on, at, *and* with *(based on Miller and Johnson-Laird, 1976, p. 391)*

Semantic conditions								
1 x (or part of x) is included in y	+	+	+	+	−	−	−	−
2 x is included in the region of the surface of y & y supports x	−	−	+	+	+	+	−	−
3 x is included in the region of y		+	+	+	+	+	+	+
4 y is included in the region of x		+	−	+	−	+	−	
Expressions								
1 x is in y	+	+	+	+				
2 x is on y			+	+	+			+
3 x is at y						+		+
4 x is with y					+	+		

Note. Each column represents a different combination of conditions, where '+' denotes the presence of a condition and '−' denotes the absence of a condition. Those combinations that correspond to *in*, *on*, *at*, or *with* are indicated by a '+' opposite the relevant expression. For example, whenever at least part of x is spatially included in y, the conditions for the expression 'x is in y' are satisfied, as in 'the spoon is in the cup', 'the train is in the station', and 'the needle is in the cushion'.

is odd even if the relation between the two corresponds to the meaning of *at*. As the decision table shows, where there is a symmetrical relation between x and y, one says *x is with y*, and there is no ordinary way in which one person can be in the region of interaction with another without the converse relation holding too. The greater acceptability of such sentences as:

The doctor is at Beryl now

said when the doctor is, say, attending her after an accident, and there is thus a functional asymmetry between them, lends further support to this analysis.

The advantage of a taxonomic organization of the lexicon is precisely that it yields vagueness in extensions – speakers are not forced to be precise in cases where they are ignorant – without a concomitant uncertainty in the communication of ideas. The only real problems that arise are when an object is 'equi-distant' from a number of prototypes in the taxonomy. A taxonomy allows for relatively simple meanings of words that can be encoded as schemata and that can be readily acquired by children. Indeed, Keil (1979) has argued that children are predisposed to taxonomize, and he has attempted to work out the order in which they master different members of the ontology of classes. The use of schemata can give rise to intensional vagueness: the 'rules of the game' are incomplete, which can be a virtue in the case of new developments in the world. If intensional vagueness begins to yield systematic difficulties in communication, it is always possible to introduce more specific technical terminology. If extensional vagueness creates a problem, it is always possible to formulate more specific predicates in the language. The beauty of the mental lexicon is that its organization is quite able to accommodate 'analytic' relations between intensions, and precise extensional specifications.

Conclusions

Are meanings in the mind or in the world? Is Realism or Psychologism right? Do concepts have necessary and sufficient conditions or not? The answer is that all of these questions appear to be false antitheses. The meanings of some words are mental constructions that are imposed upon the world in the absence of an objective correlate. Other words, however, are used to refer to classes of entity whose underlying structure is unknown. Such words pick out something in reality, but their intensions may at best be known only to a few experts. Still other words have a semantics that is stipulated or constructed as a set of necessary and sufficient conditions, which support analytic inferences. Language embodies no particular metaphysics; it embraces both Realism and Psychologism. However, psychology has the last word. Whatever the semantics of a term, its relation to the world depends on human cognitive capacity. A word with a Realist semantics would only be coined or maintained in use by virtue of its associated mental schema. Likewise, whatever the semantics of a term, it is not mentally represented in isolation. Words are taxonomically organized in the mind, and whether they have an exhaustively analytic semantics or only a stereotypical meaning, their taxonomic interrelations play a role in determining the boundaries of their extensions and, of course, in their ready use and interpretation in discourse.

10

How is the meaning of a word mentally represented?

There is a very odd phenomenon that occurs with words. Everyone is familiar with it, but it seldom draws comment from psychologists or linguists. The phenomenon is this. On the one hand, when you are taking part in normal conversation, you readily choose words appropriate to your communicative purposes, and grasp the meanings of the words in other people's utterances. I ask you, for example, 'Have you ever spent any time in Sussex?' and you understand me without any difficulty. On the other hand, if I extract one of my words from its setting and ask you what it means, then you may be extremely perplexed. What exactly is the meaning of the word *time*, which occurred in my utterance? One is reminded of St Augustine's remark: 'What, then, is time? If no one asks me I know what it is. If I wish to explain it to him who asks, I do not know.' Children have the happy knack of stumping us with such questions. Indeed, we think we understand words – we must understand a good part of them – yet we often have considerable difficulty in bringing to mind an appropriate semantic analysis of them. It is perhaps significant that one modern thinker to comment on the phenomenon was the poet Paul Valéry (1939). In a telling image, he likened it to a man crossing an abyss on a narrow plank: everything is fine if he keeps moving – the plank will just support him – but if he should stop to think, the plank will break beneath him.

An obvious consequence of the difficulty of semantic analysis is that lexicology is a preoccupation of many intellectual disciplines. We have no immediate access to the semantic content of the words we use: we have to sit and think about the matter. It *is* odd that the mind is organized so that it regularly makes use of knowledge that may pass its own understanding in this way. Such oddities should not be lightly put aside: they provide important clues to the underlying nature of human mentality.

Another notable consequence of 'the plank across the abyss' is that it raises a question to which introspection provides no guide whatsoever: how is the meaning of a word mentally represented? There are three main answers to this question in the psychological literature, and in this chapter I am going to expound each of them in turn, demonstrate their individual

205

shortcomings, and finally show that some assumptions that they have in common are grounds for a collective rejection of them.

Lexical decomposition

The theory of semantic markers

Some psychologists argue that words are represented in a mental dictionary that *decomposes* their meanings into semantic components. The origin of this idea is to be found in the linguistic theory of Katz and Fodor (1963). They assumed a version of the compositional principle: the semantic interpretation of a sentence is obtained by replacing its words with their semantic representations, and combining these representations according to the underlying syntactic structure of the sentence. They also held that the semantic representation of a word primarily comprises a structured set of elements, 'semantic markers', which decompose its meaning into more primitive semantic constituents; ultimately meanings are decomposable into a set of 'linguistically universal' and innate components. Underlying the meaning of *woman*, for example, are the fundamental concepts of *human*, *female*, and *adult*. If you look in a good dictionary, you will find such entries as:

handsome, *adjective* 1. (of actions) generous
2. (of persons or artifacts) having a pleasing appearance
3. . . .

in which each sense of the word is constrained by information about its context. Katz and Fodor elevated this lowly piece of lexicography into linguistic theory. If a word has several distinct meanings, the process of combining its meanings with those of other words is sensitive to the constraints, or 'selectional restrictions', that its different senses place upon the meanings of the other words with which it occurs. One sense of *handsome* is restricted to human beings and artifacts, and another, to conduct. Hence, neither *a handsome prince* nor *a handsome act* is ambiguous: each noun meets the selectional restrictions of only one sense of the adjective.

Table 10.1 presents a simplified example of the decompositional analysis of words together with the semantic representation of a sentence. Since the theory assumes that the meanings of words can be decomposed into

Table 10.1 *A simplified example of the analysis of meaning in terms of semantic markers*

Words in the lexicon

man	(noun)	HUMAN, ADULT, MALE
child	(noun)	HUMAN, NOT (ADULT)
lift	(verb transitive)	CAUSE (ACTIVITY X, UPWARDS (MOVE) Y),
		where X is the subject and Y is the object

The semantic representation of the sentence: 'A man lifts a child'
CAUSE (ACTIVITY (HUMAN, ADULT, MALE), UPWARDS (MOVE) (HUMAN, NOT (ADULT)))

sets of necessary and sufficient conditions, the main modification that it has undergone in its psychological versions is the introduction of a distinction between necessary and characteristic components of meaning (Smith, Shoben, and Rips, 1974) in order to cope with the phenomenon of prototypes, which I described in the previous chapter.

The quest for effects of semantic complexity

If comprehension requires the meanings of complex words to be decomposed into their semantic constituents, then, on the plausible assumption that this process should take time, the sentence 'A man lifts a boy' should be harder to understand (and perhaps occupy more space in memory) than 'An adult lifts a child'. However, there seem to be no such differences. Kintsch (1974) was unable to find any effects of semantic complexity on a number of measures, e.g., the time taken to begin to speak a sentence containing a given word. Fodor, Fodor, and Garrett (1975) recorded the time taken to evaluate such deductions as:

If practically all of the men in the room are not married, then few of the men in the room have wives.

When the word *bachelor* occurred in place of *not married*, the inference was made reliably faster, and the improvement was greater than that created by a so-called morphological negative such as *unmarried*. These authors concluded that a word such as *bachelor*, unlike *unmarried*, does not contain a negative in its semantic representation – though it ought to, according to its definition. In another study Fodor, Garrett, Walker and Parkes (1980) failed to find any evidence for a complex representation of sentences with verbs, such as *kill*, which ought to contain a causal component.

Although the negative findings suggest that decomposition is not an inevitable part of comprehension, they may fail to convince sceptics. There is no reason to suppose that the latency to make up a sentence should be affected by the semantic complexity of words (cf. the studies of definitions described later in the chapter). Kintsch's other experimental tasks might not require a subject to decompose meanings even if that were part of normal comprehension. Consider, for example, the study in which the recall of a sentence (e.g., 'John was accused of stealing') was cued by a word denoting a relevant semantic component (e.g., *guilty*). Such a cue was no better than a close associate of a word in the original sentence (e.g., *blame*). This finding could be explained without giving up the idea of decomposition: subjects may have drawn the inference that John was blamed for the theft. Likewise, Fodor, Fodor, and Garrett's conclusion – that the representation of *bachelor* does not include a negative – may not be justified by a mere difference in latency of response: a negation in a dictionary entry might be responded to faster than a morphological or explicit negation. Fodor, Garrett, Walker and Parkes (1980) may also have used a task that failed to call for the semantic decomposition of words, though it was plainly sensitive to the semantic structure of sentences.

It was with these possible objections in mind that Til Wykes and I took up the quest for effects of semantic complexity using a different experimental task. In our first experiment, the subjects were presented tachistoscopically for two seconds with a question, such as:

Who got the book from whom?

The question was replaced after a blank interval of half a second by an assertion, such as:

Mary took the book from Tom

and the subjects had to respond with the appropriate sequence of nouns (*Mary*, *Tom*) that answered the question on the basis of the information provided by the sentence. The questions were always in the active voice; half the subsequent sentences were in the active, and half were in the passive voice. On half the trials, the same verb occurred in both the question and the sentence, and on the other half the two verbs were different. We also manipulated the semantic complexity of the verbs. Both question and assertion were devised so that they could contain either one (or both) of a pair of verbs matched as far as possible for length and frequency of occurrence, but differing in semantic complexity, e.g., *move – throw, follow – chase*, and *take – steal*. The pair *take* and *steal*, for

KEY: Simple Verb in Assertion ☐
Complex Verb in Assertion ▨

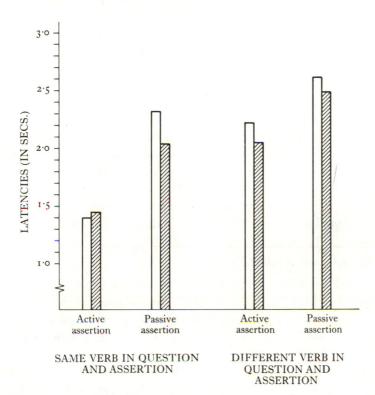

Figure 10.1 The mean latencies (in seconds) of correct responses to the assertions containing simple or complex verbs (from an unpublished experiment by Johnson-Laird and Wykes).

example, differ in complexity in the required way, because stealing necessarily implies taking, but taking does not necessarily imply stealing; according to a decompositional analysis, the semantic representation for *take* must be simpler than the representation for *steal* in order to capture this pattern of inferences.

We recorded the latency of each response from the onset of the assertion to the time the subject began speaking. Figure 10.1 presents the mean latencies for those trials on which the subjects made correct responses (the errors were minimal). As one would expect, the passive assertion produces a reliably longer latency: presumably the task of switching round the names to correspond to the order required by the active question takes an additional amount of time. Likewise, the task takes significantly longer when the verb in the question is different from the verb in the assertion: in these cases, the subjects must do some semantic processing in order to work out the answer to the question. This aspect of the task should force semantic decomposition to occur if it ever occurs, whereas when the two verbs are the same, it may be possible to answer the question on the basis of a superficial 'syntactic' strategy, i.e., merely switching round the order of the two nouns in a passive sentence to respond to the question. The difference in latencies is compatible with these explanations. If there is an effect of semantic complexity, then it should occur pre-eminently when a semantically simple verb occurs in the question and a semantically more complex verb occurs in the assertion. There was no such effect; and overall there were no effects of semantic complexity on performance of the task.

In a second experiment, Wykes and I used a slightly different procedure. An assertion was presented tachistoscopically for two seconds, and then after a blank interval of half a second a simple question was presented, such as:

Who had the book first?

The subjects' task was to produce the appropriate name on the basis of the preceding assertion. There were only two variables: whether the answer was the subject or object noun phrase of the assertion, and whether the verb in the question was simple or complex. Once again, this variable had no reliable effect on the latencies to respond.

There are several ways open to the proponents of decompositional theories to reject these findings, too. They might argue that our experiments were not sensitive enough to detect the effects of semantic complexity. The difference in meaning between such pairs of words as *take* and *steal* is indeed a relatively small one; unfortunately, pairs with a greater difference in meaning invariably differ in both length and frequency of usage. A more radical defence is simply to abandon the assumption that decomposition is a process that takes a measurable amount of time: it might be carried out almost instantaneously by an extremely efficient set of parallel processes. These defences considerably weaken the theory, especially bearing in mind the obviously detectable effects of the passive voice or of having two different verbs in the question and assertion.

Evidence that might be interpreted as consistent with the decompositional hypothesis is that sentences containing inherently negative terms tend to take longer to verify than sentences containing their affirmative counterparts. Herb Clark and his colleagues have shown such effects in a variety of ingenious studies. For example, a sentence such as 'The circle is absent' takes reliably longer to evaluate than 'The circle is present' (Clark, 1974). Similarly, Sherman (1973) found that deciding on the self-evident truth of a sentence such as:

Since she had been laughing for the last hour, we assumed she was happy

took less time than to evaluate the corresponding inherently negative sentence:

Since she had been crying for the last hour, we assumed she was unhappy.

Such effects of lexical 'marking' and negation invariably show up in verification or reasoning tasks (see Clark and Clark, 1977). But, as Clark and his colleagues allow, they do not necessarily corroborate the decompositional hypothesis, since the experimental task requires more than mere comprehension. Although negation is semantically a simple unary operator, it has the effect of changing the truth value. If p is true, then $not-p$ is false. It is this effect rather than a decompositional process that appears to cause the problem. Indeed, if a series of inherently negative words occurs in a sentence, the task of keeping track of the truth value of the simple 'atomic' proposition becomes difficult, e.g.:

Only a few attempts to repeal bans on dangerous drugs have failed.

It takes time to work out whether this assertion means that dangerous drugs tend to be banned.

On balance, the quest for effects of semantic complexity has failed so far, and this failure must count against the decomposition of lexical items as part of the process of comprehension. This conclusion, however, does not necessarily imply that the *organization* of the lexicon treats words as having no internal structure. As Miller and Johnson-Laird (1976, p. 326ff.) point out, decomposition as a necessary process in comprehension is a very different matter from the issue of whether or not there are semantic primitives. I shall return to this issue after I have considered the other semantic theories.

Semantic networks

Several psychological theories of meaning have made use of 'semantic networks', which are essentially a means for representing large numbers of interrelated facts in a way that can be readily interrogated by a computer program (Quillian, 1968). Although this work was originally conceived as an exercise in artificial intelligence, Collins and Quillian (1972) used it as the basis for a model of human performance. They assumed that the meaning of a word is its set of verbal associations, which involve a variety of different sorts of associative link, including class-inclusion, part–whole, property of, and variable relations as specified by a third defining word. The organization of the complete network supposedly reflects the way in which the information was originally acquired. People are unlikely to learn as a separate fact that, for example, poodles are animals; rather they learn that dogs are animals and, independently, that poodles are dogs. Hence, the representation of *poodle* is not linked directly to the representation of *animal*, but indirectly by way of the chain of links:

$$\text{poodle} \xrightarrow{\text{is a}} \text{dog} \xrightarrow{\text{is a}} \text{animal}$$

Once the semantic network is entered at a particular point, the retrieval of certain facts is direct (e.g., 'dogs are animals'), whereas the retrieval of other facts requires additional links to be traversed (e.g., 'poodles are animals'). The results of several experiments suggested that semantic memory does consist of a hierarchical network that can be entered with equal ease at any point (Freedman and Loftus, 1971; Loftus and Freedman, 1972), and supported the notion of a hierarchical retrieval of semantic information (Collins and Quillian, 1969; 1972). One unexpected finding was that although the closeness of items in the semantic network facilitated positive judgments about them, it impeded negative judgments: e.g., it is harder to evaluate 'a canary is an ostrich' than 'a canary is a fish'. The difference was consistently replicated (Schaeffer and Wallace, 1970; Wilkins, 1971) and constitutes a major regularity of semantic judgment: the greater the similarity in meaning between words, the easier it is to make a positive judgment, and the harder it is to make a negative one, about the semantic relation between them. The network model provided a natural account for the facilitation of positive judgments, but it is necessary to suppose that negative judgments are impeded by extraneous links between neighbouring words (Collins and Quillian, 1972).

After the apparent success of network theory in predicting the latencies of semantic judgments, the area underwent the fate of 'paradigm-driven' research: first, the central semantic regularity was given alternative explanations; second, the empirical phenomena were shown to be more complicated than was originally supposed. Schaeffer and Wallace (1970) argued that the regularity is a consequence of a process in which decompositional dictionary entries are compared. In deciding whether an item is a member of a category, the dictionary entries for both words are retrieved and compared. The comparison requires a certain amount of information to be sampled from both entries in order to satisfy a criterion of judgment. Since similar words will have some semantic elements in common, the sampling required to satisfy the criterion will be smaller for a positive judgment than for a negative one. A still simpler explanation for the facilitation of positive judgments is that an individual has to search through a list of items stored with a category label, and so the larger the category, the longer it will take. Such apparent effects of category size were discovered by Landauer and Freedman (1968), and corroborated by others (e.g., Meyer, 1970). Category size could also explain the alleged effects of direct and indirect links in a semantic network simply because position in the hierarchy tends to be confounded with category size. It may take longer to decide that a poodle is an animal than to decide that it is a dog because there are more items in the list of animals than in the list of dogs – the former contains the latter as a proper part.

Could the results of the experiments on semantic memory merely reflect Marbe's classical law of associations (see Johnson-Laird, 1974)? The law states that the more frequent the associative response to a given word, the faster it should be made; and presumably *poodle* is more likely to elicit *dog* as a response than *animal*. The law has been tested directly and emphatically sustained (Wilkins, 1971). Hierarchical effects, however, were obtained in a study that paired arbitrary digits with category names (Smith, Haviland, Buckley and Sack, 1972). Conrad (1972) similarly found that when associative frequency was held constant, hierarchical effects were present for statements about class inclusion, though absent for statements about the properties of items. There seems to be more than Marbe's law at work in categorization tasks; and of course it could never really explain the phenomena, since it predicts that *any* item with a high associative frequency should be given as an instance of a category. The law is only a statement of a correlation between frequency and latency, and it cannot account for adherence to the semantic constraints of the task.

Subsequent experimental studies have unfortunately only served to complicate the picture. A major difficulty for semantic network theory is that it fails to predict differences within categories, and yet such differences have been obtained from the very earliest of the investigations. They tend to correlate with the rated semantic distance between an instance and its category (Rips, Shoben, and Smith, 1973), and with the degree to which an instance is rated as typical of the category (Rosch, 1973). The judgments investigated in studies of semantic memory are often of the following form:

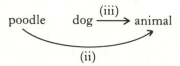

and in general (i) is found to be faster than (ii). In unpublished studies that I carried out with Diana Shapiro, and with John Morton, a comparison was made between judgments of the form:

$$\text{poodle} \qquad \text{dog} \xrightarrow{\text{(iii)}} \text{animal}$$
$$\underbrace{\qquad\qquad\qquad}_{\text{(ii)}}$$

Although the network theory predicts that (iii) should be faster than (ii), we were unable to obtain a reliable difference except by introducing low frequency subordinate terms (see Johnson-Laird, 1975b).

In summary, the semantic network theory has failed to live up to its early promise as an explanatory device for studies of categorization. Nevertheless, the theory was developed and extended, particularly within the framework of artificial intelligence, as a useful way of encoding the meanings of sentences (see, e.g., Rumelhart, Lindsay, and Norman, 1972; Findler, 1979). The initial interpretation of a sentence consists in setting up pointers to the appropriate representations of words in a semantic network. A simplified version of such a representation is illustrated in Figure 10.2. The entailments of a sentence can be captured by pursuing the links in semantic memory that emanate from the nodes initially activated – a process akin to 'spreading activation' in the network.

Semantic networks are depicted as graphs in which assertions about the same entity are gathered together at the node representing that entity, but this arrangement merely facilitates the process of search. It serves no essential semantic function: the same information could be represented in an unordered list of assertions in which co-reference is established in some other way, such as the use of the same symbol in different strings. Moreover, in the absence of any principled constraints on the processes that can be employed in setting up or interrogating semantic networks, the empirical content of the general theory of semantic networks is unclear. It may be wiser to treat them as reflecting a commitment to a certain form of computer implementation rather than to a specific psychological hypothesis.

Words in the lexicon

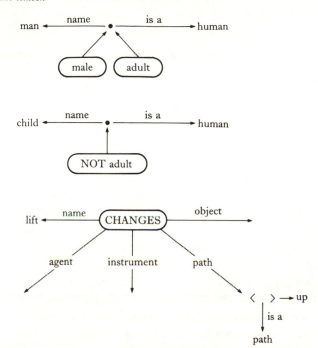

The initial representation of a sentence: "A man lifts a child".

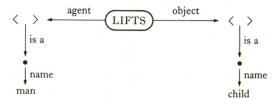

Note. Nodes represented by black dots correspond to generic nodes; nodes represented by ovals correspond to propositions that apply to other nodes; nodes represented by angle brackets represent specific instances of generic concepts. The different arguments of a verb are here, as in many network theories, assigned labels from Case Grammar (Fillmore, 1968); for some arguments against this practice, see Johnson-Laird (1977a).

Figure 10.2 An example of the representation of meaning in terms of a semantic network.

Meaning postulates

Logically speaking, a meaning postulate is an assumption that limits the set of model-theoretic interpretations of a language (see Chapter 8).

Meaning postulates were indeed originally used to specify necessary relations between predicates, e.g.:

for any x, y, and z, if x sells y to z, then z buys y from x

and they accordingly perform a useful and unexceptionable task in formal semantics. They have also been used, however, as a basis for psychological theories of meaning by Kintsch (1974), and by Fodor, Fodor, and Garrett (1975). Adherents of meaning-postulate theories – meaning postulants, as I feel tempted to call them – assume that comprehension consists in translating utterances into a mental language in which the representation of a sentence is very close to its surface form. Each morpheme in the vocabulary of natural language is accordingly represented by a corresponding unanalysed token in the mental language (*mentalese*, as it is sometimes known). The words of natural language correspond virtually one-to-one with the words of mentalese. As Janet Fodor (1977, p. 154) emphasizes, the theory proposes that a word such as *red* is not translated into components of meaning, but into a corresponding token, RED: 'language-specific words can still be represented by language-neutral semantic symbols, but the translation would not be any more DETAILED or explicit than the expression it translates. The most abstract level of representation provided by the grammar would be thus less abstract than is implied by decompositional theories.'

The entailments of sentences are captured by meaning postulates that establish the appropriate semantic relations between words, or more properly the mentalese tokens that stand in for them in the mind. It follows that in understanding a sentence such as 'A man lifts a child', a listener translates it morpheme by morpheme into a virtually isomorphic mentalese expression. In determining that the sentence entails that a human lifts a child, the listener uses a meaning postulate. Both the initial translation and the meaning postulate are presented in Table 10.2. The crucial claims of the theory are that there are no semantic primitives into which the meanings of words can be decomposed, and accordingly that there are no mental dictionary entries representing the meanings of words (see Fodor, Garrett, Walker, and Parkes, 1980). I shall examine each of these claims in turn.

Can the meanings of words be defined?

The impossibility of reflecting upon the mental representation of words has allowed the development of grossly divergent views about the feasibility of semantic analysis. On the one hand, the most extreme claim that

Table 10.2 *An example of the representation of meaning in terms of a meaning postulate theory*

Words in the lexicon

man   MAN
child   CHILD
lift   LIFT

Meaning postulates

FOR ANY X, IF X IS A MAN THEN X IS HUMAN
AND X IS ADULT AND X IS MALE.
FOR ANY X, IF X IS A CHILD THEN X IS HUMAN AND NOT
(X IS AN ADULT).
FOR ANY X AND Y, IF X LIFTS Y THEN X CAUSES Y TO
MOVE UPWARDS.

The initial representation of a sentence: 'A man lifts a child'
$((A\ MAN)_{NP}\ (LIFTS\ (A\ CHILD)_{NP})_{VP})_S$

meanings *can* be analysed into semantic elements parallels the fundamental theorem of arithmetic: just as there is only one way of decomposing a number into prime factors, so the meaning of any word can be decomposed into a unique product of semantic primitives. On the other hand, the strongest claim against analysis is that each word is a unique prime in its own right. If certain words can be defined, then their meanings at least are analysable; hence the controversy turns in part on the question of definability – the possibility of giving exact definitions of words. However, it is important to appreciate that the meaning of a word might be decomposable into ineffable components, and therefore impossible to define adequately.

Lexicographers count themselves relatively successful in the business of defining words, and the sales of dictionaries suggest that they are not wholly deluded. However, Fodor and his fellow postulants claim to the contrary that there are hardly any examples of good definitions of English words (see Fodor, 1980; Fodor, Garrett, Walker, and Parkes, 1980). One of the allegedly few acceptable definitions is that a *bachelor* is an *unmarried man*, and what is supposed to be good about this definition is that if you want to know the extension of the term *bachelor* – the set of entities that satisfy it – then it is indeed the extension of the expression *unmarried man*. Can it really be true that there are hardly any other definitions of this calibre?

A prima facie case for the feasibility of good definitions is established by the existence of *Basic English* (Ogden, 1930), which is a carefully selected set of about 900 words in which it is possible to say just about everything worth expressing, from the works of Shakespeare (which have been trans-

217

lated into Basic) to modern philosophy (which has been written in Basic). Longmans have recently published a *Dictionary of Contemporary English* that similarly defines the meanings of 55,000 words using a vocabulary of only 2000 words. Sceptics may argue that the definitions given in Table 10.3 which I have culled from this source are glaringly inadequate, but such an appeal to intuition is readily countered by the fact that the dictionary is found particularly useful by students of English.

Table 10.3 *Examples of definitions from Longman's* Dictionary of Contemporary English *(only the main senses of the verbs have been quoted)*

bring	to come with or lead
chase	to follow rapidly in order to catch
come	to move towards the speaker or a particular place
glimpse	to have a passing view of
give	to pass into someone's hands or care
hide	to put or keep out of sight; make or keep secret
lend	to give (someone) the possession or use of (something...) for a limited time
negotiate	to talk with another person or group in order to settle a question or disagreement; try to come to an agreement
own	(adding force to the idea of possession) that belongs to (oneself) and to nobody else
say	to express (a thought, intention, opinion, question, etc.) in words
search	to look at, through, into, etc., or examine (a place) carefully and thoroughly to try to find something
tell	to make (something) known in words to (someone)

The meaning postulants allow analyses of the entailments of an expression:

If x brings y then x comes with y or x leads y

but they claim that it is impossible to exhaust its meaning, i.e., to state both necessary and sufficient conditions for its application. As I argued in the previous chapter, however, different words appear to demand different forms of semantic analysis: 'natural kind' terms such as *lemon* and *tiger* call for criteria (default values) that are weaker than entailments, whereas 'analytic' terms such as *bachelor* and *warehouse-class-of-building* have both necessary and sufficient conditions. It follows that the psychological theories based on meaning postulates fall between two stools: they assume too powerful an analysis for natural kind terms and too weak an analysis for 'analytic' terms.

The difficulty of resolving the controversy is due partly to the lack of a clear concept of definition and partly to the lack of an independent index of the adequacy of a definition. If a definition is a verbal description of a schema, which can contain criteria (default values), entailments, or both necessary and sufficient conditions, then an adequate definition is one that successfully conveys the appropriate schema. There is thus a telling argument for the existence of adequate definitions: English contains many words that are acquired only from definitions. In fact, the majority of its words are known almost entirely because they are to be found in dictionaries. If they are used at all, they are used on the basis of their dictionary definitions. In order to establish this point, I carried out a simple experiment in which I selected fifty words at random from the *Shorter Oxford English Dictionary*, taking care to exclude words marked as obsolete or alien. The resulting sample is shown in Table 10.4, where it is divided into those words that are relatively familiar (of which there are twenty-two) and those that are relatively unfamilair (of which there are twenty-eight).

Table 10.4 *Fifty words selected at random from the* Shorter Oxford English Dictionary *and divided into those that are relatively familiar and those that are relatively unfamiliar (obsolete and alien words were not sampled)*

Familiar words

academe	clothes	post	shabby
alderman	cross	print	shield
alley	glass-house	purge	summer-house
antibody	honey-bird	rebuff	sweep
appendix	log-roll	repeat	
catcall	nit	sea-shell	

Unfamiliar words

absinthole	cephalization	hock-day	phraseological
araeostyle	demit	integument	pinguid
arblast	depilous	interdiffuse	puerperal
bote	ejectment	isagogic	remise
calculous	enfever	liliaceous	sial
carny	examen	meatal	sthenic
caruncle	glottology	perfectist	sweepy

Since only two of the unfamiliar words are listed in the Longmans *Dictionary*, and three of the familiar words are not, this division seems to be about right. The majority are sufficiently unfamiliar that there can be little basis for their use other than by reference to a dictionary. Table 10.5 presents definitions from the *Shorter Oxford* for some of the unfamiliar words: it is difficult to take exception to these definitions, precisely because one has no independent knowledge of the meanings of the words. It is no

Table 10.5 *Examples of words whose meanings are acquired from definitions: the definitions of unfamiliar words selected at random from the* Shorter Oxford English Dictionary

absinthole	a liquid camphor obtained from the oil of wormwood
araeostyle	of columned buildings: having the distance between the columns equal to four or more diameters of the column
arblast	a cross-bow, consisting of a steel bow fitted to a wooden shaft, furnished with special mechanism for drawing and letting slip the bowstring, and discharging arrows, bolts, stones, etc.
calculous	diseased with the stone
carny	to act in a wheedling or coaxing manner
caruncle	a small fleshy excrescence
demit	to send, put, or let down; to lower
depilous	deprived or void of hair
hock-day	the second Tuesday after Easter Sunday (or, according to some, Easter week)
integument	that with which anything is covered, enclosed, or clothed
interdiffuse	to diffuse between or among other things
isagogic	of or pertaining to isagoge; introductory to any branch of study
meatal	of or pertaining to a meatus
phraseological	using phrases or peculiar expressions; expressed in a special phrase or phrases
pinguid	of the nature of, resembling, or abounding in fat; unctuous, greasy, oily; (of soil) rich, fertile
remise	to give up, surrender, make over to another, release (any right, property, etc.)
sial	that part of the crust of the earth represented by the continental blocks

accident that these words are primarily used in literary contexts, since they were largely coined by writers.

As a final 'knock-down' argument, suppose that like Lewis Carroll I succeed in making up a new word that enters the language. Carroll invented the word *chortle* as a 'portmanteau' word that combined *chuckle* and *snort*; I coin the word *presleytizer* which means *one who proselytizes on behalf of rock music*. In the unlikely event that this word becomes commonly used, it is difficult to determine on what grounds my definition could possibly fail to be a good one – after all, it is how I choose to define the meaning of the word, and, as Humpty Dumpty almost remarked, when I coin a word it means just what I choose it to mean – neither more nor less. Words are indeed invented, and languages are made and remade by their speakers.

The spontaneous invention of language resembles in part the deliberate development of high-level programming languages. Programs written in a high-level language have to be translated into machine language by a special program known as a 'compiler'. Typically, part of the compiler is itself written in a simple 'assembly' language that maps directly into machine language. However, once the compiler has been developed sufficiently to 'lift itself up by its own bootstraps', the rest of it is written in the high-level language itself. This stratagem works because the first part of the compiler is used to translate the rest of it into machine code. It would be foolish not to use this procedure, which saves much time and trouble. It would be equally foolish to have to learn each word independently: once you have acquired a knowledge of some words from the way in which they apply to the world, that knowledge can be put to use to allow you to acquire the meanings of other words on the basis of informal definitions.

The division of the lexicon into words that are learned verbally and words that must be acquired by other, more direct, means is not clear cut. Individuals get their vocabularies in different ways. However, there is at least one general principle that follows from the distinction: the closer the meaning of a word is to some semantically primitive notion, the harder it will be to take its meaning to pieces and to re-express it in terms of other words. It follows conversely that the more complex the meaning of a word, the easier it should be to define.

Gerry Quinn and I carried out some experiments to test this prediction (Johnson-Laird and Quinn, 1976). We asked our subjects to define the meanings of a series of words in such a way that the definitions would be useful for a child or a foreigner with an imperfect grasp of the language. The materials for our experiments consisted of a set of verbs divided into four levels of complexity as shown in Table 10.6. A verb like *move* is close to expressing a primitive notion in a sentence such as 'The dot moved down the screen'; a verb like *walk* adds a component specifying the manner of movement; a verb like *bring* introduces a more complex component

Table 10.6 *The materials used in an experiment on definitions (from Johnson-Laird and Quinn, 1976)*

Primitive verbs	travel	possess	see	utter
	move	have	perceive	mean
Temporal, spatial, or manner specification verbs	come	keep	sight	speak
	walk	own	glimpse	say
Causative verbs	bring	give	show	tell
	propel	obtain	hide	ask
Intentional verbs	chase	lend	watch	lie
	emigrate	steal	search	negotiate

involving causality; finally, a verb like *chase* introduces a further intentional component in addition to causation. This hierarchy derives from the theory of the mental lexicon proposed by Miller and Johnson-Laird (1976). In the experiments, each verb was presented in a sentence designed to bring out its meaning at the appropriate level, and we asked our subjects to define the meaning that it had in the sentence.

In the first experiment, eight undergraduates each attempted to define sixteen words. Half of them received the words on the top lines of the entries in Table 10.6, and half of them received the words on the bottom lines of the entries.

The flavour of the subjects' definitions is conveyed by the following examples:

chase   to follow closely – indication of speed and urgency.

to chase is sometimes to follow it with the intention of catching up with it.

he followed the dog and tried to catch it.

The last example is one of the few cases where a subject ignored the instructions and couched the definition explicitly in terms of the sentence illustrating the meaning to be defined ('He chased the dog'). It is interesting to compare these definitions with one from a dictionary (*The American Heritage*) compiled with considerable linguistic expertise:

chase   to pursue in order to catch or overtake.

The examples are typical in that two of them capture all the essential components of meaning, analysing it in a way that might well be useful to someone with an imperfect grasp of the word. Some definitions consisted of synonyms or words with more recondite senses than the *definiendum*: they could hardly be helpful to children or foreigners. Such definitions were particularly frequent for the simple primitive verbs, accounting for just under 70% of the responses to them. This prevalence shows the difficulty of explaining the meaning of these verbs. In addition, it made it difficult to include this class when we rank-ordered the accuracy of each subject's definitions. However, it was a straightforward matter to rank the definitions of the other three categories of words.

The rankings of the accuracy of the definitions were based on formal definitions of the meanings of the words constructed from the analyses in Miller and Johnson-Laird (1976). In addition, at the end of the experiment, the subjects ranked the sixteen verbs in terms of how difficult subjectively

Table 10.7 *The results of the experiment on definitions*

Type of verb	Mean ranks of the accuracy of the definitions of each type of verb (1 = inaccurate, 4 = accurate)	Mean ranks of the subjects' subjective difficulty in defining the 16 verbs (1 = easiest verb to define, 16 = hardest verb to define)
Primitive verb	—	10·7
Temporal, spatial, or manner specification verbs	2·4	9·5
Causative verbs	2·8	8·4
Intentional verbs	3·1	5·3

they had found them to define. Table 10.7 presents the mean ranks of both sorts. The accuracy scores reliably confirmed our prediction that it is easier to define semantically complex words. The subjects' own impressions of the difficulty of the task also corroborated the prediction. Moreover, subjective difficulty was negatively correlated with the accuracy score in a highly reliable way: when a definition seemed difficult, it tended not to be very accurate. The numbers of words and clauses in a definition were not reliably related to accuracy or subjective difficulty.

The predicted order of difficulty was confirmed in two further studies. The first examined a small group of subjects' spontaneously spoken definitions: latencies to begin speaking were not affected by semantic complexity, but the definitions of more complex words were more accurate. The second study, carried out by Marla Petal, replicated the trend using written definitions of both Japanese and English words formulated by bi-lingual subjects.

Some words are evidently almost impossible to define, but other words are easy to define and hence their meanings are at least analysable (*pace* Fodor, Garrett, Walker and Parkes, 1980).

Learning the meanings of words

The existence of both definable and indefinable words suggests that there are at least two different ways in which words and their meanings can be learned: first, by encountering them in context, which may happen with either sort of word; second, by being given an explicit definition, which can happen only with definable words. If an indefinable word is picked up primarily from context, then over a period of time it is likely to have different meanings attached to it, as a function of the variety of contexts from which it is learned. Indeed, the word may be indefinable precisely because there is no common core of meaning suggested by its diverse contexts of use. If a semantically complex word can be acquired from a definition, its meaning is more likely to have crystallized, since its definition will prevent it from taking on radically new meanings. It follows that semantically simple words such as *move*, *have*, and *see* ought in general to have a greater diversity of meanings than semantically complex ones such as *chase*, *steal*, and *search*. We tested this prediction by counting the separate (numbered) meanings in *The American Heritage Dictionary* of the words that we had used in the studies of definitions. The mean frequencies of different meanings were as follows: 5·4 for intentional verbs, 8·8 for causal verbs, 10·3 for temporal–spatial verbs, and 14·8 for primitive verbs. The trend is in accordance with the prediction, but it is not quite statistically significant. Dave Haw and I selected a larger sample of words of the same categories, matching for frequency of occurrence as in the previous studies, and found that there was a significant trend in both *The American Heritage* and *The Shorter Oxford English Dictionary*: semantically simple verbs tend to have more separate meanings than semantically complex ones.

Children acquire vocabulary at so great a rate – around nine words per day on average up to the age of six years (see Templin, 1957; Miller, 1977a) – that it is unlikely that they are learning the complete meanings of the words or fixing their extensions from encountering many samples of the actual objects to which they refer. They must be able to gather a considerable amount about the meaning of a word solely from the *linguistic* context in which it occurs. This conjecture was corroborated by a study that Til Wykes and I carried out with 3- to 4-year-old children. We found that they could pick up and retain for at least a week information about the meaning of a new word merely from hearing a story such as:

John stepped out of the boat and the water mibbed his trousers, so he went to change into some dry clothes. The water had mibbed his trousers right through so Simon made him some hot tea. But John dropped his cup and the tea mibbed over the floor.

The novel verb *mib* has a transitive meaning similar to that of *soak* and an intransitive meaning similar to that of *spill*. Children evince no surprise on hearing it – there is no reason why they should, since they encounter many words they have never heard before – and it is unlikely that they merely translate it into some word they know. After two hearings of the

224

story, the children did reliably better than chance at picking out a liquid (orange juice) from a set of four alternatives in order to answer the question: 'Which one of these can mib?' They performed the same task for three other novel verbs that they had encountered in other stories. One week later they were still doing better than chance with some new alternatives (see Wykes and Johnson-Laird, 1977). Jon Davies carried out a further, unpublished, study using the same procedure and yielding complementary results: he showed that children could readily pick up information about *nouns* from their linguistic context, particularly from the verbs with which they occurred. Perhaps the most dramatic finding was obtained by Susan Carey (1978). She made the following request to nursery school children: 'Bring me the chromium tray, not the red one, the chromium one.' Since there were only two trays present – a red one and an olive-coloured one – the children readily complied. Six weeks later, however, their spontaneous use of colour words was still affected in that *green* was much less likely to be taken to refer to the olive colour that was the original referent for *chromium* in the experiment.

If children and adults pick up different aspects of the meanings of words from the contexts in which they occur, there are likely to be gaps in their knowledge. Discourse rarely depends upon speakers having complete and identical representations of the meanings of the words they use. It is perfectly possible to communicate with little or no such similarity, or else children would never learn their native tongue. Adults, too, can communicate successfully with an incomplete knowledge of meaning. When, for example, you read the sentence:

After a hearty dish of spaghetti, Bernini cast a bronze of a mastiff searching for truffles

you may understand it perfectly well even though, on reflection, you may not be entirely sure exactly what alloy *bronze* is, or what sort of *dog* a mastiff is, or what *truffles* are. Such ignorance can, of course, be notorious. One April Fool's day, BBC television broadcast a snippet of documentary film about the spaghetti harvest in Italy, and a large section of the British population was tricked into believing that peasants plucked strands of pasta from shrubs and laid them out to dry in the sun.

Graham Gibbs and I showed experimentally that speakers have systematic gaps in their knowledge of rarely used words, and that the pattern of ignorance is predictable. What you can do with something and its perceptible characteristics are, as one would expect (see Keil, 1979), more widely known than its provenance. For instance, our subjects tended to know that *pemmican* is a foodstuff, but not that it is a man-made substance. They tended to know that *turpentine* is a non-consumable liquid, but they thought erroneously that it is man-made. We found that people generally know whether or not something is consumable, and solid or liquid, but they are less well informed about whether it is natural or man-made. Exactly the same pattern was detected in the latencies with which subjects made decisions about frequently used words such as *wine*, *bread*, and *petrol* (see Johnson-Laird, 1975b).

Are there mental dictionary entries?

We have seen that some words appear to be definable and perhaps to be primarily acquired from informal definitions, whereas other words are not definable and are thus likely to be acquired from ostensive definitions or from their use in context. The question that now arises is whether semantic information about a word is gathered together in a single entry in a mental lexicon or distributed throughout a set of independent meaning postulates. At first sight, the question hardly seems open to empirical investigation, but in fact there is at least one way in which it has been addressed experimentally, though the method was originally designed for another purpose.

Some theorists, such as Gibson (1971), have suggested that when a word is processed for meaning, all of its semantic components are necessarily recovered; others have argued that an exhaustive retrieval of a word's meaning is unnecessary (Fodor, Fodor, and Garrett, 1975). The evidence in the literature appeared to be equivocal. Some studies showed that the more classification tasks subjects carry out on a word, the more likely they are to remember it (e.g., Klein and Saltz, 1976; Frase and Kammann, 1974); other studies found no such effects (e.g., Hyde and Jenkins, 1969; Hyde, 1973). Graham Gibbs, Juliet de Mowbray and I were interested in how much of a word's meaning is recovered when it is processed and whether the amount of processing that is carried out on a word determines how likely it is to be remembered. The previous studies seemed unsatisfactory because they had often not used components of the meanings of words, and because they had often confounded the number of tasks carried out with the number of categories available to act as cues to recall. Hence, we used a task in which the subjects had to detect members of a target category in a list of words of various sorts. A target category was defined in terms of a number of semantic components, and the list contained words with all, some, or none of these components. For example, if the target category is defined to be consumable liquids, then *beer* is a member of it, *petrol* and *cake* have only one of the required components, and *coal* has neither of them. We assumed that the amount of relevant processing of a word in such a task determines its memorability, and that this variable is best indexed by the number of decisions about a word that yield pertinent information. If the different semantic components of a word can be processed separately, then a word with none of the target components requires assessment on only one of them in order to be rejected, while a word with several of the target components may require processing on a number of components before it can be rejected. In general, the greater the number of components a word has in common with the target, the greater the amount of processing that it will require.

In our first experiment, the subjects listened to a list of thirty-six words and classified each of them as a positive or negative instance of a category defined on the basis of three components. The overall recall of the words on the list in an unexpected test was as follows: 57% of the target words, 45% of the words with two components of the target category, 34% of the words with one component of the target category, and 32% of the words with none of the target components. The results reliably confirmed our prediction (see Johnson-Laird, Gibbs, and de Mowbray, 1978).

In a second experiment, there were four separate groups of subjects, each assigned to a different target category: consumable liquids, non-consumable liquids, consumable solids, non-consumable solids. The same list of sixty-four words was used for each group, and it contained, in addition to the four target categories, four other categories of non-target words: utensils used for consumable liquids (e.g., *jug*), utensils used for non-consumable liquids (e.g., *vase*), utensils used for consumable solids (e.g., *plate*), and utensils used for non-consumable solids (e.g., *hammer*). Although we did not realize it at the time, these additional categories were to be of crucial importance to the question of dictionary entries. Obviously, a utensil such as *jug* does not contain *consumable* and *liquid* as direct components of its meaning, but if there is a dictionary entry for the word, they will occur embedded within its structure to represent the information that jugs are used as containers for consumable liquids. We predicted that the words would again tend to be recalled in terms of the number of components that they had in common with the particular target category. Hence, the recall of the words denoting substances would always be better

227

than the recall of words denoting utensils, but there would be the same trend within both these types of word: words with both target components would be better recalled than words with only one of them, which in turn would be better recalled than words with neither component. For example, if the target category were consumable solids, then although all of the utensils would require a negative response, a word such as *plate* should be better recalled than *jug* or *hammer*, which in turn should be better recalled than *vase*.

The percentages of the words correctly recalled are given in Table 10.8. The prediction that substance words would be better recalled than utensil words was confirmed, and likewise there were reliable trends (for both types of word) supporting the prediction that the greater the number of target components possessed by a word, the better it would be recalled.

Table 10.8 *The percentages of words correctly recalled as a function of the number of semantic components they had in common with a target category in a search task (from Johnson-Laird, Gibbs, and de Mowbray, 1978)*

	Semantic components of the target category possessed by the words			
	Both	One	Neither	Overall
Substance words	50·0	21·5	10·6	27·4
Utensil words	16·2	10·6	8·1	11·7

We argued that these results confirmed that recall was dependent on amount of processing. Brian Ross (personal communication) has carried out further experiments that have eliminated processing time as an explanation of our results. He also found that when subjects are asked to respond to an item that has *any* of the target components, then the greater the number of target components, the poorer the subjects' recall. This finding suggests that it is amount of processing which is critical, not the availability of the target components as cues for recall (though McClelland, Rawles, and Sinclair, 1981, interpret their results as favouring the latter hypothesis). We also suggested that amount of processing provided a plausible explication for the notion of 'elaboration', which Craik and Tulving (1975) introduced in order to explain the fact that items responded to positively are better remembered than items responded to negatively. For example, when subjects are asked, 'Is a shark a type of fish?' and 'Is heaven a type of fish?', they remember *shark* better than *heaven*. The advantage of using amount of processing to explicate this notion of 'elaboration' is that the number of decisions yielding pertinent information makes predictions about the differences between non-target items, e.g., deciding that a whale is not a fish requires a greater amount of processing than deciding that heaven is not a fish, and subjects should thus remember *whale* better than *heaven*. Nevertheless, all these matters are controversial.

What seems beyond doubt is that our experiment establishes that semantic information is gathered together in the form of dictionary entries. Consider, for instance, how the subjects decide that the utensil words are not members of a target category such as consumable solids. According to the theory of meaning postulates, they search for postulates of the sort:

$$\text{For any x, if x is a} \begin{cases} \text{plate} \\ \text{jug} \\ \text{hammer} \\ \text{vase} \end{cases} \text{then x is consumable.}$$

There are no such postulates for any utensil. They may also search for postulates of the sort:

$$\text{For any x, if x is a} \begin{cases} \text{plate} \\ \text{jug} \\ \text{hammer} \\ \text{vase} \end{cases} \text{then x is solid.}$$

There are postulates of this sort for every utensil. It follows that the amount of processing should be the same for all four types of utensil for a given target category, because every utensil is non-consumable and solid. Two predictions follow: first, there should be no differences in the memorability of the different types of utensil words; second, they should be better remembered when the target category is non-consumable solid than when it is any other category. Neither prediction was confirmed by our results. On the contrary, they can be explained only on the assumption that subjects consult a mental dictionary entry in order to make a decision about a word. If the target category is non-consumable solid, then the dictionary entry for a word such as *plate* contains both components embedded within it because a plate is used to serve consumable solids, but the dictionary entry for a word such as *vase* contains neither component embedded within it, since a vase is used for holding liquids that are not for consumption. The corresponding differences in the amount of processing required to reject the utensil words explain the differences in the memorability of these non-target words. Exactly the same argument, *mutatis mutandis*, can be made for the existence of dictionary entries if it turns out that the target components act as retrieval cues and that amount of processing *per se* is not responsible for increasing the memorability of words.

The three theories of meaning

The three theories of meaning that I have described all assume that meanings are represented by expressions in a mental language. They diverge on the vocabulary of that language, and on how inferences based on the meanings of words are made. The lexical decomposition theory assumes that words are represented by structured sequences of semantic markers, and that comprehension involves a process of semantic decomposition. No unequivocal evidence that this process occurs has been obtained. The meaning postulate theory assumes that words cannot be adequately defined and that they are merely translated into corresponding tokens in the mental language – tokens that also occur in the mental embodiment of meaning postulates. The evidence that I have presented also runs counter to these proposals. The main empirical claim embodied in semantic networks – the inheritance of properties – likewise appears to be an over-simplification in the light of experimental results. However, networks can always be revised to accomodate new empirical phenomena, and are perhaps best thought of as a notation rather than a strong theory of meaning.

Despite their differing inadequacies, the most important characteristic of the three theories is what they have in common. Their main scientific function is to account for the perception of semantic properties such as anomaly and ambiguity, and semantic relations such as synonymy and paraphrase. They are silent on the question of how language is related to the world.

It is easy to forget that unless a theory relates language to the world, or to a model of it, it is *not* a complete theory of meaning. The word *woman* can be decomposed into the components *human*, *adult*, *female*, or represented with links to nodes corresponding to those words, or simply translated into the token WOMAN with its associated meaning postulates, but none of these procedures actually specifies the full meaning of the word. The illusion of significance is created by an analysis that uses terms that everyone understands. Thus, for example, when Kintsch and van Dijk (1978) translate the expression *students complain* into COMPLAIN, STUDENT, they are sensitive to the potential vacuity of the step. To convince yourself of the danger, just consider the status of a semantic theory based on, say, meaning postulates but using an exotic language that you do not understand. It might well contain the following meaning postulate:

for any x, if x is a ZUG then x is a GEK and x is not a PLEK

where, say, ZUG is the token corresponding to the word *zug*. Such a postulate might well enable you to infer from *zug brochna* that *gek brochna*, but no matter how complex the system becomes, or how sophisticated the inferences that it can make, it does not provide a complete semantics. It tells you about the relations between words without telling you anything about what they pick out in the world.

This fundamental point may be easier to grasp in relation to an automaton. Imagine that there is a Turing machine that takes as input a tape containing a string of 1's and 0's, computes a specific function of this input, and produces the result as a string of 1's and 0's. The theorist who devises the set of instructions for the machine has to specify what the strings of symbols encode and the principles of the encoding. Until this essential piece of 'semantics' is provided, the function computed by the machine, though perfectly precise, is literally meaningless. It could be any one of an indefinitely large number of alternatives. It might be a function over the natural numbers, depending on how one chooses to encode them as strings of 1's and 0's; it might be a function from strings of letters to strings of letters, depending on how they are encoded; it might be a move in a game of chess, or a planned attack in a nuclear war. Only when the intended interpretation of the tapes is given can the *meaning* of the machine's operations be properly understood. Equivalently, a semantic theory that makes use of ZUG, GEK, and PLEK is just as much of a semantic analysis (and no more) than one that makes use of HUMAN, ADULT, MALE. Until we know how such components relate to the world, they are really nothing more than variables that take specific words as values. ADULT, for example, ranges over such words as *man*, *woman*, *grown-up*, *cow*, *bull*, and *horse*. The interposition of such variables between the words in one sentence and the words in another sentence is essentially an exercise in the economy of translation from one expression to another, rather than a fundamental theory of meaning. The ectoplasm in the works can be any shape, size, or colour, as long as it materializes and dematerializes in a uniform way between synonymous phrases.

There is a nice irony in the fact that model-theoretic semantics *finesses* the problem of the intensions of basic words by taking them as primitive givens, while psychological semantics avoids the problem by concentrating its attention on relations internal to language. Psychologists have followed Montague (1974) only half way. They have provided (semi-) formal languages into which sentences of natural language can be translated, but while Montague went on to give an account of truth in a model-theoretic interpretation, psychologists have stopped short of an account of the extensions of expressions.

The task for psychological semantics is to show how language and the world are related to one another in the human mind – to show how the mental representation of sentences is related to the mental representation of the world. Hence, it was a reasonable research strategy for psycholinguists to have concentrated on the representation of sentences and to have left the representation of the world to those who study perception. However, this strategic division of labour makes one cardinal assumption: it assumes that the way in which the mind copes with semantic properties such as ambiguity, and grasps semantic relations such as synonymy, can be explained without considering how expressions are mentally related to their extensions in the world. Hence, the three theories also have in common this – admittedly tacit – reliance on the psychological principle that intensions are processed autonomously. In fact, as I shall now demonstrate, the principle turns out to be mistaken, with the result that none of the theories is rich enough to provide a plausible representation of meaning.

The case against the three theories

There is one major point of agreement between proponents of all three varieties of theory and myself. We agree about the importance of psychological phenomena for semantic theory; and it is from this standpoint that my criticisms arise. My main objection is to the principle of the psychological autonomy of intensions – the thesis that semantic properties and relations are grasped by processes that operate independently of those that mediate reference. This principle leads to trouble with at least four different aspects of semantic interpretation.

Ambiguity and context

Suppose that you were to come across the following passage in a newspaper article:

The plane banked just before landing, but then the pilot lost control. The strip on the field runs for only the barest of yards, and the plane just twisted out of the turn before shooting into the ground.

You would have little difficulty in understanding it, and you would be most unlikely to realize that every single content word in the text is ambiguous. In fact, a striking feature of natural language is that, grammatical function words apart, the more frequently used a word is, the more likely it is to be ambiguous (see Miller, 1951). Plainly, if one were to design a language on a rational basis, it would be sensible to eliminate ambiguity, or at least to relegate it to the least frequently used words. There is here again an important clue to the nature of human mentality in this apparently topsy-turvy feature of language. It suggests that the processes that determine the intended sense of a word are extremely efficient. They readily bring to mind the appropriate sense of a word from the context in which it occurs. Indeed, one has the impression that it is harder to think of all the different meanings of a word presented in isolation than to retrieve a relevant sense when the word occurs in context. What, for example, are the different meanings of *plane*? The reader might like to think for a moment before consulting the following sentences:

The plane landed on the runway.
Imagine a sphere divided equally by a plane.
The carpenter smoothed the surface of the wood with a plane.
All the trees have been cut down except the tall plane at the end.

Evidently, the mind prefers to deal with a relatively small set of short, highly frequent, and ambiguous words, rather than with a relatively large set of long, less frequent, and unambiguous ones.

What psychological mechanism recovers the appropriate sense of an ambiguous word? The decompositional theory employs selectional restrictions, i.e., constraints that one sense of a word places on the meanings of other words with which it occurs. However, an *interaction* between meaning and reference is immediately apparent in the way in which disambiguation actually works. An assertion such as:

They are handsome

constrains the referent of *they*, not its meaning. Hence, if you know that *handsome* is intended to mean *generous*, then you will infer that *they* refers to acts of some sort. Of course, if instead you happen to know what *they* refers to, then you will have no difficulty in determining in what sense to take the word *handsome*. It is nonsense to suppose that the meaning of *they* is affected by a selectional restriction: what changes is its referent, and, in general, what have to be constrained are the referents of expressions.

The notion that it is possible to formulate exhaustive and definitive selectional restrictions on the different senses of words turns out to be a fiction. Consider the following sentence:

Alcock and Brown were the first to fly X from the USA to Ireland

and now ask yourself what constraints there are on the categories of things that X could refer to. The most obvious category is a vehicle of some sort:

Alcock and Brown were the first to fly an aeroplane from the USA to Ireland.

However, the sentence takes on a different meaning if another sort of vehicle is substituted:

Alcock and Brown were the first to fly a bicycle from the USA to Ireland.

It now seems that they merely took the bicycle with them, though the original sense is still possible in the case of a flying bicycle such as the one that crossed the English channel a few years ago. To separate the two interpretations, it is necessary to distinguish between flying in a vehicle and flying with a physical object. But these two possibilities do not exhaust the class of acceptable substitutions for X:

Alcock and Brown were the first to fly the Atlantic from the USA to Ireland.

An attempt can be made to capture these three different sorts of meaning using selectional restrictions. I here forego the luxury of translation into the symbolism of 'semantic markers':

x *fly* y: x controls y's path through the air (where x is human, animal or machine, and y is a vehicle).

x takes y in an aircraft (where x is human, and y is a physical object).

x travels in the air over y (where x is a physical object, and y is a geographical region of the earth's or a celestial body's surface).

234

These selectional restrictions fail to capture the correct constraints of the different senses of *fly*. To take one example, consider the sentence:

I saw the Azores flying the Atlantic.

According to the proposed selectional restrictions, this sentence is open to the interpretations:

As I was flying over the Atlantic I saw the Azores.
I saw the Azores as they were flying over the Atlantic.

The second of these interpretations is nonsensical. No normal person is likely to make such an interpretation; but how is it that one knows immediately that the Azores were not flying through the air?

This puzzle requires us to rethink the whole concept of selectional restrictions. We might try to restrict the subject of the verb *fly* to certain sorts of entities, and to rule out, at least in normal circumstances, such things as islands. We could start with a list of acceptable entities, but a moment's thought shows that such a list is not going to be easy to compile: for instance, a plane can fly, but can a *wrecked* plane fly? And what about people – can they fly? Obviously, it depends what is meant: people (outside fairy stories) cannot fly by flapping their arms, but they can fly in planes and rockets. The task is no easier if instead we try to draw up a list of things that cannot fly. These difficulties are hardly surprising: conventional selectional restrictions are really just lists of categories too. The solution appears to be to follow up the idea, suggested by Miller and Johnson-Laird (1976, p. 701), that the constraints on a particular meaning derive from that meaning itself. At least in this way we might obviate the criticism that selectional restrictions are, as Harris Savin (1973) pointed out, arbitrary excrescences tagged on to the representations of different meanings of words, with no relation in theory between the particular meaning of the word and the specific content of the selectional restriction.

The simple intransitive sense of *fly* can be glossed as follows:

x *fly*: x travel through the air.

The crucial component here is plainly travel, since the Azores cannot swim or crawl across the surface of the earth either. What a listener really does in interpreting the sentence 'I saw the Azores flying the Atlantic' is to determine whether it is *possible* for the Azores to *travel* through the air over the Atlantic. This proposition can only be decided by making an implicit inference based on general knowledge. It hinges on questions of fact, as well as on a knowledge of the meanings of words. In particular, it depends on some specific information:

An island is a land mass entirely surrounded by water.

Land masses are parts of the earth's surface that are fixed relative to other such parts (except in the case of earthquakes).

An ocean is a body of salt water that covers a large and relatively fixed part of the earth's surface.

If X is a fixed part of Y then X travels when Y travels, but X does not travel with respect to Y.

The Azores are islands in the Atlantic Ocean.

Armed with these facts, one can infer that the Azores cannot travel with respect to the Atlantic Ocean, barring earthquakes, and hence that the proper interpretation of the sentence is that the speaker was flying over the Atlantic and saw the Azores. An unexpected aspect of this analysis is that it shows that the Azores *can* fly: they fly through space as part of the earth's surface. It follows that any putative selectional restriction that eliminated them as a potential subject of the verb *to fly* would fail to provide the appropriate interpretation of the sentence:

I saw the Azores flying past as I looked out from my spaceship.

The notion that the sense of a word is selected, not by fixed semantic constraints, but by an implicit inference based on context and matters of fact violates the psychological autonomy of intensions. Such inferences often depend on the particular situation that is being referred to: e.g., in the context of a story about how the earth explodes, the Azores might well fly over the Atlantic Ocean. The evaluation of what is a *possible* referent for, say, the subject of a verb is almost invariably a matter that depends on the nature of the events to which reference is made.

A proponent of selectional restrictions, while conceding that inferences are needed in certain cases, might argue that there are nevertheless certain constraints that depend solely on the senses of expressions. The subject of the verb *to love*, for example, must be classifiable as human or animal. There is thus a semantic anomaly in the sentence:

The chair loved the table.

Yet, in a context where the dish ran away with the spoon, there may be nothing anomalous about a chair's falling in love with a table. The most that can be conceded is that some inferences become so frequent and commonplace that rather than having to make them over and over again, people keep a record of their outcome. In this way, a child may come to learn what classes of referents are invariably acceptable as the values of a verb's arguments – to learn, for instance, that *love* ordinarily demands a human subject and hence that there is something odd about a sentence like 'Sincerity loves politicians.' The idea that ambiguities are resolved by factually based inferences therefore explains how conventional selectional restrictions are acquired, and how people cope with sentences or circumstances that are outside the scope of such restrictions (see Miller, 1977b; Johnson-Laird, 1977b). However, it is always necessary to take the referential context into account, if only to establish that there is nothing untoward about it.

Once comprehension is allowed to take context into account, it is natural to try to extend the idea to cope with regularities that are factual and inductive rather than conventional or linguistic. Doctors generally cure patients rather than the converse; professors generally lecture students rather than the converse; waiters generally serve customers rather than the converse. Yet there is nothing immutable about these relations, and their converses can occur. Context is again of paramount importance. There is a similarity with selectional restrictions: both forms of constraint may help a listener to make the appropriate interpretation of an utterance, and both may serve to furnish the value that a verb's argument takes by default. Restrictions on both the probable and the possible values of an argument may be mobilized by the same inferential mechanism, and differ only in the sort of premises, linguistic or factual, on which they are based.

Instantiation and context

R. C. Anderson and his colleagues have shown experimentally that context narrows down the interpretations of words. If subjects are presented with a sentence such as:

The fish attacked the swimmer

and later asked to recall it, their memory is better when they are given a more specific and more likely term such as *shark* as a recall cue than when they are given *fish*, the general term actually used in the original sentence (see Anderson, Pichert, Goetz, Schallert, Stevens, and Trollip, 1976). In a similar study carried out by Anderson and Ortony (1975), the subjects were presented with either:

The container held the apples

or:

The container held the cola.

After a set of such sentences, the subjects were given a cued recall test. *Basket* was a better cue for the first sentence, whereas *bottle* was a better cue for the second. In these experiments, great pains were taken to ensure that the results could not be explained by associations to the retrieval cues. The tendency to make more specific interpretations is not limited to nouns. My colleague Alan Garnham compared such pairs of sentences as:

The housewife cooked the chips

and:

The housewife cooked the peas.

He found that *fried* was a better cue than *cooked* for the first sentence, whereas the converse was the case for the second sentence (see Garnham, 1979).

One way of explaining these results is to argue, as do Halff, Ortony, and Anderson (1976), that words do not have a few qualitatively distinct meanings, but rather a whole family of potential meanings – a thesis that has been advanced independently by Weinreich (1966) and Putnam (1975). The occurrence of a word in a specific linguistic context *instantiates* a specific sense which is a member of the family. This line of thought is consistent with the autonomy of intensions, but there are reasons for believing that it will not do. Suppose, for the sake of argument, that one of the original sentences in the experiment by Anderson *et al.* had been:

It attacked the swimmer

then doubtless *shark* would be a better retrieval cue than *it*. But no one would make the egregious error of arguing that *it* has indefinitely many meanings of which one is *shark*. *It* has a single meaning, but can refer to indefinitely many entities. What is being instantiated is not a specific meaning, but a specific referent. The subjects in the experiments are presumably constructing mental models based on the sentences they are given and on their general knowledge. They make implicit inferences about the entities that are being referred to. They infer that what attacked the swimmer was a shark; and hence the word *shark* provides a better cue to help them recall the sentence than the word *fish*. The advantage of this explanation over the 'instantiation' hypothesis is that it also accounts for the well-known findings of Bransford and his colleagues (e.g., Bransford and McCarrell, 1975), which show that subjects in memory experiments go beyond what is linguistically given. If, for example, they are presented with the sentence:

Three turtles rested on a floating log and a fish swam beneath them

they readily assume that the sentence asserted that the fish swam beneath the log. This result cannot be explained on the grounds that a more specific meaning was instantiated, but it is readily accounted for by assuming that a mental model of the relevant state of affairs was constructed to which the alternative sentence equally applies.

Inference and the autonomy of intensions

An inference is valid if it is impossible for its premises to be true and its conclusion false: the conclusion is true in any model of the premises. On this simple pre-theoretical notion, the following inference:

The pencil is in the box

The box is in the parcel

Therefore, the pencil is in the parcel

is valid. The psychological problem is to specify the nature of the mental machinery that makes it possible for us to recognize the truth of the conclusion given the truth of the premises. A logician would demand that the transitivity of *in* be stated explicitly, and it is plausible to suppose that there is a meaning postulate that captures the required relation:

For any x, y, and z, if x is in y and y is in z, then x is in z.

Equivalently, as Bar-Hillel (1967) once suggested, the principle of transitivity could be stated once and for all in a universal semantics, and then those relational terms to which it applies could be tagged in some way to represent this fact. The information could also be accommodated within a theory based on lexical decomposition or a semantic network.

The same strategy, however, runs into difficulties with other spatial inferences. An inference such as:

Mrs Thatcher is at her office

Her office is at 10 Downing Street

Therefore, Mrs Thatcher is at 10 Downing Street

is valid. But an inference of seemingly the same form:

Mrs Thatcher is at her desk
Her desk is at the window
Therefore, Mrs Thatcher is at the window

is not valid. One possible defence is to argue that the expression *at* designates two different relations, one transitive, one not. However, this interpretation violates the usual criteria for ambiguity. A term is generally reckoned to be ambiguous, following Zwicky and Sadock (1973), if it yields nonsensical constructions based on conjunction reduction. There are at least two senses of the verb *bank*, for example, because of the obvious anomaly in such a sentence as:

The pilot banked the airplane and the cheque from his employer.

But there is nothing wrong with the sentence:

Mrs Thatcher is at her office and her desk.

Moreover, a still more serious difficulty for any such analysis arises with such inferences as:

Matthew is on Mark's right.
Mark is on Luke's right.
Therefore, Matthew is on Luke's right.

Granted the truth of the premises, the truth of the conclusion depends on how the individuals are seated. In the case of, say, Leonardo's painting of the Last Supper, where the disciples are seated down one side of a long rectangular table, the conclusion is plainly true. But in the case of the knights of the round table, the conclusion may well be false because Matthew is opposite to Mark. One might argue that *on X's right* is ambiguous and has both a transitive and an intransitive sense. Unfortunately, this manoeuvre leads to the need for an infinite number of alternative meanings. Suppose, for instance, that there is a slightly larger number of individuals seated round a circular table; then it is entirely possible for the inference above to yield a true conclusion, but the one below to be false:

Matthew is on Mark's right.
Mark is on Luke's right.
Luke is on John's right.
Therefore, Matthew is on John's right.

On X's right would have a limited transitivity extending only over three individuals in this case. (There is likely to be a region of uncertainty, which makes it even harder to defend the use of meaning postulates with their clear-cut logic.) In fact, the extent of the transitivity of the relation varies as a function of the seating arrangements up to any arbitrary number of individuals, and would accordingly require an infinite number of different meanings in order to cope with each possible extent from zero upwards. The only way in which to accommodate this requirement within a meaning-postulate theory is to propose higher-order postulates that generate specific meaning postulates as a function of information about seating arrangements, or whatever feature of the world is relevant. But such an assumption plainly violates the psychological autonomy of intensions.

Deixis and interpretation

The examples that I have discussed show that a psychologically plausible theory of comprehension must allow for the *reference* of some expressions to play a role in determining the *senses* of other expressions. Perhaps the most striking illustrations of how reference can transcend literal meaning are some of the phenomena that Nunberg (1978) has analysed. A remark such as:

The ham sandwich is sitting at table number 5 and getting impatient

might seem to be lifted straight from a fairy-story. In fact, it is an example of the sort of *indirect reference* that a waiter might readily employ to pick out the person who ordered the ham sandwich. A listener makes sense of this sentence by recovering the appropriate referent. A theory that assumes that a set of literal meanings is first assigned to a sentence, and that context then eliminates inappropriate meanings, runs into grave difficulties with such sentences. A ham sandwich cannot literally grow impatient, and hence it would be necessary to abandon all conventional selectional restrictions. But once an autonomous system is breached in this way, plainly *anything goes*. The solution is to accept that ambiguity is only resolvable by making inferences from the context.

Conclusions

The three psychological theories of semantics that I have considered in this chapter all propose that the meanings of words are represented by expressions in a mental language; none of them explains how these expressions relate to the world. This omission might be justifiable if a satisfactory account of how speakers understand the properties of intensions and the relations between them could be given without considering how they grasp extensions. In fact, this tacit assumption of the psychological autonomy of intensions turns out to be false. Unless the retrieval of referents is taken into account, it is impossible to explain the resolution of lexical ambiguities, the instantiation of words in context, the vagaries in the logical properties of spatial relations, and a variety of deictic phenomena. Further doubt is cast on the decompositional theory by the failure to obtain experimental support for any process of decomposition, on the strong form of the network theory by the existence of marked within-category differences, and on the meaning postulate theory by the feasibility of definitions and the existence of mental dictionary entries. The primacy of referential matters is recognized by the theory to be developed in the next chapter. The theory leads to a complete reorientation in the way in which one accounts for intensional phenomena.

11

Procedural semantics and the psychology of meaning

A decade ago, experimental psycholinguists had established that individuals do not normally remember either the superficial form of sentences or their underlying syntactic structure. After reviewing this evidence, I ventured the following speculation:

It is natural to wonder whether the sentence is the largest unit normally involved in the recall of language. It is possible that from the meanings of sentences in a connected discourse, the listener implicitly sets up a much abbreviated and not especially linguistic model of the narrative, and that recall is very much an active reconstruction based on what remains of this model. Where the model is incomplete, material may even be unwittingly invented to render the memory more meaningful or more plausible – a process which has its parallel in the initial construction of the model. A good writer or raconteur perhaps has the power to initiate a process very similar to the one that occurs when we are actually perceiving (or imagining) events instead of merely reading or hearing about them. (Johnson-Laird, 1970)

This quotation contains the germ of a theory of comprehension that has been developed during the last decade. Bransford, Barclay, and Franks (1972) advanced a similar hypothesis, distinguishing between an 'interpretive' and a 'constructive' approach to semantics. An interpretive theory assumes that the semantic interpretation assigned to a sentence provides a full analysis of its meaning. A constructive theory, which these authors advocated, postulates that individuals construct interpretations that go beyond the linguistically given information. Barclay (1973) illustrated the contrast by presenting two groups of subjects with sentences that described the serial order of five animals standing in a row. One group was told to work out the order, and another group, which was not told that the sentences described a serial order, was instructed merely to memorize the sentences. In a recognition test, the first group did not distinguish reliably between the original sentences and other sentences that were true of the array, whereas the second group, the memorizers, were only able to discriminate between sentences which introduced items not originally interrelated and the remaining sentences in the memory test. For some reason, Barclay did not make a direct statistical comparison between the performance of his two groups.

Our evidence on memory for spatial descriptions (see Chapter 7) suggests a theory of comprehension in which there are two stages. In the first, a superficial understanding of an utterance gives rise to a propositional representation, which is close to the surface form of the sentence. This symbolic representation is constructed in a mental language that has a vocabulary of comparable richness to that of natural language – a hypothesis independently urged by both Kintsch (1974) and Fodor, Fodor, and Garrett (1975). Propositional representations encode sufficient information to enable verbatim information to be recalled, at least for a brief interval of time. They provide an economical way of representing discourse, especially indeterminate descriptions. They are likely to resemble surface form rather than direct phonetic (or graphemic) transcriptions of an utterance, since it is almost impossible for native speakers to suppress the process of identifying words and recovering some syntactic relations. The second stage of comprehension, which is optional, makes use of propositional representations as a partial basis for the construction of a mental model, whose structure is analogous to the state of affairs described by the discourse. Hence the recovery of a propositional representation is a necessary precursor to the construction of a mental model. The constructive process is also guided by contextual cues and implicit inferences based on general knowledge. An utterance is more like a clue to the design of a model than a blueprint.

Suppose, to take an example from Johnson-Laird (1975b), you are asked whether you understand the following sentence:

The elderly gentleman often walked the streets of the town.

If you are a reasonably proficient speaker of English, then you will have no difficulty in grasping its meaning. You know the meanings of its words and you know how to combine them according to their syntactic relations. But do you grasp the significance of the statement, that is, the proposition that it expresses? Of course not. It is merely a sentence that you have come across in a book on language. If you had read it in a town guide, however, and inferred that *the elderly gentleman* referred to Einstein and *the town* referred to Princeton, then you would not only have understood the sentence, but you would know who and what it was about. You would be well on the way to grasping its *significance*, since you would have recovered the particular proposition that it conveyed in context. Perhaps you would not arrive at its full significance until you established the writer's communicative intention. Remarks that cannot be construed within an

244

intentional framework are usually perplexing. Certainly, their illocutionary force may be obscure, and one such decision about an utterance is basic: is it intended to make a statement, ask a question, or issue a request?

The theory of mental models, as we shall see, elucidates this second stage of comprehension. The essential context of an utterance can be represented in a mental model, and the significance of the utterance is established by relating its propositional representation to this model and to general knowledge. When the referents have been identified, the new information conveyed by the utterance can then be added to the model to bring it up to date. This process, however, may well occur clause by clause, or constituent by constituent, rather than at the level of complete sentences.

Empirical evidence corroborating the two levels of representation was presented in Chapter 7. Building a mental model from a propositional representation clearly demands an extra amount of processing over that required to set up a propositional representation alone, and this difference leads to the prediction that a model should be better remembered than a proposition. Indeed, a model goes beyond the literal meaning of the discourse, because it embodies inferences, instantiations, and references; the meaning of the sentence is not recoverable from the model. The experimental findings confirmed these hypotheses. The constructive process is likely to be slowed down by any expressions that are difficult to interpret, such as negatives and semantically 'marked' words, but once a model has been constructed, these variables should have a negligible effect – a conjecture that has also been confirmed experimentally (see Glushko and Cooper, 1978).

One other phenomenon is worth noting, as it bears out the distinction between propositional representations and models. The existence and efficacy of euphemisms depends on the possibility of superficial interpretations of discourse. If a word always evoked a complete representation of its denotation, then the almost universal human propensity to call a spade, not a spade, but an 'implement for excavating earth', would serve no purpose. The exotic terminology of death and burial – so notably satirized by Evelyn Waugh in *The Loved One* – would never have been invented. Euphemisms are designed to be represented propositionally and to deter full interpretation. Obscene words in their literal meanings, however, are designed to lead straight to a model of the world. Apart from their emotive use as swear words, they are so redolent of the things they name that even adults are prey to confusing the name for the thing. Hence, in many contexts (including books on cognitive science) it is acceptable to refer to sexual intercourse, but to do so using the obscene word would be almost as shocking as a picture of the act. Unlike inventing euphemisms, it is extremely difficult to make up a new obscenity, because such an invention almost demands the creation of a new obscene act.

A theory of comprehension

The two stages of interpretation need to be developed into a comprehensive theory, and this chapter concentrates on the second and more novel stage, the mapping of propositional representations into mental models in order to represent the significance of discourse. The theory that I shall propose is based on a number of independent assumptions, and I shall review each of them briefly before going into details.

1. *The processes by which fictitious discourse is understood are not essentially different from those that occur with true assertions.* That, perhaps, is why language is so powerful a medium for creating beliefs. The way you understand, say, *War and Peace*, is much the same as the way you understand an obvious work of fiction such as your daily newspaper. This is not to say that questions of veridicality do not matter – obviously it is important to know whether or not there is a present King of France, and whether God exists. The point is that these matters do not seem to affect linguistic processing.

2. *In understanding a discourse, you construct a single mental model of it.* The discourse could of course be true of infinitely many possible states of affairs, so how can you be sure to pick the right model? (This is like Wittgenstein's (1953) question, which I cited earlier: could a single leaf be a schema for all leaves and not just represent a particular shape? Wittgenstein said yes, it could, depending on how the sample is used. Alas, he did not tell us how to use a sample in this way.) If we were concerned with how an abstract automaton constructed a model of discourse, there is a neat theoretical trick that we can use: we posit a non-deterministic device that always constructs the right models – i.e., it guesses the right answer by magic (non-determinism is explained in more detail in Chapter 13). Hence, for a plausible psychological theory, we have to 'simulate' such a device, and the next assumption concerns the nature of this simulation.

3. *The interpretation of discourse depends on both the model and the processes that construct, extend, and evaluate it.* A single model can stand for an infinite set of possible models, because although only a single model is

constructed (based on some arbitrary assumptions), it can be recursively revised in the light of subsequent discourse. It is the process of recursive revision, which will be described presently, that simulates the required non-determinism, since it can produce any of the possible models that are consistent with the discourse.

4. *The functions that construct, extend, evaluate, and revise mental models, unlike the interpretation functions of model-theoretic semantics, cannot be treated in an abstract way.* There have to be explicit algorithms for computing the functions that map propositional representations into mental models. As we shall see, this requirement has several important consequences for psychological theories of meaning based on meaning postulates, semantic networks, or decompositional dictionary entries.

5. *A discourse is true if it has at least one mental model that satisfies its truth conditions that can be embedded in the model corresponding to the world.* This formulation applies only, of course, to assertions that have definite truth conditions.

The consequence of the first assumption – that factual and fictional discourse is understood in the same way – will not become apparent until we consider the interpretation of discourse as a whole. I shall deal with the processes of constructing and evaluating mental models (the remaining assumptions) in the following section, then I shall describe a computer implementation of the theory, and finally I shall consider its implications.

A procedural semantics for mental models

The theory assumes that there are procedures that construct models on the basis of the meanings of expressions. The view derives from what is known as 'procedural semantics' – an approach to the psychology of meaning based originally on computer programming (cf. Woods, 1967; Davies and Isard, 1972; Longuet-Higgins, 1972). There is a diversity of views about the nature and purpose of procedural semantics, and unfortunately the lack of a clear consensus has led to some misunderstandings.

A trivial mistake is to assume that procedural semantics is committed to a particular position in the 'procedural–declarative' controversy that flourished a few years ago among artificial intelligencers. This argument was really about whether sentences such as 'All artists are neurotic' should be stored in the data base of a computational system as assertions in a formal language resembling, say, the predicate calculus, or as procedures that would, for example, immediately add the information that a particular person is neurotic if it is asserted that the person is an artist. It was sometimes argued that the difference is related to Ryle's (1949) celebrated distinction between *knowing that* and *knowing how*. This claim seems dubious, because there appear to be no strong empirical consequences of claiming that a certain piece of information is stored in memory procedurally as opposed to declaratively. The choice of representation largely depends on what the system is supposed to do.

A more serious misconception is that procedural semantics is necessarily based on the assumption that the meaning of a sentence is a procedure which, when it is executed, determines the truth value of the sentence. This idea derives from the Logical Positivists' doctrine of Verificationism, according to which the meaning of an assertion (other than a logical truth) is the procedure by which it is verified, and if there is no such procedure the assertion is meaningless. There are irresolvable problems with this doctrine (see, e.g., Passmore, 1967), and it is a mistake to confuse the truth conditions of an assertion with the process by which one might check whether they are satisfied. The reason should be clear: if I tell you that in the next room there is a black cat sitting on a table, then your understanding of my utterance does not require you to verify that there is something that is a black cat and something that is a table in the next room, and that the one is sitting on the other. Moreover, the actions that you would have to carry out in order to verify the assertions would plainly *not* be a part of its meaning. To suppose otherwise would be akin to the old Behaviourist blunder of identifying the meaning of a word with a conditioned response. You may salivate when someone describes a gorgeous concoction from *haute cuisine*, but your salivation is contingent upon your understanding the description; it is *not* the understanding itself.

There has been one attempt to relate language to the world procedurally. Woods (1981) has argued that the relation can be captured by *abstract* procedures. They appear to play very much the same role as the interpretation function in a model-theoretic semantics; they cannot be executable procedures because assertions may make reference to events that are remote in time or space, and because executable procedures would inevitably call for actions irrelevant to the truth conditions of assertions. Hence it is unclear what advantage is gained by replacing an abstract interpretation function by an abstract procedure. The reader should bear in mind that the present theory uses a procedural semantics to relate language, not to the world, but to mental models.

In ordinary usage a word can function in many different sorts of utterances – questions, requests, assertions, and the full panoply of illocutions. It follows that the representation of a word's meaning must fit into a range of different mental processes. Likewise, an assertion may be put to use in a variety of ways: if someone tells you 'John is standing next to the host', then you may imagine the two of them standing side by side, or you may use the information in the sentence to determine which person the host is, or to determine which person John is, or to check that John is standing next to the host. You can also use words to *formulate* a description of a given state of affairs, in making a request, and so on. All of these various processes depend on a knowledge of the meanings of words and sentences; none of them should be identified with that knowledge – they are, as I have emphasized, contingent upon it. Let us consider in more detail the process of translating an assertion into a mental model. Several general procedures are required:

1. A procedure that begins the construction of a new mental model whenever an assertion makes no reference, either explicitly or implicitly, to any entity in the current model of the discourse.

2. A procedure which, if at least one entity referred to in the assertion is represented in the current model, adds the other entities, properties, or relations, to the model in an appropriate way.

3. A procedure that integrates two or more hitherto separate models if an assertion interrelates entities in them.

4. A procedure which, if all the entities referred to in the assertion are represented in the current model, verifies whether the asserted properties or relations hold in the model.

The verification procedure may be unable to establish a truth value of an assertion : there may be no information either way about the relevant property or relation. A model of John standing next to the host, for instance, does not yield a truth value for 'John is taller than the host'. In such cases, there is:

5. A procedure that adds the property or relation (ascribed in the assertion) to the model in the appropriate way.

Since only a single model is constructed for a single assertion, the procedures that construct models will be inevitably forced to make arbitrary decisions, since ordinary assertions are always consistent with more than one state of affairs. Such a decision may be wrong in that it leads to a conflict with subsequent information in the discourse (as revealed by the verification procedure). Hence, two recursive procedures are needed to cope with the simulation of the 'non-deterministic' device that always constructs the right model. These procedures embody the fundamental semantic principle of validity:

6. If an assertion is found to be true of the current model (by the verification procedure), then the present procedure checks whether the model can be modified in a way that is consistent with the previous assertions but so as to render the current assertion false. Where no such modification is possible (without doing violence to the meaning of the previous assertions), the current assertion adds no new semantic content: it is a valid deduction from the previous assertions.

7. If an assertion is found to be false of the current model (by the verification procedure), then the present procedure checks whether the model can be modified in a way that is consistent with the previous assertions but so as to render the current assertion true. When no such modification is possible (without doing violence to the meaning of the previous assertions), the current assertion is inconsistent with the previous assertions.

If the recursive procedures for revising mental models worked exhaustively and without error, they would constitute a 'decision procedure' for any inference that could be embodied in a mental model; as the evidence presented earlier in the book shows, few individuals perform without error.

In the course of comprehension, the propositional representation of an utterance elicits one of these seven general procedures as a function of its referring expressions, the context as represented in the current mental model, and the background knowledge that is triggered by the sentence. In this way, a model is initiated, extended or evaluated according to what is known about the truth conditions of the assertion. The step by which this knowledge of truth conditions is integrated within the general procedure is therefore crucial, and one way in which it can be done will be illustrated in the next section.

A program for interpreting spatial descriptions

I have outlined the general theory of how a procedural semantics is used to produce mental models. The theory's feasibility has been tested by making a small-scale 'working model' of it in the form of a computer program. The program is not intended to simulate the complexities of

250

human performance, nor is it meant to be an exercise in artificial intelligence. Its purpose is to display the principles of the theory in a perspicuous way.

The program takes as its input propositional representations of the following sort:

Premise (Right, A, B)

which are supposed to correspond to the superficial representations of such assertions as:

A is on the right of B.

No empirical claim hangs on the particular form of these propositional representations: they could equally well have corresponded to the surface form of the sentences. Given the propositional representations corresponding to the description:

A is on the right of B
C is in front of B
D is on the left of C

the program constructs a spatial array:

$$\text{B} \quad \text{A}$$
$$\text{D} \quad \text{C}$$

which satisfies the description.

The problem of revising a model recursively is closely related to the practical problem of implementing a program that manages and maintains a data base. (A good data-base program should also include certain procedures that are not strictly necessary for semantic interpretation, e.g., a procedure for replacing a large number of separate specific assertions with one all-embracing generalization.) In general, these programs are designed to answer questions about a data base and usually have only a limited ability to cope with assertions for updating the information there. The reason for shunning assertions is precisely the problem of what to do about indeterminate or inconsistent descriptions. A question-answering program leaves that problem to the person setting up the data base, but a program that copes with assertions cannot evade it. One approach to this problem, which has been advocated by a number of workers in artificial intelligence, is to formalize a *non-monotonic* logic. In orthodox logic, when a certain conclusion follows from a set of premises, it will still follow if any additional assertion is added to the premises. When we reason by default, however, we may make an implicit inference that a subsequent assertion forces us

251

to abandon. We are told something about a dog, for instance, and we infer by default that it has four legs, but then learn that in fact it has only three. Despite several attempts to formalize the notion (see, e.g., McDermott and Doyle, 1980), it continues to present apparently irresolvable problems (Davis, 1980).

An alternative approach is to use recursive procedures for revising models, and the present program embodies both of the recursive procedures that were described in the previous section. It responds to assertions that are incompatible with its current array either by modifying its model of the previous premises to bring it into line with the current assertion, or, if this modification is impossible, by pointing out that the current assertion is incompatible with what has gone before. It responds to an assertion that corresponds to what is already in its current array by checking whether there is an alternative model of the previous sentences that is inconsistent with the current assertion. If there is such an interpretation, the program points out that hitherto the current assertion was only possibly true; if there is not, it points out that the assertion is necessarily true given what has gone before. In short, the program makes inferences from simple assertions about the spatial relations between objects, and thus in effect it is able to answer questions. If the user wishes to know whether X is in front of Y in a particular layout, then an assertion to that effect will elicit one of the following responses (provided that X and Y have both been referred to before):

The premise was previously possibly but not necessarily true.
The premise is already necessarily true.
The premise was previously possibly false but not necessarily false.
The premise is already necessarily false.

If X or Y is not in the current array, then the program assumes the truth of the assertion and carries out the appropriate construction.

The program contains a number of general procedures, corresponding to those postulated in the general theory. (One procedure is omitted: the one that is elicited when the verification procedure fails to return a truth value, since this outcome can never occur in the program's world.) The program accordingly contains:

1. A procedure that begins the construction of a new spatial array whenever it is presented with an assertion that makes no reference to any items in an existing array. It inserts the items referred to by the assertion into an array in positions that satisfy the required spatial relation.

2. A procedure which, if one item referred to by an assertion is found in an existing array, inserts another item into the array in a position that satisfies the meaning of the assertion.

3. A procedure which, if one item in an assertion is found in one array and another item in the assertion is found in a separate array, combines the two arrays into an integrated array that satisfies the meaning of the assertions.

4. If both items in the assertion are found in the same array, there is a procedure that verifies whether the required spatial relation holds between them in the array.

5. If an assertion is true of a current array, then a procedure checks recursively whether the array can be rearranged in a way that is consistent with the previous assertions but so as to render false the current assertion.

6. If an assertion is false of a current array, then a procedure checks recursively whether the array can be rearranged in a way that is consistent with the previous assertions but so as to render the current assertion true.

The details of most of these procedures are straightforward and can be left to the reader's imagination, but procedures (5) and (6) for revising an array are more complicated and merit closer inspection. When one of these procedures attempts to move one item in an array, there may be others whose positions were given in terms of it, and hence before the item can be moved it is necessary to check whether these items can be moved; but they too may have further items related to them, and so before they can be moved it is necessary to check whether these further items can be moved ... and so on. For example, if the program is given the radically indeterminate description:

A is on the right of B
C is on the left of A

it constructs the following model:

C   B   A

If it is subsequently told:

C is on the right of B

then the verification procedure (3) intially returns the value *false*. This value automatically elicits the general procedure (6) that checks whether there is any way in which the model can be rearranged so as to render the assertion true. Obviously, what the procedure must do is to check whether, if it switches round the positions of B and C, the result is still compatible with the description. (Hence, it is necessary to keep a record of the propositional representations in order to check whether a proposed alteration in the model is not directly ruled out by a particular premise.) In this particular case, there is no hindrance to the switch's taking place. Suppose, now, that the previous description had also contained an assertion to the effect that D is in front of B:

C B A

D

In this case, before B can be switched with C, it is necessary to check whether the position of D can be similarly shifted. There is, in fact, no premise to prevent such a switch and the program will construct the reorganized model:

B C A

D

However, let us consider one further example in which other, earlier, assertions had established that E is in front of C, and that E is on the left of D, yielding the model:

C B A

E D

At this point, the program is told as before that C is on the right of B. It must now first attempt to switch B and C, but it discovers that D is in front of B and that E is in front of C. Hence it must check the set of premises to determine whether D and E can be switched round; in fact, the switch is impossible because of the earlier premise that E is on the left of D. Only at this point is it plain that B and C cannot be switched, and thus the program announces that the new assertion is inconsistent with the previous description.

There is in principle no limit to the number of dependents of items in an array that might have to be followed up in order to determine whether a model can be reorganised. That is why the process is handled by a procedure that can call itself recursively. For the reader interested in technical details, Table 11.1 presents a summary of the recursive function that is used to try to remake an array so as to accommodate the current assertion – the central component of procedure (6).

The program ensures that a given sentence in a description elicits the appropriate general procedure, depending on both what the assertion refers to and the context in which it occurs. If the program is given the assertion:

A is in front of B

254

Table 11.1 *A summary of the recursive function REMAKE, used in the spatial inference program to try to reconstruct an array recursively so that it is consistent with the previous discourse and the current assertion*

The function REMAKE takes three arguments: two items X and Y in an existing array, and the direction in which X has to shift in order to create the required relation between X and Y. It contains five main steps, three of which can call the function recursively:

1. If there is a premise relating X and Y that is contrary to X's required move then return the value *false*, and Exit.

2. If there is a premise relating X to an item in the direction in which X has to move then
    If this item occupies the location to which X is supposed to move then
    If REMAKE cannot relocate the item then return the value *false*, and Exit.

3. If there is a premise relating X to an item orthogonal to the direction in which X is to move then
    If REMAKE cannot relocate this item to maintain its relative position to X then return the value *false*, and exit.

4. If there is an item in the array at the position to which X is to be shifted then
    If REMAKE cannot shift this item out of the way then return the value *false*, and Exit.

5. Shift X to its required location, return the value *true*, and Exit.

then the general procedure that is called depends on the present state of the array. If both A and B are already in the array, the program calls the verification procedure (4) to decide whether the assertion is true, and its result then elicits a procedure (either 5 or 6) to check whether the array can be rearranged. If neither A nor B is in the array, then the utterance is, as it were, starting a new topic and calls for the procedure (1) that creates a new array, though that array may ultimately be integrated into an old one should there occur an assertion that interrelates items in both of them. If only one of the items, A or B, is in the array, then procedure (2) inserts the other item into the array at the appropriate position. The particular procedure that is executed accordingly depends on the referents of the expressions in the assertion. In this respect, the program reflects a general interpretative principle, though obviously there are other factors that determine how listeners actually react to an utterance.

Once a general procedure has been selected, the meaning of the assertion has to be used in running that procedure. This step is the crucial one of integrating the meaning of the assertion into the general procedure. There are several ways in which the step could be made, but the program makes use of the device of 'freezing in' the values of a variable in a function. This process creates a new function with fewer arguments than the original function. For example, a simple arithmetical function such as addition

255

takes two variables, x and y, and when it is called during the execution of a program by an instruction such as:

$$ADD (x, y);$$

the current values of x and y are added together. A new function can be obtained from ADD by freezing in the value of one variable, i.e., fixing its value permanently. Thus, one can freeze in 5 as the value of the second variable, and then give this new function a name, say, ADD5. The programming language POP-10 allows this operation to be performed by using the following expression:

$$ADD (\% \, 5 \, \%) \to ADD5;$$

which partially applies the function ADD so as to yield the new function ADD5. The new function takes just a single variable and adds 5 to whatever its value is: e.g., the result of ADD5(2) is 7. This simple computational machinery has a natural extension that can be exploited in many ways: instead of freezing in numerical values for variables, one can freeze in functions as the values of variables. In particular, one can freeze the meaning of an expression into any one of the general procedures.

Suppose, for example, that in coping with the sentence 'A is in front of B', the general procedure that has been selected is one for inserting A into the array, i.e., B is already sitting in the current array. This general procedure is used in creating a more specific procedure that inserts the new item *in front of* the old item; and the specific procedure is created by freezing in the values of variables in the general procedure. Every general procedure has a mechanism for scanning in any arbitrary direction. It works by iteratively incrementing the two co-ordinate values of the currently scanned location. The actual increments depend on the values assigned to two parameters of the general procedure, DI and DJ, which accordingly specify the direction of the scan. Figure 11.1 illustrates the direction of the scan of the locations *in front of* the item B in an array. Since the same scanning mechanism is used by all the general procedures, the truth conditions of *in front of* can be specified in a very simple way:

```
Function Infront f;
f(% 1, 0 %);
End
```

This is the actual code in POP-10 from the program. The first line specifies that the function is called *infront* and that it takes a single argument, f, which in fact is always one of the general procedures described above.

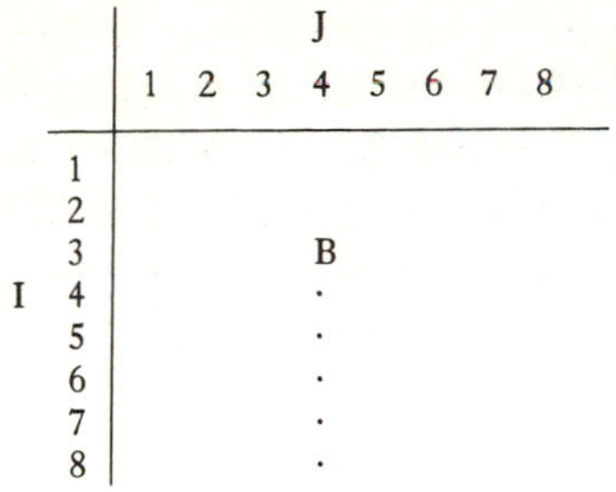

```
                        J
            | 1  2  3  4  5  6  7  8

        1   |
        2   |
        3   |        B
    I   4   |        ·
        5   |        ·
        6   |        ·
        7   |        ·
        8   |        ·
```

Given that B is located at I = 3, J = 4, then setting DI = 1 and DY = 0 causes a scan through the sequence of locations obtained by progressively incrementing the I co-ordinate by 1 whilst holding the J co-ordinate constant (incrementing it by 0). The sequence of locations scanned, as illustrated, is: (4, 4), (5, 4), (6, 4) . . . .

Figure 11.1 The sequence of locations scanned in an array that are *in front of* the item B.

The second line has the effect of freezing in the values 1 and 0 to the two rightmost parameters of the general procedure, which correspond to DI and DJ. This freeze creates a function that scans by progressively incrementing the I co-ordinate by 1 and the J co-ordinate by 0 (i.e., it holds J constant). Hence, when the function *infront* is applied to the procedure for adding a new item to the array it creates a specific procedure that adds the new item *in front of* the old item at the first available location. There is no danger of falling off the edge of the universe: an array is expanded, if need be, to accommodate a new item.

Is the lexical entry given above for *in front of* procedural or declarative? The answer is, in fact, that it is very special – almost midway between a conventional procedure and a piece of declarative information. It is a procedure that cannot be executed on its own: it takes other procedures and produces new, more specific, ones from them. Its effect is to specify the contribution of *in front of* to the truth conditions of the sentences in which it occurs, because what the new specific procedures do is to construct models that satisfy those truth conditions, to examine existing models to determine whether they satisfy them, and so on. I assume that the mental lexicon contains similar specifications that are used in the different procedures for manipulating mental models.

The program for spatial inference is, I repeat, a simplified implementation of the procedural theory of comprehension. One of its most blatant over-simplifications is that speakers do not normally require that one object lie directly in line with another in order to satisfy the truth conditions of a spatial relation. They tolerate a certain amount of vagueness, which is

257

likely to be affected by the actual shapes and sizes of the objects. Another simplification is in its treatment of referring expressions, which are always effectively proper nouns as far as the program is concerned; a more comprehensive account of reference and mental models will be given in Chapter 14. The main aspects of the program, however, are intended to be psychologically realistic.

How to eliminate meaning postulates, semantic networks, and decompositional dictionary entries

A model-theoretic semantics allows a theorist to distinguish between truth conditions and semantic relations. The contribution to truth conditions made by an expression such as *on the right of* can be specified by the interpretation function, which provides the set of ordered pairs of individuals in the model structure between which the relation holds. Its semantic properties and relations to other expressions can be captured in a set of meaning postulates, such as:

For any x, y, and z, if x is on the right of y, and y is on the right of z, then x is on the right of z.
For any x and y, if x is on the right of y, then y is on the left of z.

Thus there can be no model in which, for example, it is true that x is on the right of y, and that y is on the right of z, but false that x is on the right of z. Similarly there can be no model in which x is on the right of y, but y is not on the left of x.

Proponents of psychological theories based on meaning postulates, semantic networks, or decompositional dictionaries tacitly draw the same distinction between semantic properties and truth conditions. They argue, along with many linguists and philosophers, that the semantic representation of a sentence captures its logical or semantic form. That is to say, the entailments of the sentence are derived by operations on its semantic representation, which apply a meaning postulate, follow up an arc in a network, or compare one semantic decomposition with another. The representation of truth conditions, in virtue of which 'A is on the right of B' in the following arrangement:

B   A

is an entirely separate matter about which these theories have little or nothing to say.

258

The procedural theory, unlike a model-theoretic semantics, cannot merely assume the existence of abstract functions that map predicates into models. As we have seen, the psychological theory must contain explicit algorithms that carry out this process. A devastating consequence follows for psychological theories based on meaning postulates, semantic networks, or decompositional dictionary entries. These theories purport to capture the semantic properties and relations of expressions, but they give no account of their truth conditions. Once the interpretation function gives a full specification of truth conditions, as it must do in the procedural semantics, it is completely unnecessary to make an independent formulation of semantic properties and relations. They emerge naturally from the truth conditions. To see why, just consider the way the program treats the transitivity of *in front of*.

Given the description:

A is in front of B

B is in front of C

the program constructs the array shown in Figure 11.2. Suppose the next input is:

A is in front of C.

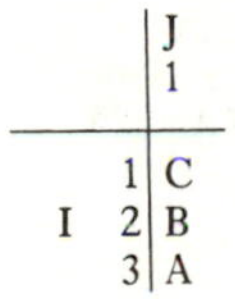

```
           | J
           | 1
 _____|_____
           | 1 | C
      I    | 2 | B
           | 3 | A
```

Figure 11.2 The array constructed by the program to represent the assertions: 'A is in front of B', 'B is in front of C'.

The program discovers that this assertion is true in the array, then attempts to reconstruct the array so as to render it false, but fails to do so and finally prints out the message:

The premise is already necessarily true.

Hence, the program makes a transitive inference even though it makes no use of any explicit information about transitivity or intransitivity.

Several theorists have claimed that the apparatus of spatial arrays smuggles in the principle of transitivity by the back door. (Both Jerry Fodor and Zenon Pylyshyn have independently made this suggestion in conversation, but it would be unfair to saddle them with a strong commitment to it.) Its plausibility rests on its confusability with a very different

259

claim, namely, that it is possible to define transitive relations over model structures that are spatial arrays. Obviously, if a transitive relation is to be represented in an array, this condition must hold. Spatial arrays, however, do not have transitivity built into them: if they did, they would be unable to represent non-transitive relations, or relations that are transitive to varying degrees. The same point emerges from a close examination of a computational example.

Consider the way in which a model might be constructed for assertions about the natural numbers $(0, 1, 2, \ldots)$. To build models that satisfy such assertions as $x > y$, we need to specify explicitly how to compute the characteristic function for this relation. Any computable function can be reduced to a combination of three basic types of basic function: the zero function, the successor function, and the identity functions (see Chapter 1). The characteristic function for $x > y$, which returns the value *true* if x is greater than y, and the value *false* otherwise, can be readily defined in terms of these functions:

$$x > y = \begin{cases} \text{true if } (x \dotminus y) \neq 0 \\ \text{false if } (x \dotminus y) = 0 \end{cases}$$

where $(x \dotminus y)$ is defined as subtraction except that it returns 0 instead of a negative number:

$$x \dotminus 0 = x$$
$$x \dotminus \text{successor } (y) = \text{predecessor } (x \dotminus y)$$

and:

$$\text{predecessor } (0) = 0$$
$$\text{predecessor } (\text{successor } (y)) = y$$

Given this full specification of the function and a model consisting of the natural numbers $(0, 1, 2, 3, \ldots)$, it is plainly not necessary to specify that the relation is transitive. For any x, y, and z, whenever the function returns the value *true* for $x > y$ and for $y > z$, it is bound to return *true* for $x > z$ too. Yet the principle of transitivity is plainly *not* expressed within any of the three types of basic function: it emerges from their particular combination in this example, but not in others.

The same argument can be carried over directly to transitivity in a spatial array. The array is a set of locations that are defined by ordered pairs of integers. The semantics of the spatial relations yields specific procedures that take an initial pair of integers, such as $(3, 4)$, and apply the successor function iteratively to them in order to produce an appropriate sequence of locations, such as: $(3, 5), (3, 6), (3, 7) \ldots$ A specific procedure for verification constructed by freezing in this semantics will examine each location to check whether it contains the required item. Hence, although the procedure may give rise to transitivity, it makes use only of basic functions, which do not in themselves contain transitivity. The principle is nowhere represented in the program; it emerges from the way the program works.

The vagaries of inference

The emergence of semantic properties from truth conditions has the great advantage of accounting for an otherwise very puzzling phenomenon – the vagaries of the inferences in daily life. The inferences discussed earlier in the book, which were based on such premises as:

Matthew is on Mark's right
Mark is on Luke's right

depend on our conception of human beings as having an intrinsic right-hand side and an intrinsic left-hand side (see, e.g., Miller and Johnson-Laird, 1976, Sec. 6.1.3). Such inferences can be readily accommodated by models that satisfy the truth conditions of the premises with respect to a frame of reference defined by the position and orientation of the relevant individuals. A simple linear semantics for *x is on y's right* will suffice. The basic idea is first to locate the relevant individual, say, Mark, then to establish a frame of reference based on his orientation, and finally to use the semantics to add Matthew to the model in a position on the right-hand side of the lateral plane passing through Mark. When this process is carried out in relation to some individuals seated at a circular table, as shown in Figure 11.3 the same simple linear semantics for *on the right* gives rise to just the vagaries of inference that are required. The transitive inference:

A is on B's right
B is on C's right
Therefore, A is on C's right

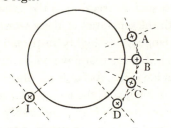

Figure 11.3 The frames of reference for a group of people seated at a table.

261

is acceptable, since A is sufficiently near to the plane passing through the locations on C's right. However, the transitive inference:

A is on B's right
B is on C's right
C is on D's right
. . .
H is on I's right
Therefore, A is on I's right

is unacceptable, since A is close to being opposite I and very far from the plane passing through the locations on I's right.

The previous section established that there was no need to capture semantic properties in meaning postulates, semantic networks, or whatever; the present exercise in procedural semantics shows that it would be a mistake to do so in certain cases, where there are marked vagaries in the validity of an inference of a given form. Change the seating arrangement, for instance, and even the deduction:

A is on B's right
B is on C's right
Therefore, A is on C's right

ceases to be valid. The criterion for validity is purely semantic, depending on the impossibility of constructing a model of the premises and their context in which the conclusion is false.

The status of semantic primitives

The theory of procedural semantics has implications for the status of semantic primitives. The meanings of basic spatial terms such as *right* and *left* cannot be lexically analysed in decompositional dictionary entries of the standard sort, because it is impossible to define these words in more primitive terms. Yet the fact that they are indefinable does not mean that they are primitives. On the contrary, the spatial program makes use of procedural primitives, such as freezing in the values of incremental parameters, in coping with the semantics of these words. The meanings of the words in the object language (a highly restricted subset of English) are formulated in procedural terms that have no simple – let alone one-to-one – relation to the object language. As far as the object language is concerned, the primitives are ineffable just as the true semantic primitives underlying our use of language are ineffable and inevitably a matter for scientific investigation. The program illustrates the need to employ such primitives in order to specify the truth conditions of expressions. It specifies them, not in relation to the real world, but in relation to *models* of the world. Human beings know how to relate expressions to models of the world; unlike the program, however, they have ways of constructing such models that are not dependent on a linguistic input.

On the basis of his mimicry theorem, Anderson (1978) has argued that any psychological behaviour based on semantic primitives can be equally well computed with the aid of meaning postulates. Although the theorem is sound, the claim is false. Meaning postulates in a psychological theory are intended to capture entailments (Fodor, 1975, p. 149). They represent the semantic properties of a word and its semantic relations to other words, but not its contribution to truth conditions. The truth conditions of many words are indeed impossible to formulate in the object language, just as, for example, there is no way to define the meaning of *on the right* and *on the left* in the language used as input to the computer program. There is thus no way to capture such truth conditions by using meaning postulates, which interrelate terms in the object language. A semantics based on procedural primitives, however, can represent truth conditions. Hence, a theory that employs semantic primitives transcends the mimicking propensities of meaning postulates.

The theory of mental models suggests that what children have to acquire are the truth conditions of expressions – more accurately, the contribution that expressions make to the truth conditions of sentences. Once they have a working knowledge of this aspect of a word they will have implicitly mastered its logical properties, given that the general skills of constructing and manipulating mental models are available to them. The intensions of words, however, are not specified in isolation. As our earlier analysis of vagueness revealed, words are organised taxonomically, and hence the route to acquiring their intensions is likely to be taxonomic too. The procedural primitives are therefore likely to be organised into a taxonomic device, such as a decision table (Miller and Johnson-Laird, 1976), that provides the structure for the relevant lexical domain. Moreover, children who reflect upon the invariant properties of a word may in time come to represent them in the form of meaning postulates. For example, many children like playing the 'opposites' game:

What is the opposite of *tall*? *Short*.
What's the opposite of *fat*? *Thin*.
And so on.

The mastery of this essentially meta-linguistic game is likely to depend on an explicit grasp of the relations between words in a taxonomy. This knowledge may well be represented by meaning postulates. If children were to learn meaning postulates first, however, it would be extremely difficult to account for the vagaries in the logical properties of many terms. They arise quite naturally from truth conditions, whose acquisition is the foundation of semantic knowledge.

Conclusions

Model-theoretic semantics maps the expressions of language into model structures, and in the case of natural language Montague (1974) and others have argued that these structures consist of 'possible worlds'. Such a semantics cannot be inserted directly into the mind, because there are infinitely many possible worlds. Both Partee (1979) and Johnson-Laird (1982) have struggled with this problem of a *rapprochement* between semantic theory and psychology. In this chapter, I have argued that there is a direct resolution of the problem: *a mental model is a single representative sample from the set of models satisfying the assertion*. The notion of *a representative sample* does not imply that the set of models satisfying the discourse is constructed and then a sample is selected from them. On the contrary, comprehension normally leads to just a single model, which is constructed by the procedural semantics from what is known about the truth conditions of an assertion. If a subsequent assertion shows that this particular model is incorrect, then recursive procedures attempt to reconstruct the model so as to satisfy the current set of assertions. The point to be stressed is that the significance of an assertion depends on both the model and the procedures for manipulating and evaluating it. These procedures treat a given model as only one of an indefinitely large set of different possibilities. Hence, the particular model stands in for the set as a whole, and, since it is constructed on the basis of default inferences from the general knowledge triggered by the discourse, it is an exemplar of the likely situation described by the discourse. But the recursive procedures can, in effect, replace one sample by another, though in practice the capacity of working memory limits the extent to which recursive reconstructions can be carried out. A mental model is finite in size, but people can also reason about sets of infinite size, such as the natural numbers. The basis of this ability is a topic that I shall defer until Chapter 15. Meanwhile, the reader should note that a mental model can represent an infinite number of different possibilities; the theory of mental models is compatible with a model-theoretic semantics for finite domains.

Even if all the semantic properties and relations of such spatial terms as *right* and *left* could be pinned down by lexical decomposition, links in a network, or meaning postulates, which were somehow able to cope with the vagaries of transitivity, then it would still be necessary to specify how these words enter into the specifications of the truth conditions of the sentences in which they occur. The procedural theory outlined in this chapter takes that goal as its starting point. What emerges from this approach is that once truth conditions have thus been taken care of there is no need to give a separate account of the semantic properties of expressions. They are emergent properties of the truth conditions.

12

Grammar and psychology

The previous chapter outlined the theory that utterances are translated into propositional representations that can be used by a procedural semantics to construct mental models; and it illustrated the way this semantics might work by describing in detail a computer program for making inferences from spatial descriptions. The time has now come to consider the initial translation into a propositional representation. This process depends on the recognition of words and intonation in the speech waveform, and on the ability to recover (and to express) grammatical relations in sentences. What makes the parsing of natural language particularly difficult to elucidate is the fact that sentences do not express their grammatical form wholly explicitly. In a formal language like arithmetic, an expression such as:

$$(x + 2)$$

has an explicit structure and a standard interpretation – carry out the operation signified by '+' on x and 2. However, a string of words such as:

two feet off the ground

is structurally ambiguous. It is a constituent of the sentence:

After the crash, the bus had its front two feet off the ground.

But it is not a constituent in the normal interpretation of the sentence:

The horse had its front two feet off the ground.

Despite the absence of explicit cues, the mental parser operates remarkably efficiently in coping with such sentences.

Earlier in the book it proved useful to distinguish between meaning (Chapter 9), the mental representation of meaning (Chapter 10), and the process by which that representation is constructed (Chapter 11). It will be similarly useful to distinguish between grammatical structure, its mental representation, and the process by which that structure is recovered. Grammatical structure is a matter for linguistic analysis; its mental representation and the process of parsing require psycholinguistic investigation. All three topics are clearly interrelated, but just how close the relation is between linguistics and psychology remains highly controversial. This chapter will consider the theory of grammar and some of its implications for psychology; the next will take up the problem of parsing.

This chapter begins with an account of transformational grammar and early work in psycholinguistics. It then re-examines progressively the basic tenets of transformational grammar in the light of recent developments in theoretical linguistics. These developments may make possible a fundamental simplification in our conception of how natural language is parsed, of how it is produced, and of how it is acquired by children.

Grammar and automata theory

Noam Chomsky (1957, 1965) radically reformulated the aims of linguistic theory. He took the initial goal of linguistics to be the framing of explicit grammatical rules of a language, which should be descriptively adequate in that they characterize the set of sentences in the language together with their appropriate syntactic structures. Since in principle there is an infinitude of descriptively adequate grammars, a further goal is the formulation of an explanatorily adequate theory that constrains the set of possible grammars. The theory in effect can construct a grammar for the language from a fragmentary sample of utterances in the same sort of way that children do. Such a theory (or hypothesis about it) concerns 'Universal Grammar', which defines the biologically determined properties of natural language; it can be tested by assessing the descriptive adequacy of the grammars that it permits. A line has to be drawn, however, between what an individual knows tacitly about the rules of the language (i.e., linguistic competence) and how the individual puts this knowledge to work in speaking and understanding (i.e., linguistic performance). A complete psychology of the grammatical aspects of language would characterize both competence (in a theory of grammar) and performance (in a theory of parsing and production). There are problems with a rigid interpretation of this division – where, for example, is one to locate a knowledge of how to cope with ungrammatical sentences? – but nevertheless, it provides a useful line of demarcation to which I shall adhere.

Chomsky argued that although languages differ superficially, their underlying form is universal and innately determined, since only this supposition could explain children's ability to construct a grammar from the fragmentary and largely positive evidence available to them. Because the primary data for a theory of grammar are judgments about what is,

267

and is not, in the language, linguists can rely on their own intuitions about their native tongues in order to construct theories.

Chomsky's concern with explicit rules reflects a mathematical conception of language owing much to the theory of automata and recursive functions. From this formal standpoint, a language can be treated as a set of strings composed from a vocabulary of signs. The set of all possible strings that can be formed from a given vocabulary is enumerably infinite, that is, the set of strings can be put into a one-to-one correspondence with the integers. A language is a subset of this set, because some strings in the set will be ungrammatical and therefore outside the language. It is easy to show that the set of all subsets of an enumerably infinite set is *not* itself enumerable, but still larger (see Boolos and Jeffrey, 1974). Hence, the set of *all* possible languages (defined on a given vocabulary) is more than merely countably infinite. When one confronts this mathematical consequence with the criterion that the grammar of a language should be an effective procedure, a striking conclusion emerges. An effective procedure can be computed by a Turing machine, and Turing machines are enumerably infinite (see Chapter 1). Hence, there are more possible languages than there are possible grammars. The argument is no mere speculation but can be readily proved, granted the assumptions about language on which it is based.

As I have argued elsewhere, the effects of the mathematical approach to linguistic theory have been profound but not altogether beneficial (see Johnson-Laird, in press). The power of mathematical proofs has forced psychologists to keep an anxious eye on the latest developments in linguistic theory, and to develop theories of performance that are perhaps too dependent on current conceptions of competence. When the linguistic theories have turned out to be misguided, the psycholinguists have had the rug pulled from beneath them. They might have been better advised to have set out independently to account for linguistic performance. Yet even today, some linguists claim that psycholinguistic studies are irrelevant because experimental facts about performance do not constrain grammar, and that the only psychological 'experiments' that therefore matter are theorists' intuitions about sentences.

The most influential of Chomsky's (1957) proofs concerns the impossibility of characterizing the grammar of a natural language by way of a *finite-state device*. One way to think of a finite-state device is as a Turing machine that has been so restricted in power that it simply shifts from one state to another as a function of its present state and the symbol that it is scanning, and cannot extend its memory (i.e., its effective number of states) by writing symbols on the tape. Equivalently, one can think of it as a device that *generates* certain symbols on an initially blank tape as it shifts from state to state, but which cannot extend its memory by use of the tape. A particular class of finite automata had always seemed to be highly pertinent to natural language, namely, those where the state of the device is determined by the last k symbols of the output sequence that has been generated, where k is some fixed integer. The behaviour of such a finite automaton can be characterized completely by either a state-diagram or a matrix of transitions as shown in Figure 12.1. This automaton is probabilistic because in certain states, namely S_1 and S_4, the particular symbol it generates is determined probabilistically.

The set of sentences produced by the device can also be specified by a set of grammatical rules, which are shown in Figure 12.1 together with an example of the 'tree' structure for a sentence that they generate. A rule such as:

$$S_0 \quad \rightarrow \quad \text{Determiner} \quad S_1$$

can be interpreted as an instruction to rewrite the symbol S_0 as the symbol Determiner followed by the symbol S_1. A rule such as:

$$S_4 \quad \rightarrow \quad \begin{Bmatrix} \text{Noun } S_5 \\ \text{Adverb} \end{Bmatrix}$$

is an abbreviation for two alternatives, rewriting S_4 as a Noun followed by S_5, or as an Adverb alone.

The device in Figure 12.1 is plainly rudimentary. The resemblance of its output to actual English would be improved by increasing the number of parts of speech that it employs, the number of its internal states, and the value of k, i.e., the number of symbols to be taken into account in determining the next state that it enters. Theorists had generally believed that if the amount of context taken into account were increased to some arbitrarily large but finite number of words, then the resulting device could produce a natural language. This view is certainly implicit in the neo-Behaviourists' assumption that grammar consists of a habit-family hierarchy of responses for each word position in a sentence.

Chomsky criticized this line of thought by arguing that no matter how many words are taken into account prior to the transition to the next word, a finite-state device could never converge completely on English. His argument rests on the assumption that a grammatical structure can be interrupted by another grammatical structure of the same sort, which, in

A state diagram:

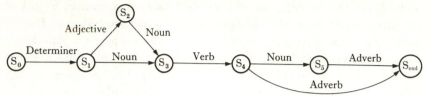

A matrix of transition probabilities:

The k + 1th symbol

		Noun	Verb	Adverb
Determiner	Adjective	1	0	0
Determiner	Noun	0	1	0
Adjective	Noun	0	1	0
Noun	Verb	0.6	0	0.4
Verb	Noun	0	0	1

The k previous symbols where k = 2

A set of grammatical rules and an example of the 'tree' they generate:

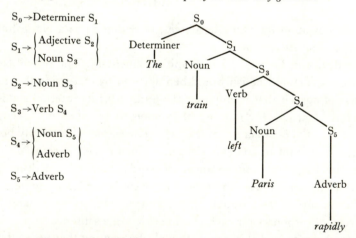

$S_0 \rightarrow$ Determiner S_1

$S_1 \rightarrow \begin{cases} \text{Adjective } S_2 \\ \text{Noun } S_3 \end{cases}$

$S_2 \rightarrow$ Noun S_3

$S_3 \rightarrow$ Verb S_4

$S_4 \rightarrow \begin{cases} \text{Noun } S_5 \\ \text{Adverb} \end{cases}$

$S_5 \rightarrow$ Adverb

Figure 12.1 A finite-state automaton represented as a state diagram, as a matrix of transitions, and as a set of grammatical rules. This particular automaton is limited by the k previous symbols of output, where k = 2, and its behaviour is probabilistic.

turn, can be interrupted in the same way ... and so on, *ad infinitum*. A sequence of self-embedded structures, such as:

The war ends the world

The war the general starts ends the world

The war the general the president ... appoints starts ends the world

gets progressively harder to understand, but according to Chomsky each of its members is grammatical. If only a finite number of embeddings is permitted in the language, a finite-state device could cope with them: the states and transitions for handling a clause could be repeated within the device the required number of times embedded within each other in the appropriate way. Figure 12.2 shows how to construct such a device for generating one embedding. But if any arbitrary number of embeddings is grammatical, then no finite-state device can cope, since by definition it has only a finite number of states and the number of embeddings in a sentence may exceed the number of states for handling embedded clauses.

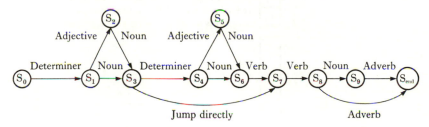

Figure 12.2 A state diagram of a finite-state automaton that handles one embedded clause.

Of course, if there were no need for the number of noun phrases in an embedded sentence to tally with the number of verbs (and to agree in grammatical 'number' with them), the sequence of embedded sentences above could be generated along with other ungrammatical ones by a relatively simple finite-state device that produced an arbitrary number of noun phrases followed by an arbitrary number of verbs.

As the reader may have realized by now, the way to handle unlimited self-embedding is, as Chomsky showed, by using a grammar that defines sentences recursively. Finite-state automata can handle simple iteration, i.e., rules of the form:

$$\text{Adjective} \rightarrow \textit{very} \quad \text{Adjective}$$

which have the effect of generating a symbol without changing state, and hence can generate an arbitrarily long sequence of symbols: *very very*

very . . . Adjective. But finite-state automata cannot handle rules that require a procedure with internal changes of state to call itself recursively. The simplest way to cope with recursive procedures is to use a push-down automaton. This device, illustrated in Figure 12.3 can be thought of as a finite-state automaton to which a special memory tape has been added. Any number of symbols can be written on or erased from the memory tape, but access is only to the most recently written symbol at the top of the 'stack', and it is therefore necessary to erase it in order to gain access to the symbol beneath it. Push-down memory thus works on a 'last in,

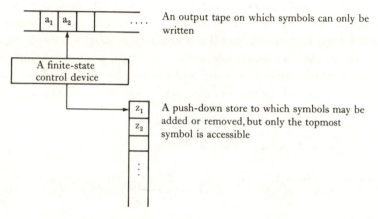

An output tape on which symbols can only be written

A finite-state control device

A push-down store to which symbols may be added or removed, but only the topmost symbol is accessible

Figure 12.3 A push-down automaton.

first out' basis like a vertical stack of symbols. Such a stack is exactly what is required in order to parse embedded structures. For example, the nesting of parentheses in mathematical formulas can be parsed by placing each left parenthesis on the stack and erasing one item from the stack for each right parenthesis: in this way the device can accept formulas with any arbitrary depth of nesting of parentheses. Although a push-down automaton is more powerful than a finite-state automaton, it is less powerful than a Turing machine, which is equivalent to a finite-state automaton equipped with *two* push-down stores.

Another way to think of a push-down automaton, illustrated in Figure 12.4, is as a 'recursive transition network' in which there is a set of separate finite automata, which can call on each other's services. Here, the device for generating a sentence immediately calls upon the services of the device for generating a noun phrase, and once the latter has generated a noun phrase, it returns control to the sentence automaton, and so on. The system

State diagrams of the finite-state devices making up the automaton:

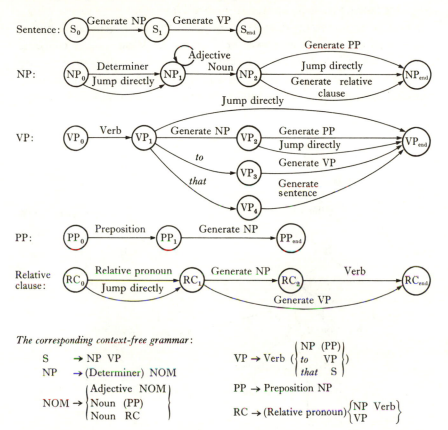

The corresponding context-free grammar:

S   → NP VP

NP   → (Determiner) NOM

$$\text{NOM} \rightarrow \begin{Bmatrix} \text{Adjective NOM} \\ \text{Noun (PP)} \\ \text{Noun RC} \end{Bmatrix}$$

$$\text{VP} \rightarrow \text{Verb } \left(\begin{Bmatrix} \text{NP (PP)} \\ to \quad \text{VP} \\ that \quad \text{S} \end{Bmatrix}\right)$$

PP → Preposition NP

$$\text{RC} \rightarrow (\text{Relative pronoun})\begin{Bmatrix} \text{NP Verb} \\ \text{VP} \end{Bmatrix}$$

Note. Items in parentheses are optional: they correspond to the choice between jumping directly and generating a symbol in the automaton. Items in braces are alternatives: they correspond to the choice between several alternatives in the automaton.

Figure 12.4 A push-down store automaton in the form of a 'recursive transition network', and its corresponding context-free grammar.

as a whole must keep track of which particular automaton it must return control to, and this requirement is satisfied by using a push-down stack.

The grammatical rules corresponding to a push-down automaton constitute what is known as a *context-free* grammar: i.e., each rule allows one symbol to be rewritten in terms of others regardless of the context in which that symbol occurs. The grammar of Figure 12.4 handles recursion: NP can be rewritten as a structure containing a relative clause, which in turn can be rewritten as a structure containing an NP. This sort of self-embedded structure is illustrated in Figure 12.5.

There is an important distinction between the weak generative power and the strong generative power of a grammar. Weak power concerns solely the set of sentences that are generated. Thus, a finite-state grammar lacks the weak generative power to specify sentences with an arbitrary number of grammatical embeddings. Strong generative power, however,

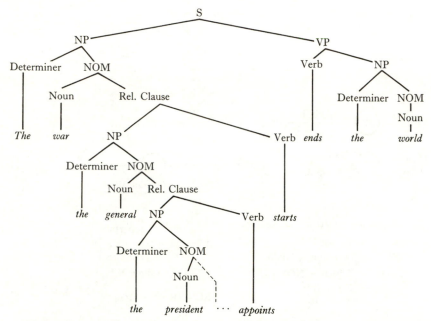

Figure 12.5 An example of a self-embedded sentence generated by the context-free grammar of Figure 12.4.

concerns the specification of the set of sentences together with their syntactic structures. A finite-state grammar again lacks the strong generative power to generate the appropriate structures for sentences since it produces the simplest possible branching structure (see Figure 12.1). It seemed intuitively obvious to Chomsky (1957) that even a context-free grammar could not give an adequate description of a natural language, in that it lacked the strong generative power to specify the correct syntactic structures of sentences, and was also unable to capture certain generalizations about the language such as the obvious relation between active and passive sentences. One particular problem is that the rules do not handle contextual constraints directly. The grammar in Figure 12.4, for example, makes no direct provision for the fact that only transitive verbs take object noun phrases. One way round this particular problem is to make use of *context-sensitive* rules that explicitly take the context of a symbol into account:

$$\text{Verb} \rightarrow \text{Verb}_{Tr}/\_\_\text{Noun phrase} \#$$
$$\text{Verb} \rightarrow \text{Verb}_{Int}/\_\_ \#$$

where ' # ' is a punctuation marker for the end of the clause. The first rule indicates that a verb is specified as transitive in a context where it precedes a noun phrase – the context is specified after the slash sign. The second rule indicates that a verb is specified as intransitive in a context where there is no following noun phrase.

Chomsky (1959) proved that context-sensitive grammars are more powerful in weak generative capacity than context-free grammars – they can generate languages that cannot be generated by context-free grammars. In general, the class of context-sensitive grammars corresponds to the class of *linear-bounded* automata, which can be thought of as Turing machines which, instead of having a potentially infinite tape on which to write and read symbols, are restricted to a portion of tape that is some linear function of the input, or equivalently, the same length as the input. They can augment their memory by freely reading and writing symbols on this portion of tape without the 'last in, first out' restriction of the push-down automaton.

Grammars that specify the structure of phrases by using trees of the sort that have been illustrated are known collectively as *phrase-structure* grammars. Although context-sensitive grammars have the weak generative power to generate a class of intricate languages, Chomsky maintained that phrase-structure grammars are inadequate for the analysis of natural languages. What is required, he claimed, are *transformational* rules, which are still more powerful, and which, instead of merely rewriting one symbol in terms of others, map whole tree structures of the sort specified by phrase-structure grammars into new tree structures. A typical transformation, the passive, consists in a formal statement of the rule:

If a grammatical structure has the form:

$$NP_1 - Aux - V - NP_2$$

then the corresponding structure:

$$NP_2 - Aux + be + en - V - by + NP_1$$

275

is also a grammatical structure (where ' + ' is used to join up expressions forming constituents, and a subsequent transformation attaches *en* to the verb to generate its passive form).

Thus, the rule takes the structure corresponding to: *Alfred – Past – eat – the cakes*, and transforms it into: *The cakes – Past + be + en – eat – by – Alfred*, which after further transformations ultimately emerges as the sentence: 'The cakes were eaten by Alfred' (see Chomsky, 1957, Sec. 5.4). The transformation establishes the general relation between active and passive sentences since it takes the structures underlying actives and transforms them into structures underlying passives. The transformational rules thus provide a natural way to capture generalizations about the language. It was also into the transformational rules that Chomsky (1957) built the recursive power of his grammar: a phrase-structure grammar produced trees, and transformational rules transformed them and could take one tree and embed it within another to generate self-embedded structures.

Transformational grammar and psycholinguistics

Modern psycholinguistics began with George Miller's (1962) hypothesis that transformational rules might correspond to mental processes in the comprehension of sentences. The initial experiments carried out by Miller and his colleagues were indeed concerned with whether there are parsing processes that correspond to undoing those transformations that take simple active declarative structures (generated by the phrase-structure grammar) and convert them into passives, negatives, interrogatives, and other such sentences. At first, it appeared that the reason that a sentence such as 'Weren't you met by the president?' is harder to understand than the sentence 'The president met you' is that the former requires three transformations in its specification that are not required in the latter's specification. However, it soon became clear that transformational complexity was not a reliable guide to psychological complexity.

In 1965, Chomsky published what is now known as the 'standard theory' of transformational grammar, which embodied a number of important modifications of the earlier theory. He introduced a lexicon which, instead of merely listing nouns, verbs, and the members of other parts of speech, links each item to a set of syntactic features: e.g., the entry for *boy* includes the features [+N, +Count, +Animate] and the entry for *sincerity* includes the features [+N, −Count, +Abstract]. The phrase-structure rules generate these 'complex symbols' at the end nodes of trees, and a word can be assigned to a node in a tree only if the word's features are consistent with the complex symbol at that node. Since different verbs occur in different linguistic contexts, the rule that introduces a verb's complex symbol into a tree is context-sensitive – in effect, it builds the particular context of the verb into its complex symbol. For example, in a tree of the form NP – Verb – NP, the complex symbol at the node for the verb has the features [+V, __NP], and only a verb with the same features, such as the transitive verb *bring*, can be assigned to this node. The most notable modification, however, was that the recursive power of the grammar was now located in the phrase-structure rules, very roughly along the lines of the grammar in Figure 12.4. This reorganization was designed to allow the trees generated by the phrase-structure rules to be treated as *deep structures* that specify the syntactic information required for the semantic interpretation of sentences. The transformation rules convert such deep structures into the *surface structures* of actual sentences, and hence the same underlying meaning can be expressed by a variety of sentences differing in their surface forms. The introduction of meaning into transformational grammar in this way turned out to be the root of many subsequent disagreements among linguists, and the 'standard theory' was subsequently revised, extended and distended. But the immediate psychological problem it presented was to find a compatible account of mental parsing.

The most influential theory was proposed by Fodor, Bever, and Garrett (1974), who argued that a key step in the perception of sentences is an active process of recovering deep structure. This claim was surprising. Deep structure is related to surface structure by a series of grammatical transformations, but there was no longer any case to be made for mental processes akin to undoing transformations, since psychological complexity did not correlate with transformational complexity. The investigators at MIT therefore proposed a number of perceptual heuristics to fill the gap left by transformations. One such heuristic treated any sequence of the form:

Noun   Verb   Noun

as a putative underlying clause. Another heuristic specified that the first noun corresponded to the subject, the second noun corresponded to the object, and the verb corresponded to the main verb of the clause. Unfortunately, there were several problems with this theory of performance. It failed to provide an effective procedure for the interpretation of sentences,

277

and imparted a slightly implausible 'hit-or-miss' flavour to the recipe for understanding them. The theory did not suffer – as Phil Gough (1971, p. 264) once put it – from premature formalization. It was almost as though the inadequacy of its procedures was to be disclaimed by labelling them 'heuristics'. Although there was experimental evidence corroborating the theory, the results were open to other plausible explanations. In particular, the evidence which suggested that deep structure is mentally represented as part of the process of interpretation could always be explained as an effect of the representation of the *meaning* of the sentence (see Johnson-Laird, 1970, 1974, for this suggestion, and Fodor, Bever, and Garrett, 1974, p. 270 for an acknowledgement of the possible confounding of deep structure effects with those of meaning). It is difficult to eliminate this confounding except by concentrating on those features of deep structure that are unique to it, but such features, as Wanner (1977) pointed out in his review of the MIT work, are motivated transformationally, and the failure to substantiate the transformational hypothesis suggests that evidence for the mental reality of such features is unlikely to be found. Indeed, my colleagues and I failed to find any evidence that the deep structures of sentences are mentally represented. A pair of sentences such as:

John liked the painting

and:

The painting pleased John

are similar in meaning, but the deep structure roles of *John* and *the painting* are completely different in the two sentences: *John*, for example is the underlying subject of the first sentence, but the underlying object of the second. We found that individuals who do not expect their memory to be tested retain the general meaning of these sentences but *not* their deep structures – i.e., they think they have heard one sentence when in fact they heard the other (Johnson-Laird and Stevenson, 1970). Of course one might argue that deep structure is nevertheless mentally represented, albeit fleetingly. However, when Mary Cooke (1975), a former student of mine, tested subjects at different intervals after the initial presentation of a sentence, she failed to find any point in time when surface structure was forgotten but deep structure retained. It seems that individuals either remember a sentence virtually *verbatim* or else remember only its meaning (cf. Dooling and Christiaansen, 1977; Jarvella, 1979). They retain either a superficial propositional representation or else just a mental model.

Our results suggested that there is no stage at which the deep structure of a sentence is mentally represented: meaning is recovered directly from surface structure. The climate of opinion at the time, however, demanded that deep structures were in the mind since the only available theory of linguistic competence demanded it too. In reviewing the literature in 1974, I searched diligently for unequivocal evidence for the use or representation of deep structure in comprehension. There was none.

The case against transformations and deep structure

The case for transformational grammar is one of the most crucial aspects of modern linguistic theory. It merits close inspection since it pulls in one direction, but, as we have seen, the experimental observations pull in another.

Chomsky (1957) advanced a number of essentially aesthetic objections to phrase-structure grammar. Its syntactic descriptions are inelegant. It provides only a clumsy treatment of conjunctions involving deletions, such as 'The liner sailed up and the tug sailed down the river.' And it is equally clumsy in its handling of discontinuous constituents such as the auxiliary verb *be* and its related affix *-en*. It fails to capture obvious generalizations about the relations between sentences, such as actives and passives. Other authors advanced still stronger arguments against phrase-structure grammar. Postal (1964) claimed that context-free grammar lacked the weak generative capacity required for the grammar of Mohawk, and that no known context-sensitive grammar could cope either. Mohawk, he argued, contains an infinite subset of sentences of the form:

$$a_1 a_2 \ldots a_n b_1 b_2 \ldots b_n$$

where the corresponding pairs $a_1 b_1, a_2 b_2, \ldots, a_n b_n$ must contain the same grammatical stem. Chomsky (1959) had proved that a language composed entirely of such strings required rules with a weak generative power greater than that of a context-free grammar. Bar-Hillel and Shamir (1960) had also noted that English constructions with *respectively* have the same property of requiring an indefinitely large series of agreements. They claimed, for example, that a string of the form:

John, Mary, David, ... are a widower, a widow, a widower, ... respectively

is grammatical if and only if the nth proper name in the initial list agrees in gender with the nth item in the widow–widower list. The case against phrase-structure grammar seemed overwhelming, and its natural replacement was transformational grammar, which had the generative capacity to cope with a language such as Mohawk, and the power to capture generalizations about a language in an elegant way.

The case for transformations is not, in fact, decisive. However, there has only recently been any general recognition that it might have been overstated. A number of independent developments were necessary before there was any scepticism about transformations on the part of those working within the generative approach to syntax.

First, Peters and Ritchie (1971, 1973a) formulated a mathematically precise definition of the class of transformational grammars, and then proved that the computations of any arbitrary Turing machine can be carried out by a transformational grammar. The intuition lying behind this proof is that the set of elementary operations that can be performed by a Turing machine, such as scanning a symbol, shifting the tape one square to the left, and so on, can all be modelled by representing tapes as tree structures and allowing transformations to shift around the constituents of such trees. Indeed, such is the power of a transformational grammar that this property of simulating any Turing machine can be achieved even if the initial trees on which the transformations operate are generated by a simple finite-state grammar in lieu of a phrase-structure grammar. This proof has a number of embarrassing consequences. It makes the task of finding empirical evidence in support of the claim that all languages have the same underlying phrase-structure grammar – the 'universal base' hypothesis – virtually impossible, because given the power of transformations, any base grammar will suffice. Similarly, a Turing machine presented with an input tape may never halt its computations, and there is no effective procedure for deciding whether or not it will halt (see Chapter 1). Hence, the same property applies to transformational grammars: if you ask whether a particular sequence of words is generated by a given transformational grammar, no answer may ever be forthcoming, and there can be no general procedure for deciding the issue. This consequence is worrying if you are of the persuasion that sentencehood ought to be a decidable matter. It is important to bear in mind, however, that a particular transformational grammar may well constitute an effective decision procedure for sentencehood: the proof applies to the class of grammars as a whole.

Second, the various arguments that had been put forward to support the need for transformations, one by one, appeared to be less than decisive.

In particular, the data on Mohawk were not as clear-cut as Postal had implied, and it was uncertain whether there were *grammatical* dependencies of so restricted a nature in the language. Likewise, the English constructions based on *respectively* do not demand syntactic agreements, but rather the expression has the semantic force of the phrase *in the order in which they are indicated* (de Cornulier, 1973). In fact, as Pullum and Gazdar (1982) point out, in dealing with all the extant arguments that English is not context-free, a sentence such as:

They live in Chicago and Columbus respectively

violates the alleged syntactic constraint, and yet is perfectly sensible in a context where *they* picks out two individuals in a specific order.

Third, Peters and Ritchie (1973b) proved a theorem showing that a seemingly innocuous assumption about the interpretation of context-sensitive rules had a striking consequence. To grasp the force of the theorem, one must appreciate the distinction between a grammar and a language. A context-free grammar, for example, may in fact generate a language that could be generated by a finite-state grammar: that is, the same language could be generated by a simpler grammar. The grammar presented in Figure 12.6 contains context-free rules, but it generates exactly the same language as the finite-state grammar of Figure 12.1. The two grammars are equivalent in their weak generative capacity; they differ only in their

The context-free grammar:

S → NP   VP

VP → Verb (Noun) Adverb

NP → Determiner (Adjective) Noun

An example of a phrase-structure tree generated by the grammar:

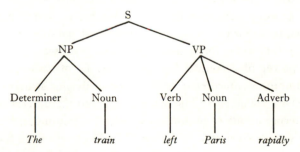

Figure 12.6 An example of a context-free grammar that generates a 'regular' language, i.e., one that can be generated by a finite-state grammar.

281

strong generative power since the structure that the context-free grammar assigns to sentences differs from the structure that the finite-state grammar assigns (compare Figures 12.1 and 12.6). The Peters and Ritchie theorem concerns the interpretation of a grammar. On the one hand, a grammatical rule can be interpreted as an instruction about how to rewrite one symbol in terms of others. The rule:

$$S \rightarrow NP \quad VP$$

can be interpreted as an instruction that allows the symbol S to be rewritten as NP VP, so that the sequence:

occurs in the formal generation of a sentence. On the other hand, a grammatical rule can be interpreted as a specification of what counts as an acceptable *analysis* of a given tree structure. Given the tree:

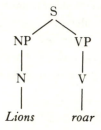

the S-node, for example, is admissible because it satisfies the rule:

$$S \rightarrow NP \quad VP$$

If every node in a tree is admissible, the tree is an analysis of the sentence according to the grammar. The two interpretations of rules had been thought to be equivalent, but Peters and Ritchie proved that they were not: any context-sensitive grammar interpreted as rules for analysing structures, rather than for generating them, possesses only the weak generative power of a context-free grammar. In other words, context-sensitive grammars interpreted as rules for analysing structures specify only context-free languages. The reader can grasp the difference between the two interpretations of grammatical rules by examining the context-sensitive grammar illustrated in Figure 12.7. The tree shown there can be analysed by the grammar; but it cannot be generated by the grammar: S can be expanded to AB, but then there is a deadlock, because the rule for

The grammar:

S → A B
A → a/__b
B → b/a__

The tree structure:

The analysis:

S in the tree is analysed as A and B in accordance with the first rule.
A is analysed as a in the context __b in accordance with the second rule.
B is analysed as b in the context a__ in accordance with the third rule.

Figure 12.7 A simple context-sensitive grammar and the way in which it analyses a tree (that it cannot generate).

rewriting A requires the context generated by the rule for rewriting B, and vice versa. Hence, the grammar fails to generate any sentences, but it does analyse at least one sentence. The important consequence of the general theorem is that a linguist can use rules that take context into account without exceeding the weak generative power of context-free grammar.

The reduction of the transformational component

The reappraisal of transformational grammar has led linguists to explore ways in which plausible constraints can be placed on the power of transformations (but cf. Chomsky, 1977; Culicover and Wexler, 1977). Others have sought to reduce the number of transformations employed by the grammar. A major recent step in this direction was made possible by Emonds (1976), who proposed a useful initial classification of transformations. He distinguished three varieties. First, there are structure-preserving transformations, which yield trees that can already be independently generated by the phrase-structure rules of the grammar. Thus, for example, the passive transformation that produces such sentences as:

The car was pushed by the chauffeur

merely shifts constituents to nodes that are generated by the phrase-structure rules which produce:

The soldier was sitting by the fence.

Second, there are root transformations, such as the inversion of subject and auxiliary verb in forming a question, which do not preserve structure and which create a node in a position in which it is immediately dominated by the topmost S-node in a tree or the S-node of an independent major clause. Third, there are 'local' transformations that merely exchange adjacent minor constituents, such as the conversion of 'He gave all of them a present' into 'He gave them all a present.'

Because a structure-preserving transformation produces a tree that can be generated by the phrase-structure rules, an obvious strategy is to drop the transformation rule, use the phrase-structure rules to generate the tree, and give an appropriate account of how the meaning of the resulting sentence relates to the meaning of a sentence in canonical form. This step was taken by Bresnan (1978). She made an interesting observation about the so-called 'cyclical' transformations, which apply in a *cycle* to each S-node in a tree, starting at the deepest S-node and working upwards to the topmost one. All the transformations in the cycle have three properties: (1), they are structure-preserving, (2), they are bounded in that they move constituents over a finitely specifiable context, and (3), they are governed by the occurrence of particular words – the passive transformation, for instance, is applicable to certain verbs such as *eat* but not to others such as *resemble*. Bresnan replaced all of these transformations by rules in the lexicon that specify the location of the verb's arguments in the syntactic structure of the sentence. The semantic components of these rules yield the proper interpretations of the structures directly generated by the phrase-structure grammar. The remaining major transformations have the effect either of deleting constituents as in the case of conjunction reduction (e.g., 'The author visited the city and was met by her publisher'), or of moving constituents as in the case of forming a question beginning with *Which* or some other Wh- word. They are not governed by particular words, they apply after the transformations in the cycle, and they do not affect the grammatical relations between noun phrases and the verb. They can be subdivided into those whose effects are unbounded, applying over any arbitrary amount of structure, and those that are bounded. Bounded transformations include the subject–auxiliary inversion that occurs in a question:

Have the police left?

Bresnan's step of directly generating a structure by phrase-structure rules can be applied to all bounded transformations by expanding the phrase-structure component of the grammar to include such rules. However, in Bresnan's view, transformational rules are indispensable for handling unbounded movements, such as shifting a topicalized noun phrase to the front of a sentence:

Dee, I know Bill likes

or shifting a Wh- noun phrase to the front to form a question:

Which book did Art ask you to give him?

The importance of unbounded movement is reflected in Chomsky's (1981) latest formulation of grammar: phrase structure rules generate the underlying structures of sentences, which are then mapped into what are called 'S-structures' by repeated applications of a single transformational rule: Move α, where α can be any grammatical category. S-structures are then assigned on the one hand a phonetic form, and on the other, a logical form. Since a transformation that moves constituents generates all sorts of ungrammatical sentences, a variety of constraints are used to filter out unwanted rubbish.

English as a phrase-structure language

Table 12.1 presents some examples of transformations that illustrate an informal classification that emerges from the work of Emonds, Bresnan, and others. Bresnan reduced the size of the transformational component of the grammar by eliminating certain sorts of transformation. The reduction of the transformational component has culminated in the proposal to abandon it altogether, along with the notion of deep structure (see Brame, 1978; Gazdar, 1979, 1981a; and unpublished work by Stanley Peters). What is important about the studies of Peters and Gazdar is that they treat English as a phrase-structure language in which the rules of the grammar are interpreted as analysing trees rather than as generating them, and that they also provide translations of sentences into an intensional logic – a lambda calculus closely related to the notation used by Montague (see Table 8.3), for which a model-theoretic interpretation can be given. There is accordingly a prima facie case that they are giving a satisfactory account of sentences and their syntactic structures: phrase-structure grammar has both the weak and the strong generative capacity to cope with English. I have deliberately omitted the semantic representations in what follows in order to concentrate on syntax.

To analyse a language using only phrase-structure rules, it is necessary to show that all those sentences apparently requiring transformations can be handled in an alternative way. The crucial problem is, of course, to do

Table 12.1 *An informal classification of transformations (with examples)*

I Local transformations

Do-insertion	Who John marry?	⇒	Who did John marry?
Quantifier postposition	All of you can go	⇒	You all can go
Complementizer deletion	He thinks that I am stupid	⇒	He thinks I am stupid

II Structure-preserving transformations (bounded, lexically governed, in the cycle)

Passive	John helped me	⇒	I was helped by John
Dative movement	She gave a book to you	⇒	She gave you a book
Subject raising	It seems that he be kind	⇒	He seems to be kind
Object raising	It is easy to amuse me	⇒	I am easy to amuse
There-insertion	A bus arrived	⇒	There arrived a bus
Equi-NP deletion	I persuaded Alf (Alf to leave)	⇒	I persuaded Alf to leave

III Root transformations that are bounded

Subject–auxiliary inversion	The police have left	⇒	Have the police left?
Participle preposing	Our man will be speaking today	⇒	Speaking today will be our man
Prepositional phrase permutation	A picture hangs in the hall	⇒	In the hall hangs a picture
Heavy NP shift	I asked the girl with the unpleasant man from Stoke to leave	⇒	I asked to leave the girl with the unpleasant man from Stoke

IV Root transformations that are unbounded

(a) Movement transformations

Wh-question	Ann likes which house?	⇒	Which house does Ann like?
Relative clause	I met the man (you like the man)	⇒	I met the man who you like
Topicalization	I know Dee	⇒	Dee, I know
Cleft	Bill hates Dai	⇒	It is Dai who Bill hates
Extraposition	The boy who was tall cried	⇒	The boy cried who was tall

(b) Deletions

Conjunction reduction	The liner sailed up the river and the liner was greeted by the villagers	⇒	The liner sailed up the river and was greeted by the villagers
Comparative deletion	Charles is taller than Mary claims David is tall	⇒	Charles is taller than Mary claims David is

Note. For simplicity, the examples show transformations operating on strings of words; in fact, of course, they map structures into structures.

286

away with transformational rules for unbounded dependencies, and in fact there are at least two ways in which they can be analysed by phrase-structure grammars.

Stanley Peters introduces the idea of there being a *link* between a node and its dislocated constituent. Figure 12.8 shows a link between a VP-node and its dislocated prepositional phrase, which has been topicalized. The

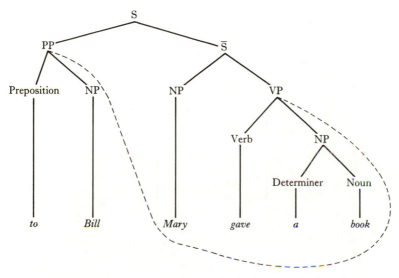

Figure 12.8 The structure assigned to a topicalized sentence by Peters's grammar.

link is shown as a broken line in the figure. The grammar can now analyse the prepositional phrase twice over, once as satisfying a rule specifically designed to cope with topicalization:

$$S \rightarrow \begin{Bmatrix} NP \\ PP \\ that \end{Bmatrix} \bar{S}$$

and once as satisfying the ordinary phrase-structure rule:

$$VP \rightarrow V \ NP \ PP$$

by virtue of the link to the VP. The latter analysis can take into account any restrictions that hold between the verb and the preposition. These restrictions are stated in the lexicon, where *give* is categorized as a verb that can occur in the context: __ NP *to* NP.

287

The same principles can be exploited in an analysis of relative clauses, as shown in Figure 12.9, which for purposes of comparison is based on

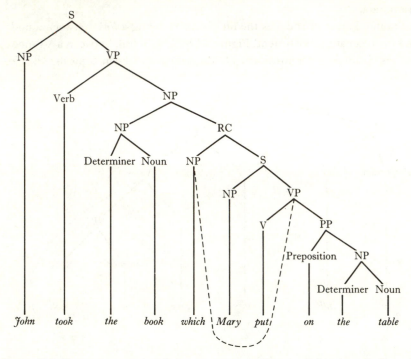

Figure 12.9 The structure assigned to a sentence containing a relative clause by Peters's grammar.

slightly different rules than those which Peters adopts. The recursive rule:

$$NP \rightarrow NP \ RC$$

introduces the relative clause RC, which is then analysed by the rule:

$$RC \rightarrow NP \ S$$

Only certain rules can be satisfied by a linked dislocated constituent, and only certain positions can be occupied by dislocated constituents – in English, for example, any node on the left of an S in a constituent can be a dislocated constituent as in topicalizations and relative clauses. In a more recent unpublished account, Peters also formulates 'barrier conditions' that prevent the formation of certain links. Thus, the ungrammaticality of examples such as:

Who did Arthur meet the man who likes?

violates the barrier that prevents a dislocated constituent linked to a node within a relative clause (cf. Ross, 1967). Barriers can be elegantly defined in terms of finite-state automata that accept, not strings of symbols, but trees (see Thatcher, 1973, for an account of such tree-automata).

In general, 'phrase-linking' grammars of the sort that Peters has specified are more powerful than context-free grammars, though they do not go beyond the scope of primitive recursion (as defined in Chapter 1). However, if there is an upper bound on the number of nodes in a subtree that can have links to dislocated constituents, then, as Peters has shown, the language generated by the grammar is context-free. In English, there can certainly be sentences with two dislocated constituents from the same clause, such as:

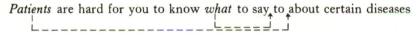

Patients are hard for you to know *what* to say to about certain diseases

where the broken lines show the links between the dislocated constituents and their related nodes. Elisabet Engdahl reports in a personal communication that her informants find the following sorts of example with three dislocations from the same clause 'strange but grammatical':

Which disease is it that *patients* are hard for you to know *what* to say to about?

This number of dislocations appears to be the upper bound, which probably arises because constructions that allow dislocated positions also create barriers.

Gerald Gazdar (1979, 1981a, b) has also proposed a non-transformational account of unbounded dependencies. His grammar provides semantic interpretations for sentences, which again, for simplicity, I shall ignore along with some of his special notational conventions. He uses a special sort of symbol to denote a syntactic constituent with a 'hole' in it. Thus, the symbol S/NP denotes a sentence with a noun phrase missing from it, such as:

Mary put t on the table,

where 't' is a symbol, or 'trace', that marks the position of the missing NP. Corresponding to each rule of a basic context-free grammar (such as the one illustrated in Figure 12.4) there are *derived* rules that make use of these derived syntactic categories. Hence, corresponding to the rule:

$$S \rightarrow NP \quad VP$$

there are rules such as the following:

$$S/NP \;\rightarrow\; NP \quad VP/NP$$
$$S/PP \;\rightarrow\; NP \quad VP/PP$$

All these rules are derived from a single meta-rule, which in effect allows a 'hole' on the left-hand side of a rule to crop up on the right-hand side. This use of meta-rules to generate new grammatical rules does not increase generative power beyond that of a context-free grammar. The rules for introducing a derived category are also specified by a general schema. For example, the schema:

$$S \;\rightarrow\; \alpha \quad S/\alpha$$

where α is a variable denoting such symbols as NP, PP, etc., produces rules for topicalization and preposing of constituents such as adjectival and adverbial phrases. The schema:

$$\alpha/\alpha \;\rightarrow\; t$$

generates rules for eliminating 'holes' of any category by replacing them with a trace, t, whose role is to prevent certain phonological contractions.

Armed with the various schemata, it is easy, for example, to derive the following rules for analysing trees:

$$S \;\rightarrow\; NP \quad S/NP$$
$$S/NP \;\rightarrow\; NP \quad VP/NP$$
$$VP/NP \;\rightarrow\; V \quad NP/NP$$
$$NP/NP \;\rightarrow\; t$$

These rules suffice to analyse a simple topicalized sentence, such as:

Tom, I like

The analysis is shown in Figure 12.10 to illustrate the rudiments of Gazdar's approach. There is a sense in which the 'hole' percolates down the tree to its rightful place, except of course that the rules are designed, not to generate a tree, but to analyse a given tree.

Gazdar also makes use of 'complex symbols' of the sort which, as I described above, consist of bundles of syntactic features that occur at nodes in trees. Certain words may also occur in such symbols. Thus, the schema:

$$PP_{[\alpha]} \;\rightarrow\; \alpha \quad NP, \text{ where } \alpha \text{ is } to, by, for, than, as \ldots$$

handles such prepositional phrases as *to Bill* and *for Mary*. In order to ensure agreement between, for example, subject and verb, the grammar

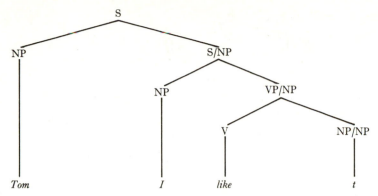

Figure 12.10 The analysis of a simple topicalized sentence by a rudimentary version of Gazdar's grammar.

allows complex symbols to be assigned to constituents e.g.

$$S \;\rightarrow\; NP_{[\alpha]} \quad VP_{[\alpha]}$$

where α ranges over permissible combinations of agreement features, such as number, and is passed to the 'heads' of the two constituents – the noun and the verb respectively. Hence, the specific rules generated by the variables include:

$$S \;\rightarrow\; NP_{\text{Nominative, Plural}} \quad VP_{\text{Plural}}$$
$$VP_{\text{Plural}} \;\rightarrow\; V_{\text{Plural}} \quad NP_{\text{Accusative}}$$

and in this way the grammar will accept the sentence:

We like him and he likes us

but reject:

Us likes he and him like we.

Gazdar adopts the elegant expedient of a lexicon in which each word is directly associated with the phrase-structure rules in which it can occur.

Figure 12.11 shows Gazdar's use of complex symbols in the structure assigned to a sentence with a topicalized prepositional phrase. The tree is specified by a sequence of rules beginning with a linking rule that introduces a derived symbol:

$$S \;\rightarrow\; PP_{[to]} \quad S/PP_{[to]}$$

representing a PP 'hole' that has the feature [to]. The derived rule:

$$S/PP_{[to]} \;\rightarrow\; NP \quad VP/PP_{[to]}$$

then in effect passes information about the 'hole' down to the VP constituent. Finally, the hole is replaced by the trace t.

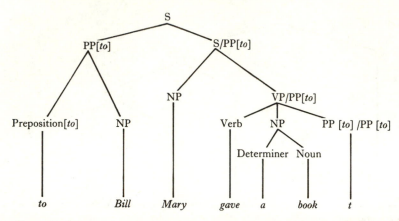

Figure 12.11 The structure assigned to a topicalized sentence by Gazdar's grammar.

Gazdar's analysis of relative clauses (See Figure 12.12) is based on the phrase-structure rules:

NP $\rightarrow$ NP RC, where RC is the relative clause category.

RC $\rightarrow$ S/NP, which introduces relative clauses that have no relative pronoun (e.g., 'The dish *he likes* . . .').

RC $\rightarrow$ $\alpha \begin{bmatrix} \text{WH} \\ \text{PRO} \end{bmatrix}$ S/α, where α is NP (as in Figure 12.12) or is PP

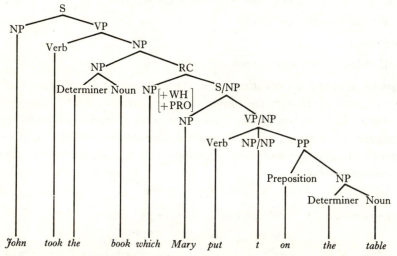

Figure 12.12 The structure assigned to a sentence containing a relative clause by Gazdar's grammar.

292

(as in '. . . to whom it was sent'), and the features on α call for a relative pronoun such as *which*.

The use of derived categories and meta-rules allows Gazdar to explain a number of hitherto perplexing phenomena at no extra cost. A simple schema analyses conjunctions and disjunctions, as follows:

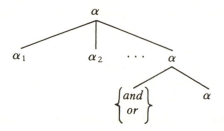

where α can be any grammatical category including a derived one. Hence, a sentence such as 'The book that she wrote and he edited has been published' can be analysed without recourse to transformations: it contains a conjunction of two S/NP nodes. In the absence of transformations, there is no need for Ross's (1967) celebrated 'co-ordinate structure constraint' to prevent the movement of one constituent out of a conjunct, as in the non-sentence, 'Who did you meet John and?' Other meta-rules enable Gazdar to handle structure-preserving constructions such as the passive, and bounded transformations such as subject–auxiliary inversion in the formation of questions (Gazdar, Pullum, and Sag, 1981).

Conclusions

To a distant and disinterested observer, there is a close relation between the recent work of Peters, Gazdar, and Chomsky. Peters has rules that introduce a dislocated constituent and he allows a link between such a constituent and its canonical position in the structure of the sentence; Gazdar has rules that introduce a dislocated constituent and he establishes the link by deriving rules from the canonical grammar that pass the 'hole' (the other end of the link) down the tree to its appropriate position; Chomsky generates the canonical structure and then uses a transformational rule to move the constituent into its dislocated position. All three theories place constraints on what can be dislocated, and on what positions can be occupied by dislocated constituents. Are the theories just notational variations on the same underlying theme? The answer is both *yes* and *no* (cf. Chomsky, 1981; Gazdar, 1981b). There are, in fact, three points of difference. First, the theories diverge on the particular grammatical rules that they employ. Second, Peters and Gazdar subscribe to the rule-by-rule principle of compositionality and provide explicit semantic rules for each of their syntactic rules; Chomsky rejects compositionality and does not provide a semantics for his grammar. Third, the three theories differ in their weak and strong generative capacity: Gazdar's grammar is a context-free phrase-structure grammar; Peters's grammar is a more powerful phrase-structure grammar though still within the bounds of primitive recursion; Chomsky's grammar is probably primitive recursive, too, but it is transformational and accordingly assigns both an underlying structure and a superficial structure to sentences. If one discounts the differences in the particular rules (the first point), and concentrates solely on questions of syntax (thereby discounting the second) then only the question of power divides the theories.

No decisive evidence against the claim that English is a context-free language has so far been discovered, but this contingency may not apply to other languages. A natural extension of Gazdar's grammar is to allow separate sets of derived rules to analyse separate 'holes' in the same sentence on similar lines to Peters's links: each dislocated constituent can be linked to its appropriate hole by an index. Such 'indexed' grammars are more powerful than context-free grammars, and, in fact, rise to the power of context-sensitive grammars (Hopcroft and Ullman, 1979, p. 390). This extension of Gazdar's grammar considerably reduces the difference between it and Peters's grammar. Chomsky's grammar, however, though it may be similar in its weak generative capacity, is clearly different in its strong generative capacity because it assigns an underlying structure to sentences.

From a psychological standpoint, the grammatical structures of any language should constitute a set that is recursively specifiable by devices of less power than unconstrained Turing machines. Certainly, the syntactic complexity of language requires recursion. But sentencehood should be decidable – i.e., a procedure for deciding whether or not a string of words is well-formed should not go into an infinite loop. If grammars are equivalent to Turing machines, then there is indeed no guarantee that they will halt with a decision about sentencehood. There are, in principle, many subsets of Turing machines for which sentencehood would be a decidable property; and there may turn out to be more relevant criteria of computational power than the familiar hierarchy defined by Chomsky.

For the time being, however, a useful conjecture midway between the lower bound of recursion and the upper bound of Turing machines is that grammatical structures can be adequately analysed by phrase-structure rules. The same conjecture is compatible with the hypothesis that grammatical sentences consist of a canonical form and any variations on that form that can be analysed using a push-down stack to store temporally displaced constituents (Ades and Steedman, 1982).

13

Parsing and performance

High-level programming languages are effectively context free. Although they contain features that technically place them outside the domain of context-free languages, such as the constraint that a procedure always has the same number of arguments whenever it occurs in a program, they can nevertheless be analysed syntactically as context free since these features are checked by other processes (see Aho and Ullman, 1972, p. 199). Many ways have been developed for compilers to parse programs in order to translate them into machine code. This knowledge has been neglected by psycholinguists (and linguists) because of the almost universal view that more powerful grammars – and parsers – are needed for natural languages. Since there are grounds, which I summarized in the previous chapter, for supposing that natural languages may have a special sort of phrase-structure grammar, a sensible research strategy is to consider what has been learned from parsing programming languages. Hence, in this chapter I am going to describe the general theory of parsers, then some of the phenomena that arise in parsing a natural language such as English, and, finally, the possible design of the parser that the mind uses to produce and to understand speech.

The theory of parsing

Parsing context-free languages

A simple context-free grammar is presented in Table 13.1 together with an example of a phrase-structure tree specified by the grammar. Of the many algorithms for parsing the sentences of such a grammar (see e.g. Aho and Ullman, 1972), one well-known method, which was pioneered by Kuno and Oettinger (1962), is to construct the tree 'top down' in the following steps starting from an initial assumption of S:

according to rule 1

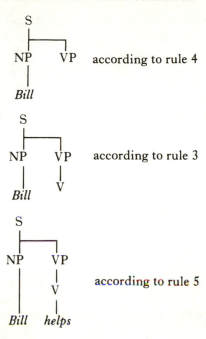

according to rule 4

according to rule 3

according to rule 5

The syntactic categories have been written in columns to help the reader to think of the customary phrase-structure tree as arranged in a table, because later we will encounter algorithms that make use of such tables.

Table 13.1 *A context-free grammar for a set of simple sentences*

1	S	→	NP	VP
2	VP	→	V	NP
3	VP	→	V	
4	NP	→	*Ann*	
			Bill	
5	V	→	*knows*	
			helps	

An example of a phrase-structure tree specified by the grammar:

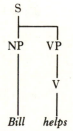

The top-down parsing procedure analyses the leftmost non-terminal symbol first, and once it reaches a terminal symbol, such as *Bill*, it goes to the next leftmost non-terminal, and so on.

An alternative parsing procedure builds the tree from the 'bottom up':

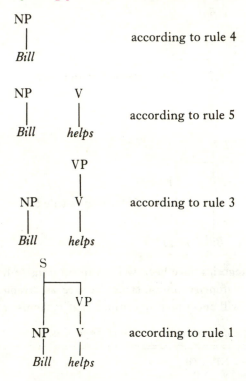

Still another procedure parses the left-hand corner of each tree (or subtree) from the bottom up and the rest of the tree (or subtree) top down:

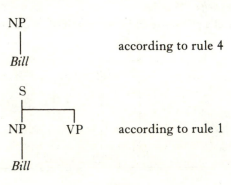

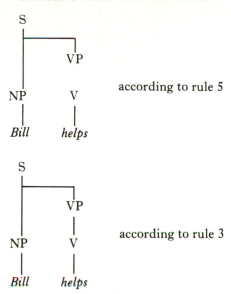

according to rule 5

according to rule 3

The procedure's name, a *left-corner* parser, derives from the fact that the first phrase to be parsed corresponds to the leftmost symbol on the right-hand side of the relevant grammatical rule. Hence, in general, with a rule of the form:

$$S \;\rightarrow\; A \quad B \quad C$$

all the nodes in the tree dominated by A – the left corner of the rule – are parsed before S is parsed, which in turn is parsed before its other descendants. There are still further ways of parsing, such as constructing the rightmost side of the tree first, or working from its left and right sides towards the middle, but rather than pursue these possibilities, I want to consider how the process of parsing can be implemented.

There is a direct correspondence between context-free grammars and push-down automata: any context-free language can be parsed by a push-down automaton. The reader will recall from the previous chapter that this device scans an input tape, which moves from left to right, and makes use of a single push-down store, on which it can read and write characters on a 'last in, first out' basis. There is a direct way to specify a 'top down' algorithm for a push-down automaton. For any rule of the grammar of the form A $\rightarrow$ α, where α denotes the symbol or string of symbols on the right-hand side of the rule, the automaton has an instruction to ignore the input tape and if A is the symbol on the top of the stack, to replace it by

α: this procedure corresponds to making a top-down prediction. For example, the symbol:

S

at the top of the stack can be replaced by :

NP
VP

according to the relevant rule in the grammar; and this step occurs without moving the input tape. For each terminal symbol, i.e., word in the language, the automaton has a conditional instruction: if the currently scanned input symbol is also on the top of the stack, then move the input tape one square to the left and erase the symbol on top of the stack. This procedure corresponds to matching a prediction with the input. For example, if the input tape is:

Ann helps #

where # is the punctuation mark for the end of a string, *Ann* is the currently scanned symbol, and the contents of the stack are:

Ann
VP
#

then the effect of such an instruction is to move the input to the next symbol:

helps #

and to erase the top symbol on the stack:

VP
#

The automaton starts in a configuration where it is scanning the leftmost symbol on the input tape, and has two symbols on its stack, a special start symbol, 'S' for sentence, and the punctuation mark ' # '. It accepts an input string and halts if all the input has been scanned and the stack is empty apart from the end-of-string symbol. Table 13.2 gives the set of instructions required to parse the language specified in the previous table; it also presents a record of the machine's performance in parsing the input string: *Ann knows Bill*. The machine has only two states: normal operation and the end state when it halts. When it is operating normally, it either makes a *top-down prediction* ignoring the input or else *matches* the current

Table 13.2 *The set of instructions for a push-down automaton that parses simple sentences in a 'top-down' manner*

	Input symbol scanned	Symbol at top of stack		New symbol(s) at top of stack
1	*Ann*	*Ann*	⇒	Erase top symbol
2	*Bill*	*Bill*	⇒	Erase top symbol
3	*helps*	*helps*	⇒	Erase top symbol
4	*knows*	*knows*	⇒	Erase top symbol
5	#	#	⇒	Erase top symbol (Machine halts)
6	Ignore input	S ...	⇒	NP VP ...
7	Ignore input	VP ...	⇒	V NP ...
8	Ignore input	VP ...	⇒	V ...
9	Ignore input	NP ...	⇒	*Ann* ...
10	Ignore input	NP ...	⇒	*Bill* ...
11	Ignore input	V ...	⇒	*helps* ...
12	Ignore input	V ...	⇒	*knows* ...

An example of the PDA's performance: its parse of 'Ann knows Bill #'

	Input tape	Contents of stack	Instruction carried out (to produce configuration)
Initial configuration:	*Ann knows Bill* #	S #	—
Subsequent configurations:	*Ann knows Bill* #	NP VP #	6 (Top down)
	Ann knows Bill #	*Ann* VP #	9 (Top down)
	knows Bill #	VP #	1 (Match)
	knows Bill #	V NP #	7 (Top down)
	knows Bill #	*knows* NP #	12 (Top down)
	Bill #	NP #	4 (Match)
	Bill #	*Bill* #	10 (Top down)
	#	#	2 (Match)
	Blank	Empty	5 (Machine halts)

input symbol with the node currently at the top of the stack and shifts the input tape one square to the left.

Top-down parsing needs the exercise of caution should the grammar contain any recursive rules of the form:

$$A \rightarrow A \ \alpha$$

where the symbol on the left occurs as the first symbol on the right, e.g.:

$$NP \rightarrow NP \ S$$

because such rules can lead to a top-down parse of the form:

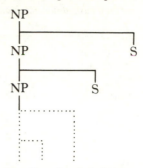

in which a new node is predicted *ad infinitum* without ever reaching a terminal symbol. It is always possible to reformulate a context-free grammar so as to eschew such rules, or else to place constraints on their use in a parsing algorithm.

A 'bottom-up' parser can be specified as a push-down automaton too. For each terminal symbol, the device has an instruction which *shifts* that symbol from the input tape to the top of the stack, and moves the input tape one square to the left. For example, if the tape is:

Ann helps #

and the content of the stack is:

#

then the effect of such an instruction is to move the input tape to the next symbol:

helps #

and to shift the previously scanned symbol to the top of the stack:

Ann
#

For each rule of the form A → α, the device has an instruction that ignores the input tape and replaces α at the top of the stack by A: the instruction in effect *reduces* α to A. For example, the symbol:

Bill

at the top of the stack can be replaced by:

NP

Similarly, the symbols on the stack:

VP
NP

which indicate that the sentence has been parsed bottom up as an NP followed by a VP, can be replaced by:

S

The device starts in a configuration in which it is scanning the leftmost symbol on the input tape, and has the punctuation mark '#' on the stack. It accepts a tape and halts after it reaches the configuration where it is scanning the end marker of the input, and has the symbol S followed by the end marker on the stack. In devising a bottom-up parser, it is best to avoid any grammar containing a rule that rewrites a symbol as the empty string, because this rule can always be applied anywhere in a bottom-up parse. However, any context-free grammar containing such a rule can always be reformulated without it and without any effect on the language it generates. Table 13.3 presents the set of instructions required for a

Table 13.3 *The set of instructions for a push-down automaton that parses simple sentences in a 'bottom-up' manner*

	Input symbol scanned	Symbols at the top of the stack (top is the rightmost symbol)		New symbol at the top of the stack
1	*Ann*	...	⇒	... *Ann*
2	*Bill*	...	⇒	... *Bill*
3	*helps*	...	⇒	... *helps*
4	*knows*	...	⇒	... *knows*
5	#	# S	⇒	Empty (Machine halts)
6	Ignore input	... NP VP	⇒	... S
7	Ignore input	... V NP	⇒	... VP
8	Ignore input	... V	⇒	... VP
9	Ignore input	... *Ann*	⇒	... NP
10	Ignore input	... *Bill*	⇒	... NP
11	Ignore input	... *helps*	⇒	... V
12	Ignore input	... *knows*	⇒	... V

An example of the PDA's performance: its parse of 'Ann knows Bill #'

	Input tape	Contents of stack (top on the right)	Instruction carried out
Initial configuration:	*Ann knows Bill* #	#	—
	knows Bill #	# *Ann*	1 (Shift)
	knows Bill #	# NP	9 (Reduce)
	Bill #	# NP *knows*	4 (Shift)
	Bill #	# NP V	12 (Reduce)
	#	# NP V *Bill*	2 (Shift)
	#	# NP V NP	10 (Reduce)
	#	# NP VP	7 (Reduce)
	#	# S	6 (Reduce)
	Blank	Empty	5 (Machine halts)

303

bottom-up parser for the simple grammar. It also provides an illustrative parse of the string *Ann knows Bill*. The stack has been represented with its topmost symbol on the right so as to make clear the direct relation between the grammar and the instructions for the machine (see instructions 6 to 12).

There is an unfortunate misconception in the psychological literature that top-down parsing is predictive but bottom-up parsing is not predictive. If a parser is deterministic, i.e., there is never more than one instruction that can be applied at any point in a parse, then it is *not* predictive whether it parses top down, bottom up, or any other way. If a parser is not deterministic and tries only one instruction at a time, then it is predictive. Hence, in this case a top-down parser predicts the next symbol down in the tree, and thus ultimately the terminal symbols in the input string. But, even though bottom-up parsing is a data driven process, it is still predictive: it predicts the next symbol up in the tree, and thus ultimately the uppermost non-terminal symbol. Granted that constituents are semantically interpreted and removed from working memory as soon as they are parsed, the two types of parser do place different 'loads' on working memory. The point can be illustrated by comparing the ways in which they parse a left-branching structure:

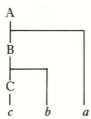

and a right-branching structure:

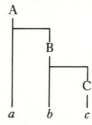

according to the following simple grammar:

$$A \rightarrow \begin{Bmatrix} Ba \\ aB \end{Bmatrix}$$

$$B \rightarrow \begin{Bmatrix} Cb \\ bC \end{Bmatrix}$$

$$C \rightarrow c$$

The algorithm for top-down parsing has to construct the whole of the left-branching tree for the input string *c b a* :

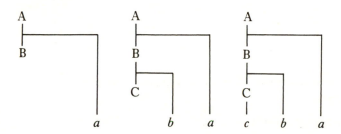

before the input can begin to be matched to the predicted terminals. This procedure places a considerable load on memory. A top-down parse of the right-branching structure is altogether easier because each prediction about an input symbol can be immediately matched:

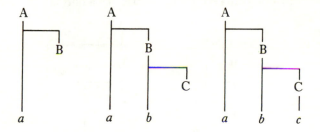

With bottom-up parsing the load is reversed. The parse of the left-branching structure copes with each input symbol immediately:

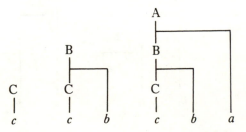

But the parse of the right-branching structure requires the earlier symbols

305

to be remembered (i.e., held on the stack) for some time prior to their analysis:

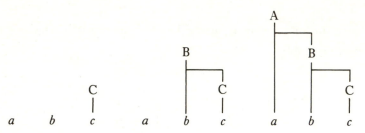

Miller and Chomsky (1963) noted long ago that left-branching constructions such as:

John's book's cover is dirty

seem to be equally easy to understand as right-branching constructions:

John has the book that has the cover that is dirty.

This observation counts against a pure top-down or bottom-up parsing strategy. However, left-corner parsing provides the best of both worlds. Its analysis of left-branching structures is just like a bottom-up parse:

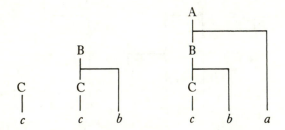

Its analysis of right-branching structures is just like a top-down parse:

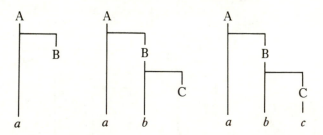

The algorithm for left-corner parsing that I shall describe is not the standard one (cf. Aho and Ullman, 1972, p. 310) but a more direct integration of top-down and bottom-up parsing. It makes use of four sorts of instruction, which correspond to the *shift* and *reduce* instructions of a bottom-up parser and the *prediction* and *match* instructions of a top-down parser. It uses special symbols on its stack consisting of ordered pairs, e.g. [NP VP], [X NP], where X is a variable ranging over non-terminals and thus in effect allows several instructions to be expressed in one. The first symbol in a pair, such as [S NP], stands for a top-down prediction, and the second symbol stands for a non-terminal parsed bottom up. Table 13.4 presents the instructions for an automaton that carries out the required left-corner parse. First, for each terminal symbol, there is an instruction that *shifts* the terminal from the input tape to the top of the stack, and moves the input tape one square to the left (see instructions 1 to 4). Second, for each terminal symbol, there is an instruction that *reduces* the terminal when it is at the top of the stack to the appropriate non-terminal (see instructions 6 to 9). Thus, if the stack contains the symbols:

Ann

S

#

the effect of such an instruction is to replace the two symbols at the top

Table 13.4a *The set of instructions for a push-down automaton that carries out a 'left corner' parse by combining a bottom-up and top-down procedure*

	Input symbol scanned	Symbols at the top of the stack (top on the left)		New symbols at the top of the stack
1	*Ann*	. . .	$\Rightarrow$	*Ann* . . .
2	*Bill*	. . .	$\Rightarrow$	*Bill* . . .
3	*helps*	. . .	$\Rightarrow$	*helps* . . .
4	*knows*	. . .	$\Rightarrow$	*knows* . . .
5	#	#	$\Rightarrow$	Erase top symbol (Machine halts)
6	Ignore input	*Ann* X . . .	$\Rightarrow$	[X NP] . . .
7	Ignore input	*Bill* X . . .	$\Rightarrow$	[X NP] . . .
8	Ignore input	*helps* X . . .	$\Rightarrow$	[X V] . . .
9	Ignore input	*knows* X . . .	$\Rightarrow$	[X V] . . .
10	Ignore input	[X NP] . . .	$\Rightarrow$	VP [X S] . . .
11	Ignore input	[X V] . . .	$\Rightarrow$	NP [X VP] . . .
12	Ignore input	[X V] . . .	$\Rightarrow$	[X VP] . . .
13	Ignore input	[X X] . . .	$\Rightarrow$	Erase top symbol

Table 13.4b *An example of the PDA's performance : its parse of* 'Ann knows Bill #'

Input tape	Contents of stack (top on the left)	Instructions carried out
Initial configuration:		
Ann knows Bill #	S #	—
knows Bill #	*Ann* S #	1 (Shift)
knows Bill #	[S NP] #	6 (Reduce)
knows Bill #	VP [S S] #	10 (Top down)
Bill #	*knows* VP [S S] #	4 (Shift)
Bill #	[VP V] [S S] #	9 (Reduce)
Bill #	NP [VP VP] [S S] #	11 (Top down)
#	*Bill* NP [VP VP] [S S] #	2 (Shift)
#	[NP NP] [VP VP] [S S] #	7 (Reduce)
#	[VP VP] [S S] #	13 (Match)
#	[S S] #	13 (Match)
#	#	13 (Match)
Blank	Empty	5 (Machine halts)

of the stack by the symbol:

$$[S \quad NP]$$
$$\#$$

which indicates that S is still predicted but an NP has been parsed bottom up. Third, there are instructions that reduce non-terminals and, where possible, make a top-down *prediction* (see instructions 10 to 12). The symbol at the top of the stack:

$$[S \quad NP]$$
$$\#$$

is thereby replaced by the symbols:

$$VP$$
$$[S \quad S]$$
$$\#$$

which reduce the NP to an S and make a top-down prediction of a VP:

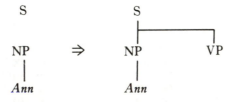

The pair [S   S] indicates a top-down prediction of S and a bottom-up parse of S that occurs in this case if the VP on the top of the stack is parsed. Finally, such a *match* of a predicted and parsed non-terminal node is handled by instructions that allow any pair of the form [X   X] to be erased (see instruction 13).

The best way to understand how the left-corner parser works is to go through the process of parsing *Ann knows Bill* # as illustrated in Table 13.4. The parser starts with the goal of parsing a sentence, and its stack accordingly has the contents:

S

#

It then shifts the first input symbol, *Ann*, onto the stack and reduces it to an NP. It is therefore still predicting S but has recognised a noun phrase, and the stack accordingly contains:

[S   NP]

#

It can now make a top-down prediction that the next constituent will be a VP, indicating this prediction by replacing the top symbol on the stack by the symbols:

VP

[S   S]

#

which specify that if a VP is parsed, then the predicted S will have been parsed bottom-up. Next, *knows* is shifted and reduced to a verb, and a top-down prediction of a noun phrase is made. *Bill* is shifted and reduced to an NP that satisfies this prediction. The predicted VP is thereby obtained, and thus finally the predicted S is parsed.

How to cope with non-determinism by backtracking

Consider an automaton that is scanning a particular symbol in a particular state with a particular symbol at the top of its stack. If it has a choice between two or more alternative actions, it is known technically as a *non-deterministic* device: there are at least two different instructions that it could carry out. The top-down parser of Table 13.2 is non-deterministic because it has more than one way of expanding certain nodes – for example, there are two ways to expand verb phrases and there is no means of predicting which particular one will be correct for a given input string. The bottom-up parser of Table 13.3 is non-deterministic because whenever it can reduce one symbol to another, e.g., V to VP, it has to choose either

309

to reduce the symbol or else to shift a new input symbol onto the stack, and there is no means of predicting which is the correct choice. The left-corner parser is non-deterministic because it has both sorts of choices. In the sample parses illustrating these devices, each has in effect guessed which were the correct choices. Non-determinism here has thus nothing to do with unpredictable or random behaviour; it is a convenient fiction that allows a theorist to assume that a machine automatically hits on the right moves to make within its repertoire of possibilities. Plainly, no real machine can guess the correct answers: real machines are deterministic. If a non-deterministic device is to be effectively implemented, then its non-determinism has to be simulated in some way.

Although there are deterministic push-down automata, they are not as powerful as non-deterministic ones, and not every context-free language can be parsed by a deterministic device. Moreover, there are grounds for supposing that natural language requires a non-deterministic automaton: its grammar is ambiguous in that it assigns more than one syntactic structure to certain sentences, and so it will be necessary to simulate a non-deterministic parser. The one argument to the effect that natural language can be parsed deterministically turns out, as we shall see, to be unconvincing. There are two chief ways of simulating non-determinism: either every possible choice is used to build up a *table* or parallel analyses, or else a system of *backtracking* is employed. I shall deal with backtracking in this section and with the tabular methods in the next section.

In backtracking, a device tries one choice, and if ultimately the choice leads nowhere, it returns to the choice point and tries another. If there is no remaining alternative, it backs up to the previous choice point and makes a different choice there. If, eventually, it gets back to the beginning of the input and has run out of choice points, it has exhausted all possible analyses. One effective backtracking procedure for top-down parsing has been described by Aho and Ullman (1972, p. 289). The parser has three states: it is either operating normally, backtracking, or coming to a halt. It makes use of two push-down stores: a *history* stack, which contains the history of the alternative choices of grammatical rules used in the parse, together with the input symbols that they parsed; and a *parse* stack, which contains the currently active nodes in the parse. The history stack is thus the essential record required for backtracking, and the parse stack is identical to the stack used by the non-deterministic parser. The parser takes as its input a context-free grammar and an input string of symbols terminating with the punctuation mark #. It starts in its normal state of operation, with its scanner on the first symbol of the input tape. It has an empty history stack, and its parse stack contains the initial symbol, S, followed by the punctuation mark #. The different rules for each non-terminal symbol in the grammar must be numbered, e.g.:

$$VP_1 \text{ for the rule } VP \rightarrow V \quad NP$$
$$VP_2 \text{ for the rule } VP \rightarrow V$$

There are six sorts of step in the algorithm, which is summarized in Table 13.5. An example of its performance is presented in Table 13.6.

Backtracking algorithms for other styles of parsing are equally easy to devise. However, backtracking can be an expensive business. The space required for the parse in Table 13.6 is only a linear function of the number of symbols in the input, but the time the parse takes may be an exponential function of the number of input symbols. This particular parser is so short-sighted that it even tries rules that require more symbols than are in the input. There are ways to speed up backtracking: the amount of it that is allowed can be restricted, and the rules of the grammar can be

Table 13.5 *The six sorts of step in a top-down backtracking parsing algorithm (based on Aho and Ullman, 1972)*

1 Tree expansion: if the grammatical rule $A \rightarrow \alpha$ is the first rule in the grammar for A, and A is at the top of the parse stack, then put A_1 on top of the history stack, and replace A by α on the parse stack.

2 If the symbol scanned on the input tape matches the terminal symbol on top of the parse stack, then remove it from the parse stack, shift the input tape one square to the left, and place the input symbol on the history stack.

3 If the symbol scanned on the input tape fails to match the terminal symbol on top of the parse stack, then shift into the backtracking state of operation.

4 Backtracking on input: where there is a terminal symbol on top of the history stack, shift the input tape back one square to the right, remove the terminal symbol from the top of the history stack and place it on top of the parse stack.

5 Try the next alternative grammatical rule: where A_i is on top of the history stack and α is on top of the parse stack. If the next alternative rule for A is $A \rightarrow \beta$, then replace A_i by A_{i+1} on the history stack and α by β on the parse stack, and return to normal state of operation. If the parser is scanning the very first symbol on the input tape and S is the special initial symbol, and there are no alternative rules for S left to try, then halt: the input cannot be parsed. Otherwise, remove A_i from the history stack, replace α by A on the parse stack, and continue backtracking.

6 Successful conclusion: if the parser is scanning # on the input, is in its normal state of operation, and # is on top of the parse stack, then shift to end state and erase # from stack.

The parse can be recovered from the history stack by erasing all the terminal symbols to leave the list of grammatical rules that were used in the successful parse of the input.

Table 13.6 *An example of the performance of the top-down backtracking algorithm (of Table 13.5)*

Given the grammar:

S	→	NP VP	(Rule S_1)
VP	→	V NP	(Rule VP_1)
VP	→	V	(Rule VP_2)
NP	→	*Ann*	(Rule NP_1)
NP	→	*Bill*	(Rule NP_2)
V	→	*knows*	(Rule V_1)
V	→	*helps*	(Rule V_2)

and the input: *Ann knows* #

Input tape	Parse stack (top on the left)	History stack (top on the left)	Instruction carried out (Table 13.5)
Ann knows #	S #	Empty	—
Ann knows #	NP VP #	S_1	1
Ann knows #	*Ann* VP #	$NP_1 S_1$	1
knows #	VP #	*Ann* $NP_1 S_1$	2
knows #	V NP #	VP_1 *Ann* $NP_1 S_1$	1
knows #	*knows* NP #	$V_1 VP_1$ *Ann* $NP_1 S_1$	1
#	NP #	*knows* $V_1 VP_1$ *Ann* $NP_1 S_1$	2
#	*Ann* #	NP_1 *knows* $V_1 VP_1$ *Ann* $NP_1 S_1$	1
	Backtrack		3
#	*Bill* #	NP_2 *knows* $V_1 VP_1$ *Ann* $NP_1 S_1$	5
	Backtrack		3
#	NP #	*knows* $V_1 VP_1$ *Ann* $NP_1 S_1$	5
knows #	*knows* NP #	$V_1 VP_1$ *Ann* $NP_1 S_1$	4
knows #	*helps* NP #	$V_2 VP_1$ *Ann* $NP_1 S_1$	5
	Backtrack		3
knows #	V NP #	VP_1 *Ann* $NP_1 S_1$	5
knows #	V #	VP_2 *Ann* $NP_1 S_1$	5
knows #	*knows* #	$V_1 VP_2$ *Ann* $NP_1 S_1$	1
#	#	*knows* $V_1 VP_2$ *Ann* $NP_1 S_1$	2
Blank	Empty	*knows* $V_1 VP_2$ *Ann* $NP_1 S_1$	6

The history stack now contains the correct parse of the input sentence:

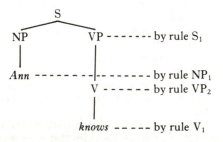

ordered so that the most likely ones are tried first. Parsers can even be devised that 'lookahead' at the next k input symbols to determine which rule applies. By looking ahead far enough, of course, it may be possible to construct a deterministic parser for certain languages, though in the case of a natural language such as English it is easy to see that for a fixed value of k, no matter how large, there will always be certain syntactic ambiguities that remain unresolved.

The notion of 'lookahead' has inspired Marcus (1981) to argue that natural language can be parsed deterministically without ever having to discard any structure assigned by the parser. The parser that he has implemented employs both a push-down store that holds incomplete constituents and a separate buffer that holds complete constituents that have yet to be integrated at a higher level. Marcus's idea is to use the buffer as a way of looking ahead, not at some fixed number of words, but at a fixed number of constituents, which may each contain any number of words. His basic claim is that the parser need only look ahead at three constituents; the buffer in fact has five places in order to allow the structure of NP's to be constructed in a way that can be inspected by the rules that apply to clauses, but only three places are used at any one time. The parser works partly bottom up and partly top down by matching sets of grammatical rules with some of the constituents in the buffer and the accessible nodes in the push-down store. For example, a sentence that begins 'Have the boys . . .' may either be an imperative:

Have the boys take the exam today

or a question:

Have the boys taken the exam today?

By waiting until the buffer contains the constituents

Word	NP	Word
Have	*the boys*	*take*

the parser can determine that the clause must be an imperative. The details of the parser need not detain us – it assumes a transformational grammar – since the only point at issue is whether the claim about determinism is correct. In fact, it fails in at least two ways. First, a sentence may lead the parser up the garden path. Marcus (1977) acknowledges this fact, and his real claim is accordingly that 'All sentences which people can parse without conscious difficulty can be parsed strictly deterministically.' But this claim is empty since we have no independent characterization of what can be

313

parsed without conscious difficulty. Marcus is saying little more than that all sentences can be parsed deterministically apart from those that cannot be parsed deterministically. Second, such sentences as:

Tom, I like to tell jokes to

which seem easy to understand cannot have their local ambiguities resolved merely by storing three constituents in the buffer:

NP	NP	Word
Tom	I	like

It should be noted that the string *like to tell jokes* cannot be entered as the third constituent in the buffer because the 'hole' corresponding to *Tom* may occur after *like* or after *tell*, and these possibilities are eliminated only by the final dangling preposition. We have no option but to abandon Marcus's hypothesis – a view that has been independently urged by Kaplan (1980).

How to cope with non-determinism by constructing tabular analyses

A different way to simulate non-determinism is to build up a record of all possible analyses in parallel. Two of these methods – the Cocke–Younger–Kasami (CYK) algorithm and the Earley algorithm – accommodate any context-free grammar and can parse any input string of n symbols in a space that is proportional to n^2 and in a time that is proportional to n^3 (see Hopcroft and Ullman, 1979). They rely on the essential characteristic of context-free grammar; the internal analysis of a constituent does not depend on the context in which it occurs. Hence, once a constituent has been analysed as, say, a noun phrase, it is never necessary to recompute this analysis. A natural strategy is accordingly to keep a tabular record of all analyses. These records are sometimes known as 'well-formed substring tables', but I shall refer to them simply as 'tables'.

The idea underlying the CYK algorithm is to construct a table representing all possible analyses of the input string working bottom up. It is a special case of a technique known as 'dynamic programming' in which a program calculates the solution to all subproblems, stores their answers in a table, then calculates the solutions to the problems at the next level up, stores their answers in the table, and so on (see Aho, Hopcroft and Ullman, 1974). The technique is feasible only if it is never necessary to recalculate a solution to a subproblem in the light of subsequent information. It is therefore particularly suitable for parsing context-free languages.

314

In the CYK table, the entries representing the syntactic categories of the input words are entered first. Thus, in parsing the sentence, *Ann helps Bill*, according to the grammar in Table 13.1, the initial entries are:

NP	V	NP
Ann	*helps*	*Bill*

The next level is constructed by considering all the alternative ways in which these categories can form constituents according to the grammar:

—	VP	
NP	V	NP
Ann	*helps*	*Bill*

The general principle of computing the entry for a cell is to consider each pair of entries that could possibly divide up the string lying along the edge of the triangle below that cell. In the following case, for example, the input to be considered for cell U is the substring *bcd*. This substring could be analysed by the pair of entries in cells X and W, or by the pair of entries in cells V and Z:

	U		
	V	W	
	X	Y	Z
Input	*a*	*b*	*c*	*d*

If there is a grammatical rule that reduces either pair of entries (in XW or VZ) to another symbol, then that symbol can be entered in cell U. Obviously, this algorithm only works if the grammar contains at most two non-terminal symbols on the right-hand side of any rule. However, the algorithm can be generalized to cope with grammars of a different form and even to deal with grammars that are more powerful than context free (see Kay, 1967, for an account of such 'chart'-parsers).

The time and space required for the CYK algorithm are apparent from its mode of operation. The size of the table is proportional to n^2 where ń is the number of symbols in the input; the number of operations to compute the value of a cell is proportional to n, and so the time required for the parse is proportional to n^3. However, if each cell were a separate finite-state automaton, then the construction of the table for a context-free grammar could be carried out in parallel in a time proportional to the length of the input (cf. Guibas, Kung, and Thompson, 1979).

Earley's (1970) method of 'tabular' parsing works top down. It maintains a table of all the rules in the grammar that match the string so far, and all the rules that might start to match from the current point in the parse. Each column in the table corresponds to an input symbol, and the rules that match are entered into the appropriate column together with the number of the column in which the match began, and an index of how many symbols on the right-hand side of the rule have so far been matched to the input. The following entry in the second column of Table 13.7, for example:

$$VP \rightarrow V \cdot NP, 1$$

indicates that the rule $VP \rightarrow V\ NP$ was introduced in column 1 and that V matches the input string. The '·' punctuation thus divides the right-hand side into those symbols that have been matched and those that have yet to be matched.

There is a systematic way to fill in the contents of the table:

1. Matches: If a is the current input symbol and there is a rule in the previous column of the form $A \rightarrow \alpha \cdot a\beta$ where α and β may be null, then the rule obviously continues to match the input, and should be added to the current column in the form:

$A \rightarrow \alpha a \cdot \beta$.

2. Completions: If there is any entry in the current column indicating that a rule is now completely matched, i.e., of the form: $B \rightarrow \gamma \cdot$, and there is an entry in a previous column that requires a B constituent to be parsed, e.g., $A \rightarrow \alpha \cdot B\beta$, then the information that this constituent has now been parsed is added to the current column: $A \rightarrow \alpha B \cdot \beta$.

3. Top-down predictions: If there is any entry in the current column requiring a particular non-terminal symbol to be parsed next, e.g., $C \rightarrow \gamma \cdot D$, then add all the rules in the grammar that rewrite D to the current column, indicating the constituent that should match the next input symbol, e.g., $D \rightarrow \cdot \alpha$.

316

Table 13.7 *An example of a parse table generated by Earley's algorithm*

Given the grammar:

$$
\begin{array}{lll}
1 & S & \rightarrow & NP & VP \\
2 & VP & \rightarrow & V & NP \\
3 & VP & \rightarrow & V \\
4 & NP & \rightarrow & Ann \\
5 & NP & \rightarrow & Bill \\
6 & V & \rightarrow & knows \\
7 & V & \rightarrow & helps
\end{array}
$$

and the input: *Bill helps Ann*, the algorithm generates the table:

Columns

	0	1	2	3
Input	—	*Bill*	*helps*	*Ann*
	Predictions: S → · NP VP, 0 NP → · Ann, 0 NP → · Bill, 0	Matches: NP → Bill ·, 0 Completions: S → NP · VP, 0 Predictions: VP → · V NP, 1 VP → · V, 1 V → · knows, 1 V → · helps, 1	Matches: V → helps ·, 1 Completions: VP → V · NP, 1 VP → V ·, 1 S → NP VP ·, 0 Predictions: NP → · Ann, 2 NP → · Bill, 2	Matches: NP → Ann ·, 2 Completions: VP → V NP ·, 1 S → NP VP ·, 0

The presence of S → NP VP ·, 0 in the last column indicates that the input is accepted by the parser. Its analysis can be readily recovered in a rightmost derivation working backwards from this entry in the table:

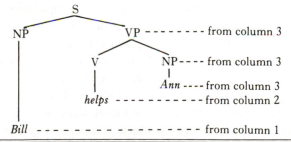

In order to initiate the parsing process, a column 0 is constructed to precede the input string. It consists of a top-down specification of all the rules in the grammar that might start to match the initial input symbol: first, all the rules with the S-symbol on the left-hand side, such as:

$$S \rightarrow \cdot NP \ VP$$

317

then any rules that expand the leftmost constituent, such as:

$$NP \rightarrow \cdot \text{ Determiner N}$$

and then any rules that expand *their* leftmost constituents, and so on. An input string is parsed if and only if there is an entry in the column corresponding to its last symbol that indicates that a rule expanding S, which was introduced in column 0, has been completely matched against the input, e.g.:

$$S \rightarrow NP \, VP \cdot , 0$$

Table 13.7 shows the way in which Earley's algorithm sets up a parse table for a simple sentence. One incidental feature of its performance that distinguishes it from a direct top-down parser is that it yields all possible analyses of the sentence up to any arbitrary point, and it is therefore not so crucial to know at which point the current sentence ends and the next one begins. Kaplan has developed an 'active chart parser' that is a generalization of the Earley algorithm designed to cope with a transformational grammar (see Ford, Bresnan, and Kaplan. In press).

The key to the efficiency of the CYK and Earley algorithms is, as Sheil (1976) has shown, *not* their method of parsing, but their reliance on a well-formed substring table. This property is sufficient in itself to ensure that a parse can be carried out in proportion to at most some polynomial function of the length of the input, such as n^3, rather than an exponential function of it, such as 3^n. One reason why such a record speeds up a parse is that once a constituent's analysis is entered into the table, it never has to be re-analysed regardless of the number of alternative trees that it may be used in. The table thereby avoids redundant computations by storing the results of successful parses of sub-constituents of the tree. Likewise, the parser can treat all analyses of a given constituent as, say, an NP as equivalent for the rest of the parse. It follows, as Sheil demonstrates, that there is nothing inherently exponential about backtracking. He presents a top-down parser that backtracks recursively and that in virtue of its use of a table is as efficient as the CYK or Earley algorithms. It is restricted to grammars that have no rule in which there are more than two non-terminals on the right-hand side of the rule. The way the parser works is to examine the table to check whether it has an entry for the current constituent. If it has, that entry is retrieved, otherwise each rule for which the constituent is a left-hand side is considered in turn. If the right-hand side of the rule matches the input string, then this parse is entered in the table. If the right-hand side of the rule contains one non-terminal, the

Customer name: Nuttall, Louise Ann

Title: The psychology of attention / Elizabeth A. Styles.
ID: 100582020X
Due: 01 Jul 2013 23:59

Title: Mental models : towards a cognitive science of language, inference, and consciousness / P.N. Johnson
ID: 1000635375
Due: 01 Jul 2013 23:59

Total items: 2
20/12/2012 15:59

All items must be returned before the due date and time.
The Loan period may be shortened if the item is requested.

WWW.nottingham.ac.uk/is

parsing routine is called recursively to see whether it matches the relevant portion of the input string. And if the right-hand side of the rule contains two non-terminals, say, B and C, the parser cuts the input string into two pieces, starting with the smallest possible left-hand piece and working progressively through to the largest possible left-hand piece, and for each such 'cut' it makes a recursive call to try to parse the left-hand piece as B and a recursive call to try to parse the right-hand piece as C.

The psychological problems of parsing

If English is a phrase-structure language, the question naturally arises as to which of the many possible systems for generating and parsing it the mind employs in speaking and understanding. This problem is not just a matter of matching an existing parser to human performance, because natural language has a number of special features. In particular, the grammar of English permits sentences with dislocated constituents, and it is also ambiguous in that it assigns more than one syntactic structure to many sentences. Even if a sentence has only a single syntactic analysis, it may nevertheless contain portions that are 'locally ambiguous' and that are only resolved later in the sentence. A standard example illustrates this phenomenon:

The boy told the story passed it on to us.

A plausible analysis construes the first part of the sentence as a simple main clause:

The boy told the story

and only later does it become clear that an alternative analysis involving a relative clause is the correct one:

The boy (who was) told the story passed it on to us.

As I have already demonstrated, the relation between a dislocated constituent and its corresponding 'hole' may also be locally ambiguous:

Tom, I like to tell jokes to.

It is not until the final dangling preposition that one knows for certain where the 'hole' corresponding to *Tom* is located.

These facts of English imply that the parser must simulate non-determinism. It must be mentally realized in a system that employs backtracking, or tabular analyses, or lookahead, or some combination of such techniques.

The facts of human performance, however, place some constraints on these various possibilities.

It is useful to distinguish the internal operations of the parser from the way in which it relates to other components of performance, particularly the semantic system. I shall consider each of these matters in turn, dealing first with three aspects of its internal design: (1), the general operating procedure of the parser, (2), the way in which it copes with non-determinism, and (3), whether it uses any specific parsing heuristics; and then with the parser's external relations to other processes underlying comprehension.

The general operating procedure of the mental parser

The human parser might work top down, bottom up, or in both directions. But since left-branching and right-branching structures are of comparable difficulty, it is unlikely that the parser operates wholly top down or wholly bottom up. It certainly seems to need to make predictions in order to cope with dislocated constituents: as soon as such a constituent is identified, the parser must be sensitive to the subsequent occurrence of a potential 'hole', because such 'holes' often have no explicit syntactic cue to their presence (Frazier and Fodor, 1978).

There are in principle several types of prediction that a parser might make. It could predict that the next constituent will be of a particular category. This type of prediction is regularly made by a standard left-corner parser, as in the step from:

to:

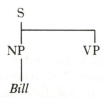

which was illustrated earlier. It could predict that a particular constituent must definitely occur at *some* later point in the sentence, though not necessarily as the next constituent. The occurrence of *the* predicts a subsequent noun though it may not be the next word, and the occurrence of a dislocated constituent predicts a subsequent 'hole' that corresponds to it. Finally, the parser could make either sort of prediction with respect to optional constituents. For example, given the occurrence of a verb that can be used transitively or intransitively, it could predict that the next constituent is optionally a noun phrase.

The point of making predictions is to increase efficiency. If too many predictions are made, however, the system will collapse under its own processing load. It would thus be folly to design a system that made top-down predictions about, say, occurrences of conjunctions, or adverbs like *only*, or any other constituent that is ubiquitous. Such predictions would have to be made after almost every word in a sentence and mostly would fail to be fulfilled. It follows that the sensible way to deal with ubiquitous constituents is bottom up: whenever one is encountered, it initiates a bottom-up analysis (cf. Winograd, 1972).

Granted a parser that employs both top-down and bottom-up procedures, the next problem is to determine how they divide up the work between them. A conjecture that is worth exploring is that the beginnings of constituents cannot be predicted top down, but once a constituent has been recognized, there may be useful redundancies in the language that enable top-down predictions to be made. In English, this principle certainly applies at the level of sentences. A sentence may be a declarative:

Alfred burnt the cakes

an imperative:

Burn the cakes!

a Yes/No question:

Did Alfred burn the cakes?

or a Wh-question:

Who burnt the cakes?

It would be pointless to make top-down predictions about the first constituent of a sentence, but once that constituent has been recognized bottom up, it is often possible to identify the type of sentence and to make various predictions: a declarative has a subsequent VP, an imperative with a transitive verb has an NP, a Yes/No question has an NP and a VP, and a Wh-question has a subsequent VP. The occurrence of an NP is also relatively hard to predict top down, but once the beginning of one has been recognised from the presence of a determiner, a subsequent noun can be predicted. Likewise, once the beginning of a VP has been identified from the occurrence of a verb, the type of VP depends on the particular verb that occurred. The general principle is: it is harder to predict the beginning of a constituent (and its particular sub-category) than to predict what follows (and its sub-category). Although there are other ways of combining top-down and bottom-up parsing, this particular principle is, of course, embodied in a left-corner parser.

How the parser copes with syntactic ambiguity and dislocated constituents

The second major issue is the way in which the parser copes with non-determinism arising from the need to parse ambiguous expressions. In order to implement efficient backtracking it would need to keep a record of previous choices in a push-down store. Hence, the crucial question is whether humans have a memory organised like a 'stack'. And the answer is: almost certainly not. The evidence from the figural effect in syllogistic reasoning suggested that, on the contrary, working memory operates according to a 'first in, first out' principle. Moreover, if a stack were available for parsing, then self-embedded sentences, such as:

The war the general the president appoints starts ends the world

should not be difficult to understand. Likewise, a sentence such as:

They told the boy that the girl liked the story

should be equally often interpreted as an embedded construction:

They told the boy (that the girl liked) the story

as it is interpreted as a non-embedded construction:

They told the boy (that the girl liked the story).

In fact, the non-embedded interpretation is more likely (Wanner, Kaplan, and Shiner, 1975). It is true that some self-embedded sentences are easier to understand than others. Kimball (1975) cites the example:

The guy whom the secretary we fired slept with is a real lucky dog

where there are both explicit syntactic and semantic cues to aid comprehension. It is also true that there are a variety of explanations of why self-embedding creates difficulties. They include: the difficulty of having to call a procedure whilst in the midst of executing that procedure, i.e., a recursive procedure call (Miller and Isard, 1964); the impossibility of working on more than two clauses at any one time (Kimball, 1973); the load on memory of having to hold a dislocated constituent until its 'hole' is parsed (Wanner and Maratsos, 1978); the tendency to group words superficially, which disrupts the parsing of dislocated constituents (Frazier and Fodor, 1978). All these hypotheses are tantamount to the rejection of an efficient push-down store. Conversely, there are cases where people are *not* limited to the 'first in, last out' principle that they would be constrained to if their memory consisted solely of a stack (see Engdahl's examples, 1981, to be discussed later in the chapter). Hence, the evidence suggests that people do not have a 'stack'-like memory at their disposal. It follows that they are unlikely to be able to backtrack to any great depth.

With backtracking eliminated as a general procedure for coping with ambiguity, a second possibility is the use of lookahead. But this procedure is similarly constrained both by its theoretical inadequacies, which I discussed earlier, and by an obvious aspect of linguistic performance: the speed at which comprehension occurs. Listeners do not have to wait until the end of a constituent in order to start to understand it, but can normally cope with it from word to word. Marslen-Wilson has shown in a series of studies that many people understand much of a sentence with a lag of only about a syllable after hearing each word. His technique is to ask subjects to listen to a tape-recorded passage and to 'shadow' what they hear, that is, to speak out aloud the same words with as little a lag as possible. Certain individuals are able to do this with a delay of only about 250 msec between what they hear and what they say. However, even though they are shadowing so rapidly, when they make an error it almost invariably (i.e., 98%) fits the context both syntactically and semantically (Marslen-Wilson, 1973). For example, several subjects repeated back the sentence 'He had heard at the Brigade . . .' as 'He had heard *that* the Brigade . . .' Such a change could even lead to an appropriate modification later in the sentence: the actual sentence 'He had heard at the Brigade that the Austrians . . .' was repeated as 'He had heard *that* the Brigade *had* the Austrians . . .' Likewise, when Marslen-Wilson (1975) inserted deliberately anomalous words into the materials to be shadowed, the subjects' perform- ance was disrupted: they were sensitive both to syntactic and semantic anomalies. And when deliberate mispronunciations were introduced, they were corrected so as to make sense in context. Hence, the process of parsing (at least up to the point of constructing a propositional representation) must be very rapid. If errors are interpreted so quickly, a process of lookahead is almost certainly ruled out: there would be no time to wait for the subsequent words (or constituents) to disambiguate syntactic structure while continuing to shadow and to correct speech with a delay of only a syllable.

A third possibility is that the mental parser builds up a table of all possible analyses of a sentence. This possibility is corroborated by experimental findings on the accessibility of alternative interpretations of ambiguous sentences (cf. Garrett, 1970). But it appears to be ruled out as a general procedure by the fact that certain sentences, like the earlier examples, lead one 'up the garden path' syntactically. Crain and Steedman (1981), however, have resisted this claim. They argue that the parser builds up different *semantic* interpretations in parallel and that it is the semantic component that selects amongst them and is responsible for the garden-path effect. It follows that when a sentence such as:

The teachers taught by the Berlitz method passed the test

is presented in isolation, readers are unlikely to perceive the phrase:

The teachers taught by the Berlitz method . . .

as a noun phrase with a relative clause, because this interpretation requires additional presuppositions to be made about the particular class of teachers to which reference is made. Crain and Steedman corroborated this hypothesis by showing that readers are much less likely to be led up the garden path by sentences of the form:

Children taught by the Berlitz method passed the test

where the indefinite plural 'children' carries fewer presuppositions and is also more plausibly construed as the head of this particular relative clause. Similarly, if a previous sentence had established a plausible referent for the noun phrase with the relative clause, the subjects were less likely to be led up the garden path. However, as Crain and Steedman allow, the parser could build up the alternative interpretations serially. It could propose a syntactically driven interpretation of a constituent of a sentence, which is either accepted or rejected in the light of information in the current mental model of the discourse.

The phenomena of dislocated constituents are equally equivocal. As Janet Fodor (In press) has emphasized, it is often easy to detect the presence of a dislocated constituent, but difficult to determine the corresponding 'hole' to which it is related. The point is illustrated by considering the following sequence of topicalized sentences, where '*t*' indicates the position of the 'hole' to which the initial noun phrase relates:

i. Tom, I like *t* to tell jokes.

ii. Tom, I like to tell *t* jokes.

iii. Tom, I like to tell jokes to *t*.

iv. Tom, I like *t* to tell jokes to the audience.

v. Tom, I like to tell jokes to the audience about *t*.

vi. Tom, I like *t* to tell jokes to the audience about mothers-in-law.

Examples (i) and (ii) are, of course, two different interpretations of the same sentence. The sequence as a whole shows that a definite relation between the dislocated phrase and the trace cannot be established until the very end of the clause. Frazier, Clifton and Randall (In press) timed how long their subjects spent in reading two such types of sentence. The sentences were presented on a video-display at a rate comparable to normal reading, and the subjects were asked to press a button as soon as possible after the end of the sentence to indicate that on a quick intuitive basis they had understood the sentence without having to reread it. Sentences of the form:

This is the girl the teacher wanted to talk to

were understood reliably faster (100 msec) than sentences of the form:

This is the girl the teacher wanted to talk.

Frazier *et al.* predicted this result from the hypothesis that when the parser detects a 'hole' it initially and rapidly assigns the most salient – here, the most recent – potential dislocated constituent to it. The first sentence is correctly parsed according to this principle:

This is *the girl the teacher* wanted *t* to talk to *t*.

The second sentence is initially mis-parsed according to this principle because *the teacher* is erroneously assigned to the 'hole', when in fact the correct analysis is:

This is *the girl* the teacher wanted *t* to talk.

These results, however, do not necessarily imply that the parser assigns one analysis at a time. There are two qualifications to be borne in mind.

First, the task may not reflect a genuine comprehension of the sentences. On a third of the trials at random, the subjects were asked a subsequent question about the content of the sentence, such as:

Who was wanted to talk?

There was no reliable difference in the percentages of correct answers to the two questions. Another result bears on the same point: when the main verb in the sentence permitted only the assignment of the distant filler to the 'hole', as in:

This is the girl the teacher forced to talk

there was no reliable decrease in initial 'comprehension' time, but there was a significant improvement in the subjects' ability to answer the subsequent questions. Hence, the syntactic constraints of a verb are evidently taken into account after the initial 'comprehension' response. Second, Frazier *et al.* assume that the cause of the difficulty is in identifying which particular noun phrase fills the 'hole'. An alternative possibility is that the problem arises in finding the hole in the first place (cf. Fodor, 1978). The sentence:

This is the girl the teacher wanted to talk to

has an alternative syntactic cue – the dangling preposition – to the presence of a 'hole'. The sentence:

This is the girl the teacher wanted to talk

has no explicit cue to the location of the 'hole'.

Taken together, these two qualifications suggest an alternative explanation: the subjects make their initial response, not on the basis of a full syntactic analysis which should be sensitive to the constraints of the main verb, but on the basis of a rapid, intuitive and task-oriented check that where there is a dislocated noun there is also a corresponding 'hole'. This check takes less time for those sentences in which there is an explicit cue to the 'hole'. Subsequently, the subjects carry out a complete syntactic analysis of the sentences, which enables them to answer the questions about 80% of the time; and this analysis takes the syntactic constraints of the verb into account and is unaffected by whether the distant or recent filler is the correct assignment, since it builds up a table of both possible analyses.

The parsing of sentences with dislocations depends on three component processes: first, the detection of potentially dislocated constituents; second, the detection of potential 'holes'; and, third, the marrying of the right dislocations with the right 'holes'. The detection of potentially dislocated

326

constituents is not always easy (*pace* Fodor) as the following example illustrates:

Tom, Bill and Mary want to give presents to.

In this case *Tom* is topicalized and *Bill and Mary* is the subject of the main verb. However, it is reasonable to suppose that dislocations are usually easy to detect. For example, as soon as the following string has been parsed:

Tom, I like . . .

Tom can be assigned an analysis as a topicalized noun phrase. If Frazier *et al.* are correct in assuming that an initial and rapid syntactic analysis is made, then presumably there should be some principle governing the detection and marriage of 'holes'. A principle in accord with the idea of a fast initial analysis is to assign the *first* potential hole to the most recent potential filler. This principle yields the following analysis:

i, Tom, *I* like *t* to . . .
    └ _ _ _↟

If the sentence continues: 'Tom, I like to tell jokes', then the principle yields a further assignment:

ii, *Tom, I* like *t* to tell *t* jokes.
    │   └ _ _↟   ⋀
    └ _ _ _ _ _ _ _ _ ⌐

Hence, this analysis should be preferred over the other possible interpretation of the complete sentence:

iii, *Tom, I* like *t* to tell jokes.
     └ _ _ _ _ ↟

Indeed, in an informal survey, I got people to read the sentence and then I asked them who tells the jokes; there was an overwhelming bias in favour of interpretation (ii). According to these principles, however, the sentence: 'Tom, I like to tell jokes to', will lead the parser up the garden path, because the initial analysis:

iv, *Tom, I* like *t* to tell *t* jokes to
    │   └ _ _↟   ⋀
    └ _ _ _ _ _ _ _ _ _ ⌐

fails to work and the sentence has to be reparsed:

v, *Tom, I* like *t* to tell jokes to *t*.
   │   └ _ _↟   ⋀
   └ _ _ _ _ _ _ _ _ _ _ _ _ _ ⌐

Unfortunately, as the reader will have noticed, these principles lead to the prediction that sentences such as (v) should be harder to parse than sentences such as (ii), and this prediction is exactly the opposite to Frazier *et al.*'s results. Hence, even if their salient filler hypothesis is correct, it is difficult to sustain the notion of an initial rapid single parse of 'holes'; a more plausible assumption is that a record is kept of all potential 'holes'.

This conclusion is corroborated by the results of a study carried out by Engdahl (1981) with native speakers of Swedish. In Swedish, the sentence equivalent to the following:

Herring, this knife is impossible to gut *t* with *t*

is perfectly grammatical, and Engdahl's subjects readily interpreted it in this way, thereby showing that they were *not* restricted to a 'stack'-like memory for dislocated constituents. A sentence with the same syntactic structure but with a verb whose semantic constraints are different was interpreted in a 'nested' way:

This pan, the cake is easiest to bake *t in t*.

This effect of semantics on syntactic analysis suggested to Engdahl that perhaps the parser computes both analyses in parallel and then the semantics selects between them.

Although a record of all the potential 'holes' in a sentence is likely to be maintained, the question of whether the parser builds up parallel analyses of all ambiguous expressions has yet to be resolved decisively. If it does not, and is genuinely led up the garden path, its process of recovery remains to be established. Granted that memory does not function like a push-down store, systematic backtracking is unlikely. A plausible alternative is to reparse the sentence from the start of a local ambiguity trying to avoid the analysis that failed to make sense. Frazier and Rayner (1982) report just the regressive eye movements that one would expect in this case from their study of how people read ambiguous sentences. As I will show in the final part of the chapter, this reparsing procedure and the parallel representation of potential 'holes' can be readily implemented using a table of well-formed substrings.

328

Are there specific parsing heuristics?

There are allegedly a number of specific parsing heuristics that reflect the natural characteristics and memory limitations of the mental parser; and several phenomena have been interpreted as evidence for these heuristics. A sentence such as:

Kay said that Andy had called on Wednesday

is theoretically ambiguous in that *on Wednesday* may modify *Kay said* or *Andy had called*. In the absence of information to the contrary, readers generally interpret the adverbial as modifying the most recent phrase. The bias may reflect the greater load on working memory if *Kay said* has to be held there in order to be syntactically related to *yesterday* (Kimball, 1975), or, alternatively, there may be a restricted 'window' within which words are initially grouped together syntactically (Frazier and Fodor, 1978). However, the same bias occurs with:

Kay said Andy called yesterday

where the sentence is sufficiently short to lie within such a window (Wanner, 1980). Hence, if there is a parsing principle underlying the phenomenon, it appears to be one that creates a bias towards attaching constituents to the rightmost of the previous nodes (Kimball, 1973, 1975; Wanner, 1980; Fodor and Frazier, 1980). But the phenomenon may not reflect the operations of the parser at all: it could be an indirect consequence of the unambiguity of such sentences as:

Kay said on Wednesday that Andy had called.

The fact that a writer has eschewed this unambiguous sentence in favour of an ambiguous counterpart may lead readers to infer that the other interpretation is intended. This hypothesis is consistent with the intuition (of Frazier and Fodor, 1978) that there is no difference in the likelihood of the two interpretations of:

John said that Martha claimed that 1984 will be blissful yesterday

where the adverbial applies equally to *John said* or *Martha claimed*. Here, the writer has eschewed both of the unambiguous counterparts:

John said yesterday . . .
John said that Martha claimed yesterday . . .

and so there is nothing to choose between them.

A sentence such as:

John bought the book for Susan

329

appears to violate the alleged bias towards attaching constituents to the rightmost previous node. Its natural interpretation is that the book was bought for Susan:

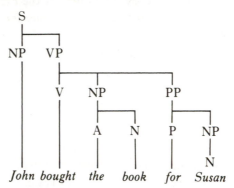

rather than that the-book-for-Susan was bought:

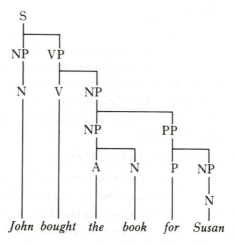

but it is this second structure that attaches *for Susan* to the rightmost node of the previous analysis, i.e., the NP. The bias here may reflect parsimony – a desire for the simplest syntactic analysis in terms of the number of nodes (Frazier and Fodor, 1978), and a reluctance to modify a syntactic structure that has already been established (Kimball, 1973; Fodor and Frazier, 1980) – the second structure demands an additional NP to be inserted before the PP can be added. A rather different possibility is that the V NP PP analysis of the first structure is an optional prediction from the verb *bought*, whereas there is no sensible way of predicting that an NP consists of an NP followed by a PP.

The putative bias for parsimonious structures fails to apply altogether in the case of the sentence:

Joe bought the book on the most beautiful Hindu temples as a birthday gift for Susan.

Frazier and Fodor argue that the mechanism giving rise to parsimony therefore does not work over long distances and instead that there is a local attachment reflecting the restricted 'window' of the initial parsing mechanism. But here, too, the attachment may depend merely on its plausibility in the light of the specific content of the sentence. Hence, the alleged bias towards an attachment to the verb reappears in the following sentence:

Joe bought the book on the most beautiful Hindu temples in India for Susan.

Ford, Bresnan, and Kaplan (In press) similarly propose that parsing is sensitive to the structure of grammatical functions favoured by specific lexical items. Thus, according to their theory, the following functional structure of the clause:

(SUBJECT) (OBJECT) (PREPOSITIONAL COMPLEMENT)

is favoured by the verb *bought* over the structure:

(SUBJECT) (OBJECT)

It is this preference that accounts for the salient interpretation of 'John bought the book for Susan.' They argue that only such specifications of grammatical functions can explain the bias, because a specification based merely on the rule:

VP → NP PP

leaves out the subject of the sentence and applies only to 'untransformed' sentences. This argument loses its teeth, however, if transformational grammar is abandoned in favour of phrase-structure grammar, since each surface form is then directly specified by phrase-structure rules and each rule for expanding the verb phrase is directly associated with the specific verbs to which it applies. Hence, one can accept the general claim that specific lexical items favour this or that structure without having to adopt Ford, Bresnan, and Kaplan's particular theory.

These various phenomena are difficult to understand because they are open to so many alternative interpretations. There is an abundance of parsing principles that have been proposed to explain them: Table 13.8

Table 13.8 *Some possible heuristics used by the mental parser*

1 Right association	Example: 'Tom said Andy called yesterday', in which there is a bias to attach a new node to the rightmost node of the current structure assigned to the sentence (Kimball, 1973). Frazier and Fodor (1978) suggest that the principle is a consequence of the limited size of the 'window' of the parsing mechanism that initially groups words together; Fodor and Frazier (1980) take it to be a general principle that applies both to the initial and the ultimate assignment of structure.
2 Minimal attachment	Example: 'John bought the book for Susan', in which the constituents are parsed so as to yield a parsimonious structure with the fewest possible nodes (Frazier and Fodor, 1978). It may in part be a consequence of the fixed-structure heuristic.
3 Local association	Example: 'Joe bought the book on the most beautiful Hindu temples as a birthday gift for Susan', in which nearby words are grouped together syntactically as a result of the limited size of the initial parsing 'window' (Fodor and Frazier, 1980).
4 Early closure	Example: 'The boat floated on the water sank', is hard to understand because the structure assigned to an expression is closed as soon as possible, i.e., unless the next node parsed is an immediate constituent of the expression (Kimball, 1973).
5 Late closure	Example: 'Since Jay always jogs a mile seems like a short distance to him' is hard to understand because items are preferably parsed as constituents of the phrase currently being analysed (Frazier, 1981).
6 Fixed structure	It is costly to have to reanalyze an expression (Kimball, 1973); an analysis is revised only as a last resort, i.e., when it ceases to be compatible with the input (Fodor and Frazier, 1980).
7. Two sentences	It is impossible for the parser to cope with the analysis of more than two clauses at any one time (Kimball, 1973).

summarizes just some of them. However, as we have seen, the examples that are supposed to establish the principle of *right association* are equivocal and may reflect instead the contrast in the use of an ambiguous and an unambiguous sentence; the examples that appear to motivate *minimal attachment* and *local attachment* may arise from the limited capabilities of working memory, or from optional predictions based on specific lexical items. When these and other principles are deployed in an informal account of parsing, it is easy to lose track of all the ways in which they might interact, and it is almost impossible to evaluate the various principles in isolation. It is the theory as a whole that needs to be assessed, ideally from a computer implementation of it. For the time being, it seems prudent to keep an open mind about the principles in Table 13.8.

Does the mental parser operate autonomously?

Syntactic analysis is just part of the process of comprehension, and one is bound to wonder about how it relates to other parts of the process. The conventional view in psycholinguistics, as I pointed out in the previous chapter, is that the parser yields a syntactic structure, perhaps constituent by constituent or clause by clause, which is then used by the semantic component to build up an interpretation of the sentence. In fact, there is no need and no evidence for any representation of syntactic structure, because meaning can be recovered directly from a syntactically driven analysis of the sentence. Indeed, the efficiency of comprehension is perhaps attributable to the direct construction of a propositional representation and to the parser's ability to take all relevant information into account. If you hear an utterance of the ambiguous sentence 'The firm bosses like the unions', its timing and intonation is likely to provide a very good clue to its correct analysis. The contour:

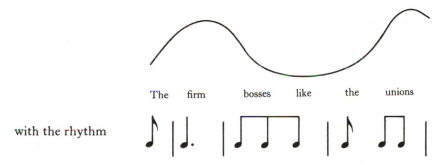

suggests the parsing (The firm) (bosses like the unions). The contour:

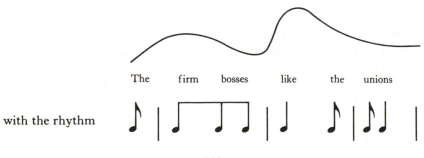

333

suggests the parsing (The firm bosses) (like the unions). Likewise, if you overhear the conversation:

A: Anne was first into the room.
B: No, Anne was preceded by Jane.
C: No! It was Mary whom Anne was preceded by

your grasp of the prior context makes the task of understanding the final utterance easier than when it occurs in isolation. (The effect should be apparent just in reading these sentences; there appear to be no experiments demonstrating this point.)

Other potential influences on the process of parsing a sentence are the meaning and reference of its previous constituents, the mental model of the context in which it occurs, and the general knowledge which the sentence triggers. A number of psycholinguists, however, have argued that syntactic processing is autonomous, by which they mean that these semantic and pragmatic factors have no effect on syntactic processing (see, e.g., Forster, 1974; Fodor, Bever, and Garrett, 1974; Garrett, 1976). The fact that these various processes are separate enterprises does not of course imply that they must operate autonomously – indeed, the question of autonomy versus interaction can only be raised on the assumption that they are separate enterprises – and I shall argue against autonomy and in favour of an interaction between the processes. There is evidence that is consistent with autonomy in that the manipulation of syntactic and semantic variables had only 'additive' effects on the performance of four main tasks: the completion of ambiguous or unambiguous fragments of a sentence (Bever, Garrett, and Hurtig, 1973), the detection of a particular target phoneme in a sentence, the accurate perception of sentences displayed using the so-called 'RSVP' technique in which the words of the sentence are presented one after another in a rapid sequence, and the classification of sentences as meaningful and well-formed (see, e.g., Forster and Olbrei, 1973; Forster, 1976; Garrett, 1976). None of these tasks involves just the simple ordinary comprehension of sentences. Moreover, additive results in studies that manipulate two or more independent variables are merely consistent with the null hypothesis of autonomy, which of course cannot be proved. My colleagues and I, however, have consistently obtained evidence which suggests that this null hypothesis should be rejected (see Steedman and Johnson-Laird, 1977, for some preliminary findings).

The most striking results have been obtained by my former student, Scott Warman. In his experiments, the subjects first see an informative sentence (on the visual display of a microcomputer) for a period of four seconds, e.g.:

In the park, the man saw the boy who waved at him.

They are then presented with a question about the content of the sentence to which they have to answer 'Yes' or 'No'. In one experiment, Warman compared the effects of the presence or absence of an explicit syntactic cue to a relative clause, e.g., the question:

Did the boy that the man saw wave?

as opposed to:

Did the boy the man saw wave?

As the results in Table 13.9 show, the question that lacks the cue takes longer to answer. However, the additional time is almost entirely eradicated

Table 13.9 *The mean latencies to answer four sorts of question about a previous assertion (from an unpublished study carried out by Warman)*

	Type of question	Mean latencies (seconds)
No semantic cue	{ Did the boy that the man saw wave?	2·39
	{ Did the boy the man saw wave?	2·55
Semantic cue	{ Did the dog that the bus hit die?	1·86
	{ Did the dog the bus hit die?	1·85

when there is a good semantic cue to the respective roles of the two noun phrases, as in the questions:

Did the dog that the bus hit die?

and:

Did the dog the bus hit die?

where it is plain that only the dog, and not the bus, can die. In order to ensure that the subjects were not responding solely on the basis of whether or not dogs can die, the trials on which the answer to the question was 'no' consisted of equal numbers of questions containing an inappropriate subject (e.g., *cat*), an inappropriate main verb (e.g., *live*), an inappropriate noun in the relative clause (e.g., *car*), and an inappropriate verb in the relative clause (e.g., *missed*). A purely pragmatic cue based on the relative likelihoods of the two noun phrase referents engaging in a particular activity, e.g., the question:

Did the bather (that) the lifeguard saved collapse?

335

also eliminated the difference between responding to the two constructions, though not quite so effectively.

In a further study using the same technique, Warman established that a semantic cue would even virtually eliminate the retarding effect of a deliberate grammatical error. The results are shown in Table 13.10. Subjects are slower in answering a question such as:

Did the boy the that [sic] man saw wave?

but, remarkably, they very rarely notice any error – they simply take longer to respond than to a corresponding grammatical question. However, the retarding effect of ungrammaticality is all but eliminated by the presence of a semantic cue, as in:

Did the dog the that [sic] bus hit die?

Table 13.10 *The mean latencies to answer grammatical and ungrammatical questions about a previous assertion (from an unpublished study carried out by Warman)*

	Type of question	Mean latencies (seconds)
No semantic cue	⌠Did the boy that the man saw wave?	2·23
	⌡Did the boy the that man saw wave?	2·67
Semantic cue	⌠Did the dog that the bus hit die?	1·61
	⌡Did the dog the that bus hit die?	1·69

A defender of autonomy might argue that interactions occur because normal syntactic processing cannot cope with the experimental materials and must be supplemented by special 'problem-solving' strategies (cf. Forster, 1979). This assumption reduces the empirical content of the autonomy hypothesis to a dangerous degree, and it is more fruitful to assume that the results establish that there are genuine interactions, and to explore the possible underlying mechanism. In fact, there appear to be several sources of interaction between syntactic and semantic processing.

First, lexical entries contain information not merely about the most likely syntactic frame, but also about potential referents for the different arguments. Selectional restrictions, default values, and factual information for the use of an inferential component, may all be used to make predictions, and sentences that conform to them will be easier to interpret than those that do not.

Second, there may be similar effects at the level of constituents: for instance, the propositional representation of one constituent could help to determine the proper analysis of other constituents. Likewise, the identification of the referents of expressions could influence the process of parsing (cf. Winograd, 1972). A request such as:

Put the blue pyramid on the block in the box

is ambiguous since it is unclear whether the object to be moved is the blue pyramid or the blue pyramid on the block. A special procedure in Winograd's program interrupts the parse to check whether there is a unique blue pyramid on the block, or one that has been recently mentioned, and the outcome of this search determines the interpretation of the sentence. The implausibility of the interpretation of a sentence as a whole may also lead to the rejection of its propositional representation.

The general mechanism underlying such interactions must simulate a non-deterministic automaton. Since, as I argued earlier, there is no independent syntactic representation, the automaton cannot select between alternative syntactic structures on the basis of semantic cues, but must rather choose between propositional representations. It must build up the correct propositional representation of a sentence on the basis of a concurrent syntactic and semantic analysis. The systematic use of lookahead has already been ruled out, and hence there are only two standard methods available: the construction of parallel interpretations using a tabular procedure, or the construction of a single analysis at a time with some provision, such as backtracking, for recovery from error. In either case, there are two general methods for organizing the concurrent decisions: the process could be syntactically driven and semantic cues could be used to eliminate inappropriate interpretations, or the process could be semantically driven and syntactic analysis could be used to eliminate inappropriate interpretations. The idea of independent syntactic and semantic analyses that are then compared is difficult to reconcile with the assumption that no syntactic representation is constructed: a purely syntactic analysis could hardly yield a set of putative propositional representations. Since the lexical items of most sentences can probably be fitted together to yield many possible candidate propositional representations when syntax is not taken into account, there are good grounds for supposing that the interpretative process is syntactically driven. The parser uses the grammar to build up a propositional representation based on the lexical semantics. Whenever it has a choice, it can be guided by further semantic information in the lexicon, by the mental model of the discourse, or by general knowledge. In the case of a tabular method, this guidance would reduce the number of alternative interpretations entered into the table. In the case of a serial method, it would select the most plausible single interpretation at each stage in the process. What remains possible is that the interactive effects occur only after an initial choice of propositional representation. In a study of eye movements, Frazier (1981) found that when subjects read a sentence beginning in the following way:

The spy saw the man with a revolver . . .

the reading time per character was significantly longer in the region following the prepositional phrase in comparison with a sentence beginning:

The spy saw the man with the binoculars . . .

Frazier suggests that the parser initially follows the minimal attachment heuristic (see Table 13.8). In the case of the first sentence, the parser thus uses a V NP PP analysis that is incompatible with the preferred frame, V NP, for the verb *see*. It is therefore necessary for the parser to reanalyse the prepositional phrase as a constituent of the noun phrase, whereas no such reanalysis is required for the second sentence. Unfortunately, there is no direct evidence that the sentence is reparsed: not even regressive eye movements are definitive sign of reparsing, because readers may instead be choosing an alternative analysis from a set computed in parallel. Moreover, if Frazier is correct, then a sentence beginning in the following way:

The spy wanted the revolver in the gunsmiths . . .

should also need to be reparsed, whereas a sentence beginning:

The spy wanted a revolver in his pocket . . .

is correctly parsed by minimal attachment. In any event, there is only one feasible conclusion, which is supported by other independent evidence (e.g., Tyler and Marslen-Wilson, 1977): the process of interpretation is syntactically driven, but the parser can and does make use of semantic information to aid it in its processing. The only point at issue is whether it does so in constructing an initial interpretation or a subsequent interpretation of a sentence.

The design of the mental parser

The evidence places four principal constraints on the feasible designs of the mental parser:

1. The parser delivers an almost immediate propositional representation of a sentence constituent by constituent, or word by word. (It does not set up a representation of syntactic structure.)

2. It uses semantic information from several sources to help it to parse.

3. It uses both top-down and bottom-up procedures, perhaps integrated within a left-corner parsing system.

4. It copes with local ambiguity arising from dislocated constituents either by maintaining a table of possible analyses, or by reparsing the ambiguous constituent. (It does not make a systematic use of either backtracking or lookahead.)

No current parser satisfies all four of these desiderata. In sketching the design for a parsing mechanism, I shall make use of two separate parsers that have been implemented in computer programs. The first, which was developed some years ago in collaboration with Mark Steedman, was designed to meet the first two desiderata (see Steedman and Johnson-Laird, 1977; Johnson-Laird, 1977a). The second and more recently developed parser was designed to meet the last two desiderata.

A semantic transition network

The starting-point of the first parser was an attempt to do 'psycholinguistics without linguistics' (Johnson-Laird, 1977a). I took the view (for the reasons outlined earlier) that the experimental evidence had failed to support the need for the mental representation of deep structure, and I suggested instead that comprehension consisted in mapping a sentence directly into a semantic representation, and that speaking consisted in mapping a semantic representation directly into a sentence. This direct link between utterance and meaning made it easier to accommodate an interaction between syntax and semantics, and accounted for the rapidity of speech and comprehension. The question was: what mechanism could achieve the desired mapping? A plausible answer was: an *augmented transition network*.

In Chapter 12, the notion of a recursive transition network was introduced as one way in which to represent a parser for context-free languages (see Figure 12.3). Such devices can be *augmented* by the addition of various actions so that they are able to cope with transformational grammars (Thorne, Bratley, and Dewar, 1968; Woods, 1970): indeed, they become equivalent in power to unrestricted Turing machines. Specific ATN's, however, have been used to model various perceptual heuristics for parsing

339

(Kaplan, 1972), and to codify alternative processing strategies (Wanner and Maratsos, 1978). A typical ATN is illustrated in a simplified form in Figure 13.1. The device is essentially a non-deterministic top-down parser in which each transition has a condition (above the arcs in the figure) and an action that is carried out (below the arcs in the figure) if the condition is satisfied. The way the parser works can be illustrated by an example.

Sentence network:

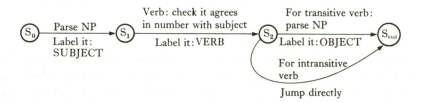

Noun phrase network:

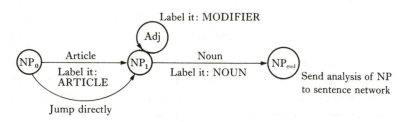

Figure 13.1 A simple augmented transition network (ATN).

Suppose the input sentence is our familiar example: *Bill helps*. The sentence network predicts the occurrence of an initial NP and accordingly passes control to the NP-network. This network predicts an initial occurrence of an article, or (by a direct jump to its next state) a noun, and the noun may be preceded by an arbitrary number of adjectives. In practice, such a non-deterministic choice is simulated by scheduling an order in which to try each of the arcs leading out from a given state. If the schedule prefers, for example, to parse a noun rather than an NP, and in general follows an ordering based on the closeness of a constituent to a terminal symbol, then it will automatically follow the heuristics of *right association* and *minimal attachment* (see Wanner, 1980; Ford, Bresnan, and Kaplan, In press). To return to our example, *Bill* satisfies the test for a noun and is accordingly so labelled. This analysis is then labelled as an NP and

340

returned to the sentence network where it is in turn labelled as the SUBJECT. The next word is a verb which agrees in number with the subject of the sentence, and, since it is intransitive and the last word of the input, the analysis of the sentence as a whole is assembled:

(SENTENCE: SUBJECT = (NP: NOUN = *Bill*)
               VERB   = *helps*)

The notation labels each constituent of the sentence according to its underlying syntactic function. The ATN's processor uses a stack to keep track of where it is working so that it can return an analysis to the appropriate network, and an ATN that can handle a richer fragment of the language will allow recursion: e.g., the NP network can make a recursive call to the sentence network in order to parse a relative clause.

My aim was to forego the luxury of an underlying syntactic structure (on the grounds that there was no evidence for its mental representation) and to devise a *semantic transition network* that yielded the meaning of the sentence directly. The device would not produce an explicit analysis of syntactic relations, but would be immediately responsive to them in building up a semantic representation. This principle can be epitomized in a variant of Occam's razor: if you can read the signposts, you don't need a map. Understanding a sentence is indeed like following a series of syntactic signposts, and you can reach your destination without having to keep a record of the directions in which they point. The STN, which was described in Johnson-Laird (1977a), had actions on each arc that built up semantic interpretations. It exploited the fact that a cyclical transformation merely shifts constituents around within a set of nodes generated by the base grammar (see Chapter 12). For example, its syntactic analysis of the passive *by*-phrase is identical to its analysis of an ordinary prepositional phrase, and the two diverge only in their semantic interpretation. The STN could be used for *producing* utterances by in effect switching round the conditions and actions on each arc – for instance, a referent elicits the action of constructing a noun phrase.

A model of an STN was implemented in a computer program developed by Mark Steedman (see Steedman and Johnson-Laird, 1977). The program answers questions about a simple one-dimensional universe of discourse that consists in 'particles' moving to and fro, colliding with each other, and so on. Since it builds up, not a syntactic representation of a sentence, but a special kind of propositional representation, it is a simple matter to use the device to produce the answers to the questions.

341

A typical history of the universe for the program consists of the following set of propositional representations in a data base:

[Y AT A 0]
[X AT B 0]
[Z AT C 0]
[E1 Y MOVE FROM A TO B START 1 FINISH 2]
[E2 X MOVE FROM B TO C START 2 FINISH 3]
[E3 Z MOVE FROM C TO D START 3 FINISH 4]

where, for instance, the first item means that object Y is at location A at time 0, and the fourth item means that event E1 consists in Y moving from location A to location B starting at time 1 and finishing at time 2. The data base was set up using the programming language PICO-PLANNER (Anderson, 1972), which allows the goal of finding a fact in the data base to be satisfied either directly by a match with a proposition represented there or, if that fails, by deducing the fact from others in the data base. This system and its semantic representations were used for convenience; no claim that they correspond to the mental representation of meaning was intended.

As the program parses a question such as:

Did X hit Z at location C?

it operates in exactly the same way as an ATN except that instead of constructing a syntactic representation of the sentence, it sets up a series of goals in a propositional representation:

EVENT HIT SUBJ X: Find an event that has X as the subject of a
                 hitting.
EVENT HIT OBJ Z: Check that the event has Z as its object.
EVENT HIT AT C: Check that the location of the event is C.

Each goal is evaluated with respect to the data base. Higher-level descriptions of events, such as *hitting*, are not directly represented there, and answers to questions about them are inferred from the data base. With the present question, each goal is satisfied by the history of the universe above:

E2 HIT SUBJ X: Event E2 has X as the subject of a hitting,
E2 HIT OBJ Z: and Z as its object,
E2 HIT AT C: and occurred at location C.

In this case, the program simply responds 'Yes'.

342

If a goal fails to be satisfied, the program constructs a 'helpful' answer. There are two such sorts of answer, depending on the nature of the goal that fails. A failure may occur in a goal that corresponds to 'given' information in the question, that is to say, the questioner has taken for granted something that is in fact false. For example, the question:

Did X hit Y at location C?

takes for granted that X hit Y and queries the location of the event. The program returns the following answer with respect to the illustrative history of the universe:

No, X did not hit Y, X hit Z.

The information for this answer is obtained by noting that a goal corresponding to a 'given' constituent has failed and then determining what X actually hit. In reality, the division of sentences into 'given' and 'new' information is a complicated business depending on surface order, intonation, and context. The program takes a very simple view of the matter: all the initial goals are taken as 'given', and only the last goal is 'new'. The passive question:

Was Z hit by X at location A?

accordingly fails on the 'new' goal, which corresponds to the location of the event. In this case, the program responds with a second type of 'helpful' answer:

No, Z was hit by X at location C.

The information underlying this response is obtained by generating a new goal to find the location of the given event. The surface order of the answer is the same as that of the question, because the STN is also used to generate the answer from the evaluation of the goals produced in parsing the question: the tests and actions on the STN arcs are swapped round so that it tests for certain sorts of semantic content, and acts by producing words in an appropriate order. In particular, the evaluation of the goals set up by the question 'Was Z hit by X at location A?' yields the following information from the data base:

E2 HIT OBJ Z
E2 HIT SUBJ X
E2 HIT AT C

where the last item is generated after the initial failure to find the required event at location A. These three 'assertions' are then fed into the STN after the initial failure has triggered the response 'No'. The effect is as follows:

E2 HIT OBJ Z   elicits the printing of the value of the variable: Z. The presence of OBJ fails the arc corresponding to the active, but satisfies the arc corresponding to the passive. Hence it elicits the printing of the passive form of the verb: *was hit.*

E2 HIT SUBJ X elicits the passive prepositional phrase and the printing of the value of the variable: *by X*.

E2 HIT AT C   elicits the printing of a prepositional phrase: *at C*.

The main way in which the STN uses semantics to help the process of parsing can be illustrated by considering how it handles passives. Its syntactic component analyses:

X was pushed by Y

where 'Y' denotes an individual, in exactly the same way as:

X was pushed by A

where 'A' denotes a location. The two sentences are distinguished in setting up their respective goals only by taking into account knowledge about individuals and locations: an individual, Y, can be the subject of an action like pushing but a location, A, cannot play this role. Hence, 'by A' must refer to a location, whereas 'by Y' may refer to the subject of an action or to a location. The program, in fact, treats the latter as an unambiguous reference to the subject of the action.

Another aspect of semantic processing emerged in the actual development of the program. The problem arose as to whether each goal procedure should be executed as it was set up, or, alternatively, stored until the end of the question when all of the procedures could be executed. As far as a computer is concerned, it makes little difference, but what do people do? Our intuition was that listeners can start to answer a question as they hear it rather than waiting for its end, and that even when they have decided that they will not answer, it may be difficult for them to prevent the answer coming to mind. If someone starts to ask a question, 'Does your father . . . ?' it is difficult to prevent your father coming to mind even if you decide that the question is impertinent and refuse to answer it. (There is a children's 'double bind' that is similarly effective: 'Don't think of elephants!') for these reasons, the program was arranged to evaluate goals as it set them up.

This principle has a consequence that we did not at first appreciate: if a question is based on a false assumption, then once this failure has been revealed, it is pointless to set up any further goals representing the question, although other procedures may well be run in order to deal with the false assumption. In the case of the question:

Was Y hit by X at location C?

if Y wasn't hit by X, it is futile to try to determine whether the putative event took place at location C. Hence, once a false assumption has been detected, no further processing of the constituents of the question need occur. Charles Bethell-Fox and I indeed found that subjects have a poor memory for such questions in comparison to their memory for questions that can be answered 'Yes' or 'No' in a straightforward way (Johnson-Laird and Bethell-Fox, 1978). Evidently, the likelihood of recalling a question depends on how much of it is processed, and the amount of processing of one part of a question depends on the outcome of the semantic processing of its earlier constituents.

A left-corner parser for English

The semantic transition parser had a deliberately restricted syntactic capability: it was only a working demonstration of the feasibility of a system that made direct mappings between sentences and propositional representations. The purpose of the left-corner parser that I have designed is to investigate the division of labour between top-down and bottom-up processes, and the use of a table of possible analyses. The parser constructs a left-corner analysis of a sentence following the general principles of the procedure summarized in Table 13.4. But instead of a push-down store with its cumbersome notation for left-corner parsing, the parser uses a well-formed substring table. It treats dislocated constituents by building up a table of parallel analyses. The same strategy could, of course, be adopted for all local ambiguities. The phenomena of garden-path sentences suggests that there are cases where the correct interpretation is not made at first, though this conclusion has been resisted by Crain and Steedman (1981). The issue, as I pointed out earlier, has yet to be resolved. Hence, in designing the parser, I have opted for a system that is a compromise in that it uses parallel analyses for dislocations but otherwise builds up a single analysis of local ambiguities (on the basis of a simple ordering of the grammatical rules for analysing each syntactic category). My motive was a frank curiosity about how such a system might be made to work.

The parser is not concerned with semantic matters; its input is a string of words (and a context-free grammar) and its output is the syntactic structure, if any, assigned to the input by the grammar. In a psychologically plausible parser, of course, the parse would be guided by semantic information, including the interpretation of previous constituents and the current mental model of the discourse – factors that would eliminate certain otherwise possible parses. These constraints have not been implemented in the parser. I shall describe first the main components of the algorithm for constructing the parse table, and then how it has been extended to deal with dislocated constituents and local ambiguities.

The shift function. The purpose of the shift function is to look up an input word in the lexicon and to put the word and its syntactic categories into the parse table.

In detail, the shift function carries out the following operations:

If the input word is in the lexicon then it is put into the parse table at level 0 of the current input column; and its syntactic categories are put into the parse table at level 1 of the current input column;
else an error message is returned to the user that a word outside the vocabulary of the parser has been used.

Entries in the lexicon. An entry in the lexicon specifies a word, its major syntactic categories, and for each such category its sub-categories as defined by the rules of the grammar. In addition, there is information about the tense and number of a verb, the number of a noun, and so on. The entry for *sends*, for example, specifies that it is a verb which can be used in the following numbered rules for expanding the verb phrase:

$$
\begin{array}{llll}
\text{VP5:} & \text{VP} & \rightarrow & \text{V} \quad \text{NP} \\
\text{VP6:} & \text{VP} & \rightarrow & \text{V} \quad \text{NP} \quad \text{PP} \\
\text{VP7:} & \text{VP} & \rightarrow & \text{V} \quad \text{NP} \quad \text{NP}
\end{array}
$$

The entry also specifies that *sends* is in the present tense and singular in number:

[sends [V5, 6, 7 pres sing]]

It would be relatively simple to rank the rules according to their likelihood for the specific verb, and this ranking could be used to determine the order in which the parser made use of the rules. Likewise, general scheduling principles of the sort advocated by Wanner (1980) could also be implemented in a straightforward way.

346

The main parsing function. There are a number of separate processes to be carried out by the main parsing function. I shall illustrate each of them in turn.

First, the function can reduce a node dominating the current input symbol to a higher node according to the rules of the grammar:

where V1 indicates a verb to which the following rule applies:

VP1:   VP → V

The function can also reduce more than one existing node in the table to a single higher node:

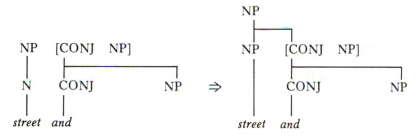

Second, where there is a rule in the grammar that allows one symbol to be reduced to another and a subsequent symbol to be predicted, then a top-down prediction can be made by the function:

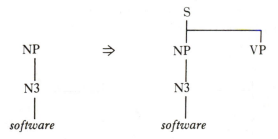

It is important to note that rules are initiated by a node that dominates the current input column, i.e., a node that is linked from a higher level to the node in the input column. Such a dominating node need not be in

347

the same column as the current input. Hence, the function can carry out the following construction:

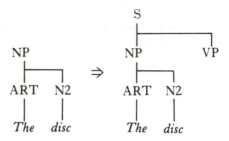

These procedures occur when there is no prediction in the current input column. Where a prediction has been made, they can be carried out, but they are executed in a modified form that is contingent upon a match between the input category and the prediction. The first case arises when there is a simple match between the two nodes:

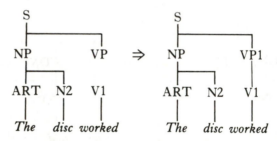

On the assumption that the semantics is going to be driven by the parser on a rule-by-rule basis, it is helpful to carry sub-category information up the tree in the way illustrated in this example. This information is provided by the parser as it builds up the tree.

The second case arises where the input node matches the predicted node, but in addition enables a prediction to be made about the next constituent in the sentence:

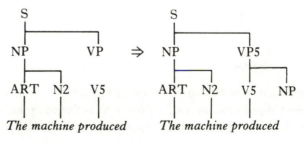

I shall now present an informal account of the function corresponding to the general parse procedure:

If there is no predicted node in the current input column and Bn is the node dominating the current input column, then for the first 'available' rule (in the grammar) of the form: A → B1 B2...Bn z, where the nodes B1 through Bn correspond to a sequence of nodes to be found in the parse table, and z is a string of symbols which may be null, then add A to the parse table so that it is above B1 and linked to all the B nodes and to the symbols in z, which are placed as predictions in the columns following the current input word;

else if there is a predicted node, P, in the current input column and Bn is the node dominating the current input column then for the first available rule (of the grammar) of the form: P → Bn z, where z may be null, then link P to Bn and to the symbols in z, which are placed as predictions in the columns following the current input word; carry the sub-category information up the tree from Bn to P;

else if there is no rule of the form P → Bn, i.e., the input fails to match the prediction, then indicate in the parse table that the prediction P has failed.

A schematic example corresponding to the first part of this rule is:

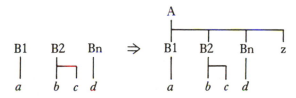

A schematic example corresponding to the second part of the rule, which applies when the input column contains a predicted node, is:

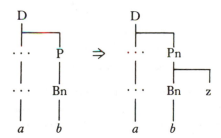

Parsing 'dislocated' constituents. The parser works on the principle, which I defended earlier, of not assigning a definite interpretation to a sentence such as:

John, I like to tell jokes to

until it has parsed the entire sentence. Once it has detected the presence of a dislocated constituent, it keeps its options open, noting the possible sites of 'holes' so that all but the relevant one can be immediately eliminated as soon as a definitive assignment is possible. Hence, in the case of dislocated constituents, the table is used to build up the set of possible analyses in parallel. The parser constructs the following initial representation:

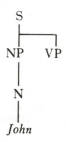

It looks up *I* in the lexicon and discovers that it is a pronoun, which fails to match the predicted verb phrase:

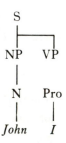

In order to handle the possibility that the start of VP has simply been postponed, the parser checks whether there is a rule of the form:

$$S \rightarrow NP \quad Pro \quad VP$$

There is no such rule, and the top-down prediction is abandoned because there is no other syntactic category for the pronoun. When a prediction fails in this radical way, the parser shifts temporarily into a mode where it carries out only simple reductions on the 'affected' nodes:

NP   NP
| |
N   Pro
| |
John *I*

350

before going back into its normal mode of operation. The verb is now
shifted into the table and elicits a prediction:

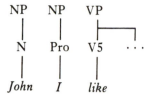

A reduction is also possible:

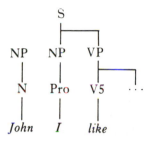

This configuration can be further reduced by a special 'dislocation' rule
of the sort postulated by Peters and Gazdar (see Chapter 12):

$$S \rightarrow (NP) \ S$$

where the circle indicates that the node is dislocated. Such rules are not
used to predict S-clauses following NP's. They are only used in reductions:

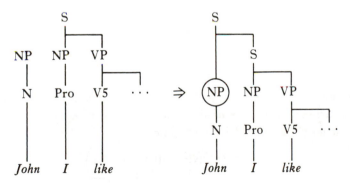

Whenever a dislocated node is entered into a table, every subsequent
possible 'hole' of the same category is parsed as such. In the present case,
of course, the actual 'hole' can be decisively located only after the last

word of the sentence has been shifted into the table:

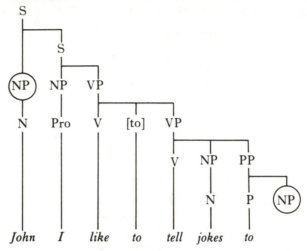

John   I   like   to   tell   jokes   to

If a language is context free and the links between dislocated constituents and their 'holes' are nested, the parser can operate merely by stacking up the constituents and assigning them to holes on a 'last in, first out' basis. If a language requires a more powerful grammar and the links can cross one another as in Engdahl's example above, then the parser can violate the stacking constraint and use an indexing system to keep track of its assignments. Hence it is by no means restricted to context-free grammars.

After two initial NP's have been parsed in a sentence (and the initially predicted VP eliminated):

Tom Dick

it is always possible that the sentence turns out to contain a conjunction. The occurrence of *and* or *or* elicits a prediction of a constituent of the same category that precedes the conjunction:

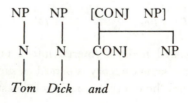

Tom   Dick   and

and these constituents are reduced to one of the same category:

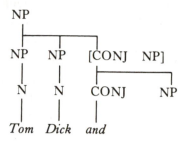

How the parser recovers from errors. A major source of potential error for the parser is treating a word as the wrong part of speech. A word such as *like*, for example, is initially shifted into the table as being either a verb or a preposition. If the input column is dominated by the prediction of a VP, it will be interpreted as a verb. If, ultimately, the prediction turns out to have been false, it will be necessary to recover from the error and to assign *like* to its other syntactic category. In general, errors arise because a prediction fails to be fulfilled. For example, a rule for analysing verb phrases, such as VP → V NP, is triggered by a specific verb, but the NP prediction is falsified by the occurrence of the preposition *to*. Here there is an immediate remedy – the rule is replaced by one that allows for a complement, such as VP → V *to* VP. Such a recovery is immediate and does not require any constituent to be reparsed.

In the case of garden-path sentences, the parser has been designed to explore the process of an intelligent recovery from error. Hence, unlike its treatment of dislocated constituents, it parses according to one rule at a time. In the case of a sentence such as:

The boy told the story cried

the failure to parse the sentence as a whole is apparent only on shifting the last word into the table. In my view, the most plausible procedure for recovery takes into account two types of information: facts about the parse that failed, and facts about which constituents of the sentence have a definitive analysis. In the present case, the word *cried* is shifted into the table, assigned the category V, which is then reduced to VP, and then the parse fails. The record of those constituents that have been parsed deterministically, that is, with no other possible analysis, shows that there is no alternative analysis to treating *the boy* as an NP because both lexical items are syntactically unambiguous and cannot be combined in any other way. But the verb *told*, which has been treated as active in order to match

353

the prediction of a VP, could be in the passive form, and so its analysis was not definitive. Granted that the grammar contains the following rule for forming subject relative clauses in the passive voice:

$$RC \quad \rightarrow \quad (NP_{[\substack{+WH \\ +PRO}]} \quad AUX_{[+BE]}) \quad VP_{[+PASSIVE]}$$

where the first two constituents are optional, the correct reanalysis will be discovered. The string *told the story* is a VP corresponding to a relative clause, and the constituents NP RC can be reduced to an NP. This complex NP together with the VP corresponding to *cried* can be reduced to an S.

Conclusion

There are two general strategies to the problem of specifying the way in which the mind recovers the grammatical relations inherent in a sentence. On the one hand, one can argue that the parser should operate with a minimum of computational power and perhaps even lack sufficient power to analyse the complete language. Kimball (1975) took just such an approach in advocating a 'lookahead' parser for natural language, which he believed required a transformational grammar. Never mind, he said, if the parser can't always cope: human beings can't either. A psychologically plausible parser *must* fail from time to time. On the other hand, one can argue that the grammar should be of a minimal power, but the parser should employ as many resources as possible. This is the approach that I have advocated in this chapter. A grammar that is restricted, say, to context-free rules may be entirely adequate for specifying the syntactic structures of English sentences, and, since such a grammar does not need deep structure, it is immediately compatible with the psychological evidence. It becomes feasible to establish a direct mapping from utterances to semantic representations, and vice versa. The efficiency of speaking and understanding can at least be envisaged within such a theory. They become still more conceivable if one abandons the notion that the parser should be a push-down automaton, and equips it instead with a table in which to record possible analyses. The table makes it easier to handle dislocated constituents and to search for alternative syntactic structures in parallel. I strongly suspect that the unconstrained use of such a table confers the power of a Turing machine on a parser, but I see no reason to doubt that in principle the mind has this power, always accepting that there is ultimately a limitation on the amount of potential memory. And if the context-free conjecture turns out to be inadequate, then for once a psycholinguistic model is not immediately overturned by the failure of a linguistic theory.

What form does the design of the mental parser take? The answer appears to be that it is a device that follows a left-corner analysis of sentences, taking into account the rule preferences of specific verbs and using both the semantic interpretation of the context of a constituent and the mental model of the discourse to bias those preferences. Its output, however, is not a structural description but an immediate propositional representation. The parser sets up this representation in a table rather than in a push-down store, and such a table is in effect a semantically interpreted tree. Like a line of code in a programming language, it serves as the input to the procedural semantics (cf. Davies and Isard, 1972) which has the option of beginning to construct a model even before the table is complete. Should an initial parse fail radically, in that a top-down prediction is at first confirmed only to be disconfirmed later, the information in the table is used to guide the parser in its reanalysis of the sentence.

This chapter completes my account of the linguistic processing of sentences; but sentences never occur in isolation. They are always uttered and interpreted in a context. The context may consist of other sentences, but even an expression uttered in isolation stands in a context defined by the specific circumstances of its utterance and the general background of knowledge of the participants in the discourse. My final task in analysing the psychology of language is to consider what the nature of discourse is and how it depends on context.

14

The coherence of discourse

What is discourse? What is it that makes a sequence of sentences into a coherent whole as opposed to a chaotic assemblage? The difference between a typical passage of prose and a randomly selected sequence of sentences leaps out at you from the page. Here is a fragment of text:

It was the Christmas party at Heighton that was one of the turning-points in Perkins' life. The duchess had sent him a three-page wire in the hyperbolical style of her class, conveying a vague impression that she and the Duke had arranged to commit suicide together if Perkins didn't 'chuck' any previous engagement he had made. And Perkins had felt in a slipshod sort of way – for at that period he was incapable of ordered thought – he might as well be at Heighton as anywhere . . . (from *Perkins and Mankind* by Max Beerbohm)

And here is a fragment of untext:

Scripps O'Neil had two wives. To tip or not to tip? Dawn crept over the Downs like a sinister white animal, followed by the snarling cries of a wind eating its way between the black boughs of the thorns. When I had reached my eighteenth year I was recalled by my parents to my paternal roof in Wales.

The most salient feature of the contrast is that the sentences of the text are connected whereas the sentences of the untext are not. Even if you do not understand completely what is being said you can still recognize that sentences are related to one another:

The purpose of this scheme is to present a taxonomic dichotomization which would allow for unilinear comparisons. In this fashion we could hope to distinguish the relevant variables which determine the functional specificities of social movements. Any classificatory scheme is, essentially, an answer to some implicit other scheme. In this instance, it is an attempt to answer the various hylozoic theories which deny that social categories can be separable.

Before you protest that this passage makes perfect sense, you should know that it is an extract from a deliberate spoof by the eminent sociologist Daniel Bell; apparently, some of his colleagues treated it seriously (see Macdonald, 1960). However, even manifest nonsense can appear to have structure:

The field buys a tiny rain. The rain hops. It burns the noisy sky in some throbbing belt. It buries some yellow wind under it. The throbbing belt freezes some person on it. The belt dies of it. It freezes the ridiculous field.

These sentences were individually generated by a program written by Ben Johnson-Laird, for testing simple grammars.

Does discourse have a structure?

One way to find out the extent to which discourse is structured is to use the traditional method for generating statistical approximations to English, but with a larger basic unit. The original procedure closely resembles the game 'The exquisite corpse', invented by the Surrealists, in which a group of people each contribute one word to a sentence without knowing what the others have written. The first sentence produced in this way was: 'The exquisite corpse drinks the red wine' (See Germain, 1978). In the procedure used by psychologists, a series of subjects generate the successive words of a sentence. For a second-order statistical approximation, each subject sees one previous word and adds one new word of his or her own, while for a third-order approximation each subject sees the two previous words and adds a third word, and so on (see Miller, 1951). Statistical approximations to English do indeed often have a surrealist flavour. In order to generate approximations, not to sentences, but to discourse, the same basic technique can be used except that the subjects now read a number of sentences and then add one sentence of their own. Here is an example of a story that is a second-order approximation – i.e., each subject read one previous sentence and then added a new one:

The baying of the hounds and the screaming of the chickens echoed below me, as I quickly scanned the tracks leading towards the hole – this was going to be a hectic breakfast. I thought I'd better eat a full meal because of the task ahead and the difficulties I might encounter. But it was only when I had cooked myself a steak, and that piece of shark meat that had been ignored by everyone, that I discovered that I could only pick at these titbits, having, as I now recalled, breakfasted, lunched and dined to repletion already. Rather than throw the food away, I rang up my husband at work and asked him to bring home some colleagues to dine with us.

And here is an example of a second-order approximation to dialogue in which each subject read one previous remark and then added the next speaker's response:

A: If you think I'm going to crucify myself again in order to salvage your self-esteem, it's time for some kind of a fundamental adjustment.

357

B: I never said you had to crucify yourself just for my sake, but simply that you'd have to make some sacrifices to preserve my sanity.

A: Why should I be responsible for your mental state?

B: I didn't suggest you should be – anyway you're incapable of looking after your own.

A: Well, I wouldn't mind that – a busdriver's not a bad job – just because I've never got a job it doesn't mean I can't look after my own.

The interest of the technique, which was first used in an unpublished study by Kenneth Pease, is not that it generates genuine statistical approximations to discourse – there is not enough real discourse and too many possible sentences for the idea of a transitional probability from one sentence to another to be anything more than an abstract fiction – but rather that it introduces a 'window' of a variable size through which anaphoric references have to operate. With a second-order approximation, anaphora and ellipsis cause problems. In the conversational example, one subject contributed the sentence:

B: I didn't suggest you should be – anyway you're incapable of looking after your own.

where it is clear from the previous sentence that what is at issue is B's mental state. The next subject, who obviously had no way of recovering this reference, makes the plausible inference that *your own* refers to A's family, and adds the sentence:

A: Well, I wouldn't mind that – a busdriver's not a bad job – just because I've never got a job it doesn't mean I can't look after my own.

The resemblance to real discourse naturally increases with higher-order approximations. Here is a fourth-order approximation to narrative:

What point was there? The dog knew her as a friend and not as an insurgent worth barking over. Anyway the last time they had met, the dog's enthusiastic warning had been rewarded with a kick. She had bent down to pat his head and whispered a few reassuring words, then walked over to the door. He lowered his body and shuffled into the corner of the room, and curled up, watching. 'Stupid animal', she thought. His ears followed her down the stairs and into the silence beyond. As soon as he was sure she was gone he jumped up. He would show her who was stupid. No one was going to talk to him like that.

The only thing that goes seriously wrong is the Kafka-like metamorphosis from dog into person. Fourth-order approximations to conversations are still more realistic, perhaps because their major referents tend to be the conversationalists themselves:

A: Again – is this the nineteenth breakdown?

B: Don't be so facile – I'm asking you to help.

A: I'm sorry, but I think that being depressed is just a state of mind.

B: It's my mind, OK? It's in a mess, so help me!

A: I really think you enjoy going through this every so often.

B: But I had thought you were the only person who could understand why I felt like this now.

A: You've become addicted.

B: Now that really is unfair. How can you be so cruel as to term friendship and love just an 'addiction'?

At the level of a sixth-order approximation, the texts seem wholly convincing. The following example might almost be an extract from a Russian novel:

'I'm not afraid you know', Rubashov cried out. The door remained silent and unyielding. It was true, he was next, after Yoshenko. He had heard Yoshenko in the night, crying out. He had listened for the words, but could not make them out, like all the other nights. Had he known it would be his turn next? Of course he did. They all did, secretly, privately. He knew it himself, and like a fly caught in the palm of a hand he was just waiting to be crunched. And there was nothing he could do.

And this sort of conversation – a sixth-order approximation – seems commonplace:

A: You still haven't answered my question.

B: I became an adult at seventeen when my father died.

A: How can you be so precise?

B: First you force me to answer in your terms, then you criticize me for it.

A: I just don't understand your insistence on the importance of change.

B: You don't understand because you think of a change to maturity as a once and for all step.

A: But is change what we ought to focus on?

B: What alternative is there?

A: Surely maturity is when you're aware you're an adult?

B: Doesn't it also involve having all the emotional capabilities and strengths that go with the responsibilities of adulthood?

Prose almost certainly has tighter constraints than conversation, but even it can vary considerably, as a simple demonstration establishes. The procedure derives from an engaging study also carried out by Pease (1969). He was interested in the extent to which different politicians stuck to the point in answering questions put to them by interviewers. He took transcripts of interviews and cut them up into separate sentences, and then asked a panel of subjects to try to match up the questions with their actual answers. The extent to which the subjects were able to carry out this task provided a measure of the degree to which the politicians stuck to the point. As a nostalgic note for older British readers, here is the politician who achieved the highest index of 'evasion' in characteristic vein:

Norman Hunt: So that when you were talking about making No. 10 a power-house and not a monastery, you were really meaning that you wanted to strengthen both No. 10 and the cabinet secretariat. What sort of people have you, in fact, brought in to strengthen them?

Harold Wilson: No. 10 has not been expanded greatly in size. I have referred to the political secretariat, to which I attach enormous importance particularly for its links with the parliamentary party, the party in the country ...

What the experiment showed was not only that some politicians were more evasive than others, but also that some interviewers allowed greater evasion than others.

For many years, we have carried out a study based on a similar technique in laboratory classes. Extracts from three different sorts of prose passage – a recipe, a story, and an anthropological argument, as shown in Table 14.1 – are cut up into separate sentences, and the students' task is to reassemble each passage into its original order. Not surprisingly, it is much easier to reconstruct the recipe – though no one has ever got it exactly right – than to reconstruct the sociological argument, which is also slightly harder than the extract from the story.

All of these phenomena bear out the existence of structure in discourse. The question is: on what basis is this structure to be explained? The answer provides us with a general theory about the interpretation of discourse.

Table 14.1 *Texts that differ in the ease with which the original order of their sentences can be reconstructed*

An extract from a Mrs Beeton recipe for puff pastry

Wash and squeeze the butter in cold water, dry well in a floured cloth, shape into a square about the size of sandwich bread, and keep in a cool place while the paste is being prepared. Sieve the flour on to a marble slab, or board, make a well in the centre, put in the lemon-juice, and add water gradually until a smooth paste is formed. The condition of the butter determines the consistency; when soft, the paste must be equally so. Knead the paste until smooth, then roll it out into a strip a little wider than the butter, and rather more than twice its length. Place the butter on one half of the paste, fold the other half over, enclosing the butter entirely, and press the edges together with the rolling pin. Let it remain in a cool place for about 15 minutes, then roll out to about 3 times the original length, but keeping the width the same, and fold exactly in three. Turn the paste round so that the folded edges are on the right and left, roll and fold again, and put aside for 15 minutes. Repeat this until the paste has been rolled out 6 times. The rolling should be done as evenly as possible, and the paste kept in a long narrow shape which, when folded, forms a square. Each time the paste is rolled out it may be well sprinkled with flour, but it must be evenly distributed with a paste-brush, and all the loose flour carefully brushed off before beginning to roll. When the paste has had its 6th roll it is ready for use. It should be baked in a hot oven, and until the paste has risen and become partially baked, the oven door should not be opened, because a current of cold air may cause the flakes to collapse on one side.

An extract from Dashiell Hammett's story "The gutting of Couffignal'

My feet sometimes on the edge of the pebbles, sometimes in the water, I went on up the shore line. Now I saw a boat. A gently bobbing black shape ahead. No light was on it. Nothing I could see moved on it. It was the only boat on that shore. That made it important. Foot by foot, I approached. A shadow moved between me and the dark rear of a building. I froze. The shadow, man-size, moved again, in the direction from which I was coming. Waiting, I didn't know how nearly invisible, or how plain, I might be against my background.

An extract from Durkheim and Mauss (1963, *originally published* 1903)

Primitive classifications are not singular or exceptional, having no analogy with those employed by more civilized people. On the contrary, they seem to be connected, with no break in continuity, to the first scientific classifications. In fact, however different they may be in certain respects from the latter, they nevertheless have all their essential characteristics. First of all, like all sophisticated classifications, they are systems of hierarchized notions. Things are not simply arranged by them in the form of isolated groups, but these groups stand in fixed relationships to each other and together form a single whole. Moreover, these systems, like those of science, have a purely speculative purpose. Their object is not to facilitate action, but to advance understanding, to make intelligible the relations which exist between things. Given certain concepts which are considered to be fundamental, the mind feels the need to connect to them the ideas which it forms about other things. Such classifications are thus intended, above all, to connect ideas, to unify knowledge; as such, they may be said without inexactitude to be scientific, and to constitute a first philosphy of nature. The Australian does not divide the universe between the totems of his tribe with a view to regulating his conduct or even to justify his practice. It is because, the idea of the totem being cardinal for him, he is under a necessity to place everything else that he knows in relation to it. We may therefore think that the conditions on which these very ancient classifications depend may have played an important part in the genesis of the classificatory function in general.

A critique of story grammars

There are several hypotheses about what it is that provides a structure to discourse. One conjecture, independently proposed by several psychologists, is that there are *story grammars* that formally specify the large-scale structure of certain stereotyped varieties of story, such as folk-tales, in much the same way that grammars of a language analyse the well-formed sentences of the language and their syntactic structures. The difficulties with this hypothesis can be illuminated by considering a story grammar

361

that I have constructed as a caricature of the enterprise. My grammar contains a rule that applies to any story:

STORY → (BEGINNING) (MIDDLE) (END)

When the full rule is used, one obtains what might be called the Aristotelian 'well-made' story with a beginning, a middle, and an end, since it was Aristotle who advanced this rule in his *Poetics* – the first work to analyse the structure of plots. Some stories start in the middle (Joyce); some have no middle at all (Borges); and some are all middle (Gertrude Stein). Hence, each constituent in the rule is optional. Moreover, in order to account for 'flashbacks' and 'flashforwards', there are movement transformations that shift constituents around.

What this mock example shows is that it is all too easy to invent grammars if you are not concerned with offering explicit analyses of such categories as BEGINNING, MIDDLE, and END, or with justifying a recourse to the power of context-free or transformational grammars. Moreover, if a story were found that violated the rule above, I could always claim that it was a new variety of story to which the grammar was not intended to apply. Obviously, actual story grammars are more plausible than mine. Table 14.2 presents an early version of a story grammar devised by Rumelhart (1975); the syntactic and semantic structures that the grammar assigns to a simple story are illustrated in Figures 14.1 and 14.2. There are a number of minor problems with this example, which need not detain us, because Rumelhart and other story grammarians have proposed more advanced grammars. A real difficulty, however, is to know what counts as an instance of such categories as SETTING, EVENT, REACTION. No story grammarian has ever formulated an effective procedure for determining the membership of such categories. It is clear that they cannot be defined in terms of the proposition that a sentence expresses. Consider, for example, the sentence 'Margie cried and cried'. In the story of Figure 14.1 it is categorized as an OVERT RESPONSE. In the following brief story:

> Margie cried and cried. No one knew why. Eventually her husband divorced her. Margie stopped crying.

the sentence is presumably the SETTING of the story or an EVENT that INITIATES a REACTION. The very fact that one is not certain about its category illustrates the problem. In a grammar for a language, the

Table 14.2 *A simple example of a story grammar based on Rumelhart's (1975) pioneering formulation*

The syntactic rules

1 Story	→	Setting + Episode
2 Setting	→	(State)* [i.e., an arbitrary number of states]
3 Episode	→	Event + Reaction

4 Event → $\begin{cases} \text{Episode} \\ \text{Change-of-state} \\ \text{Action} \\ \text{Event + Event} \end{cases}$

5 Reaction	→	Internal response + Overt response

6 Internal response → $\begin{cases} \text{Emotion} \\ \text{Desire} \end{cases}$

The semantic rules (*corresponding to each syntactic rule*)

1 Setting ALLOWS episode, i.e., makes it possible.
2 State AND State AND . . . , i.e., logical conjunction of the states.
3 Event INITIATES reaction, i.e., an external event causes a mental reaction.
4 Event CAUSES event, or event ALLOWS event. (No semantic rule is required for the first three options in the syntactic rule.)
5 Internal response MOTIVATES overt response, i.e., the response is a result of the internal response.
6 No semantic rule required.

---

categories NOUN, VERB, ADJECTIVE, and so on, can be defined by enumerating the sets of nouns, verbs, adjectives, and so on; the non-terminal categories are then defined by the grammatical rules. If, however, there is no way of specifying the lowest categories in the trees generated by story grammars, then these grammars have little explanatory value.

Theorists can propose the sort of analysis illustrated in Figures 14.1 and 14.2 only because they understand the story; such analyses cannot be derived without the exercise of intuition based on such an understanding. Similarly, the semantic relations associated with the rules, which appear to boil down to logical conjunction and varieties of causation, can be selected only on the basis of the grammarian's knowledge about the likely relation between the specific events referred to in the story. Given two events in the context of a story . . . $E^1 E^2$ . . . , there is no way of assigning the appropriate relation between them unless one knows what those events are. Only then by relying on general knowledge may it be possible to construe their causal relation correctly. The problem arises even in the

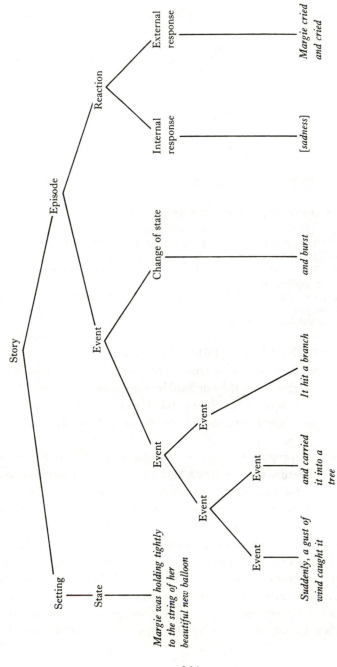

Figure 14.1 The syntactic structure of a story according to the story grammar of Table 14.2

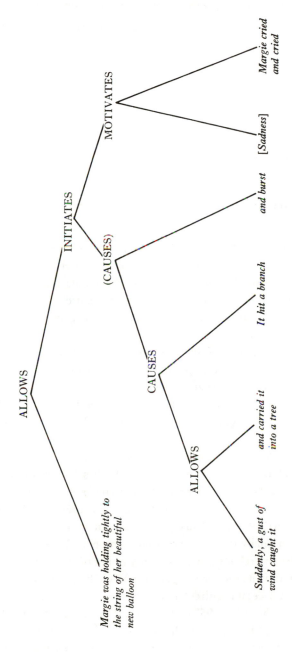

Figure 14.2 The semantic structure of a story according to the story grammar of Table 14.2

interpretation of simple conjunctions, as I pointed out some years ago (see Johnson-Laird, 1969c). The contrast between such conjunctions as:

James had worked hard in the morning and he went for a walk in the afternoon

and:

James went for a walk in the afternoon and he had worked hard in the morning

depends primarily on knowing that such references to morning and afternoon apply to the same day. There is an obvious causal interpretation between the two events referred to in the sentence:

He had taken the drug and he died

but a very different interpretation to the similar sentence:

He died and he had taken the drug.

The first sentence suggests a case of poisoning, whereas the second suggests a medicine that failed. If the interpretation of conjunctions depends on a knowledge of the typical relations between the events that they refer to, then *a fortiori* it is impossible to state adequate semantic rules for interrelating the EVENTS in stories unless one can appeal to general knowledge about the nature of such events.

Although the semantics of story grammars is unworkable at present, could their syntactic rules perhaps be of use? The grammar in Table 14.2 contains context-free rules that involve recursion: e.g., Episode can be rewritten as Event + Reaction, and Event can in turn be rewritten as Episode. However, story grammarians have never offered any very convincing evidence of the need for context-free grammars. There is admittedly a genre of children's stories that have a repetitive structure of the sort illustrated in Table 14.3. After the scene has been set, each story contains a sequence of events of the same sort involving a series of individuals A,B,C . . . N, then there is an event that acts as a bridge to a briefer series in which the various individuals participate in a mirror-image order, N . . . C,B,A, and finally there is a coda-like sentence. A language in which each well-formed expression consists of any string of symbols from a finite alphabet followed by its mirror-image, e.g., ABCCBA, cannot be generated by a finite-state device: it requires a context-free grammar and a push-down store parser (see Chomsky, 1957). However, this abstract language is very different from the structure of the stories: the language tolerates no exceptions, but stories of this genre may well allow an exception, in which

Table 14.3 *Examples of children's stories with a 'mirror-image' structure*

'*Mr Gumpy's Outing' by John Burningham*

Mr Gumpy owned a boat and his house was by a river.
One day Mr Gumpy went out in his boat.
'May we come with you?' said the children.
'Yes', said Mr Gumpy, 'if you don't squabble.'
'Can I come along, Mr Gumpy?' said the rabbit.
'Yes, but don't hop about.'
. . .
. . .
'May I join you, Mr Gumpy?' said the goat.
'Very well, but don't kick.'
For a while they all went along happily but then
The goat kicked
. . .
. . .
The rabbit hopped
The children squabbled
The boat tipped
And into the water they fell . . .

'*The Fat Cat', A Danish Folktale, translated by Jack Kent*

. . . When the old woman came back, she said to the cat, 'Now what has happened to the gruel?' 'Oh,' said the cat, 'I ate the gruel and I ate the pot, too. And now I am going to also eat YOU.'
And he ate the old woman.
    He went for a walk and on the way he met Skohottentot.
And Skohottentot said to him, 'What have you been eating, my little cat? You are so fat.' And the cat said, 'I ate the gruel and the pot and the old woman, too. And now I am going to also eat YOU.' So he ate Skohottentot.
. . .
    Next he met a woodcutter with an axe. 'My! What have you been eating, my little cat? You are so fat!' 'I ate the gruel and the pot and the old woman, too, and Skohottentot . . . . And now I am going to also eat YOU.' 'No.
You are wrong, my little cat.' said the woodcutter.
He took his axe and cut the cat open.
And out jumped
. . .
. . .
and Skohottentot.
And the old woman took her pot and her gruel and went home with them.

'*The Old Woman and her Pig' as retold by Vera Southgate*

. . . The old woman said to the pig, 'Pig! Pig! Jump over the stile, or I shan't get home tonight.'
But the pig would not jump over the stile.
    So the old woman went a little further along the road, to look for help. Soon she came to a dog. She said to the dog 'Dog! Dog! Bite pig! Pig won't jump over the stile, and I shan't get home tonight.'

continued on next page

367

continued from previous page

But the dog would not bite the pig.

. . .

. . .

So the old woman went a little further along the road, to look for help. Soon she came to a rat. She said to the rat, 'Rat! Rat! Gnaw rope! Rope won't hit butcher, . . . , dog won't bite pig, pig won't jump over the stile, and I shan't get home tonight.' But the rat would not gnaw the rope.

So the old woman went a little further along the road, to look for help. Soon she came to a cat. She said to the cat, 'Cat! Cat! Kill rat! Rat won't gnaw rope, rope won't hit butcher, . . . , dog won't bite pig, pig won't jump over the stile, and I shan't get home tonight.' And the cat said to her, 'If you will go over to that cow and bring me a bowl of milk, I will kill the rat.'

So the old woman went to the cow and asked for some milk. The cow said to her, 'If you will go over to that haystack and bring me a handful of hay, I will give you some milk.'

So the old woman went to the haystack, for a handful of hay and brought it to the cow. As soon as the cow had eaten some of the hay, she gave the old woman some milk.

Then the old woman took the milk to the cat.

As soon as the cat had lapped up the milk –

the cat began to kill the rat,

the rat began to gnaw the rope,

. . .

. . .

the dog began to bite the pig,

the pig jumped over the stile,

and the old woman *did* get home that night!

---

case they could be generated by a finite-state grammar. Moreover, the stories typically contain a sequence of different referring phrases, e.g., ABCDE . . . N, and their mirror-image sequence; and it would be reasonable to assume that the sequence is, say, never greater than 100. This constraint makes it possible to generate the required sequence using a finite-state grammar of the sort illustrated in Figure 14.3. Table 14.4 presents a simple finite-state story grammar as an alternative to Rumelhart's formulation; the table also shows the structure that is assigned to a story. A more complicated set of rules would be needed to handle the stories in Table 14.3, but they could be finite state, too. The only way to prove that a context-free grammar is essential would be by restricting the domain to a very narrow set of unusually structured stories.

The main virtue of story grammars is that they have stimulated research into the comprehension and memory of stories (Mandler and Johnson, 1977; Thorndyke, 1977). But all the story grammars in the literature share

Table 14.4 *A finite-state story grammar*

The syntactic rules:

1. STORY → Setting   EPISODE

2. EPISODE → $\begin{cases} \text{Event} \quad \text{(EPISODE)} \\ \text{Change of state} \quad \text{EPISODE} \\ \text{Internal response} \quad \text{Overt response} \end{cases}$

The syntactic structure of a story according to the grammar:

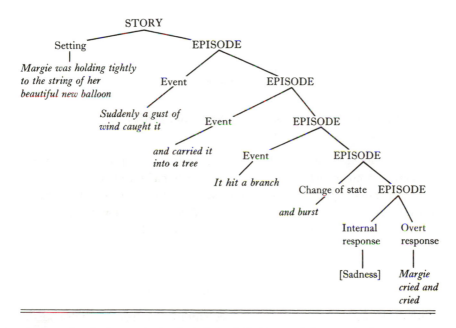

---

these major faults – a lack of explicit definitions of the terminal categories, a semantics based on an unacknowledged reliance on general knowledge; and an unmotivated use of context-free rules (Garnham, Oakhill, and Johnson-Laird, 1982). They depend on what the theorist using the grammar brings to it, and they either fail to make explicit, or else are not intended to make explicit, much that would be required in an effective procedure for interpreting stories. Their major theoretical claim is that certain stories have a definite structure, which is independent of their content, and which people know and use in the course of comprehension (Mandler and Johnson, 1980). As an intuition, this claim may be true, but if the set of stories to which it is supposed to apply is small, it becomes

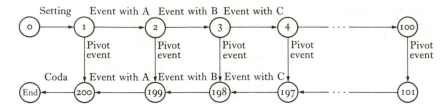

The corresponding grammar:

$$Story \rightarrow Setting\ S_1$$
$$S_1 \rightarrow Event\ with\ A\quad S_2$$
$$S_2 \rightarrow \begin{Bmatrix} Event\ with\ B\quad S_3 \\ Pivot\ event\ S_{199} \end{Bmatrix}$$

. . . .

$$S_{199} \rightarrow Event\ with\ A\quad S_{200}$$
$$S_{200} \rightarrow Coda$$

Figure 14.3 A finite-state automaton for producing 'mirror-image' stories.

almost vacuous. For example, if the set is restricted to just a single story, then any grammar that generates that story can claim to have captured its structure independently of its content. When the set is enlarged to a more sensible size, then, as we have seen, it is difficult to see how the categories of SETTING, EPISODE, etc. can be made to work independently from content.

Discourse and mental models

With the failure of story grammars to account for the structure of discourse, there is an obvious alternative hypothesis: a necessary and sufficient condition for discourse to be *coherent,* as opposed to a random sequence of sentences, is that it is possible to construct a single mental model from it (Johnson-Laird, 1980; Garnham, Oakhill, and Johnson-Laird, 1982). Coherence must be distinguished from *plausibility,* since a discourse may be perfectly coherent yet recount a bizarre sequence of events. The possibility of constructing a single mental model depends on the principal factors of co-reference and consistency. Each sentence in a discourse must refer, explicitly or implicitly, to an entity referred to (or introduced) in another sentence, since only this condition makes it possible to represent the sentences in a single integrated model. Likewise, the properties and relations ascribed to referents must be consistent, that is, compatible with one another and free from contradiction. Plausibility depends on the possibility of interpreting the discourse in an appropriate temporal, spatial, causal, and intentional framework – a framework that, as Miller and Johnson-Laird (1976) argued, cross-classifies all semantic fields. When subjects generate approximations to discourse or reconstruct the order of a passage of prose, they make use of clues about both plausibility and co-reference.

The one substantial hypothesis about the organization of the knowledge underlying plausibility is the notion of a *script* (cf. Minsky, 1975; Schank and Abelson, 1977). A script represents the normal sequence of events in some relatively stereotyped activity such as dining at a restaurant. Schank and Abelson have written computer programs that both implement such scripts and use them in making inferences about stories. The possession of a script allows a speaker to leave many things unsaid with the certainty that the listener will be able to fill them in by default. For example, it is unnecessary to state explicitly that a customer in a restaurant eats the food that he has ordered. In accordance with the conversational conventions delineated by Grice (1975), it is only necessary to describe such untoward circumstances as, say, the customer refusing to eat his meal. If enough is said to elicit the appropriate script, then it can be used to fill in unspoken detail.

The main difficulty with the doctrine of scripts is that knowledge is also used to understand discourse about events that are *not* stereotyped. You can understand Kafka's *The Trial* without having a script for the persecution of an individual by an anonymous bureaucracy. Indeed, the novel is perhaps the original 'script' for all such encounters. Likewise, if I tell you a story about an aristocratic ski-instructor trying to get a permit to work in Oregon, I can rely on your general knowledge to support many inferences that do not derive from scripts. Schank (1980) is, of course, sensitive to these problems and to the need to account for the acquisition of scripts, but there is still much work to be done to explain the automatic and rapid retrieval of *relevant* information underlying the plausibility of a discourse.

The coherence of prose depends primarily on its pattern of co-reference. Narrative texts usually have a chain of co-reference linking one assertion to the next, whereas descriptive texts may have a series of references back to the same common topic. One of the main sources of evidence in support of story grammars is that jumbled versions of stories are much harder to remember than the original versions. However, when the order of the

371

sentences in a story is randomized, the continuity of reference is also destroyed. Consider, for example, this brief story (cf. Table 14.1):

Margie was holding tightly to the string of her beautiful new balloon. She had just won it and was hurrying home to show her sister. Suddenly, a gust of wind caught it and carried it into a tree. It hit a branch and burst. Margie cried and cried.

When the order of the sentences is randomized, referential continuity is disrupted:

She had just won it and was hurrying home to show her sister. Suddenly, a gust of wind caught it and carried it into a tree. Margie was holding tightly to the string of her beautiful new balloon. Margie cried and cried. It hit a branch and burst.

It ceases to be clear quite what the story is about: the first sentence refers to *she* and *it*, and the reader is likely to imagine a girl with some sort of prize. Later, when Margie and her balloon are introduced, it seems that reference is being made to a new individual with a new possession. It is simple enough to restore referential continuity by modifying the noun phrases in an appropriate way whilst maintaining the same randomized order of sentences:

Margie had just won a beautiful new balloon and was hurrying home to show her sister. Suddenly, a gust of wind caught it and carried it into a tree. Margie was holding tightly to the string of her balloon. She cried and cried. It hit a branch and burst.

Now the text merely reports a slightly implausible sequence of events. Margie seems to have been holding on to the string of her balloon after it was carried into the tree. Alternatively, the author may have meant to write 'Margie *had been* holding tightly to the string of her balloon.'

This simple illustration should clarify the distinction between coherence and plausibility. The fact that coherence is important in the interpretation of discourse has been demonstrated experimentally by Garnham, Oakhill, and Johnson-Laird (1982). In one experiment, the subjects were given three versions of stories and descriptive passages: the original version, a randomized version, and a randomized version that had been revised in order to restore referential continuity. Of course, a subject read only one version of any particular story. Table 14.5 shows the length of the recall protocols, expressed as proportions of the number of words in each passage. The original stories were better remembered than the random versions, but the restoration of referential continuity reliably ameliorated the effects of randomization. The descriptive passages, however, had little referential

Table 14.5 *The length of the recall protocols, expressed as proportions of the number of words in each type of passage, in an experiment reported by Garnham, Oakhill, and Johnson-Laird (1982). Each entry is summed over twenty-four subjects and three passages*

| | Version of the text | | |
Type of passage	Original	Revised random	Random
Story	0·71	0·43	0·30
Description	0·32	0·30	0·32

continuity from one sentence to the next – they referred back to the same underlying topic – and, as we predicted, the effects of randomization on their memorability were negligible. The subjects' ratings of the comprehensibility of the various passages yielded exactly the same pattern of results.

In a second experiment, a group of skilled, and a group of less skilled readers were selected from a population of 7- to 8-year-old children. The major difference between the two populations was known to be their inferential ability in reading texts. Both groups read a series of short stories presented in the same three versions as used in the previous experiment. Their recall performance was scored in terms of the number of major 'ideas' (as assessed by an independent panel of judges) that they remembered. Table 14.6 presents the mean number of ideas that the two groups recalled for each type of story. As we predicted, the ameliorating effects of restoring referential continuity in a randomized story were confined to the group of skilled readers. They have sufficient inferential ability to re-establish co-reference even in the context of a somewhat bizarre sequence of events.

Table 14.6 *The mean number of major 'ideas' (max. = 9) recalled by skilled and less skilled readers for three versions of stories. The subjects were 8-year-olds, and the experiment was reported by Garnham, Oakhill, and Johnson-Laird (1982).*

| | Version of the story | | | |
	Original	Revised random	Random	Overall
Skilled readers	7·3	6·1	4·8	6·1
Less skilled readers	5·2	3·5	3·9	4·2

The most direct way in which to disrupt referential continuity is to insert material between the original identification of an entity and a subsequent reference to it. Rather than interpolate wholly extraneous material, Kate Ehrlich and I simply reordered the sentences in short descriptions to produce the required condition (Ehrlich and Johnson-Laird, 1982). Our subjects listened to three sentences about the spatial relations between four common objects, e.g.:

The knife is in front of the spoon
The spoon is on the left of the glass
The glass is behind the dish

and then attempted to draw a diagram of the corresponding layout using the names of the objects. On the assumption that the subjects would attempt to construct a mental model of the layout, the task should be straightforward if the assertions (as in the example) permit the model to be built up continuously. But if the sentences are in a discontinuous order such as:

The glass is behind the dish
The knife is in front of the spoon
The spoon is on the left of the glass

in which the first two assertions refer to no item in common, then the task should be very much harder. In this case, a subject must either construct two mental models and then combine them in the light of the third assertion, or else represent the premises in a propositional form until the time comes to make the drawing – and this form is known to be harder to remember (see the experiments reported in Chapter 7). The results showed a striking confirmation of the prediction: 69% of the diagrams based on continuous descriptions were correct, whereas only 42% of the diagrams based on discontinuous descriptions were correct. The crucial factor, however, should be the presence or absence of an item in a mental model to which subsequent reference can be made. This thesis was tested by using a third 'semi-continuous' ordering of the assertions:

The spoon is on the left of the glass.
The glass is behind the dish.
The knife is in front of the spoon.

Here, the third assertion has nothing in common with the second, but the lack of a common referent should not matter, because the third assertion refers to the spoon, which should be in the mental model as it was introduced in the first assertion. This ordering of the assertions yielded 60% correct diagrams, a proportion that was not reliably different from performance with the continuous descriptions.

374

The same phenomena occur, as one would expect, if the subjects read the sentences. This technique made it possible to record the reading times for each sentence. The mean reading times are shown in Table 14.7. The main finding of interest is the interaction between the continuity of a description and the position of a sentence, an interaction which is largely explained on the grounds that the third sentence only takes longer to read in a discontinuous description. The reason for the additional three seconds in this case is presumably that the subjects are attempting to combine their interpretations of the two previous assertions in the light of the information they obtain from the third assertion. This process is, of course, unnecessary in the case of the continuous and semi-continuous descriptions.

Table 14.7 *The effect of referential continuity on the time subjects take to read spatial descriptions before drawing a correct diagram of them (from Ehrlich and Johnson-Laird, 1982). The means are in seconds*

| | | Type of description | |
	Referentially continuous	Referentially semi-continuous	Referentially discontinuous
1st sentence	5·7	6·3	5·6
2nd sentence	7·1	6·3	6·5
3rd sentence	5·4	6·5	9·4
Overall mean	6·1	6·3	7·1

The plausibility of a story also affects its comprehensibility and its memorability, as Paul Freeman and I have shown in an unpublished study. Lacking a good theory of plausibility, we devised an operational technique for manipulating it. We took six original stories (of the sort typically used in experiments) and stripped them of all their verbs and other relational expressions. Hence, the following extract from one of the stories:

No one knew how to kill the turtle but somebody suggested that they kill it with hatchets. The turtle said that hatchets were useless against its thick shell. So then the people of the village had to think again, someone suggested that they kill it with sharp stones . . .

yielded the skeletal framework:

No-one . . . the turtle . . . somebody . . . they . . . it . . . hatchets. The turtle . . . hatchets . . . its . . . shell . . . the people of the village . . . someone . . . they . . . stones.

The skeletal sentences comprising the whole story were presented to members of a separate panel of subjects whose task was to fill in the missing words with whatever they thought appropriate. In the 'zero-order' condition, each member of the panel filled in a separate sentence in isolation from the rest of the story. The result was a referentially coherent sequence of sentences that is highly implausible:

No one had told the turtle that somebody had said they had given it a number of very sharp hatchets. But of course the turtle knew that even hatchets could cut its thick but soft shell very easily. And then the people of the village waited silently until someone shouted loudly and then they threw jagged stones . . .

In the 'third-order' condition, each member of the panel read the two previous completed sentences of the story and then filled in the sentence that came next. The result seemed to be less implausible:

No one wanted the turtle to live a moment longer so somebody yelled very loudly and then they quickly killed it with sharp hatchets. Then the turtle bled venomously and profusely because the hatchets had cleaved right through its thick shell. Then all the people of the village cheered at the sight, next someone suggested that they throw stones . . .

Finally, we added further adjectives to some of the stories in order to balance their lengths. These materials were then used in the experiment proper. A separate group of subjects read two of the original stories, two 'third-order' approximations, and two 'zero-order' approximations. The materials were rotated over the subjects so that each of the six basic stories from which all the materials had been generated occurred equally often in the three versions. The subjects' free recall of the stories reliably confirmed the effects of plausibility. The lengths of the recall protocols expressed as proportions of the number of words in each text were as follows: 0·75 for the original stories, 0·68 for the 'third-order' approximations, and 0·58 for the 'zero-order' approximations. There was also an equally reliable trend in the same direction for the rated comprehensibility of the stories.

Both coherence and plausibility evidently affect the interpretation and memorability of discourse. The two factors are theoretically entirely distinct. Coherence is a property of discourse since it depends on the occurrence of co-referential expressions and the ascription of logically consistent predicates to them. Plausibility, however, concerns more than discourse, since an actual sequence of events will be more or less plausible depending on how readily it can be construed within a temporal, causal, or intentional framework. A typical sequence, for example, might consist of a physical event that creates a particular state of mind in an observer; this state of mind then yields an intention; the intention issues in an action; and the action has an effect on the world. People are highly familiar with such sequences, and can use their knowledge to interpret events, whether they be real, depicted, or described.

Is all discourse both coherent and plausible? Plainly not. One·special form of text sometimes goes out of its way to avoid these ideals, perhaps because it is a higher-order form that derives from prosaic discourse. Consider the following lines:

Swiftly the years, beyond recall.
Solemn the stillness of this spring morning.

They are, in fact, from one of Arthur Waley's translations of a Chinese poem. William Empson (1961, p. 24) comments:

Lacking rhyme, metre, and any overt device such as comparison, these lines are what we should normally call poetry only by virture of their compactness; two statements are made as if they were connected, and the reader is forced to consider their relation for himself. The reason why these facts should have been selected for a poem is left for him to invent; he will invent a variety of reasons and order them in his own mind. This, I think, is the essential fact about the poetical use of language.

One kind of representation for discourse, or two?

Earlier in the book, I argued that there are two kinds of representation for discourse, a superficial propositional format close to linguistic form, and a mental model that is close to the structure of the events or states of affairs that are described in the discourse. At least one influential theory, however, makes use of just a single format. Kintsch and van Dijk (1978) claim that discourse is interpreted propositionally. Thus, the following extract:

A series of violent, bloody encounters between police and Black Panther Party members punctuated the early summer days of 1969. Soon after, a group of Black students I teach at California State College, Los Angeles, who were members of the Panther Party, began to complain of continuous harassment by law enforcement officers can be represented as a set of separate propositions, written in predicate–argument notation:

1. (SERIES, ENCOUNTER)
2. (VIOLENT, ENCOUNTER)
3. (BLOODY, ENCOUNTER)
4. (BETWEEN, ENCOUNTER, POLICE, BLACK PANTHER)
5. (TIME: IN, ENCOUNTER, SUMMER)
6. (EARLY, SUMMER)
7. (TIME: IN, SUMMER, 1969)

and so on. The first stage in interpreting the text is to establish what Kintsch and van Dijk call its 'microstructure': the referential links between propositions. The process that carries out this operation can hold only a certain number of the propositions in its memory buffer and can consider only a certain chunk of propositions in the text – the actual values depend on the particular individual and the nature of the text. If the processor finds the same argument in both the buffer and the input chunk, it links them together as co-referential. If there is no argument in common, it searches through the propositions in long-term memory (or in the written text) to find such a relation. This search takes time and effort. If it fails, an inference has to be made in order to create a proposition that connects the input chunk to those propositions that have already been processed.

The co-referential links form a graph between the propositions. The proposition at the highest level is supposedly selected to reflect the topic of the text and to ensure that the resulting graph will be simple. In the case of the example, the first cycle of processing takes in the initial chunk of seven propositions and constructs the graph shown in Figure 14.4. Because referential links are established solely on the basis of the occurrence of the same argument, the initial proposition is linked to four other

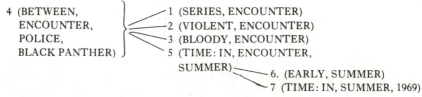

Figure 14.4 The construction of the 'microstructure' of a text according to Kintsch and van Dijk (1978).

propositions in virtue of their common argument: ENCOUNTER. Some propositions will participate in more than one processing cycle and they should therefore be more memorable. A number of factors are supposed to affect the likelihood of a proposition's being held in the memory buffer, including both its recency and its level in the graph. The authors adopt what they call the 'leading edge' strategy: the propositions in the buffer consist of the most recent propositions that lie along the graph's lower edge. If there is any room left, then the buffer contains the most recent propositions from the next level up, and so on. In the case of Figure 14.4, if there were a limit of four propositions in the buffer, then propositions 4, 5, 7, and 3, would be in the buffer after the first chunk of the text was processed. The final result of representing the whole text in this way is to produce a graph representing all the referential links between the propositions. Kintsch and his colleagues have found that the number of cycles in which a proposition was in the memory buffer predicts the memorability of the proposition. This corroboration of the theory would be more impressive if the propositional analysis and the construction of the graph were less of an exercise of the theorists' intuitions.

In an earlier work on 'text grammar', van Dijk (1977) argued that a chain of co-references was not enough to render a discourse well-formed. It must also have a 'macrostructure'. Thus, the following sequence of sentences is co-referential:

My daughter works in a library in London. London is the home of a good museum of natural history. The museum is organized on the basis of cladistic theory. This theory concerns the classification of living things. Living things evolved from inanimate matter

but it lacks an acceptable macrostructure, a unifying topic around which it is organized. In order to explain the recovery of the topic of a text and such phenomena as the retention of gist, Kintsch and van Dijk (1978) propose that various operations are carried out on the microstructure of a text in order to yield its macrostructure. These operations, or 'macrorules', are applied under the control of a schema that corresponds to the reader's goals. The schema is used to classify each proposition in the microstructure as either relevant or irrelevant to the topic. If a proposition is irrelevant, it is not entered into the macrostructure. There are other macrorules for generalizing a proposition, and for constructing global facts which enter the macrostructure in place of specific propositions in the text. Kintsch and van Dijk have not specified the way in which these inferential rules work.

Many forms of discourse are supposed to possess schemata, and, according to Kintsch and van Dijk, when the schema for a psychological report is applied to the propositions in the example above, it elicits various macrorules. The first such operation is to form 'generalizations' of the propositions. Thus the first proposition:

(SERIES, ENCOUNTER)

is generalized to:

(SOME, ENCOUNTER)

The seventh proposition:

(TIME: IN, SUMMER, 1969)

is generalized to:

(IN, EPISODE, SIXTIES)

It appears that the process of generalization consists in the insertion of quantifiers, though there is no notational machinery for coping with their scope. The schema is then applied to determine which propositions are relevant. It picks out the generalized setting statements. The macrorules are applied in several cycles with ever more stringent criteria of relevance (we are not told how this machinery is to be implemented) until, at the top level of macrostructure, there is only a single macroproposition corresponding to the topic of the text. The long-term recall of a text is assumed to be based on the propositions in its macrostructure.

There are many criticisms of the representation and processes postulated by Kintsch and van Dijk that might be made: I have struggled – not altogether successfully – to suppress them so that the one major defect of the theory should stand out clearly, namely, its reliance on a single propositional format for the representation of both microstructure and macrostructure. The first point at which this format effectively destroys the credibility of the theory concerns co-reference. It simply will not do to assume that if two arguments overlap, they are co-referential. The principle works in the example: (SERIES, ENCOUNTER) and (VIOLENT, ENCOUNTER) are co-referential, but there are many cases where it would fail disastrously. The text:

Roland's wife died in 1928. He married again in 1940. His wife now lives in Spain

contains two propositions about ROLAND'S WIFE, but despite this overlap in argument, they are obviously not co-referential. This failure of the theory is a symptom of an ultimately fatal debility. The real difficulty is that two propositional representations that have no overlap in their arguments can nevertheless be co-referential – for instance, *the prime minister*, *Maggie*, *Mrs Thatcher*, and *that woman*, may all refer to the same individual. A superficial propositional representation is necessary to capture the linguistic form of these descriptions, but it cannot do double duty and represent what they refer to.

The distinction between a representation of the sense of a text and a representation of its significance (including what it refers to) is no mere philosophical trifle. It is crucial to the way in which people understand and recall discourse, a point that has been demonstrated experimentally by my colleague Alan Garnham (1981). His subjects listened to a story that included the sentence:

The man standing by the window shouted to the host

where it was clear from the context that the initial noun phrase was co-referential with an earlier noun phrase, *the man with the martini*, in the story. Another sentence contained the noun phrase *the woman with the diamond brooch*, which plainly referred to an individual who had previously been described as *the woman smoking the perfumed cigarette*. When the subjects were given an unexpected recognition test of sentences in the story, they were unable to identify which noun phrases had occurred in the original sentences. They readily confused co-referential descriptions. When the subjects were warned that their memory would be tested, they had little difficulty in performing the task accurately. It seems that there are at least two things to be represented about a discourse: its sense and its significance. Both may well be ultimately represented as strings of symbols at the level of machine code, but, as I argued in Chapter 7, at a higher level there are both structured and functional differences between a propositional representation that captures sense and a mental model that captures significance.

Once models have been introduced as representations of discourse, they appear to be equally plausible candidates for representing the large-scale structure of discourse – the skeletal framework of events that corresponds to the 'plot' of a narrative, the 'argument' of a non-fiction work, and so on. Kintsch and van Dijk's proposal that there are 'macrorules' for constructing high-level representations could apply *mutatis mutandis* to mental models. It is not yet clear, however, that special rules are needed to induce this level of representation.

If discourse is represented initially at a propositional level and sub-sequently at the more profound level of a mental model, then there should be a number of linguistic phenomena that bear out the two kinds of representation. There are indeed many aspects of reference that appear to depend on the contrast between propositional representations and mental models, and in the remainder of the chapter I am going to consider the following topics: definite and indefinite descriptions, referential and attributive descriptions, pronouns, elliptical expressions and other anaphors. In sketching an account of these phenomena, I am more than conscious that I am treading in the footsteps of others. Many of the same sort of ideas can be found in the work of Stenning (1977) and Webber (1978) on descriptions, Sag and Hankamer (1980) on anaphors, and Kamp (1980) on pronouns.

Definite and indefinite descriptions

The principles governing the interpretation of descriptions can be summarized in terms of indefinite and definite descriptions. A sentence containing an indefinite description which introduces a referent requires a token to be put into the discourse model to represent a specific member of the relevant class. Individual entities can be unique within a discourse model even when no individuating information is known about them. Consider, for example, a discourse model of the assertion:

Ann is in a shop.

It will contain a token corresponding to Ann, a token corresponding to a shop, and a relation between them signifying the appropriate spatial relation. An individual with a vivid imagination may construct a three-dimensional model, or an image, of Ann in a prototypical shop with goods on display, a till, a shop assistant, and so on. If Ann is known to the person constructing the model, the procedural semantics can relate the token representing *Ann* to the repository of individuating knowledge about her. The recursive procedures for revising models (see Chapter 11) can treat the token standing for *a shop* as a representative sample from the set of shops because there is no individuating information about it, but this token will be unique within the discourse model even if nothing else is so far known about the shop. Ignoring the potential richness of the model, it has a structure of the form:

Ann → shop

382

where *Ann* stands for the individual known to the listener, the arrow stands for a representation of the appropriate spatial relation, and *shop* stands for a token designating a member of the set of shops.

Stenning (1977, 1978) has argued that an indefinite description does not necessarily lead to the introduction of a discourse referent, because such texts as:

Ann was in a shop. In fact, she visited several. The shop was a tobacconist's

are incoherent: The incoherence of the definite description, however, follows from the introduction of more than one token corresponding to a shop in order to represent the second sentence. What is true is that there are some indefinite descriptions (concerning individuals) that do not require a new token to be introduced. These are cases of the predicative use of an indefinite, such as:

Ann is a teacher.

This assertion requires a relation of identity to be established between the token representing Ann and a token representing a member of the class of teachers:

Discourse model		Background knowledge
		teacher
Ann	=	teacher
		. . .
		teacher

The reason for the incoherence of the discourse:

Ann is a teacher. The teacher caught a bus

is precisely that there is no unique token for a teacher in the current discourse model. The role of background knowledge can be critical in the interpretation of discourse, as the following example, which I owe to John Marshall, makes clear:

This is a story about a man who was a war correspondent in the Boer war, a man who became Prime Minister, and a man whose wife burnt his portrait by Graham Sutherland.

If you recognize that all three indefinite descriptions could refer to the same individual, then you will introduce a single token; otherwise you will probably introduce three separate tokens representing three different men into your model of the discourse, and perhaps at some later stage be forced to form identities between them.

Once a token has been introduced into a discourse model, a definite description can be used to refer to the corresponding individual. But definite descriptions are often used without a prior introduction of the relevant individual. The following discourse:

Ann was in a shop. She was talking to the assistant

requires the introduction of a token for a member of the class of shop assistants. Such a token may have been introduced as part of the representation of a prototypical shop. If not, the utterance can trigger its introduction by way of an inference based on a knowledge of prototypical shops. In the latter case, it is reasonable to assume that it will take longer to interpret the sentence, and this prediction has been confirmed by Haviland and Clark (1974). In the absence of an explicit reference, a discourse may nevertheless almost certainly lead to the introduction of the relevant token. Sanford and Garrod (1981) report that the time taken to read the second of two sentences of the form:

Mary dressed the baby
The clothes were made of pink wool

was not reliably longer than in the case of:

Mary put the baby's clothes on.
The clothes were made of pink wool.

But there was a detectable increase in the reading time of the second sentence in the pair:

Mary put the baby's clothes on
The material was made of pink wool

where the context presumably elicits a prior representation of clothes, but not of their material. These effects seem to depend on whether or not the discourse evokes a model containing a representation of the relevant token.

Under what conditions is a discourse likely to lead to the introduction of tokens corresponding to entities that have *not* been referred to explicitly? Once again the answer surely depends on background knowledge, but also on the specific content of the predicates and relations ascribed to those entities that are designated explicitly. The discourse:

Ann was in a florist's
The flowers were overwhelming in their fragrance

can be interpreted more smoothly than the discourse:

Ann was in a shoe shop.
The flowers were overwhelming in their fragrance.

384

Both, however, seem more natural and less surprising than:

Ann was in a tobacconist's.
The flowers were overwhelming in their fragrance.

Referential and attributive descriptions

Definite descriptions have long been known to give rise to a special problem, and it too can be elucidated by the concept of a discourse model. If a speaker asserts:

Ann was in a shop and talking to the assistant

no one would ordinarily take this usage to entail (*pace* Russell, 1905) or to presuppose (*pace* Strawson, 1950) that there is one and only one assistant in the shop. The speaker is rather referring to the only assistant who is relevant, or who is going to be relevant, in the immediate context. As Alan Garnham and I pointed out in discussing such examples:

Uniqueness in a model rather than in reality is what controls the use and interpretation of definite descriptions. If a speaker is to communicate felicitously, then he must consider whether an entity will be unique in his listener's model. Utterances need seldom be more than clues about how to change a discourse model: they depend for their interpretation on what a listener knows, but that interpretation in turn modifies or extends the discourse model. A discourse model is a surrogate for reality. Indeed, it is sometimes convenient to speak as if language were used to talk about discourse models rather than the world. (Johnson-Laird and Garnham, 1980, p. 377)

The specific problem of definite descriptions, which Garnham and I examined, is the distinction between their referential and attributive uses. This contrast was originally drawn by Donnellan (1966). He pointed out that a description such as *the murderer of Smith* can be used by a speaker who intends a listener to pick out the particular individual about whom he is speaking: this usage is referential. Alternatively, the speaker's intention may be merely to pick out whoever satisfies the description: this usage is attributive. The contrast is clear in the use of such descriptions as *the winning captain* : after the match, the description may be used to pick out the relevant individual; before the match, it may be used to designate whoever will satisfy it. It is natural to suppose that in an attributive use there must be someone or something that does satisfy the description, or else the assertion will be vacuous; but where a description is used referentially, such a failure is not so critical, since a listener may nevertheless be able to discern the speaker's intentions and recover the appropriate referent even though it is misdescribed. Despite the plausibility of this argument, we showed that there is a flaw in it.

Suppose that a friend of yours has been to the cinema, and you ask his wife:

How did John enjoy the film he saw last night?

where your usage is plainly attributive since you know nothing about the film and can designate it in no other way. John's wife might reply:

He enjoyed it

using the pronoun attributively, too. But now consider a rather different case. John has told everyone that he is going to see *The Sound of Music*, which he does indeed see, but then he makes a clandestine visit to another cinema showing a very different sort of film. You believe that his wife has found out about this second visit but that John does not realize that she has discovered his misdemeanour. You accordingly ask John's wife:

How do you think John enjoyed the film that he doesn't know that you know he saw last night?

where your intention is again plainly attributive – you are picking out whichever film it was that John doesn't know that his wife knows that he saw. Unfortunately, you are mistaken: there is no such film, because John knows that his wife has found him out, and she knows that he knows. Nevertheless, your attributive designation will be perfectly intelligible to her. She can readily reconstruct her model of your beliefs so that it contains a film that her husband does not know that she knows he saw. What makes this step so easy for her, of course, is that the existence of such a film was precisely her husband's original intention.

The moral of this example, which vitiates other accounts of the referential – attributive distinction (e.g. Stalnaker, 1972; Kaplan, 1977; Kripke, 1977), is that discourse models are constructed on the basis of inferences from general knowledge and from a specific knowledge of context. It is a mistake, however, to talk of *the* context of an utterance: there is one context for the speaker, and another for the listener. Potential discrepancies between the two models are important both for motivating discourse in the first place (cf. Steedman and Johnson-Laird, 1980) and for their effects on a speaker's referential intentions. For example, a speaker may deliberately intend to make it clear that there is such a discrepancy:

I don't want to tell you anything about the person I met yesterday.

Here, the definite description is probably intended to be referential for

386

the speaker but attributive for the listener. Conversely, the instruction:

Double the number you're thinking of

contains a description that is probably intended to be attributive for the speaker but referential for the listener. Garnham and I accordingly argued that the distinction in usage must be made twice over – once for the speaker and once for the listener. It depends on the knowledge that the speaker intends to be relevant to the interpretation of the utterance. In an attributive use, no other unique descriptions that fit the designatum are intended to be relevant to the interpretation of the utterance, even if they are known to the speaker and to the listener. Hence, the only constraint on the token in the mental model is that normally it satisfies the description; the recursive procedures can replace one token by another that in addition satisfies other subsequently divulged descriptions. In order to use a description referentially, a speaker must have a certain minimal knowledge about what it designates. A speaker might intend to refer to an individual as, say, *the murderer of Smith* even though he has no other way of picking out that individual, but it is difficult to envisage circumstances in which such an intention could arise. So we suggested that the speaker must have sufficient information to pick out the individual in at least one other independently individuating way. The idea here is that speakers can intend to refer only to those entities on which they can take at least two independent 'cross-bearings', since they are committed in a referential usage to the substitution *salva veritate* of other designations of the entity. The listener may therefore take into account any individuating knowledge of the relevant entity in constructing a model of the discourse: the token cannot be freely replaced by another that merely satisfies the description.

Pronouns

A speaker's referential intentions affect not just the use of descriptions but all forms of referring expressions. For example, grammarians have sometimes argued that a pronoun cannot refer to the same individual as any other noun phrase within the same clause. Thus, in the sentence:

Only Mary loves her

they would say that *Mary* and *her* must refer to different individuals. This claim is false, because the speaker may unwittingly have used *her* to refer to Mary. The putative constraint actually applies to the intended referents:

speakers must not use a pronoun (other than a reflexive), if their intention is to pick out the same individual twice within a clause:

Only Mary loves Mary.

The major puzzle about pronouns, however, is the apparent diversity of their behaviour. They can be used in at least five seemingly distinct ways:

1. Pronouns have a *deictic* use where the referent depends on context. Suppose, for instance, that someone throws a bottle at the screen in the cinema; the lights come on and the manager appears; and at that moment, a member of the audience rises to his feet, points to the person next to him, and declares:

He did it!

Plainly, the speaker purports to identify the perpetrator of the deed. The referent of *he* is the individual at whom the accusing finger is pointed, and the referent of *it* is the preceding bottle throwing.

2. Pronouns can be used to refer to entities that are introduced by other expressions in the discourse. A pronoun may refer back *anaphorically* to a previously identified entity:

John had a gold watch. *He* gave *it* away.

Alternatively, a pronoun may refer forward *cataphorically*:

When *they* had finished the dessert, the waiter brought the guests tea.

3. A pronoun may occur following a quantifier in a sentence such as:

Every man loves a woman who loves *him*

where it need not be taken to refer to a particular individual, but rather behaves like a *bound variable* in a logical expression:

For any x that is a man there is some y that is a woman such that x loves y and y loves x.

4. There are what I shall call Evans-pronouns – in memory of the late Gareth Evans (1980), who drew special attention to them. They, too, occur following a quantifier, but they cannot be analysed as bound variables. A typical Evans-pronoun occurs in the sentence:

Some tories are still monetarists, but *they* are members of the government.

If this pronoun functioned as a bound variable then the sentence could be analysed as:

There are some x, such that x are tories and x are still monetarists and x are members of the government.

388

This assertion is clearly different, however, because it does not imply that tory monetarists are only to be found in the government. Another standard illustration of an Evans-pronoun occurs in the much discussed conditional examples, such as:

If Alex has a car, then he drove *it* to work.

The occurrence of *it* cannot be treated as a simple anaphoric pronoun, because the discourse has not clearly established the existence of anything for it to refer to. The pronoun cannot be treated as a bound variable unless the sentence is taken to have the form:

For any x, if x is a car and Alex has x, then Alex drove x to work

but an indefinite description should surely correspond to an existentially quantified expression. The analysis:

If there is some x such that x is a car and Alex has x, then Alex drove x to work

is inadequate since the final occurrence of the variable is outside the scope of the quantifier, which is restricted to the antecedent of the conditional:

$$((\exists x)\,(Car(x)\,\&\,Has(Alex, x))) \rightarrow Drove\text{-}to\text{-}work(Alex, x)$$

The force of the pronoun is evidently to refer to *the car that Alex has*, if he has one.

5. There are pronouns that merely stand in place of earlier *expressions* in a sentence, as in this example from Karttunen (1969):

The man who gives his paycheque to his wife is wiser than the man who gives it to his mistress

where *it* stands in for the expression *his paycheque*. This category is a special case of what Geach (1962, pp. 124–5) called 'pronouns of laziness', and, following Partee (1978), I shall restrict the label to this use of pronouns.

The variety of pronominal usage presents a challenge to linguists searching for underlying principles, and they have proposed a number of competing theories that purport to reveal the unity beneath the diversity. Some have followed Lasnik (1976) in believing that anaphoric and cataphoric pronouns can be treated as special cases of deictic pronouns, where the referents are to be found in the text rather than in the world. Others have followed Evans (1980) in rejecting this thesis, because it obscures the relation between bound-variable and anaphoric pronouns. In fact, the behaviour of pronouns can be explained in terms of the theory that discourse has two levels of representation.

389

The interpretation of the deictic pronouns in the sentence:

He did it

depends on the prior existence of the corresponding referential tokens in the mental model of the circumstances of the utterance. Listeners recover the intended referents on the basis of inferences: they know that it is wrong to throw bottles at the screen, and they use that knowledge to infer that *did it* refers to this event, which is represented in their model of what has just happened in the cinema. A Martian or other alien who lacked such knowledge might well take *did it* to refer to the switching on of the house lights in the cinema. Anaphoric pronouns are treated in a similar way, except that their referents are introduced into the model as a result of interpreting the earlier discourse. The process of finding the corresponding token is aided by syntactic cues, such as gender and number. Indeed, my former student Kate Ehrlich showed experimentally that the time taken to identify the referent of a pronoun is reliably faster if gender suffices to eliminate all but one candidate in the linguistic context (Ehrlich, 1980). This result suggests that factually based inferences may be employed if grammatical cues are insufficient to determine reference. There are, of course, other syntactic cues to pronominal reference. Since cataphoric pronouns are like blank cheques – they are not much use until their values are filled in – they seldom occur outside subordinate clauses:

When he came into the room, John saw the safe was open

where the fact that the clause is subordinate presumably signals that the pronoun's referent will be supplied imminently. However, this syntactic constraint is less powerful when the pronoun is the object of the initial clause, as shown by the acceptability of the sentence:

The waiter brought them tea when the guests had finished the dessert.

Since quantified assertions can be interpreted as mental models, it follows that when a pronoun functions like a bound variable it takes its referent in such a model. The assertion:

Every man loves a woman

can be represented in a mental model of the form:

man → woman
man → woman
(woman)

390

where the arrow stands for the appropriate relation. The interpretation of the assertion:

Every man loves a woman who loves him

builds on the previous model to produce:

$$man \leftrightarrow woman$$
$$man \leftrightarrow woman$$
$$(woman)$$

This interpretation, as Evans desired, closely corresponds to the interpretation of a sentence containing an anaphoric pronoun:

John loves a woman who loves him.

The model that would be constructed for this assertion:

$$John \leftrightarrow woman$$

is created for each individual in the set representing every man. Even with a small number of tokens, there are obviously a variety of alternative models that would satisfy such assertions, which may explain the increased difficulty of understanding them (as can be demonstrated experimentally, see Johnson-Laird, 1969a). Where there are many possibilities, a single mental model functions as a representative sample from the set of alternatives. It is a prototype that represents the meaning of the assertion in the simplest way. A model such as:

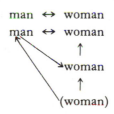

obscures the essential meaning of the assertion by violating the simple symmetry of the previous model. The Evans-pronoun that occurs in the sentence:

Some tories are still monetarists and *they* are in the government

likewise takes its reference from the mental model representing the initial clause of the sentence:

$$tory = monetarist$$
$$tory = monetarist$$
- - - - - - - - - -
$$tory$$
$$tory$$

(I have here assumed that the force of the word *still* in the sentence is that some tories are not now monetarists, and for simplicity I have ignored the barely imaginable possibility that some monetarists are not tories.) The resulting model of the sentence as a whole accordingly has the form:

tory = monetarist = member of the government
tory = monetarist = member of the government
(tory   = member of the government)
tory

In contrast, the following sentence, which though it contains no pronoun has an interpretation equivalent to a sentence with a bound variable:

Some tories are still monetarists and in the government

yields a model in which there may be tory monetarists who are not in the government:

tory = monetarist = member of the government
(tory = monetarist)
(tory   = member of the government)
tory

The critical difference between bound-variable pronouns and Evans-pronouns is accordingly that the reference of a bound-variable pronoun is the same in the model as that of its antecedent noun phrase, whereas the reference of an Evans-pronoun is the same as the set of entities that satisfy the clause in which its antecedent occurs. Both, of course, depend on the presence of a quantifier in the antecedent noun phrase, so how are their occurrences to be distinguished? Evans (1980) suggests the following general principle: a pronoun is interpretable as bound by a quantifier phrase only if the quantifier phrase precedes and c-commands it, where the syntactic relation 'c-commands' means that the pronoun is dominated by the first branching node that dominates the quantifier. The relation accordingly seems to be the syntactic analogue of the logical scope of a quantifier. Hence, a pronoun can be interpreted as a bound variable only if it is within the scope of its antecedent, which is a quantified noun phrase; otherwise it refers to whatever entities have been inserted into the model to satisfy the description of the antecedent.

Pronouns of laziness are distinct from the previous classes in that they take their reference not directly from a referring expression in the sentence, but rather use the propositional representation of their antecedent to pick out a new referent. So the sentence:

392

The man who gives his paycheque to his wife is wiser than the man who gives it to his mistress

is interpreted as though the earlier noun phrase were simply repeated:

The man who gives his paycheque to his wife is wiser than the man who gives his paycheque to his mistress.

Once such a substitution has been made, the noun phrase can be interpreted in the usual way.

Anaphora and ellipsis

There are many kinds of anaphors in English. Their fundamental function is presumably to enable speakers to avoid wasting breath and listeners to avoiding wasting energy on unnecessary verbiage. If a reference or sense has already been established, it can be communicated either by a pro-form or by a manifest 'gap' in an utterance. As I established in the previous section, pronominal anaphors accordingly depend either on a propositional representation of sense or else on a mental model of significance. As Sag and Hankamer (1980) have shown, this distinction applies to all anaphors including those that depend on ellipsis, that is, the deliberate omission of material from a sentence.

The commoner species of elliptical anaphors are illustrated by the following examples in which 'ø' marks the position of ellipsed material:

	but I don't ø	(Verb-phrase ellipsis)
	and ø hug Jane	(Conjunction reduction)
Eric wants to	and Tim ø Anna	(Gapping)
kiss Pearl	but ø not ø here	(Stripping)
	but I don't know why ø	(Sluicing)
	and she'll let him ø	(Null complement)

Sag and Hankamer originally distinguished between 'surface' and 'deep' anaphora. A surface anaphor, such as a verb-phrase ellipsis:

Eric wants to kiss Pearl but I don't ø

appears to relate directly to an earlier part of the surface structure of the sentence. But, as these authors point out, an example such as:

Person A: I wonder if they'll like me.
Person B: I'm sure they will ø

393

requires access not to the surface form of *like me*, but to its sense, which yields an analysis equivalent to B's having said 'I am sure they will like you.' Certainly, however, such anaphors establish the need to keep a record in the propositonal representation of the superficial linguistic form of the sentence. The discourse:

The Romans were beating the Gauls. The Britons were ø, too

plainly means that the Britons were beating the Gauls. However, if the ellipsis is preceded by a sentence that is synonymous with the original but in the passive voice:

The Gauls were being beaten by the Romans. The Britons were ø, too

then the effect is to change the interpretation of the elliptical sentence, which now means that the Britons were being beaten by the Romans. It follows that contrary to what has sometimes been assumed in psycholinguistic theories of processing, the superficial form of a sentence cannot be discarded immediately it has been interpreted. It may be needed in the interpretation of a subsequent sentence.

Deep anaphors do not depend on the superficial form of a sentence, but take their reference either deictically or from other referring expressions in the discourse. Apart from pronominal anaphors, this category includes one major species of ellipsis, the null complement anaphors. Suppose, for example, that you are at an airport security check and that the guard beckons you to pass through the doorway of the metal detector. You could declare:

No, I refuse ø   (Null complement)

and your remark would be linguistically acceptable, because the ellipsed material can be established from a mental model of the situation. But, had you declared instead:

No, I will not ø

then your remark would hardly be acceptable, because verb-phrase deletion depends on the sense of the previous discourse, and in this case there is no previous discourse. Of course, there are occasions when people deliberately break the rules for stylistic effect:

It is a spottily hilarious and technically brilliant cavort through art, using actors and animated pictures and starting with the Arnolfini family by Van Eyck. Oh yes you do. The one where the bride wears her wedding dress so oddly bunchy over her stomach. (Nancy Banks Smith in the *Guardian*, 5 September 1980)

Here, Miss Smith in her inimitably chatty prose anticipates that the reader will respond to her reference to the Van Eyck picture by retorting:

I don't know it.

And it is to this imaginary remark that she replies elliptically:

Oh yes you do [know it]. [It is] the one [i.e., the picture] where the bride . . .

In this case, the reader's mental model must represent an imaginary sentence in order for the discourse to work.

Conclusions

The chapter began with the question of what makes sentences into discourse. There appear to be two principal factors: referential coherence, and plausibility within a framework of general causal knowledge. Both of these factors have been corroborated experimentally. Reference can be properly analysed only by an account that, unlike the theory of text grammar, distinguishes at least two levels of representation: a representation of the sense of a discourse, and a representation of its significance (including what it refers to). This distinction is precisely what is captured in the theory of propositional representations and mental models; and it has been borne out by linguistic analyses of definite and indefinite descriptions, pronouns, and other anaphoric expressions.

Is there any other sort of structure to be found in discourse and to which the human interpretative apparatus is sensitive? I argued earlier that the theory of story grammars is defective, but it is clear that here at least it makes a testable claim. If coherence and plausibility have been accounted for, then folk-tales should still produce structural effects on comprehension and recall that do not occur with texts outside the genre. The critical comparison for the theory of story grammars is accordingly between folk-tales and other forms of narrative balanced for coherence and plausibility. Unfortunately, this stringent test has not yet been carried out.

Finally, I argued that referential usage depends on a speaker's intentions, and that they will be reflected in the constraints on revising mental models in the light of subsequent descriptions of entities. The notion of intention, however, remains to be elucidated; I shall return to this topic only after I have tried to clarify the nature of mental models.

15

The nature of mental models

In Chapter 2, I described the following scenario:

Person A asks: Where's the university?

Person B replies: Some of those people are from there.

Person A goes up to the group of people indicated by B and asks them the same question. As I pointed out, A's behaviour depends on a chain of inferences including the syllogism:

Some of those people are from the university.

Any person from the university is likely to know where the university is.

∴ Some of those people are likely to know where the university is.

My goal of accounting for the processes of inference, which I took to be a useful test case for cognitive science, has now been attained. Of course, I have not explained every mental process that underlies A's behaviour, but I have shown how the meanings of words can be mentally represented, how sentences can be parsed to form a propositional representation, how a propositional representation can be treated as the input to a procedural semantics that constructs mental models, how a unitary mental model of a discourse, such as the premises of the syllogism, can be formed on the basis of co-reference, and how reasoning follows the fundamental semantic principle of validity in a search for counter-examples to putative conclusions.

In some areas of cognition, it is possible to formulate a theory of competence that specifies what has to be computed and why, and then to define a psychologically plausible algorithm for computing it. The theory of grammar, as we saw in Chapter 12, characterizes the syntactic structure of sentences, and the theory of parsing specifies an algorithm for computing that structure. This approach to psychology is powerful though double-edged, in that a correct theory of competence is an invaluable constraint on theories of performance, but an incorrect theory of competence can seriously mislead researchers. In the case of inference, no one has successfully formulated what exactly the mind computes, and the resulting theoretical gap has been filled by a largely tacit (and accordingly potent) assumption that formal logic constitutes the theory of competence. The fundamental shortcoming of this doctrine is that most inferences in daily life depend on drawing spontaneous conclusions, and reasoners do not draw just any valid conclusion – and sometimes do not draw a valid conclusion at all. It is therefore misleading to assume that what has to be computed is the set of valid deductions, since spontaneous valid deductions are only a subset of this class. In Chapter 2, I argued that an essential constraint on everyday inference is that deductions which depend only on the relations between propositions must express the same semantic content as their premises in a more parsimonious form; and in Chapter 3, I described two algorithms that could in principle carry out the necessary computations, though only the second of them was psychologically plausible. The subsequent development of the theory to cope with inferences based on quantifiers was less straightforward, because there was no obvious way of formulating a theory of competence. It was necessary to observe what conclusions people actually draw from syllogistic premises. Strangely, despite seventy years of research on these problems, no previous investigator had carried out such a study – a testament to the potency of the idea that logic characterizes what the mind computes, and thus that there is no need to make observations to answer this question.

Mental models emerged as theoretical entities from my attempts to make sense of inferences, both explicit and implicit. They replaced the formal rules of a hypothetical mental logic. Subsequently, I was able to give a better explanation of meaning, comprehension, and discourse, by postulating mental models in place of other forms of semantic representation. The theory developed piecemeal, but it was extended and corroborated by computer implementations and experimental investigations. It is now plausible to suppose that mental models play a central and unifying role in representing objects, states of affairs, sequences of events, the way the world is, and the social and psychological actions of daily life. They enable individuals to make inferences and predictions, to understand phenomena, to decide what action to take and to control its execution, and above all to experience events by proxy; they allow language to be used to create representations comparable to those deriving from direct acquaintance with the world; and they relate words to the world by way of conception and perception.

Yet the reader may wonder what exactly mental models are intended to be, and how they differ from other postulated forms of mental representation. Schemata and prototypes, for example, appear to be special cases of procedures for constructing mental models, but we cannot be certain until we have an explanatorily adequate theory that specifies the set of all possible mental models, and comparable theories from the proponents of schemata and prototypes. At present, no complete account can be given – one may as well ask for an inventory of the entire products of the human imagination – and indeed such an account would be premature, since mental models are supposed to be in people's heads, and their exact constitution is an empirical question. Nevertheless, there are three immediate constraints on possible models. The first of them follows from the doctrine of functionalism:

1. The principle of computability: Mental models, and the machinery for constructing and interpreting them, are computable.

This is a weak constraint, but it at least entails that there are no more than a denumerably infinite number of possible mental models (see Chapter 1). The second constraint follows from the assumption that the brain is a finite organism:

2. The principle of finitism: A mental model must be finite in size and cannot directly represent an infinite domain.

The third constraint arises from the primary function of mental models, which is, of course, to represent states of affairs. Since there are a potentially infinite number of states of affairs that could be represented, but only a finite mechanism for constructing them, it follows that models must be built out of more basic constituents:

3. The principle of constructivism: A mental model is constructed from tokens arranged in a particular structure to represent a state of affairs.

This constraint raises a number of fundamental questions:

— How do mental models represent the external world? In other words, how do tokens function as symbols for entities, how do properties of tokens symbolize properties of entities, and how do relations between tokens symbolize relations between entities?

— What processes construct and interpret mental models?

— What concepts are embodied in mental models? This question is an ontological one. It concerns the sorts of entities, properties, and relations – whether concrete or abstract – that can be symbolized in mental models. It also concerns the conceptual primitives of the procedural semantics, and how the primitives combine to form more complex concepts.

— What are the basic structures of mental models, and how do they differ from those of other postulated mental representations?

In this penultimate chapter, I intend, not to summarize what the book has had to say about mental models, but to approach them from a different angle so as to answer these four questions. The answers will yield principles that place further constraints on the set of possible models, and accordingly lead to a first approximation to an explanatorily adequate theory. This theory will be crystallized in a classification of types of mental models. I shall then consider how a mental model can represent a mental model. This problem concerns assertions about knowledge and belief, and, as we shall see, its solution leads to a straightforward semantics for such 'propositional attitudes'. The existence of a solution is crucial, of course, for the feasibility of cognitive science. I shall also propose a way in which large or infinite domains, such as the natural numbers, can be mentally represented. Finally, I shall consider the question of truth, since the truth of a discourse depends on the relation between its mental model and reality. This relation is problematical, however, in the case of discourse with incomplete truth conditions. Nevertheless, it will be possible to bring about a *rapprochement* between the theory of mental models and model-theoretic semantics.

How do mental models represent the external world?

The question of what makes a mental entity a representation *of* something has plagued philosophers but has largely passed psychologists by. In consequence, as I remarked in the Prologue, psychological theories of meaning have almost invariably failed to deal with reference. Like any matter concerning explanatory adequacy, the question must ultimately have a biological answer: in nature, there is no representation without evolution, and perhaps there is no evolution beyond a certain point without the capacity to represent the world.

Consider the lowly bacterium, which is older and simpler than the protozoa and the higher animals and plants. A bacterium such as *Salmonella typhimurium*, which can cause food poisoning, or the biologist's favourite, *Escherichia coli*, which can cause diarrhoea, is able to detect a chemical gradient equivalent to a difference of only 1 part in 10 over the length of its body (approximately 2 microns), and to modify its behaviour so as to migrate up a nutrient gradient and down a toxic gradient. This behaviour might be thought to display perception, memory, and choice, but, as Koshland (1977) and others have shown, the reality is rather different. Migration depends on the rate at which the bacterium tumbles, which in turn depends on the direction in which its flagellae rotate: when they rotate anti-clockwise they push the organism forward in a straight line, but when they rotate clockwise they fly apart and cause it to tumble over and over. If a bacterium is moving in the 'right' direction, its rate of tumbling is suppressed and it continues to move in a straight line; if it is moving in the 'wrong' direction, its rate of tumbling is increased and it ceases to move in that direction. Hence its path is a random walk that is biased by its ability to detect ambient chemical stimuli. They are, in fact, detected by special receptor proteins that can bind (according to the shape of the molecule) a variety of substances including glucose, galactose, and oxygen. Their reception affects a regulator that shifts the 'gear' controlling the direction in which the flagellae rotate. The process is transient and unless further stimuli are detected the direction of the rotation simply alternates. In this way, the bacterium is able in effect to 'compare' the strength of a chemical substance over the time it takes to swim a distance of somewhere between 20 to 100 times its own body length.

The unicellular organism *Paramecium* swims through the water by the co-ordinated beating of its cilia. If it bumps into an obstruction, it reverses the direction of its ciliary beat, backs off, and then swims away in a new direction. This behaviour seems as if it depends on an ability to make a decision based on a perceptual representation of the world, but once again there is an alternative explanation. Mechanical stimulation causes the membrane of the organism to depolarize. The sequence of ensuing electro-chemical events leads to the cilia's reversing the direction of their power strokes. When the membrane recovers a few seconds later, the further change in ion conductance results in the resumption of normal swimming (Quinn and Gould, 1979).

Bacteria and protozoa appear to move through their respective worlds in a thoughtful way, but in reality they are what I shall call *Cartesian* automata. As Figure 15.1 illustrates, there is a direct, physically mediated, causal link from stimulus to response. Cartesian automata are a Behaviourist's dream: they respond to the world, yet their responses are based not on representations of the world, but on direct causal interaction with it. They are 'open loop' systems, and their responses have perhaps come down to higher organisms in the form of unconditioned reflexes that are not controlled by feedback.

Even in the simplest of organisms, however, feedback plays a role, because theoretically it occurs whenever the value of a variable depends upon itself in an analogue of recursion. Consider the following standard

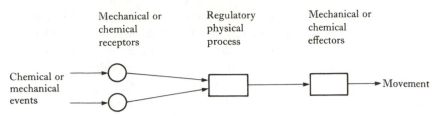

Figure 15.1 A block-diagram of the causal chain of events in a Cartesian automaton.

example. When water flows out of a cistern, the rate of outflow is proportional to the volume of water in the cistern; but this volume in turn depends on the rate of outflow (as well as on the rate of inflow). The system is defined by an equation in which outflow depends on its own value:

$$\text{Outflow} = k \int (\text{Inflow} - \text{Outflow}) \, dt$$

Net flow is integrated with respect to time to yield the volume of water in the cistern, and the volume is multiplied by a constant, k, that depends on the bore of the outflow pipe. Although it is modelled by a feedback loop, the cistern itself obviously has no device monitoring the outflow and feeding back its value.

The teleological use of feedback is sometimes said to depend on a representation of a goal or desired state, its comparison with current performance, and the maintenance or modification of behaviour in the light of that comparison (Wonham, 1976). But this claim is not perhaps as straightforward as one might have thought. Biological processes in everything from bacteria to human beings are ultimately governed by protein molecules – sensory receptors are proteins, antibodies that protect organisms from infection are proteins, enzymes that control chemical reactions in the organism are proteins – and feedback plays a part in all of these processes. For example, when you ingest glucose, it can either be oxidized immediately to provide energy in the form of adenosine triphosphate (ATP) or it can be stored in the form of glycogen. The enzymes that control these processes are turned on or off by the amount of ATP in the system, and the molecules that activate one process inhibit the other. This is a chemical equivalent of feedback, but it does not depend on a representation: the ATP in the system does not represent the amount of available energy, it *is* that amount. Hence, in such cases feedback is a direct consequence of biochemical reactions. Other biochemical reactions may, perhaps, represent the world, because, as Oatley (1974) has argued, the feedback processes in them may give rise to the non-linear oscillations that underlie 'biological clocks' – the internal timing devices that enable organisms to synchronize their activities with time and tide.

The simplest organisms have no mental life. Their behaviour, as we have seen in no way depends on internal representations of the external world. More advanced organisms, however, do not merely react physically to their immediate environment, but seek to anticipate it since it is advantageous to avoid obstacles before bumping into them. With the evolution of nervous systems, organisms developed sensory transducers sensitive to stimuli from distant objects. These transducers convert impinging energy into nerve impulses, and these impulses in turn are the input to a computational process that leads to the construction of representations of the world. Such representations can then be used in much the same way that a navigator uses a map to avoid danger and to reach a desired destination in safety. The richer and the more veridical the internal model, the greater will be the organism's chances of survival.

You may say that you perceive the world directly, but in fact what you experience depends on a model of the world. Entities in the world give rise to the patterns of energy that reach the sense organs. The information latent in these patterns is used by the nervous system to construct a (partial) model of the entities that gave rise to the energy in the first place. Some theorists argue that all the information that is needed impinges on the sensorium; others, that the recovery of the 'world' depends on a large body of a priori knowledge. On the one hand, if we were suddenly to become sensitive to infra-red in our visible spectrum, the world we experienced would be very different from how it is now. It so happens that when I view the world monocularly, my right eye yields colours of greater intensity than my left eye. Which eye perceives the correct colours? There is no answer to this question – not even if we could swap our subjective experiences – a representation can be a representation of a real thing, but it is not the real thing itself. Hence, the nature of the mind and its perceptual system exert a decisive effect on the world we perceive. On the other hand, if there ceased to be any objects emitting or reflecting light, the world we experienced would again be very different. In short, our view of the world is causally dependent both on the way the world is and on the way we are. There is an obvious but important corollary: all our knowledge of the world depends on our ability to construct models of it. Since this ability is a product of natural selection, our knowledge indeed depends on our biological make-up as well as on things-in-themselves. I take this thesis to be the essential moral of Kant's philosophy.

What counts as a representational model of the world? It is clearly not a matter of the ultimate medium of the representation, since all biological processes finally depend on protein molecules. Similarly, it is not merely a matter of the organism's interacting with the world in an appropriate causal way, since Cartesian automata interact with the world but make no use of internal models. The essential characteristic of a model is its functional role. A model is a high-level representation in what is, from a functional point of view, an arbitrary symbolic notation. The interpretive system treats an element in this notation, A′, as corresponding to an entity, A, in the world. The organism avoids an obstruction, A, in virtue of its representation, A′. There is no direct physical correspondence, because the pattern of neural events underlying A′ is quite different from the aggregate of molecules comprising A. There may be a structural resemblance, however, because the structure of a spatial model may be related to the corresponding physical structure. The trouble is: we have no way of knowing what the structure is (or even of whether the notion makes sense) that is independent from the way in which we conceive the world.

An organism that makes use of a representation of the external world is what I shall call a *Craikian* automaton. It can be constructed from a Cartesian automaton by adding both a sensorium that encodes impinging stimuli and the machinery to use this information to construct a representation of the world, which guides its behaviour. Figure 15.2 presents a block-diagram of a Craikian automaton.

Part of the functional structure of a Craikian automaton is illustrated perspicuously in a simple robot devised by my colleague Christopher

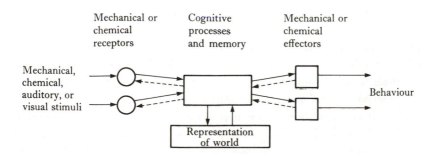

Figure 15.2 A block-diagram of a Craikian automaton (showing feedback loops).

Longuet-Higgins. The robot moves freely on the surface of a table, but whenever it reaches an edge it rings an alarm bell to summon its human keeper to rescue it from disaster. It possesses neither pressure sensors for detecting edges, nor any sort of electronics. How then does it respond to the edge of the table? The answer turns – literally – on a model. As the robot travels around the table, its main wheels drive two small wheels that hold a piece of sandpaper up underneath its baseplate. The paper is the same shape as the table, and as the small wheels turn they move the paper around beneath the baseplate. In fact, their position on the paper at any moment corresponds exactly to the robot's position on the table. There is a ridge at the edge of the paper (corresponding to the edge of the table) so that whenever one of the small wheels is deflected by it, a simple circuit is closed to ring the alarm. The large wheels in effect act as perceptual organs (as well as a means of transport) that register the robot's movement through its environment. The small wheels and the piece of sandpaper are not intrinsically a model, but they become a model in the robot because of their function as an arbitrarily selected symbolic notation that is used to register the position of the robot in its world. There are many other symbolic notations that could have been used in the robot. The rotation of the large wheels could have been used as an input to a microprocessor that manipulated a symbolic array representing the table-top. It is what *all* such mechanisms have in common, namely, their functional structure, that renders them models of the world. Of course, the robot is not a complete Craikian automaton, because it does not construct its own model of the table-top – it merely employs a God-given model, which if wrong puts the robot at risk.

The use of a model allows a Craikian automaton to avoid certain classes of entities, either because it is innately pre-programmed to avoid them or because it can learn to avoid objects that give rise to noxious proximal stimuli like mechanical shocks, intense pressures and temperatures, and toxic reactions. A still more advanced method of avoiding such dangers depends on communication. Craikian automata could in principle use an *external* symbolic notation to communicate the contents of their models. For instance, they could be pre-set to make a distinctive noise whenever they perceived a precursor to a noxious stimulus, and they could be pre-set to respond appropriately to this noise when it was produced by another member of the species. The noise would be symbolic because it would not be a necessary physical consequence of the situation: its choice would be arbitrary (cf. de Saussure, 1960).

Nature contains an abundance of self-reproducing Craikian automata, of which the most obvious examples are the insects, but their perceptual systems vary in the extent to which they yield rich models of the world. The house-fly's visual system, for example, controls its flight pattern by way of a set of automatic mechanisms (Reichardt and Poggio, 1981). The fly tracks a mate using a system that is sensitive to a small black patch moving in relation to the background. This system provides the values of two critical variables: the angle of the patch in the visual field, and its angular velocity. Another system automatically puts the fly into its landing routine if its visual field expands rapidly because the fly is approaching a surface. Hence, the fly's visual mechanisms provide little information about the state of the world: its behaviour is directly controlled by properties of the visual field. The bee, however, appears to have access to a richer representation of the world. When a foraging worker bee returns from a supply of nectar, she conveys to other workers its distance by the proportion of time that she spends wagging her tail in a special dance usually carried out on a vertical honeycomb within the hive. She also communicates the direction of the nectar in relation to the sun's position by the angle to the vertical of the wagging portion of her dance (von Frisch, 1966).

There is no doubt that the bee constructs a model of the spatial location of the food source, and is able to transmit the salient features of this model to her fellow workers. Her dance signals the direction of the food, not the direction she has flown, should the two conflict because of an obstacle. The bee uses a symbolic response, A'', that corresponds to an element in an internal representation, A', that corresponds to a state of affairs, A, in the world. The symbol accordingly corresponds to the state of affairs. Yet bees do not possess a language in which symbols refer to the world in the way in which human beings can make reference to it. Reference certainly requires representations that correspond to elements in the world, but it is a mistake to confuse reference with mere correspondence. The use of natural language to communicate depends on an *intentional* correspondence between a symbolic expression and a state of affairs. Bees convey the location of nectar, but presumably they do so without any communicative intentions. Bees cannot tell lies. People, however, use linguistic expressions with the intention of picking out certain states of affairs. Successful communication may transcend literal failures of reference, as we saw in the previous chapter, because a listener may be able to recover a speaker's referential intentions. Human communication therefore depends on a tacit understanding that symbolic expressions can either correspond or fail to correspond to reality.

Computer programs can be written which embody this notion of correspondence but which perform without in any way recognizing that their behaviour is controlled by it. Indeed, I have described several such programs in this book. They are nothing more than Craikian devices that abide by the principle of correspondence in much the same way that a bee abides by it – neither program nor bee can help itself, because its behaviour is governed by the laws of its respective universe. Human beings, in contrast, need to understand the notion of intentional correspondence in order to refer and to make use of natural language. Intentionality is wrapped up in the notion of consciousness, and I shall attempt to unwrap it in the final chapter of the book.

What processes construct and interpret mental models?

Mental models owe their origin to the evolution of perceptual ability in organisms with nervous systems. Indeed, perception provides us with our richest model of the world. The late David Marr (1982) and his colleagues have outlined a computational theory of vision that largely accounts for the derivation of perceptually based models of the world. The theory postulates three principal forms of representation: first, the 'primal sketch', which is a symbolic representation of the disposition of intensity changes in the visual image, their local geometry, and the structure in the underlying reflectance distributions; second, the '$2\frac{1}{2}$-D sketch', which is a viewer-centred representation of the depth and orientation of surfaces, including contours and discontinuities; and third, the three-dimensional model of an object, which is based on an object-centred set of co-ordinates and primitives that make the space-filling shape of the object explicit. The account of 3-D models applies only to certain classes of objects, but it is clear that the basic ideas should be extensible to all objects and to scenes in which there are spatial relations between objects. Marr and his colleagues have developed algorithms for computing the various representations, corroborated some of them in the light of experimental evidence, and in some cases have even been able to identify appropriate neurophysiological mechanisms for carrying out the actual computations. It is therefore safe to assume that a primary source of mental models – three-dimensional kinematic models of the world – is perception.

Mental models can take other forms and serve other purposes, and, in particular, they can be used in interpreting language and in making inferences. These roles are a natural extension of their perceptual function: if the perception of the world is model-based, then discourse about the world must be model-based, and the ability to make inferences from what we perceive or from what we are told enables us to anticipate even quite remote events. Discourse, however, may be about fictitious or imaginary worlds, and hence our propensity to interpret it by building models of the states of affairs it describes frees us from the fetters of perceptual reality.

The comprehension of discourse depends on three principal levels of representation: first, there is a phonemic (or graphemic) representation that encodes the sounds (or letters) of an utterance; second, there is a propositional representation, which is close to the surface form of the utterance; third, there is a mental model. The mental model is constructed on the basis of the truth conditions of the propositions expressed by the sentences in the discourse. The meaning of a sentence, according to the principle of compositionality, is a function of the meanings of its words and the syntactic relations between them (see Chapter 8). Meaning, however, is an abstract notion that reflects only what is determined by a knowledge of the language. The significance of an utterance goes beyond meaning because it depends on recovering referents and some minimal idea of the speaker's intentions. The truth conditions of the proposition expressed by a sentence therefore depend on the meaning of the sentence, its context of utterance (as represented in the current mental model), and the implicit inferences that it triggers from background knowledge.

The main procedures required for constructing and interpreting mental models were outlined in Chapter 11, which also described an algorithm for carrying them out. The principal procedures for interpreting models generate descriptions (or other illocutions) based on them. Since there is a procedure that verifies assertions with respect to mental models, and the relevant model may derive from perception, discourse is readily related to the world.

If a mental model derives from visual perception, it will be a single entity corresponding to a single, perhaps unique, state of affairs. If, however, it is based on discourse, there is a problem. Discourse is almost invariably indeterminate and compatible with many different states of affairs. It is natural to suppose, however, that any mental representation should be as parsimonious as possible, and this assumption leads to the following constraint on models of discourse:

4. The principle of economy in models: A description of a single state of affairs is represented by a single mental model even if the description is incomplete or indeterminate.

In theory, the single model should be constructed by a non-deterministic device that always produces the correct model; in practice, non-determinism has to be simulated by a procedure that constructs an initial model on the basis of plausible, though sometimes arbitrary, assumptions, and recursively revises the model should such an assumption turn out to be wrong. Hence, the content captured in a mental model – its significance – is a function of both the model and the processes that evaluate it. A single mental model can stand for an infinite number of possible states of affairs, because the model can be revised recursively. For most communicative purposes indeterminacies do not matter, because conversation works according to a Gricean convention that a speaker will be precise if necessary and will give the relevant information in an order that will enable a listener to cope with it without having to carry out too much revision. But should a subsequent assertion turn out to be inconsistent with the current model, the model can be revised, if possible, so as to accommodate the new assertion.

The procedures for making inferences work in essentially the same way. If a conclusion is true of a current model, attempts are made to modify the model recursively in a way that is both consistent with the premises and inconsistent with the conclusion. If the procedure fails, then of course the inference is valid.

There are limits, of course, on the revision of a mental model. The process is ultimately governed by the truth conditions of the discourse on which the model is based. Ideally, it would be useful to be able to build the restrictions on reconstruction directly into the mental model itself. But, again, the notion of economy of representation constrains what is possible. In the case of an assertion such as:

All the husbands are liars

it is economical to represent the fact that there may be liars who are not husbands by introducing a special token into the mental model:

$$h = 1$$
$$h = 1$$

(1)

which indicates that such liars may, or may not, exist. This convention does not lead to an explosive combinatorial problem, because anything that is predicated of liars will apply to the liars in this category, too, and will not increase the possible states of affairs. Suppose, however, that indeterminacies concerning spatial relations were to be captured in a spatial model. For example, an assertion of the form:

A is on the right of B, which is on the left of C

might be represented in a spatial array either by duplicating tokens representing the same entity:

B   (A)   C   (A)

or by introducing propositional-like links:

B $\overleftarrow{}$→ C   A

In either case, the addition of further indeterminacies leads rapidly to an intractable growth in the number of possible interpretations of the model. In effect, it ceases to be a model at all. Indeed, the semantic content of the links in the diagram is entirely equivalent to that of the initial propositional representation of the sentence. Representational economy therefore leads to the following constraint:

5. Mental models can directly represent indeterminacies if and only if their use is not computationally intractable, i.e., there is not an exponential growth in complexity.

In many cases, there is no effective way of restricting recursive revision apart from going back to the original assertions or to their propositional representations. If, however, people constructed only propositional representations and made no use of mental models, there would be no way of relating discourse to the world and no way of accounting for inference without recourse to a mental logic.

The functions that construct, interpret, and revise mental models should suffice for any finitely representable discourse, since an assertion can only call for a new model, or modifications to existing models. But these functions cannot be treated in an abstract way as in model-theoretic semantics. They require explicit algorithms that can map propositional representations into mental models. This need for explicitness has, as we saw in Chapter 11, a striking and unforeseen consequence. Once the truth conditions of a word have been formulated in the lexicon, there is no longer any need to specify its semantic properties and relations to other words, which emerge directly from its truth conditions. Hence, analyses

409

of the mental lexicon in terms of decompositional dictionary entries, semantic networks, or meaning postulates, are otiose.

What concepts are embodied in mental models?

Since mental models can take many forms and serve many purposes, their contents are very varied. They can contain nothing but tokens that represent individuals and identities between them, as in the sort of models that are required for syllogistic reasoning. They can represent spatial relations between entities, and the temporal or causal relations between events. A rich imaginary model of the world can be used to compute the projective relations required for an image. Models have a content and form that fits them to their purpose, whether it be to explain, to predict, or to control (cf. the studies of expertise reported in Gentner and Stevens, In press). Their structure corresponds to the perceived or conceived structure of the world, and is accordingly more constrained than their contents. The possible contents, of course, constitute an ontology.

Our conception of what exists is a function of the world and the human conceptual apparatus. It is most unlikely that natural science will ever achieve an explanatorily adequate ontology. As Monod (1972) argued, the class of living things consists of entities that are compatible with biological principles but not predictable from them; even *Homo sapiens* is a contingent rather than necessary species. What we can know of the world, however, depends on our conceptual apparatus, and it might be possible to discover constraints on what the mind can conceive, so tying down one end of the ontological problem. Certainly, a number of theorists have attempted this manoeuvre.

One way to construct an ontology is to consider the concepts that underlie the meanings of everyday expressions. Our basic ontology according to this criterion contains things and substances, their properties, and relations between them. It should also admit properties of properties, relations between properties, relations between relations, and so on, in a system that has no a priori limit to the construction of higher-order properties and relations. Yet, concepts must be constrained by the nature of the human cognitive apparatus. I shall consider three such constraints here, each of which affects the possible contents of mental models. The first goes some way towards explaining why certain concepts are natural and represented in mental models and why other classes are unnatural and are not normally represented in mental models. The second constraint con-

cerns the nature of the primitives from which mental models are constructed. The third concerns the organization of concepts.

Several authors (see Keil, 1979) have argued that concepts are governed
by the following constraint on the applicability of predicates:

6. The predicability principle: one predicate can apply to all the terms
to which another applies, but they cannot have intersecting ranges of
application.

Thus, for example, *animate* and *human* apply to certain things in common,
animate applies to some things to which *human* does not apply, but there
is nothing to which *human* applies and *animate* does not. There are prima
facie counter-examples to the principle, e.g., *intelligent* applies to both
person and *action*, and *tall* applies to both *person* and *tree*, but *intelligent*
does not apply to *tree*, and *tall* does not apply to *action*. But these counter-
examples are probably more apparent than real. An intelligent action is
one that is carried out with intelligence, i.e., by an agent, such as a person,
capable of intelligence. There is, in other words, no uniform compositional
principle for the interpretation of adjective + noun constructions, and this
fact must be borne in mind in assessing the predicability constraint. The
virtue of the constraint is, of course, that it explains what counts as an
artificial or unnatural concept. A concept that is extensionally defined as,
say, the following set: {42, a shoe, Father Christmas, beer, blue, the House
of Lords, elbows} is artificial, because its members have nothing in common: that is to say, such sets readily violate the predicability constraint,
and they themselves are not subsets of sets that conform to it.

What are the conceptual primitives on which all mental models are
constructed? The second constraint rules out a large number of candidates:

7. The innateness principle: All conceptual primitives are innate.

Some theorists, notably Fodor (1980), have argued that *all* concepts are
innate, though some concepts may only be 'triggered' by experience –
much as the duckling's innate 'following'-response is released by the first
large moving object that it encounters. This claim appears to be primarily
based on the thesis that conceptual learning is impossible. I rejected this
extreme form of Nativism in Chapter 6, and defended an analogy between
conceptual learning and the construction of computable functions. Any
computable function can be constructed from a set of primitive functions
(the zero, successor, and identity functions) using three sorts of building-
block (composition, primitive recursion, and minimization). If conceptual
learning occurs in an analogous way, it follows that no acquired concept

is primitive, but constructed from primitives or from previously acquired concepts. Hence, primitives cannot be acquired, and must be innate.

The case for conceptual learning overwhelms all but the most obdurate of Nativists. It is hard to believe that the concepts of, say, H-bombs, the Gorgons, and Mrs Thatcher, are all innate and merely waiting for the right (or the wrong) experience to 'trigger' them. Similarly, the fact that some words, can be informatively defined in terms of others (as I demonstrated in Chapter 10) corroborates the existence of acquired concepts. Nevertheless, it is a mistake to assume that indefinable words correspond one-to-one with primitive concepts. There are words that can be defined but that correspond to primitive concepts. Motion, for instance, is one of the givens of the phenomenal world, it is detected in the visual field in the early stages of perception, and it lies at the core of an important semantic field (Miller, 1972). It is a conceptual primitive, which a sophisticated thinker may none the less analyse as a continuous change of location over time. Indefinability is a sufficient condition, not a necessary one, for identifying primitive concepts.

The problem of conceptual analysis is similar to the problem of isolating the ultimate constituents of action. The act of walking, for example, is not such a constituent, so the argument goes, because walking consists of taking one step after another. And perhaps a step is not an ultimate constituent, either, because it consists in pushing a foot against the ground to propel the body forward, shifting the weight onto the other leg, lifting the foot and swinging it forward, and so on. Voluntary control begins to peter out at the level of contracting a major muscle, yet the primitive constituents of action remain unclear. In a similar way, a concept such as location is hardly susceptible to further conceptual analysis, but its comprehension depends on still more basic cognitive operations, just as contracting a muscle depends on synergies and muscle spindles. The analogy is apt in another way. There appears to be a hierarchy of motor control so that higher-order instructions can be couched in general terms without having to worry about the details, which can be interpreted more specifically at the next level down, with the consequence that it is only occasionally necessary to take voluntary control of fine movements. Likewise, comprehension usually requires conscious attention at most to high-level notions. When an individual constructs a mental model, the business of mobilizing the basic procedures is taken care of as automatically as the tuning of muscles.

In Chapter 6, I pointed out that the meaning of a relation such as *on*

412

the left is so basic that there is no ready way of defining it using the ordinary predicates of English, and I described one way in which its semantics could be handled procedurally for the construction and evaluation of mental models. The procedural primitives have no ready expression in the object language. They are outside conscious awareness; they cannot be easily described; and they cannot be acquired from experience, because the mental representation of experience already demands the ability to construct models of reality on the basis of perception. These primitives are indeed innate. They underlie our ability to represent the world, to carry out actions based on those representations, and to envisage alternative possibilities: primitives underlie perceptual experiences, motor abilities, and cognitive skills. The meanings of semantically simple words consist of semantic primitives, as in the procedural representation of the expression *on the left*. The meanings of semantically complex words are likewise composed from such primitives, acquired from the meanings of semantically simple words. Hence, there are three major levels of conceptual analysis: primitives, simple concepts, and complex, definable concepts.

A lexicological analysis carried out by Miller and Johnson-Laird (1976) yields a third constraint on the nature and organization of semantic primitives and hence on the constituents of mental models:

8. There is a finite set of conceptual primitives that give rise to a corresponding set of semantic fields, and there is a further finite set of concepts, or 'semantic operators', that occur in every semantic field serving to build up more complex concepts out of the underlying primitives.

The semantic fields revealed by the analysis include shape, colour, person, kinship, motion, perception, cogitation, emotion, bodily action, possession and communication. Each field is reflected in the lexicon by a large number of words sharing a common concept at the core of their meanings. Verbs of visual perception, for example, include: *sight*, *glimpse*, *spy*, *view*, *scrutinize*, and *watch*, which all contain an underlying core corresponding to the simple concept of seeing. The semantic operators include concepts of :

Time
Space
Possibility
Permissibility
Causation
Intention

Thus, for example, if people *watch* something, they focus their eyes on it for an interval of time with the intention of seeing what happens.

We do indeed organize our experience in terms of temporal and spatial locations, within frameworks of what is possible and permissible, and within a nexus of causes and intentions. The semantic operators provide precisely the framework (to which I alluded in the previous chapter) around which we organize the general knowledge underlying the plausibility of discourse. Semantic fields provide us with our conception of the furniture of the world – of what exists – and the semantic operators provide us with our concept of the various relations that may inhere between these objects. Time and space are primitives that are merely simulated in mental models. Possibility and permissibility depend on our capacity to construct models of situations that are alternatives to reality and to evaluate them with respect to our knowledge of the 'laws' of nature or morality. Hence, we judge that something is possible (in a given context) if we can construct a model (based on the context and the 'laws' of the relevant domain) that leads to that event, or if at least we are unable to rule out the existence of such a scenario (see Johnson-Laird, 1978). Causality and intentionality can be analysed into more basic concepts (see Miller and Johnson-Laird, 1976), in much the same way that motion can, but they lie at the right descriptive level for formulating the main domains of mental models. Hence, a dynamic model of, say, the description of a game of football calls for a temporal sequence of events at various locations, for causal relations between the events, and for the representation of individuals, interacting physically and socially, governed by physical laws and constrained by the 'laws' of the game and social conventions, and motivated by various intentions.

In what ways can concepts be combined so as to form more complex concepts? The analogy with recursive functions can be usefully pursued by treating concepts, whether primitive, simple or complex, as *characteristic* functions that deliver a truth value (see Chapter 8). The concept of x seeing y, for instance, yields the value *true* if x does indeed see y in the relevant context. A striking feature of Miller and Johnson-Laird's lexical analysis can now be stated succinctly: nearly all complex concepts corresponding to words can be constructed from simpler concepts by the operation of composition. This phenomenon can be illustrated by a slightly more formal analysis of the verb *to watch*. Given the concepts corresponding to *see* and *look at*, and the semantic operators corresponding to causation and intention, the characteristic function for *x watches y* can be constructed by composition:

$$\text{cause } ((\text{intend } (x, \text{see } (x, y))), \text{look at } (x, y))$$

that is, x intends to see y, and this intention causes x to look at y (for some interval of time). This account is deliberately simplified (cf. Miller and Johnson-Laird, 1976, p. 610), but the full analysis does not call for any operation other than composition. There are, however, at least some words that correspond to concepts that can only be defined recursively, and I shall discuss one example in a moment.

Whenever I have talked about mental models, audiences have readily grasped that a layout of concrete objects can be represented by an internal spatial array, that a syllogism can be represented by a model of individuals and identities between them, and that a physical process can be represented by a three-dimensional dynamic model. Many people, however, have been puzzled about the representation of abstract discourse; they cannot understand how terms denoting abstract entities, properties, or relations can be similarly encoded, and therefore they argue that these terms can have only 'verbal' or propositional representations. Of course such representations are used, if only as a first stage in the process of comprehension, and perhaps it is even true that we all walk around happily using some words and concepts that are built on air. But concepts without foundation can hardly underlie all abstract sentences; as long as individuals have clear intuitions about how the world would have to be for an assertion to be true, they must have transcended a purely propositional representation. If the sceptics were correct, the only way in which an abstract sentence could be represented would be as a sequence of symbols in a mental language, or as a set of nodes in a semantic network; but such a representation would be without truth conditions, and meaningless unless some semantic component provided an interpretation for it. Granted my argument that all our knowledge of the world depends on an ability to construct models, such a semantic interpretation would have to map the expression into a model of the world. There is no other possibility if one is to account for the truth conditions of abstract sentences.

There is an interesting and subtle question about abstract discourse: if an assertion is true, then to what does it correspond in the real world? This ontological issue, rather than mental representation, is the fundamental problem about abstraction. A term is abstract because it denotes

415

something that is not a physical entity, or a physical property, or a physical relation (or *a fortiori* perceptible). Ownership, for example, is abstract, since it does not correspond to a physical relation though it can hold between physical entities. Yet ownership is plainly not a hypothetical entity like the continuum of real numbers. To understand an assertion such as:

I own a car

is to know what has to hold in the real world for the assertion to be true – and what *that* is remains just as puzzling for a theory based on propositional representations or semantic networks as it is for the theory of mental models.

In Chapter 9, I described some words, in contradistinction to natural kind terms, as having a 'constructive' semantics that is imposed on the world. The verb *to own* is precisely of this character. Human beings have a concept of inherent possession, which is one of the pivots of their social life. Social interactions have physical consequences – an exchange of ownership, for example, usually demands utterances of various sorts, and a physical exchange of goods and money – but ownership can no more be reduced to such observable responses than a mental model can be reduced to protein molecules. To make either step is to commit the fallacy of reductionism. The inherent possession of property could not exist in a species incapable of communication, since the concept is defined by a set of conventional rights and duties that exist in their purest form as beliefs, that is, as mental entities. These beliefs are common to societies of individuals, because they can be communicated in speech and writing, and in this way they constitute a code of conduct that is intended to govern behaviour by mutual agreement. Such a code concerns what is permissible and what is not permissible. Hence, the essence of ownership can be described (see Miller and Johnson-Laird, 1976, Sec. 7.2) in four principles:

i. If I own something then it is permissible for me to use it, and it is not permissible for you to prevent me from using it, e.g., I can use it as an instrument for carrying out some action, I can consume it, I can transform it, I can make it into something else, I can destroy it, and so on.

ii. If I own something, then it is permissible for you to use it if I give you permission to use it.

iii. If I own something, then it is permissible for me to give you permission to use it.

Such conditions hold prima facie, but there are obvious exceptions to them. There is one other important aspect of inherent possession: if I own

416

something then I can transfer its ownership to someone else. This condition is an example of a concept that requires a recursive definition:

iv If I own something, then it is permissible for me to act so as to cause you to own it (and me to cease to own it).

Once the institution of property has been defined in this way, the regulative rules of society govern what things can be owned, what property can be conveyed and the mode of conveyance, and so on.

If you own a car, then prima facie all of the propositions above hold for the relation between you and the car. Certain physical relations can hold between you and the car, e.g., you can drive it, and such relations can be judged as permissible in virtue of the abstract relation of ownership. Likewise, certain physical relations can be judged as evidence for your ownership of the car, or as evidence for your having transferred its ownership to someone else. Can you own the car without knowing it? Of course. Can you own the car without anyone knowing it? Yes, because certain events that establish your ownership may have occurred outside everyone's cognizance. But, if ownership is not a physical relation and no one is aware of the relation, then surely, a Platonist would argue, there must be an Ideal realm of abstract relations, because there is nowhere else for your relation of ownership to exist. The difficulty with this view, as with the analogous claim about numbers, is how human beings are able to interact with such a domain and to apprehend its contents. Moreover, what exactly *is* different about the world after the events that establish your ownership? The answer is, by definition, that there is no effect on the course of either physical or mental events: your unknown ownership has no causal bearing on the world whatsoever. For example, if you were to use the car that you in fact own, you might be judged to have acted improperly. It is only when the events that established your ownership come to light that matters change: you will no longer be judged to have acted improperly. In short, ownership is a moral concept; concepts are mental entities; mental entities exist. What distinguishes the concept of ownership from many other concepts, and indeed frees it from the taint of subjectivism, is that it is common to societies of individuals and that it manifestly regulates interactions between them. It is a conceptual relation that is entailed by the occurrence of certain physical events with a symbolic significance, and that entails certain judgments about other behaviours. People do not merely impose the relation on the world as a 'constructive' device for making sense of events, but also impose it on themselves as a

417

regulative principle of social behaviour. And they can impose it retrospec-
tively, as in the case of your unknown ownership of the car.

Regardless of whether the details of this analysis are correct, they suggest
a conspectus for the treatment of abstract relations. Mental models contain
some elements, A', that correspond to physical elements, A, in the world.
These elements constitute an ontology of the physical contents of the
world. Certain abstract relations, however, hold between these entities
ultimately in virtue of the contents of mental models. That is to say, people
act towards the entities in the world in particular ways, and make judge-
ments about them, because of certain relations that exist only in their
models of the world. Although these relations do not correspond to
anything in the physical situation, they do depend for their existence on
the occurrence of certain physical events: ownership cannot be created
merely by an act of imagination.

The procedures for constructing and evaluating models of abstract
relations depend on access to the relevant background knowledge. For
example, a mental model of the assertion:

I sold my car to Stuart for a hundred pounds

requires a kinematic sequence in which the first 'frame' represents me as
the owner of a car and Stuart as the possessor of a hundred pounds:

$$Phil \rightarrow car \qquad Stuart \rightarrow £100$$

where the arrow denotes a relation between the tokens that represents the
relation of possession. In the next frame, which represents a later time,
there has been an exchange of the two entities:

$$Phil \rightarrow £100 \qquad Stuart \rightarrow car$$

The model must also represent the fact that the cause of the exchange is
a pair of reciprocal and intentional actions on the part of Stuart and myself.
(Various aspects of this model are assumed by default, i.e., to be taken
for granted unless there is evidence to the contrary.) Background knowledge
about ownership can then play a role in the interpretation of subsequent
discourse. If I assert that after I sold the car, I drove it without Stuart's
permission, the addressee will know that I have done something that is
not normally permissible.

As theorists, our notion of what we can imagine is too often limited to
what we can visualize. Fortunately, our imaginations are not as limited as
we imagine. We cannot perceive an abstract relation such as ownership,
but only states of affairs that might count as evidence for the existence of

such a relation. How then do we know about ownership, and how are we able to envisage particular instances of it? The answer that I have given treats such relations as in essence constitutive theories about the world – theories that in themselves bring about the existence of certain relations, since those relations are deontic. As social animals, we regulate our society by conventions that govern the physical transactions between us, but these transactions only make sense in a conceptual world of social conventions. We create (or acquire) the conventions, and, most importantly, we can describe both them and our behaviour in the light of them to one another. When we talk about them, our descriptions make contact with our repository of knowledge, and this knowledge lies behind the models of discourse that we construct.

The structure of mental models

Although mental models are an old idea that goes back at least to Craik's (1943) programmatic work, they are, in comparison to current psychological theories of meaning, a new sort of representation with a new sort of form, and in this section I am going to spell out how a constraint on their structure distinguishes them from other forms of representation postulated by other theories of meaning. The constraint derives, in part, from the notion that representations should be economical, and hence that every element in a mental model, including its structural relations, should play a symbolic role. There should be no aspects of structure that are vacuous or lacking in significance. I have tacitly followed this principle in that the structure of the models I have presented has depended wholly on the relations that they are intended to represent. This principle, together with my earlier argument that all our knowledge of the world depends on mental models, leads to the following constraint:

9. The principle of structural identity: The structures of mental models are identical to the structures of the states of affairs, whether perceived or conceived, that the models represent.

One consequence of this constraint is that mental models differ from truth tables, Euler circles and Venn diagrams, which all have structures that are not identical to the states of affairs they represent. Truth tables capture only the truth-functional relations between propositions; Euler circles and Venn diagrams map descriptions of finite sets into infinities of points. They have artificial structures invented by logicians and acquired by learning (see Chapters 3–5). Likewise, mental models differ both from the propositional representations that I have advocated, which are close to the linguistic form of sentences, and from the more general sorts of propositional representation, which embrace a wide variety of formats from the predicate calculus to semantic networks. To substantiate this claim, I shall compare mental models with semantic networks.

For a semantic network to represent the content of a sentence such as:

Every man owns a car

it is necessary to introduce some special machinery lacking in earlier versions of network theory. Thus, Hendrix (1979) uses a system of partitioned networks of the sort illustrated in Figure 15.3 to cope with quantified assertions. The basic idea is that an *isa* pointer from the representation of a sentence (in 'scratch' space) to a node such as MEN (in background knowledge) corresponds to: x is a man. If a node occurs in both the antecedent partition and the consequent partition of a sentence, then it represents the variable x in a sentence of the form:

If x is a so-and-so, then x is a such-and-such

and by convention the variable can be treated as universally quantified:

For any x, if x is a so-and-so, then x is a such-and-such.

The sentence 'Every man owns a car' likewise depends on partitioning the sentence into an antecedent and a consequent as shown in Figure 15.3. The antecedent x is a man is represented by an *isa* pointer to the node MEN. The consequent x owns a car consists of a node with an *isa* pointer to the representation of OWNINGS, and the node has two other arguments: an agent consisting of the node in the antecedent, and an object consisting of a node with an *isa* pointer to the representation of CARS. Hence, the representation as a whole is equivalent to:

For any x, if x is a man, then x owns a y which is a car.

Such a representation, however, is not a natural mental model, because it violates the structural constraint, i.e., its structure does not correspond to that of the state of affairs described by the sentence. In that state of affairs, there is a certain number of men and each man owns a car. Hence, in general terms, there are two sets of entities and a mapping between them. The semantic network has a very different structure comprising a set of four partitions containing eight nodes with various links between them. The network representation is not isomorphic to our conception of the particular situation that it describes. In the case of a mental model of the

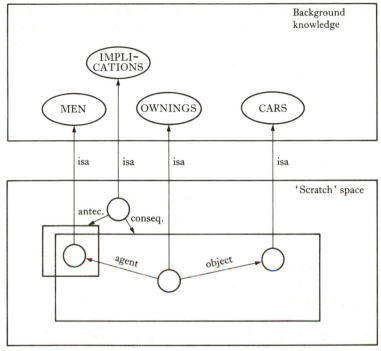

Note: The '*isa*' links between nodes denote class-membership. If a node occurs in both the antecedent and the consequent space of an implication, it represents a universally quantified variable.

Figure 15.3 The representation of 'Every man owns a car' using a partitioned semantic network (Hendrix, 1979).

assertion, however, there is a direct structural correspondence:

$$man \rightarrow car$$
$$man \rightarrow car$$
$$(car)$$

The model has a set of tokens that corresponds to the set of men, a set of tokens that corresponds to the set of cars, and a mapping between the two sets of tokens that corresponds to the mapping between the two sets of entities. The cardinalities of the corresponding sets in the two domains may be different, but this difference, as I shall show subsequently, is of no account.

Mental models also differ in *function* from representations in a semantic network. A network representation is functionally equivalent to an uninterpreted formula in the predicate calculus: a semantic network has no machinery for assigning a truth value to an assertion. Ironically, a semantic network requires a semantic interpretation. Hence, a network representation of a sentence is like a propositional representation: it is a description of a set of models – those that would be assigned to it by the semantic component, if one were provided. A mental model, however, is functionally equivalent to that set of models, since it is a representative sample from them.

A typology of mental models

In the previous sections of this chapter, I have considered a number of fundamental questions about mental models with a view to clarifying their theoretical status. The answers to these questions have revealed a number of constraints on possible mental models. In particular, I have shown that mental models can contain tokens that correspond to entities in the world, that the properties of these tokens and the relations between them correspond to our conception of the states of affairs that the models represent, and that this correspondence applies to abstract relations such as ownership. My aim here is to formulate an explanatorily adequate account by using the constraints to specify the types of possible mental model. The typology is informal and tentative, but I believe that its essentials are correct. There is an important distinction between what I shall call 'physical' models and 'conceptual' models. Physical models represent the physical world; conceptual models represent more abstract matters. I shall begin by considering the six major types of physical models.

A simple *relational* model is a static 'frame' consisting of a finite set of tokens representing a finite set of physical entities, a finite set of properties of the tokens representing the physical properties of the entities, and a finite set of relations between the tokens representing physical relations between the entities.

A *spatial* model consists of a relational model in which the only relations between the entities are spatial, and the model represents these relations by locating tokens within a dimensional space (typically of two or three dimensions). A spatial model can satisfy the properties of ordinary metric space; in particular, its dimensions can be psychologically continuous in that the array is fine-grained, and all distances can satisfy the triangle inequality, i.e., the distance between any two points is never greater than the sum of the distances between each of them and some third point.

A *temporal* model consists of a sequence of spatial 'frames' (of a constant dimensionality) that occurs in a temporal order corresponding to the temporal order of events (though not necessarily in real time).

A *kinematic* model consists of a temporal model that is psychologically continuous. The model accordingly represents changes and movements of the depicted entities with no temporal discontinuities. Such a model may of course run in real time, and will certainly do so if the model derives from perception.

A *dynamic* model is a kinematic model in which, in addition, there are relations between certain frames representing the causal relations between the events depicted.

An *image* is similar to the '$2\frac{1}{2}$-D sketch' postulated by Marr in the process of vision, except that its source is visual imagination. It consists of a viewer-centred representation of the visible characteristics of an underlying three-dimensional spatial or kinematic model. It therefore corresponds to a view of (or projection from) the object or state of affairs represented in the underlying model.

There is no precise line between perception and conception, but it is plausible to assume that perception normally produces a dynamic, metric, 3-D model of the world, in which each 'frame' characterizes the volumetric shapes of objects and the spatial relations between them, in terms of an object-centred co-ordinate system (cf. Marr, 1982). The only controversial aspect of this claim concerns causation; it is an abstract relation, but the perceptual system appears to be sensitive to cues to it (cf. Miller and Johnson-Laird, 1976, Sec. 2.6). Hence, these six types of model may be classified under the general heading of 'physical' models in that, with the exception of causality, they correspond directly to the physical world. They can represent perceptible situations, but they cannot represent either abstract relations or anything other than determinate physical descriptions.

Mental models apart from those deriving from perception may be intended to represent a true situation, a possible situation, or an imaginary situation (see Chapter 3). Individuals must keep in mind the status of a model, but they can do so easily because they can remember what led to the construction of the model in the first place. Such models may be either physical or conceptual, though most discourse calls for a conceptual model.

Conceptual models demand the existence of machinery for their own recursive revision. They also require a way of representing various connectives, though conjunction can be represented directly by co-presence within a model. Negation can be accommodated by a one-place relation associated with a model, or a component of a model; the relation is treated by the procedures for interpreting models as signifying that the model, or the component of the model, does not correspond to the relevant state of affairs. Thus, if a token is negated, the entity that it represents does not exist; and if a relation is negated, the corresponding entities are not in that relation. Disjunction can be accommodated by a two-place relation between models, or components of models, signifying a disjunction of the states of affairs they represent. Thus, an inclusive disjunction between tokens indicates that at least one of the entities exists; and a disjunction between relations indicates that at least one of them holds for the relevant entities. Unfortunately, disjunction violates the constraint (5) on the representation of indeterminacies: a sequence of disjunctions soon leads to a computationally explosive number of possibilities. This fact presumably lies at the heart of the well-established difficulty of absorbing disjunctive information (cf. Bruner, Goodnow, and Austin, 1956).

The use of connectives in mental models is straightforward if their truth conditions are elementary. The interpretation of conditionals, however, depends on constructing a mental model of a scenario in which the antecedent is realized – a process that is sensitive to the information in the consequent – and then interpreting the consequent with respect to this model (see Chapter 3). Hence, if a conditional as a whole is to be represented *de novo*, it is necessary to construct the antecedent model and the consequent model, and then form a relation between them corresponding to the relation conveyed by the conditional. As we saw, conditionals can express a variety of relations – from material implication to causation – depending on their constituent propositions and the particular background knowledge that they elicit in comprehension.

Conceptual models also need machinery for quantifiers. Monadic models are used for syllogistic reasoning, and the reader should by now be familiar with their broad outlines. Thus, for example, to represent the assertion:

All sculptors are artists

a model of the following form was proposed in Chapter 5:

$$sculptor = artist$$
$$sculptor = artist$$
$$(artist)$$

where the token 'sculptor' is here a notational device to show that the corresponding mental token represents an individual as being a sculptor. The notation of enclosing a token within parentheses likewise corresponds to a special device in conceptual models which represents that it is uncertain whether or not the corresponding individual exists (in the model's domain).

424

This notation is obviously arbitrary: how such tokens are actually represented in the mind is unlikely ever to be known. Models must also be able to represent: identity, non-identity, and a lack of information either way. My notation follows the principle that two tokens of the same type represent different individuals, and that otherwise the three possibilities are respectively represented by an identity symbol, its negation, and the absence of either symbol.

Although there appears to be an important ontological difference between entities and their properties, and the two are certainly distinguished in perceptual models, there are no crucial differences in their logical behaviour. I have therefore treated them uniformly in conceptual models. (If it were desirable to distinguish them, then it would be necessary to introduce machinery for conjoining properties to tokens representing individuals, for negating them, and so on.) There are four major types of conceptual model.

A *monadic* model represents assertions about individuals, their properties, and identities between them. It consists of three components:

   i. a finite number of tokens representing individual entities and properties.

  ii. two binary relations, identity ($=$) and non-identity ($\neq$), either of which may hold between any pair of individual tokens from two different sets to indicate that the corresponding individuals are, or are not, identical. Non-identity is the negation of the identity relation.

 iii. a special notational device (to which the recursive revision is sensitive) indicating that it is uncertain whether there are any entities of a particular sort.

A monadic model can accommodate only one-place predicates denoting properties, and identities and non-identities. For more general assertions, it is necessary to employ:

A *relational* model, which introduces in addition a finite number of relations, possibly abstract, between the tokens in a monadic model.

Certain terms in natural language denote functions, and hence a special case of a relational model is one that contains a finite set of mappings (many-to-one or one-to-one) from the tokens of one set to the tokens of another. Such a model is required to represent an assertion such as:

There are more a's than b's

425

which calls for a mapping of the form

$$a\text{----}b$$
$$a\text{----}b$$
$$a$$

The machinery that has so far been introduced suffices for the construction of finite models of assertions with variables that range over individuals. It also suffices for handling proper names, definite and indefinite expressions, and all the customary types of referring expression in natural language which were discussed in the previous chapter. Quantifiers of the form *more than half of the* X can be handled by admitting more complex truth conditions that guide recursive revision. Thus, the assertion 'More than half of the X are Y' can be represented in the standard form of a relational model:

$$x = y$$
$$x = y$$
$$x = y$$
$$x \quad y$$

but the truth conditions of the assertion constrain revisions of the model so that indeed more than half of the x's are identical to y's.

There are conceptual equivalents, of course, to the various types of physical models: that is, abstract entities, properties, and relations, can be represented in static 'frames', spatial, temporal, kinematic, and dynamic models. Conceptual models, however, also require a number of novel features. A great gain in their representational power derives from recursion, which is manifest in several different ways. One case arises in discourse about discourse. In order to represent such discourse, it is necessary to introduce mental models of the relation between symbols and their corresponding entities in the world:

A *meta-linguistic* model contains tokens corresponding to linguistic expressions, and certain abstract relations between them and elements in a mental model of any type (including a meta-linguistic model). The abstract relations include key semantic ones such as *refers to* and *means*.

An assertion such as:

One of the men is called 'Jim'

requires the following sort of meta-linguistic model:

$$\begin{array}{ccc} & & m \\ \text{'Jim'} & \rightarrow & m \\ & & m \end{array}$$

426

where quotation marks are used to signify a token representing a linguistic expression, and the arrow denotes the relation of reference.

The definition above of meta-linguistic models is recursive, and so one model can be embedded within another. In theory, human beings possess the ability to relate a symbolic expression 'P' to a corresponding model that satisfies it:

where 'P' designates, not the sixteenth letter of the alphabet, but some arbitrary assertion. The ability to construct meta-linguistic models makes it possible to form a mental model of this very relation. A special case arises in the meta-linguistic model of an assertion of the form:

'P' is true.

In this case, the mental model relates 'P' to a mental model that can be mapped into the real world:

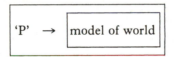

where the arrow designates the relation of truth. Here, I am not trying to advance an analysis of truth, but merely to illustrate the recursive embedding of mental models. Thus, in order to represent an assertion of the form:

what ' "P" is true' means is that 'P' corresponds to the world

it is necessary to introduce a meta-meta-linguistic model:

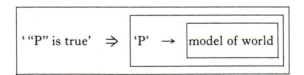

where the double arrow designates the relation of meaning. We shall encounter another form of self-embedding in the subsequent section on propositional attitudes.

Recursion also occurs with set-membership. The basic relation is represented by an identity between an individual token and one token in a set. A set as a whole, however, can be a member of another set. Earlier, in Chapter 6, I represented this relation by using the notation:

$$\left.\begin{array}{c} a \\ a \\ a \end{array}\right\} = \begin{array}{c} b \\ b \\ b \\ b \end{array}$$

which shows that the set of a's is a member of the set of b's. The set of a's, however, can be treated as an entity in its own right, and this possibility is admitted within the theory:

A *set-theoretic* model contains a finite number of tokens directly representing sets. It may also contain a finite set of associated tokens designating the abstract properties of a set, and a finite set of relations (including identity and non-identity) between the tokens designating sets.

This machinery allows quantification over sets. The danger is that it may give rise to the paradoxes of naive set theory, e.g., Russell's celebrated paradox of the class of all classes that are not members of themselves. A simple way to illustrate the problem is to consider the assertion:

Some bibliographies list themselves and some do not.

A mental model of the form:

$$b1 = \left\{\begin{array}{c} \text{‘b1’} \\ \text{‘b2’} \\ \text{‘b3’} \end{array}\right.$$

represents the fact that a bibliography, b1, consists of three names including its own. Hence, the bracket is equivalent in force to the standard notation of set theory:

$$b1 = \{\text{‘b1’, ‘b2’, ‘b3’}\}$$

We can similarly define a bibliography of the bibliographies that do not list themselves:

$$b6 = \{\text{‘b3’, ‘b4’, ‘b5’}\}$$

But, consider the expression 'a bibliography that lists all and only bibliographies that do not list themselves'. Does b6 satisfy the truth conditions of this expression? Plainly not, because it omits at least one bibliography that does not list itself, namely, b6 itself. Yet obviously, if we rectify this omission:

$$b6 = \{\text{‘b3’, ‘b4’, ‘b5’, ‘b6’}\}$$

we violate the truth conditions of the expression, because b6 is no longer a bibliography of just those bibliographies that do not list themselves: it contains at least one bibliography that does list itself, namely, b6 itself. It follows, of course, that there cannot be a bibliography of all and only bibliographies that do not list themselves. Such a conclusion is hardly disturbing: there are many other self-contradictory descriptions that cannot be satisfied by any entity. A parallel argument, however, establishes the irreducibly paradoxical nature of the set of all sets that are not members of themselves. Should this set include itself as a member? If it doesn't, then it should, because it will be a set that is not a member of itself. If it does, then it shouldn't, because it won't be a set that is not a member of itself. This is a disastrous result given the goal of formulating a system for manipulating sets that is free from internal contradictions.

Should the theory of mental models admit such contradictions? One might be tempted to allow them. After all, even logicians have been known to espouse inconsistent theories, and some way of representing the meaning of self-contradictory expressions would seem to be necessary. However, the representation of self-contradictory expressions depends, not on having an inconsistent system, but on determining, as in the bibliographical example, that there cannot be any mental model that satisfies the expression. Moreover, if the system of thought itself were intrinsically irrational, then it would be impossible to account for either valid inference in daily life or the development of rational disciplines such as mathematics and logic. There is, however, a crucial constraint on the conceptual operation of forming sets that preserves the machinery of mental models from intrinsic inconsistencies:

10. The principle of set formation: If a set is to be formed from *sets*, then the members of those sets must first be specified.

That, of course, is the conceptual significance of the bracketting operation that I described above. The general principle is that before a set can be represented as a member of a set, its own members must be determined. It is therefore impossible to construct a model of a set that is (or is not) a member of itself. This constraint suffices to prevent the paradoxes: the mind is not intrinsically inconsistent.

There may be types of mental model that have eluded this classification and that will be discovered only as a result of further investigations. Nevertheless, the typology has revealed the essential character of mental models: they derive from a relatively small set of elements and recursive operations on those elements; their representational power depends on a further set of procedures for constructing and evaluating them. The major constraints on mental models derive from the perceived and conceived structure of the world, from the conceptual relations governing ontology, and from the need to maintain a system free from contradictions.

Propositional attitudes and the embedding of mental models

Because language is used to create worlds by proxy, it does not matter, as far as psychological processes are concerned, whether these worlds are real or imaginary. The processes by which discourse is produced or understood do not differ strikingly between factual assertions and fictitious ones. These matters do not even seem to affect linguistic usage in many languages, though perhaps there are languages where existence/non-existence has a morphological reflex.

Since even little children can understand assertions about beliefs, hopes, and other propositional attitudes, one might imagine that the semantic analysis of such expressions is easy. Infants chat about who still believes in fairies, perhaps without even a tacit knowledge of scope and opacity. In fact, propositional attitudes present severe problems for model-theoretic semantics as described in Chapter 8. The difficulty is perhaps not surprising, because that attempt to relate language to models eschews the notion of the human mind's acting as an intermediary between the two. When language explicitly refers to mental attitudes towards propositions, the theory has no apparatus for such matters. What I want to show is how the machinery for embedding one mental model within another readily copes with the semantics of propositional attitudes.

If the meaning of a sentence is constructed compositionally, then replacing one expression by another that is synonymous with it should have no effect on the meaning of the sentence overall. This principle breaks down with propositional attitudes: when one expression is replaced by another with the same extension, the resulting sentence may have a different truth value. For example, the sentence 'Mrs Thatcher thinks that the man who leaked Cabinet secrets is a traitor' may be true, but 'Mrs Thatcher thinks that her husband is a traitor' may be false, even if the two noun phrases are co-referential. This phenomenon is not critical for a model-theoretic analysis since the two co-referential expressions have different intensions: there are possible worlds in which they pick out different individuals. The real difficulty arises when one expression is replaced by another with the same intension. Such examples arise when one necessary

430

truth (or self-contradiction) is replaced by another, since they have the same truth value in all possible worlds. Nevertheless, one cannot be substituted for another with impunity; for instance, 'John believes that $2 + 2 = 4$' may be true, but 'John believes that there is no decision procedure for the predicate calculus' may be false. The same problem can arise when one expression is replaced by another that it entails, e.g., 'Mary believes that every integer has a successor' may be true, but 'Mary believes that there are a denumerably infinite number of integers' may be false.

Theorists have tried three main approaches to the problem of propositional attitudes. First, some philosophers have adopted what Robert Stalnaker calls the 'heroic' solution: they have ignored the facts of ordinary discourse. Hintikka (1962), for instance, formalized a concept of knowledge in which individuals are said to 'know' the logical consequences of their 'knowledge'. Another heroic solution, the so-called doctrine of 'eliminative materialism', argues that the folk psychology entrenched in propositional attitudes is simply wrong: its assumptions are mistaken, its ontology an illusion, and the advance of neuroscience will lead us to abandon our current languages in favour of new languages that have no place for propositional attitudes (Churchland, 1981). The fact remains, however, that people ascribe truth values to sentences, and, if it is conceded that there is nothing suspect about this practice, then it is difficult to see how there could be anything dubious about the notion that an individual holds that an assertion is true (or false). Such claims are certainly sensible to most speakers, and should accordingly be susceptible to semantic analysis.

Second, philosophers who are sceptical about possible worlds and intensions – those 'creatures of darkness', as Quine once called them – have attempted to analyse assertions about propositional attitudes as relations between individuals and sentences. Quine (1960) himself tried to treat clauses describing beliefs as though they were direct quotations of sentences, e.g.:

The police chief believes-to-be-true: 'The hijackers are still in the plane.'

Unfortunately, this analysis hardly applies in such cases as: 'The Martian believes-to-be-true "We are friendly" ', since the Martian may not speak English. Likewise, Quine's alternative tactic of treating the propositional verb and its complement as a simple unitary predicate:

The police chief believes-that-the-hijackers-are-still-in-the-plane

abandons the principle of compositionality. Another strategy is to hold that beliefs are relations holding between individuals and sentences in the language of the mind, and this doctrine has been espoused both by philosophers (Field, 1978; Lycan, 1981) and by artificial intelligencers (Moore and Hendrix, 1982). Any verbally expressed proposition can certainly be an object of belief, but the converse principle is open to doubt. A sentence such as:

What Meister Eckhart believed about God could not be expressed in words

seems sufficiently sensible not to be judged as necessarily false. Hence, there are problems for this approach if the language of the mind is supposed to map directly into natural language – an assumption that is often made.

Third, theorists have introduced more fine-grained notions of meaning – of several different varieties – so that necessary truths cease to be equivalent to each other. 'Why be difficult when with a little more effort you can be impossible?' runs the old adage, and one way to specify a more refined semantics is to introduce *impossible* worlds (see Hintikka, 1975). This stratagem allows the intension of a sentence to be defined as a function from the set of possible and impossible worlds to a truth value, and one contradiction is then distinguished from another by virtue of the fact that they are true in different impossible worlds. The problem with impossible worlds, apart from the fact that they *are* impossible, is that they complicate even the simplest operations of model-theoretic semantics. Another method of developing a more refined semantics has been advocated by Bigelow (1978) and Cresswell (1980). It takes into account the way in which the intension of a sentence is derived from the intension of its parts (cf. Lewis, 1972) and can accordingly distinguish between two sentences with the same intension. Still another method, advocated by Klein (1979), makes use of the idea, which I described in Chapter 8, of using two sets of possible worlds, one to represent the meanings of propositions and the other to represent the contexts that determine which proposition a particular use of a sentence expresses. Finally, one can take propositions as primitive and unanalysed, and postulate that they are sufficiently fine-grained to inhibit the substitution *salva veritate* of expressions that are merely intensionally equivalent (see Thomason, 1981). All of these approaches seem to lead to over-refinement. There is nothing wrong in principle with the semantic mill grinding ever finer grains of meaning, but its work will be redundant for most assertions that do not express propositional attitudes.

In the framework of mental models, there is a straightforward solution to the problem of propositional attitudes. A propositional attitude is a relation between an individual and that individual's mental model of the relevant state of affairs. To represent a propositional attitude, it is merely necessary to allow a recursive embedding of mental models, such as occurs in meta-linguistic models, but based on abstract relations including beliefs, hopes, and thoughts:

A mental model can represent an abstract relation between a token representing an individual and a mental model (of any sort) representing a state of affairs.

This specification is recursive and accordingly allows for an arbitrary degree of embedding of mental models within mental models. In practice, the capacity of working memory curtails the degree of embedding.

An assertion such as:

The police chief believes that the hijackers are in the plane

is represented by translating the clause expressing the object of the attitude:

the hijackers are in the plane

into a mental model in the usual way. This model is then embedded within a model representing the appropriate relation – here, belief – between the police chief and the embedded model.

The essential phenomenon about (other) people's beliefs is that they may be mistaken. They may believe that Santa Claus exists or that Bianca Jagger is a figment of a press agent's imagination. They may believe that Euthanasia is a country somewhere in South-East Asia, or that insecticide is the lemming-like collective suicide of a colony of social insects. They may believe that $\sqrt{2}$ is a rational number, or that a quantity of liquid is increased by pouring it from a broad beaker into a narrow one. When you mentally represent someone else's beliefs, you can insulate them totally from your own. But usually, of course, there is some communality, which will be represented in your mental model. If, for instance, you believe that all the members of the government are monetarists, and I believe that at least some of them are, the relevant part of your model of the world will correspond to the following state of affairs:

$$g = m$$
$$g = m$$
$$g = m$$
$$(m)$$

433

where 'g' denotes a member of the government and 'm', a monetarist. My model will correspond to this sort of state of affairs:

$$g = m$$
$$g = m$$
$$(g) \quad (m)$$

In your model of my beliefs, you can represent the fact that there is a certain individual about whom we agree, as is illustrated in Figure 15.4, by an identity between a token in your model and a token in your model of my model.

Your beliefs:
1. All the members of the government (g) are monetarists (m).
2. Phil (p) believes ($\rightarrow$) that at least some members of the government are monetarists.
3. We both believe that the chancellor of the exchequer (c) is a monetarist.

Your beliefs:

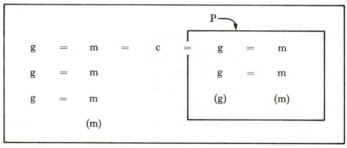

Figure 15.4 An example of a nested set of beliefs within a mental model.

This analysis can certainly accommodate the traditional cases of substituting one term for another co-referential with it. Suppose, for example, I remark:

I want to meet the man who lives at 221b Baker Street

using the description attributively (see Chapter 14). You, who know perfectly well that there is no one who lives at that address, can report my state of mind:

Phil would like to meet the man who lives at 221b Baker Street

without being committed to the existence of such an individual except in your model of my wants. What is less obvious is that even when a description is used referentially, there may be a failure of reference in such a context that does not affect the truth of the assertion. If I share the allegedly common delusion of believing that Sherlock Holmes is a real person, who lives at 221b Baker Street, who is a great detective, and so on, then you, who know all about my beliefs, may instead report my remarks in the following words:

Phil would like to meet Sherlock Holmes.

Your designation is referential by the usual criteria: you are committed to the substitution *salva veritate* of other designations that pick out the same individual in your model of my beliefs, e.g.

Phil would like to meet Professor Moriarty's mortal enemy.

Yet you do not intend to refer to an actual person. Hence, the referential–attributive distinction is independent of propositional attitudes (*pace* Hintikka, 1969, and Cole, 1978).

One unexpected consequence of the theory is that it brings to light some new problems with indefinite descriptions. Suppose, for example, Diana wants to marry a particular individual, who happens to be a snob. She may know that he is a snob, or she may not. In either case, the assertion:

Diana wants to marry a snob

can be analysed as:

There exists a snob that Diana wants to marry

though this analysis may be slightly misleading where Diana is ignorant of the man's true nature. Now, consider a different case. Diana wants to marry an English aristocrat; she has no specific individual in mind; and unfortunately she does not know that they are all snobs. You, who are fully aware of this situation, can truly assert:

Diana wants to marry a snob, though she doesn't know it.

This assertion implies neither that there exists a snob that Diana wants to marry nor that Diana wants there to exist such a snob. Hence, the analysis above fails, and so does the standard 'notional' or opaque analysis:

Diana wants there to exist a snob that she marries.

It is easy to see what is going on in terms of mental models. A model of Diana's wants contains a model in which she marries an (arbitrary) aristocrat: i.e., the model can be recursively revised to pick out any aristocrat, within reason. Diana has no belief to the effect that all aristocrats are snobs. The speaker's mental model has this model of Diana's mind embedded within it, but in addition contains the speaker's belief that all aristocrats are snobs. Hence, the speaker can argue validly:

> Diana wants to marry an aristocrat.
> All aristocrats are snobs, but Diana doesn't know it.
> ∴ Diana wants to marry a snob, but doesn't know it.

This conclusion holds in all recursive revisions of the speaker's mental model.

From a psychological perspective, the treatment of propositional attitudes in the philosophical literature seems odd because it has concentrated on single isolated beliefs. People do not have such beliefs: they have systems of belief; they have ideologies. This point leads to another unexpected consequence of the present theory: far from wanting finer grains of meaning, there are cases where a coarser grain is required in order to accommodate propositional attitudes that hinge on systems of belief. Consider the following example:

> Albert knows that only some numbers are primes.

What follows validly in virtue of its specific complement? Of course, many things could follow, but it is quite impossible to answer the question without further information. It is necessary to know about Albert's theory of arithmetic – his system of beliefs about it – before you can determine the consequences of the assertion. Hence, if Albert is under the delusion that infinite sets behave just like finite sets, then it may be valid to infer:

> Albert thinks that there are more numbers than primes.

Indeed, the two assertions may be synonymous as far as Albert is concerned. So we need coarser grains of meaning here, because the two embedded propositions are not even extensionally equivalent – one is true, and the other is false. A special case, which I have discussed elsewhere (Johnson-Laird, 1982), arises when an individual has erroneous beliefs about the meanings of words. Speakers often have only an imperfect grasp of their language, and this fact must be allowed for in the analysis of discourse about their ignorance. For example, the assertion:

> My friend thinks that transvestites are monks

could describe either an error of fact (men who dress up in women's clothes are members of some religious order – they have unusual habits, let us say) or an error of meaning (the word *transvestite* means *a member of a religious order*).

One person can have an attitude about another person's propositional attitude, and so on indefinitely:

Maggie knows that I hope that Eddie believes that his wife thinks that . . . you are here

and such assertions are accommodated by the recursive embedding of mental models within mental models. But there are constraints imposed by the nature of particular propositional attitudes. The following sentence, for example, is nonsensical:

I was aware that I was unconscious.

A special sort of embedding can arise when person A has beliefs about person B, including beliefs about B's beliefs about A, beliefs about B's beliefs about A's beliefs about B, and so on *ad infinitum*. Philip Cohen (1978) has devised a computer program that uses partitioned semantic networks nested in this way. He prevents embarrassing infinite recursions by adopting an idea from David Lewis's (1969) analysis of conventions: the regress can be stopped once there is no difference between A's belief about something and what A believes B believes A believes about it. In this way a mutual belief (see Schiffer, 1972) can be represented with finite means.

One final question: which verbs characterize propositional attitudes? The answer tends to take the form of an *ad hoc* list. But a case can be made to show that they are all verbs that contain a particular semantic primitive – one that corresponds to the idea of constructing a mental model (cf. Miller and Johnson-Laird, 1976, Sec. 7.3).

The theory of mental models solves the problems that cause difficulties for model-theoretic semantics. One person can possess a mental model of another person's belief system, and part of the representation of those beliefs can be information about their misconceptions. Assertions about an individual's propositional attitudes warrant at most those inferences that can be made from them on the basis of that person's system of beliefs and knowledge of the language. Propositional attitudes may be analysable within a model-theoretic semantics, but the simplest method of analysis depends on introducing mental models as intermediaries between language and the world. Once they are introduced, there is no need whatsoever for any special semantic machinery for propositional attitudes: all the unusual phenomena arise from embedding one model within another representing an individual's attitude towards the situation represented in the embedded model. Tokens in the embedded model may not correspond to anything in (a speaker's model of) the world, and the significance of the model may be in blatant contradiction to a veridical model, and yet an assertion describing the contents of the model will be true if the model is indeed an appropriate part of the relevant individual's own mental model.

Truth and mental models

A contingent assertion is true if it corresponds to reality; false if it conflicts with reality. We can judge an assertion to be true by evaluating it in relation to a model of the world or by establishing that it follows necessarily from other assertions known to be true. We can judge an assertion to be false by evaluating it in relation to a model of the world or by establishing that it is necessarily inconsistent with other assertions known to be true. Both correspondence and coherence thus have a role to play in verification. The evaluation of an assertion with respect to a coherent body of knowledge requires no more than the inferential machinery that I modelled in the program for interpreting spatial descriptions (see Chapter 11). The comparison of an assertion with reality is a more problematical enterprise, particularly because of the fundamental incompleteness of knowledge.

What does it mean to say that a discourse is true because it corresponds to reality? The heart of the problem is to show how language relates to the world through the agency of the mind. The line of research that seems most promising might be termed the 'psychologizing' of model-theoretic semantics – the recognition that many aspects of comprehension are best thought of as constructive processes that yield models of discourse. This approach is most discernible in Hans Kamp's (1980) work on discourse models. The same tendency (though with an underlying Realist philosophy) can be found in Jon Barwise's (1980) theory of situation semantics. Barwise uses model-theoretic techniques to give a semantic interpretation of a sentence that consists, not of truth values in a set of possible worlds, but of types of situation in which the sentence is true. A *situation*, as in common parlance, consists of a number of individuals, possessing certain specific properties and lacking others, and related in certain specific ways and not in others. Like a mental model, however, a situation is usually incomplete, failing to specify whether or not an individual within it has certain properties or enters into certain relations. A situation is accordingly more like the way in which we perceive or conceive the world than an abstract world model.

438

Kamp (1980) argues independently that certain phenomena can be properly analysed within a model-theoretic semantics only by using both a model of the discourse and a model of the world. Since a discourse represents just a part of what the world would be like if the discourse were true, Kamp formulates the following definition of truth. A text represented in a discourse model is true provided that there is a mapping of the individuals and events in the discourse model into the real world model in a way that preserves their respective properties and the relations between them.

This approach provides an elegant account of temporal reference. Most previous theorists have assumed an underlying semantics for time consisting of an infinite sequence of durationless moments over which such relations as *later than* can be defined (see Chapter 8). Kamp (1979) proposes instead that the hearer constructs a discourse model in which tensed verbs and other temporal expressions refer to events of finite duration. On the assumption that two events overlap each other in time or else one of them wholly precedes the other, the linear sequence of durationless moments can be reconstructed for the real world as an idealized limit. Thus, a given event can be treated as both 'punctual' in the discourse model and as extending over a divisible period of time in the real world model. This twofold analysis appears to be precisely what is needed for the semantics of temporal expressions.

Kamp has introduced a device new to model-theoretic semantics – a discourse model that mediates between language and model-structure – in order to give a fuller account of the truth conditions of connected discourse. The need for such intermediary models reflects the fact that natural language is both made and used by human beings, who certainly rely on representations of discourse. In some respects, however, Kamp's discourse models themselves remain abstract idealizations; to take one example, they are formulated so that they never have to be revised in the light of subsequent information in the discourse.

The way to define truth for mental models is to take advantage of Kamp's notion of an appropriate mapping and to combine it with the idea that a mental model is a representative sample. As we saw earlier, the assertion 'Every man owns a car' yields a model of the form:

$$man \rightarrow car$$
$$man \rightarrow car$$
$$(car)$$

439

This model is merely a representative sample from an infinite set of possible models, from which an illustrative subset has been drawn and depicted in Figure 15.5. Any member of the set could in theory be generated by the recursive procedures for revising the representative sample. At the heart of the theory of mental models lies the following idea: a mental model represents the *extension* of an assertion, i.e., the situation it describes, and the recursive machinery for revising the model represents the *intension* of the assertion, i.e., the set of all possible situations it describes. Of course,

	2	3	4	...
0	m → c	m → c	m → c	...
	m → c	m → c	m → c	...
		m → c	m → c	...
			m → c	...
1	m → c	m → c	m → c	...
	m → c	m → c	m → c	...
	c	m → c	m → c	...
		c	m → c	...
			c	...
2	m → c	m → c	m → c	...
	m → c	m → c	m → c	...
	c	m → c	m → c	...
	c	c	m → c	...
		c	c	...
			c	...
...	...	...	...	...
...	...	...	...	...
...	...	...	...	...

Figure 15.5 A subset of the denumerably infinite set of models corresponding to an assertion of the form 'Every man owns a car.' The number of men (m) owning (→) cars (c) is taken to be at least two, and the number of other cars in the domain of discourse is assumed to range from zero upwards.

one needs a non-deterministic device to deliver the actual extension, and it is simulated by the recursive machinery. Supposing that the assertion 'Every man owns a car' is true, one of the models in the set of possible models will correspond exactly to reality and even the cardinalities of the sets of tokens and the sets of entities will be identical. In terms of Montague's model-theoretic analysis (see Chapter 8), if the sentence is true, the actual set of persons owning cars (of type $\langle e, t \rangle$), comprising, say, the individuals j, k, 1, will be a member of the set denoted by every man, i.e., the set of all sets containing every man (of type $\langle \langle e, t \rangle, t \rangle$). If j and 1 are the only men in the universe of discourse, then the extension of every man is: $\{\{j, 1\}, \{j, k, 1\}, \{j, k, 1, m\}, \ldots\}$. The set of persons owning cars

440

{j, k, l} is indeed a member of this set, and the sentence is accordingly true on this model-theoretic interpretation.

In principle, we can assume that a discourse is true if and only if there is at least one mental model of it that can be mapped into the real world model in a way that preserves the content of the mental model – i.e., the individuals represented in the mental model occur in the real world with the same properties and the same relations holding between them. This definition, however, is only a first approximation to what is needed.

The reader will recall from Chapter 9 that natural kind terms have incomplete intensions, which may not even be fixed. For example, a doctor observing a peculiar fever that he has never encountered before may say to himself, 'I am going to call this condition "Ebstein's fever".' (His name is Ebstein.) He intends to pick out a particular condition, whatever its ultimate underlying structure turns out to be. He thereby introduces a new natural kind term into the language, which he can convey to others by describing the stereotypical features of the condition and, of course, by exhibiting patients suffering from it. Communication about Ebstein's fever is entirely feasible – if it were not, then it would be unlikely that anyone could improve our knowledge of it. Mental models can be constructed on the basis of whatever is known about the meaning of the term, even on a mere stereotype associated with it. Ignorance of an intension, even if that ignorance is universal, is no bar to successful communication: a token can be introduced into a mental model to stand for something known to be subsumed by a term that has only the merest clue to its intension. If you are a Platonic realist, you can argue that it none the less has an intension that picks out the same entity in every possible world. (Such views are perfectly all right amongst consenting philosophers in private.) But, as I suggested, these intensions are idle wheels in the intellectual traffic of the world. As doctors encounter more cases of Ebstein's fever, talk about their findings, and so on, they may change their minds about the term. They may decide that it denotes not a unitary disease but several with similar signs and symptoms, or that it denotes no disease whatsoever and that Ebstein was deluded (cf. Asher, 1972), or that it indeed denotes, say, a new viral disease. There need not be a simple causal chain by which natural kind terms pass from one speaker to another; they may even change their extensions. Such changes are possible only because although their intensions are not in the mind, people can communicate what is to be found there.

There are terms that do not have a fixed extension, and hence that do not have a fixed intension either. There are terms that have only an incomplete intension, and in this case a linguistic community may cope with them in a way that parallels the recursive revision of mental models – plumping for an interpretation that it may be necessary to revise subsequently. The basic working principle for the interpretation of discourse is that individuals construct mental models on the basis of what they know about the meanings of words and what they know they do not know. Where everyone is ignorant, the recursive procedures for reconstructing the model will obviously admit a wider range of possibilities. If, for instance, I say in that splendid language coined by Anthony Burgess in *A Clockwork Orange*:

The gloopy malchicks are scatting razdrazily to the mesto

the model you are likely to build will be rather impoverished, but it will rule out some possibilities.

It is now clear how to formulate a more comprehensive definition of truth than the one offered above. If a discourse has complete truth conditions, it is true with respect to the world if and only if it has at least one mental model that can be mapped into the real world. If a discourse has only partial truth conditions (like the assertion about the gloopy malchicks), it is false with respect to the world if it has no mental model that can be mapped into the real world. If its truth conditions are not fixed or not known, then, to use Russell's aphorism about mathematics, we never know what we are talking about, nor whether what we are saying is true. Indeed, we cannot know.

Such an analysis of truth does not, of course, tell one anything about how to verify assertions. It suggests, however, that if you wish to verify a discourse directly, you must get yourself into a position in which you can compare a model of the discourse with reality. It is relatively rare that speakers are in a position to make such a comparison; more often, they can compare a discourse with an independent, though indirect, model of the world. Language is primarily used to communicate the content of a model from one individual to another. There is not often much point in communicating information that is perceptually available to the addressee.

The size of mental models and the representation of infinity

If you see a crowd of spectators at a football match and you are told that it contains 50,492 people, you cannot see that there are 50,492 people there. You may have learned to estimate the size of crowds, but this skill depends on perception rather than underlies it, and besides, you are hardly likely to estimate so precise a number. If you are asked to imagine a crowd of 50,492 people, you may be able to form an image of a sea of faces, but you will be similarly unable to determine how many individuals your image contains. In vision, you can subitize only a small number of individuals; in imagery, you can knowingly represent only a small number, too. This restricted ability to imagine specific numbers of entities has led critics to assume that images, and by implication mental models, have only a limited role in the interpretation of discourse. A mental model could not represent an assertion such as:

Two hundred men are driving cars

because it is impossible to set up a representation of so many individuals. Yet, most people have no difficulty in understanding assertions about two hundred individuals.

How does one understand such an assertion? The answer depends on its meaning, which is that there is a set of men who are driving cars and that the set can be mapped one-to-one into the positive integers up to and including the number 200. This information can be grasped without having to construct a mental model containing the complete mapping. One way of thinking of the representation of the sentence is therefore as a propositional representation that is set up but never actually used in a procedure to construct a mental model. It is a cheque that is not presented for payment, but which, if presented, would be honoured. Of course, the procedure could be used to produce a scaled-down mental model in which a manipulable number of tokens is taken to represent the set of two hundred individuals. This stratagem would be particularly useful if it were necessary to make an inference based on the assertion. The model could be used to produce a conclusion that could be scaled back up to the appropriate numerical quantity. Another possibility is to use the procedure to construct a fragment of the model depicting a set of men driving cars, with the part of the procedure representing the number 200 functioning as a propositional-like label attached to the model. Just such a representation seems to be called for when you look at the crowd at the football match after you have been told that it contains 50,492 individuals.

Mental models of discourse are used in order to experience vicariously the events that are described, to make inferences from them, or to compare them with reality. In the case of assertions about large numbers, a vicarious experience does not depend on an exact representation: an inference can usually be made by recourse to the method described above or to formal mathematical techniques, but a comparison with reality does require the cheque to be cashed either by laboriously counting the relevant entities or by some alternative method for enumerating them. It is hardly essential to capture the precise number in the mental model itself.

Mental models can contain only a finite number of entities, but we can reason about infinite quantities and sets of infinite size such as the natural numbers. There is accordingly a distinction between naive or intuitive reasoning, which is directly based on mental models, and mathematical reasoning, which relies on other mechanisms. It is not my task in this book to account for mathematical reasoning, but a few remarks about it would seem to be appropriate. Outside mathematics, most conceptions of infinity are vague, confused or erroneous; within mathematics, it was not until the work of Cantor and other nineteenth-century mathematicians that infinity was put upon a secure foundation, and not until 1961 that Abraham Robinson provided a precise formulation of infinitesimals. Common sense, which is commonly nonsense, suggests that there must be twice as many numbers as even numbers; and yet each number can be paired with an even number in the mapping:

$$
\begin{array}{cccc}
1 & 2 & 3 & \ldots & n \\
| & | & | & & | \\
2 & 4 & 6 & \ldots & 2n
\end{array}
$$

This seemingly paradoxical state of affairs led some earlier mathematicians to conclude that infinite numbers could not exist. The resolution of the paradox is simple: if one set is part of another, then for infinite sets it does not follow that they are of different sizes.

Our ability to grasp and to reason about infinite quantities is puzzling. Consider, for instance, how we understand the proposition that every natural number has a successor. Plainly, we can represent this assertion by constructing a mental model of it, using a propositional label (like the familiar string of dots) that corresponds to 'infinity'. Such a label, however, requires elucidation, and the problem – as we found in the analysis of abstract concepts – is an ontological one. If assertions about infinite sets are true, to what in the real world do they correspond?

Our first intuitions about infinity probably derive from our conception of the negation of a finite process, as in the contrast between mortality and immortality. We can grasp that every number has a successor by learning, first, how to name numbers using the standard decimal system of numerals, and second, how to form the numeral that is the successor of any numeral. We can readily imagine a simple machine that accepts any integer written in the decimal system of numerals and produces an output of the decimal equal to the successor of the numeral. We can think of this procedure working iteratively and applying to its own output, and imagine that it starts with 1 and stops at 200. We can think of the same procedure, and imagine that it does not stop.

Modern mathematicians tend to be Realists and to assume that numbers exist and that their nature is independent of the operations of the mind. This philosophy is an appealing working hypothesis for anyone who reflects daily about numbers and their properties. Yet the invention of mathematics and the apprehension of numbers must depend on the properties of the mind. If we accept Realism, we are committed to an extraordinary Platonic domain of numbers whose existence is mysterious. We also have a considerable problem in explaining how entities in this domain can be grasped by human beings. If we reject Realism, we seem to have a problem in explaining the objectivity of mathematics. Its proofs endure for all time, and this fact seems hard to explain if mathematics is merely the product of the mind. It was for just such reasons that Frege launched his great attack on Psychologism (see Chapter 9).

There is, however, a third possibility, which is to revive and to revise Intuitionism. Intuitionists take the view that mathematics is a mental construction, and that the *procedures* by which infinite sequences are generated constitute the essential topic of the mathematical investigation of infinity. They couple this view with some unnecessary and unacceptable constraints on mathematical methods (e.g., the banning of proofs about infinite sets that rely on the law of the excluded middle). None the less, a modified philosophy of an Intuitionistic character can be defended. The ability to devise mathematics depends on the capacity to make valid deductions, to invent symbolic languages, and to define the hypothetical truth conditions of terms in them. In particular, the truth conditions of a term can be defined independently of whether or not anything in the real world satisfies them. Moreover, these definitions can be made without grasping the logical properties of the terms so defined. Mathematics is the systematic working out of the informative valid consequences of the hypothetical truth conditions of sets of consistent assumptions.

A simple instance of the ability to frame the truth conditions of terms designating hypothetical entities is provided by an example that I have used before. A lawyer might make the following stipulative definitions:

A *warehouse building* is a manufactory, brewery, distillery, or any other building exceeding 150,000 foot cube which is not open to the general public.

A *public building* is a hotel, hospital, school, or any building open to the general public exceeding 250,000 foot cube.

A *domestic building* is one that is not a warehouse or a public building.

Granted these definitions, it follows that:

If an *alcázar* is a building exceeding 150,000 foot cube and not open to the general public, it is not a domestic building.

The truth of the proposition does not depend on the existence of *alcázars* or any other class of buildings, though their existence may help us to grasp its truth. With appropriate care in framing the initial assumptions, such truths can be as enduring as mathematical truths. They differ principally in that they have no intrinsic interest and that no one is likely to postulate the initial assumptions unless such terms as *building* denote actual physical entities.

The flaw in the Realist critique is analogous to the flaw in nativist critiques of learning: both theories confuse what is known with how it is known. Humans can construct propositions that assert necessary truths about hypothetical entities even though the methods by which they come by them may be subjective, idiosyncratic, or superstitious. It is ironical that Frege took such pains in distinguishing between the truth conditions of a proposition and the mental processes by which one becomes conscious of them, and yet failed to see that this distinction frees one from having to postulate a realm of Platonic ideals.

Conclusions

The theory of mental models is intended to explain the higher processes of cognition and, in particular, comprehension and inference. It suggests a simple three-part inventory for the contents of the mind: there are recursive procedures, propositional representations, and models. The procedures are ineffable. They carry out such tasks as the mapping of propositional representations into models. They also project an underlying model into another special form of model – a two dimensional view or image. There are presumably many other forms of procedure that play a part in thinking. Prototypes and other schemata, for example, are procedures that specify by default the values of certain variables in mental models. Likewise, analogies may depend on procedures that apply a model of one phenomenon to another. But are there any other forms of mental representation? Apart from the sensory precursors to models produced by the perceptual system, there are no grounds for supposing that higher cognitive processes depend on other forms of representation. Thus what we remember consists of images, models, propositions, and procedures for carrying out actions. The major remaining problems for this analysis are why so many procedures are inaccessible to introspection, and what underlies intentions, which play so critical a role in action and communication. These phenomena, however, are a part of a larger puzzle that I shall attempt to solve in the final chapter.

16

Consciousness and computation

How can body and mind be accommodated within the same explanatory framework? Philosophers adopt almost every conceivable posture on this issue. Materialists like Watson and Carnap deny the reality of mind and argue that behaviour has not mental, but physical causes. Idealists like Berkeley and McTaggart deny the reality of body and argue that only mental phenomena exist. Others, however, do not doubt that both body and mind exist. Amongst them, on one side, Monists like Kant and Köhler claim that the two are identical, or just different aspects of some *tertium quid* (Spinoza), or different arrangements of the same sort of stuff (Hume, James, Russell). And, on the other side, Dualists argue that the two are radically different and separate entities that either just happen to run along in parallel like two clocks keeping perfect time (Leibniz) or else causally interact by way of the pineal gland (Descartes), the cerebral hemispheres (Popper and Eccles), or the good offices of God (Malebranche). As the old adage has it: *What is mind? No matter. What is matter? Never mind.*

The mind–body problem is, of course, a psychological problem too, and metaphysical issues can be obviated by Craik's (1943) 'functionalist' hypothesis: mental phenomena depend not on the particular constitution of the brain but on how it is functionally organized. The digital computer is the metaphor, immanent in Craik's work, but manifest in subsequent formulations of the functionalist doctrine by Miller, Galanter, and Pribram (1960), Putnam (1960), and Fodor (1968). As the software of the computer stands to its hardware, so the mind stands to the brain. Only one major problem remains for this doctrine, but it is unfortunately the most central and the most puzzling of all the phenomena of mental life – consciousness.

No one really knows what consciousness is, what it does, or what function it serves. There is, however, a clear series of alternatives. Either consciousness is wholly mysterious or else it is open to scientific explanation. Either Turing's thesis that effective procedures are computable is correct or else consciousness may depend on hitherto unknown effective procedures that are not computable. Either the doctrine of functionalism is correct or else mental life depends not only on the way the brain works but also on its

448

particular physical properties. Hence, consciousness must fall into one of four categories:

1. It is a supernatural phenomenon – a real 'ghost' in the machine that is totally beyond scientific explanation.

2. It can be explained, but only by recourse to as yet unknown non-computable effective procedures.

3. Like the weather, it is explicable by theories that can be simulated by computer programs, but it can no more be embodied within a computer than can an actual anti-cyclone: only organisms with brains can be conscious.

4. It is computable: computers can in principle be programmed so as to be conscious.

Of course, separate aspects of consciousness might be in different categories. If any aspect of it were truly supernatural, then any other component interacting with it would be problematical – there would be a new mind–body problem (in this case a spirit–mind problem) lodged within consciousness. The first of the four possibilities is accordingly not of any scientific interest. The second possibility is obviously a remote one, because all formulations of an effective procedure have so far turned out to be computable (see Chapter 1). The choice between the remaining possibilities, however, is subtle.

The idea that machines might be fashioned to be conscious is as old as Western civilization. In Homer's *Iliad*, one reads that Hephaestus, the artificer of Olympus, made some mechanical girls of gold to help him:

They looked like real girls and could not only speak and use their limbs but were endowed with intelligence and trained in handiwork by the immortal gods. (E. V. Rieu's translation, 1950, p. 348)

The coming of the computer has renewed speculation on the topic (see, e.g., Gunderson, 1971; Dennett, 1978; Sloman, 1978). Only one point has emerged with any certainty: the issue will not be settled until there is a feasible theory of consciousness.

Psychologists have, of course, proposed theories of consciousness. They have tried to account for it in terms of the evolution of more complex brains (e.g., John, 1976), or more complex behaviours culminating in linguistic communication and society (e.g., Mead, 1934; Humphrey, 1977). But consciousness is hardly a consequence of merely more neurones with more connections between them; we can be conscious of very simple acts; and if language and society could have evolved without consciousness, why should they need, and how would they be able, to awaken the slumbering minds of sleeptalkers? Psychologists have also identified consciousness with the contents of a limited capacity processing mechanism (Posner and Boies, 1971), with a device that determines what actions to take and what goals to seek (Shallice, 1972), and with a particular mode of information processing that affects the mental structures governing actions (Mandler, 1975). These claims are plausible, but the conditions they describe might all, perhaps, be satisfied by a controller on a central heating boiler, or a program written in the high-level language PLANNER. These conditions are hardly sufficient to engender consciousness, and neither explain, nor are intended to explain, how self-awareness and intentionality depend on consciousness.

The functionalist alternative is that consciousness depends on the computations of the nervous system. These computations require a brain of a certain size and complexity, for two reasons. First, computational power depends on memory: e.g., the difference between a finite-state automaton and a Turing machine, for example, is not their basic operations, but how these operations can be extended by access to memory. Second, computational speed depends on the size of the units that can be processed at the same time, i.e., the number of processors that can be brought to bear on the task. Computational power is important since it governs the potential complexity of an organism's behaviour: language and society ultimately depend on the mental ability to compute recursively defined linguistic structures. Computational speed is important, because conscious decisions occur in real time. Indeed, consciousness is a temporal phenomenon: it exists in time and through it we become aware of the phenomenal 'present'. A philosophical sceptic might argue that an organism could be conscious in 'slow motion', being aware of reality only very sluggishly (cf. Block, 1978). However, a slow apprehension of events might lead to a cumulative divergence between the world and the mind with the contents of consciousness lagging further and further behind reality. If the perceptual system were 'switched off' in order to catch up with events, then consciousness would assume an intermittent character contrary to the continuity of normal experience. A retarded or intermittent consciousness would be unlikely to serve any adaptive purpose. Hence, for a computer to be conscious, it would be necessary for it to operate in real time.

An implicit goal of the present book has been to give a functionalist explanation of consciousness, since in my view it depends on a special form of mental model. Such an account is needed to explain the nature of intentions, which, as we saw in the previous chapter, are an essential part of human communication because they distinguish between reference and mere correspondence between a symbol and reality. In this final chapter, I shall approach mental models and recursive processes from a different angle in order to analyse consciousness, self-awareness, and intentionality. I shall start by bringing together three clues to the nature of the mind.

Three clues to human mentality

1. *The mind employs different levels of organization.* This principle is easiest to discern in language. In particular, language is organized at the level of speech sounds, morphemes, sentences, and discourse. Distinctive features combine to form speech sounds; speech sounds combine to form morphemes, which have meanings; sentences have grammatical structures that enable their meanings to be constructed compositionally from those of their morphemes; and inferences from meanings lead to models of discourse.

2. *Mental processing at each level takes context into account.* Speech is not a series of sounds one after the other, but a sequence of overlapping events: a slice through continuous speech at one moment in time usually contains information about adjacent sounds laid out like geological strata, and the perceptual effect of any given cue depends heavily on the context in which it occurs (Liberman, Cooper, Shankweiler, and Studdert-Kennedy, 1967). The identification and interpretation of words also depends on context; for instance, the occurrence of one word can affect the recognition of another (see, e.g., Meyer and Schvaneveldt, 1971), a particular sentential context can affect the recognition of a word (Morton and Long, 1976) and the retrieval of specific aspects of its meaning (Tabossi and Johnson-Laird, 1980). Similarly, although the grammar of English may be context free (see Chapter 12), the processing of grammatical relations is not independent of context; a left-corner parser works on the assumption that the right-hand side of constituents can be predicted top down (see Chapter 13). Above all, the significance of an utterance and the way in which it is interpreted depend on which referents are already represented in the discourse model – a phenomenon that was simulated in a rudimentary way by the computer program for interpreting spatial descriptions (see Chapter 11). Few utterances are wholly without a deictic component, which depends for its interpretation on the context and circumstances of utterance.

451

The inferences that are made to 'flesh out' the bones of discourse are likewise highly dependent on context.

3. *Processing at different levels is not autonomous, but interactive.* The most frequently used words in the language tend to be the most ambiguous. It is thus plausible to suppose that the processes of comprehension can rapidly establish the intended sense of a word from the context in which it occurs. I have outlined a theory of how the intended meaning depends on inferences from factual knowledge, though these inferences may ultimately be transmuted into linguistic 'selectional restrictions' (see Chapter 10). The intended sense of one expression may be determined by the reference of other expressions; conversely, the intended reference of an expression may be determined by the sense of other expressions. Similarly, though more controversially, syntactic analysis may be aided by semantic processes: the difficulty of parsing an ungrammatical string or a difficult construction can be eased by the presence of good semantic cues (see Chapter 13). Both syntactic and semantic cues also appear to affect the identification of words, and there may be interactive processing here too (see Marslen-Wilson and Welsh, 1978; Tyler and Marslen-Wilson, 1982; though cf. Forster 1979; Norris, 1982). Most theories of word recognition that incorporate effects of context postulate that the recognition of one word facilitates the recognition of other semantically related words (e.g., Forster, 1979; but cf. Norris, in press). However, an idea embodied in a mental model, rather than a word or set of words, may also aid the process (see Tabossi, 1982). Speech and comprehension undoubtedly rely on separate 'modules' operating at different levels. These modules, however, do not function as closed autonomous processes, but interact. The system is unlikely to depend on one module directly modifying the inner workings of another, since such interactions would produce highly unstable and unpredictable consequences. A more plausible form of interaction relies on the processes of one module being sensitive to information from other modules. These messages could take the form of predictions, constraints on or outcomes of processing, and other such 'interrupts'. A system of this sort could readily account for the observed statistical interactions between the syntactic and semantic variables manipulated in experiments.

These three phenomena – the different levels of organization, the dependence on context, and the interaction between levels of processing – all point to one essential, though hardly novel, principle: *mental processes occur in parallel.* There are different levels of organization because separate processors can operate on different levels simultaneously; at a given level, one processor works on one item whilst others work on its context; and communication between processors at different levels allows them to interact. What we must now consider are the advantages of parallel computation, its latent dangers and how they can be obviated.

The organization of parallel computation

The chief advantage of parallel computation is speed. Consider the major stages of comprehension: speech perception, word identification, parsing, semantic interpretation, and inference. If each stage takes on average t units of time and there are m stages, the complete process takes mt units of time. If the stages are arranged like an assembly line (Johnson-Laird, 1977a) and all of them operate concurrently, then the output of the system will be one item in every t units of time. Some computer systems designed for specialized streams of data operate in just this way, which is known as 'pipelining'. Computation can be speeded up still more, of course, in what might be called 'totally parallel processing', where each process operates on the *same* item at the same time: the overall time to process the input in this case shrinks to t units, but the cost is an increase in the number of processors proportional to nm, where n is the average number of items at a stage and m is the number of stages.

There are some problems – the parsing of certain abstract languages, for example – that can be shown to be solvable in principle but not in practice: they are to computation what Malthus's doctrine of population growth is to civilization. A problem is inherently intractable when any algorithm for it takes a time that grows exponentially with the size of the input. For an input of n, where n is small an algorithm may be feasible, but even if the time it takes is proportional, say, to 2^n, then, because such exponentials increase at so great a rate with an increase of n, a computer the size of the universe operating at the speed of light would take billions of years to compute an output for a relatively modest input. Parallel processing is of no avail for rendering such problems tractable. What it does is to speed up the execution of algorithms that take only a time proportional to a polynomial of the size of the input, i.e., a term or sum of terms in which n is raised to a constant power and multiplied by a constant coefficient. For example, the CYK algorithm for parsing context-free grammars (see Chapter 13) requires a time proportional to n^3 in its serial version, but this time can be reduced to one proportional to n in a parallel version (Guibas, Kung, and Thompson, 1979).

453

An irresolvable impediment to totally parallel processing is the dependence of one process on the outcome of another. The syntactic combination of meanings, for instance, cannot begin until there are meanings to combine, and there cannot be any meanings until words have been at least partially identified; comprehension must therefore depend on some pipelining of processes. A major analytical problem is to determine which components of an algorithm can in principle be executed in parallel. Consider, for example, a simple iterative procedure for searching for a word in a list of n words. Figure 16.1 presents a flow diagram of a serial

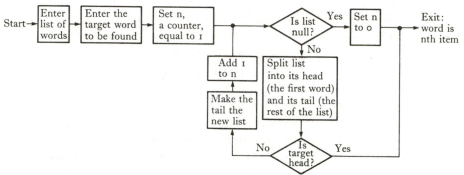

Figure 16.1 A flow diagram of a simple serial procedure for searching for a word in a list of words. If the target word is not in the list, then the procedure returns the value 0; otherwise, it returns the ordinal position of the word in the list.

procedure for carrying out the search. As the diagram shows, the algorithm consists of a set of functions ordered in a particular way. Hence a distinction can be drawn between calculation and flow of control. The flow diagram specifies both components, but a flow diagram in which the boxes were empty would specify only the flow of control. Parallel computation requires control to be divided into a number of independent components, which subsequently merge again into unitary control. Thus, it is clear that in the search algorithm the three main computations in the loop – the decision about whether the target word matches the head of the list, making the tail of the list into the new list, and incrementing the counter – can be carried out in parallel. Similarly, the three initial steps of the computation – entering the list of words, etc. – can be carried out together. Whenever operations are independent of one another, they can be carried out in parallel. This condition is not equivalent to commutativity: if the order of the calculations in the loop in Figure 16.1 is swapped round, the resulting

454

procedure would be defective. A parallel algorithm for searching is sum-marized in the flow-diagram of Figure 16.2. The arrows between com-ponents still indicate the flow of control, which divides in the case of parallel computations and unites after them (as indicated by the small circles in the diagram). If the maximum number, n, of iterations required in the loop is known prior to entering it, i.e., the loop is primitive recursive (see Chapter 1), then the set of m operations in the loop can be farmed out to nm separate parallel processors. The resulting algorithm is totally parallel once the list and the target word have been entered: all n items in the list are examined simultaneously. The algorithm is accordingly very rapid. If n is greater than the number of available processors, then the list can be examined in a series of chunks, with each item in a chunk examined simultaneously.

These examples of parallel processing establish a point that is easily overlooked: certain algorithms can be executed only by parallel processors. Thus, an algorithm for primitive recursion in which all n processes are carried out simultaneously plainly cannot be executed by a serial device, which is forced to employ a loop. Any function that can be computed can indeed be computed serially, but not all algorithms for computing such functions are serial. There are many algorithms, such as the search process in Figure 16.2, that can be executed only by a parallel processor.

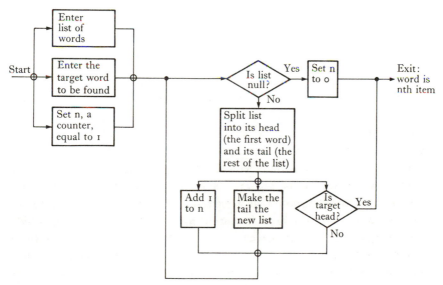

Figure 16.2 A flow diagram of a parallel procedure for searching for a word in a list of words.

The most general architecture for a parallel processing system consists of a set of finite-state processors with channels between them for communicating the values of parameters and global variables. Each processor starts to compute as soon as it receives the values of the parameters etc. that it needs. Other parallel systems are special cases of this design, e.g., systems in which only information about level of activation is passed from one processor to another (Anderson and Hinton, 1981), systems in which all the processors are synchronized by reference to an internal clock (Kung, 1980), vector machines in which all the processors carry out the same procedure (Kozdrowicki and Theis, 1980), and so on.

A variety of 'pathological' phenomena can occur in executing parallel programs unless care is taken to avoid them. Several processors may contend for the same information in memory. If this problem is avoided by providing each processor with its own memory cache, then the processors may independently modify the contents of their memories so that inconsistencies arise. If checks for consistency are carried out, then the speed of the system is reduced. There are other more serious problems, which I shall illustrate using a new sort of diagram that shows the flow of information from one parallel processor to another. (Other notations for investigating parallel processing, such as Petri nets, Peterson, 1981, are too abstract for my purposes.) Suppose that two processors, A and B, yield outputs to the same processor, C, as depicted in the following information-flow diagram:

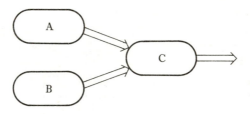

where the arrows represent channels through which the values of parameters, variables, and other data, are communicated from one processor to another. Now, suppose that what processor C does depends on which of the two, A or B, produces its output first. In this case, there is a 'race' between A and B, and the system may produce wholly different outputs for a given input from one occasion to another depending on which processor wins the race. If the 'winner' of the race is determined not by the nature of the computations carried out by A and B, but by completely extrinsic factors, such as, say, the number of cosmic rays that happen to bombard the two processors, then the system will not be deterministic. This sort of indeterminism may well be a feature of the brain, and would contribute to the unpredictability of behaviour. It might well render an actual computer unfit for use. Where the outcome of a race depends on the intrinsic nature of the computations carried out by A and B, then the system is obviously deterministic, and corresponds to the sort of 'race' models that are sometimes proposed in psychological theories.

A disastrous possibility for brain and computer alike is that there are two processors, B and C, that require an input from each other in order to start computing:

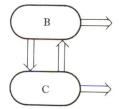

Here, B cannot compute until it receives information from C, and C cannot compute until it receives information from B. The processors are in deadlock: they are crippled by a 'deadly embrace' from which neither can escape. Another pathological configuration occurs in the case of the following sort of loop:

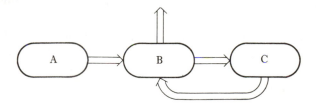

Everything is fine once the system is in operation, but there is an initial 'hangup': there is no way in which computation can begin, because B requires an input from both A and C, but C cannot deliver an output because it requires an input from B. Finally, of course, a direct 'conflict' can arise if two separate processors yield different values for the same variables, which are not compared by any error-correcting procedure:

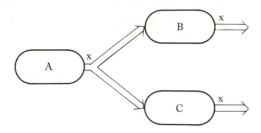

Given a parallel processing system consisting of a set of finite-state automata that can be connected in a network that allows them to interact, we want to specify what counts as a system that is wholly free of such pathological phenomena, and we also want to know how to implement such a system, that is, how to introduce programs into the processors in a way that will not lead to disastrous states of affairs. The parallel processors must obviously communicate with one another in order to pass the values of variables around, and I shall assume that the system is asynchronous, i.e., instead of a clock to keep operations in phase, each processor begins to compute as soon as it has the information it needs. It is the flow of information between processors that can lead to anomalous configurations, and therefore criteria need to be laid down to exclude deadlocks and other inconsistencies. Plainly, it is safe to assume that a set of basic functions, including the zero, successor, and identity functions, can be implemented. What have to be formulated are the principles governing parallel versions of composition, conditionals, and *while*-loops, or some other equivalent set of building-blocks that suffice for all effective procedures (see Chapter 1).

Composition is accommodated by allowing the output values of a set of processors to be the input values for another processor, but in order for parallel computation to occur, it is necessary to admit the following sort of flow of information:

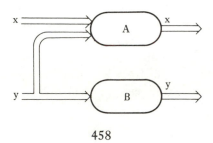

Thus, the value of a variable can be communicated to any number of processors, and so arrows can divide. It is also necessary to allow for arrows to merge, but they cannot do so merely as a result of the composition of functions, or else there would be a 'collision' between different pieces of data. If two processors are to yield results that merge, as in the configuration:

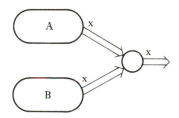

then in order to avoid a collision, it will be necessary to introduce a conditional with an outcome that determines whether A or B is to compute the value of the variable. The composition of functions should likewise not lead to loops, since they open up the possibility of deadlocks and other 'pathologies'. Hence, the admissible configurations created by composition are loop-free directed graphs.

The ability to handle conditional decisions lies at the heart of all computational devices from abstract Turing machines to actual digital computers, and conditionals are needed in order to introduce loops. There are important, and psychologically relevant, differences between the serial and parallel implementations of conditionals. In a serial system, a conditional such as:

If word = target then print value of n;
Else n + 1 → n;

consists of an antecedent condition depending on the values of variables, and one consequent procedure is executed if the antecedent is true, and another consequent procedure is executed if the antecedent is false. This sort of conditional translates into a parallel implementation in a straightforward way to be described presently. In the case of a serial conditional that has no 'else' clause:

If word ≠ target then n + 1 → n;

there is no instruction to be executed when the antecedent is false, and in a serial program control merely passes to the next instruction. In the parallel implementation of this conditional control does *not* pass to the

459

next instruction when the antecedent is false: nothing whatsoever happens, and the processor handling the conditional falls idle until it receives another input. Thus, the flow of information for this simple conditional has the following form:

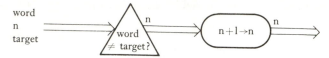

where the triangle symbolizes the processor carrying out the antecedent test. There is a subjective counterpart to this type of conditional. There are many occasions where the mind reacts to the presence of some stimulus, but not to its absence, e.g., noticing your name if it is mentioned in another conversation at a cocktail party. If a serial program is written to model such a phenomenon, it has to include a loop which repeatedly checks for the occurrence of the critical stimulus. The perpetual testing of auditory input to determine whether it corresponds to your name is implausible psychologically, because you are conscious only of a positive outcome to the test, not a negative one. In a parallel program, however, the simple conditional can be in a state of complete quietus until aroused by an occurrence of the event that satisfies its antecedent: there is no need for a loop or for any explanation of why a negative outcome of the test passes unnoticed.

The antecedent of a conditional may be any Boolean function of a number of truth values, i.e., it can be defined in terms of the conjunction, disjunction, and negation, of a set of basic properties and relations. The separate constituents of an antecedent consisting of a conjunction or disjunction can be evaluated in parallel, and the process can take advantage of the fact that any conjunction is false if one of its conjuncts is false, and of the fact that any (inclusive) disjunction is true if one of its disjuncts is true – in this way, action can be taken without necessarily having to wait for the evaluation of all the constituents of the Boolean expression. (Something similar happens in certain serial programming languages: as soon as information arrives that establishes the truth value of the antecedent, action is taken; but the antecedent is of course evaluated in the serial order of its components.) In general, a conditional of the form:

If condition 1 and condition 2 then procedure A
else procedure B;

has a straightforward parallel implementation. The values of the required variables are conveyed to conditions 1 and 2, and passed on for use by procedures A and B. Conditions 1 and 2 can be executed in parallel and their resulting truth values passed on to the conditional (as indicated by the shaded channels), which evaluates the appropriate Boolean function of them:

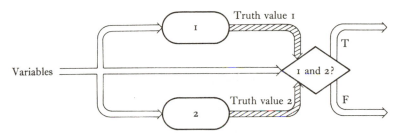

If the test *1 and 2?* yields the result *true*, then the relevant variables are passed to procedure A; if the test yields the result *false*, then the relevant variables are passed to procedure B. The complete conditional has the following form:

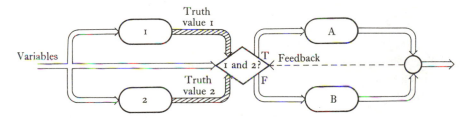

In an asynchronous system, it is always possible that there could be a 'race' or a 'clash' when alternative values of variables are computed: procedure A may take so much longer than procedure B that the results of two separate calls to the conditional might emerge in the wrong order, or even simultaneously. One way to prevent such pathological outcomes is to arrange for a feedback signal to be sent from the point at which the channels merge (indicated by the circle in the diagram) to the antecedent test. As soon as the antecedent test passes on variables to one or other of the procedures contingent upon it, it enters a refractory period in which it cannot pass on the results of the next test until it receives the 'all clear' signal from the merge. The signal indicates that the previous results of procedure A or procedure B have been cleared from the system.

If there are sufficient processors, a primitive recursive loop can sometimes be implemented, as we have seen, by a parallel algorithm that carries out n procedures simultaneously. Such a stratagem is impossible for a while-loop because the number of passes through the loop cannot be determined beforehand. The parallel implementation of while-loops is a straightforward matter. A set of procedures, A, computes the initial conditions and truth values for the conditional test; and a further set of procedures, B, is executed in the body of the loop. At least some of these procedures may be carried out in parallel. Only when the resulting values of the variables satisfy the test is the loop terminated. At this point, a feedback signal is sent to unlock the loop for a new input from A. This scheme is shown in the following diagram:

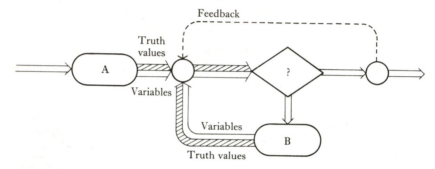

The same procedure can be readily modified to cope with primitive recursive loops that need a larger number of iterations than there are available processors.

Armed with these schemes for parallel computation, there is a natural recursive definition of a well-formed system that is free of pathological configurations. A well-formed system is one that consists of any of the following:

1. A basic function.
2. A loop-free directed graph of well-formed systems.
3. A parallel conditional composed of well-formed systems.
4. A parallel primitive recursive-loop or while-loop composed of well-formed systems.

The mental implementation of parallel processing

The problem of implementing a parallel program can be solved in a number of ways. In a completely distributed system, where each processor is on a par with the others, there is no way in which one processor can contain

462

the program and communicate instructions to the others. There has to be a fixed program that is 'wired in' to the processors. Networks of neurones can presumably develop in this fashion: their functional architecture is laid down genetically, and natural selection weeds out designs that are not well formed. Since the computations carried out by a single processor must inevitably be simple, and the information immediately available to a processor must derive from only some of the other processors in the network, the performance of the system as a whole is unlikely to be optimal. It will be capable of only a limited degree of flexibility in behaviour. The system, however, should be free of deadlocks and other anomalies, and it should be able to deal with local failures: it should contain sufficient redundancy to cope with a limited degree of damage or degradation. These characteristics, of course, are notable amongst such organisms as the coelenterates (e.g., sea anemones and jellyfish) and the echinoderms (e.g., starfish and sea urchins), which have a distributed or radial nervous system but no central brain. A graphic illustration of the dangers of parallel computation is provided by the cutting of the radial nervous system of a starfish into two separate arcs: the starfish may literally tear itself apart in trying to move in opposite directions.

Another method of implementing a parallel system is based on a central processor that runs the main program and farms out particular instructions to independent processors. Such a design does not appear to have been used by nature, but it was employed in the early days of automation – a single main computer ran a production line by way of a number of local sensors and actuators. A degree of flexibility is possible, but the drawbacks of the system are clear: the main program has to be very complex, and the system is slow to react to emergencies and unable to cope should the central computer fail.

What is needed ideally is a system that has flexibility, resistance to degradation, and a rapid response to emergencies. Such a system needs the benefits of both a centralized and a distributed organization: a high-level processor that monitors and controls the overall goals of lower-level processors, which in turn monitor and control the processors at a still lower level, and so on in a hierarchy of parallel processors, which at the lowest level govern sensory and motor interactions with the external world. The notion of a hierarchical organization of the nervous system has been urged by neuroscientists from Hughlings Jackson to H. J. Jerison (see Oatley, 1978, for the history of this idea), and Simon (1969) has argued that it is an essential feature of an intelligent organism. From a computational

463

standpoint, the highest level should contain the operating system. In a digital computer, the operating system is a suite of programs that allow a human operator to control the computer. There are instructions that enable the operator to recover a program stored on a magnetic disk, to compile it, to run it, to print out its source code, to call an editing program, and so on. When the computer is switched on, its resident monitor is arranged to load the operating system either automatically or as a result of some simple manual instructions. The mind's operating system has considerable autonomy, though it is responsive to demands from other processors, and can be switched on and off by the mechanisms controlling sleep. It depends on a second level of processors for perceiving, understanding, acting, remembering, communicating, and thinking. These processors in turn depend on lower-level processors for passing down more detailed control instructions or for passing up partially interpreted sensory information. Doubtless, there are interactions between processors at the same or different levels, and facilities that allow priority messages from a lower level to interrupt computations at a higher level. One of the most important functions, which the operating system can evidently call for, is the development of new programs to cope with novel situations.

Totally distributed systems that are simple can solve the problem of pathological configurations by natural selection. The computational system embodied in the human brain, however, can develop and run its own programs and has no such protection. Just as the mental 'programs' that individuals produce for solving problems may have notable 'bugs' within them (see Sussman, 1973), so their implementation may also lead to anomalous configurations between processors. A primal form of consciousness may originally have emerged from the web of parallel processors as a way of overriding deadlocks and other pathological interactions. The virtue of a centralized system is that one operating program can govern the system as a whole, including the development of new programs, their assignment to other processors, and the monitoring of their execution. The virtue of a distributed system is that the operating program can be relatively simple: it does not need to be concerned with the detailed implementation of the instructions that it sends to lower-level processors. It specifies what the processors have to do (e.g., recall the Prime Minister's name, tell someone the time, estimate the cost of the Brighton Royal Pavilion), but not how they are to carry out the necessary computations. It receives information from lower-level processors about the results of computations (e.g., Mrs Thatcher, 2.30 p.m., half a million pounds), but not about how they are obtained. Indeed, there is no reason to suppose that the same computational code is necessarily used at the different levels, provided that they can communicate effectively.

Conscious and unconscious processes

On the basis of purely computational considerations, I have argued that there is a division in the mind between a high-level operating system and a hierarchical organization of parallel processors. The best psychological evidence for this division comes from a further clue to human mentality: the distinction between what one can be conscious of, and what one cannot be conscious of. This evidence is relevant to the assumption that the contents of consciousness are the current values of parameters governing the high-level computations of the operating system. The operating system, as I argued in the previous section, can receive such values from other processors, but it cannot inspect the internal operations of these processors. Natural selection has ensured that they are necessarily unconscious.

When people speak to you, you can be conscious of the words that they use, and of whether or not you understand their utterances. You can be conscious of whether or not what they assert is true, of what answer to give to a question they ask, and of how to fulfil a request they make. And, if none of this information is available to you, you can be aware of that, too. More generally, you can be conscious at least to some degree of what you perceive, of your feelings and attitudes, of your goals, intentions, and motives, and of your memories, expectations, hopes, and fears. Consciousness ranges from the transcendental to the trivial – from the inevitability of death to the inescapability of taxes. In short, you can be conscious *that p*, where *p* may be wanting a meal, seeing a restaurant, remembering you have no cash, and hoping that a credit card will be acceptable; but the specific contents of consciousness are ineffable – the particular pangs of hunger on one occasion, for instance, cannot be uniquely distinguished in words.

Although there is much that you can be aware of, there is also much that is permanently unavailable to you. Indeed, you can never be completely conscious of how you exercise any mental skill. Even in the most deliberate of tasks, such as the deduction of a conclusion, you are not aware of how you carried out each step in the process. Similarly, you are not aware of the underlying nature and mechanism of mental representations: you are conscious of what is represented and of whether it is perceived or imagined, not of the inherent nature of the representation itself.

465

The division between conscious and unconscious processes is the best available clue to the structure of the mind, but we are so familiar with it, and have been so much distracted by the content of Freudian conceptions, that we fail to see how informative it is. Why is it that people are conscious of the contents of the operating system? They might have been designed so that they were ordinarily conscious of the minutiae of mental life and of the mechanisms underlying their representations of the world, but unconscious of their attitudes and intentions. It is hard to imagine this state of affairs, but it is logically possible. If linguistic communication were still under conscious control, it would be reduced to pointless exchanges about scenes and bodily movements, and would bear no relation to the reasons for people's actions. This hypothetical organization would be maladaptive. If organisms are going to communicate, it is to their mutual advantage that they talk about those matters that govern their behaviour, that is, the contents of the operating system. Likewise, if they were aware that their visual world is a representation, they would be more likely to doubt its veridicality and to treat it as something to be pondered over – a potentially fatal debility in the case of danger. Some psychologists, notably J. J. Gibson (1979), have argued that there are no mental representations. Until they formulate their theories as effective procedures, though, they may be deemed to have been deceived by the adaptive nature of consciousness. Psychology is difficult precisely because of the evolutionary advantage of seemingly direct contact with the world – a phenomenon that makes the task of discovering the machinery of the mind that much harder.

The demarcation between what is accessible and what is inaccessible to consciousness is related to the difference between knowing *that* something is the case and knowing *how* to do something (Ryle, 1949). Knowing *that* p implies that one has conscious access to the proposition that p is true. Knowing *how* to do p may depend on conscious access to some of the parameters controlling performance, but it also depends on low-level processors with internal operations that cannot be inspected by the operating system. To try to become cognisant of precisely what one is doing can accordingly be an extremely taxing business. Consider, for instance, the difference between whistling a tune and writing it down in musical notation. A computer program devised to carry out one of these tasks could be readily modified to carry out the other, since they both use an internal representation of a melody to control behaviour. Yet whistling is a habit of errand boys, while the ability to take musical dictation is a prerogative

466

of skilled musicians. Whistling, like speaking, is mastered with little exercise of conscious control; in particular, one has no access to the 'melodic' representation that governs pitch. This representation is generated by a low-level processor for use in controlling the vocal apparatus, and there is no possible way in which the action of writing musical notation can gain access to it. Written notations can be mastered only by a lengthy process of learning controlled by the operating system. Once the appropriate software has been developed, it may be farmed out, perhaps in a compiled form, to a lower-level processor, which can operate automatically. There always remains, however, a distinction between our concept of music – as reflected in our notation (see Longuet-Higgins, 1979), and the mental representations that directly control singing, whistling, and musical performance. When you learn to whistle a new tune, you learn without being conscious of what it is that you are learning. If you doubt this proposition, whistle the opening bars of any tune, and then ask yourself what you did in order to change the pitch of the notes. You changed the shape of mouth and tongue, but in what way precisely? Mere introspection is unlikely to tell you.

All learning depends on unconscious processes, but this dependence is most marked in learning *how* to do things. Consider, for example, a musician learning how to improvise melodies to given harmonic sequences. Certain aspects of the skill can be matters of conscious knowledge: a teacher can point out that some notes in an improvisation sound well whereas others invariably clash with the harmonic accompaniment – for example, E consorts well, but C poorly, with a chord of B minor 7th. Musicians discover how to improvise partly by acquiring such principles and putting them into practice, partly by slavishly imitating other improvisers, and partly by experimenting. They learn to improvise by improvising. Great improvisers develop a characteristic style, which is often recognizable after only a few bars. Hence, there must be some original principles underlying their performances. Yet no one knows what these principles are, because they are embodied in processors that are inaccessible to the operating system. They have to be so embodied, because when musicians improvise they do not make a conscious decision about each note – there is not enough time for that. The fascination of improvisation is that musicians may surprise *themselves* by what they play.

Learning to exercise any creative skill is just like learning to improvise. Exactly the same amalgam of conscious and unconscious practice goes into learning to use language, to reason and to solve problems, to play games, to create works of art or scientific theories. In learning to speak, for instance, children pick up grammatical constraints and the meanings of words by listening to other people's utterances, by occasionally learning that one form of words consorts poorly with another, and by experimenting. By speaking, they learn to speak. Once they have mastered the skill, they can do so without the least idea of the principles governing their performance, whether they be general rules of grammar that reflect universal and innate principles or idiosyncratic habits that mark their personal styles.

It is harder to investigate unconscious learning than the explicit learning of propositional knowledge. According to the present computational hypothesis, however, any attempt to use introspection in order to become conscious of something that is normally unconscious is unlikely to succeed. Not only is the information inaccessible, but also an essentially parallel process has to be grasped by the serial deliberations of the operating system. The result is that the intrinsic nature of the process is distorted. When as lay theorists we consciously characterize concepts, we isolate them in a cold-blooded systematic way that is very different from the parallel taxonomic system that is actually in the mind. We think of speech as an alphabet of sounds strung together like beads on a string. We take categories and meanings to be invariably defined by necessary and sufficient conditions. (We consciously coin words to work in this way.) We analyse complex concepts as Boolean functions of simple concepts. We hold inferences to be governed by mental rules of logic. But, as I have tried to show, all of these doctrines are delusions. The conclusion is clear: the structure of the concepts on which cognition depends is not open to conscious inspection.

There are several clinical syndromes that corroborate the present hypothesis about the division between conscious and unconscious processes. I shall consider three examples. The first is the phenomenon of 'blindsight' (Weiskrantz, Warrington, Sanders, and Marshall, 1974). After damage to the visual cortex, certain patients report that they are blind in parts of the visual field, and their blindness is apparently confirmed by clinical tests. Yet more subtle testing shows that the patients are able to use information from the 'blind' part of the field. It seems that their sight in the affected regions has continued to function but no longer yields an output to the operating system: they see without being conscious of what they see. The second example is the dissociation between the operating system and the multiple processors that can occur in automatisms after epileptic attacks. In this condition, patients function apparently without

468

consciousness and without the ability to make high-level decisions. For example, they may be capable of driving a car, but unable to respond correctly to traffic lights (Penfield, 1975). The third example is the well-attested illness of hysterical paralysis. Prolonged stress may lead to paralyses that have, unbeknown to the patient, no neurological explanation. They appear to be a reaction that is outside the knowledge or control of the operating system. They can often be cured by similarly duping the individual into believing that electrical stimuli will overcome the reaction (see Adrian and Yealland, 1917). This last category of dissociations establishes an important qualification to the computational hypothesis as I have so far described it. I have talked of the operating system governing the computations that occur in the multiple processors. Evidently, it does not have complete control over them. There are many phenomena that suggest that certain lower-level processors retain considerable autonomy. Love, hate, laughter, and tears, for instance, may be consciously feigned, but they cannot be genuinely invoked by a deliberate decision. Similarly, an individual may have a real intention, say, to give up smoking, but the operating system may fail to impose the decision on the lower-order processors. The withdrawal effects of nicotine addiction may lead the multiple processors to transmit parameter values back to the operating system that in turn evoke a conscious decision to start smoking again. One says either that the withdrawal effects are too extreme or that the smoker lacks the *will-power* to succeed. There appear to be genuine differences from one domain to another in the ease with which intentions can be put into effect. The notion of will-power, which is so potent in 'folk psychology', presumably arises from perceived differences between individuals in the extent to which the operating system can enforce its decisions. It certainly seems that some people are able to exert a tight control on themselves, whereas others, like Oscar Wilde, can resist everything except temptation.

Let us take stock of the argument so far. The division between conscious and unconscious processes is a consequence of parallelism. The evolutionary advantages of a parallel hierarchy are fourfold. (1) Parallel processing allows organisms to evolve specialized sensory, cognitive, and motor systems, which operate rapidly, since each such component can work at the same time. (2) The hierarchy is relatively resistant to failure – if one processor should fail, others can take over its work. (3) Control by the operating system enables decisions to be made rapidly and flexibly. (4) The parallel hierarchy allows the world to be presented directly to the operating system without any awareness of the processes of symbolic

representation. These advantages depend on a hierarchy of control governed by an operating system that can monitor the other processors, and on
limiting its interactions to the exchange of information so that is is unable
to gain access to the internal operations of other processors. Our introspective conceptions are accordingly very different from their unconscious
counterparts: we tend to force intrinsically parallel notions into a serial
strait-jacket.

Granted the distinction between the serial computations of the operating
system and the parallel computations of the multiple processors, one might
nevertheless ask why the former give rise to the unique phenomenon of
consciousness. Couldn't there merely be two forms of computation carried
out by the brain with no particular subjective experience associated with
them? Certainly, there could be. The theory as it has so far been developed
accounts only for a bare awareness of the world, such as might be found
in neonates or other species. Once a monitor mediating such awareness of
the world had evolved, however, it could plainly develop further so as to
take on additional functions. It is the most important of these functions
– the capacity for self-awareness, which underlies the unique subjective
experience of consciousness – to which the rest of the chapter is devoted.

Self-awareness in automata that understand themselves

At the beginning of this book, I raised the perplexing argument that the
mind must be more complicated than any theory of it: however complex
the theory, a device that invented it must be still more complex. Obviously,
cognitive scientists aim to understand the mind – to have a mental model
of a device that makes mental models. There is a striking similarity between
this goal and the achievement of self-awareness: the mind is aware of the
mind. It understands itself at least to some extent, and it understands that
it understands itself . . . The idea seems both central to the subjective
experience of consciousness and paradoxical. It resembles the puzzle of
the inclusive map: if a large map of England were to be traced out in
accurate detail on the middle of Salisbury Plain, then it should contain a
representation of itself, which in turn should contain a representation of
itself, and so on *ad infinitum*. Such a map is impossible, because an infinite
regress cannot be captured in a physical representation. (Leibniz thought
that the mental regress was equally impossible and hence a decisive
objection to Locke's theory of the mind.) However, a recursive procedure
for representing a map can easily be contrived so as to call itself to draw

the map on a smaller scale. Such a procedure could in principle run forever, continually drawing the same map within the map on a progressively smaller scale. There would inevitably come a point where the physical realization of the map would become too small to be perceived or to be physically drawn, but the values of the variables that were computed could, in principle, go on diminishing perpetually.

Psychology may indeed be trying to bite off its own head, but I believe that there is a similar recursive solution to the paradox of the mind trying to understand the mind. The construction of a mental model is a computational process, and the way out of the riddle of cognition can be found by considering what it means to say that a computer program understands itself. This is a deep question, which has seldom been asked and has yet to be answered satisfactorily.

It is possible to devise a Turing machine which, when it is presented with a blank tape, prints out its own description in a general notation such as the one described in Chapter 1. The specification of such a machine requires considerable ingenuity: a simple-minded approach that relies on formulating instructions to print out instructions is doomed because it takes several instructions to print out each instruction and so the length of the machine – like Tristram Shandy's life – increases at a faster rate than it can be described. The trick is to make use of two special machines as illustrated in Table 16.1. Although some computer scientists consider a machine that describes itself to be 'introspective', it can hardly be said to understand itself. It produces a complete description of itself that is useful for self-reproduction, but it no more understands this description than a molecule of DNA can be said to understand genetics. Minsky (1968) once suggested in a brief but brilliant essay that a self-describing Turing machine could contain an 'interpretative' program that could use its own description to calculate what it itself would do under some hypothetical circumstance. In other words, the program would use a complete description of itself as its own model. This is an ingenious but inadequate account of consciousness. Self-imitation is not the same as self-awareness: no Turing machine, as we shall see, can be conscious.

In the previous chapter, I described Craikian automata as devices that can construct internal models of the external world. In order for a Craikian automaton to be conscious and to have intentions, it must be enhanced by the crucial component of self-awareness. If the power to form mental representations of the relations between mental representations is realized by a recursive procedure, then, as in the inclusive map, there is in theory

Table 16.1 *The principles of a self-describing Turing machine (based on Thatcher, 1963)*

Two special machines are needed to construct a self-describing machine:

1 A Turing machine, A, which if given a string of binary digits, prints out the description of a *machine* that would print out that string. Hence, if the string 0110 is fed into A, its output is a string of symbols that constitute a description of a Turing machine which, if started with a blank tape, prints out 0110:

$$0110 \longrightarrow \boxed{A} \longrightarrow \text{Description of Turing machine that} \\ \text{prints the string, 0110.}$$

2 A Turing machine, B, which merely prints out the description of machine A:

$$\boxed{B} \longrightarrow \text{Description of Turing machine A}$$

The effective procedure for a self-describing Turing machine consists of the following instructions:

1 Go to 4.
2 Run machine A, which prints a description of a machine that prints everything on the tape so far, i.e., it prints the description of a machine equivalent to instruction 4.
3 Print a description of the instruction 'Go to 2'; Stop.
4 Print a description of the instruction 'Go to 4'; Run machine B, which prints a description of machine A; Print a description of the instructions: 'Print a description of the instruction "Go to 2"; Stop.'
5 Go to 2.

The effect of executing this procedure is to produce a tape that is a description of instructions 1 to 5 inclusive. The program jumps to instruction 4, which outputs the following items on the tape:

A description of 'Go to 4', i.e., a description of instruction 1.
A description of machine A, i.e., a description of instruction 2.
A description of 'Print a description of "Go to 2"; Stop', i.e., a description of instruction 3.

It then jumps to instruction 2, which runs machine A. This machine adds to the tape:

A description of a machine that prints out everything on the tape so far, i.e., a description of instruction 4.

Finally, instruction 3 adds:

A description of 'Go to 2', i.e., a description of instruction 5.

It is relatively straightforward to modify any Turing machine, including a Universal one, so that it becomes self-describing. This manoeuvre is a crucial part of the theory of self-reproducing automata.

no barrier to an arbitrary number of embeddings of models within models. Hence, one component of the solution to the cognitive paradox is the recursive construction of mental models: at stage 0, the program can construct a model of a proposition p; at stage 1, it can construct a model of itself as a program operating at stage 0; and, in general, at any stage it can construct a model of itself operating at the previous stage.

Once the recursive embedding of models has been introduced, its ubiquity in the phenomena of consciousness is obvious. Such embeddings are required for the representation of propositional attitudes (see Chapter 15). An individual can, for example, perceive that something is the case, be aware that he is perceiving it, become aware that he is aware that he is perceiving it . . . Likewise, genuine intentionality depends on the embedding of mental models. A programming language such as PLANNER (Hewitt, 1971) makes it possible to devise a program that sets up goals, which then govern the behaviour of the program: it is designed to achieve them by simulating a non-deterministic process. But such a program does not act intentionally – it merely acts as *though* it had intentions. The missing component is self-knowledge. An intention is a conscious decision to act so as to try to achieve a particular goal. An organism can have an intention only if it has an operating system that can elicit a model of a future state of affairs, and decide that it *itself* should act so as to try to bring about that state of affairs. A crucial part of having an intention is precisely an awareness that the system itself is able to make such decisions. The system has to be able to represent the fact that it can itself generate models of future states of affairs and decide to try to bring them about. Granted a goal-directed planning ability and the recursive machinery to embed models within models, the operating system only needs access to a model of itself in order to have intentions.

The model that individuals have of themselves includes memories of how they have felt or behaved in the past; memories of how they interacted with others; and a knowledge of their tastes, preferences, and proclivities. They also know much about the high-level realities of their own minds: their ability to perceive, remember, and act; their mastery of this or that intellectual skill; their imaginative and ratiocinative abilities. Of course, they have access only to an incomplete (and perhaps partially erroneous) model of their own mental abilities. Their model has no information about the inner workings of the multiple parallel processors or about the processes that underlie its own representation. The model that they possess is essentially a model of the options available to the operating system. In principle, this idea of a model of the self could be wholly mistaken, as some materialists have argued (e.g., Churchland, 1981), but it is difficult to believe that the framework of intentions, motives, reasons, and causes, by which we attempt to explain and to predict our own and others' behaviour, is not a genuine reflection of mental life. Moreover, models need be neither complete nor wholly accurate to be useful; and what our limited knowledge of our own operating system gives us is a sense of self-identity, continuity, and individuality.

There are, as we have seen, three main levels in the phylogeny of automata. At the first level, there are the Cartesian machines, which make no use of symbolism either internally or externally. They act without awareness. At the second level, there are the Craikian automata, which construct symbolic models of the world in real time. They are aware in the way in which young babies and other animals are aware. They may also communicate using a semantics that relates external symbolic responses to their models of the world. Finally, at the third level, there are devices that have the recursive ability to embed models within models, that possess a model of their own operating system, and that can apply the one to the other. They are *self-reflective* automata that can act and communicate intentionally. They are indeed autonomous though they contain no entelechy or mysterious teleological force. Are such automata conscious? The conditions that I have described would certainly seem to be necessary: full human consciousness depends on intentionality and self-awareness; and they in turn depend on a simple Craikian awareness and a recursive embedding of a model of the self within the self so that the different embeddings are accessible *in parallel* to the operating system. Whether such conditions suffice for consciousness remains an open question, if only because the term is a pre-theoretical one that at present has no clear meaning.

In defence of functionalism

Consciousness is the one remaining problem for the functionalist doctrine that mental phenomena correspond to the computations of the brain. Some philosophers have defended the more specific thesis that mental states, such as pain, correspond to the states of a Turing machine (see Putnam, 1960). However, since a Turing machine is a serial device, it could only simulate a theory of consciousness; the actual algorithm for consciousness, as I have argued, must be a parallel one. Even so, one might still doubt whether it could achieve consciousness. The philosophical sceptic might well wonder how the subjective experience of, say, pain could be identified with a computational state. Consider the example, cited by Dennett (1978), of a computational model of the mind simulated by a group of people communicating with each other by telephone – perhaps, as Block (1978) has suggested, the entire population of China might be used in the simulation. Could such a model really have a conscious sensibility? Could it experience the feeling of pain or the phenomenal appearance of the spectrum?

Although such questions have something of the metaphysical flavour of 'How many angels can dance on a pin's head?', I think one would be trading functionalism for sanity to answer them affirmatively. Happily, a negative answer does not require functionalism to be abandoned. To see why, it is only necessary to turn the argument round. Granted that the Chinese 'collective computer' cannot have conscious sensations, and that functionalism is correct, it follows that there must be certain computational states into which a human simulation cannot enter. Perhaps no group of people *can* carry out the computations of a self-reflective automaton. There are at least two aspects of this device that they are unlikely to be able to cope with. First, they might not interact quickly enough to maintain its real-time properties. For Block, speed of response is irrelevant, since he envisages conscious beings whose mental operations are very much slower than ours, and with whom we could communicate only by time-lapse photography. Such beings may be possible, but, as I argued earlier, a retarded or intermittent consciousness is hardly viable. A serial device such as a Turing machine could not exist in real time if its environment changed at a faster pace than the rate at which it could analyse events; it would rapidly lose all contact with reality. Second, a group of people may not be capable of the degree of parallel interaction required for consciousness. To perceive the world, to be aware that one is perceiving the world, to be aware that one is aware that one is perceiving the world, and so on, at one and the same time, must require a very high degree of parallel processing, with each processor handling many inputs simultaneously, so that the embedded mental models are available in parallel to the operating system. An individual in a group simulation would not be able to cope with this demand, and hence it would not be possible to run a human simulation of the parallel algorithm for consciouness. Paradoxically, the conscious human mind, which is a serial operating system, is not capable of the degree of parallel processing required to give rise to consciousness. The moral of these deliberations is simple. Consciousness is a property of a particular class of algorithms, not of the functions that they compute: *it's not what you do, it's the way that you do it.*

This conclusion has an interesting corollary. There may be no decisive test to tell whether an organism is conscious. Consciousness might have no obvious hallmarks in behaviour, if behaviour depends on the functions that are computed and not on how they are computed. They can always be computed by a serial device, such as a Turing machine, which cannot be conscious. There would be, at best, only suggestive diagnostics for consciousness.

Our brains have evolved to enable us to use language and thus to engage in a richer and more varied social life than any other species. Our conscious minds tend to model our world at its highest level – a world of people with intentions, a world of objects and events in causal relations – so that we can make conscious decisions about those matters that govern our behaviour. We also, of course, have a comparable model of ourselves – of what sort of persons we are: our traits, our likes and dislikes, our skills and shortcomings, our previous experiences, our long-term goals. Such models, as both Humphrey (1977) and Oatley (1981) have emphasized, assist us in understanding other people. We assume that others, too, have the same sorts of conscious experiences, and the same sorts of reasons for their actions. This assumption helps us to understand our families, friends, and peers; it eases the social transactions of daily life. (Our understanding of other people may also, of course, help us to understand ourselves.) But consciousness has conferred on us at least one other capacity. As many ethologists have argued, deception is fundamental to animal communication; and human interchanges also require, as Paul Valéry remarked, that brains be as impenetrable as banks. The best deception is a self-deception, since it precludes involuntary tell-tale signs that might give the deceiver away. To deceive oneself, however, presupposes that one part of the mind is inaccessible to another. Self-deception is made possible by the division of the mind into a conscious operating system and an unconscious battery of parallel processors. A capacity for self-deception is accordingly a suggestive diagnostic sign of a conscious organism. It shows itself in repression, perceptual defence, and hysterical illness.

Epilogue

At the beginning of the book, I raised a number of questions about human mentality: Why is it that we cannot think everything at once but are forced to have one thought after another? Why are there silences when we think aloud? Why can't we become aware of the rules of language and thought by introspection? And so on. These questions have all been answered in terms of a computational theory. The mind can be modelled by a parallel automaton that contains a model of itself. Parallel computation confers speed and flexibility, but it is liable to various 'pathologies' such as deadlocks. These configurations can be weeded out by natural selection in the case of simple systems, but in those that are able to implement new programs some other form of protection is required. Consciousness may originally have emerged as a processor promoted to be an operating system and to monitor other processors so as to override pathological configurations. The division between the conscious and unconscious components of the mind bears out this distinction: the contents of consciousness appear to be the values of parameters that serve as the input and output to the operating system. The particular subjective experience of consciousness depends on self-awareness, which arises from both the recursive ability to embed mental models within mental models and the mind's possession of a high-level model of the capabilities of its own operating system. The argument is, of course, suggestive rather than decisive, and it will remain so until an effective procedure for self-awareness is developed. If the functionalist argument is correct, however, consciousness is a property of a certain class of parallel algorithms. Computers can be conscious, though no direct behavioural evidence for their consciousness may ever be obtained.

For many people, the computational theory of consciousness may be distasteful. Surely, they will say, the human mind is a transcendental creation, and any attempt to explain away its mystery and to reduce it to computation is a wicked travesty. They have misunderstood my argument. Of course there may be aspects of spirituality, morality, and imagination, that cannot be modelled in computer programs. But these faculties will remain forever inexplicable. Any scientific theory of the mind has to treat it as an automaton. This is in no way demeaning or dehumanizing, but a direct consequence of the computability of scientific theories. Above all, it is entirely consistent with the view that people are responsible agents. It *is* a proposition, however, that may lead us in time to revise our concept of computation. At the moment that I am writing this sentence, I know that I am thinking, and that the topic of my thoughts is precisely the ability to think about how the mind makes possible this self-reflective knowledge. Such thoughts begin to make the recursive structure of consciousness almost manifest, like the reflections of a mirror within a mirror, until the recursive loop can no longer be sustained.

Suggestions for further reading

These suggestions are designed to help readers to follow up some of the technical aspects of computation, syntactic theory, logic, and model-theoretic semantics. Except where indicated, I have tried to select works that require a minimum of technical knowledge.

Computational theory

Turing's (1936) account of his machines is worth reading, though his formulation of them is different in detail from modern specifications. Davis (1958) and Rogers (1967) are standard references on Turing machines, recursive functions, and the theory of computability, but they presume considerable mathematical experience on the part of the reader. Boolos and Jeffrey (1980) provide a briefer and more accessible account; they also deal with logic at a fairly technical level. For the reader who is prepared to put some effort into the book, Minsky (1967) is highly stimulating.

There is only one way to become familiar with computer programming itself, and that is to learn to program. BASIC is undoubtedly the most accessible programming language, but it too readily allows the neophyte to develop bad habits, e.g., writing code with so many GOTO instructions that it is all but impossible to understand. LOGO is easy to learn but only just becoming generally available. Many high-level programming languages, such as ALGOL, C, and PASCAL, naturally inculcate a more structured form of programming (cf. Dahl, Dijkstra, and Hoare, 1972). Programs for modelling mental processes are easier to write in languages that allow list-structures to be manipulated. The two main list-processing languages are POP-2 (Burstall, Collins, and Popplestone, 1971) and LISP (Winston and Horn, 1981). POP-2 and its descendants are used mainly in the UK; LISP in various dialects is more international. Inexpensive interpreters for LISP are available for certain types of microcomputer.

I know of no good introductory text on the theory of parallel computation. Peterson (1981) provides a readable account of the theory of Petri nets; Kung (1980) surveys some aspects of the field and includes a useful

479

bibliography; Dennis (1980) describes the implementation of data flow programs.

Anyone frightened of computers should read T. H. Nelson's book, *Computer Lib*, with its splendid motto, 'You can and must understand computers NOW.' (Fear often manifests itself in the sufferer's mind as disdain.) Anyone not frightened by the potential misuse of computers should read Weizenbaum (1976).

Syntactic theory

The abstract theory of syntax and its relation to automata theory is described in Hopcroft and Ullman (1979); although this book necessarily employs a large amount of mathematical symbolism, it does not take for granted much mathematical knowledge. There are several good textbooks on transformational grammar (e.g., Bach, 1974; Culicover, 1976). Of Chomsky's technical works, *Syntactic Structures* is the most accessible and should be read by every student of natural language. His recent books are more approachable, but often less devoted to matters of pure grammatical theory (cf. Chomsky, 1980). Brame (1978) has written an elementary account of his theory of phrase-structure grammar for natural language, but unfortunately there are as yet no books on the work of Peters, Gazdar, and their colleagues. The theory of parsing context-free languages is surveyed magisterially in Aho and Ullman (1972), but that book makes few concessions to readers unused to formal notation.

Logic and model-theoretic semantics

Introductory textbooks on logic abound: Lemmon (1965) provides an excellent starting-point; Hughes and Cresswell (1968) deal with modal logic (and its model-theoretic semantics) in a congenial way; Jeffrey (1967) gives an introduction to logic from the standpoint of 'natural deduction'.

The book by Dowty, Wall, and Peters (1981) assumes only a rudimentary knowledge of set theory and provides a thorough grounding in model-theoretic semantics and Montague grammar. For those who prefer a shorter treatment, which takes a little more for granted, Partee (1975) is excellent.

Bibliography

Ades, A. E. and Steedman, M. J. (1982) On the order of words. *Linguistics and Philosophy*, **4**, 517–58.

Adrian, E. D. and Yealland, L. R. (1917) The treatment of some common war neuroses. *Lancet* (June), 3–24.

Aho, A. V., Hopcroft, J. E. and Ullman, J. D. (1974) *The Design and Analysis of Computer Algorithms*. Reading, Mass.: Addison-Wesley.

Aho, A. V. and Ullman, J. D. (1972) *The Theory of Parsing, Translation, and Compiling*. Vol. 1: *Parsing*. Englewood Cliffs, NJ: Prentice Hall.

The American Heritage Dictionary of the English Language (1969) Edited by William Morris. Boston: American Heritage Publishing Co. and Houghton Mifflin.

Anderson, D. B. (1972) Documentation for LIB PICO-PLANNER. School of Artificial Intelligence, Edinburgh University.

Anderson, J. A. and Hinton, G. E. (1981) Models of information processing in the brain. In G. E. Hinton and J. A. Anderson (eds.) *Parallel Models of Associative Memory*. Hillsdale, NJ: Erlbaum.

Anderson, J. R. (1978) Arguments concerning representations for mental imagery. *Psychological Review*, **85**, 249–77.

Anderson, R. C. and Ortony, A. (1975) On putting apples into bottles – a problem of polysemy. *Cognitive Psychology*, **7**, 167–80.

Anderson, R. C., Pichert, J. W., Goetz, E. T., Schallert, D. L., Stevens, K. V. and Trollip, S. R. (1976) Instantiation of general terms. *Journal of Verbal Learning and Verbal Behavior*, **15**, 667–79.

Asher, R. (1972) *Talking Sense*. London: Pitman.

Austin, J. L. (1961) Ifs and cans. In J. L. Austin *Philosophical Papers*. Oxford: Clarendon Press.

Bach, E. (1974) *Syntactic Theory*. New York: Holt.

Baddeley, A. D. and Hitch, G. (1974) Working memory. In G. H. Bower (ed.) *The Psychology of Learning and Motivation*, Vol. 8. New York: Academic Press.

Baker, G. P. (1974) Criteria: a new foundation for semantics. *Ratio*, **16**, 156–89.

Barclay, J. R. (1973) The role of comprehension in remembering sentences. *Cognitive Psychology*, **4**, 229–54.

Bar-Hillel, Y. (1967) Dictionaries and meaning rules. *Foundations of Language*, **3**, 409–14.

Bar-Hillel, Y. (1970) Argumentation in pragmatic languages. In Y. Bar-Hillel, *Aspects of Language*. Amsterdam: North-Holland.

Bar-Hillel, Y. and Carnap, R. (1952) An outline of a theory of semantic information. Technical report No. 247 of the Research Laboratory of Electronics, MIT. Reprinted in Y. Bar-Hillel, *Language and Information*. Reading, Mass.: Addison-Wesley. Jerusalem: Jerusalem Academic Press, 1964.

Bar-Hillel, Y. and Shamir, E. (1960) Finite-state languages: representations and adequacy problems. *The Bulletin of the Research Council of Israel*, 8f(3).

Barwise, J. (1980) Scenes and other situations. In J. Barwise and I. A. Sag (eds.) *Stanford Working Papers in Semantics*, Vol. 1. Cognitive Science Group, Stanford University.

Barwise, J. and Cooper, R. (1981) Generalized quantifiers and natural languages. *Linguistics and Philosophy*, **4**, 159–219.

Baylor, G. W. (1971) Programs and protocol analysis on a mental imagery task. *First International Joint Conference on Artificial Intelligence*, n.p.

Beerbohm, M. (1912) *A Christmas Garland*. London: Heinemann.

Beeton, I. (1906) *Mrs. Beeton's Household Management*. London: Cape (originally published in 1861).

Bennett, D. C. (1975) *Spatial and Temporal Uses of English Prepositions: An Essay in Stratificational Semantics*. London: Longman.

Berlin, B. and Kay, P. (1969) *Basic Color Terms: Their Universality and Evolution*. Berkeley and Los Angeles: University of California Press.

Beth, E. W. and Piaget, J. (1966) *Mathematical Epistemology and Psychology*. Dordrecht: Reidel.

Bever, T. G., Garrett, M. F. and Hurtig, R. (1973) The interaction of perceptual processes and ambiguous sentences. *Memory and Cognition*, **1**, 277–86.

Bigelow, J. G. (1978) Believing in semantics. *Linguistics and Philosophy*, **2**, 101–44.

Block, N. (1978) Troubles with functionalism. In C. W. Savage (ed.) *Perception and Cognition: Issues in the Foundations of Psychology*. Minnesota Studies in the Philosophy of Science, Vol. 9. Minneapolis: University of Minnesota Press.

Boolos, G. and Jeffrey, R. (1974) *Computability and Logic*. Cambridge: Cambridge University Press (second edition, 1980).

Bower, G. H. (1972) Mental imagery and associative learning. In L. Gregg (ed.) *Cognition in Learning and Memory*. New York: Wiley.

Bracewell, R. J. and Hidi, S. E. (1974) The solution of an inferential problem as a function of stimulus materials. *Quarterly Journal of Experimental Psychology*, **26**, 480–8.

Braine, M. D. S. (1978) On the relation between the natural logic of reasoning and standard logic. *Psychological Review*, **85**, 1–21.

Braine, M. D. S. (1979) On some claims about *if–then*. *Linguistics and Philosophy*, **3**, 35–47.

Brame, M. K. (1978) *Base Generated Syntax*. Seattle: Noit Amrofer.

Bransford, J. D., Barclay, J. R. and Franks, J. J. (1972) Sentence memory: a constructive versus interpretive approach. *Cognitive Psychology*, **3**, 193–209.

Bransford, J. D. and McCarrell, N. S. (1975) A sketch of a cognitive approach to comprehension: some thoughts about understanding what it means to comprehend. In W. B. Weimar and D. S. Palermo (eds.) *Cognition and the Symbolic Processes*. Hillsdale, NJ: Erlbaum.

Bresnan, J. (1978) A realistic transformational grammar. In M. Halle, J. Bresnan and G. A. Miller (eds.) *Linguistic Theory and Psychological Reality*. Cambridge, Mass.: MIT Press.

Broadbent, D. E. (1958) *Perception and Communication*. London: Pergamon.

Brooks, L. (1967) The suppression of visualization by reading. *Quarterly Journal of Experimental Psychology*, **19**, 280–99.

Brown, C., Keats, J. A., Keats, D. M. and Seggie, I. (1980) Reasoning about implication: a comparison of Malaysian and Australian subjects. *Journal of Cross-Cultural Psychology*, **11**, 395–410.

Bruner, J. S., Goodnow, J. J. and Austin, G. A. (1956) *A Study of Thinking*. New York: NY Science Editions, Inc.

Bryant, P. E. and Trabasso, T. R. (1971) Transitive inferences and memory in young children. *Nature*, **232**, 456–8.

Burgess, A. (1962) *A Clockwork Orange*. London: Heinemann.

Burningham, J. (1970) *Mr. Gumpy's Outing*. London: Cape.

Burstall, R. M., Collins, J. S. and Popplestone, R. J. (1971) *Programming in POP-2*. Edinburgh: The Round Table and Edinburgh University Press.

Campbell, R., Donaldson, M. and Young, B. (1976) Constraints on classificatory skills in young children. *British Journal of Psychology*, **67**, 89–100.

Carey, S. (1978) The child as word learner. In M. Halle, J. Bresnan and G. A. Miller (eds.) *Linguistic Theory and Psychological Reality*. Cambridge, Mass.: MIT Press.

Chapman, I. J. and Chapman, J. P. (1959) Atmosphere effect re-examined. *Journal of Experimental Psychology*, **58**, 220–6.

Chihara, C. S. and Fodor, J. A. (1965) Operationalism and ordinary language: a critique of Wittgenstein. *American Philosophical Quarterly*, **2**, 281–95. Reprinted in G. Pitcher (ed.) *Wittgenstein: The Philosophical Investigations*. London: Macmillan, 1968.

Chomsky, N. (1957) *Syntactic Structures*. The Hague: Mouton.

Chomsky, N. (1959) On certain formal properties of grammars. *Information and Control*, **2**, 137–67.

Chomsky, N. (1965) *Aspects of the Theory of Syntax*. Cambridge, Mass.: MIT Press.

Chomsky, N. (1977) *Essays on Form and Interpretation*. Amsterdam: North-Holland.

Chomsky, N. (1980) *Rules and Representations*. Oxford: Blackwell.

Chomsky, N. (1981) Knowledge of language: its elements and origins. *Philosophical Transactions of the Royal Society of London*, Series B, **295**, 223–43.

Churchland, P. M. (1981) Eliminative materialism and the propositional attitudes. *Journal of Philosophy*, **78**, 67–90.

Clark, H. H. (1974) Semantics and comprehension. In T. A. Sebeok (ed.) *Current Trends in Linguistics*. Vol. 12: *Linguistics and Adjacent Arts and Sciences*. The Hague: Mouton.

Clark, H. H. and Clark, E. V. (1977) *Psychology and Language: An Introduction to Psycholinguistics*. New York: Harcourt Brace Jovanovich, Inc.

Cohen, L. J. (1981) Can human irrationality be experimentally demonstrated? *Behavioral and Brain Sciences*, **4**, 317–70.

Cohen, P. (1978) On knowing what to say: planning speech acts. Ph.D. Dissertation, Technical Report No. 118, Department of Computer Science, University of Toronto.

Cole, P. (1978) On the origins of referential opacity. In P. Cole (ed.) *Syntax and Semantics*. Vol. 9: *Pragmatics*. New York: Academic Press.

Collins, A. M. and Quillian, M. R. (1969) Retrieval time from semantic memory. *Journal of Verbal Learning and Verbal Behavior*, **8**, 240–7.

Collins, A. M. and Quillian, M. R. (1972) How to make a language user. In E. Tulving and W. Donaldson (eds.) *Organisation and Memory*. New York: Academic Press.

Conan Doyle, Sir Arthur (1905) *The Return of Sherlock Holmes*. London: Murray.

Conrad, C. (1972) Cognitive economy in semantic memory. *Journal of Experimental Psychology*, **92**, 149–54.

Cooke, M. de Z. (1975) An investigation of the memory for sentential meaning. Unpublished Ph.D. Thesis, University College London.

Cooper, G. S. (1968) A semantic analysis of English locative propositions. Report 1587. Cambridge, Mass.: Bolt, Beranek, and Newman.

Cornulier, B. de (1973) But if 'respectively' meant something? *Papers in Linguistics*, **6**, 131–4.

Cox, J. R. and Griggs, R. A. (1982) The effects of experience on performance in Wason's selection task. *Memory and Cognition*, **10**, 496–502.

Craik, F. I. M. and Tulving, E. (1975) Depth of processing and the retention of words in episodic memory. *Journal of Experimental Psychology: General*, **104**, 268–94.

Craik, K. (1943) *The Nature of Explanation*. Cambridge: Cambridge University Press.

Crain, S. and Steedman, M. J. (1981) On not being led up the garden path: the use of context by the psychological parser. Paper presented to the Sloan Conference on Modelling Human Parsing, University of Texas at Austin.

Cresswell, M. (1980) Quotational theories of propositional attitudes. *Journal of Philosophical Logic*, **9**, 17–40.

Culicover, P. W. (1976) *Syntax*. New York: Academic Press.

Culicover, P. W. and Wexler, K. (1977) Some syntactic implications of a theory of language learnability. In P. Culicover, T. Wasow and A. Akmajian (eds.) *Formal Syntax*. New York: Academic Press.

Dahl, O. J., Dijkstra, E. W. and Hoare, C. A. R. (1972) *Structured Programming*. New York: Academic Press.

Davies, D. J. M. and Isard, S. D. (1972) Utterances as programs. In D. Michie (ed.) *Machine Intelligence*, Vol. 7. Edinburgh: Edinburgh University Press.

Davis, M. (1958) *Computability and Unsolvability*. New York: McGraw-Hill.

Davis, M. (1980) The mathematics of non-monotonic reasoning. *Artificial Intelligence*, **13**, 73–80.

Dennett, D. C. (1978) Toward a cognitive theory of consciousness. Chapter 9 in *Brainstorms*. Vermont: Bradford Books.

Dennis, J. B. (1980) Data flow supercomputers. *Computer*, **13**, 48–56.

De Soto, C. B., London, M. and Handel, S. (1965) Social reasoning and spatial paralogic. *Journal of Personality and Social Psychology*, **2**, 513–21.

Dickens, C. (1854) *Hard Times* (republished, London: Nonesuch edition, 1938).

Dickstein, L. S. (1978) The effect of figure on syllogistic reasoning. *Memory and Cognition*, **6**, 76–83.

Dijk, T. van (1977) *Text and Context: Explorations in the Semantics and Pragmatics of Discourse*. London: Longman.

Donaldson, M. (1978) *Children's Minds*. London: Fontana.

Donnellan, K. S. (1966) Reference and definite descriptions. *Philosophical Review*, **75**, 281–304.

Dooling, D. J. and Christiaansen, R. E. (1977) Levels of encoding and retention of prose. In G. H. Bower (ed.) *The Psychology of Learning and Motivation*, Vol. 11. New York: Academic Press.

Dowty, D. R., Wall, R. E. and Peters, S. (1981) *Introduction to Montague Semantics*. Dordrecht: Reidel.

Dummett, M. (1959) Wittgenstein's philosophy of mathematics. *Philosophical Review*, **68**, 324–48.

Durkheim, E. and Mauss, M. (1963) *Primitive Classification*. London: Routledge and Kegan Paul (originally published in 1903).

Duyne, P. C. van (1974) Realism and linguistic complexity in reasoning. *British Journal of Psychology*, **65**, 59–67.

Duyne, P. C. van (1976) Necessity and contingent in reasoning. *Acta Psychologica*, **40**, 85–101.

Earley, J. (1970) An efficient context-free parsing algorithm. *Communications of the Association for Computing Machinery*, **13**, 94–102.

Ehrlich, K. (1980) The comprehension of pronouns. *Quarterly Journal of Experimental Psychology*, **32**, 247–56.

Ehrlich, K. and Johnson-Laird, P. N. (1982) Spatial descriptions and referential continuity. *Journal of Verbal Learning and Verbal Behavior*, **21**, 296–306.

Einstein, A. and Infeld, L. (1938) *The Evolution of Physics*. New York: Simon and Schuster.

Emonds, J. (1976) *A Transformational Approach to English Syntax: Root, Structure-Preserving and Local Transformations*. New York: Academic Press.

Empson, W. (1961) *Seven Types of Ambiguity*. Harmondsworth, Middx: Penguin (originally published 1930).

Engdahl, E. (1981) Interpreting sentences with multiple filler–gap dependencies. Mimeo, Max Planck Institut für Psycholinguistics, Nijmegen.

Erickson, J. R. (1974) A set analysis theory of behavior in formal syllogistic reasoning tasks. In R. Solso (ed.) *Loyola Symposium on Cognition*, Vol. 2. Hillsdale, New Jersey: Erlbaum.

Evans, G. (1980) Pronouns. *Linguistic Inquiry*, **11**, 337–62.

Evans, J. St B. T. (1982) *The Psychology of Deductive Reasoning*. London: Routledge and Kegan Paul.

Feuerstein, R., Hoffman, M. B. and Miller, R. (1980). *Instrumental Enrichment*. Baltimore: University Park Press.

Field, H. (1978) Mental representation. *Erkenntnis*, **13**, 9–61.

Fillmore, C. J. (1968) The case for case. In E. Bach and R. T. Harms (eds.) *Universals in Linguistic Theory*. New York: Holt, Rinehart and Winston.

Findler, N. V. (ed.) (1979) *Associative Networks: Representation and Use of Knowledge by Computers*. New York: Academic Press.

Finocchiaro, M. A. (1980) *Galileo and the Art of Reasoning*. Dordrecht: Reidel.

Fisher, S. C. (1916) The process of generalizing abstraction; and its product, the general concept. *Psychological Monographs*, **21**, No. 2 (whole No. 90).

Fodor, J. A. (1968) *Psychological Explanation*. New York: Random House.

Fodor, J. A. (1975) *The Language of Thought*. Hassocks, Sussex: Harvester Press.

Fodor, J. A. (1980) Fixation of belief and concept acquisition. In M. Piattelli-Palmarini (ed.) *Language and Learning: The Debate between Jean Piaget and Noam Chomsky*. Cambridge, Mass.: Harvard University Press.

Fodor, J. A., Bever, T. G. and Garrett, M. F. (1974) *The Psychology of Language*. New York: McGraw-Hill.

Fodor, J. A., Garrett, M. F., Walker, E. C. T. and Parkes, C. H. (1980) Against definitions. *Cognition*, **8**, 263–367.

Fodor, J. D. (1977) *Semantics: Theories of Meaning in Generative Grammar*. New York: Crowell.

Fodor, J. D. (1978) Parsing strategies and constraints on transformations. *Linguistic Inquiry*, **9**, 427–73.

Fodor, J. D. (1982) The mental representation of quantifiers. In S. Peters and E. Saarinen (eds.) *Processes, Beliefs, and Questions*. Dordrecht: Reidel.

Fodor, J. D. (In press) *Parsing, Constraints and the Freedom of Expression*. Montgomery, Vermont: Bradford Press.

Fodor, J. D., Fodor, J. A. and Garrett, M. F. (1975) The psychological unreality of semantic representations. *Linguistic Inquiry*, **4**, 515–31.

Fodor, J. D. and Frazier, L. (1980) Is the human sentence parsing mechanism an ATN? *Cognition*, **8**, 418–59.

Ford, M., Bresnan, J. W. and Kaplan, R. M. (In press) A competence-based theory of syntactic closure. In J. W. Bresnan (ed.) *The Mental Representation of Grammatical Relations*. Cambridge, Mass.: MIT Press.

Forster, K. I. (1974) The role of semantic hypotheses in sentence processing. In *Problèmes actuels en psycholinguistique* (Colloques Internationaux du CNRS No. 206). Paris.

Forster, K. I. (1976) The autonomy of syntactic processing. Paper delivered at the Convocation on Communications, 9–10 March 1976, MIT.

Forster, K. I. (1979) Levels of processing and the structure of the language processor. In W. E. Cooper and E. C. T. Walker (eds.) *Sentence Processing: Psycholinguistic Studies presented to Merrill Garrett*. Hillsdale, NJ: Erlbaum.

Forster, K. I. and Olbrei, I. (1973) Semantic heuristics and syntactic analysis. *Cognition*, **2**, 319–47.

Fraassen, B. van (1969) Presuppositions, supervaluations and free logic. In K. Lambert (ed.) *The Logical Way of Doing Things*. New Haven: Yale University Press.

Frandsen, A. N. and Holder, J. R. (1969) Spatial visualization in solving complex verbal problems. *Journal of Psychology*, **73**, 229–33.

Frase, L. T. (1968) Associative factors in syllogistic reasoning. *Journal of Experimental Psychology*, **76**, 407–12.

Frase, L. T. and Kammann, R. (1974) Effects of search criterion upon unanticipated free recall of categorically related words. *Memory and Cognition*, **2**, 181–4.

Frazier, L. (1981) Processing sentence structure. Paper delivered at the Sloan Workshop on Eye Movements in Reading. Amherst, Massachusetts.

Frazier, L., Clifton, C. and Randall, J. (In press) Filling gaps: decision principles and structure in sentence comprehension.

Frazier, L. and Fodor, J. D. (1978) The sausage machine: a new two-stage parsing model. *Cognition*, **6**, 291–325.

Frazier, L. and Rayner, K. (1982) Making and correcting errors during sentence comprehension: eye movements in the analysis of structurally ambiguous sentences. *Cognitive Psychology*, **14**, 178–210.

Freedman, J. L. and Loftus, E. F. (1971) Retrieval of words from long-term memory. *Journal of Verbal Learning and Verbal Behavior*, **10**, 107–15.

Frege, G. (1879) *Begriffsschrift, eine der Arithmetischen nachgebildete Formelsprache des reinen Denkens*. Halle: Nebert.

Frege, G. (1892) Über Sinn und Bedeutung. *Zeitschrift für Philosphie und philosophische Kritik*, **100**, 25–50. Translated in P. T. Geach and M. Black (eds.) *Philosophical Writings of Gottlob Frege*. Oxford: Blackwell, 1952.

Frege, G. (1953) *The Foundations of Arithmetic*. Translated by J. L. Austin. Second revised edition. Oxford: Blackwell (originally published 1884).

Frisch, K. von (1966) *The Dancing Bees*. Second edition. London: Methuen.

Gale, R. M. (1967) Propositions, Judgments, Sentences, and Statements. In P. Edwards (ed.) *The Encyclopedia of Philosophy*. New York: Macmillan.

Garnham, A. (1979) Instantiation of verbs. *Quarterly Journal of Experimental Psychology*, **31**, 207–14.

Garnham, A. (1981) Mental models as representations of discourse and text. Unpublished D.Phil. Thesis, University of Sussex.

Garnham, A., Oakhill, J. and Johnson-Laird, P. N. (1982) Referential continuity and the coherence of discourse. *Cognition*, **11**, 29–46.

Garrett, M. F. (1970) Does ambiguity complicate the perception of sentences? In G. B. Flores d'Arcais and W. J. M. Levelt (eds.) *Advances in Psycholinguistics*. Amsterdam: North-Holland.

Garrett, M. F. (1976) The organisation of sentence processors. Paper delivered at the Convocation on Communications, 9–10 March 1976, MIT.

Gazdar, G. (1979) English as a context free language. Unpublished paper, Mimeo, University of Sussex.

Gazdar, G. (1981a) Unbounded dependencies and coordinate structure. *Linguistic Inquiry*, **12**, 155–84.

Gazdar, G. (1981b) On syntactic categories. *Philosophical Transactions of the Royal Society of London*, Series B, **295**, 267–83.

Gazdar, G., Pullum, G. K. and Sag, I. (1981) *Auxiliaries and Related Phenomena in a Restrictive Theory of Grammar*. Bloomington, Indiana: Indiana University Linguistics Club.

Geach, P. (1962) *Reference and Generality*. Ithaca, New York: Cornell University Press.

Gentner, D. and Stevens, A. (eds.) (In press) *Mental Models*. Hillsdale, NJ: Erlbaum.

Germain, E. B. (ed.) (1978) *English and American Surrealist Poetry*. Harmondsworth, Middx: Penguin.

Gibson, E. J. (1971) Perceptual learning and the theory of word perception. *Cognitive Psychology*, **2**, 351–68.

Gibson, J. J. (1979) *The Ecological Approach to Visual Perception*. Boston: Houghton Mifflin.

Gilhooly, K. J. and Falconer, W. A. (1974) Concrete and abstract terms and relations in testing a rule. *Quarterly Journal of Experimental Psychology*, **26**, 355–9.

Glushko, R. J. and Cooper, L. A. (1978) Spatial comprehension and comparison processes in verification tasks. *Cognitive Psychology*, **10**, 391–421.

Golding, E. (1981) The effect of past experience on problem solving. Paper presented at the Annual Conference of the British Psychological Society, Surrey University.

Gough, P. B. (1971) Experimental psycholinguistics. In W. O. Dingwall (ed.) *A Survey of Linguistic Science*. University of Maryland: Linguistics Program.

Grice, P. (1975) Logic and conversation. In P. Cole and J. L. Morgan (eds.) *Syntax and Semantics*. Vol. 3: *Speech Acts*. New York: Academic Press.

Griggs, R. A. and Cox, J. R. (1982) The elusive thematic-materials effect in Wason's selection task. *British Journal of Psychology*, **73**, 407–20.

Griggs, R. A. and Cox, J. R. (In press) The effect of problem content on strategies in Wason's selection task. *Journal of Experimental Psychology: Learning, Memory, and Cognition*.

Guibas, L. J., Kung, H. T. and Thompson, C. D. (1979) Direct VLSI implementation of combinatorial algorithms. *Proceedings of the Caltech Conference on Very Large Scale Integration: Architecture, Design, Fabrication*. Pasedena: California Institute of Technology.

Guilford, J. P. (1959) Three faces of intellect. *American Psychologist*, **14**, 469–79.

Gunderson, K. (1971) *Mentality and Machines*. New York: Anchor.

Guyote, M. J. and Sternberg, R. J. (1978) A transitive-chain theory of syllogistic reasoning. Technical Report No. 5, Department of Psychology, Yale University. Revised version in: *Cognitive Psychology*, **13**, 461–525, 1981.

Hacker, P. M. S. (1972) *Insight and Illusion: Wittgenstein on Philosophy and the Metaphysics of Experience*. Oxford: Clarendon Press.

Halff, H. M., Ortony, A. and Anderson, R. C. (1976) A context-sensitive representation of word meanings. *Memory and Cognition*, **4**, 378–83.

Hammett, D. (1966) The gutting of Couffignal. In *The Dashiell Hammett Omnibus*. London: Cassell.

Haviland, S. E. and Clark, H. H. (1974) What's new? Acquiring new information as a process in comprehension. *Journal of Verbal Learning and Verbal Behavior*, **13**, 512–21.

Hendrix, G. G. (1979) Encoding knowledge in partitioned networks. In Findler, N. V. (1979).

Henle, M. (1978) Foreword to R. Revlin and R. E. Mayer (eds.) *Human Reasoning*. Washington, DC: Winston.

Hewitt, C. (1971) Description and theoretical analysis (using schemas) of PLANNER: a language for proving theorems and manipulating models in a robot. Ph.D. dissertation, MIT.

Hintikka, J. (1962) *Knowledge and Belief: An Introduction to the Logic of the Two Notions*. Ithaca, NY: Cornell University Press.

Hintikka, J. (1963) The models of modality. *Acta Philosophica Fennica*, **16**, 65–82.

Hintikka, J. (1969) *Models for Modalities: Selected Essays*. Dordrecht: Reidel.

Hintikka, J. (1973) *Logic, Language-games, and Information*. Oxford: Oxford University Press.

Hintikka, J. (1974) Quantifiers vs. quantification theory. *Linguistic Inquiry*, **5**, 152–77.

Hintikka, J. (1975) Impossible possible worlds vindicated. *Journal of Philosophical Logic*, **4**, 475–84.

Hinton, G. (1979) Imagery with arrays. Commentary on S. M. Kosslyn, S. Pinker, G. E. Smith and S. P. Shwartz, 'On the demystification of mental imagery'. *The Behavioral and Brain Sciences*, **2**, 555–6.

Hitch, G. J. and Baddeley, A. D. (1976) Verbal reasoning and working memory. *Quarterly Journal of Experimental Psychology*, **28**, 603–21.

Homer. (1950) *The Iliad*. Translated by E. V. Rieu. Harmondsworth, Middx: Penguin.

Hopcroft, J. E. and Ullman, J. D. (1979) *Formal Languages and their Relation to Automata*. Reading, Mass.: Addison-Wesley.

Hughes, G. E. and Cresswell, M. J. (1968) *An Introduction to Modal Logic*. London: Methuen.

Hull, C. L. (1920) Quantitative aspects of the evolution of concepts. *Psychological Monographs*, **28**, whole No. 123.

Hume, D. (1896) *A Treatise of Human Nature*, Vol. 1. Edited by L. A. Selby-Bigge. Oxford: Clarendon Press.

Humphrey, N. (1977) Nature's psychologists. The Lister Lecture delivered to the British Association for the Advancement of Science. Reprinted in B. Josephson and V. S. Ramachandran (eds.) *Consciousness and the Physical World*. Oxford: Pergamon (1979).

Hunt, E. B., Lunneborg, C. E. and Lewis, J. (1975) What does it mean to be high verbal? *Cognitive Psychology*, **7**, 194–227.

Hunter, I. M. L. (1957) The solving of three term series problems. *British Journal of Psychology*, **48**, 286–98.

Huttenlocher, J. (1968) Constructing spatial images: a strategy in reasoning. *Psychological Review*, **75**, 550–60.

Hyde, T. S. (1973) Differential effects of effort and type of orientating task on recall and organization of highly associated words. *Journal of Experimental Psychology*, **97**, 111–13.

Hyde, T. S. and Jenkins, J. J. (1969) Differential effects of incidental tasks on the organization and recall of a list of highly associated words. *Journal of Experimental Psychology*, **82**, 472–81.

Inhelder, B. and Piaget, J. (1958) *The Growth of Logical Thinking from Childhood to Adolescence*. London: Routledge and Kegan Paul.

Jarvella, R. J. (1979) Immediate memory and discourse processing. In G. H. Bower (ed.) *The Psychology of Learning and Motivation*, Vol. 13. New York: Academic Press.

Jeffrey, R. (1967) *Formal Logic, Its Scope and Limits*. New York: McGraw-Hill.

John, E. R. (1976) A model of consciousness. In Schwartz, G. E. and Shapiro, D. (eds.) *Consciousness and Self-Regulation: Advances in Research*, Vol. 1. London: Wiley.

Johnson-Laird, P. N. (1967) An experimental investigation into one pragmatic factor governing the use of the English language. Unpublished Ph.D. thesis, University College London.

Johnson-Laird, P. N. (1969a) On understanding logically complex sentences. *Quarterly Journal of Experimental Psychology*, **21**, 1–13.

Johnson-Laird, P. N. (1969b) Reasoning with ambiguous sentences. *British Journal of Psychology*, **60**, 17–23.

Johnson-Laird, P. N. (1969c) '&'. *Journal of Linguistics*, **6**, 111–14.

Johnson-Laird, P. N. (1970) The perception and memory of sentences. In J. Lyons (ed.) *New Horizons in Linguistics*. Harmondsworth, Middx: Penguin.

Johnson-Laird, P. N. (1974) Experimental psycholinguistics. *Annual Review of Psychology*, **25**, 135–60.

Johnson-Laird, P. N. (1975a) Models of deduction. In R. J. Falmagne (ed.) *Reasoning: Representation and Process in Children and Adults*. Hillsdale, NJ: Erlbaum.

Johnson-Laird, P. N. (1975b) Meaning and the mental lexicon. In A. Kennedy and A. Wilkes (eds.) *Studies in Long Term Memory*. London: Wiley.

Johnson-Laird, P. N. (1977a) Psycholinguistics without linguistics. In N. S. Sutherland (ed.) *Tutorial Essays in Psychology*, Vol. 1. Hillsdale, New Jersey: Erlbaum.

Johnson-Laird, P. N. (1977b) Procedural semantics. *Cognition*, **5**, 189–214.

Johnson-Laird, P. N. (1978) The meaning of modality. *Cognitive Science*, **2**, 17–26.

Johnson-Laird, P. N. (1980) Mental models in cognitive science. *Cognitive Science*, **4**, 71–115.

Johnson-Laird, P. N. (1982) Formal semantics and the psychology of meaning. In S. Peters and E. Saarinen (eds.) *Processes, Beliefs and Questions*. Dordrecht: Reidel.

Johnson-Laird, P. N. (In press) Linguistics and psychology. In M. H. Bornstein (ed.) *Cross Currents in Contemporary Psychology*.

489

Johnson-Laird, P. N. and Bara, B. (1982) The figural effect in syllogistic reasoning. Mimeo, Laboratory of Experimental Psychology, Sussex.

Johnson-Laird, P. N. and Bethell-Fox, C. (1978) Memory for questions and amount of processing. *Memory and Cognition*, **6**, 496–501.

Johnson-Laird, P. N. and Garnham, A. (1980) Descriptions and discourse models. *Linguistics and Philosophy*, **3**, 371–93.

Johnson-Laird, P. N., Gibbs, G. and de Mowbray, J. (1978) Meaning, amount of processing, and memory for words. *Memory and Cognition*, **6**, 372–5.

Johnson-Laird, P. N., Legrenzi, P. and Legrenzi, M. S. (1972) Reasoning and a sense of reality. *British Journal of Psychology*, **63**, 395–400.

Johnson-Laird, P. N. and Quinn, J. G. (1976) To define true meaning. *Nature*, **264**, 635–6.

Johnson-Laird, P. N. and Steedman, M. J. (1978) The psychology of syllogisms. *Cognitive Psychology*, **10**, 64–99.

Johnson-Laird, P. N. and Stevenson, R. (1970) Memory for syntax. *Nature*, **227**, 412.

Johnson-Laird, P. N. and Wason, P. C. (1970) Insight into a logical relation. *Quarterly Journal of Experimental Psychology*, **22**, 49–61.

Johnson-Laird, P. N. and Wason, P. C. (eds.) (1977) *Thinking: Readings in Cognitive Science*. Cambridge: Cambridge University Press.

Kamp, J. A. W. (1971) Formal properties of 'Now'. *Theoria*, **37**, 227–73.

Kamp, J. A. W. (1975) Two theories about adjectives. In E. L. Keenan (ed.) *Formal Semantics of Natural Language*. Cambridge: Cambridge University Press.

Kamp, J. A. W. (1979) Events, instants and temporal reference. In R. Bäuerle, U. Egli and A. von Stechow (eds.) *Semantics from Different Points of View*. Berlin: Springer-Verlag.

Kamp, J. A. W. (1980) A theory of truth and semantic representation. Report of Center of Cognitive Science, University of Texas at Austin.

Kant, I. (1787) *The Critique of Pure Reason*. Second edition. Translated by J. M. D. Meiklejohn. London: Dent, 1934.

Kaplan, D. (1977) Demonstratives: an essay on the semantics, logic, metaphysics and epistemology of demonstratives and other indexicals. Paper read to March 1977 meeting of the Pacific division of the American Philosophical Association.

Kaplan, R. M. (1972) Augmented transition networks as psychological models of sentence comprehension. *Artificial Intelligence*, **3**, 77–100.

Kaplan, R. M. (1980) Computational resources and linguistic theory. In G. Lavendel (ed.) *A Decade of Research*. New York: Bowker.

Karttunen, L. (1969) Pronouns and variables. In R. I. Binnick, A. Davison, G. Green and J. Morgan (eds.) *Papers from the Fifth Regional Meeting of the Chicago Linguistics Society*, 1969. Chicago, Illinois: University of Chicago.

Katz, J. J. and Fodor, J. A. (1963) The structure of a semantic theory. *Language*, **39**, 170–210.

Kay, M. (1967) Experiments with a powerful parser. Memorandum RM–5452–PR, The RAND Corporation, Santa Monica, California.

Keil, F. (1979) *Semantic and Conceptual Development: Ontological Perspective*. Cambridge, Mass.: Harvard University Press.

Kent, J. (Translator) (1972) *The Fat Cat*. London: Hamish Hamilton.

Kimball, J. (1973) Seven principles of surface structure parsing in natural language. *Cognition*, **2**, 15–47.

490

Kimball, J. (1975) Predictive analysis and over-the-top parsing. In J. Kimball (ed.) *Syntax and Semantics*, Vol. 4. New York: Academic Press.

Kintsch, W. (1974) *The Representation of Meaning in Memory*. Hillsdale, NJ: Erlbaum.

Kintsch, W. and van Dijk, T. A. (1978) Towards a model of text comprehension and reproduction. *Psychological Review*, **85**, 363–94.

Klein, E. (1979) On sentences which report beliefs, desires and other mental attitudes. Unpublished Ph.D. thesis, University of Cambridge.

Klein, K. and Saltz, E. (1976) Specifying the mechanisms in levels-of-processing approach to memory. *Journal of Experimental Psychology: Human Learning and Memory*, **2**, 671–9.

Kneale, W. and Kneale, M. (1962) *The Development of Logic*. Oxford: Clarendon Press.

Koshland, D. E. Jr (1977) A response regulator model in a simple sensory system. *Science*, **196**, 1055–63.

Kosslyn, S. M. (1980) *Images and Mind*. Cambridge, Mass.: Harvard University Press.

Kozdrowicki, E. W. and Theis, D. J. (1980) Second generation of vector super-computers. *Computer*, **13**, 71–83.

Kratzer, A. (1978) Conditional necessity and possibility. Unpublished paper, Max-Planck-Gesellschaft, Nijmegen.

Kripke, S. (1963a) Semantical analysis of modal logic: I: normal propositional calculi. *Zeitschrift für mathematische Logik und Grundlagen der Mathematik*, **9**, 67–96.

Kripke, S. (1963b) Semantical considerations on modal logics. *Acta Philosophica Fennica*, **16**, 83–94.

Kripke, S. (1972) Naming and necessity. In D. Davidson and G. Harman (eds.) *Semantics of Natural Language*. Dordrecht: Reidel.

Kripke, S. (1977) Speaker's reference and semantic reference. *Midwestern Studies of Philosophy*, **2**, 255–76.

Kung, H. T. (1980) The structure of parallel algorithms. In M. C. Yovits (ed.) *Advances in Computers*, Vol. 19. New York: Academic Press.

Kuno, S. and Oettinger, A. G. (1962) Multiple-path syntactic analyzer. *Information Processing*, **62**, 306–12.

Lakoff, G. (1972) Hedges: a study of meaning criteria and the logic of fuzzy concepts. In *Papers from the Eighth Regional Meeting of the Chicago Linguistics Society*. Chicago: Chicago Linguistics Society.

Landauer, T. K. and Freedman, J. L. (1968) Information retrieval from long-term memory: category size and recognition time. *Journal of Verbal Learning and Verbal Behavior*, **7**, 291–5.

Lasnik, H. (1976) Remarks on coreference. *Linguistic Analysis*, **2**, 1–22.

Leech, G. N. (1969) *Towards a Semantic Description of English*. London: Longman.

Lemmon, E. J. (1965) *Beginning Logic*. London: Nelson.

Levy, P. (1973) On the relation between test theory and psychology. In P. Kline (ed.) *New Approaches to Psychological Measurement*. London: Wiley.

Lewis, D. K. (1969) *Convention: A Philosophical Study*. Cambridge, Mass.: Harvard University Press.

Lewis, D. K. (1972) General semantics. In D. Davidson and G. Harman (eds.) *Semantics of Natural Language*. Dordrecht: Reidel.

Lewis, D. K. (1973) *Counterfactuals*. Cambridge, Mass.: Harvard University Press.

Liberman, A. M., Cooper, F. S., Shankweiler, D. P. and Studdert-Kennedy, M. (1967) Perception of the speech code. *Psychological Review*, **74**, 431–61.

Lipman, M. and Sharp, A. M. (1978) *Growing up with Philosophy*. Philadelphia: Temple University Press.

Locke, J. (1961) *An Essay concerning Human Understanding*. Reprint of fifth edition, edited by J. W. Yolton, 2 vols. London: Dent (fifth edition originally published 1706).

Loftus, E. F. and Freedman, J. L. (1972) Effect of category-name frequency on the speed of naming an instance of the category. *Journal of Verbal Learning and Verbal Behavior*, **11**, 343–7.

Longman Dictionary of Contemporary English (1978) Editor-in-chief: Paul Proctor. Harlow: Longman.

Longuet-Higgins, H. C. (1972) The algorithmic description of natural language. *Proceedings of the Royal Society of London*, B, **182**, 255–76.

Longuet-Higgins, H. C. (1979) The perception of music. *Proceedings of the Royal Society of London*, B, **205**, 307–22.

Lucy, J. A. and Shweder, R. A. (1979) Whorf and his critics: linguistic and nonlinguistic influences on color memory. *American Anthropologist*, **81**, 581–615.

Lunzer, E. A., Harrison, C. and Davey, M. (1972) The four card problem and the generality of formal reasoning. *Quarterly Journal of Experimental Psychology*, **24**, 326–39.

Luria, A. R. (1977) *The Social History of Cognition*. Cambridge, Mass.: Harvard University Press.

Lycan, W. G. (1981) Toward a homuncular theory of believing. *Cognition and Brain Theory*, **4**, 139–59.

McClelland, A. G. R., Rawles, R. E. and Sinclair, F. E. (1981) The effects of search criteria and retrieval cue availability on memory for words. *Memory and Cognition*, **9**, 164–8.

McDermott, D. and Doyle, J. (1980) Non-monotonic logic I. *Artificial Intelligence*, **13**, 41–72.

Macdonald, D. (1960) *Parodies: An Anthology from Chaucer to Beerbohm – and After*. London: Faber and Faber.

Mandler, G. (1975) *Mind and Emotion*. New York: Wiley.

Mandler, J. M. (1981) Structural invariants in development. In L. S. Liben (ed.) *Piaget and the Foundation of Knowledge*. Hillsdale, NJ: Erlbaum.

Mandler, J. M. and Johnson, N. J. (1977) Remembrance of things parsed: Story structure and recall. *Cognitive Psychology*, **9**, 111–51.

Mandler, J. M. and Johnson, N. J. (1980) On throwing out the baby with the bathwater: a reply to Black and Wilensky's evaluation of story grammars. *Cognitive Science*, **4**, 305–12.

Mani, K. and Johnson-Laird, P. N. (1982) The mental representation of spatial descriptions. *Memory and Cognition*, **10**, 181–7.

Manktelow, K. I. and Evans, J. St B. T. (1979) Facilitation of reasoning by realism: effect or non-effect? *British Journal of Psychology*, **70**, 477–88.

Marcus, M. P. (1977) A theory of syntactic recognition for natural language. Ph.D. Thesis, MIT.

Marcus, M. P. (1981) A computational account of some constraints on language. In A. K. Joshi, B. L. Webber and I. A. Sag. (eds.) *Elements of Discourse Understanding*. Cambridge: Cambridge University Press.

Markham, E. M. and Seibert, J. (1976) Classes and collections: internal organisation and resulting holistic properties. *Cognitive Psychology*, **8**, 561–77.

Marr, D. (1977) Artificial intelligence – a personal view. *Artificial Intelligence*, **9**, 37–48.

Marr, D. (1982) *Vision: A Computational Investigation in the Human Representation of Visual Information*. San Francisco: Freeman.

Marslen-Wilson, W. D. (1973) Linguistic structure and speech shadowing at very short latencies. *Nature*, **244**, 522–3.

Marslen-Wilson, W. D. (1975) Sentence perception as an interactive parallel process. *Science*, **189**, 226–8.

Marslen-Wilson, W. D. and Welsh, A. (1978) Processing interactions and lexical access during word-recognition in continuous speech. *Cognitive Psychology*, **10**, 29–63.

Mead, G. H. (1934) *Mind, Self and Society from the Standpoint of a Social Behaviourist*. Edited by C. W. Morris. Chicago: University of Chicago Press.

Mehler, J. and Bever, T. G. (1967) Cognitive capacity of very young children. *Science*, **158**, 141–2.

Meyer, D. E. (1970) On the representation and retrieval of stored semantic information. *Cognitive Psychology*, **1**, 242–300.

Meyer, D. E. and Schvaneveldt, R. W. (1971) Facilitation in recognizing pairs of words: evidence of dependence between retrieval operations. *Journal of Experimental Psychology*, **90**, 227–334.

Miller, G. A. (1951) *Language and Communication*. New York: McGraw-Hill.

Miller, G. A. (1962) Some psychological studies of grammar. *American Psychologist*, **17**, 748–62.

Miller, G. A. (1972) English verbs of motion: a case study in semantics and lexical memory. In A. W. Melton and E. Martin (eds.) *Coding Processes in Human Memory*. Washington, DC: Winston.

Miller, G. A. (1977a) *Spontaneous Apprentices: Children and Language*. New York: Seaburg Press.

Miller, G. A. (1977b) Practical and lexical knowledge. Reprinted in P. N. Johnson-Laird and P. C. Wason (eds.) *Thinking: Readings in Cognitive Science*. Cambridge: Cambridge University Press. (From E. Rosch and B. B. Lloyd (eds.) *Cognition and Categorization* Hillsdale, NJ: Erlbaum, 1978).

Miller, G. A. (1979) Images and models, similes and metaphors. In A. Ortony (ed.) *Metaphor and Thought*. Cambridge: Cambridge University Press.

Miller, G. A. and Chomsky, N. (1963) Finitary models of language users. In R. D. Luce, R. R. Bush and E. Galanter (eds.) *Handbook of Mathematical Psychology*, Vol. 2. New York: Wiley.

Miller, G. A., Galanter, E. and Pribram, K. (1960) *Plans and the Structure of Behavior*. New York: Holt, Rinehart and Winston.

Miller, G. A. and Isard, S. (1964) Free recall of self-embedded English sentences. *Information and Control*, **7**, 292–303.

Miller, G. A. and Johnson-Laird, P. N. (1976) *Language and Perception*. Cambridge: Cambridge University Press. Cambridge, Mass.: Harvard University Press.

Minsky, M. L. (1967) *Computation: Finite and Infinite Machines*. Englewood Cliffs, NJ: Prentice-Hall.

Minsky, M. L. (1968) Matter, mind, and models. In M. L. Minsky (ed.) *Semantic Information Processing*. Cambridge, Mass.: MIT Press.

Minsky, M. L. (1975) Frame-system theory. In R. C. Schank and B. L. Nash-Webber (eds.) *Theoretical Issues in Natural Language Processing*. Pre-prints of a conference at MIT (reprinted in Johnson-Laird and Wason, 1977).

Monod, J. (1972) *Chance and Necessity*. London: Collins.

Montague, R. (1974) *Formal Philosophy: Selected Papers*. New Haven: Yale University Press.

Moore, R. C. and Hendrix, G. G. (1982) Computational models of belief and the semantics of belief sentences. In S. Peters and E. Saarinen (eds.) *Processes, Beliefs, and Questions: Essays on Formal Semantics of Natural Language and Natural Language Processing*. Dordrecht: Reidel.

Morton, J. and Long, J. (1976) Effect of word transition probability on phoneme identification. *Journal of Verbal Learning and Verbal Behavior*, **15**, 43–51.

Mostowski, A. (1957) On a generalization of quantifiers. *Fundamenta Mathematicae*, **44**, 12–36.

Nelson, T. H. (1974) *Computer Lib*. Copies available from 702 So Michigan So Bend., Indiana 46618.

Newell, A. (1981) Reasoning, problem solving and decision processes: the problem space as a fundamental category. In R. Nickerson (ed.) *Attention and Performance*, Vol. 8. Hillsdale, NJ: Erlbaum.

Newell, A. and Simon, H. A. (1972) *Human Problem Solving*. Englewood Cliffs NJ: Prentice-Hall.

Norman, D. A. and Rumelhart, D. E. (1975) Memory and knowledge. In D. A. Norman, D. E. Rumelhart, and the LNR Research Group, *Explorations in Cognition*. San Francisco: Freeman.

Norris, D. G. (1982) Autonomous processes in comprehension: a reply to Marslen-Wilson and Tyler. *Cognition*, **11**, 97–101.

Norris, D. G. (In press) Word recognition: context effect without priming. Laboratory of Experimental Psychology, University of Sussex.

Nunberg, G. (1978) *The Pragmatics of Reference*. Bloomington: Indiana University Linguistics Club.

Oakhill, J. (1982) Constructive processes in skilled and less skilled comprehenders' memory for sentences. *British Journal of Psychology*, **73**, 13–20.

Oatley, K. (1974) Circadian rhythms and representations of the environment in motivational systems. In D. J. McFarland (ed.) *Motivational Control Systems Analysis*. London: Academic Press.

Oatley, K. (1978) *Perceptions and Representations: The Theoretical Bases of Brain Research and Psychology*. London: Methuen.

Oatley, K. (1981) Representing ourselves: mental schemata, computational metaphors, and the nature of consciousness. In G. Underwood and R. Stevens (eds.) *Aspects of Consciousness*. Vol 2: *Structural Issues*. New York: Academic Press.

Ogden, C. K. (1930) *Basic English: A General Introduction with Rules and Grammar*. London: Kegan Paul, Trench, and Trubner.

Osherson, D. N. (1975) Logic and models of logical thinking. In R. J. Falmagne (ed.) *Reasoning: Representation and Process in Children and Adults*. Hillsdale, NJ: Erlbaum.

Osherson, D. N. and Smith, E. E. (1981) On the adequacy of prototype theory as a theory of concepts. *Cognition*, **9**, 35–58.

Paivio, A. (1971) *Imagery and Verbal Processes*. New York: Holt, Rinehart and Winston.

Palmer, S. E. (1975) Visual perception and world knowledge: notes on a model of sensory-cognitive interaction. In D. A. Norman, D. E. Rumelhart, and the LNR Research Group, *Explorations in Cognition*. San Francisco: Freeman.

Paris, S. G. and Carter, A. Y. (1973) Semantic and constructive aspects of sentence memory in children. *Developmental Psychology*, **9**, 109–13.

Partee, B. H. (1975) Montague grammar and transformational grammar. *Linguistic Inquiry*, **6**, 203–300.

Partee, B. H. (1978) Bound variables and other anaphors. In D. L. Waltz (ed.) *Theoretical Issues in Natural Language Processing* Vol. 2. New York: Association for Computing Machinery.

Partee, B. H. (1979) Semantics – mathematics or psychology? In R. Bäuerle, U. Egli and A. von Stechow (eds.) *Semantics from Different Points of View*. Berlin: Springer-Verlag.

Pascal, B. *Pensées*. Translated by A. J. Krailsheimer. Harmondsworth, Middx: Penguin, 1966.

Passmore, J. (1967) Logical Positivism. In P. Edwards (ed.) *The Encyclopedia of Philosophy*. New York: Collier-Macmillan.

Pease, K. (1969) The great evaders. *New Society*, (Oct.), 507–9.

Penfield, W. (1975) *The Mystery of Mind*. Princeton: Princeton University Press.

Peters, P. S. and Ritchie, R. W. (1971) On restricting the base component of transformational grammars. *Information and Control*, **18**, 483–501.

Peters, P. S. and Ritchie, R. W. (1973a) On the generative power of transformational grammars. *Information Sciences*, **6**, 49–83.

Peters, P. S. and Ritchie, R. W. (1973b) Context-sensitive immediate constituent analysis: context-free language revisited. *Mathematical Systems Theory*, **6**, 324–33.

Peterson, J. L. (1981) *Petri Net Theory and the Modeling of Systems*. Englewood Cliffs, NJ: Prentice-Hall.

Piaget, J. (1962) The stages of the intellectual development of the child. *Bulletin of the Menninger Clinic*, **26**, 120–8. Reprinted in P. C. Wason and P. N. Johnson-Laird (eds.) *Thinking and Reasoning*. Harmondsworth, Middx: Penguin, 1968.

Pollard, P. (1981) The effect of thematic content on the 'Wason selection task'. *Current Psychological Research*, **1**, 21–9.

Pollard, P. and Evans, J. St B. T. (1981) The effects of prior beliefs in reasoning: an associational interpretation. *British Journal of Psychology*, **72**, 73–81.

Popper, K. R. and Eccles, J. C. (1977) *The Self and its Brain*. Berlin: Springer-Verlag.

Posner, M. I. and Boies, S. J. (1971) Components of attention. *Psychological Review*, **78**, 391–408.

Postal, P. (1964) *Constituent Structure : A Study of Contemporary Models of Syntactic Description*. Bloomington, Indiana: Research Center for the Language Sciences.

Prior, A. N. (1960) The runabout inference-ticket. *Analysis*, **21**, 38–9.

Pullum, G. K. and Gazdar, G. (1982) Natural languages and context-free languages. *Linguistics and Philosophy*, **4**, 471–504.

Putnam, H. (1960) Minds and machines. In S. Hook (ed.) *Dimensions of Mind*. New York: New York University Press.

Putnam, H. (1970) Is semantics possible? *Contemporary Philosophic Thought: The International Philosophy Year Conferences at Brockport*. Vol. 1. *Languages, Belief and Metaphysics*, edited by H. Kiefer and M. Munitz. New York: State University of New York Press.

Putnam, H. (1973) Explanation and reference. In G. Pearce and P. Maynard (eds.) *Conceptual Change*. Dordrecht: Reidel.

Putnam, H. (1975) The meaning of 'meaning'. In K. Gunderson, (ed.) *Language, Mind and Knowledge*. Minnesota Studies in the Philosophy of Science, Vol. 7. Minneapolis: University of Minnesota Press.

Pylyshyn, Z. W. (1973) What the mind's eye tells the mind's brain: a critique of mental imagery. *Psychological Bulletin*, **80**, 1–24.

Pylyshyn, Z. W. (1981) The imagery debate: analogue media versus tacit knowledge. In N. Block (ed.) *Imagery*. Cambridge, Mass.: MIT Press.

Quillian, M. R. (1968) Semantic memory. In M. Minsky (ed.) *Semantic Information Processing*. Cambridge, Mass.: MIT Press.

Quine, W. V. O. (1953) *From a Logical Point of View: Nine Logico-philosophical Essays*. Cambridge, Mass.: Harvard University Press.

Quine, W. V. O. (1960) *Word and Object*. Cambridge, Mass.: MIT Press.

Quinn, W. G. and Gould, J. L. (1979) Nerves and genes. *Nature*, **278**, 19–23.

Ramsey, F. P. (1931) General propositions and causality. In F. P. Ramsey, *The Foundations of Mathematics and other Logical Essays*. London: Routledge and Kegan Paul.

Reich, S. S. and Ruth, P. (1982) Wason's selection task: verification, falsification, and matching. *British Journal of Psychology*, **73**, 395–405.

Reichardt, W. E. and Poggio, T. (1981) Visual control of flight in flies. In W. E. Reichardt and T. Poggio (eds.) *Theoretical Approaches in Neurobiology*. Cambridge, Mass.: MIT Press.

Rescher, N. (1969) *Many-Valued Logic*. New York: McGraw-Hill.

Revlis, R. (1975) Two models of syllogistic reasoning: feature selection and conversion. *Journal of Verbal Learning and Verbal Behavior*, **14**, 180–95.

Rips, L. J. (1982) Cognitive processes in propositional reasoning. Unpublished paper, University of Chicago.

Rips, L. J., Shoben, E. J. and Smith, E. E. (1973) Semantic distance and the verification of semantic relations. *Journal of Verbal Learning and Verbal Behavior*, **12**, 1–20.

Rogers, H. (1967) *Theory of Recursive Functions and Effective Computability*. New York: McGraw-Hill.

Rosch, E. (1973) On the internal structure of perceptual and semantic categories. In T. M. Moore (ed.) *Cognitive Development and the Acquisition of Language*. New York: Academic Press.

Rosch, E. (1976) Classification of real-world objects: origins and representations in cognition. In S. Ehrlich and E. Tulving (eds.) *La Memoire semantique*. Paris: Bulletin de psychologie (reprinted in Johnson-Laird and Wason, 1977).

Ross, J. R. (1967) Constraints on variables in syntax. Ph.D. dissertation, MIT.

Rumelhart, D. E. (1975) Notes on a schema for stories. In D. G. Bobrow and A. M. Collins (eds.) *Representation and Understanding: Studies in Cognitive Science*. New York: Academic Press.

Rumelhart, D. E., Lindsay, P. H. and Norman, D. A. (1972) A process model for long-term memory. In E. Tulving and W. Donaldson (eds.) *Organisation and Memory*. New York: Academic Press.

Rumelhart, D. E. and Norman, D. A. (1981) Analogical processes in learning. In J. R. Anderson (ed.) *Cognitive Skills and their Acquisition*. Hillsdale, NJ: Erlbaum.

Russell, B. A. W. (1905) On denoting. *Mind*, **14**, 479–93.

Russell, B. A. W. (1927) *An Outline of Philosophy*. London: Allen and Unwin.

Ryle, G. (1949) *The Concept of Mind*. London: Hutchinson.

Sag, I. A. and Hankamer, J. (1980) Toward a theory of anaphoric processing. In J. Barwise and I. A. Sag (eds.) *Stanford Working Papers in Semantics* Vol. 1. Cognitive Science Group, Stanford University.

Sanford, A. J. and Garrod, S. C. (1981) *Understanding Written Language: Explorations of Comprehension Beyond the Sentence*. Chichester: Wiley.

Saussure, F. de (1960) *Course in General Linguistics*. London: Peter Owen.

Savin, H. (1973) Meanings and concepts: a review of Jerrold J. Katz's Semantic Theory. *Cognition*, **2**, 213–38.

Schaeffer, B. and Wallace, R. (1970) The comparison of word meanings. *Journal of Experimental Psychology*, **86**, 144–52.

Schank, R. C. (1980) Language and memory. *Cognitive Science*, **4**, 243–84.

Schank, R. C. and Abelson, R. P. (1977) *Scripts, Plans, Goals and Understanding*. Hillsdale, NJ: Erlbaum.

Schiffer, S. R. (1972) *Meaning*. Oxford: Clarendon Press.

Scribner, S. (1977) Modes of thinking and ways of speaking: culture and logic reconsidered. In R. O. Freedle (ed.) *Discourse Processes: Advances in Research and Theory*. Vol. 1. *Discourse Production and Comprehension*. Norwood, NJ: Ablex. Reprinted in Johnson-Laird and Wason, 1977.

Sells, S. B. (1936) The atmosphere effect: an experimental study of reasoning. *Archives of Psychology*, **29**, 3–72.

Shallice, T. (1972) Dual functions of consciousness. *Psychological Review*, **79**, 383–93.

Sheil, B. (1976) Observations on context free parsing. *Statistical Methods in Linguistics*, 71–109.

Shepard, R. N. (1978) The mental image. *American Psychologist*, **33**, 125–37.

Sherman, M. A. (1973) Bound to be easier? The negative prefix and sentence comprehension. *Journal of Verbal Learning and Verbal Behavior*, **12**, 76–84.

Shorter Oxford English Dictionary (1945) Third edition prepared by H. W. Fowler and J. Coulson, revised by C. T. Onions. Oxford: Oxford University Press.

Simon, H. A. (1969) *The Sciences of the Artificial*. Cambridge, Mass.: MIT Press.

Simon, H. A. (1972) What is visual imagery? An information processing interpretation. In L. W. Gregg (ed.) *Cognition in Learning and Memory*. New York: Wiley.

Sloman, A. (1978) *The Computer Revolution in Philosophy: Philosophy, Science and Models of Mind*. Hassocks, Sussex: Harvester Press.

Smith, E. E., Haviland, S. E., Buckley, P. B. and Sack, M. (1972) Retrieval of artificial facts from long-term memory. *Journal of Verbal Learning and Verbal Behavior*, **11**, 583–93.

Smith, E. E. and Medin, D. L. (1981) *Categories and Concepts*. Cambridge, Mass.: Harvard University Press.

Smith, E. E., Shoben, E. J. and Rips, L. J. (1974) Structure and process in semantic memory: a featural model for semantic decisions. *Psychological Review*, **81**, 214–41.

Smoke, K. L. (1932) An objective study of concept formation. *Psychological Monographs*, 42, whole No. 191.

Southgate, V. (1973) *The Old Woman and Her Pig*. Loughborough: Ladybird Books.

Stalnaker, R. C. (1968) A theory of conditionals. In N. Rescher (ed.) *Studies in Logical Theory*. Oxford: Blackwell.

Stalnaker, R. C. (1972) Pragmatics. In D. Davidson and G. Harman (eds.) *Semantics of Natural Language*. Dordrecht: Reidel.

Steedman, M. J. and Johnson-Laird, P. N. (1977) A programmatic theory of linguistic performance. In P. T. Smith and R. N. Campbell (eds.) *Advances in the Psychology of Language: Formal and Experimental Approaches*. New York: Plenum.

Steedman, M. J. and Johnson-Laird, P. N. (1980) The production of sentences, utterances and speech acts: have computers anything to say? In B. Butterworth (ed.) *Language Production*. Vol. 1. *Speech and Talk*. London: Academic Press.

Stenning, K. (1977) Articles, quantifiers, and their encoding in textual comprehension. In R. O. Freedle (ed.) *Discourse Processes: Advances in Research and Theory*. Vol. 1. *Discourse Production and Comprehension*. Norwood, NJ: Ablex.

Stenning, K. (1978) Anaphora as an approach to pragmatics. In M. Halle, J. Bresnan, and G. A. Miller (eds.) *Linguistic Theory and Psychological Reality*. Cambridge, Mass.: MIT Press.

Stenning, K. (1981) On remembering how to get there: how we might want something like a map. In A. M. Lesgold, J. W. Pellegrino, S. D. Fokkema and J. Glaser (eds.) *Cognitive Psychology and Instruction*. New York: Plenum.

Störring, G. (1908) Experimentelle Untersuchungen über einfache Schlussprozesse. *Archiv für die gesamte Psychologie*, **11**, 1–27.

Strawson, P. F. (1950) On referring. *Mind*, **59**, 320–44.

Sussman, G. J. (1973) A computational model of skill acquisition. AI Report TR–297, AI Laboratory, MIT.

Tabossi, P. (1982) Sentential context and the interpretation of unambiguous words. *Quarterly Journal of Experimental Psychology*, **34A**, 79–90.

Tabossi, P. and Johnson-Laird, P. N. (1980) Linguistic context and the priming of semantic information. *Quarterly Journal of Experimental Psychology*, **32**, 595–603.

Tarski, A. (1956) The concept of truth in formalized languages. In *Logic, Semantics, Metamathematics: Papers from 1923 to 1938*. Translated by J. H. Woodger. Oxford: Oxford University Press.

Templin, M. C. (1957) *Certain Language Skills in Children: Their Development and Interrelationships*. Minneapolis: University of Minnesota Press.

Thatcher, J. W. (1963) The construction of a self-describing Turing machine. In J. Fox (ed.) *Mathematical Theory of Automata. Microwave Research Institute Symposia*, Vol. 12. Polytechnic Institute of Brooklyn, New York: Polytechnic Press.

Thatcher, J. W. (1973) Tree automata: an informal survey. In A. V. Aho (ed.) *Currents in the Theory of Computing*. Englewood Cliffs, NJ: Prentice-Hall.

Thomason, R. H. (1981) A model theory for propositional attitudes. *Linguistics and Philosophy*, **4**, 47–70.

Thorndyke, P. W. (1977) Cognitive structures in comprehension and memory of narrative discourse. *Cognitive Psychology*, **9**, 77–110.

Thorne, J. P., Bratley, P. and Dewar, H. (1968) The syntactic analysis of English by machine. In D. Michie (ed.) *Machine Intelligence*, **3**, New York: American Elsevier.

Turing, A. M. (1936) On computable numbers, with an application to the Entscheidungsproblem. *Proceedings of the London Mathematical Society*, Series 2, **42**, 230–65, (corrections, *ibid.*, **43**, 544–6.

Turing, A. M. (1950) Computing machinery and intelligence. *Mind*, **59**, 433–60.

Tyler, L. K. and Marslen-Wilson, W. D. (1977) The on-line effects of semantic context on syntactic processing. *Journal of Verbal Learning and Verbal Behavior*, **16**, 683–92.

Tyler, L. K. and Marslen-Wilson, W. (1982) Conjectures and refutations: a reply to Norris. *Cognition*, **11**, 103–7.

Valéry, P. (1939) *Poetry and Abstract Thought*. Oxford: Clarendon. Reprinted in *The Collected Works of Paul Valéry*. Vol. 7: *The Art of Poetry*. London: Routledge and Kegan Paul.

Vygotsky, L. S. (1962) *Thought and Language*. Cambridge, Mass.: MIT Press.

Wanner, E. (1977) Review of J. A. Fodor, T. G. Bever and M. F. Garrett, *The Psychology of Language*. *Psycholinguistic Research*, **6**, 261–70.

Wanner, E. (1980) The ATN and the sausage machine: which one is baloney? *Cognition*, **8**, 209–25.

Wanner, E., Kaplan, R. and Shiner, S. (1975) Garden paths in relative clauses. Unpublished paper, Harvard University.

Wanner, E. and Maratsos, M. (1978) An ATN approach to comprehension. In M. Halle, J. Bresnan and G. A. Miller (eds.) *Linguistic Theory and Psychological Reality*. Cambridge, Mass.: MIT Press.

Wason, P. C. (In press) Rationality and the selection task. In J. St B. T. Evans (ed.) *Thinking and Reasoning*. London: Routledge and Kegan Paul.

Wason, P. C. and Johnson-Laird, P. N. (1972) *Psychology of Reasoning*: *Structure and Content*. Cambridge, Mass.: Harvard University Press; London: Batsford.

Wason, P. C. and Shapiro, D. (1971) Natural and contrived experience in a reasoning problem. *Quarterly Journal of Experimental Psychology*, **23**, 63–71.

Waugh, E. (1948) *The Loved One*. London: Chapman and Hall.

Webber, B. L. (1978) Description formation and discourse model synthesis. In D. L. Waltz (ed.) *Theoretical Issues in Natural Language Processing* – 2. New York: Association for Computing Machinery.

Weinreich, U. (1966) Explorations in semantic theory. In T. A. Sebeok (ed.) *Current Trends in Linguistics*, Vol. 3. The Hague: Mouton.

Weiskrantz, L., Warrington, E. K., Sanders, M. D. and Marshall, J. (1974) Visual capacity in the hemianopic field following a restricted occipital ablation. *Brain*, **97**, 709–28.

Weizenbaum, J. (1976) *Computer Power and Human Reason*. San Francisco: Freeman.

Wertheimer, M. (1961) *Productive Thinking*. Enlarged edition, edited by Michael Wertheimer. London: Tavistock.

Wetherick, N. E. (1970) On the representativeness of some experiments in cognition. *Bulletin of the British Psychological Society*, **23**, 213–14.

Whimbey, A. and Lochhead, J. (1980) *Problem Solving and Comprehension*: *A Short Course in Analytical Reasoning*. Second edition. Philadelphia: The Franklin Institute Press.

Whorf, B. L. (1956) *Language, Thought and Reality*. New York: Wiley.

Wilkins, A. J. (1971) Conjoint frequency, category size, and categorization time. *Journal of Verbal Learning and Verbal Behavior*, **10**, 382-5.

Wilkins, M. C. (1928) The effect of changed material on the ability to do formal syllogistic reasoning. *Archives of Psychology*, **16**, No. 102.

Winograd, T. (1972) *Understanding Natural Language*. New York: Academic Press.

Winston, P. H. and Horn, B. K. P. (1981) *LISP*. Reading, Mass.: Addison-Wesley.

Wittgenstein, L. (1922) *Tractatus Logico-Philosophicus*. London: Routledge and Kegan Paul.

Wittgenstein, L. (1953) *Philosophical Investigations*. Translated by G. E. M. Anscombe. New York: Macmillan.

Wonham, W. M. (1976) Towards an abstract internal model principle. *IEEE Transactions on Systems, Man, and Cybernetics*, Vol. SMC–6, **11**, 735–40.

Woods, W. A. (1967) Semantics for a question-answering system. Mathematical linguistics and Automatic Translation report NSF–19, Harvard Computational Laboratory.

Woods, W. A. (1970) Transition network grammars for natural language analysis. *Communications of the Association for Computing Machinery*, **13**, 591–606.

Woods, W. A. (1981) Procedural semantics. In A. K. Joshi, I. Sag and B. L. Webber (eds.) *Elements of Discourse Understanding*. Cambridge: Cambridge University Press.

Woodworth, R. S. and Sells, S. B. (1935) An atmosphere effect in formal syllogistic reasoning. *Journal of Experimental Psychology*, **18**, 451–60.

Woodworth, R. S. and Schlosberg, H. (1954) *Experimental Psychology*. Revised edition. London: Methuen.

Wykes, T. (1981) Inference and children's comprehension of pronouns. *Journal of Experimental Child Psychology*, **32**, 264–78.

Wykes, T. and Johnson-Laird, P. N. (1977) How do children learn the meanings of verbs? *Nature*, **268**, 326–7.

Youniss, J. (1975) Inference as a developmental construction. In R. J. Falmagne (ed.) *Reasoning: Representation and Process in Children and Adults*. Hillsdale, NJ: Erlbaum.

Zukav, G. (1979) *The Dancing Wu Li Masters: An Overview of the New Physics*. New York: Morrow.

Zwicky, A. M. and Sadock, J. M. (1973) Ambiguity tests and how to fail them. *Working Papers in Linguistics, Ohio State University*, **16**, 1–34.

Name index

Abelson, R. P., 371
Ades, A. E., 295
Adrian, E. D., 469
Aho, A. V., 296, 306, 310–11, 314, 480
Anderson, D. B., 342
Anderson, J. A., 456
Anderson, J. R., 149–51, 263
Anderson, R. C., 198, 237–8,
Aristotle, 6, 9, 64, 70, 76, 122, 133, 134, 142, 362
Arrow, K., 58
Asher, R., 441
Augustine, St, 205
Austin, G. A., 186, 190, 424
Austin, J. L., 55

Bach, E., 480
Baddeley, A. D., 117
Baker, G. P., 188–9
Bara, B., 94, 102–4, 110, 111, 119
Barclay, J. R., 243
Bar-Hillel, Y., 36, 126, 239, 279
Barwise, J., 140, 175, 438
Baylor, G. W., 147
Beerbohm. M., 356
Beeton, I., 360–1
Bell, D., 356
Bennett, D. C., 196
Berkeley, G., 448
Berlin, B., 190
Beth, E. W., 25, 34
Bethell-Fox, C., 162, 345
Bever, T. G., 122, 277–8, 334
Bigelow, J. G., 432
Block, N., 450, 475
Boies, S. J., 450
Boole, G. 186
Boolos, G., 17, 268, 479
Borges, J., 143, 362
Bower, G. H., 147
Bracewell, R. J., 33
Braine, M. D. S., 29, 55–6
Brame, M. K., 285, 480
Bransford, J. D., 239, 243
Bratley, P., 339
Bresnan, J., 284–5, 318, 331, 340

Broadbent, D. E., 105
Brooks, L., 147
Brouwer, L. E. J., 187–8
Brown, C., 32
Bruner, J. S., 186, 190, 424
Bryant, P. E., 122
Buckley, P. B., 213
Bull, D., 122
Burgess, A., 442
Burningham, J., 367
Burstall, R. M., 479

Campbell, R., 186
Cantor, G., 17, 59, 444
Carey, S., 225
Carnap, R., 36, 448
Carroll, L., 220
Carter, A. Y., 130
Chapman, I. J., 74–5
Chapman, J. P., 74–5
Charniak, E., 127
Chihara, C. S., 189
Chomsky, N., 11, 66, 169, 178, 267 *et seq.*, 274–7, 279–80, 283, 285, 293–4, 306, 366, 480
Christiaansen, R. E., 278
Church, A., 179
Churchland, P. M., 152, 431, 473
Clark, E. V., 111, 211
Clark, H. H., 111, 211, 384
Clifton, C., 325 *et seq.*
Cocke, J., 314–16, 453
Cohen, L. J., 31
Cohen, P., 437
Cole, P., 435
Coleridge, S. T., 61
Collins, A. M., 212
Collins, J. S., 479
Conrad, C., 213
Cooke, M. de Z., 278
Cooper, F. S., 451
Cooper, G. S., 197
Cooper, L. A., 245
Cooper, R., 140
Cox, J. R., 32–3
Cornulier, B. de, 281

501

Subject index